ISBN 978-1-331-90024-5
PIBN 10251585

This book is a reproduction of an important historical work. Forgotten Books uses
state-of-the-art technology to digitally reconstruct the work, preserving the original format
whilst repairing imperfections present in the aged copy. In rare cases, an imperfection in
the original, such as a blemish or missing page, may be replicated in our edition. We do,
however, repair the vast majority of imperfections successfully; any imperfections that
remain are intentionally left to preserve the state of such historical works.

1 MONTH OF
FREE
READING

at

www.ForgottenBooks.com

By purchasing this book you are eligible for one month membership to ForgottenBooks.com, giving you unlimited access to our entire collection of over 700,000 titles via our web site and mobile apps.

To claim your free month visit:
www.forgottenbooks.com/free251585

English
Français
Deutsche
Italiano
Español
Português

www.forgottenbooks.com

Mythology Photography **Fiction**
Fishing Christianity **Art** Cooking
Essays Buddhism Freemasonry
Medicine **Biology** Music **Ancient**
Egypt Evolution Carpentry Physics
Dance Geology **Mathematics** Fitness
Shakespeare **Folklore** Yoga Marketing
Confidence Immortality Biographies
Poetry **Psychology** Witchcraft
Electronics Chemistry History **Law**
Accounting **Philosophy** Anthropology
Alchemy Drama Quantum Mechanics
Atheism Sexual Health **Ancient History**
Entrepreneurship Languages Sport
Paleontology Needlework Islam
Metaphysics Investment Archaeology
Parenting Statistics Criminology
Motivational

HIS GRACE THE STEWARD
AND TRIAL OF PEERS

HIS GRACE THE STEWARD

AND

TRIAL OF PEERS

A NOVEL INQUIRY INTO A SPECIAL BRANCH
OF CONSTITUTIONAL GOVERNMENT

FOUNDED ENTIRELY UPON ORIGINAL SOURCES OF
INFORMATION, AND EXTENSIVELY UPON
HITHERTO UNPRINTED MATERIALS

BY

L. W. VERNON HARCOURT

LONGMANS, GREEN, AND CO.
39 PATERNOSTER ROW, LONDON
NEW YORK, BOMBAY, AND CALCUTTA
1907

PREFACE

THE Steward of England still is, and, according to popular tradition, always has been the first officer of state in the kingdom. True, no historian has so far discovered much reliable evidence of his ancient greatness, while in modern times he is seldom with us : his only present duty, if we except coronation pageantry, is to preside at certain state trials ; as, for example, when a peer of the realm is arraigned for treason or felony. Peers, fortunately, are not specially addicted to such offences ; therefore a permanent judge is not required for them, and the office in question is only called out of abeyance when occasion arises.

But even if the steward makes no great figure in modern history, his career is well worth studying ; being as he is, and was, first officer of state, the story of his rise and fall necessarily contains matter of some constitutional moment. The subject has never been seriously investigated. Some contributions to a mythology of the steward are to be met with in Hearne's Curious Discourses, Somers' Collection of Tracts, Thoms' Book of the Court, etc. ; and a few isolated references naturally occur in standard works like the Complete Peerage, or the Dictionary of National Biography, but they are merely the *obiter scripta* of persons engaged upon other inquiries. For these and other reasons it is time for the steward to render an account of his stewardship.

In the first six chapters of this book I have set forth the history of the office, from its origin to the period when it ceased to exist as an hereditary dignity. The steward by this time had acquired certain duties connected with royal coronations, and had asserted various unfounded pretensions of a rather formidable character. The subsequent history of the stewardship is chiefly important in connection with trial by peers, and is dealt with accordingly in the second part of this book. Hitherto there have been two explanations of the steward's association with such trials: one view is that he has enjoyed his present functions from time immemorial, or at least ever since the date of the Norman Conquest; the other view is that he succeeded to some of the duties of the justiciar when that office was abolished. The former hypothesis has no foundation in fact, the latter may be traced to the careless reading of a thirteenth-century law-book.

The true story is somewhat remarkable and will, I think, be found by no means a dry subject, or deficient in matters of general interest. A few details are still rather obscure, but the main outlines are sufficiently established by the evidence which has been collected.

The remainder of the book deals with the trial of peers of the realm by their peers, the origin of the practice and its development. This again, I venture to affirm, is a subject which has never so far received adequate historical investigation; and yet it is a subject of the highest importance. When the Entstehung der Schwurgerichte by Heinrich Brunner made its appearance, it was justly hailed in England as an epoch-making treatise. The jury system has long formed an integral portion of our constitutional government, it has become endeared to us by an abiding though fabulous tradition; but, until Brunner's work appeared, there had been no sufficient research into the history of its origin, and existing ideas were extremely erroneous.

Even if the same importance cannot be claimed for the present subject of inquiry on account of its limited scope, still trial by peers of the realm and trial by jury are clearly to some extent complementary institutions, and therefore a study of the one is incomplete without a study of the other. Moreover, is the scope of an institution the proper test of its importance? Surely a system established to protect the lives and dignities of the nobility is at least as important a subject-matter for investigation as the corresponding system which guards the proletariat.

The privilege of trial by peers of the realm affords a remarkable study in sociology : it is full of surprises ; and the critical point in its evolution contains a mystery, which would perhaps be considered as romantic as any historical problem, but for the fact that the central figure is only a man, and not a foolish, beautiful woman like Mary queen of Scots. I claim to have solved the mystery. It is my contention that a break occurred in the uniform development of the system in question ; and that the modern practice is largely founded upon a gross fraud, *une impudente supercherie*, committed apparently by or on behalf of Henry the Seventh.

The question turns on the fate of John Holand, earl of Huntingdon, who died some time in January, 1399–1400. Did this man meet his fate at Pleshy in Essex, without any process of law, finding a lingering death at the hands of a squire with an unskilful sword ; or did he, on being arraigned before the steward of England in Westminster Hall, present the peers of the realm and all the justices, duly confess his treason and receive sentence of death according to law? If the earl died at Pleshy uncondemned, as I hold to be the fact, then the conclusions above indicated are fairly proved ; and the importance of those conclusions can hardly be questioned. It is on such materials as this that the sociologist must decide whether our chief political institutions are to be credited or debited to the account of modern English civilization.

I wish to acknowledge my indebtedness to the many friends who have given me assistance; it would be difficult to name those who have helped me most, but I owe especial gratitude to my uncle, Mr. H. S. Brandreth, and to my friends, Mr. J. G. Wood and Mr. W. J. Hardy, for assistance in various ways, and to the officials of the Record Office and British Museum for their kindness and courtesy.

L. W. VERNON HARCOURT.

7 New Square,
    Lincoln's Inn, W.C.,
        March, 1907.

CONTENTS

PART I

THE ORIGIN OF THE STEWARDSHIP OF ENGLAND

CHAPTER I

The Dapifers:—History of the office of dapifer or seneschal, in France and England, from early times down to the end of the reign of Henry I . . . . *pages* 1-29

Appendix:—The Colchester tract; The style given to the chief officer of Normandy in the Très Ancien Coutumier . 29-32

CHAPTER II

The Dapifers, the hereditary Dapifers, and the provincial Seneschals:—History of these officers from the commencement of the anarchy down to the reign of Richard I . 33-55

Appendix:—Charter to Geoffrey de Mandeville, earl of Essex; Charter to Humphrey de Bohun; Charter to Robert earl of Leicester; Charter to Robert, son of Robert earl of Leicester; Confirmation charter to Robert earl of Leicester; Charter to Hugh Bigod; Charter to Walter Fitzalan; References in various chronicles to the stewardship of France, the charter of Saint-Julien de Tours, the contest between the countesses of Champagne and Flanders 56-71

CHAPTER III

How the House of Montfort became sole hereditary stewards of the household:—A history of the office from the accession of Richard I to the year 1239, when Simon V was duly invested with the earldom of Leicester 72-86

CONTENTS

Appendix:—Charter to Roger Bigod; Records showing the devolution and partition of the Leicester estates; Confirmation charter to the earl of Winchester; Records connected with the disseizin of Simon IV and the management of his moiety of the estates, the accounts of Robert de Ropeley and William de Cantilupe; Writs on behalf of the earl of Chester; Records of dealings with the Leicester estates from the accession of Henry III to the advent of Simon V; Records showing how Simon V obtained the stewardship and estates . *pages* 87–114

CHAPTER IV

Evolution of the hereditary stewardship in the hands of Simon earl of Leicester:—The history of the office continued to the death of Simon at Evesham 115–128

Appendix on the alleged use of the style "justiciar" by Simon de Montfort 128–137

CHAPTER V

The Lancastrian Stewards:—Edmund of Lancaster and Edward I; Thomas of Lancaster and Edward II . . . 138–153

Appendix:—Various grants to Edmund of Lancaster; Letters-patent of Edmund renouncing all claim to an estate of inheritance in the stewardship of England; Letters-patent of Edward II granting the stewardship of England to Thomas and the heirs of his body; The Lancastrian tract on the stewardship of England; the tract on the stewardship of Normandy; De casibus et judiciis difficilibus, in the Modus tenendi parliamentum 154–169

CHAPTER VI

The Lancastrian Stewards (*continued*):—Henry earl of Lancaster; Henry duke of Lancaster; John of Gaunt; and Thomas duke of Clarence, the last holder of the office . . 170–192

Appendix:—The Hinckley tracts on the stewardship of England; Coronation roll of Henry IV; Appointment of Richard earl of Warwick as steward, in place of the duke of Clarence, for the coronations of Henry V and queen Katharine . . 192–201

PART II

THE TRIAL OF PEERS

CHAPTER VII

Judgment of Peers, early principles and Magna Charta *pages* 205–236

Appendix:—A comparative analysis of the language and provisions in chapter xxxix of Magna Charta . . 236–244

CHAPTER VIII

John Lackland and the Peers of France; Judgment by Peers in
France in the thirteenth century . . . 245–275

CHAPTER IX

Judgment of Peers in the Thirteenth and Fourteenth Century:—
The development of the principle during the reigns of
Henry III, Edward I, and Edward II . . . 276–308

Appendix:—Records illustrating the procedure adopted against
peers spiritual and temporal, and peeresses, during the reigns
of Richard I, John, Henry III, and Edward I; Proceedings
against Thomas earl of Lancaster; Repeals of the proceedings
against the Despencers, Thomas earl of Lancaster, Roger
Mortimer, and Bartholomew de Badlesmere; Petition for the
reversal of the proceedings against Andrew Harcla earl of
Carlisle 308–334

CHAPTER X

Trial of Peers in the Fourteenth Century:—The causes célèbres of
the reigns of Edward III and Richard II . . 335–359

Appendix:—The Statute of 15 Edward III; Proceedings in the
King's Bench for annulling the outlawry of Thomas earl of
Warwick 359–361

CHAPTER XI

Trial of Peers in the Fifteenth Century; The Court of Chivalry:—
A history of procedure down to the year 1497, when lord
Audeley was sentenced by a court of chivalry for his share in
the Cornish rising 362–399

Appendix:—Proceedings in the court of chivalry against Roger
Damory; Appointment of a deputy constable and deputy
marshal in consequence of archbishop Scrope's rebellion;
Commission of oyer and terminer in consequence of the same;
Proceedings against Richard earl of Cambridge and lord
Scrope of Masham for treason; Patent appointing John Tiptoft, earl of Worcester, to be constable of England; Patent
appointing earl Rivers and his son to be constable of England
successively for life; Patent reappointing the earl of Worcester;
Patent appointing a steward of England to execute judgment
on the duke of Clarence; Patent appointing commissioners
to exercise the office of constable and marshal for the trial of
lord Audeley   .   .   .   .   *pages* 399–415

CHAPTER XII

The Institution of the Court of the Lord High Steward:—The
report in the Year Book for the first year of Henry IV; the
evidence that this report is a forgery; The proceedings against
the earl of Warwick, lord Dudley, and the duke of Buckingham   416–443

Appendix:—William Peion's account of Huntingdon's flight; The
escheators' accounts of Huntingdon's personal property, seized
at Leigh in the Hundred of Rochford; Reference to a judgment against Huntingdon on the rolls of the Exchequer;
Confession of John Pritewell; Huntingdon's capture and death
as related by the chroniclers; The Year Book account of
Huntingdon's trial; Letters-patent appointing a steward of
England for the trial of the earl of Warwick; Trial of the earl
of Warwick; Letters-patent appointing a steward of England
for the trial of lord Dudley; The Year Book report of the
duke of Buckingham's trial   .   .   .   444–470

Index   .   471–500

PART I
THE ORIGIN OF THE STEWARDSHIP OF ENGLAND

CHAPTER I

THE DAPIFERS

DURING the latter half of the eleventh century a remarkable development took place in the royal household of France, culminating at the beginning of the twelfth
century in the establishment of five great officers of state—
the dapifer (or seneschal), the chancellor, the butler, the
chamberlain, and the constable.[1] The dapifer then became
the first great officer of state, and so continued until the
suppression of the office. The evolution of the French
household can be traced in the royal charters of the period
under consideration. Thus the gradual division of the royal
household into state officers and purely domestic officers is
marked in the diplomatic instruments by the gradual dis-
appearance of lesser officials, such as marshals and cooks,
from among the attesting witnesses. In the same way the
growing influence of the dapifer is evidenced by the order
of precedence adopted in attesting.

During the final stage all royal charters are attested exclusively by the dapifer, butler, chamberlain and constable,
in the order named, and expedited by the chancellor. The
presence of each official ceases to be indicated by his attestation, but if an office is actually vacant a special formula is
employed. If, for example, there is no dapifer, the words
dapifero nullo take the place of the dapifer's attestation.[2]

---

[1] For modern authorities see Luchaire, Institutions de la France,
i, pp. 163, 173–81; and Luchaire, Louis VI, pp. xliv–liii, app.
pp. 303–4; Viollet, Institutions de la France, ii, pp. 109–12.

[2] See Delisle, Catalogue des Actes de Philippe-Auguste, pp.
lxxviii–lxxxviii: Luchaire, Études sur les Actes de Louis VII,
pp. 44–6.

The following are the formal parts of a fairly typical French charter of the twelfth century :—

In nomine sancte et individue Trinitatis, amen.   Ego Ludovicus, Dei gratia Francorum rex.   Sciant universi presentes et futuri quod. . . .

Actum publice apud . . . anno Dominice Incarnationis [e.g.] millesimo centesimo quinquagesimo quarto, astantibus in palatio nostro quorum subtitulata sunt nomina et signa.

Signum comitis Theobaudi, dapiferi nostri.   Signum Guidonis, buticularii.   Signum Mathei, camerarii.   Signum Mathei, constabularii.   Data per manum Hugonis, cancellarii.

The above-mentioned Thibaud count of Blois was the last holder of the dapifership.[1]   The office, though not at once abolished, was never regranted after the count's death in 1191.   During the last few years of its actual existence the post declined considerably in importance, but at the zenith of its fame the dapifership had attained a position of portentous power recalling that of the ancient mayors of the palace who founded the Carolingian dynasty.   While, indeed, a Rochefort or a Garland was tenant of the office the dapifer was the second personage in the realm, a kind of viceroy invested with well-nigh all the prerogatives of monarchy.

To some extent I have been anticipating events which will have to be noted later on in greater detail, but it is essential that the main facts relating to the French dapifership should be stated at the outset.   The important point now to determine is when and in what capacity did this functionary make his appearance, and when did he establish his precedence over the other officers of the court.

The name *seneschal* occurs at a very early date in history :[2] the name *dapifer* appears to be of more recent origin, but it is to be found in documents belonging to the reign of Charles Magnus.[3]   We need not, however, carry our inquiries back so far as this.   In early times, and perhaps until the end of the

---

[1] Delisle, Catalogue des Actes de Philippe-Auguste, pp. lxxxi–lxxxii.

[2] See, for example, Vitae SS. Ord. S. Bened., iv, pp. 558, 560; and generally, Ducange, s.v. Senescallus.

[3] Muratori, Antiquitates, i, p. 929 (A.D. 878); Waitz, Verfassungsge⁶, iii, s. 416.

tenth century, the functions of the dapifer or seneschal were discharged by two or more officials of that name. After the accession of Hugh Capet there is no evidence of even dual tenure of the office; and it seems reasonably certain that, in the ordinary process of development, the office had by the beginning of the eleventh century become entrusted to a single dapifer, with no doubt a staff of minor officials under him.[1]

After the year 1047 a functionary so styled begins to appear frequently on Capetian charters, and becomes an important officer of the household.[2] At first his correct title appears to be indifferently *seneschal* or *dapifer*, but towards the close of the eleventh century his definite official style is *dapifer*.

His duties to begin with are not of an extensive or very important character. He is primarily, as the name dapifer implies, the chef-du-service or the caterer for the royal banqueting table and nothing more. He is not an officer of state properly so called, and prior to the year 1070 he is most certainly not the first even of the household officers.[3] From the year 1070 to the close of the century the rise of the French dapifership is undoubtedly rapid; and, the development being due not to the office but to the officer, the various stages of the development closely correspond with the dates when the office changed hands. For the present we need carry our inquiries no further than the year 1066. By that date, at any rate, the French dapifer had not yet attained a position of any pre-eminence; nor did he attain such a position until some years after William the Bastard had won the decisive battle of Hastings.[4]

Now it has been asserted by Stapleton, who was in his

---

[1] Luchaire, Institutions de la France, i, p. 176 n.; cf. Bouquet, H. F., vol. xi, p. clv.

[2] Luchaire, Manuel des Institutions, p. 521.

[3] Luchaire, Institutions de la France, i, p. 175; Manuel, p. 521.

[4] For example, Charter of 1067—Signa Philippi Francorum regis, Husgonis Melaudis comitis, Hugonis de Puteolo, Frederici de Curbeio, Gauterii Constabularii, Guillelmi prepositi Carnotensis ecclesie, Baudwini dapiferi. . . . (Transcribed from original, R.O. Transcripts, 140 B., vol. i, p. 79.)

day the highest authority on Anglo-Norman politics, that the petty court of Normandy took its model from the superior court of France.[1] Something of the kind we should naturally expect. We should equally expect to find, in point of development, the petty court lagging somewhat behind the model court; indeed to assert the converse case would be a contradiction in terms; and we might, even in the absence of better evidence, reasonably infer that at the date of the battle of Hastings duke William's dapifer was a quite unimportant functionary. Stapleton, however, on the contrary held that he was first officer of state; and Stubbs and a host of other historians have accepted Stapleton's view. I think we might acquit the last-named writer of illogical inference, because he probably fixed the date when the French dapifer attained his paramount position much earlier than is now known by charter evidence to be the true date; but I propose to convict him of a serious error in fact.

A comparison of the witnesses and signatories of the Norman ducal charters with those of the French royal charters affords the most trustworthy evidence obtainable of the household officers from time to time attached to the respective courts; for it appears to be a feature, common to all charters of this period, that household officials of every grade are occasionally present and attest, however humble their station. Now the French charters of the period evidence the existence of a large, highly organised household permanently maintained by the sovereign: the Norman charters warrant no such conclusion. Such household officers as do appear attached to the Norman court undoubtedly affect styles identical with some one or other of the French officials,[2] and to this extent it is clear that the petty Norman court modelled itself on the French court; but it is none the less clear that the former was in a far more primitive and

---

[1] Rotuli Scaccarii Normanniae, vol. i, p. xvii.

[2] For dapifers see below. Constabularius; France Cal. R.O., no. 1422. Camerarius and Butteilerius (Buticularius); ibid., no. 1167. Pincerna; ibid., no. 73. Cubicularius; ibid., no. 711. Marescallus; Cartulaire de S. Trinité du Mont (Doc. Inéd., Cartulaire de S. Bertin.), nos. 2, 32. Camerarius and Pincerna; ibid., nos. 38, 39, etc.

undeveloped state than the latter. Indeed it seems highly probable that such Norman officials as had acquired a permanent existence and style, had as yet, with one or two exceptions, no settled, definite or very important functions. So much for the Norman household generally. We will now consider the dapifership in particular.

During the period A.D. 1030 to A.D. 1066 it is fairly clear upon the evidence that there were at least two dapifers or seneschals always attached to the Norman court. Osbern son of Herfast,[1] Anfred,[2] and Gilbert[3] appear as dapifers to Duke Robert; and Osbern son of Herfast,[1] Osbern,[4] Herluin (?),[5] Gerald,[6] and Stigand[7] as dapifers to duke William. The list is probably far from complete. When the various persons named were appointed and how long they held office it is impossible to say, but at all events during the years 1061–6 the duke's dapifers were Gerald and Stigand. The most notable person among them all was Osbern son of Herfast, with whom we shall have to deal at some length. The only other dapifer of sufficient importance to be mentioned in the chronicles was Gerald: this man and Hugh de Grentmaisnil are said by Ordericus Vitalis to have been given the custody of the castle of Neufmarché, where they

[1] Osbern, son of Herfast, dapifer, mentioned: France Cal. R.O., nos. 75, 85; Cartulaire de S. Trinité du Mont, no. 6; Ordericus Vitalis (Soc. de l'Hist. de France), i, pp. 179–80, ii, p. 369; and infra.

[2] Signa Osberni dapiferi . . . Anfredi dapiferi (circa A.D. 1031): France Cal. R.O., no. 1422.

[3] Signa Osberni dapiferi . . . Gisleberti senescalli (circa A.D. 1030–5): Cartulaire de S. Trinité du Mont, no. 5.

[4] Teste Osberno dapifero (A.D. 1055): Gallia Christiana, xi, app. col. 13.

[5] See Cartulaire de S. Trinité du Mont, no. 46.

[6] Signum Geraldi senescalci (A.D. 1055): France Cal. R.O., no. 1167. Signum Giraldi senescalli (A.D. 1066): ibid., no. 73. Geraldus dapifer (circa A.D. 1066): Gallia Christiana, xi, app. col. 59. See also Cartulaire de S. Trinité du Mont, no. 39; Migne, cxlix, col. 1374, etc.

[7] Signum Stigandi dapiferi (A.D. 1061): France Cal. R.O., no. 711. Also A.D. 1066: Martène, Thesaurus Novus, i, 196. Stigandus dapifer: Monasticon Anglicanum, vi, 1100–1. Also A.D. 1071: France Cal. R.O., no. 91.

did good service in pacifying the surrounding country.[1]
Gerald, dapifer, is also mentioned as contributing ships for
the transport of William's invading army.[2] Stigand continued to act as dapifer after the conquest,[3] but very little is
known about him.

Osbern son of Herfast appears to have been a man of
considerable wealth and position in Normandy : he was
nephew to Gunnor,[4] and married Emma daughter of Ralph
count of Ivri.[5] By his wife he had two sons, William Fitz-
Osbern, afterwards earl of Hereford, and Osbern who became
bishop of Exeter. Osbern, dapifer (circa A.D. 1040), is called
by William of Jumièges *procurator principalis domus*, which
means that he was the chief officer of the household, and
perhaps implies that he was the principal guardian of the
young duke's person, but he was certainly not an officer of
state. Probably he would never have been mentioned by the
chroniclers, but for the fact that, while tending little William
at Vaudreuil, he was foully murdered in the ducal night-
nursery. William of Jumièges relates the affair after this
fashion —:

Deinde Turoldus, teneri ducis paedagogus, perimitur a perfidis
patriae desertoribus. Osbernus quoque, procurator principalis domus,
Herfasti Gunnoris comitissae fratris filius, quadam nocte, dum in
cubiculo ducis cum ipso in valle Rodoili securus soporatur, repente
in stratu suo a Willelmo Rogerii de Montegumeri filio jugulatur.[6]

He then proceeds to describe how Osbern's faithful servant
avenges the murder with scrupulous attention to the principles
of retaliation.

Ordericus Vitalis suggests a rather different scene, not a
stealthy assassination at dead of night, but a sanguinary

[1] Ordericus Vitalis, ii, p. 113.
[2] Brevis Relatio, ed. Giles, p. 22. This famous list of ships
belongs to romance and not to history, but it is something to be
a hero of romance.
[3] France Cal. R.O., no. 91.
[4] Ibid., nos. 702, 704; and see below.
[5] Cartulaire de S. Trinité du Mont, passim; Monasticon Anglicanum, vi, 1101; France Cal. R.O., nos. 77, 81, 85; William of
Jumièges, ed. Migne, cxlix, col. 875.
[6] William of Jumièges, ed. Migne, cxlix, col. 847.

affray in which a dozen or more took part, and where those who fell at all events died sword in hand.

Tunc Turchetillus de Novo-Mercato et Rogerius de Toenia et Osbernus dapifer Normanniae et duo filii Rogerii de Montegomerici, Guillelmus et Hugo, Rodbertus de Bellomonte, Galchelinus de Ferrariis et Hugo de Monteforti et alii plures in armis potentes alterutrum se peremerunt.[1]

The learned editor of this ecclesiastical history aptly describes the incident as one of those intestine quarrels which made a shambles of the young duke's court. One of Osbern's followers, severely pricked both in body and conscience, assumed the monk's habit at S. Trinité du Mont, and with the assent of Osbern's heirs made liberal donations to that monastery.[2] Such is the story of Osbern's death. Of his life we know nothing, for he was a mere household official, procurator and dapifer,[3] not an officer of state.

William of Jumièges leaves us in no doubt as to who were in fact the chief officers of state in Normandy. These were not dapifers or procurators, but persons styled *tutores* by the chronicler; and, as might be expected from the name, such tutors were not permanent officials, but appointed temporarily during the minority or incapacity of the duke. During the minority of Richard the First, Ralph (Torte), Bernard (called *the Dane*) and Anslech were appointed by duke William— totius Normannici ducatus tutores.[4] The procurator at this

---

[1] Ordericus Vitalis, ii, p. 369; see also ibid., i, pp. 179–80.

[2] Cartulaire de S. Trinité du Mont no. 6:—Tempore quo Osbernus dapifer a suis hostibus est interemptus, Gulbertus filius Erchembaldi vicecomitis, fidelis ejus, cum eo graviter est vulneratus.

[3] For this combination cf. a charter of William I, printed by Rymer, Foedera R.C., i, p. 2:—Willielmus rex Anglorum . . . Sciatis me concessisse et confirmasse donationem quam Gilbertus abbas et monachi de Westmonasterio concesserunt in hereditate Hugoni de Coleham et heredibus suis, videlicet, ut ipse Hugo totius predicte abbatie sit dapifer, et sub abbate procurator, et heredes sui post eum. . . .

[4] Ed. Migne, cxlix., col. 811. Compare the following references to the position of Ralph Torte.

Praefectum comitatui praefecit Rodulphum agnomento Tortam qui vectigalia annuatim a subditis exigeret et tota hac in provincia jura ac quaelibet negocia decerneret (ibid., col. 814).

Eo namque tempore erat quidam Rodulfus cujus agnomen Torta

time was Osmund, a person of no great standing in Normandy.[1] During the minority of William the Bastard, Alan count of Brittany was appointed tutor of Normandy, but succumbed to poison.[2] Gilbert count of Brionne succeeded him and was assassinated.[3] Ralph de Wac was thereupon appointed tutor by William :—ex consultu majorum sibi tutorem eligit et principem militiæ Northmannorum constituit.[4] These appointments more than cover the whole period of Osbern's dapifership and procuratorship under William.

The above data are fatal to the view that the Norman dapifer was an official of any pre-eminence.[5] Taking the

vocabatur, qui totius Northmanniae honorem post mortem Willelmi altius caeteris comparibus sibi vendicabat. . . . (Dudo de St. Quentin, ed. Duchesne, p. 127.)

Great political changes had taken place before Wace wrote his Roman de Rou.   Wace describes this same Ralph thus :—

> Dan Raoul, un vassal ki Torte ert apelez
> Mananz esteit, . . .
> A cil livra li reis totes li prevostez
> De Cax e de Roem e des altres citez.
>
> . . . .
>
> Cil ki ert seneschal Raol Torte aveit non,
> Mult par esteit tenu por encrisme felon.

(Ed. Pluquet, vv., 3575, 3830.)   Wace died circa 1175. In my opinion it was not merely an anachronism to call Ralph seneschal, it was an absolute error.

[1] Quidam tyro (Dudo, p. 117). Cf. Ordericus Vitalis, ii, p. 363 :—Sed ille nutu Dei et prudentia Osmundi nutritoris sui exivit.

[2] In Normannia his temporibus multa mala nequiter patrata sunt. Alanum enim comitem Britonum, suique ducis tutorem, Normanni veneno peremerunt, et successorem ejus Gislebertum comitem, Godefridi filium, crudelibus armis prostraverunt, . . . (Ordericus Vitalis, ii, p. 369).

[3] Gislebertus comes Ocensis filius Godefridi comitis, callidus et fortis, tutor Willelmi pueri, . . . (William of Jumièges, col. 847).

[4] Ibid., col. 849.

[5] On the existing evidence, I think we may conclude that after William attained his majority it was the chamberlain, if anyone, who became the chief officer of the duke's household. Ralph de Tancarville is called magister aulae Willelmi ducis.   This style should be compared with the major domus regiae, an expression which we subsequently find employed on certain occasions to designate the

contemporary evidence as a whole, it is reasonably certain that this particular functionary had at most acquired some of the household functions discharged by the French dapifer in the earliest stages of his development under the Capetian dynasty. But although it turns out on close investigation that even Osbern, nephew to Gunnor the duchess, was nothing more than head nurse of the palace and sewer in the ducal household : still, to give him his due, he was nothing less than the protagonist of his grace the Lord High Steward of England as hereafter will appear.

The facts above set forth strictly accord with the evidence furnished by charters and all contemporary chroniclers,[1] but they do not accord with the views expressed by later chroniclers and by Ordericus Vitalis in particular. On the contrary, these subsequent writers make William Fitz-Osbern, on the death of his father Osbern dapifer, succeed to the paternal post, and as dapifer Normanniae become first officer of state in Normandy. For example, when dealing with the episode of Emma's marriage, at which Roger earl of Hereford drunk with the bride-ale of Norwich plotted to his own destruction against the king, Ordericus Vitalis is moved to eloquence, and concludes with this perfervid lament.

Vere gloria mundi ut flos foeni decidit et arescit, ac velut fumus deficit et transit. Ubi est Guillelmus, Osberni filius, Herfordensis comes et regis vicarius, Normanniae dapifer et magister militum bellicosus.[2]

Wace, in his Roman de Rou, makes William address Fitz-

dapifer of France. See Bouquet, H.F., xii, p. 76 ; Ordonnances, vii, p. 414. See also R.O. transcripts 140 A No. 31, where Ralph is called— *Willelmi regis magister et summus camerarius.*

[1] There, is, however, a passage in William of Poictiers worth noting :—Quadam vero die, dum custodiam navium viseret dux, indicatum est forte spatianti prope navalia monachum Heraldi legatum adesse. Ipse protinus illum convenit ingeniosa hac elocutione :— "Proximus," infit, "ego sum Willelmi comitis Normannorum ac dapifer. Eum alloquendi nisi per me copiam habere non poteris, quod affers mihi narra. Libens ille cognoscet idem per me, quia neminem suorum cariorem habet me. . . ." (Giles, p. 128.)

[2] Vol. ii, p. 265. Ordericus Vitalis died circa 1142. His history was compiled circa 1123–41, or more than fifty years after the death of Fitz-Osbern.

Osbern as " my seneschal." [1] In the postscript to the Brevis Relatio, William dapifer the son of Osbern is said to have provided sixty ships for the conquest of England.[2] Henry of Huntingdon calls Fitz-Osbern "dapifer ducis" ;[3] and so forth.

Now William Fitz-Osbern, even before he came to England, was one of the foremost Normans of his time, and his position and fortunes were considerably furthered by the conquest. At the beginning of the year 1067 he had probably already received the earldom of Hereford and large grants of land in England.[4] In the same year Fitz-Osbern and the bishop of Bayeux were appointed joint regents of England during the absence of William in his duchy, and at a later date the earl occupied for a short time the same position in Normandy.[5]

The first-mentioned regency is dealt with by Stubbs as quoted below, and his observations on the subject show the importance of definitely deciding (if possible) Fitz-Osbern's claim to the office of dapifer.   Stubbs writes as follows :—

The office [of Justiciar] appears first as the lieutenancy of the kingdom or viceroyalty exercised during the king's absence from England. In this capacity William Fitz-Osbern the steward of Normandy and Odo of Bayeux acted during the Conqueror's visit

[1] Ed. Pluquet, ii, pp. 54, 199. Ed. Andresen, ii, pp. 207, 333. Written circa 1160–74. Wace died circa 1175.

[2] Ed. Giles, Caxton Soc., p. 22. Temp. Henry I (?).

[3] Rolls Series 74, p. 199; cf. Rolls Series 82, iv, p. 36; and Gallia Christiana, xi, col. 123. See also Diceto, Rolls Series 68, i, p. 195. Henry of Huntingdon died circa 1155.

[4] See Mr. Round's article in Dict. of Nat. Biog. s.v. Fitz-Osbern ; and the Complete Peerage s.v. Hereford.

[5] Compare the following passages in Ordericus Vitalis.—Intra moenia Guentae, opibus et munimine nobilis urbis et mari contiguae, validam arcem construxit, ibique Guillermum Osberni filium in exercitu suo praecipuum reliquit, eumque, vice sua, toti regno versus Aquilonem praeesse constituit. Doveram vero totamque Cantiam Odoni fratri suo commendavit, qui multa liberalitate et industria saeculari pollebat. His duobus praefecturam Angliae commisit. . . . (Vol. ii, p. 166.)

Willelmo dapifero Normanniae Osberni filio insulam Vectam et comitatum Herfordensem dedit. (Vol. ii, p. 218.)

Anno quinto regni sui Guillelmus rex Guillelmum Osberni filium misit in Normanniam, ut cum Mathilde regina tueretur provinciam. (Vol. ii, p. 234.)

to the continent in 1067 : they were left according to William of Poictiers, the former to govern the north of England and the latter to hold rule in Kent in the king's stead *vice sua;* Florence of Worcester describes them as *custodes Angliae* and Ordericus Vitalis gives to their office the name of praefectura. It would seem most probable that William Fitz-Osbern at least was left in his character of Steward, and that the Norman seneschalship was thus the origin of the English justiciarship.[1]

Even if Stubbs is right in his assumption that Fitz-Osbern was a dapifer or steward of Normandy, there is still much to be said against his conclusion in view of the insignificance of this office. The first question, however, to determine is whether or not Fitz-Osbern was in fact one of the duke's dapifers.

The only evidence of a diplomatic character which, so far as I am aware, has ever been advanced as proving Fitz-Osbern's dapifership is an extract from a cartulary[2] recording a grant to the S. Trinité du Mont at Rouen. This extract is as follows :—

Regis regum, Christi gratia largiente, qui cuncta semper pio gubernat moderamine, Willelmus dux Normannorum, regnum adeptus Anglorum, cum esset in villa regia quae Anglica lingua Guentha[3] dicitur, consilio et suggestione fidelis sui Willelmi filii Osberni dapiferi qui comes erat palatii, dedit Sanctae Trinitati de Monte in perpetuam hereditatem terram quae Anglice Hermodesodes nuncupatur cum ecclesia et omnibus sibi pertinentibus, scilicet in agris pratis pascuis molendinis aquis humectis silvis ceterisque hujusmodi eidem villae contiguis, presente abbate Raynerio cum duobus monachis Nicholao et Guillelmo. Haec donatio facta est per unum cultellum quem prefatus rex joculariter dans abbati quasi ejus palmae minatur infigere; "ita," inquit, "terra dari debet". Hoc ergo evidenti signo multorumque nobilium qui regio lateri astabant testimonio facta est haec donatio. Anno Dominicae incarnationis MLXVIIII. Signa :—Willelmi Regis, Mathildis Reginae, Willelmi filii Osberni, Willelmi episcopi Londoniae, Goisfredi episcopi Constantiae, Rotberti filii Guimar, Ricardi filii Torstein Goiz, Erfasti tunc capellani postea episcopi, Hugonis de Sillevilla."[4]

Upon this extract Stapleton says :—"Thus dapifer or

---

[1] Const. Hist., i, p. 374.

[2] Printed among the Documents Inédits as an appendix to the Cartulaire de S. Bertin.

[3] Gueritho in printed cartulary, see p. 455.

[4] See Stapleton, Rot. Scacc. Norm., i, p. xvii.

senescallus Normanniae, the usual title of the chief justiciar
of Normandy, is rendered comes palatii in a cartulary written
towards the close of the eleventh century." Stubbs goes
further :—" Normandy," he says, " had its steward or seneschal
for whom even the name of comes palatinus is claimed,"
and in a note he refers to the cartulary I have cited as speaking of "William Fitz-Osbern, 'dapiferi qui comes erat palatii'."
Stubbs's phraseology down to this point suggests that he
entertained some doubt as to the validity of this claim, but
a few lines below he writes quite definitely :—" At the time
of the conquest William Fitz-Osbern was, as his father had
been, dapifer and comes palatii."[1]

The above assertions of Stapleton and Stubbs are, I
venture to contend, not one of them warranted by the
evidence. Approaching the question, as we are entitled to
do, with the knowledge that Osbern held the office of dapifer
but in uncertainty as to whether his son held the office, it is
obvious that the cartulary cited decides nothing. But let us
beg the question of Fitz-Osbern's dapifership and read the
extract as if it ran : " Willelmi (filii Osberni) dapiferi qui
comes erat palatii." Even thus the passage, in my opinion,
unquestionably suggests the reverse of what Stapleton con-
tends : it suggests the conclusion I desire to emphasise as the
true one, that the office of dapifer and comes palatii had nothing to do with each other. Take by way of illustration the
sentence following :—" Eudo dapifer qui erat vice-comes."
Could anyone contend that the statement is untrue, or even
that it contains the smallest suggestio falsi, implies that is
to say a connection between the office of dapifer and sheriff?
Such a contention would be quite unarguable.

The question about the dapifership is fortunately concluded by the cartulary itself, which makes it clear that the
style *dapifer* is applied to Osbern and not to his son.[2] It
is only in this one extract that any ambiguity arises. As

[1] Stubbs, Constitutional History, i, p. 372.
[2] The editor of this cartulary quite rightly punctuates the
passage as follows: Willelmi, filii Osberni dapiferi, qui comes erat
palatii, dedit. . . . Cf. no. 55 : . . . Willelmus comes, filius Osberni
dapiferi, cum domino suo . . .; and no. 49 : . . . Emma, Osberni
dapiferi uxore, et filiis ejus Willelmo et Osberno. . .

regards the style comes palatii, which is given to Fitz-Osbern, very little need be said. It may refer, either to the earl's regency, or to the fact that he was at the time indicated exercising palatinate jurisdiction over a large portion of England, having Winchester for its chief centre. Odo of Bayeux in precisely similar circumstances is called earl palatine by Ordericus Vitalis,[1] and the term is a perfectly appropriate one; besides, it must be remembered that the extract under discussion is not a formal charter, but a very informal notification of one, in which the scribe does not think it out of place to relate how William the Conqueror had a playful jest with the abbot. There is not the slightest foundation for the assertion that Osbern the father was ever comes palatii.

The other existing diplomatic evidence is all opposed to Fitz-Osbern's dapifership. Both before and after the conquest Fitz-Osbern constantly figures in charters, but he never attests other people's charters as dapifer, and never so describes himself in his own.

The chronicle evidence, as already stated, is almost equally unfavourable to the claim, the statements of later writers being quite outweighed by the silence of contemporaries upon the subject. There is, it is true, a Cottonian manuscript[2] of very uncertain authority, in which a curious story

---

[1] Quid loquar de Odone Baiocasino praesule, qui consul palatinus erat, et ubique cunctis Angliae habitatoribus formidabilis erat, ac veluti secundus rex passim jura dabat? Principatum super omnes comites et regni optimates habuit, et cum thesauris antiquorum Cantiam possedit, . . . (Ordericus Vitalis, ii, p. 222).

Odo nimirum, ut supra-dictum est, palatinus Cantiae consul erat, et plures sub se comites virosque potentes habebat (ibid., iii, p. 270).

[2] Printed Monasticon Anglicanum, vol. iv, 607; and see appendix to this chapter. The terms in which the office of dapifer is mentioned are worth special attention :—Rex Willielmus junior civitatem Colecestriae cum suis pertinentiis tradidit servandam Eudoni qui erat major domus regiae quod nos vulgariter senescallum vel dapiferum vocamus.

I incline to the opinion that this tract was composed in the interests of Geoffrey de Mandeville earl of Essex: it must be taken into account in tracing the development of the dapifership during and after the anarchy; and should be compared with the Angevin tract on the stewardship of France, and the Lancastrian tract on the stewardship of England.

is told about the dapifership, with a view to explaining how Eudo dapifer got possession of that office after the conquest. The story runs somewhat as follows. Fitz-Osbern was in attendance on the king at the banqueting table, and serving up the dishes in his capacity of dapifer. The imperious Norman is represented as being little suited to his task, for he set before the king the flesh of a scarcely half-roasted crane. The king's gorge rose at the nauseating sight; he turned round, clenched his fist, and aimed a lusty blow at the offending dapifer. At this Eudo, who was close at hand, thought it desirable to interpose, and the blow failed to reach its intended destination. Fitz-Osbern, however, had had more than enough, he declined to continue in office and suggested that Eudo should take his place. I fear no reliance whatever can be placed on this story for the purpose of elucidating the true history of the dapifership during the eleventh century.

No doubt it may be observed that, if these stories of Fitz-Osbern's dapifership are all untrue, it is difficult to account for their existence. When however the facts are summarised, and we see that Fitz-Osbern, the son of a dapifer, acted as vicegerent both in England and Normandy, and as such exercised functions comparable in many respects to those subsequently exercised by the French dapifer but without apparently any recognised official style by which chroniclers could designate him,[1] it would be surprising not to find some later writer giving him the title in question.[2]

[1] Upon this point see Stubbs, Const. Hist., i, 374–7.

[2] Ample corroboration of this argument is afforded by an analysis of the occasions on which Master Wace makes use of the term 'seneschal':—

Vol. 1, p. 113, line 2043.
> Dan[s] Bernart li Daneis out la seneschalcie,
> Les terres e les rentes e l'altre manantie

Vol. 1, p. 150, line 3089.
> Cil ki ert seneschals, Raoul Torte aueit nun,

Vol. 2, p. 61, line 801.
> Gentil furent li cunestable
> E bien puissant e bien aidable;
> Gentil furent li senescal,
> Gentil furent li marescal,
> Gentil furent li butteillier,

Fitz-Osbern, we must conclude, was never dapifer to William ; and, this fact once proved, many an argument

> Gentil furent li despensier ;
> Li chamberlenc e li ussier
> Fuit tuit noble cheualier.

Vol. 2, p. 150, line 2985.

> A Alain, ki esteit sis huem,
> Par l'arcevesque de Ruem
> Liura sa terre en cumandise,
> Cume a senescal e justise.

Vol. 2, p. 207, line 4413.

> Le filz Osber, son seneschal,
> Guill. out non, noble uassal

Vol. 2, p. 253, line 5587.

> En la terre out un senescal,
> Heraut out nom, noble uassal,
> Por son pries e por sa bonte
> Out el regne grant poeste ;
> Li plus forz hoem fu del pais,
> Fort fu d'omes e fort d'amis,
> Engleterre out en sa baillie
> Come hoem qui a seneschaucie ;

Vol. 2, p. 264, line 5897 ; p. 265, line 5908.

> Eis uos atant le seneschal,
>
> E li seneschal dist itant :

Vol. 2, p. 333, line 7673.

> E Guill. mis seneschaus,
> Li filz Osber, un boens vassaus

Vol. 2, p. 369, line 8550.

> E li seneschals de Corcie

Vol. 2, p. 370, line 8571.

> L'ancestre Hue le Bigot,
> Qui aueit terre a Maletot
> E as Loges et a Chanon ;
> Le duc soleit en sa maison
> Seruir d'une seneschaucie,
> Mult out od lui grant compaignie.
> En fieu esteit sis seneschals,
> E mult esteit noble uassals

The citations are from Andresen. Heraut is the ill-fated Harold : the Courcies and the Bigods we shall encounter presently. I have only two observations to make : the seneschals of Master Wace and those who attest charters as such are, period for period, totally different persons ; when he gives a list of officials, he places the constable first.

c

founded on the contrary assumption falls to the ground. But even if a charter should be subsequently produced in which the earl of Hereford is so styled, such evidence would be utterly insufficient to rehabilitate those same arguments : it would merely add very incongruously one distinguished name to the existing list of undistinguished holders of an undistinguished office ; and the true inference from such a discovery would probably be that here was an early example of the curious practice of appointing eminent persons to exercise menial offices on special occasions.

During the same period the Anglo-Saxon household under Edward the Confessor appears to have reached a fair state of development, different in construction[1] and inferior in organisation to that of France, but decidedly superior to that of Normandy. At the Saxon Court the dapifer is unquestionably a mere household officer of no pre-eminence. By the year 1060 the number of dapifers in regular attendance was probably as large as three, two being assigned to the king and one to the queen.[2]

On Christmas day 1066 William the Conqueror, by virtue of election and divine unction, became king of the English : thenceforth he had two turbulent countries to rule instead of one, and these divided by a broad strip of sea which wind and waves often rendered impassable to the mightiest Nor-

[1] The chief officer of the household appears to be styled praefectus or praepositus (A.S., heah-gerefa) rather than major or magister. The gerefa was the vicecomes or sheriff. Whatever may have been the functions of the praefectus, his Anglo-Saxon style suggests a ministerial rather than a domestic officer. The advent of the Normans very naturally led to occasional confusions of style of the most absurd description. Thus the vicegerent is sometimes called praefectus, and the sheriff is sometimes called dapifer, e.g. . . . Ricardi de Belmesio, qui tunc dapifer hujus comitatus erat. (Cartulary of St. Peter's Abbey, Shrewsbury, Coll. Top. et Geneal, i, p. 24.)

[2] If discifer is merely another name for the dapifer, and such evidence as the chronicle of the Monastery of Abingdon may be so far trusted, there had been several dapifers attached to the Saxon court for at least a hundred years before the conquest. See Chron. Mon. Abingdon, Rolls Series [2], i, p. 84 (A.D. 926): Wulfhelm discifer regis a witness. Ibid., i, p. 119 (25th May, 946): De morte Edmundi regis et successione Edredi fratris sui.—Iste vero rex

man vessels. To meet the requirements of this new situation it was obvious that William must delegate the royal authority in one or other of his divided dominions to one or more supreme officers of state. The Conqueror must also have found it equally imperative to enlarge very considerably the staff of his household, and more thoroughly organise the several functions of its members. For these purposes, if a model was wanted, William had the French and English courts to copy from. But clearly neither of these could offer him much assistance in his peculiar predicament. He wanted a suitable array of household officers to have with him wherever he went, and efficient officers of state to leave behind him : consequently it was idle to look to courts where household and state functions were indiscriminately discharged by the same officials.

In short William was in a position for which there was no precedent; and the natural result was that he appointed as occasion required temporary vicegerents of England or Normandy who were not household officers, and cannot possibly be identified, either as regards style or functions, with any then existing English or French officer of state. William's consort and Roger de Montgomery in Normandy were not dapiferi : Odo and Fitz-Osbern in England were not praefecti. Their successors in office were eventually styled justiciarii, an entirely novel designation for a supreme officer of state.

Eadmundus cum in die festivitatis Augustini Anglorum doctoris, in regia villa quae Anglice Pichile Chirche nuncupatur, curiam suam cum magnatibus suis festive teneret, accidit ut coram eo pincerna suus primo conviciis deinde lethaliter in suum insurget dapiferum ; quod cum rex moleste tulisset volens dapiferum suum ex mortis eripere confinio, ictu detestabili a pincerna suo nomine Leofwine interfectus diem clausit extremum. Ibid., i, p. 206 (A.D. 956): Elfheah discifer, Elfsige discifer and Elfsige discifer are witnesses to a charter. Oliver, Monasticon Exon., p. 9 (c. A.D. 943). Oddo discifer and Helpine discifer witness an infeudation of Ethelstan.

See Kemble, Codex, iv, p. 143 (A.D. 1060): Raulfus regis dapifer and Asgarus regis dapifer attest as witnesses. Ibid., p. 159 (A.D. 1062): the following among others attest as witnesses—Esgarus regiae procurator aulae, Radulfus regis aulicus, Bundinus regis palatinus, Regenbaldus regis cancellarius, Wigodus regis pincerna, Herdingus reginae pincerna, Adzurus regis dapifer, Yfingus regis dapifer, Godwinus reginae dapifer. Cf. Engl. Hist. Rev., xix, p. 90.

With this one inevitable exception William organised his staff of great officers according to existing methods, probably more closely following in some cases the French, in others the Saxon model. We are only here concerned with the dapifership, and in this instance it is sufficiently clear that William adopted the practice common to himself as duke and his English predecessor. He appointed several dapifers, two being probably the normal number in attendance on the king, and one on the queen. The list of dapifers to the king includes the following: Stigand,[1] Eudo,[2] Hamo,[3] Ralph de Montpinçon,[4] and probably several others, such as Roger Bigod,[5] Hubert,[6] Godric,[7] Heltho,[8] and another Eudo.[9] There is no evidence that some of these were appointed to act only in Normandy, others to act only in England: any such theory is negatived by the fact that the better-known among them are found witnessing charters as dapifers both in England and Normandy.

There is no indication of any settled order of precedence among the household officers during the reign of William the Conqueror. The dapifers were certainly not the chief household officers; on the other hand it cannot be asserted positively that they ranked below any particular members of that body, although their average position in the list of witnesses

---

[1] See above.

[2] Domesday passim; Gallia Christiana, xi, app. 66; France Cal. R.O., nos. 92, 94; Cartae Antiquae A., no. 3, CC., no. 16; Ramsey Cartulary, Rolls Series; etc.

[3] Domesday passim; Wharton, Anglia Sacra, i, 338; Monasticon Anglicanum, i, 164, 237, and iv, 666; Ramsey Cartulary; etc.

[4] France Cal. R.O., no. 919; Ordericus Vitalis, ii, pp. 435–6. There is a Radulfus dapifer mentioned in Domesday.

[5] Gallia Christiana, xi, app. 228; cf. Monasticon Anglicanum, ii, 267; and Charter Roll 6 Edward III, no. 18.

[6] Gallia Christiana, xi, app. 67; Monasticon Anglicanum, vi, 1003.

[7] Domesday R.C., ii, 7b., 125, 188, etc.; Monasticon Anglicanum, iii, 87.

[8] Domesday R.C., i, 2b.; Gallia Christiana, xi, app. 71.

[9] The better-known Eudo was son of Hubert de Rie; the other Eudo was son of Turstin Haldup. See France Cal. R.O., no. 921; Ordericus Vitalis, ii, p. 108; Gallia Christiana, xi, 917, app. 224; Engl. Hist. Rev., xiv, p. 428.

is not high.[1]   A useful indication of the estimation in which
the office was held in this reign is afforded by cases of
plurality.   Some of the dapifers, notably Eudo and Hamo,
we find appointed sheriffs (*vicecomites*) of counties; and
while so acting they frequently, but not invariably, drop the
title "dapifer" and style themselves "vicecomes."[2]   This at
once precludes the idea that the dapifership was looked upon
as a superior dignity to that of sheriff.

During this period (1066–87) the dapifership shows no trace
of development in any direction.   The holder of the office is
ex officio the dish-thane and caterer, probably nothing more.

Under William Rufus the occasional vicegerent during the
king's absence develops into a permanent officer of state, but
apparently not yet distinguished by any particular official
title.   There can be no possible doubt, however, as to this
officer's identity with the justiciar of subsequent reigns.
This statesman has no connection with the household, and
his pre-eminence over all the household functionaries is unquestionable.   These facts accepted, we are not for the
present any further concerned with the development of the
justiciarship, and Stubbs's account of it may be accepted as
correct, except that when he says "the High Steward on the
other hand sees every one of his really important functions
transferred to the justiciar"[3] he is attributing vision to a
myth.   The high steward had not yet come into existence,
and the important functions acquired by the justiciar were
acquired directly and not by transference.

[1] The household officials in England do not attest in any official
capacity: their attestations simply occur here and there amongst a
number of other witnesses; nevertheless the precedence inter se of
such household officials as are found attesting charters of William I
is worth noting.   Chamberlain, Butler, Seneschal (circa 1055);
France Cal. R.O., no. 1167.   Seneschal, Chamberlain, Butler (circa
1066); Cart. de S. Trinité du Mont, no. 39.   Dapifer, Chamberlain
(circa 1066); Cart., Eccles. Baioc., i, p. 10.   Dapifer last of a long
list of other witnesses (circa 1074); ibid., i., p. 6.   Chancellor,
Butler, Dapifer; Monasticon Anglicanum, i, 144.   Butler, Dapifer
(circa 1071); France Cal. R.O., no. 91.   Chancellor, Dapifer (ante
1086); ibid., no. 92.   Dapifer, Dispenser; ibid., no. 94.   Butler,
Dapifer; Monasticon Anglicanum, vi, 1101.

[2] Gallia Christiana, xi, app. 72, 74, 228; Monasticon Anglicanum,
i, 164; Hamo in Domesday, etc.   [3] Const. Hist., i, p. 374.

The following must be included in the list of William the Second's dapifers. Eudo[1] and Hamo,[2] who apparently held office during the whole of this reign, Roger Bigod,[3] Ranulf brother of Ilger,[4] Ivo,[5] William,[6] and Ordric.[7] There is no trace of any development in the dapifership during this reign, no evidence, for instance, that with some holders it has acquired an hereditary character.

Vastly different is the history of the French dapifership during the period covered by the reigns of William and his son Rufus. From about the year 1071 onwards the French dapifer heads the list of witnesses to royal charters, but it is not until the closing years of the century that his pre-eminence appears fully established. The office was at that time in the hands of Guy of Rochefort, and during his tenure it acquired a preponderating control over well-nigh all the departments of mediæval government. The dapifer, in fact, became director-general of the palace, commander-in-chief of the army, chief justice of the kingdom, superintendent of local government officials, and so forth, a veritable viceroy in short, assisting or rather supplanting the king in the exercise of all the highest functions of sovereignty.

Twice during the opening years of the twelfth century a Rochefort was hurled from this post, the first time only to return with an increased power, which was maintained by Guy and his son up to the year 1107. Then Prince Louis challenged their supremacy with the sword ; and, amidst a blaze of civil war, the dapifership of France was wrested from the Rocheforts and bestowed on the Garlands as the price of their assistance. Little good did the change bring to Philip ;

---

[1] Monasticon Anglicanum, i, 602 ; ii, 267 ; vi, 1295. France Cal. R.O., no. 1177. Rymer, Foedera R.C., i, p. 5. Cartae Antiquae F., no. 17. See also Ramsey Cartulary, Rolls Series, etc.

[2] Monasticon Anglicanum, i, 164 ; ii, 267 ; iv, 16. Charter Roll 3 Edward III, no. 51. Charter Roll 9 Edward II, no. 37. Cartulary of St. Augustine's, Canterbury, fol. 152, etc.

[3] Monasticon Anglicanum, ii, 267 ; Charter Roll 6 Edward III, no. 18 ; Gallia Christiana, xi, app. 228 ; Wace, Roman de Rou, ed. Andresen, ii, p. 370.

[4] Ramsey Cartulary, Rolls Series [79], ii, p. 259, etc.

[5] Monasticon Anglicanum, ii, 267 ; vi, 1295.

[6] Ibid., ii, 267.   [7] Ibid., i, 601–2 ; sed quaere.

his yoke had been grievous before, the new-comers added to it, doubtless with the deliberate intention of ultimately doing what the mayors of the Merovingian palace had done before them.

In England during the reign of Henry the First a certain development of the dapifership is observable. The staff of dapifers appears to have been increased, and the list of Henry's appointees is consequently a large one. Amongst them may be noticed the following: Eudo,[1] Hamo,[2] Ranulf brother of Ilger,[3] Roger Bigod,[4] Roger's eldest son William Bigod (o.s.p. 26th of November, 1120),[5] Roger's second son Hugh Bigod,[6] Robert de la Haie,[7] William de Pirou,[8] William de Courci,[9] Robert de Courci,[10] Humphrey de Bohun,[11] Adam de Port,[12] Gerald [13] and Ralph.[14]

[1] Monasticon Anglicanum, i, 164; ii, 267; vi, 1083. France Cal. R.O., no. 167. Charter Rolls 3 Edward I, no. 2; 6 Edward III, no. 18. Chron. Abingdon, Rolls Series [2], ii, passim.

[2] Rymer, Foedera R.C., i, 8. Ramsey Cartulary, Rolls Series [79], passim. Cart. of St. Augustine's, Canterbury, fols. 151, 152. Charter Rolls 6 Edward II, no. 3; 20 Edward II, no. 6; 3 Edward I, no. 2; 6 Edward III, no. 18; France Cal. R.O., nos. 5, 167; Monasticon Anglicanum, ii, 65, etc.

[3] Vide supra.

[4] Charter Roll 6 Edward III, no. 18.

[5] Monasticon Anglicanum, v, 148: a charter of William Bigod, dapifer regis. Matthew Paris, Rolls Series, vi, p. 36.

[6] Charter Roll 3 Edward I, no. 2. Confirmation Roll 1 Henry VIII, pt. 5, no. 13; Monasticon Anglicanum, vi, 53. Engl. Hist. Rev. (1893), p. 80. Monasticon Anglicanum, v, 121. France Cal. R.O., nos. 373, 609.

[7] France Cal. R.O., nos. 373, 724: Robert was nephew of Eudo son of Turstin Haldup.

[8] Ordericus Vitalis, iv, p. 418. Confirmation Roll 1 Henry VIII, pt. 5, no. 13. Matthew Paris, vi, p. 36.

[9] France Cal. R.O., no. 1196. Chron. Abingdon, ii, pp. 52–4. Charter Roll 6 Edward III, no. 18.

[10] France Cal. R.O., no. 609.

[11] Pipe Roll 31 Henry I: Unfrid. de Bohun reddit compotum de xxij li.–xs. pro relevatione terre patris sui et de cccc m. arg. ut sit dapifer regis. Monasticon Anglicanum, vi, 1271. France Cal. R.O., nos. 373, 609.

[12] Pipe Roll 31 Henry I, p. 18. Monasticon Anglicanum, iii, 66.

[13] Exch. Miscell. K.R., no. 1, p. 13.

[14] Charter Roll. Cal., vol. ii, p. 102.

The office is clearly becoming hereditary in some families, notably in that of Bigod and Courci. Still it shows no sign of any advance in dignity, no trace of pre-eminence over other household functionaries. The precedence of the witnesses to charters still affords almost the only reliable evidence,[1] but there exists for this reign one other singular piece of direct testimony.

Shortly after the death of Henry the First the famous *Constitutio domus regis*[2] was compiled. It purports to represent the fees, food, and other allowances of the various members of the royal household under the last-mentioned king, and these allowances are set out in considerable detail. The document is a curious one, but there is no reason to doubt its genuineness and substantial accuracy. According to the rules there laid down, the dapifers in attendance, if they take their meals outside the palace, have the same allowance as the Chancellor, Dispensers, Butler, Master Chamberlain, Treasurer and Constables, namely 5 solidi a day, certain allowances of simnels and wine, one large wax candle and forty candle-ends. If they take their meals in the palace their allowances are less, but presumably they are permitted to feast sumptuously at the royal board.

This ordinance exhibits the royal household in a very primitive condition, for the great officers are mentioned together with cooks, scullions, larderers, and other back-stair menials of low degree. In truth the English royal household appears to be in much the same condition as the French household was nearly a century earlier, when the names of dapifer and queux, connétable and sommelier, chambrier and sous-voyer jostle each other on the royal charters.

It should be mentioned that the justiciar, first officer of

---

[1] France Cal. R.O., no. 5 (A.D. 1111–16)—Chancellor, Chamberlain, Butler, Dapifer. Matthew Paris vi, p. 36 (dated 1116)—Chancellor, Dapifers, Butler, Constable, Sheriff. France Cal. R.O., no. 373 (dated 1131)—Dapifers, Constable. Monasticon Anglicanum, vi, 1271 (dated 1132) — Chancellor, Constable, Dapifer, Chamberlain.

[2] Printed in the Liber Niger Scaccarii, ed. Hearne; also in the Liber Rubeus de Scaccario, Rolls Series; also Pegge, Curialia Miscellanea.

state and now occasionally referred to as "secundus a rege," does not figure at all in the *Constitutio*. This statesman never became connected with the household.

A circumstance of some importance in the development of the dapifership was the reunion in Henry's reign of Normandy with England. After the conquest of England in 1066 William undoubtedly governed Normandy during his absences in the same way as in like cases he governed England, namely by appointing one or more vicegerents[1]; and there is no evidence that the Norman vicegerents, any more than the English, had any formal style or designation. We may pass over the period of Robert's rule or misrule, which terminated suddenly and finally at the fatal fight before Tenchebray, and take up the thread of Norman affairs at the period of Henry's assumption of the dukedom. The question is who were Henry's chief officers of state in Normandy, and there can be little doubt now as to the correct answer. They were persons designated as the king's justiciars or chief justiciars, and not functionaries styled dapifers or seneschals of Normandy as has been commonly assumed.[2]

[1] They might still, perhaps, be most appropriately referred to as *tutores*. See Ordericus Vitalis, ii, p. 234:—Anno quinto regni sui Guillelmus rex Guillelmum Osberni filium misit in Normanniam, ut cum Mathilde regina tueretur provinciam. Ibid., ii, pp. 177–8 :—' Rex igitur Mathildi conjugi suae filioque suo Rodberto adolescenti principatum Neustriae commisit, et cum eis religiosos praesules et strenuos proceres ad tutandam regionem dimisit . . . Rex in illa transfretatione Rogerium de Montegomerici (quem tutorem Normanniae, dum ad bellum transmarinum proficisceretur, cum sua conjuge dimiserat) secum minavit.

[2] . . . Nemo autem justitiariorum cogat abbatem ad placitandum extra curiam suam coram aliquo, nisi coram me vel coram proprio justitiario qui super omnes alios vice mea justitiam tenet. Nullus etiam praesumat abbatiam vel homines abbatiae namnis inquietare, nisi clamore prius facto ad abbatem, et si justitiam et rectitudinem in curia sua facere noluerit, tunc proprius justitiarius meus inde requiratur. . . . (Charter of Henry I to St. Pierre sur Dive. See Gallia Christiana, xi, app. 156–7.)
. . . Nemo autem justitiariorum meorum praesumat violenter cogere abbatem ad placitandum extra curiam suam, nisi tale placitum fuerit, quod in praesentia mea debeat terminari; nullus etiam praesumat abbatiam namnis inquietare, nisi clamore facto apud abbatem, et illo justitiam et rectitudinem facere nolente, meus

The names of Henry's justiciars in Normandy are some of them easily ascertainable, but the times during which these justiciars held office is extremely doubtful. We find occasionally as many as five persons acting concurrently in this capacity; possibly in such cases one was always regarded as *capitalis* or at least as *primus inter pares*, certainly the most notable justiciar was John bishop of Lisieux. The following persons are shown by the evidence to have been at some time or other, jointly or severally, members of the supreme court of Normandy:—John bishop of Lisieux, Robert de la Haie, Hugh de Montfort, Geoffrey de Sablé and Roger Marmion; this is represented as constituting a full court[1]: John bishop

proprius justitiarius inde requiretur, qui super omnes alios vice mea justitiam tenet. . . . (Same to same; ibid., app. 157–8.)

. . . Precipio quod juste faciatis habere . . . et nisi feceritis, justicia Normannica faciat fieri. . . . (Writ· of Henry I; Cart. Eccles. Baioc., no. 37.)

Deinde justiciarii regis Ebroicensem consulatum et omnes fundos proditorum invaserunt, et dominio regis mancipaverunt. (Ordericus Vitalis, iv, p. 453.)

The evidence afforded by the structure of the ancient custumal of Normandy is very striking and well worth studying; see appendix to this chapter.

M. Ch. de Beaurepaire has noticed the fact, but failed to draw the true conclusion. "Aussi son nom était-il moins celui de sénéschal ou de dapifer que celui de justicia capitalis, ou tout simplement, de justicia." (La sénéchaussée de Normandie, Rouen. 1883.)

[1] Rogerius filius Petri de Fonteneto in castello Cadomi, in presentia totius justitiae reddidit S. Stephano terram illam et omnes decimas illas quas ipse sanctus a Godefrido suo (sic) illius et a patre suo habuerat easque eidem sancto deinceps firmiter in perpetuum tenendas concessit. . . . Testes Joannes scilicet Lexoviensis episcopus, Robertus de Haia, Hugo de Monteforti, Gaufridus de Subiis, Rogerius Marmio. (Analyse d'un ancien Cartulaire de S. Etienne de Caen, pp. 47–8.)

The above use of "justitia" is very noticeable. Compare ibid. p. 52—Joannes filius Guarini occupaverat injuste super S. Stephanum unam masuram in quarraria quam Guillelmus abbas super eum occupavit, ita quod Joannes eam dimisit S. Stephano et omnino clamavit quietam in castello Cadomi coram justicia regis qui condonavit ei emendam hujus forisfacti [etc.]. Also see below.

If numbers are any guide, here is another full court also presided over by bishop John.—Emit Eudo abbas a Willelmo de Capella

of Lisieux, Robert de la Haie and Geoffrey de Sablé[1]: John bishop of Lisieux and Roger de Mandeville; also these same two in conjunction with William fitz Ansgar[2]: John bishop of Lisieux in conjunction with Robert earl of Gloucester, Ranulf earl of Chester and Robert de la Haie[3]:

molendinum de Dottione juxta Divam 22 libris in prima emptione. De quo molendino desaisitus per Robertum Frellam dedit praefatus abbas praedicto Willelmo alias 22 libras ut ipsum molendinum contra praedictum Robertum disratiocinaret et Stephano adquietaret quae disratiocinatio et adquietacio facta fuit apud Argenteium ante regem Henricum. Testes Johannes Luxoviensis episcopus, Robertus de Curceio, Willelmus de Tancardivilla, Willelmus Penrellus, Rainaldus de Argenteio. (Analyse, p. 44.)

[1] Homines de Siccavilla recepti in societate monasterii Sancti Stephani dederunt eidem sancto (duas) partes decimarum suarum. Hujus autem ville ecclesiam quam Sanctus Stephanus antiquitus in magna pace tenuerat Hebertus quidam clericus ei modis quibuscumque poterit auferre querens abbatem et monachos inde diu fortiter vexavit. Quorum vexationi Henricus rex finem imponere decernens utriusque ante se in castello Cadomi diem constituit placitandi. Die igitur quo constituto abbas et monachi cum omnibus que eis necessaria erant ipsi regi et justicie suum placitum obtulerunt. Heberto autem ibi in audientia regis et totius justicie necnon et baronum deficiente, de prefata ecclesia ipsius regis et justicie judicio Sanctus Stephanus saisitus remansit nemini deinceps amplius inde responsurus. Testes hujus rei ipse rex Henricus et justicia, Johannes videlicet Luxoviensis episcopus, Robertus de Haia, Gaufridus de Sublis, et barones Radulfus Taisso, Rogerius Marmio, Willelmus Patricus, Robertus Carbonellus. (Pancarta of St. Stephen Caen; cited Delisle, Bibl. de l'École des Chartes, 2nd series, t. v, p. 273 n.: Inspex. Charter of Henry II, R.O. Transcripts 140 B., vol. i, p. 174; and Analyse d'un ancien Cartulaire, p. 48.)

[2] H. rex Angl. Johanni Luxoviensi episcopo et Rogero de Magnavilla et Willelmo filio Ansg. salutem. Precipio vobis ut ita faciatis habere Ricardo episcopo Baiocensi justicias episcopatus. . . . Et quicunque ei vel ministris suis inde aliquid detinuerit, vos ei plenam faciatis justiciam. Teste (etc.) (Cart. Eccles. Baioc., no. 29 (1107–33).

Henricus rex Anglorum Johanni episcopo Lexoviensi et Rogerio de Magn[avilla] salutem. Precipio vobis ut facietis tenere [etc.]. (Analyse d'un ancien Cartulaire de S. Etienne de Caen, p. 18.)

[3] Ibid., no. 34 (1121–34). This is a writ precisely similar to the last. For Ranulf's position see Ordericus Vitalis, iv, p. 453: Familias vero suas cum praecipuis ducibus per castella disposuit, eisque contra praedones tutelam provinciarum commisit. Nam Ranulfum Baiocensem constituit in Ebroarum turri, . . . ; and see ibid., p. 456.

John bishop of Lisieux and Robert de la Haie[1]: the same
and Stephen count of Mortain[2]: Robert earl of Gloucester[3]:
Richard de la Haie.[4] Probably if all available evidence was
collated, a fairly complete list of justiciars could be obtained,
but the details given above are sufficient for our present
inquiry.

With the death of Henry the First may be said to close
the initial stage in the history of the stewardship of England.
From this point the evolution of the office proceeds more
rapidly and can be much more easily traced.

Before going further, however, it is necessary to follow the
history of the French dapifership during the period we have
been considering. The rule of the Garlands did not last long.
In 1127 Louis le Gros decided on a coup d'état. Etienne de
Garland the then holder of the dapifership was expelled from
the palace, his houses in Paris were rased to the ground, his vine-
yards destroyed. The measures adopted were undoubtedly
vigorous, but it took the king five years of hard fighting to
bring his dapifer to submission ; and, as the affair terminated
by Etienne de Garland being entrusted with the chancellor-
ship, one seems justified in thinking it was rather a Pyrrhic
victory for the king. At all events France had learnt a lesson ;

[1] . . . quam ante placitum istud disracionaverat per judicium
episcopi Luxoviensis et Roberti de Haia et multorum aliorum ad
scaccarium. (Engl. Hist. Rev., xiv, p. 426, ante 1130).

[2] Writ of Henry I, inserted by Ordericus Vitalis in his chronicle,
vol. iv., pp. 435–6, addressed to John bishop of Lisieux and
Stephen count of Mortain and Robert de la Haie. For the
position of John bishop of Lisieux, see also Cartulary of S. Evroul
in the Bibl. Nat., and Ordericus Vitalis, iv, p. 303.

[3] H. rex Angl. justiciis. . . . Precipio quod juste faciatis habere
Reginaldo filio Roberti nep. decimam suam quam Radulfus de Rais
illi detinet . . . sicut illam disrationavit in curia mea, ne audiam
inde clamorem pro penuria justiciae et recti. Et nisi feceritis
justicia Normannica faciat fieri. Teste comite Gloucestriae, apud
Arch. (Cart. Eccles. Baioc., no. 37 (1121–35 : 1135?) Henricus
rex Anglie fecit inquiri de feodis . . . [ecclesie Baioc.] . . . Hoc
autem factum est coram Roberto comite Glocestrie filio regis qui ad
hoc audiendum ab ipso rege missus est apud Baiocas statim post
mortem Ricardi episcopi filii Sansonis. (R.O. Transcripts, 140 B.,
vol. i, p. 53.)

[4] Cart. Eccles. Baioc., no. 8 (A.D. 1133–5). A writ similar to no. 37.

the dapifership remained vacant for a season, and was then conferred on Ralph count of Vermandois, who, on account of his connection with the royal house and for other reasons, was not a person to be feared. Ralph held the office till his death in the year 1152.[1]

APPENDIX TO CHAPTER I

THE FIRST TRACT ON THE STEWARDSHIP OF ENGLAND

MS. Cotton Nero D. VIII, 345.[2] *Printed Monasticon Anglicanum, vol. iv, p.* 607

Rex Willielmus junior civitatem Colecestrie cum suis pertinentiis tradidit servandam Eudoni qui erat major domus regie quod nos vulgariter senescallum vel dapiferum vocamus. Fecit autem hoc, civium Colecestrensium postulatione, qui hoc ab eo impetravere grandi exenio, tam victualium quam impendiorum transmare delato. Acceperat autem Eudo hunc honorem ab Willielmo seniore, pro sui patris suaque in regalem familiam devotione. Pater vero ejus erat Hubertus de Ria, qui internuntius et sequester inter ducem Normannie et regem Anglie extiterat . . . [His visit to Edward the Confessor is described] . . . Peracto colloquio et mandatis acceptis, reversus ad ducem, detulit insignia quibus Willielmus declarabatur heres Edwardi regis Anglorum; spatam scilicet cum capulo in quo erant incluse sanctorum reliquie, cornu de auro venatorium et caput ingens cervinum. Pro hiis etiam laudatus a duce, promissionem habuit dapiferatus: sed veniente Willielmo in Angliam accipere sibi regnum, quoniam a Cinomanica regione suspicabatur tumultus, Hubertus, quia erat promptus manu et consilio bonus, missus est illic pretendere et servare pacem. Secuti sunt autem ducem quatuor filii ejus: Radulfus cui commissa est custodia castelli et comitatus Notingeham, Hubertus cui commissa est turris Norwici post

---

[1] See Luchaire, Institutions de la France, i, pp. 176 et sqq., and the authorities there cited.

[2] This is only a modern transcript. It is entitled "Marianus libro tertio de Monasterio Colecestrensi et ejus fundatore."

fugam Radulfi de Waer, et Adam qui magnas possessiones habuit in Cantia. Eudo vero adhesit servitio regali. Erat tunc temporis major domus regie Willelmus filius Osberni, habens hunc honorem ex successione procerum Bretuliensium. Is cum quodam festo die regi carnem gruis semicrude, adeo ut sanguis exprimeretur, apposuisset, et a rege objurgatus; tandem licet stomachans manum porrexisset, ictum ferientis regis subjecta manu Eudo excepit, nec sine dolore quam lachrime, licet invite, prodiderunt. Itaque iratus Willielmus cessit ab officio, rogans ut illud Eudoni contraderetur : ita tam pro sui patris merito, quam pro suo officio, quam etiam Willielmi postulatione, dapiferatus Eudoni traditur. Post hec decumbente rege Willielmo apud Cadomum, Eudo arrepta occasione ex paterna concessione Willielmum juniorem aggreditur, et ut negotio insistat hortatur. Inde in Angliam transvecti, appliciti Porcestrie, comparato sibi favore Willielmi de Ponte Arce, claves thesauri Wintonie suscipiunt, quarum idem Willielmus custos erat. Deinde Eudo impiger castellum Dobrie adiit, fideque et sacramento custodes obligat nemini nisi suo arbitrio claves munitionis tradituros. Hoc ipsum apud Pevenesen, hoc ipsum apud Hastingas facit ceteraque maritima castella, pretendens regem in Normannia moras facturum, et velle de omnibus munitionibus Anglie securitatem habere, per se scilicet qui senescallus erat. Acceleratoque negotio Wintoniam rediit, et tunc demum regem obiisse propalat. Ita dum ceteri proceres de regni successione tractant in Normannia, interim studio et opera Eudonis Willielmus junior in regem eligitur, consecratur, confirmatur in Anglia. . . .

TRÈS ANCIEN COUTUMIER[1]
(c. A.D. 1199)

(Cap. 2.) . . . Duce vel ejus capitali justicia . . .
       . . . Duci vel ejus justicie capitali . . .

(Cap. 12.) . . . Postea vero in tempore guerre, Ricardo rege possidente.

(Cap. 15.) . . . nisi manu justicie regis . . .

[1] Printed by the Société de l'Histoire de Normandie, edited by M. Tardif.

(Cap. 21.) . . . coram justicia . . .

(Cap. 25.) Nulla fiet recognitio, nisi per breve ducis, vel ejus justicie . . .

(Cap. 30.) Si aliquis dominus homini suo in curia sua rectum facere noluerit, et preceptum ducis, vel ejus justicie, habuerit rectum faciendi in curia ducis . . . per justiciam ducis . . .

(Cap. 31.) Nullus hominum audeat versus alium guerram facere, sed de injuria sibi illata duci, vel ejus justicie, conqueratur : . . .

(Cap. 33.) . . . par l'assentement le duc et a sa justice.

(Cap. 36.) . . . nec dux nec justicia sint ausi pecuniam accipere . . .

(Cap. 50.) . . . incontinenti festinare [debet] ad primam justiciam ducis quam invenire poterit.[1]

(Cap. 57.) . .. tamen multociens inter dominum Rhotomagensem archiepiscopum et Willelmum senescallum [placitum] inde audivimus.

(Cap. 59.) . . . sed quoniam justicia ducis, qualiter receptavit . . .

(Cap. 60.) . . . In tempore Willelmi senescalli statutum fuit . . . Postea vero, pluribus annis elapsis, perventum est ad aures senescalli quod . . . Penituit ergo senescallum fecisse hoc statutum.

(Cap. 61.) . . . De hoc dicit senescallus, quod . . .

(Cap. 62.) Quaestio mota fuit coram senescallo, . . . De hoc dicit senescallus . . .

(Cap. 64.) . . . Cum igitur perventum fuisset ad aures senescalli, prefato Rogero conquerente, dixit senescallus . . . Iratus vero senescallus jussit quod . . .

(Cap. 65.) . . . absque precepto justicie . . . absque precepto justicie, et ita clericus justicie . . .

The rest of the tract is clearly of somewhat later origin, and the style justiciar rarely occurs. A charter of Henry the First is, however, cited :— . . . et si inde convictus fuerit, episcopus ille, in cujus diocesi hoc factum est, emendam

---

[1] So far no mention has occurred of an official styled seneschal or dapifer.

suam, id est ix li[bras], de pecunia convicti, per manus justicie mee habebit . . . (see Tardif, p. 66).

In the year 1199, or the approximate date of the first part of the custumal, William Fitz-Ralph was seneschal of Normandy (see infra, chapter II), he succeeded the bishop of Winchester who was styled justiciar or chief justice of Normandy. This custumal, I contend, clearly indicates that a change of style had taken place, and that originally the vicegerent was styled neither dapifer nor seneschal, but simply justiciar.

CHAPTER II

THE DAPIFERS, THE HEREDITARY DAPIFERS, AND THE PROVINCIAL SENESCHALS

DURING the anarchy the English dapifership undergoes a rapid development. All offices of the household are tending to become hereditary, and the dapifership is no exception to the rule. Amongst Stephen's dapifers may be mentioned Hugh Bigod,[1] Humphrey de Bohun,[2] William Martel,[3] Robert Fitz-Richard,[4] Robert Malet,[5] and Simon de Beauchamp.[6] Amongst those of the empress may be included Humphrey de Bohun,[7] Geoffrey earl of Essex,[8] and Robert de Courci.[9] Both Bigod and Courci are by this time familiar names in connection with the household office in question, and it might fairly be said that the dapifership had already become hereditary in both families, though not so far as we know by express grant.

In two cases, however, during this period the office was

[1] Statutes of the realm, i, 3 ; also see Bémont, Chartes 8-10, and McKechnie, Magna Carta, p. 568.   [2] Ibid.

[3] Colchester Chart., i, p. 143 ; ibid., p. 168 ; Robert of Torigni, Rolls Series [82], iv, p. 144 ; Henry of Huntingdon, Rolls Series [74], p. 276 ; Hearne, Liber Niger Scacc., pp. 808-10 ; and Round, Geoffrey de Mandeville, pp. 262-3.

[4] Somerset Record Soc., vii, p. 58, and Round, Geoffrey de Mandeville, pp. 262-3.

[5] Hearne, Liber Niger Scacc., pp. 808-10 ; and Round, Geoffrey de Mandeville, pp. 262-3.   [6] Ibid.

[7] See below; also Brit. Arch. Ass. Journal, xxxi, p. 392, no. 11 ; p. 394, nos. 16 and 17.   [8] See Appendix.

[9] The charter granting the dapifership to the earl of Essex is attested by Robert de Courci as dapifer. See also Brit. Arch. Ass. Journal, xxxi, p. 391, No. 9.

expressly conferred by charter of the empress to hold as an office of inheritance. The earl of Essex was granted the dapifership of Eudo to hold hereditably as being his of right:—"Et do ei totam terram que fuit Eudonis dapiferi in Normannia et dapiferatum ipsius. Et haec reddo ei ut rectum suum, ut habeat et teneat hereditabiliter. . . ."[1]

Also Humphrey de Bohun was granted his dapifership in England and Normandy—dapiferatum suum in Anglia et Normannia—to hold to himself and his heirs as a serjeanty appertaining to certain lands.[1] The last-mentioned grant is made by the empress and her son jointly, but otherwise calls for no particular comment: there seems not the smallest reason to doubt that the intention was to exact the active duties attaching to the post of dapifer from Humphrey de Bohun and his heirs, as the service to be rendered for the possession of particular properties.

It is almost inconceivable that anything of the kind was intended in the case of so great a magnate as Geoffrey de Mandeville earl of Essex. There are other possible suppositions: that conferring the dapifership on the earl was a mere diplomatic fiction added by way of compliment to Eudo's memory; or that it was intended to confer an honorary dapifership on the earl, involving services similar to those exacted from the hereditary dapifers in the reign of Henry the Second. More probably the donee in this instance wanted and asked for the office because he had special ideas on the subject, ideas born of an acquaintance with the French and Angevin dapifers. We shall have to recur to this problem later on. Geoffrey's connection with the dapifership is an isolated incident: the arch-traitor and sinner died outlawed and excommunicate, his possessions and dignities perished with him.

The government of Normandy under Stephen was still entrusted to one or more justiciars. William de Roumare and Roger Fitz-Nigel vicomte du Contentin acted in this capacity.[2] But before long the duchy transferred its allegiance to Anjou; and, with the arrival of Geoffrey Plantagenet on

[1] See Appendix.

[2] Neustriae vero justiciarios Guillelmum de Rolmara et Rogerium vicecomitem aliosque nonnullos constituerat . . . (Ordericus Vitalis, vol. v, p. 91).

the scene, Angevin principles began to exert an immediate influence upon existing Norman institutions. In Anjou the chief officer of state was the dapifer[1]; and, besides this individual, there were other subordinate dapifers placed in control of towns or districts.[2] These circumstances very naturally produced certain results in Normandy. No ostensible change was made by count Geoffrey in the form of government. He appointed ministers who were still styled justiciars, but the very names of these justiciars indicate a new development. Eight persons at least can be mentioned as having held such office during Geoffrey's administration : they are the count of Mellent,[3] Reginald de St. Valery,[4] William de Vernon,[5] Robert de Neufbourg,[6] Robert de Courcy,[7]

[1] See Glasson, Institutions de la France, iv, p. 722 ; Beautemps-Beaupré, Recherches sur les Juridictions d'Anjou et du Maine ; and the same writer's Anciennes Coutumes d'Anjou et du Maine.

[2] See Beautemps-Beaupré, op. cit. Hugh de Clers, a name famous in the literature of the French dapifership, was for some time dapifer of La Flèche ; as such he attests charters of Henry II, see France Cal. R.O., p. 467.

[3] [G.] duci Normannie et comiti Andegavie Guillelmus (sic) comes Mellenti, uti caro domino, salutem. Sciatis quod precepto vestro fecimus recognosci per sacramentum, etc. . . . (Cart. Eccl. Baioc., no. 89.)

[4] Almost identical report from Robertus (sic) de Sancto Walerico. (Ibid., no. 90.)

Dux Normannorum . . . Raginaldo de Sancto Walerico, Roberto de Novo Burgo et omnibus justiciariis suis de Normannia salutem. Volo et concedo . . . Si quis vero ei inde resistere voluerit, precipio vobis quod firmam justiciam inde faciatis. Testibus Hugone archiepiscopo, Ricardo cancellario, Reginaldo de Sancto Walerico, Roberto de Novo Burgo. Apud Rhotomagum. (Ibid., no. 17.)

Dux Normannorum . . . Raginaldo de Sancto Walerico, Willelmo de Vernone, Roberto de Novo Burgo et omnibus justiciis et proceribus suis Normannie salutem. Sciatis quod ego concedo . . . sicut recognitum fuit et juratum in choro Baiocensis ecclesie quod . . . astantibus ibidem per preceptum nostrum Roberto de Curceio dapifero nostro, Ricardo de Haia et aliis quam pluribus . . . [Same witnesses as no. 17]. (Ibid., no. 19.)

[5] Vide supra.

[6] . . . recognita est . . . coram Roberto de Novoburgo et coram Roberto de Curceio justiciis meis juramento. . . . (Ibid., no. 39.) For two reports of these same justiciars see ibid., nos. 43 and 44.

[7] Vide supra.

Richard de la Haie,[1] Enjuger de Bohun (?)[2] and G. de Sablé.[3] Of these five are known to have been dapifers, or at all events are occasionally so styled, and a sixth (Enjuger de Bohun) was closely connected with the dapifership.[4] This cannot have been mere coincidence. But, notwithstanding the practice here indicated of combining the two offices, there is not the slightest indication of an intention to fuse them.

The chief justiciars were probably the count of Mellent and Reginald de St. Valery: the subordinate justiciars appear to have had special districts or bailiwicks assigned to them.[5] Geoffrey's administration did not last long; his failing health unfitted him for the task of governing Normandy, and he ceded the province to his son Henry Fitz-Empress.

As duke of Normandy Henry appears to have had a large establishment of household officers, including a chancellor,

[1] Dux Normannorum. . . . Enjugero de Buhun salutem. Mando tibi et precipio quod dimittas episcopo Baiocensi in pace feudum militis quod Robertus Marinus de ipso tenebat Wireville et feudum suum quod Willielmus de Moiun de ipso apud Mummartin tenere debet quod huc usque injuste occupasti, quod nisi feceris precipio quod justicia mea Ricarde de Haia secundum assisiam meam recognosci faciat predictum feodum episcopi quomodo. . . . Et te, Engengere, precor ne de aliquo injuste fatiges episcopum quia ego non paterer quod de jure suo aliquid injuste perderet. Tibi etiam, Ricarde de Haia, precipio quod per totam bailiam tuam secundum assisiam meam recognosci facias feudum episcopi Baiocensis et ipsum in pace tenere, sicut recognitum fuerit secundum assisiam meam. Teste. . . . (Ibid., no. 24.)

[2] The only authority I can give is Stapleton, Rot. Scacc. Norm., vol. i, p. xxxiv. After citing the last-mentioned extract he says :— " Richard de Haia (Haie-du-Puits) was dapifer Normanniae under Geoffrey and with him were associated as justices this Engelger de Bohun, Robert de Neufbourg and Robert de Courcy." The statement about Richard de Haie is incorrect, and the writ in question is no authority for the assertion, being merely addressed to Bohun as a deforciant. See, however, Cart. Eccles. Baioc., i, p. 47.

[3] Dux Normannorum . . . G. de Sableio et Roberto de Curceio justiciis suis salutem : Mando vobis . . . (Cart. Eccl. Baioc., no. 25).

[4] For Robert de Courcy vide p. 35, note 4: for the rest I can only cite charters of Henry, q.v. infra. We have seen, however, that Robert de la Haie and Humphrey de Bohun were dapifers to Henry I.

[5] e.g. Richard de la Haie, supra.

constable, numerous dapifers,[1] and chamberlains. The dapifers usually in attendance were probably Humphrey de Bohun and Manasser Bisset. The justiciar, and chief officer of state, during this administration was Arnulf bishop of Lisieux.[2] Robert de Neufbourg,[3] Richard de la Haie,[4] and William Fitz-John[5] appear as subordinate justiciars, and there were probably others. Joslen of Tours was at this time dapifer and, as such, chief officer of state in Anjou.[6]

Geoffrey Plantagenet died on the 7th September, 1151, and in 1153 Henry landed in England with the avowed object of wresting the crown from Stephen. He did not defeat Stephen, he never even fought him in a pitched battle, but he secured by the treaty of Wallingford the right to succeed to the throne.

During this period Henry visited Bristol, and there gave charters to Robert Beaumont earl of Leicester and Robert his son, conceding to the earl, his son and heirs certain lands in England and Normandy, together with the dapifership of both countries (dapiferatum Anglie et Normannie).[7] I have only succeeded in finding a transcript of the duke's charter to earl Robert[8]: the original charter to his son is extant, and has been a source of quite unnecessary perplexity to genealogists. On the occasion in question grants to other persons

---

[1] The following were dapifers to duke Henry: Humphrey de Bohun, Robert de Courci, Manasser Biset (Rymer, Foedera R.C., i, p. 16); Richard de la Haie (Cart. Eccl. Baioc., no. 7, and France Cal. R.O., nos. 518, 519); Manasser Biset and Hubert (Monasticon Anglicanum, vol. vi, 366). Indications of the following precedence, viz. constable, dapifer, chamberlain, are becoming numerous. See, for example, Berkeley Castle Charters, ed. Jeayes, nos. 1 and 2.

[2] Henricus dux Normannie . . . Arnulfo Lexoviensi episcopo et Ricardo de Haia dapifero, et omnibus aliis justiciis suis salutem. Sciatis quod Gaufridus de Clintonia recognovit coram me . . . (Cart. Eccl. Baioc., no. 7; France Cal. R.O., no. 1441; and Mem. Soc. Antiq. Norm., 1st series, vol. 8, p. 437 [circa Oct., 1154]).

[3] France Cal. R.O., no. 127.

[4] Ibid., no. 523.   [5] Ibid., no. 516.

[6] Ibid., no. 1160 (circa A.D. 1152). Joslen of Tours attests as dapifer comitis Andegavorum, his attestation is followed by those of the constable and chamberlain of Anjou.   [7] See Appendix.

[8] The existence of this transcript appears to be unknown to genealogists.

were similarly supplemented by a grant to their heirs apparent, with the obvious idea that two charters would serve better than one to ensure the loyalty of the particular family. The Beaumont charters, technically ultra vires the duke, were undoubtedly confirmed by Henry after his coronation, although in this instance the only evidence that can be produced is a copy of Henry's confirmation to the earl.[1] In only a few cases (for example, the grants to Robert Fitz-Harding and his son, which are preserved among the muniments at Berkeley castle) are all four instruments of the series known to be still in existence.[2]

It is not, however, by reason of its form only that this grant of an hereditary dapifership to the Beaumonts calls for special comment. We have already had to chronicle and comment upon a grant in fee of the same office to Geoffrey earl of Essex.[3] Each earl was at the time he received his grant one of the most powerful magnates in England, and their allegiance was therefore a matter of especial moment to the Angevin cause. Moreover, just as earl Geoffrey was claiming to stand in the shoes of Eudo dapifer, earl Robert in right of his wife Amicia was claiming to represent Fitz-Osbern earl of Hereford.[4] Thus the two cases present singular and significant analogies. The explanation of both grants is probably the same; both certainly require explaining.

The truth, in my opinion, is this: that both grantees particularly asked for an hereditary dapifership because, having regard to the constitutions of France and Anjou, they both thought this office well worth cultivating. I also think it is

---

[1] See Appendix.   [2] See Berkeley Castle, Charters, ed. Jeayes.
[3] Vide supra, p. 34.
[4] See the observations of Mr. Round on this point in Geoffrey de Mandeville, p. 153: the charter of Stephen granting the earldom of Hereford to Robert earl of Leicester with special reference to the possessions of Fitz-Osbern is preserved among the royal charters of the duchy of Lancaster. Practically speaking, Amicia was the heiress of William Fitz-Osbern :—[Itta (or Amicia)] nupsit Roberto comiti Legrecestrie, filio Roberti comitis Mellenti. Unde factum est ut Lire, Glot, Britolium et plurimam partem terrae quam Willelmus filius Osberni avus (sic) uxoris suae habuerat in Normannia, post mortem Willelmi de Britolio avunculi uxoris suae, idem comes haberet. (Continuator of William of Jumièges, Duchesne, p. 300.)

highly probable that both earls attempted to further their designs by recourse to deliberate forgery of title.

The story of how Eudo acquired his office from Fitz-Osbern has been already told : that story may without hesitation be described as an obvious fabrication. We are not justified in so characterising the allusions to Fitz-Osbern's dapifership in Ordericus Vitalis and Henry of Huntingdon ; not, however, because they are any the less untrue, but because, as I have pointed out, these allusions are susceptible of an innocent explanation. Still it does not follow that the innocent explanation is the right one. It is certainly rather a remarkable coincidence that the one story should emanate from Essex, the other from St. Evroul where the Beaumonts were chief patrons. The suggestion certainly covers the facts. How this tampering with history (if any) was accomplished we need not consider ; many ready methods suggest themselves. Historical forgeries were not uncommon in those days, and the explanation I have suggested is *à priori* only too probable.

About the same time Henry Fitz-Empress was himself laying claim to the hereditary dapifership of France ; and his example was followed by Philip count of Flanders.[1] That the claim of the former was supported by at least one most barefaced forgery, no modern historian pretends to dispute.[2] Both claimants were in a measure successful.[3] What these hoped for from the dapifership of France it is not easy to understand ; but, if we admit there were designs on the English office such as I have indicated, the method and purpose in the latter instance seem obvious enough. The object in view must have been to show that the justiciarship, or chief office of state, was a post appertaining to the hereditary dapifer : hence the advantage of deducing a title from Fitz-Osbern, who was in effect one of the first justiciars of England, and at all events the son of a famous dapifer, a combination of offices possessed by no other family in England. Stephen died on the 25th of October, 1154, and

[1] For an account of these claims see Appendix.
[2] I refer to the first part of the famous treatise De Senescalcia Franciae, stated by the author of that tract to be the work of Foulques le Jérosolimitain. [3] See below, and Appendix.

on the 19th of December Henry was hallowed king at Westminster.

Although Humphrey de Bohun continued for some time after the accession of Henry the Second to act as a royal dapifer, it does not appear that the hereditary grant of the empress was ever confirmed by her son, in spite of the fact that he had joined with her in making the grant. On the other hand, the Bigod claim to the dapifership was expressly recognised by Henry in his charter creating Hugh Bigod earl of Norfolk:—"Et dapiferatum suum ei ita libere et quiete concedo habendum sicut Rogerus pater suus melius vel liberius habuit tempore regis Henrici avi mei. . . ."[1] It will be noticed that the earl of Leicester's office is described as *dapiferatum Anglie et Normannie*, the earl of Norfolk's office as simply *dapiferatum suum*, but this difference of language does not import any difference whatever in the offices conferred.

It does not appear that Henry the Second expressly granted an hereditary dapifership to any other person, and indeed the earls of Leicester and Norfolk were almost certainly at the very outset placed on a totally different footing to the other dapifers. In the case of the ordinary dapifers, the office still shows a tendency in one or two isolated instances to descend from father to son ; but, in opposition to this tendency, the practice of appointing dapifers to act during pleasure comes into vogue, and after Henry the Second's time no trace of any other practice is observable.

The following persons, amongst others, acted from time to time as dapifers to Henry : Hugh Bardolf,[2] Manasser Biset,[3]

---

[1] See Appendix. An hereditary dapifership was about the same time established in Scotland. See Appendix.

[2] Monasticon Anglicanum, v, 565, 662 ; vi, 2, 1097 ; Cart. Antiq. P., DD.; Wombridge Chart., no. 423 ; Madox, Formulare, no. ccclvii; France Cal. R.O., no. 949 ; Ramsey Chart., Rolls Series, i, 123 ; see Stapleton Rot. Scacc. Norm., i, p. 116 ; Charter Roll Cal., vol. ii, p. 96, etc.

[3] Rymer, Foedera R.C., i, 42 ; Monasticon Anglicanum, iv, 111, 539; v, 101, 479; vi, 116, 639, 1296; Cart. Antiq. K., no. 4, D., no. 42, S., no. 23, T., P., X, L, Q, V, DD, EE, FF, OO; France Cal. R.O., nos. 15, 129, 480, 525, 685, 748, 882, 1067; etc.

Henry Biset,[1] Humphrey de Bohun,[2] Robert de Courci(?),[3] William de Courci,[4] William Fitz-Aldelm,[5] William Fitz-John,[6] Gilbert Fitz-Reinfrid,[7] Henry de Hereford,[8] Gilbert Malet,[9] William Malet,[10] Hugh de Morewich,[11] Robert de Neufbourg(?),[12] William Ruffus,[13] Alured de St. Martin,[14] Robert de Watteville.[15] The general position of these officers with regard to the other members of the household is now becoming more clearly defined : so far, that is to say, as the chancellor, constables, dapifers, chamberlains, and butlers are

[1] Cart. Antiq. S.S., no. 12.

[2] Rymer, Foedera, R.C., p. 41 ; Monasticon Anglicanum, v., 385 ; vi, 157, 1296 ; Cart. Antiq., Q., V. ; etc.

[3] Probably Robert de Courci never acted as dapifer after Henry's accession: he was killed at Counsylth in 1157 when William Courci appears to have succeeded to his dapifership.

[4] Hist. Abingdon, ii, 223 ; Monasticon Anglicanum, v, 363 ; vi, 818 ; Cart. Antiq. M., P., no. 10 ; Rymer, Foedera R.C., i, 30 ; France Cal. R.O., nos. 24, 173, 302, 482, 530, 551, 685, 754, 867 ; Benedict of Peterborough, Rolls Series 49, i, p. 99 ; Antiq. of Shropshire, viii, 153-4 ; William de Courci was also sometime justiciar of Normandy, but apparently never the chief justiciar: see post, p. 49.

[5] Monasticon Anglicanum, ii, 228 ; iii, 314 ; iv, 325 ; v, 73, 363 ; vi, 374 ; Rymer, Foedera, R.C., i, 30, 36 ; Godstow Chartulary fol. 165 ; Madox, Formulare, p. 48 ; Memorials of Fountains Abbey, p. 8 ; France Cal. R.O., nos. 419, 756, 757 ; see Dict. Nat. Biog., xix, p. 103.

[6] Cart. Eccl. Baioc., no. 46.

[7] Monasticon Anglicanum, vi, 920 ; see Hist. de G. le Maréchal, iii, 119.

[8] Gloucester Chartulary, ii, 106.

[9] Rymer, Foedera R.C., i, 30 ; Monasticon Anglicanum, ii, 228 ; iv, 85 ; Cart. Antiq. F., T., P. ; France Cal. R.O., nos. 551, 754, 867.

[10] Madox, Formulare, no. lxxviii ; Duchy of Lanc., Grant to Eustace Cade ; Cart. Antiq. T. dors. ; Camden Soc., Chron. de Brakelond, p. 120 ; Monasticon Anglicanum, vi, 644 ; France Cal. R.O., nos. 344, 861, 1163, 1216.

[11] Monasticon Anglicanum, v, 564, 662 ; vi, 2, 612 ; Madox, Formulare, no. ccclvii ; Cart. Antiq. P., DD. ; Wombridge Chartulary, no. 423 ; France Cal. R.O., nos. 191, 554 ; see also Stapleton, Rot. Scacc. Norm., i, p. 116 ; Charter Roll Cal., vol. ii, p. 96.

[12] See below.

[13] Rymer, Foedera R.C., i, 40.

[14] Rymer, Foedera R.C., i, 30 ; Benedict of Peterborough, Rolls Series, 49, i, p. 99.   [15] Gloucester Chartulary, ii, 106.

concerned, these persons normally take precedence in the order given.[1]

The position of the earls of Leicester and Norfolk calls for special attention. *They never attest charters as dapifers.* Legally speaking they appear to have been grand serjeants, liable, apart from custom, to be summoned at any time to act as dapifers. In practice they were only summoned, if at all, for high festivals. For example at the end of the year 1186, when the king kept Christmas in state at Guildford, we find both the hereditary dapifers and William earl of Arundel, hereditary butler, called upon to discharge the duties of their respective offices.[2] The principle was a simple one. The regular members of Henry's household were in almost every case men of secondary rank, the best that could be desired or obtained for ordinary occasions. For special state func-

---

[1] The order is by no means invariable : the dapifer frequently attests after the chamberlain : e.g. Cart. Antiq. K., no. 4 ; Monasticon Anglicanum, v, 479 ; vi, 639, Charter Roll Cal., vol. ii, p. 132. Still on the whole I incline to the opinion that the dapifership was at this time regarded as the more important of the two.

The above list of dapifers might possibly be somewhat amplified. The name of Oger dapifer, for example, figures very frequently on the Pipe Rolls ; but so far as I am aware the only charters he attests as dapifer are those of Richard de Luci the justiciar, and therefore Oger's real position remains conjectural. In the Pipe Roll for 1174–5 (Pipe Roll Soc., vol. xxii) Oger dapifer is mentioned, pp. 113, 115 ; a Thomas dapifer occurs p. 69 ; and the names of William fitz Aldelm dapifer and Gilbert Malet dapifer also appear ; see pp. 190, 191 and 213 ; and 210. See also Eyton's Itinerary of Henry II passim.

[2] Anno MCLXXXVII, qui est annus tricesimus tertius regni Henrici regis Secundi, idem rex Henricus filius Matildis imperatricis, tenuit sollemne festum die Nativitatis Dominicae, quae quinta feria evenit, in Anglia apud Gedefordam. Cui interfuit Johannes filius ejus et Johannes Cumyn archiepiscopus Divelinensis, Gaufridus Eliensis episcopus, David frater regis Scotiae comes de Huntedona, Robertus comes de Leycestria, Willelmus comes de Arundel, Rogerus Bigot comes. In illo vero festo predicti comites de Leicestria et de Harundel et Rogerus Bigot servierunt ad mensam regis de servitio quod ad illos pertinebat in coronationibus et sollemnibus festis regum Angliae. (Benedict of Peterborough, Rolls Series 49, ii, p. 3.) These honorary services appear, not infrequently even at this time, to have been the subject of disputes. See Walter Map, De Nugis Curialium (Camden Soc.), pp. 231–5.

tions something more was wanted to give pomp and lustre to the king's court, and accordingly the great magnates of the realm were ordered for the nonce to take the places of the ordinary household officers.

We have here no new custom due to the ingenuity of Henry the Second, but a custom already in vogue on the continent.[1] Honorary services, once inaugurated, became extraordinarily popular. The great charm of the English coronation ceremonies lay in the fact that, for this one occasion, the chief families in the realm were summoned to attend in splendid apparel and perform various domestic and other services for their king: carry his regalia, fetch him water to wash, bring him a towel, offer him wine, distribute his alms, defy his enemies and so forth. It would perhaps be untrue to say that Henry the Second was the first to introduce this fashion into England, but he undoubtedly assisted in establishing it.

The general principle was obviously incapable of being systematically elaborated in this country. Honorary dapifers, chamberlains, and butlers were all very well; but an hereditary high constable, for example, with duties confined to state pageants was at that time an impossible official.

It is important to consider who were the chief officers of state in England and Normandy during the reign of Henry the Second.

The king remained in England after his coronation until January, 1155-6. During most of this period Arnulf bishop of Lisieux and Robert de Neufbourg were acting as justiciars of Normandy: both ministers, however, appear to have been

[1] e.g. Flanders 25th December, 1171.—Iste quidem novus comes sollempnitatem natalis Domini primo in Valencenis cum Marghareta uxore sua in gaudio celebravit, in qua curia fuerunt milites 500, ubi Egidius sepedictus de sancto Oberto, vir magne probitatis magnique nominis ubicumque terrarum, dapes tanquam summus Hanoniensis dapifer amministravit, et cum eo milites et servientes qui in officio illo jus hereditarium habebant. Arnulphus vero vir nobilis de Landast, qui mortuo Egidio de Aunoit summo Hanonie pincerna, uxorem illius duxerat, vinum tanquam summus pincerna propinavit, et cum eo milites et servientes qui in officio illo jus hereditarium habebant. (Gislebert de Mons, Chronicon Hanoniense (ed. 1904), p. 107; see also ibid., p. 116 (25th December, 1174).)

present at Henry's coronation, and were possibly absent from Normandy for some weeks.[1] During this interval it is probable that the empress mother was entrusted with the administration of the duchy.[2] Meanwhile Robert earl of Leicester was appointed chief justiciar of England[3]; and, on Henry's return to France, this earl and Richard de Luci were charged with the government of the kingdom. The king's choice proved

[1] Robert of Torigni, Rolls Series 82, iv, app. p. 333, no. 9.—Eodem anno abbas Robertus dirationavit sedèm unius molendini in Constantino pago in villa que dicitur Sancte Marie Ecclesia, per duellum contra Ricardum episcopum Constanciensem. . . . Et hoc fuit factum in assisa apud Karentun, in presentia Arnulfi episcopi Lexoviensis et Roberti de Novo Burgo, qui tunc erant magistri justicie totius Normannie. Testes Robertus de Novo Burgo, Willelmus de Vernone, Willelmus de Verdun, Johannes de Gabreio, Robertus prefectus de Fulchereville, Ricardus de Halvilla. (The date appears from the context to be 1155.)

Ibid. no. 10.—Eodem anno cum Robertus abbas vellet tenere unum duellum de honore Sancti Paterni apud Montem Sancti Michaelis, et Guillelmus de Sancto Johanne prohiberet ne bellum de honore Sancti Paterni duceretur extra ipsum honorem, idem abbas in assisa apud Danfrontem ostendit hoc verbum Arnulfo episcopo Lexoviensi et Roberto de Novo Burgo qui erant justicie regis, et consideratione curie regis adjudicatum est quod. . . . Testes Robertus de Novo Burgo, Hasculfus de Folligneio, Gislebertus de Campellis et alii multi. (See France Cal. R.O., no. 734.)

Cart. Eccles. Baioc., no. 10.—Writ of facias habere: Henricus rex. . . . Willelmo Patricii salutem. Precipio. . . . Et nisi feceris precipio quod justicia mea faciat ei habere. . . . Teste Ernulfo episcopo Lexoviensi, apud Baiocas.

[2] See France Cal. R.O., no. 131. Writ of Henry II addressed to his justices and bailiffs of Normandy and John count of Eu and earl Walter Giffard directing seizin of certain lands to be given to the church of Fécamp—and unless this is done his lady and mother the empress will cause it to be done.

[3] See Cart. Antiq. W., where the earl of Leicester is referred to as "tunc temporis capitali justicia mea totius Anglie." The Dialogus de Scaccario furnishes valuable evidence of his powers and functions. For a biography of this earl with a list of authorities see Dict. of Nat. Biog., s.v. Beaumont.

This combination of the offices of hereditary dapifer and chief justiciar is particularly worthy of note. The same combination occurs in Scotland. See Monasticon Anglicanum, vi, 1154: Charter of Alexander dated 3rd February, anno regni 17 apud Clacmannan. Tested by "Waltero filio Alani seneschallo et justiciario Scotiae."

an excellent one in every respect. Both men were extremely able, unswervingly loyal, and during their joint lives no change was made either in the justiciarship or in the occasional regency of England. For the time being, therefore, we may confine our attention to affairs in Normandy.

At the end of the year 1155 the bishop of Lisieux was despatched on a mission to Rome, and during the greater part of the next four years Robert de Neufbourg probably acted as chief justiciar.[1] This Robert was the son of Henry earl of Warwick and first cousin to the same Robert earl of Leicester whom I have ventured to accuse of an attempt to

---

[1] Cart. Eccles. Baioc., no. 27; and France Cal. R.O., no. 1443 (October 1156); writ of facias recognosci:—Henricus rex . . . Willelmo filio Johannis salutem. Precipio tibi quod facias recognosci . . . Et nisi feceris, Robertus de Novo Burgo faciat. Teste Toma cancellario apud Lemovicas.

Cart. Eccles. Baioc., no. 35 (April 1157): writ of faciatis habere: —Henricus rex . . . Willelmo filio Johannis . . . Precipio vobis quod faciatis habere Philippo episcopo Baiocensi . . . sicut recognitum fuit precepto meo coram Roberto de Novo Burgo et Willielmo filio Johannis et Godardo de Vallibus et Petro de Lacon et Etardo Pulcino per sacramenta . . . et nisi feceritis justicia mea faciat fieri. Teste Roberto de Novo Burgo apud Barbifluctum in transfretatione regis.

Compare the above with the following English writs:—

Rievaulx Chartulary, Surtees Soc., 83, p. 148; writ of Henry II addressed to the sheriff and officers of Yorkshire:— . . . Precipio quod . . . faciatis recognosci . . . et nisi feceritis comes Legrecestrie faciat.

Regist. Malmesbury, Rolls Series 72, p. 335:—Regina Angliae . . . militibus qui tenent de feodo ecclesiae de Malmesburia salutem. Precipio vobis quod faciatis abbati de Malmesburia servicium de feodis vestris integre et plenarie sicut recognitum fuit ante regem et ante justiciarios apud Wygorniam. Teste Roberto comite Leicestrie apud Wygorniam.

As to the official style of Robert de Neufbourg see further the following:—

Cart. Eccles. Baioc., no. 36: writ of facias recognosci:—Henricus rex . . . Willelmo filio Johannis salutem. Precipio tibi quod . . . et facias recognosci quomodo . . . quod nisi feceris justicia mea Normannica faciat fieri. Teste Roberto de Novoburgo apud Mirebellum in obsidione.

Cart. Eccles. Baioc., no. 12:—Henricus rex . . . Etardo Pulet salutem. Precipio quod episcopus Baiocensis teneat in pace . . .

exploit the dapifership in England. The case against the earl is, in my opinion, a strong one. The case against his cousin of making a similar attempt in Normandy is incontestable. The following are some of the styles assumed by Robert de Neufbourg : *dapifer et justicia totius Normannie ; dapifer ;* and *dapifer Normannie ;* and, on one occasion at least, he appears on a copy of the record of a judgment of assize with a quasi-regal precedence by attesting in front of three bishops.[1]

No doubt count Geoffrey had done something to pave the way for a conversion of the Norman justiciar into the French

quod nisi feceris justicia mea Normannica faciat fieri. Teste Roberto de Novoburgo apud Mirebellum in obsidione.

See also Cart. Eccles. Baioc., no. 32 ; and France Cal. R.O., no. 1445 : writ of faciatis tenere ; but correct "coram nobis et coram Roberto de Curceio" by substituting "vobis" for "nobis"; and compare with nos. 43 and 44. See finally France Cal. R.O., no. 454 : writ of Henry II confirming the decision of Robert de Neufbourg in the king's court, circa 1156–9.

Note the writ referred to by Eyton at p. 25 of his Itinerary of Henry II, from which it might be inferred that William de Vernon was chief justiciar of Normandy in 1157. This is due to an error in D'Anisy's Normandy Transcripts, ii, p. 180 : compare France Cal. R.O., no. 882.

[1] Robert of Torigni, Rolls Series 82, iv app., p. 339, no. 35 :— Eodem anno in assisa apud Cadomum . . . diffinitum in plenaria curia regis, utpote in assisa ubi erant barones iiij comitatuum Baiocasini, Constantini, Oximini, Abricatini, quod. . . . Hoc judicium approbaverunt et confirmaverunt Robertus de Novo Burgo dapifer et justicia totius Normannie, Philippus episcopus Baiocensis, Arnulfus Lexoviensis, Ricardus Constanciensis, Willelmus Talevat comes Ponthivi, Ingergerius de Bohun . . . et alii multi. And see France Cal. R.O., no. 824 (circa 1157).

Compare Robert of Torigni, app. p. 337, where Robert de Neufbourg is made to attest before the bishop of Bayeux.

Ibid., no. 34 :—Eodem anno rex Anglorum Henricus apud Cadomum pro pace monachorum fecit recognoscere per jusjurandum legalium hominum utrum . . . an. . . . Et sicut juratum fuerat preceptum est. Testes Robertus de Novo Burgo dapifer, Willelmus filius Johannis, Robertus filius Bernardi prepositus Cadomi . . . And see France Cal. R.O., no. 734.

The abbey of Mont S. Michel is a suspicious source : so too is the abbey of Préaux. See Cartulaire de Préaux, fol. 39, no. 78, where Robert de Neufbourg describes himself as dapifer of Normandy in connection with a quit-claim in the king's court :—In

and Angevin dapifer, and it would seem that Henry himself was not unwilling to foster some connection between these offices whenever it suited his plans. But there is no evidence that the king approved or in any way recognised the styles assumed by Robert de Neufbourg.[1]

During some portion of the period under discussion this man must have been more or less superseded in the government of Normandy, for we find Philip bishop of Bayeux presiding over the king's court.[2] In 1159 Robert de Neuf-

curia regis cum ego Robertus de Novo Burgo dapifer essem Normannie . . . et quoniam hoc ante meam presentiam in regis curia et ante regis barones factum est sigilli mei munimento confirmo (France Cal. R.O., no. 341; Brunner, Die Entstehung der Schwurgerichte, s. 148). But there are other instances. See France Cal. R.O., no. 824 (Savigny), Charter of Henry II (circa 1157)—original not preserved. Testibus [inter alios] Roberto de Novo Burgo tunc dapifero Normannie. Also ibid., no 1254 (Vendômes et Chartres), an entry in which Robert is styled "seneschal of Normandy." Also Analyse d'un ancien Cartulaire de l'Abbaye de St. Etienne de Caen, p. 18—Carta Rogeri (sic) De Novo-Burgo dapiferi totius Normanniae data in plena assisia apud Abrincas in qua recognitum fuit quod homines abbati Cadomi de manerio de Vei quitanciam suam habent de omnibus rebus venditis et emptis in Abrincis excepto die mercati. Ibid., p. 42. Carta Roberti de Novo-Burgo dapiferi totius Normannie . . . circa litem inter Willelmum abbatem et Anselmum de Caburgo. . . . This is a seventeenth-century analysis or transcript; the original cartulary is lost. See also a Confirmation Charter of Richard I, R.O. Transcripts, 140 B, vol. i, p. 183: Concedimus et confirmavimus quod portus Dive proprius est Sancti Stephani (totive) cum omnibus consuetudinibus venientium et recedentium per mare quod per juramentum recognitum fuit coram Roberto de Novo-Burgo senescallo Normannie. . . .

[1] The words "tunc dapifero Normannie" in the Savigny chartulary, cited above, must be regarded as unofficial embellishment. I have found no royal charter or writ in which Robert de Neufbourg is referred to as dapifer Normannie, nor any original royal charter attested by him as such. The existing evidence points almost conclusively to two things: (1) that the official style of the king's chief minister in Normandy was still "justiciar"; (2) indications of an unauthorised or at least unofficial change of style, in the case of Robert de Neufbourg, from justiciar to dapifer.

[2] France Cal. R.O., no. 132: Charter of Henry II confirming to Henry abbot of Fécamp and the abbey the port of Fécamp, to which they proved their right in the king's court before Philip bishop of Bayeux and Robert de Neufbourg at Rouen. Such

bourg's health failed, he became a monk at Bec, and prepared with all haste for heaven by distributing his then useless possessions among the poor and the churches. He probably died the same year. The chroniclers, in relating his death, describe him in various ways : one calls him *dapifer et justicia totius Normannie*[1] ; by another he is named *totius Normannie vicecomes aut vicedominus, id est dapifer.*[2]

Rotroc bishop of Evreux succeeded his brother Robert as chief justiciar, Reginald de St. Valery being associated with him.[3] The bishop remained in office till 1164, and probably

evidence, however, by itself is inconclusive. (Compare Register of Osmund, Rolls Series 78, i, p. 207 : Charter of Henry II (A.D. 1155–62) :—Henricus rex . . . Sciatis me concessisse . . . ecclesiam de Godelming cum terris et decimis ejusdem ecclesiae adjacentibus, videlicet . . . et illas quas tenuit in Godelming, Tywesleia et Hendena quas Rogerus archidiaconus Wiltesir. dirationavit apud Norhamton in curia mea coram Roberto episcopo Lincolniensi et Roberto comite Leycestrie justiciario meo ecclesiae de Godelming adjacere. . . . Testibus Roberto Exoniensi episcopo et Thoma cancellario, Roberto comite Leycestrie, apud Gloucestriam.) See also Analyse d'un ancien Cartulaire de S. Étienne de Caen, p. 43 :— Carta Henrici regis Angliae et ducis Normanniae et Aquitaniae et comitis Andegavensis qua concedit concordiam quae facta fuit coram se inter abbatem de Cadomo et Jordanum de Veeris et Heldefeudem uxorem ejus de feodis Roberti de Villeio et Radulfi de Hotot. Testes Philippus Bajocensis, Robertus de Novo Burgo, Jordanus Taisso, Engelgerius de Bohon, Ricardus de Haia, Godardus de Vallibus. Also R.O. Transcripts, 140 B., vol. iii, p. 24, Writ of teneat in pace : . . . et nisi feceritis justicia mea fecerit. Teste Philippo episcopo Baioc. Apud Argentonium.

[1] Robert of Torigni, Rolls Series 82, iv, p. 203 : Mense Julio Robertus de Novoburgo, dapifer et justicia totius Normanniae, adversa valetudine tactus, gibbum cameli deposuit, videlicet in-numeras divitias ecclesiis et monasteriis et pauperibus dividens. . . .

[2] See three extracts printed in the Genealogist N.S., vol. x, p. 13. Compare Neustria Pia, p. 479:—Robertus de Novoburgo vicecomes totius Normannie.

[3] Mem. de la Soc. des Antiquaires de Normandie, xv, p. 197b. Assise at Bayeux circa 1160 :—Rotroldus episcopus Ebroicensis et R. de Sancto Walerico omnibus ballivis Henrici regis totius Normannie salutem. Sciatis quod recognitum fuit ante nos in assisia apud Baiocas quod terra quam tenuit Ivo Boz in Crisetot et terra quam tenuit Ricardus filius Hervei in Crisetot . . . sunt de feodo Sancti Stephani de Cadomo. See ibid., vol. 7, p. 275 : Rotroc bishop of Evreux and R. de St. Valery give judgment in the assises

continued to act for a short period after his translation to Rouen.[1] He apparently was succeeded by Henry bishop of Bayeux and William Fitz-John (dapifer),[2] these in their turn being succeeded by William de St. John as chief justiciar

of Henry II at Bayeux. France Cal. R.O., no. 641 : Charter of Henry II referring to judgment before Rotroc bishop of Evreux then his justice for all Normandy. Robert of Torigni, Rolls Series 82, iv, p. 217 :—Rotrocus episcopus Ebroicensis et Rainaldus de Sancto Walerio fecerunt in Normannia recognoscere jussu regis per episcopatus legales redditus et consuetudines ad regem et ad barones pertinentes (circa 1163). Bouquet H.F., vol xvi, p. 66, prints two official letters of Reginald de St. Valery to Louis of France. See also ibid., p. 111; and Duchesne H.F. Script, iv, pp. 633, 635 : letters of Hugh bishop of Soissons to Louis :— . . . colloquium habuimus cum episcopo Ebroicense et aliis Normannis, et cepimus cum eis diem in quo debemus obsides recredere [etc.] :— . . . Convenimus ad diem nominatum episcopus Belvacensis et comes Bellimontis, . . . ex parte vestra. Ex altera parte fuerunt episcopus Ebroicensis, R. de Sancto Walerico, . . . et multi alii. Proposuimus eis responsum vestrum, sicut vestri barones dederant vobis in consilio. . . . France Cal. R.O., no. 491 : writ of Henry II dated at Worcester and addressed to Rotroc bishop of Evreux and Reginald de St. Valery. See also ibid., nos. 133, 134, and 340. Cart. Eccles. Baioc. no. 9 : writ of Henry II :—Henricus rex . . . Ectardo Pochin salutem. Precipio tibi quod facias habere et tenere Philippo Baiocensi episcopo banlevam suam de Cambremer . . . et nisi feceris justicia mea faciat. Teste Rotrodo Ebroicensi episcopo. Charter of Henry II in the Pancarta of St. Stephen's Caen (cited by Delisle, Bibl. de l'Ecole des Chartes, Ser. ii, t. 5, p. 267, n. 4) :—Testibus Rothrodo Ebroicensi episcopo justicia Normannie. . . . However, in a Confirmation Charter of Richard I, R.O. Transcripts 140 B., vol. i, p. 183, we find :—Recognitum fuit coram Rothrodo Ebroicensi episcopo dapifero Normannie.

[1] France Cal. R.O., no. 910 : writ of Henry II addressed to the bishop of Coutances . . . the archbishop of Rouen is to see to it if the bishop does not, Teste Arnulfo episcopo Lexoviensi apud Sanctum Laudum.

[2] Cart. Eccles. Baioc., no. 46 : report of a judicial recognition :— Notum sit omnibus tam presentibus quam futuris quod precepto Henrici regis Anglie recognita fuit consuetudo de Isigneio et de Nuilleio coram Henrico episcopo Baiocensi et Guillelmo filio Johannis dapifero per juramentum. . . .

R.O. Transcripts 140 B., vol. iii, p. 22 :—. . . Sciatis quod ego Radulfus de Hamard coram Henrico Baioc. episcopo et Willelmo filio Radulfi [?] et coram baronibus sedentibus ad scaccarium concessi. . . .

E

and William de Courci (dapifer),[1] the latter remaining in office until his death in 1176. Robert de Neufbourg's attempt to convert the governor of Normandy into a dapifer seems for the time being to have died with him : I can find no further trace of any such movement. William de Courci, although he was a quasi-hereditary dapifer, never so far as I am aware styled himself dapifer Normannie : it appears to have been well recognised in his case that the two posts he held of justiciar in Normandy and dapifer regis had no connection whatever with each other.[2]

We must now turn for a moment to England. In 1168 Robert earl of Leicester,[3] hereditary dapifer of England and

[1] Robert of Torigni, Rolls Series 82, iv, p. 253 (December 25th, 1171): Et ut appareat multitudo eorum qui interfuerunt cum Willelmus de Sancto Johanne Normanniae procurator et Willelmus filius Hamonis senescallus Brittanniae qui. . . .

Procurator became the popular term for the vicegerent of Normandy. Compare Giles, Arnulfi Lexoviensis Epistolae, no. 110 :— Ad dominum papam Alexandrum ; and no. 117 :—Ad Petrum cardinalem. "Major procurator regis" is the phrase used in these letters by the bishop of Lisieux when referring to William fitz Ralph (q.v. infra).

France Cal. R.O., no. 456 : this refers to the "king's justiciars William de St. John and William de Courcy." See also ibid., no. 406 : Charter of Henry II granting exemption from shire courts, hundred courts, aids, scutages, and carrying services, as enjoyed in the time of Henry I, also prompt justice for infringement—Testibus Willelmo de Sancto Johanne et Willelmo de Curci dapifero apud Argentonum. Hoveden, Rolls Series 51, ii, p. 100 (A.D. 1176): Eodem anno obiit Willelmus de Curci justiciarius Normanniae. . . . Benedict of Peterborough, Rolls Series 49, i, p. 125: Willelmus de Courci justicia Normanniae obiit eodem anno. The Norman Pipe Roll of A.D. 1180 refers three times to events—*de tempore Willelmi de Curceio.*

William de St. John was probably in office at least as early as July 1166 when he heads the list of witnesses to a Final Concord between Rualend de Genest and the abbot of Mont S. Michel. (See R.O. Transcripts 140 B., vol. ii, p. 290.)

[2] Because, however, William de Courci was a dapifer it has been commonly assumed that he and not St. John was the chief justiciar : the assumption is erroneous. See also France Cal. R.O., no. 1218 (A.D. 1172–4), and note order of attestation ; and (contra) Benedict of Peterborough, Rolls Series [49], i, 124, cited infra p. 52, n. 3.

[3] The statement in Knighton that this earl—de consensu Amiciae

Normandy and chief justiciar of England, died, and his son
Robert Blanchemains succeeded to the earldom. If Henry
had ever entertained the idea of making the earls of Leicester,
in the capacity of dapifers, hereditary chief officers of state,
the advent of Robert the Third must have speedily convinced
him of his folly. The grandfather and father had been men
of exceptional ability and integrity. Robert the First, earl of
Mellent, was a capable warrior, and withal a great statesman,
"cold and crafty, the Achitophel of his time"; men appealed
to him, it has been said, as to the oracle of God. His son
Robert the Second, earl of Leicester, was in every way his
equal if not his superior, and we have the contemporary
evidence of the Exchequer *Dialogus* to testify to his enormous
power and influence in England. "He must be a great
person," wrote Fitz-Nigel, "who is interested with the concerns
of the whole kingdom as also with the king's heart, for it is
written — 'where your treasure is there shall your heart
be also.'"[1]

Robert the Third differed vastly from his aforesaid predecessors alike in character and capacity. He had little skill
as a soldier, no statecraft whatever. He was witless enough
to turn traitor and bring over a body of Flemings to try
conclusions with the English levies. Had Henry not entertained a deep affection for the justiciar, his son would quite
possibly have forfeited his life. As it was he received lenient
enough treatment: Henry kept him in gentle durance until
he had learnt discretion, and then pardoned him. As for the
justiciarship, it was entrusted to the sole care of Richard de
Luci, who, with the help of Humphrey de Bohun (son of the
dapifer) the king's principal constable, achieved very creditable
success in the administration and pacification of the country.

uxoris suae sumpsit in abbatia ista de Pratis Leycestriae habitum
nostrae religionis vivens juste et sancte quindecim annis et amplius
—is a myth invented most probably on behalf of John of Gaunt
in the latter half of the fourteenth century.

[1] The Dialogus de scaccario was completed in 1178 or 1179. See
Madox, Hist. of the Exchequer, Appendix; Stubbs, Select Charters
(1895), 168–248; E. F. Henderson, Select Historical Documents,
20–134 (a translation).

Indeed it was these two who, "in the twinkle of an eye," routed Robert Blanchemains' Flemings.[1]

From this point the English justiciarship has scarcely any bearing on the subject under consideration: it was never again held by an hereditary dapifer. The case of Normandy is different.

On the death of Courci in 1176 William de Malpalud may have been appointed to succeed him: he was certainly acting as a justiciar at about this time.[2] In the autumn, however, of 1176 a new administration was formed in Normandy with Richard bishop of Winchester, chief justiciar, and Simon de Tournebu, Robert Marmion, William de Glanville, and others as assistant justices.[3] This can hardly have been intended to be more than a temporary arrangement, and the bishop was, in fact, recalled in 1178.[4] He was the last justiciar

---

[1] Benedict of Peterborough, Rolls Series 49, i, p. 62: . . . percusserunt aciem in qua comes Leicestriae erat. Et in momento, in ictu oculi, victus est ille comes et captus, et uxor sua. . . .

We are told by Jordan Fantosme how the countess took part in the battle.

v. 1006.　Ore oiez, seignurs, baruns, de Deu la grant venjance
　　　　　Qu'il fist descendre sur Flamens e sur la gent de France.
　　　　　Li cuens de Leircestre fud de grand puissance;
　　　　　Mes trop fud de curage jofne e d'enfance
　　　　　Quant il par Engleterre volt aler en oiance,
　　　　　Fesant sa roberie senz aver desturbance,
　　　　　E fait armer sa femme, porter escu e lance:
　　　　　La sue grant folie prendrad dure neissance.

[2] France Cal. R.O., no. 34.
[3] See the Pipe Roll of 1176; and Eyton, Itinerary, p. 206.

France Cal. R.O., no. 517 (A.D. 1176):—Actum est autem hoc publice in aula regis in castello Cadomi coram judicibus regis ad scaccarium sedentibus anno ab incarnatione Domini 1176. Super hoc autem testes sunt dominus Ricardus Wintoniensis episcopus qui tunc tempore erat capitalis justicia. . . .

Ibid., no. 1446: Notification by Richard bishop of Winchester, Simon de Tournebu, Robert Marmion, and William de Glanville that while they were in assise at Caen, etc.

Benedict of Peterborough, Rolls Series 49, i, p. 124: Et misit in Normanniam Ricardum Wintoniensem episcopum, et constituit eum justitiam Normanniae loco Willelmi de Curci, et fecit saisiri in manu sua omnia castella comitum et baronum suorum Normanniae.

[4] His return is referred to in the Pipe Roll of that year.

of Normandy. From this period, until the loss of the province by John, Normandy was placed under the control of an officer styling himself *senescallus Normannie*, with an organised staff of justices and other officials under him. William Fitz-Ralph was the first seneschal of Normandy: he remained in office during the rest of Henry's reign, and during the whole of the reign of Richard.[1]

Uniformity was probably the object aimed at in effecting this change in the style of the chief officer of Normandy. Nearly all French provinces in which England was then, or afterwards, interested, had by this time a seneschal as chief officer of state—the synonymous term dapifer was rapidly becoming obsolete. Stephen of Tours was seneschal of Anjou[2]: Ralph de Fougères was seneschal of Brittany[3]: Fulk of Mastac and William of Mengoti were seneschals of Poitou[4]: Gascony had its seneschal[5]: in fact, throughout France the chief dignitary of the vassal courts was almost invariably the seneschal. Flanders had a seneschal[6]: the chief officer of Champagne was styled dapifer till 1157, then seneschal[7]: Burgundy had its seneschal—under Hugh the

---

[1] It is, invariably I believe, as senescallus Normannie that Fitz-Ralph attests charters. In the Pipe Roll of 1180, however, the chief officer is always styled justiciar; except that, when Fitz-Ralph is mentioned by name, he is styled *William Fitz-Ralph Dap[ifer]*. The later rolls adopt the new diplomatic style.

William Fitz-Ralph died the 9th of June, 1200 (Bouquet, H.F., xxiii, p. 463): he was succeeded by Warin de Glapion, who held office till May–June, 1202: he was succeeded by Ralph Tesson, who held office till July–August, 1203: he finally was succeeded by William Crassus. Philip Augustus after some hesitation suppressed the office; it was revived by Henry V, and retained after the final reconquest of Normandy. It was again suppressed in 1499, but Louis de Breszé and even Diane de Poitiers retained the title.

[2] France Cal. R.O., nos. 1068, 1074, 1075, 1078, etc.

[3] France Cal. R.O., no. 838; cf. Monasticon Anglicanum, vol. v, p. 306; Glasson Instit., iv, p. 688, etc.

[4] France Cal. R.O., nos. 1245, 1286, 1288.

[5] Ibid., p. 450.

[6] Hellin de Wavrin: see A. du Chesne, Hist. gén. de la maison de Béthune.

[7] Glasson Instit., iv, p. 543; D'Arbois de Jubainville, Hist. des comtes de Champagne.

Second, two seneschals equal in rank.[1] The singularity of Normandy in being so long governed by a justiciar was the result of the conquest of England. Had William the Bastard rested content with the dukedom of a French province it can hardly be doubted that his dapifers would have developed like the rest from menial servants into officers of state, and there would have been seneschals of Normandy long before the time of Fitz-Ralph: these too would have been the official descendants of Stigand and Gerald instead of having, in fact, a totally different parentage.

William Fitz-Ralph, as regards precedence, appears to have ranked below the king's constables, William de Humez included, throughout the reign of Henry; but after Richard's accession William de Humez assumed the style of constable of Normandy and the seneschal then took precedence.[2]

The history of the French dapifership during this period may be very briefly told. Shortly after the death of the count de Vermandois in 1152, Thibaud the Fifth, count of Blois, was appointed to succeed him ; and, except for a short vacancy caused by this count's treasonable relations with Henry of England, the dapifership was held by Thibaud till his death in 1191. During this period the popular, and to some extent the official, term for the office is seneschal instead of dapifer : it is only in the attestation of charters that the latter style is always preserved.

So much for the French official dapifership; but, as in England under Henry the Second, so in France under Louis the Seventh, an honorary dapifer or seneschal makes his appearance. In 1169, at a state banquet in Paris, the young Henry of England waited on the French king at table as seneschal of France.[3] At the coronation of Philip Augustus, the count of Blois was superseded for the occasion by Philip

---

[1] See Plancher, Hist. de Bourgogne, ii, 253–83; Seignobos, Le régime féodale en Bourgogne, c. vii.

[2] The order in which Humez and Fitz-Ralph attest royal charters, although there is no absolute uniformity, sufficiently justifies the statement in the text. For such charters see Eyton, Itinerary of Henry II, and France Cal. R.O. passim.

[3] Robert of Torigni, Rolls Series [82], iv, p. 240; Hist. Comitum Andegav., printed Chron. des Comtes d'Anjou, p. 346.

count of Flanders : it was Philip who carried the sword at
the sacring of the king, and Philip who presented the dishes
at the great coronation feast.[1] The parallelism with England
is very striking. The Plantagenets claimed by ancient hereditary right. So did the Beaumonts. In neither case had
their immediate ancestors occupied the ordinary post of
dapifer, and they themselves were not claiming to do so.
Philip of Flanders, on the contrary, claimed in right of his
wife to succeed the count of Vermandois as hereditary dapifer
of France, but count Raoul was in every respect an ordinary
dapifer. The earl of Norfolk, except that he claimed by
direct descent, was in precisely the same position. Even the
subsequent disputes between the earls of Leicester and Norfolk[2] have their exact counterpart in the rival claims of the
countesses of Champagne and Flanders at the coronations of
Louis VIII and Louis IX.[3] If the Angevin claim had any
real foundation in antiquity, the idea at the root of it was
probably the same as that which prompted Henry to make
his own magnates officers of the household for special occasions. At one time the dapifership in France had been as
insignificant a post as it was then in England, and the rank
of the holders no doubt corresponded. Even the Garlands
can only have held a secondary rank amongst the nobility of
France. In the front rank were the great provincial feudatories, such as the counts and dukes of Flanders, Aquitaine,
Burgundy, Normandy, Toulouse, and Champagne, who subsequently formed the six lay peers of the realm : to these
had to be allotted the chief parts in the religious pantomime
at Reims.

The seneschal of France, as a coronation official, survived
the accession of Louis the Ninth. Ultimately the constable
of France took his place.[4]

---

[1] See Appendix.   [2] See post, chap. iii.   [3] See Appendix.

[4] Postmodum rex a solo archiepiscopo gladio cum vagina accingi-
tur. Quo accincto statim idem gladius de vagina ab archiepiscopo
extrahitur, vagina super altare reposita, et datur ei ab archiepiscopo
in manibus : quem debet rex humiliter afferre ad altare, et statim
resumere de manu episcopi : et incontinenti dare senescallo
Franciae ad portandum ante se et in ecclesia usque ad finem missae,
et post missam cum ad palatium vadit. (Coronation Order temp.

APPENDIX TO CHAPTER II

CARTA M. IMPERATRICIS FACTA COM. GAUFREDO ESSEXIAE DE PLURIBUS TERRIS ET LIBERTATIBUS
(A.D. 1142)

M. Imperatrix Henrici regis filia et Anglorum domina archiepiscopis episcopis abbatibus comitibus baronibus justi-ciariis vicecomitibus ministris et omnibus fidelibus suis Francis et Anglis totius Anglie et Normannie salutem. Sciatis me redidisse et concessisse comiti Gaufredo Essexe omnia tene-menta sua sicut Gaufredus avus suus aut Willelmus pater suus aut ipsemet postea unquam melius vel liberius tenuerit aliquo tempore in feodo et hereditate sibi et heredibus suis ad tenendum de me et de heredibus meis videlicet in terris et turribus in castellis et bailliis et nominatim Turrim Lundonie cum castello quod subtus est ad firmandum et efforciandum ad voluntatem suam et vicecomitatum Lundonie et Middlesex. per ccc libras sicut Gaufredus avus ejus tenuit et vicecomi-tatum Essex. per ccc libras sicut idem Gaufredus avus ejus tenuit et vicecomitatum de Heortfordscira per lx libras sicut avus ejus tenuit et preter hoc do et concedo eidem Gaufredo quod habeat hereditabiliter justiciā Lund[onie] et Middelsex. et Essex. et de Hertfordscira ita quod nulla alia justicia placitet in hiis supradictis vicecomitatibus nisi per eis et concedo illi ut habeat illas c libratas terre quas dedi illi et servicium illorum xx militum sicut illud ei dedi et per aliam cartam meam confirmavi et illas cc libratas terre quas rex Stephanus et Matildis regina ei dederunt et illas c libratas terre de terris eschaetis quas idem rex et regina ei dederunt et servicium militum quod ei dederunt sicut habet inde cartas illorum. Et do ei totam terram que fuit Eudonis dapiferi in Normannia et dapiferatum ipsius et hec reddo ei ut rectum

Louis VIII.) See Godefroy, Le Cérémonial Francais, t. i, pp. 13, 18. For a similar coronation order temp. Louis IX, see ibid., p. 28. And see Varin, Archives Administratives de Reims, i, pt. 2, p. 529 n. ; ii, pt. 1, p. 571 n.; MS. Cotton. Tib. B., viii, Sacre des Rois de France. See finally the appendix to this chapter.

suum ut habeat et teneat hereditabiliter ita ne ponatur inde in placitum versus aliquem. Et si dominus meus comes Andegavie et ego voluerimus, comes Gaufredus accipiet pro dominiis et terris quas habet eschaetis et pro servicio militum quod habet totam terram que fuit Eudonis dapiferi in Anglia sicut tenuit ea die qua fuit et vivus et mortuus quia hoc est rectum suum . . . .

. . . .

Apud Oxineford. Sub magno sigillo dicte Matildis Imperatricis.

(Original missing; printed in full from a collation of several existing transcripts by Round, Geoffrey de Mandeville, pp. 166–72.)

GRANT TO HUMPHREY DE BOHUN
(A.D. 1144)

Duchy of Lancaster Royal Charters, No. 19. (Original, no seal)

M. Imperatrix Henrici regis filia et Anglorum domina Et Henricus filius comitis Andegavorum archiepiscopis episcopis abbatibus comitibus baronibus justiciis vice-comitibus ministris et omnibus fidelibus suis Francis et Anglis totius Anglie salutem. Sciatis nos redidisse et concessisse Unfrido de Buhun totam terram suam unde fuit tenens die qua rex Henricus fuit vivus et mortuus et dapiferatum suum in Anglia et Normannia sine hoc quod non ponatur inde in placitum sicut melius tenuit tempore Henrici regis. Et preter hoc dedimus ei et concessimus pro servicio suo Melchesiam cum appendiciis suis et burgum Malmesberie sine fortitudine facienda ibidem et Boczam que fuit Gaufr. de ***** et Stokes que fuit Everard. de Calna. Haec omnia supradicta dedimus ei et concessimus tenenda in foeudo et hereditate sibi et heredibus suis de nobis et de heredibus nostris. Et pro hiis supradictis devenit homo noster ligius contra omnes homines. Quare volumus et firmiter precipimus quod bene et in pace et libere et quiete et honorifice et plenarie teneat in forestis et fugaciis in bosco et plano in pratis et pasturis in aquis et molendinis in viis et semitis in foris et feriis infra burgum et extra in civitate et extra et in omnibus locis cum

soca et saca et toll et team et infangenethef et cum omnibus
aliis consuetudinibus et libertatibus et quietudinibus. Testibus
Bernardo episcopo de sancto DD. et Gisleberto abbate Gloecestrie et Roberto comite Gloecestrie et Rogero comite Herefordie et Radulpho Pagan[ello] et Gos[celino] de Doia et
Willelmo de Bellocampo et Willelmo de Doura conestabulario
et Unfrido filio Odonis, Roberto de Dunestanvilla et Willelmo
Paganello et Hugone filio Ricardi **** Apud [Devizes].

(Printed Round, Ancient Charters, Pipe Roll Soc., x, p. 45.
Also Birch, Brit. Arch. Journ., xxxi, p. 398.)

GRANT TO ROBERT EARL OF LEICESTER
(A.D. 1153)

Transcipt. Antiq.;[1] *MS. Cotton. Vesp. Dx, fol.* 132

H. dux Normannie et Aquitanie et comes Andegavie omnibus archiepiscopis episcopis comitibus baronibus vicecomitibus
et fidelibus et amicis suis Normannie et Anglie salutem.
Sciatis me redidisse et concessisse in feodo et hereditate
Roberto comiti Leycestrie et heredibus suis totam terram
quam tenuit Robertus comes Mellent pater suus in Anglia
sicut ipse Robertus comes de Mellent eam melius et liberius
tenuit die qua fuit vivus et mortuus exceptis terris R. comitis
de Mellent de Sturmenstre et cum pertinentiis. Concessi
eciam ei omnia illa que Henricus rex avus meus dedit illi.
Insuper reddidi et concessi ei Britolium cum toto honore et
cum omnibus pertinentiis sicut predictus (sic) Willelmus de
Britolio melius et liberius tenuit die qua fuit vivus et mortuus.
Preterea dedi et concessi in feodo et hereditate Pasci cum
toto honore et totam terram quam Willelmus de Pasci tenuit
in Anglia et in Normannia in feodo de me et de quococumque
(sic) eam tenuisset et dapiferatum Anglie et Normannie.
Quare volo et precipio quod predictus Robertus et heredes
sui omnia ista predicta de me et heredibus meis teneant ita
bene et libere et quiete et honorifice cum omnibus libertatibus

---

[1] Late thirteenth century. This is one of a large collection of
charters, transcribed probably for the purposes of an action between
Edmund of Lancaster and the crown.

et consuetudinibus liberis in terris in aquis in bosco in plano
in pratis in pascuis in viis in semitis et in omnibus aliis rebus
sicuti antecessores sui de antecessoribus meis unquam melius
tenuerunt. Concedo eciam et confirmo concambium quod
idem Robertus comes Leycestrie et Rogerus comes Warrwici
fecerunt de terris et hominibus suis. Hiis testibus etc.—
sine dat.

GRANT TO ROBERT, SON OF ROBERT EARL OF LEICESTER

(A.D. 1153)

*Original (sealed), Trésor des Chartes, Conches et Breteuil,
No. 1 carton J. 219*

Henricus dux Normannie et comes Andegavie omnibus
archiepiscopis episcopis comitibus baronibus vicecomitibus et
omnibus fidelibus et amicis suis Normannie et Anglie salutem.
Sciatis me redidisse et concessisse in feudo et hereditate
Rodberto filio comitis Legrecestrie et heredibus suis totam
terram Rodberti comitis patris sui de Anglia sicut comes
Rodbertus de Mellend avus suus die qua fuit vivus et mortuus
eam melius et liberius tenuit. Insuper reddidi ei et concessi
Britolium cum toto honore et cum omnibus pertinentiis sicut
Willelmus de Britolio melius et liberius et quietius tenuit die
qua fuit vivus et mortuus. Preterea dedi ei et concessi in
feudo et hereditate Pasci cum toto honore et totam terram
quam Willelmus de Pasci in Anglia et in Normannia tenuit
in feudo de me et de quocumque eam tenuisset et dapiferatum
Anglie et Normannie. Quare volo et precipio quod predictus
Rodbertus et heredes sui omnia ista predicta de me et de
heredibus meis teneant ita bene et libere et quiete et honorifice cum omnibus libertatibus et consuetudinibus in terris in
aquis in bosco in plano in pratis in pascuis in viis in semitis
et in omnibus aliis rebus sicuti antecessores sui de antecessoribus meis unquam melius tenuerunt. Testibus: Willelmo
comite Gloecestrie, R. comite Cornubie, R. de Humez, Philippo
de Columbers, R. de Dunstanvilla, Willelmo filio Johannis,
R. de Govitio, Waltero de Herefort, Guarino filio Geroldi,

Henrico suo fratre, Maneser Biseth dapifero, Willelmo filio Hamundi et Willelmo Patricio, Willelmo de Crevecor, Willelmo de Angervilla, Galfrido de Briencurd, Rogero de Gratepance, Rodberto de Watervilla, Raginaldo de Bordineio, Gaufrido abbate. Apud Bristou.[1]

(Printed Delisle, Cartulaire Normand, no. 7; see also Calendar R.O. France, no. 464; Genealogist, vol. x, p. 12.)

CONFIRMATION TO ROBERT EARL OF LEICESTER
(A.D. 1154–68)
Duchy of Lancaster, Miscellanea 1/35. *Ancient Calendar of Charters*

De Breteuil, Pascy et la seneschalcie Dengleterre. Item Carta regis Henrici Secundi per quam reddidit et concessit in feodo etc. Rodberto comiti Leyrecestrie et heredibus suis totam terram quam Rodbertus comes de Mellent pater suus tenuit in Anglia extra terra G. comitis de Mellent de Sturmenistre et eis pertinentiis. Concessit eciam illi Roberto omnia illa que Henricus avus suus dedit illi. Insuper reddidit et concessit Britollium cum toto honore et pertinentiis sicut Willelmus de Britolio melius et liberius tenuit. Preterea dedit ei et concessit in feudo et hereditate Pascy cum toto honore et totam terram quam Willelmus de Pascy tenuit in Anglia et in Normannia de rege et de quocumque alio eam tenuisset et dapiferatum Anglie et Normannie etc. Concedens eciam et confirmans concambium quod idem rex comes Leyrecestrie et Rogerus comes Warewicie fecerunt de terra et hominibus suis etc.

GRANT TO HUGH BIGOD
(A.D. 1154–5)
Carta Antiqua S. 13

Henricus rex Anglie et dux Normannie et Aquitanie et comes Andegavie archiepiscopis episcopis abbatibus comitibus justitiariis baronibus vicecomitibus ministris et omnibus fidelibus suis Francis et Anglis tocius Anglie et Normannie salutem.

[1] Indorsed: H. dux Normannie et comes Andegavie reddit et concedit filio comitis Legrecestrie certas terras hic contentas.

Sciatis me fecisse Hugonem Bigot comitem de Norfolcia scilicet de tercio denario de Nordwico et de Norfolcia et volo et precipio quod ipse et heredes sui ita libere et quiete et honorifice teneant de me et de meis heredibus sicut aliquis comes Anglie melius vel liberius comitatum suum tenet. Et dapiferatum suum ei ita libere et quiete concedo habendum sicut Rogerus pater suus melius vel liberius habuit tempore regis Henrici avi mei. Et sciatis me recognovisse rectum suum de iiij maneriis scilicet de Evesham et de Walesham et de Alvergate et de Aclay cum Berkariis et hec iiij maneria predicta cum omnibus pertinenciis suis ei reddidi dedi et concessi sibi et heredibus suis de me et de heredibus meis tenenda cum socha et sacha et thol et theam et ynfangenetheof et dom et som et cum omnibus libertatibus et liberis consuetudinibus et quietanciis predictis maneriis pertinentibus. [Et] concedo ei omnia tenementa sua de cujuscumque feodo sint que racionabiliter adquisivit. Quare volo et firmiter precipio quod ipse et heredes sui habeant et teneant omnia predicta in pace et libere et quiete et honorifice cum omnibus libertatibus et liberis consuetudinibus et quietanciis que ad predicta tenementa pertinent in bosco et plano in pratis et pascuis in aquis et molendinis in vivariis et piscariis et mariscis in viis et semitis in warennis et fugacionibus infra burgum et extra et in omnibus rebus et in omnibus locis. Testibus Teobaldo Cant. archiepiscopo, Henrico Winton. episcopo, Philippo Baioc. episcopo, Arnulfo Lexov. episcopo, Nigello Elyens. episcopo, Toma cancellario, Reginaldo comite Cornubie, Henrico de Essex. constabulario, Ricardo de Humez constabulario, Ricardo de Luci, Warino filio Geroldi camerario, Manesero Biset dapifero, Willelmo filio Hamonis, Roberto de Dunstanvilla, Joscelino de Baillol. Apud Norh.

(Printed Rymer, Foedera, R.C., i, p. 42.)

CARTA HEREDITARII OFFICII SENESCALLATUS SCOTIE ET DE DIVERSIS TERRIS
(24TH JUNE, A.D. 1158)

Malcolmus rex Scottorum episcopis abbatibus comitibus baronibus justiciis vicecomitibus prepositis ministris cunctisque aliis probis hominibus clericis et laicis Francis et Anglis

Scotis et Gallowidensibus totius terre sue tam presentibus quam futuris salutem. Notum sit vobis omnibus quod priusquam arma suscepi concessi et hac mea carta confirmavi Waltero filio Alani dapifero meo et heredibus suis de feodo et hereditate donationem quam rex David avus meus ei dedit scilicet Renfrew et Passeleth et Polloc et Talahec et Kerkert et le Drep et le Mutrene et Englisham et Lochinauche et Innerwick cum omnibus istarum terrarum pertinentiis. Et similiter ei hereditarie dedi et hac mea carta confirmavi senescalliam meam tenendam sibi et heredibus suis de me et heredibus meis liberaliter in feodo et hereditate ita bene et ita plenarie sicut rex David ei Senescalliam suam melius et plenarius dedit et concessit et sicut ipse eam melius et plenarius ab eo tenuit. Preterea ego ipse eidem Waltero in feodo et hereditate dedi et hac eadem carta confirmavi pro servitio quod ipse regi David et mihi ipsi fecit Prethe quantum rex David in manu sua tenuit et Inchenan et Steintum et Halestonesden et Legardsuode et Birchinsyde. Et preterea in unoquoque burgo meo et in unaquaque dominica gista mea per totam terram meam unum plenarium toftum ad hospitia sibi in eo facienda et cum unoquoque tofto viginti acras terre. Quare volo et precipio ut idem Walterus et heredes ejus in feodo et hereditate teneant de me et heredibus meis in capite omnia prenominata tam illa que ipse habet ex donatione regis David quam illa que ex mea habet donatione cum omnibus eorum pertinentiis et rectitudinibus et per rectas divisas omnium prenominatarum terrarum libere et quiete honorifice et in pace cum sacca et socca cum tol et them et infangtheefe in villis in scallingis in campis in pratis in pascuis in moris in aquis in molendinis in piscariis in forestis in bosco et plano in viis in semitis sicut aliquis ex baronibus meis liberius et quietius feudum suum de me tenet : Faciendo mihi et heredibus meis de illo feudo servitium quinque militum. Testibus Ernaldo episcopo sancti Andree, Herberto episcopo de Glasgow, Johanne abbate de Kelkow, Willelmo abbate de Melros, Waltero cancellario, Willelmo et David fratribus regis, comite Gospatric, comite Duncano, Richardo de Morevill, Gilberto de Umphramvill, Roberto de Bruis, Radolpho de Soulis, Philipo de Colveill, Willelmo de Sumer.

villa, Hugone Riddell, Davide Olifard, Valdero filio comitis Gospatric, Willelmo de Morevill, Baldwino de la Mar, Liolfo filio Maccus. Apud arcem de Roxburgh in festo Sancti Johannis Baptiste anno regni nostri *v*to.

(Printed Acta Parliamentorum Scotiae, i, 92; Burgh of Paisley, ed. Metcalfe, app. p. 1.)

REFERENCES IN GIRALDUS CAMBRENSIS TO THE STEWARDSHIP OF FRANCE

Item comes Andegavie Gaufredus regina Alienora, quando senescallus Franciae fuit, abusus fuerat; . . . (Rolls Series [21], viii, p. 300).

In primis itaque post patris obitum, Philippi Flandrensium comitis praecipue fultus auxilio . . . proprios avunculos et matrem reginam, ducem quoque Burgundiae cognatum suum, totumque genus illud de Bleys, Flandrensibus infestum olim et exosum, armis impetiit, in primis duci Burgundiae Alexandro, consanguineo suo, castella plurima, reginae Alae, matri suae, dotalitium suum totum et propter nuptias donationem, comiti Theobaldo Franciae totius seneschalliam aliisque munitiones et terras amplas auferendo.

Cum autem comes Philippus, seneschallia Franciae, quam ab uxoris parte de Viromannia oriundae adeptam, comiti Theobaldo sub se quasi vicario jure concesserat, ad manum revocata, jam seneschallus per se, immo plus quam rex occupavit, ad cujus quippe nutum a rege cuncta fiebant, aliquandiu fuerit; quoniam cor ante ruinam exaltari solet, comitissa Flandriae, filia scilicet Radulfi comitis de Perrona, per quam comitatui Flandriae Viromanniam viriliter adjecerat et ditionem suam in Franciam procul extenderat, subito casu et inopinato citra haeredis solatium in fata decessit. Quod audientes avunculi regis et stirps Blessensis, idonea tam talionis et vindictae occasione captata, ad regem accesserunt, jus suum in Viromannia eidem, extinctis haeredibus, aperientes et, ut tantum honorem ad manus ejus de jure devolutum, Anglorum regis Henrici fultus auxilio, ab injusto detentore revocaret suoque dominico et mensae regali potenter adjiceret, persuadentes. Rex autem, quanquam aetate puer, mente maturior et consilio, gratiaque praecipue desuper adjutus, honoris sui et emolumenti monita non respuens, Anglorum regem tanquam pro patre suscepit ejusque in hoc articulo se consiliis ex toto submisit. Unde et ad ejus nutum in primis seneschalliam iterum comiti Theobaldo, et matri suae reginae dotalitium suum integre restituit (viii, pp. 228–9).

Haec etenim fuerat regis Henrici natura perversa, quod summo opere discordias inter filios et suscitabat et fovebat, solum sibi ex eorum discordia pacem sperans et quietem. Comes itaque Gaufredus adeo Philippi regis procerumque Franciae cunctorum sibi jam animos allexerat, ut unanimi omnium voto seneschallus Franciae crearetur. Qui cum in tanta jam potestate tantaque regis familiaritate constitutus fuisset, adeo Francorum regem totamque Franciam communiter in patrem suum et fratrem verbis persuasoriis, ut erat eloquentissimus pariter et amantissimus, jam excitaverat, ut inquietudinem tantam quantam, nisi morte praeventus fuisset, antea non viderant eis procul dubio comparasset (viii, p. 176).

REFERENCES IN ROBERT OF TORIGNI TO THE STEWARDSHIP OF FRANCE

Comes Carnotensis Tedbaudus despondit filiam Ludovici regis Franciae, et ideo rex ei concessit dapiferatum Franciae quem comes Andegavensis antiquitus habebat, unde etiam nostris temporibus Radulfus de Parrona pro eo serviebat, et, inde ei homagio faciens, ut dominum honorabat. (Rolls Series 82, iv, p. 222. The editor observes in a note that this and the next entry appear to belong to 1154. These entries, however, occur under date 1164, or ten years after the count's appointment to the regular office.)

In Epiphania Domini concordati sunt rex Francorum et rex Anglorum. Henricus, filius Henrici regis Anglorum, fecit homagium regi Francorum, socero suo, de Andegavensi comitatu, et de ducatu Brittanniae, quem rex concessit eidem genero suo. Nam de Normannia fecerat ei antea homagium et concessit ei rex Francorum ut esset seneschallus Franciae quod pertinet ad feudum Andegavense. (Ibid., p. 240, A.D. 1168–9.)

In purificatione Beatae Mariae fuit Henricus filius regis Anglorum Parisius, et servivit regi Francorum ad mensam ut senescallus Franciae. Hanc senescalciam, vel, ut antiquitus dicebatur, majoratum domus regiae, Robertus rex Francorum dedit Gaufrido Grisagonella comiti Andegavorum propter adjutorium quod ei impendit contra Othonem imperatorem Alemanniae.[1] Dedit etiam ei quicquid habebat in episcopatu Andegavensi. Postea vero, cum Gaufridus comes Perticensis et David[2] comes Cenomannensis essent rebelles eidem Roberto regi Francorum, praedictus rex Francorum, Gaufrido Grisagonella ferente sibi auxilium, obsedit munitionem Moritoniae et cepit. Et quia David comes Cenomannorum, evocatus a rege, ad eum venire contempsit, dedit rex Gaufrido Grisagonella homagium illius et ipsam civitatem, et quicquid habebat in episcopatu Cenomannensi. (Ibid., p. 240, A.D. 1168-9.)

GERVASE OF CANTERBURY AND THE STEWARDSHIP OF FRANCE

MCLVIII-IX. Rex Henricus transfretavit et Parisius profectus a rege Franciae Ludovico in magna gloria et honore susceptus est; filiam ejus filio suo Henrico petiit et accepit. Eo tempore, per industriam Thomae cancellarii a Londonia, rex Angliae a rege Francorum Christianissimo, viro tamen nimis simplici, optinuit, ut quasi senescallus regis Francorum intraret Britanniam, et quosdam ibidem inter se inquietos et funebre bellum exercentes coram se convocaret et pacificaret, et quem inveniret rebellem violenter coherceret. Hic fuit primus ingressus ejus super Britones edomandos, et sic civitatem de Nantes ad jus suae dominationis inflexit. . . . (Rolls Series [73], i, p. 166.)

[1] Robert, Geoffrey, and Otho were not contemporaries; for further details see below.

[2] This David is unknown to history.

F

THE CHRONICLES OF ANJOU[1] AND THE STEWARDSHIP OF FRANCE

Chronica de Gestis Consulum Andegavorum.[2] *Chron. Anjou,* p. 76. Siquidem nequitia Herberti, comitis Tricacensis, non potuit sustinere prosperitatem Roberti regis . . . exercitum rex congregavit. Obsedit Meledunum[3] . . . vocato Gosfrido[4] cum Andegavensibus suis. . . . Videntes autem Andegavi quod nullum possent habere hospitium, induunt arma, prorumpunt per medium exercitum, transmeant fluctus Sequanae, dant assultum oppido, virtute consueta capiunt castrum, et quod exercitus non potuit per septem menses, isti dimidiae diei spatio adepti sunt. . . . Videns autem tanti principis strenuitatem et ipsum praevalere in regno, tam armis quam consilio, et quae hic et alibi bene meruerat, sibi et successoribus suis, jure hereditario, majoratum regni et regiae domus dapiferatum, cunctis plaudentibus et laudantibus, exinde donavit.

Historia Comitum Andegavensium.[5] *Chron. Anjou,* p. 323. DCCCCLXXVIII. Gaufridus, quartus comes Andegavensium.[6] Hic filius Fulconis Boni, ob insignia summi et singularis meriti, a rege Roberto in praeliis signifer et in coronatione regum dapifer, tam ipse quam ejus heredes constituuntur.

Ibid., p. 346.[7] MCLXIX. Henricus, filius Henrici regis Angliae, fecit homagium regi Francorum, socero suo, de Andegavensi comitatu et de ducatu Britanniae, quem rex concessit eidem genero suo, nam de Normannia fecerat ei antea homagium ; et concessit ei rex Franciae ut esset

---

[1] The references are to the edition published by the Soc. de l'Hist. de France. A new edition is badly needed. This one would be worthless but for the introduction.

[2] The subjoined extract occurs, it is believed, only in the fourth recension of this chronicle. The date of this recension is given as A.D. 1169–70.

[3] A.D. 1001.

[4] Died on the 21st July, 987, during the reign of Hugh Capet.

[5] Known as the Victorine MS., and conjectured to be extracts from materials collected by Ralph de Diceto.

[6] This passage appears word for word in Diceto, i, p. 154.

[7] Compare with Robert of Torigni; no similar passage occurs in Diceto.

senescalus Franciae, quod pertinet ad feudum Andegavense. In purificatione sanctae Mariae, fuit Henricus filius regis Angliae Parisius, et servivit regi Franciae ad mensam ut senescalus Franciae. Hanc senescalciam vel, ut antiquitus dicebatur, majoratum domus regiae, Robertus rex Francorum dedit Gaufrido Grisagonella, comiti Andegavorum propter adjutorium quod sibi impendit contra Othonem imperatorem Alemanniae. Dedit . . .[1] Cenomannensi.

Historia Abbreviata Consulum Andegavorum. Chron. Anjou, p. 357. De Gaufrido Grisa Tunica. Iste militiae peritus. . . . Qui ob insignia . . .[2] heredes constituuntur.

Scriptum Huonis de Cleeriis de Majoratu et Senescalcia Franciae Comitibus Andegavorum Collatis.[3] Hoc scriptum fecit Fulco comes, Jerosolimitanus . . . [The story of Robert, Otho, and Geoffrey is told.] . . . Nequitia comitis Tricacensis . . .[4] dapiferatum, cunctis applaudentibus et laudantibus, exinde constituit. . . . Huc usque sunt scripta Fulconis Jerosolimitani. Vos autem qui ista scripta audieritis, scitote quod ego, Huo de Cleeriis, vidi scripta Fulconis comitis Jerosolimitani in ecclesia Sancti Sepulchri de Lochis de majoratu et senescalcia Franciae sibi et suis antecessoribus a rege Rotberto collatis.[5]

Inter regem Ludovicum, Philippi regis filium, et Fulconem comitem, qui postea factus est rex Jerusalem, magna erat dissensio. Fulco enim comes nolebat ei servire, rex enim Ludovicus dederat majoratum et senescalciam Franciae Anselmo de Garlanda, et postea Guillermo de Garlanda, de

---

[1] Substituting "dictus" for "David," this passage is identical with that in Robert of Torigni.

[2] This is substantially identical with the passages in the Historia Comitum Andegavensium and in Diceto.

[3] Printed in full, Chron. Anjou, p. 387; Baluze Misc., vol. iv; Bouquet, vol. xii; Duchesne, vol. iv, etc.; the MS. belongs to the twelfth century. Hugh de Clers is a well-known person, a contemporary of Geoffrey le Bel and Henry II, and was for some time dapifer of la Flèche.

[4] Apart from verbal differences this is substantially identical with the passage in the Chron. de Gestis Consulum Andegavorum.

[5] Here the first part of the tract ends, and this portion, at all events, is a tissue of falsehoods.

quibus Fulco comes suas redhibitiones et sua hominia habere non poterat. . . . [Louis, at war with Henry I, desires Fulk's assistance. The author of this tract arranges a conference.] . . . . Cumque dies instaret colloquii, dominus rex Ludovicus et Fulco comes ad locum constitutum venerunt, cum suis consultoribus; ibique recognita sunt jura comitis, videlicet majoratus et senescalcia Franciae. Guillelmus de Garlanda, tunc Franciae senescallus, recognovit in illo colloquio hominium se debere comiti Fulconi de senescalcia Franciae et unde fuit in voluntate comitis. Post Guillelmum, fuit senescallus Stephanus de Garlanda, qui fecit hominium comiti; post Stephanum, Radulfus comes Peronae qui similiter fecit hominia et servitium. Ille enim qui senescallus erit Franciae faciet hominium, et talia alia. . . . Si vero ad coronamenta regis comes ire voluerit, senescallus praeparare et liberare faciet hospitia quae comes habet propria et dedita. Cum autem, die suae coronae, ad mensas rex discubuerit, scannum pulcherrimum fultro pallii aut tapeto coopertum senescallus praeparabit, ibique, et sui comites, quousque fercula veniant sedebit. Cum vero primum venerit ferculum, comes, se defibulans, e scanno surget; et de manu senescalli ferculum accipiens, ante regem et reginam apponet .   .
.   .   .   .[1]

De caetero comes appellatur Major in Francia, propter prae-tutelam et retutelam quam facit in exercitu regis. Item quando erit in Francia, quod et curia sua judicaverit firmum erit et stabile. Si vero contentio aliqua nascetur de judicio facto in Francia, rex mandabit quod comes veniat illud emendare; et si pro ea mittere noluerit, scripta utriusque partis comiti transmittet, et quod inde sua curia judicabit firmum erit et stabile. Ego Huo de Cleeriis vidi multocies judicia facta in Francia in Andegavia emendari, sicut fuit de bello apud sanctum Audomarum facto, et de pluribus aliis placitis et judiciis. Haec vidi et multi alii mecum.[2]

[1] The passages here omitted refer principally to the Count's military duties and privileges.

[2] The authenticity of this famous treatise has been critically dis-cussed by M. Bémont, Études d'Histoire du Moyen Age, dédiées à Gabriel Monod (1896), pp. 253-60; this writer considers the second part has a distinct historical value: also by M. Luchaire,

OTHER REFERENCES TO THE STEWARDSHIP
OF FRANCE

Diceto, Rolls Series [68], i, *p*. 438. Philippus itaque rex Francorum, in coronatione sua, tam in gladio praeferendo, quam in regiis dapibus apponendis, Philippum Flandriae[1] comitem privilegiatum habuit ministerialem, utentem duplici jure, paterno videlicet et uxorio. Henricus rex, Henrici regis Angliae filius, et Philippi regis Francorum sororius, regiae consecrationi Remis interfuit. . . . (We know, be it remembered, from extant coronation ceremonials, that it was the steward who carried the sword and served at the banquet.)

Hoveden, Rolls Series [51], ii, *p*. 194. Henricus autem rex Angliae filius, in progressione a thalamo usque in ecclesiam, ipso die coronationis, ibat ante illum gestans coronam auream de jure ducatus Normanniae, qua predictus Philippus coronandus erat. Et Philippus comes Flandriae praeibat ferens ante illum gladium regni.

Gislebert de Mons, *p*. 127. Eodem anno Domini 1179 Ludovicus sepedictus Francorum rex filium suum unicum Philippum, . . . Remis in festivitate omnium sanctorum in regem coronari fecit. Ad hoc coronamentum et regis edictum, cum omnes Francie principes accederent, Philippus Flandrie et Viromandie comes potentissimus, qui in gestamine gladii regalis jus reclamabat, cum armis et militibus multis venit. . . . Sicque Philippus cum summa veneratione et reverentia inunctus et in regem coronatus fuit. Ibique comes Flandrie gladium regale gestavit.

Bibliothèque de la Faculté des Lettres, iii, Mélanges d'Histoire du Moyen Age (1897), pp. 1-38. The latter rejects the entire story and concludes as follows: " Tout porte à croire que l'écrit composé au nom de Hugue de Clers a été produit en 1158, au moment où la chancellerie de Henri II négociait avec la court de France pour faire attribuer au roi d'Angleterre la fonction de sénéschal, en vue de son expédition de Bretagne."

[1] Le Ménestrel de Reims (ed. Wailly, p. 8) says: "Et à son disner, le servi li rois Henris d'Angleterre à genoux et tailla devant lui." Perhaps Philip, like Henry, occasionally had two honorary hereditary dapifers in attendance.

Note :—Walter Map (Cam. Soc., p. 106) tells a proverb about a —" miles quidam, haereditarius Franciae senescallus."

Ibid., p. 130. Philippus autem rex Elizabeth duxit uxorem in castro comitis Flandrie Bapalmis feria secunda post octavam pasche anno Domini 1180, quam ipse rex in sequenti die festo ascensionis Domini eodem anno apud sanctum Dyonisium in Francia inungi et regia corona insigniri qua decuit veneratione fecit. Ubi ipse, ad sue nupte noveque regine honorem, regalem cum ea gestavit coronam, . . . astante eciam ipsius regine avunculo Philippo Flandrie et Viromandie comite et ibidem gladium regalem gestante.

Rigord, Gesta Philippi Augusti, p. 20. Anno dominice incarnacionis mclxxx, quarto Kalendas Junii . . . idem rex Philippus secundo imposuit sibi diadema, et tunc inuncta fuit Elizabeth uxor ejus venerabilis regina, filia Baldwini illustris comitis Haenuensis, neptis Philippi magni comitis Flandrensium, qui ea die, prout moris est, ensem ante dominum regem honorifice portavit.

The Charter of Saint-Julien de Tours.[1]

Henricus rex Anglie et dux Normannie et Aquitanie et comes Andegavensis omnibus fidelibus suis salutem. Sciatis quod rex Francie Aurelianis in communi audientia recognovit quod custodia Abbatie sancti Juliani Turonensis ad me pertinet ex dignitate dapiferatus mei unde servire debeo regi Francie sicut comes Andegavensis ita quod archiepiscopus Turonensis nullam habet in ea potestatem preter episcopalia sicut in ceteris. His audientibus, Joscio scilicet tunc Turonensi archiepiscopo,[2] abbate sancti Evurcii, abbate sancti Benedicti super Ligerim, Gaufrido et Stephano capellanis, Richardo thesaurario, Johanne camerario, Vend. B.[3] fratre regis Francie, Willelmo sil. Ham.,[4] Roberto de Novoburgo,[5] Hugone de Cleeriis. (MS. 2669, Bibl. Colbert.[6] Reg. Phil. Aug.—Printed Baluz, iv, 12.)

[1] Date 1157–9, (?) 1158.   [2] Elected 1157.
[3] Recte "P."; read Vendocinensi Philippo.
[4] Recte "filio Hamonis."
[5] Obiit 1159.
[6] A vidimus of the bailli de Tours, R. Barbou, dated 1288. See Luchaire, op. cit., pp. 24–7. The authenticity of this charter is doubtful.

Chronique de Philippe Mouskes.

Vers. 24241.   Et s'ot mainte cose nommée
Pour porter l'ensègne et l'espée.
Mais, pour oster ire et desroi,
Le porta li frères le roi.
    (Sacre de Louis viii a Reims.)

Vers. 27707.   Si vint la dame de Campagne
Et vint la contesse Jehane
De Flandres, qui sa nièce estoit.
Si fisent demander pour droit
A porter l'espée le roi.
Mais pour abaiscier le desroi,
Saus tos drois, le porta méismes
Li quens de Boulogne Felipres,
Ki fu oncles à cel enfant.
    (Sacre de Louis ix a Reims, 29 Nov., 1226.)

Le Nain de Tillemont, vie de Saint Louis i, pp. 434-5

Après la cérémonie, il y eut contestation à qui porteroit l'épée royale entre des femmes, ce qui est étrange, sçavoir entre les comtesses de Champagne et de Flandre, qui prétendoient chacune avoir ce droit au nom de leurs maris. Pour les appaiser on donna l'épée au comte de Boulogne, sans préjudice du droit des comtesses, ce qui ne s'accorde pas avec le cérémonial du P. Labbe, qui porte que le roy donna l'épée au sénéschal qui la porta jusqu'au palais. Il y avoit longtemps qu'on ne parloit plus de sénéschal en France Le même comte de Boulogne l'avoit déjà portée au sacre de Louis viii pour oster aussi les disputes.

CHAPTER III

HOW THE HOUSE OF MONTFORT BECAME SOLE HEREDITARY STEWARDS OF THE HOUSEHOLD

ON the accession of Richard the First the style *dapifer* for the ordinary stewards of the household began to drop out of use, the style seneschal taking its place.[1] A slight tendency in this direction was noticeable during the previous reign. The same change of style took place in the case of the hereditary stewards of the household: thus in the king's charter to Roger Bigod, making him earl of Norfolk and restoring to him his hereditary office,[2] the word used is *senescalcia*.

Robert *Blanchemains*, earl of Leicester, the other hereditary steward, was present at Richard's coronation and carried a sword in the royal procession.[3] As the dapifer for the occasion at a French coronation also carried a sword, the incident is suggestive. This earl married, before 1159,[4]

---

[1] France Cal. R.O., no. 56, Charter of Richard I, dated 2nd March, 1190.—Testibus [inter alios] Rogero de Pratellis et Stephano de Longo Campo, senescallis nostris. But the old style is still frequently used, e.g. ibid., no. 1346. Charter of Richard I, dated 17th December, 1189.—Testibus [inter alios] Rogero de Pratellis, Stephano de Longo Campo dapiferis. See also Rymer, Foedera, R.C., i, pp. 49-50. [2] See Appendix.

[3] Deinde venerunt David frater regis Scotiae, comes de Huntedun, et Johannes comes Moretonii frater ducis, et Robertus comes Leicestriae portantes tres gladios regios sumptos de thesauro regis quorum vaginae desuper per totum auro contectae erant, medius autem illorum ibat comes Moretonii (Hoveden, Rolls Series [51], iii, p. 9; Benedict of Peterborough, Rolls Series [49], ii, p. 81).

[4] The Complete Peerage gives 1168 as the date of Robert III's marriage, but see France Cal. R.O., no. 1062, Charter (A.D. 1155-9) of Robert earl of Leicester to Nuneaton, which is tested by "Roberto filio meo" and "Petronilla uxore filii mei."

Petronilla (Parnel), an heiress of the family of Grandmaisnil, a circumstance to which we shall have to revert later on. Shortly after Richard's coronation he went on a pilgrimage to Palestine, and died in Greece on his way back in the year 1190. His son Robert *Fitz-Parnel* succeeded him, and was formally invested with the earldom by Richard at Messina during the following year.[1]

Robert *Fitz-Parnel* does not figure large in English history. In 1193 he was captured and imprisoned by the king of France, and was not liberated till 1196. He was therefore incapable of taking part in king Richard's second coronation, at which presumably Roger Bigod officiated as steward.

On the accession of John, the earl of Leicester disputed Roger Bigod's right to act as steward at the coronation. No particulars of this dispute have as yet come to light, but it is known that the matter was there and then compromised by Roger withdrawing all future claims to the stewardship in consideration of ten knights' fees to be assigned to him by the earl of Leicester.[2] Accordingly, but only under pressure of legal process, the latter earl named Roger de la Zouche for four knights' fees, Robert de Furnival for three fees, Reginald de Leiham for two fees, and Richard Gubiun for one fee.[3] He did not, however, in fact assign all these knights' fees to the earl of Norfolk, and was still

---

[1] For the history of the Beaumont earls of Leicester see generally —The Complete Peerage, s.v. Leicester; The Genealogist, vol. x, p. 1; The Dict. of Nat. Biog., s.v. Beaumont; Planché, The Genealogy and Armorial Ensigns of the Anglo-Norman Earls of Leicester. The views expressed by these authorities on the subject of the stewardship are quite unreliable.

[2] Rotuli Curie Regis, ii, p. 184. (Suff.) Comes Rogerus ponit loco suo Milonem ***** vel Rogerum de Braham versus Willelmum filium Alani de . . . et idem ponit eosdem et Robertum Capellanum et Ricardum de Senges versus comitem Legrecestrie ad recipiendum x milites et cirographum suum. That this matter has any connection with the stewardship we only know from subsequent events.

The final concord between earl Roger and Fitzalan is preserved, but I have searched vainly for the one relating to the stewardship.

[3] Rotuli Curie Regis, ii, p. 194. Hii sunt milites quos comes Leicestrie assignavit comiti Rogero Bigot, Rogerum de la Zuche

in default when he died ; but the result of the compromise was, none the less, to leave the earls of Leicester sole hereditary stewards of the household.

Robert *Fitz-Parnel* married a lady named Lauretta, but died without issue in 1204. He had, however, two brothers : Roger bishop of Salisbury ; and William, a leper and monk ; also two sisters : Amicia (the elder), who married Simon the Third of Montfort ; and Margaret, who married Saer de Quincy. Amicia's husband was dead, and her eldest surviving son, Simon the Fourth, an alien in the allegiance of France. Accordingly Saer de Quincy, in consideration of a fine of 1000 marks, was granted possession of all the Leicester estates ; except the castle of Munsorell which the king retained, and the dower lands belonging to the countesses Petronilla and Lauretta, but without prejudice to any future claim by the countess Amicia. This was in the year 1205.[1]

A claim must have been promptly made by Simon the Fourth, not only to the lands but also to the earldom ; for in August of the following year Simon is referred to as earl of Leicester, and on the 10th of March the king confirmed a division of the Beaumont estates made between Simon the Fourth of Montfort, as earl of Leicester, and Saer de Quincy, then earl of Winchester, which reserved to the former earl the third-penny of the county of Leicester, the chief messuage of Leicester and the stewardship of the household :— *salvis predicto comiti Simoni tertio denario comitatus Leicestrie unde ipse comes est et capitali mesagio Leicestrie et senescalcia nostra.* On the deaths of the countesses Petronilla and Lauretta the outstanding dower lands were also to be divided.[2]

de feodis iiij militum, feodum Roberti de Furnuvalle pro iij militibus et feodum Reginaldi de Leiham pro ij militibus et feodum Ricardi Gubium pro j milite.

[1] See Appendix. I ought perhaps to add that when I say "Quincy in consideration of a fine of 1000 marks was granted possession," I mean what I say and no more : it is not an elaborate way of stating that he paid 1000 marks and obtained possession ; he neither paid in full, nor did he obtain possession of all the estates.

[2] See Appendix.

In this way the earldom and honours of Leicester passed to the great house of Montfort; but Simon the Fourth, that renowned warrior, the scourge of the Albigenses, although he appears to have visited England to take seizin of his possessions,[1] was only permitted for a very brief time, if at all, to receive the rents and profits of his estates. In February of 1206-7 the king had seized his possessions,[2] nominally for a debt due to the crown; and, notwithstanding the statements of some recent writers, we have the strongest possible evidence that they were never restored to him.[3] The partition above mentioned appears to have been highly unfavourable to Saer de Quincy, from which we may conclude that John never intended anyone but himself to enjoy Simon's moiety. The earl of Winchester, be it noted, did not submit: he appealed, the partition suit was referred back to the Bench, and the original decree varied in his favour."[4]

The value of the Leicester estates, and the way they were managed or mismanaged, after Simon's dispossession, by the royal officers to whom they were entrusted, are matters of no small moment. According to the younger Simon's own statement, a great amount of voluntary waste was perpetrated in the interests of John[5]; while the modern biographers of this same earl have made some rather remarkable suggestions on the same subject. Fortunately the accounts are extant; and the rents, profits and outgoings, the extent of the waste, the loss on the second partition and such-like items may be calculated to the last obolus.[6] The restoration of Simon was one of the papal conditions of 1213, which, two years later, John so far complied with as to

---

[1] See Appendix. It is said by some authorities to be very doubtful whether this Simon ever set foot in England, but, in view of the very precise statements on the close rolls of Henry III that he did do so, I think the doubt must be dismissed.

[2] Appendix. The custodians were (1) Robert de Ropeley, (2) William de Cantilupe.

[3] The custodians' accounts date from the 2nd of February; see Appendix.   [4] Appendix.

[5] Bibl. Nat. de Fr. Clairembault, 1188, fol. 80; printed from the original by Bémont, S. de Montfort, p. 333.   [6] Appendix.

entrust the Leicester fiefs to Randolf earl of Chester as custodian in Simon's behalf[1]; and so matters remained till the accession of Henry the Third.

John's reign clearly marks another stage in the evolution of the stewardship. The three great houses of Bigod, Montfort and Quincy had each acquired some title to the office. Bigod sold his right for ten knights' fees, and as between the other claimants the alien house was preferred. a preference almost amounting to a suppression of the office. Not that there was much to suppress, merely the privilege of serving at the royal table on special occasions, with perhaps the additional right of carrying a sword at coronations.

It is worth noticing that ultimately the ousted claimants, including the Bohuns who retired from the contest in the days of Henry the Second, all received compensation in kind. The Bohuns became hereditary constables of England; the house of Quincy hereditary constables of Scotland; while the Bigods acquired the hereditary marshalship of England.

On the day of St. Simon and St. Jude in the year 1216 Henry the Third was crowned at Gloucester. It was a sorry pretence at a coronation, for England was virtually under the dominion of France. Two years later Simon de Montfort the crusader died before Toulouse. [2]

Thanks to the interference of the papal see Henry's prospects speedily improved; and in the year 1220, on Whitsunday, the king was crowned a second time, at Westminster. It seems probable that on this occasion the earl of Norfolk again claimed to act as steward, his claim being opposed by the earl of Chester as custos of the Leicester fiefs. At any rate Hugh Bigod, on behalf of his father, brought the matter before the king in council at Oxford the following Christmas day, complaining that earl Roger had only received some of the knights' fees representing the

---

[1] Appendix.
[2] The actual date was the 27th of June, 1218. In consequence of Simon's death the Marshal ordered the honour of Leicester to be seized into the king's hands: it was restored to the earl of Chester on October 4th, 4 Henry III; and granted to him for life by letters patent dated May 18th in the eleventh year. See Appendix.

consideration for his withdrawing all claims to the steward-ship, and it was then agreed fhat the earl of Chester should specifically perform the agreement. The earl of Chester, however, did nothing ; and on the 1st of May in the follow-ing year a writ of *fi. fa.* was issued against him.[1] This process proved abortive, evidently owing to the death of the earl of Norfolk.

Simon the Fourth of Montfort had died, leaving several sons and daughters surviving him. His heir was Amaury the Sixth, who, notwithstanding his position in France and the hostile relations of that country with England, appears to have frequently pressed his claims to the Leicester earldom and honours. He certainly adopted the title, styling himself prior to the cession of his southern possessions duke of Narbonne, count of Toulouse and Leicester, lord of Mont-fort, and subsequently count of Montfort and Leicester.

It is not unimportant to notice that Amaury was created constable of France, and must have been fairly well ac-quainted with the recent history of French offices of state : the royal charters he attested still bore the legend *dapifero nullo.* He was certainly also aware that an hereditary stewardship was attached to the Leicester honour, and we have good ground for supposing that he regarded this office as analogous to the suppressed dapifership of France. The count, therefore, may possibly have conceived the wild idea of being chief officer of state in England as well as constable of France. Be this as it may, the divided allegiance of the count of Montfort would have suited neither sovereign, and

---

[1] *De senescalcia hospitii domini regis.*—Rex R. comiti Cestrie et Lincolnie salutem. Sciatis qualiter convenerit inter vos et Hugonem le Bigod filium et heredem comitis Rogeri le Bigod coram nobis et consilio nostro apud Oxoniam ad Natale proximum preteritum de senescalcia hospicii nostri de qua contencio fuit inter comitem Leicestrie preteritis diebus et ipsum comitem Rogerum videlicet quod vos tanquam custos honoris Leicestrie faceretis ipsi comiti Rogero et heredibus suis habere id quod ei restat de feodis x militum pro eadem senescalcia. Et ideo vobis mandamus quod ipsi comiti Rogero id quod de eisdem feodis x militum ei restat faciendum sine dilatione fieri faciatis. Teste H. etc. apud Westmonasterium primo die Maii. (Close Roll 5 Henry III, m. 12, A.D. 1221.)

the count eventually withdrew his own claims in favour of Simon his younger brother.

Simon the Fifth of Montfort appears first on the scene about the year 1229, seemingly as a fugitive from France, having provoked the ire of the queen-regent.[1] He presented himself to Henry, ingratiated himself with that monarch whose besetting sin was a love of foreigners, and asked for the earldom of Leicester. Simon brought with him a letter of introduction from Amaury : "I have often besought your royal majesty," the letter runs, "humbly and devoutly to restore me my property [and so forth]." He makes, in fact, a final appeal on his own behalf, but concludes with one for Simon : "If this be not pleasing to you, I send to your lordship's feet my brother Simon who holds nothing of the French king : If you restore him my property I shall hold myself well satisfied." The letter is dated at Paris in the month of February.[2]

Simon so far found favour with the king that he had a promise of the earldom and honour of Leicester together with the stewardship so soon as the lands ceased to be held by the earl of Chester ; a promise duly confirmed by letters patent of the 6th of February, 1230, attested by Randolf earl of Chester himself.[3]

Simon was far from satisfied with so nebulous a grant, and returned to France, as he expressed it, "sans grace trouver."[4] Henry, too, evidently doubted whether he had been sufficiently gracious, for on the 8th of April, 1231, he despatched Simon a letter referring to the earldom as a mere question of time, and stating that meanwhile he had granted Simon an annuity of 400 marks.[5]

Perhaps it was this letter which spurred Simon de Montfort to fresh efforts in a new direction : in the same year he visited the real obstacle to his ambitions, the earl of Chester,

---

[1] W. Nangis, see Bouquet, H.F., vol. xx, p. 548 ; and Trevet, Eng. Hist. Soc., p. 226.

[2] See Appendix.   [3] See Appendix.

[4] Bibl. Nat. Clairembault 1188, fol. 80 ; printed from the original by Bémont, Simon de Montfort, app. no. xxxiv.

[5] See Appendix.

at his castle of St. Jean Beveron, in Brittany, and pleaded for the restoration of his father's heritage.[1] Simon probably remained with Randolf till the conclusion of a three years' truce with France: certainly he accompanied the earl to England immediately afterwards, arriving early in August.

According to Simon's own story Randolf was complaisant and agreed to surrender the Leicester fiefs. It is further stated that Randolf admitted Simon's superior title to these estates; himself requested the king to take Simon's homage in respect of them, which was done; and thereupon Simon was let into possession.[2] These statements, however, though made by or on behalf of Simon in 1261, must be accepted with some caution.

We know for certain that Simon did homage for the Leicester honour in August 1231; and mandates were accordingly sent to the sheriffs of four counties directing them to give Simon, as heir to his father, seizin of his father's estates.[3] These mandates apparently were not complied with. Either the earl of Chester had repented of his complaisance, or other magnates were moving strenuously in the matter, for there are clear indications that somebody promptly advanced and maintained the objection that Simon had no valid title to the property.

One cannot help suspecting that Randolf was the chief source of the difficulty. A man who could not be brought to disgorge a few knights' fees at the suit of an earl of Norfolk is not *prima facie* likely to have readily surrendered entire estates to a penniless foreigner however just his claims:

---

[1] L'autre an apres, mi sires le Rais passa en Bretaigne et le conte de Cestre aveqe li qi mon eritage tenait; e j'alai au conte a un chastiau q'il tenait Saint Jaque de Beveronne. (Bémont, app. no. xxxiv.)

[2] La li priai qe je puisse sa grace trovair d'avoir mon éritage, e il, seue merci, s'i acorda, e, en l'aoust apres, me mena-il aveqe li en Engleterre, e pria le Rai q'il me receust a home de l'eritage mon pere, a quieu j'avaie greigneur drait qe li, si comme il disait, e tot le don qe li Rais li avait doné en cele chose il li quita, par issi q'il me receust a home. E einssinc mi sires li Rais prist mon homage, e me fu ma terre rendue. . . . (Bémont, app. no. xxxiv.)

[3] See Appendix.

moreover, it is difficult to see how anyone else~ could have effectively intervened.[1]

The first objection seems to have been that, assuming Simon was the heir, his father did not die seized of the estates in question, and amended mandates were accordingly sent out on the 22nd of September following.[2] Simon, as heir to his father, was to be put into possession of all property belonging to the honour of Leicester of which his father was seized when he left England, and which thereupon came into the hands of the crown.

At this stage the objectors must have shifted their ground and taken the point that Simon was not heir to his father. This was really an unanswerable objection in law, and left only two courses open : to proceed by forfeiture and regrant, or to appeal to Amaury, the real heir ; and we know that the latter was the course actually adopted. It seems, however,

---

[1] The opposition, probably, chiefly manifested itself in the refusal of a large number of tenants to attorn. The earl of Winchester's position in John's time was fairly analogous, and his difficulties did not end even after the judgment on appeal in his partition action. Compare the following :—

Assisa venit recognoscere si Robertus comes Leicestrie frater Margarete uxoris comitis Wintonie seizitus fuit in dominico suo ut de feodo de c acris terre cum pertinentiis in Swithelond die qua obiit et si predicta Margareta propinquior heres ejus sit, quam terram Willielmus Falconer tenet, qui venit et dicit assisam inde non debere quia predicta Margareta habet sororem que adeo magnum jus haberet in terra sicut ipsa Margareta de qua non fit mencio in brevi etc. (Placitorum Abbreviatio, p. 99.)

Willielmus de Turevill summonitus fuit ad ostendendum quare ipse non fecit Sahero comiti Wintonie servicium suum quod ei adjudicatum fuit in curia domini regis coram justiciariis suis de banco unde idem comes ostendit quod servicium suum scilicet de duobus militibus ei aretro est a tempore quo particio terrarum facta fuit coram eisdem justiciariis per preceptum domini regis inter eum et comitem Leicestrie per quam particionem predictus Willielmus ei attornatus fuit de predicto servicio duorum militum. Et Willielmus venit et dicit quod per particionem primam ipse attornatus fuit comiti Simoni et, postquam terra ejusdem comitis Simonis seisita fuit in manu domini regis, fecit ipse plenarium servicium domino regi, et si placuerit domino regi vel ejus justiciariis libenter faciet eidem comiti Sahero quod facere debet. (Trin. 15 John; Placitorum Abbreviatio, p. 88.)   [2] See Appendix.

that the difficulty may to some extent have been anticipated, for in August, 1231, Amaury had despatched another letter to Henry requesting that Simon might be given seizin of the Leicester estates: upon this being done, he, Amaury, undertook to duly release his claims, reserving only to himself the remainder expectant upon a failure of heirs of the body of Simon.[1] Perhaps on the strength of this epistle, the king, by letters patent dated the 27th of May, 1232, and expressed to be granted on the petition of the count of Montfort, confirmed to Simon the property in question—que ad ipsum Aumaricum jure hereditario pertinebat; thus abandoning the pretence that Simon was the heir, and following the terms of the conditional grant of two years before.[2] These letters patent were legally quite valueless; Simon had as yet no title which could be confirmed. On the 15th of June, 1232, further letters patent were issued granting Simon de Montfort the Norman escheats within his fief.[3]

In the same month Amaury responded to the appeal made to him by executing a document.[4] This instrument is dated at Paris, and is in form a grant of the property to Simon and the heirs of his body (de uxore sua desponsata exeuntibus), with remainder to the donor and his heirs in fee. It also purports to assign the portentous office of steward of the whole of England (senescalcia Anglie totius). A more impudent piece of conveyancing it would be difficult to imagine. No doubt a grant was the proper form of instrument to convey the land, as Henry, and not the donor or donee, was in possession; but confirmation by the king was, in such cases, essential to perfect the grant. The case of the stewardship was altogether different: the pretentious language in which it is described should alone have precluded confirmation of the assignment. Compared, however, with the attempt to assign the office, its description sinks to a mere peccadillo of drafting. Such an office was wholly inalienable; the right to it, and the services incident to its possession, could with

---

[1] Appendix.
[2] Appendix. See also (ibid.) the letters close of January 10th, 1232, which throw some light on what was taking place.
[3] Appendix.   [4] Appendix.

the king's consent be surrendered and released, but that was all. A confirmation therefore of the grant in question would have been highly derogatory to the king.

The document is in some other respects a curious one, and was probably not the work of an English conveyancer. But there is no need for further criticism. Amaury's grant of June, 1232, was never confirmed and never acted upon. Simon de Montfort was as far off as ever from obtaining the beatitude of lawful seizin, and in this unsatisfactory state his title to the honour and earldom of Leicester remained for several years.

Now why was there all this bother? The king might have proceeded by forfeiture and regrant, a most simple and expeditious course to which no exception could have been taken. Why was this not attempted? One and only one reason can be assigned which will cover the facts. Simon was bent on getting possession of the estates in right of his father, and not as a grantee direct from the crown. Only if he came in by succession could he establish his position as an Englishman, and render himself proof against the charge of being an alien. Ultimately he succeeded in this.

In October of the year 1232 Randolf earl of Chester, last relic of the old feudal aristocracy, died at Wallingford. Probably this man's demise materially affected Simon's position and prospects.

On the 20th of January, 1236, Eleanor, consort of Henry the Third, was crowned at Westminster with the greatest pomp and splendour, and once again a Bigod claimed to act for the occasion as steward of the household. A sharp contest for the office took place on the actual day of the coronation between Roger earl of Norfolk and Simon de Montfort, and this time the latter appears well versed in the legal technicalities of his situation.

Simon's argument, recorded in the Exchequer Red Book, is terse and to the point. Roger claimed prior title: Simon pleaded the agreement between their predecessors: Roger replied that two knights' fees and a half were still due and owing. To this Simon rejoined that the other's remedy for the default lay in the court of the lord king; that Roger, by his reply, had admitted the agreement and possession of seven fees and a half, and had therefore no right to hinder him in the enjoyment of the office. This plea the earl of Norfolk could not rebut, and there the incident closed, this time finally.[1]

So Simon de Montfort served that day as steward without let or hindrance. With the assistance of the citizens of Winchester he superintended the royal kitchen and made arrangements for the coronation banquet.[2] This feast took place in Westminster Hall in the evening, directly after the religious ceremony at the abbey. As soon as Henry had seated himself at the banqueting table Simon, arrayed in robe of office, gave him water in a basin to wash his hands. When all was over the master-cook obtained the steward's robe as his customary perquisite.[3]

Possibly there were other ceremonies in which the steward figured on this occasion; but our chronicler, Matthew Paris, when he comes to the banquet, wearies of his tale of pageantry and gives no further details of the day's proceedings. However, the above particulars afford us quite a sufficient

[1] Servivit autem ea die de senescalsia comes Simon de Monteforti comes Legecestrie cui de jure competit illud officium, licet contradiceret Rogerus de Bigot comes Norfolcie qui dicebat suum esse jus illud a veteri, ad quod respondit dictus Simon quod tempore regis Johannis facta inter eorum predecessores contencio super hoc et hoc modo pacificata quod comes Leycestrie dedit comiti Norfolcie servicia x militum, et comes Rogerus Norfolcie remisit ei totum clamium quod habuit in senescalsia: ad quod replicavit alius quod adhuc restabant ei assignanda duo feoda et dimidium de predictis x feodis: ad quod respondit comes Simon quod secundum legem terre bene potuit consequi sua arreragia alias in curia domini regis nec propter hoc debuit impediri, maxime cum confiteretur comes Rogerus illam convencionem et se seisitum de vij feodis et dimidio pro illa convencione; et sic libere servivit comes Simon ea die. (Red Book of the Exchequer, fol. 232.)

Note, however, that the Liber Regalis contains the following rubric:—Serviit ea die de senescallia comes Leycestrie, licet comes Norfolchie illud sibi vendicaverit obsequium. (See Legg, Engl. Coronation Records, p. 108.)

[2] . . . sicuti et civitas Wyntonie de coquina in auxilium senescalli. (Red Book of the Exchequer.)

[3] Magister cocorum coquine regis semper in coronacione recipit robam senescalli tanquam jus suum. (Ibidem.)

idea of the duties appertaining to the hereditary stewardship, and perhaps it might be said with truth that the office had declined in importance, for certainly Simon carried no sword at this ceremony like his Beaumont predecessor did at the coronation of Richard the First.[1]

Simon de Montfort clearly entertained the idea that vastly different and more important functions properly appertained to this office, functions of which Henry was unjustly depriving him ; and this was part of his plaint to the French king in 1261.[2] If Louis of France ever investigated this branch of the matter, Henry may have found it difficult to convince him that the sole duty properly belonging to Simon de Montfort as hereditary steward was the business of chief sewer at particular state banquets. Nevertheless such was the case, and moreover there was nothing intrinsically strange in the matter. The strangeness lay rather in the circumstance that the French and other dapifers had soared to precedence over all other functionaries, than in the fact that the English dish-thegn was a dish-thegn still.

It is more than probable that Simon had looked to the English stewardship as a ready-made foundation on which he might easily build up his political power to the measure of his political aspirations. If so, these expectations were never realised: the converse was what actually occurred. Simon raised the stewardship to a position of considerable importance on the foundation of his own achievements.

To a man in Simon de Montfort's position the question of marriage was one of prime importance. Anything almost was possible. He might wed a kingdom, or fetter himself to dowerless nonentity ; and, according to his choice, his wife would either crown or extinguish his ambitions.

About the year 1234 Simon made a bold attempt at matrimony and captured the elderly affections of the countess of Boulogne. This was viewed as a menace to the French

---

[1] Perhaps it was the earl of Chester who had usurped this privilege.

[2] . . . e de la seneschaucie pluseurs draiz me retient, e sovent l'ei requis q'il me feist drait, mes unqore ores ne m'en a rien fet. (Bémont, app. no. xxxiv.)

crown; the match was vigorously opposed, and the countess yielded to pressure. She was subsequently solaced by an alliance with Alfonso, the king of Portugal's brother. Simon then attached himself to Jeanne of Flanders, who had been a widow since 1233 and would have passed anywhere for his grandmother. But this affair was even less palatable to Louis, who promptly intervened, or at all events with as much promptness as the special circumstances necessitated. One may suspect that the bride had already consented, for they took an oath of her that she had not married Simon, which if true was surely unnecessary.

Simon de Montfort did not permit these failures to curb his ambitions, and in the end he achieved what few would have ventured to attempt. On the 7th of January, 1237–8, with Henry's consent and approbation, he was married secretly to the princess Eleanor, Henry's own sister. This clandestine affair was naturally regarded as a piece of gross discourtesy to the nation, besides being, on account of Eleanor's vows of continence, a scandalous breach of Church discipline. Clandestine the marriage had to be or it would never have taken place, but the step was critical in the extreme, so fierce was the storm of popular and ecclesiastical resentment which it aroused.

Popular hostility was headed by no less a person than Richard earl of Cornwall. On the 8th of March Henry, so to speak, confessed his sins and vowed he would sin no more. Simon, on the contrary, faced the situation unabashed. By honey-tongued flattery he achieved much: for the rest, even the earl Richard had his price, which Simon, pauper though he was, could easily pay. But ecclesiastical hostility had also to be dealt with, and apparently in the same month of March Simon de Montfort set out for Rome. By the influence of his royal connection and a judicious expenditure of borrowed money he obtained a dispensation from the Pope and returned to England in October.

On the 28th of November, 1238, the countess of Leicester gave birth to a son: the king stood sponsor to the infant and named him Henry. The crisis was now over: Simon's hotly assailed marriage had had a happy issue: the earl stood high in the royal favour. Now was the time for him to consolidate his position as successor to his father's title and estates.

Early in the year 1238–9 we find the count of Montfort in England, probably in response to an urgent appeal from his brother; and on the 2nd of February, 1238–9, Simon at last was duly invested with the earldom of Leicester and the stewardship, and given seizin of the estates, the presence of Amaury enabling all legal formalities to be strictly complied with.[1] Simon having thus got seizin of the property, Amaury, by charter dated the 11th of April, released the Leicester estates to Simon and the heirs general of his body subject to the performance of all services incident to such estates, the service of steward included (*faciendo inde eis debitum servitium ad illam partem pertinens tam in senescalcia domini regis Henrici predicti quam in aliis servitiis*), reserving, however, to the grantor and his heirs the fee simple expectant on the determination of the estate tail.[2] This charter was confirmed by the king on the 17th of April, 1239, thus legally perfecting Simon's title to the property.[3] Amaury's charter of 1239 is in striking contrast to the document of 1232; and especially noticeable are the facts that in the later instrument the stewardship is referred to in proper and unpretentious terms, and the absurd pretence of assigning that office is altogether dropped.

In this way the hereditary stewardship in England became vested in Simon de Montfort, earl of Leicester, and the heirs of his body.

[1] Die vero purificationis beatae virginis contulit dominus rex comitatum Legrecestriae Simoni de Monteforti et investivit, vocato prius comite Almarico primogenito fratre ejus et pacificato, ne super hoc aliquando moveret quaestionem. (Matthew Paris, Rolls Series, iii, p. 524.)

[2] See Appendix. This charter appears in Rymer's Foedera erroneously dated A.D. 1232.

[3] See Appendix.

APPENDIX TO CHAPTER III

GRANT TO ROGER BIGOD
Carta Antiqua S. 14

Ricardus Dei gratia rex Anglie dux Normannie et Aquitanie comes Andegavie archiepiscopis episcopis abbatibus comitibus baronibus justiciariis vice-comitibus et omnibus ministris et fidelibus suis Francis et Anglis salutem. Sciatis nos fecisse Rogerum Bigot comitem de Norfolcia scilicet de tertio denario de Norwico et de Norfolcia sicut comes Hugo pater ejus melius unquam fuit tempore domini regis Henrici patris nostri et volumus et precipimus quod ipse et heredes sui ita libere et quiete et honorifice teneant de nobis et de heredibus nostris sicut aliquis comes Anglie melius et liberius et honorabilius comitatum suum tenet. Sciatis etiam nos reddidisse ei senescalciam suam et heredibus suis ita libere et quiete integre et honorifice habendam sicut Rogerus Bigot avus suus et comes Hugo pater suus melius et liberius vel integrius illam habuerunt tempore domini regis Henrici avi patris nostri vel tempore patris nostri. Sciatis etiam nos recognovisse ei rectum suum de iiij maneriis scilicet de Evesham et de Walesham et de Alvergate et de Aclay cum Bercariis et ea ei sicut recto heredi et sicut jus suum cum omnibus pertinentiis suis reddidisse. Preterea reddidimus eidem Rogero et presenti carta confirmavimus totam terram que fuit Albrede de Insula trans Humbrum et citra Humbrum sicut recto heredi scilicet Setringetonam et Holebroch cum omnibus aliis pertinentiis suis et nominatim illas terras que non fecerunt servicium castello de Belvario tempore regis Henrici avi patris nostri. Concessimus etiam eidem Rogero et heredibus suis et presenti carta confirmavimus omnes terras suas et tenementa de cujuscunque feodo sint habenda et tenenda sicut carte donatorum testantur. Quare volumus et firmiter precipimus quod prefatus Rogerus et heredes sui habeant et teneant omnia predicta de nobis et heredibus nostris cum socha et sacha et tol et theam et ynfangenetheof et dom et som bene et in pace libere et quiete integre plenarie et honorifice in bosco et plano in viis in semitis in pratis et pascuis in aquis et molendinis in vivariis et piscariis et stagnis in mariscis et trubariis in warennis et fugacionibus infra burgum et extra in homagiis et servitiis et releviis cum advocatione ecclesiarum et in omnibus aliis locis et rebus cum omnibus libertatibus et quietanciis et liberis consuetudinibus suis. Testibus H. Dunelm, H. Sarum, episcopis, comite Willielmo de Arundell, comite Alberico, comite Ricardo de Clare, Alberico de Ver, Johanne Marescallo, Willielmo Marescallo, Rogero de Toony, Ricardo de Clare, Ricardo de Muntfichet, Rogero de Pratell. dapifero, Willielmo de Pratell., Roberto de Witefeld, Willielmo filio Aldelin. Data apud Westmonasterium xxv die Novembris — per manum Willielmi Elyen. electi cancellarii nostri, regni nostri anno primo.

(Printed by Rymer, Foedera R. C., vol. i, p. 49.)

Fine Roll, 6 *John, m.* 10

Petronilda comitissa.Leircestrie dat domino regi tria millia marc. pro habenda Leircestria cum pertinentiis cum feodis et dominicis omnibus que pertinent ad honorem de Grantemeynill infra comitatum Leircestrie et extra sicut jus suum et hereditatem ita quod domino regi remaneant omnes terre Normannorum que sunt de eodem feodo et quod domus de Withewich committatur cui dominus rex voluerit qui de fideliter serviendo domino regi obsides dabit et predicta comitissa omnia predicta que dominus rex ei reddidit tenebit nisi per judicium curie domini regis dissaisiatur. Preterea domus de Withewic commissa est Willielmo de Senevilla et ipse Willelmus dabit Johannem filium et heredem suum in obsidem de fideliter serviendo et Ricardum filium suum alium si voluerit. Et de bruillio de Luttegarhal quod fuit ipsius comitisse faciet dominus rex voluntatem suam. Termini infra Purificacionem beate Marie anno &c. vjto. D. marc. in Pascha D. marc. in festo Sancti Johannis Baptiste D. marc. et in festo Sancti Michaelis D. marc. in Natali sequenti CCL. marc. in Pascha sequenti CCL. marc. in festo Sancti Johannis Baptiste CCL. marc. et in festo Sancti Michaelis CCL. marc.

Fine Roll, 6 *John, m.* 1

Saherus de Quincy dat mille marc. per sic quod dominus rex committat ei totam terram que fuit comitis Leicestrie in Anglia tam in dominicis quam in feodis excepto honore de Gretenmenill. et exceptis dotibus comitissarum tam matris quam uxoris ipsius comitis et excepto castello de Munsorell. cum hiis que pertinent ad castellum quod dominus rex retinet in manu sua quamdiu ei placuerit ita quod si forte Avicia comitissa de Monteforti soror uxoris ipsius Saeri venerit et partem suam in terra illa reclamaverit et si consideratio curie domini regis viderit expedire tota predicta terra tam in dominicis quam in feodis reveniet in manu domini regis sine aliqua contradictione ad faciendum utrique hoc quod judicium curie sue dederit. Et de hiis omnibus idem Saherus fecit litteras suas patentes domino regi. Et si forte predicta comitissa venerit et per judicium curie domini regis partem suam inde recuperaverit ipsa reddet secundum porcionem quam inde habebit porcionem predicti finis. Et per hunc finem concessit dominus rex quod per sacramentum legalium hominum declarabitur que terre et feoda sint de honore de Grantemenill et que de aliis honoribus quos comes tenuit.

Close Roll, 6 *John, m.* 11

Rex etc. vicecomiti Leircestrie. Precipimus tibi quod diligenter inquiri facias quantum terre de honore de Grentemenvill R. comes Leircestrie dedit episcopo Lincoln. in escambium terre sue extra Leirc. et quantum de honore predicto idem episcopus habet tantum ad valentiam sine dilatione facias habere Petronille comitisse Leircestrie de predicta terra que fuit episcopi extra Leirc. quia ipsa finem facit nobiscum pro habendo plenarie predicto honore. Teste me-ipso apud Meskesh. xxvij die Dec.

Ibid., m. 6

Rex etc. vicecomiti Gloc. etc. Scias quod commisimus dilecto et fideli nostro Saero de Quency totam terram que fuit comitis Leircestrie que est in manu nostra tam in dominicis quam in feodis. Et ideo tibi precipimus quod ei plenariam saisinam inde habere facias in balliva tua. Et precipe

omnibus militibus et liberis tenentibus de feodo illo qui sunt
in manu nostra in balliva quod eidem Sahero in omnibus sint
intendentes salva fide nostra. Teste domino Cantuar. apud
Abbedon. xxx die Marc.

Sub eadem forma scribitur aliis vicecomitibus in quorum
ballivis comes Leircestrie habuit terram vel feoda que fuerunt
in manu domini regis excepto castello de Montsorell quod
dominus rex retinuit in manu sua quamdiu ei placuerit.

Ibid., m. 3

Rex vicecomiti Leicestrie etc. Mandamus tibi quod sine
dilatione facias habere dilecto et fideli nostro Sahero de
Quency Baggewrde Westan et Seneby que fuerunt comitis
Leicestrie unde mandatum nostrum recepisti quod ea liberares
comitisse Leicestrie in custodia retinenda quamdiu nobis
placeret si non sint de honore de Grentemenvill nec de dote
predicte comitisse quia ea predicto Sahero commisimus in
custodia donec aliud ei inde fecerimus. Teste me-ipso apud
Turrim Lond. xxviij die April.

Sub eadem forma scribitur vicecomiti Bercscire de manerio
de Hungerford.

Ibid., m. 3.

Rex vicecomiti Leicestrie etc. Precipimus tibi quod sine
dilatione facias habere dilecto et fideli nostro Saero de Quency
terram extra mur. Leirc. que fuit comitis Leicestrie quia ei
commisimus eam in custodiam si non sit de honore de
Grentemeinvill nec de dote comitisse Leirc. Salva comitisse
Leic. terra quam ei reddi precepimus in escambium terre
de honore Grentemeinvill quam idem comes dedit domino
Lincoln. per concordiam inter eos factam pro terra illa et
salva canonicis Leic. terra quam idem comes dedit eis in ligia
potestate sua quam eis reddi precepimus. Teste meipso apud
Turrim London. xxviij die April.

Ibid., m. 2

Rex vicecomiti Wiltes. etc. Precipimus tibi quod sine dilatione facias habere Amicie comitisse de Muntford manerium
de Winterburstok. cum pertinentiis quod fuit datum ei in

maritagium quod commiseramus Sahero de Quency. Teste
G. filio Petri apud Windesor xxx die April. per Philippum
de Lucy.

Pipe Roll, 6 John, m. 17*d*

Petronilla comitissa Leircestrie reddit compotum de mmm
marc. pro habendo Leycestriam cum pertinentiis cum feodis
et dominicis omnibus que pertinent ad honorem de Grent-
meisnill infra comitatum et extra sicut jus suum et hereditatem
ita quod regi remaneant omnes terre Normannorum que sunt
de eodem feodo et quod domus de Wittewich commitatur cui
rex voluerit quod [de] fideliter regi serviendo obsides dabit et
predicta comitissa omnia predicta que rex ei reddidit tenebit
nisi per judicium curie regis dissaisietur. Termini. Infra
purificationem beate Marie anno regis vjto d marc. In
Pascha d marc. In festo sancti Johannis Bapt. d marc. Et
in festo S. Michaelis d marc. Et in Natali sequenti cc et
l marc. In Pascha sequenti cc et l marc. In festo sancti
Johannis Bapt. cc et l marc. Et in festo S. Michaelis cc et
l marc. ∫ resp. infra.

Petronilla comitissa Leicestrie reddit compotum de mmm
marc. pro habendo Leircestriam sicut supra continetur. In
thesauro d marc. Et ipsi regi in camera sua d marc. per
breve G filii Petri. Et debet mm marc.

Saerus de Quenci reddit compotum de m marc. per sic
quod rex committat ei totam terram que fuit comitis Leycestrie in Anglia tam in dominicis quam in feodis excepto
honore de Grentemeisnil et exceptis dotibus comitissarum
tam matris quam uxoris ipsius comitis et excepto castello de
Montesorel cum his que pertinent ad castellum quod rex
retinet in manu sua quamdiu ei placuerit. Ita quod si forte
Amicia comitissa de Monteforti soror uxoris ipsius Saeri
venerit (et partem suam in terra illa clamaverit et si consideratio curie regis viderit expedire tota predicta terra tam
in dominicis quam in feodis reveniet in manu)[1] in manu
regis sine aliqua contradictione ad faciendum utrique hoc
quod judicium curie sue dederit. Et de his omnibus idem
Saherus fecit litteras suas patentes regi. Et si forte predicta

---

[1] Interlined.

comitissa venerit et per judicium curie regis partem suam inde recuperaverit ipsa reddet secundum porcionem quam inde habebit porcionem predicti finis. Et per hunc finem concessit rex quod per sacramentum legalium hominum declarabitur que terre et feoda sint de honore de Grentemais-nill et que de aliis honoribus quos comes tenuit. In thesauro nichil et in perdonis ipsi Saiero c et lxxix li.–iij s.–iiij d. per breve regis quod attulit de perdonando ipsi ccc marc. (quod est in forulo marescalli). Et debet cccc et quater xx et vij li.–x s. quare resp. inde in rotulo ix.[1]

Fine Roll, 7 John, m. 11

Saherus de Quency dat v millia marc. pro habenda tota terra et omnibus feodis de honore de Grentemesnyll cum pertinentiis que dominus rex tradiderat Petronille comitisse Leicestrie et postea cepit in manu sua salvis inde eidem comitisse catallis et bladis et manerio de Wares. et feodis trium militum unde Rad. de Martiwas tenet feodum j militis de (etc.) . . . que idem Saherus concessit eidem comitisse tenenda quamdiu vixerit et salvis utrique comitisse Leicestrie dote sua. Et mandatum est vicecomiti Suhampton. quod sine dilatione habere faciat prefato Sahero plenariam saisinam sicut predictum est de hiis que inde sunt in balliva sua.

(Note, this entry is repeated on the Pipe Roll for 7 John, Northampton, m. 21.)

Close Roll, 7 John, m. 23

Rex etc. vicecomiti Leicestrie salutem. Scias quod recognitum est in curia nostra coram nobis que terre et feoda que continentur in scripto quod tibi mittimus sub sigillo nostro inclusa sunt de feodo de Grentemesnill et debent remanere comitisse Leicestrie. Et ideo tibi precipimus quod alias terras et feoda que comes Robertus tenuit et unde saisitus fuit in dominico suo ut de feodo in balliva tua die qua obiit liberes sine dilatione Sahero de Quency salva predicte comitisse dote sua quia ea cum alia terra quam habet tradidimus ei in custodia quamdiu nobis placuerit. Teste me-ipso apud Clarendon xxviij die Maii.

[1] The whole of the above entry is crossed out on the roll.

Ibid., m. 16

Rex archidiacono Stafford. et Roberto de Roppell etc. Mandamus vobis quod quater xx et xij libratas terre que sunt in Leicestria unde nobis mandastis assignetis comitisse Leicestrie juniori in dotem et viij libratas terre que restant ei alibi assignetis. Ita quod integre habeat centum libratas terre. Teste me-ipso apud Ivelcestr. xxv die Aug.

Mandatum est archidiacono Stafford. et Roberto de Roppell quod faciant habere L. comitisse Leicestrie bladum hujus autumpni de centum libratis terre ei assignatis per eos in dotem.

Ibid., m. 15

Rex etc. archidiacono Stafford. et Roberto de Roppell custodibus honoris de Grentemenill salutem. Mandamus vobis quod ad quater viginti et xij libratas terre quas Loretta comitissa Leicestrie habet in balliva vestra faciatis ei habere viij libratas terre ita quod per totum habeat c libratas terre sicut vobis alia vice precepimus. Teste me-ipso apud Merleberg. xv die Sept.

Pipe Roll, 7 John, m. 3

Comes Leircestrie debet iiij li.–viij d. de firm. de Belegrave cum redditu j domus que fuit Ricardi Rollos.

(The amount is pardoned on the next roll.)

Petronilla comitissa debet mm marcas pro habenda Leircestria sicut continetur ibidem. ∫; recordatum est per breve filii Petri et per barones quod non potuit habere terras pro quibus finivit quia Saierus de Quenci finivit pro eisdem terris per v millia marc. et ideo non debet predicta comitissa amplius summoniri de predictis mm marc.

Saierus de Quency cccc et quater xx et vij li. et x s. per sic quod rex committat sicut continetur ibidem quare resp. inde in rotulo ix.

Robertus de Roppelai reddit compotum de . . . lij li.–iiij s.– de honore de Leycestria de termino S. Michaelis. . . .

Close Roll, 8 John, m. 5

Rex etc. G. filio Petri etc. Mandamus vobis quod sine dilatione faciatis habere Simoni comiti Leicestrie c m. terre de terris quas Alanus filius Comitis tenuit vel in aliis escaetis nostris de terris Normannorum ad respondendum nobis inde si voluerimus. Et ponatis in respectum demandam finis quem comitissa mater comitis Leicestrie nobiscum fecit quousque sciamus qualiter fiat particio terrarum pro qua finivit. Teste me-ipso apud Muilleron xxviij die Aug.

Ibid., m. 3

Rex vicecomiti Wiltes. etc. Precipimus tibi quod facias habere dilecto nostro Sahero comiti Wintonie saisinam de viginti libratis terre cum pertinentiis in Winterburnestok que remanserunt Simoni comiti Leicestrie et matri sue qñ triginta librate terre assignate fuerunt predicto Sahero in eodem manerio quia volumus quod illas viginti libratas terre habeat ad proficiendum xl libratas terre que illi assignari debuerant in comitatu Leicestrie unde nondum ei assignate fuerunt nisi viginti librate tantum. Teste me-ipso apud Oxon. x die Feb. per (etc.).

Patent Roll, 8 John, m. 3

Rex omnibus militibus et libere tenentibus de honore comitis Leicestrie etc. Sciatis quod commisimus Roberto de Roppell custodiam tocius terre comitis Simonis de Monteforti in Anglia ad faciendum inde commodum nostrum de redditibus et vendicionibus bosci et aliis exitibus terre illius quousque habuerimus inde denarios quos idem comes nobis debet et volumus quod duo milites de eodem honore videant receptam illam et quantum nobis inde de predictis denariis solvatur. Et ideo vobis mandamus quod eidem Roberto interim tanquam ballivo nostro ad hoc sitis intendentes. Teste me-ipso apud Wudestok xiij die Feb. anno etc. viij.

CARTA SAIERI COMITIS WINTONIE
Carta Antiqua, K. 17

Johannes Dei gratia rex Anglie etc. Sciatis nos concessisse et presenti carta nostra confirmasse partitionem factam coram nobis et baronibus nostris per Simonem de Monteforti comitem Leircestrie et Saiherum de Quenci comitem Wintonie de omnibus terris et honoribus qui fuerunt

comitis Roberti de Leircestria die qua obiit cum omnibus
pertinentiis suis ita scilicet quod tota medietas illarum
terrarum et honorum in dominicis et feodis et omnibus aliis
rebus et locis integre remaneant uni illorum comitum et
altera medietas alteri salvis predicto comiti Simoni tertio
denario comitatus Leicestrie unde ipse comes est et capitali
mesag. Leicestrie et senescalcia nostra. Ita etiam quod
quadraginta librate terre de parte comitis Simonis remane-
bunt prefato comiti Saihero preter partem suam quousque
simul deliberaverit eidem comiti Saihero rationabilem partem
suam de terra que fuit prenominati comitis Roberti in
Normannia. Post obitum vero comitissarum Petronille matris
ejusdem comitis Roberti et Laurent. quondam uxoris ipsius
Roberti que dotate sunt de predicto honore dotes illarum
sicut diliberabuntur dividentur et una medietas inde remanebit predicto Simoni et altera medietas prefato Saihero.
Quare volumus et firmiter precipimus quod predictus comes
Saiherus et heredes sui habeant et teneant imperpetuum
predictam partem suam cum omnibus pertinentiis suis bene
et in pace libere et quiete integre et honorifice sicut predictum est. Testibus domino W. London., domino P. Winton.,
episcopis; G. filio Petri comite Essex, Alberico de Ver
comite Oxon., Rogero de Lasci constabulario Cestrie. Data
per manum Hugonis de Well. archidiaconi Well. apud
Illingbr. decimo die Marcii anno regni nostri octavo.

(Printed Rymer, Foedera,[1] R. C., i, p. 96. The Charter
Roll for this year is missing.)

Close Roll, 8 John, m. 7

Rex etc. baronibus de Scaccario etc. Mandamus vobis
quod de ccc marc. quas perdonavimus Sahero de Quency
anno etc. vij apud Dertem. quas ei locastis in mille marc.
quas nobis primo promiserat ut dicitur ei locari faciatis in
totali debito suo scilicet in sex millibus marc. per quas finivit

---

[1] In the Foedera this charter is headed "Pro Simone de Monteforti comite Leicestr. et Sahero de Quenci comite Winton [etc.]."
This is a misleading blunder. This is the earl of Winchester's
charter and is so headed in the roll: it is most unlikely that Simon
de Montfort was granted a corresponding charter.

nobiscum pro habenda terra que fuit Roberti comitis Leicestrie que eum contingit ex parte uxoris sue et pro habendo honore de Hinkel. Ita tamen quod de scaccario in scaccarium locentur ei ille ccc marc. scilicet ad quodlibet scaccarium c marc. Teste me-ipso apud Porcestr. xxv die Maii anno etc. viij.

Ibid., m. 1

Rex baronibus de Scaccario etc. Sciatis quod Robertus de Roppell pacavit in camera nostra apud Windlesor die Veneris ante Florid. Pasch. quater viginti marc. et decem marc. de exitibus honoris Leicestrie qui est in custodia sua. Et ideo vobis mandamus quod de tanto quietus sit. Teste W. Briw. apud Windlesor xiiij die April. anno regni nostri viij. per dominum Winton.

Rex baronibus suis de Scaccario etc. Computate Rob. de Roppell septies viginti et sex li. et xiij s. et iiij d. quos liberavit in camera nostra die Lune proxima post festum sancti Dunstan. apud Dunham. de exitibus terre Simonis de Monteforti de honore Leicestrie. Teste Roberto de Veteri Ponte apud Gringel. xxij die Maii anno regni nostri viij. per (etc.)

Close Roll, 9 *John, m.* 17

Rex baronibus de Scaccario etc. Computate Roberto de Roppell centum marc. quas liberavit in camera nostra apud Lameh. die apostolorum Petri et Pauli anno regni nostri ix de exitibus terre comitis Simonis de Monteforti quam habet in custodia. Teste me-ipso apud Lameh. xxix die Junii per etc.

Ibid., m. 14

Rex baronibus de Scaccario etc. Allocate Willelmo Briw. sexties viginti libr. quas comes Leircestrie recepit de catallis que fuerunt Roberti de Duvr. et ponatis inde in debitum Saherum comitem Wintonie et Simonem comitem Leircestrie unum eorum de una medietate et alterum de alia et illas ab eis exigatis. Teste G. filio Petri apud Westmonasterium viij die Octobris per dominum Winton.

Ibid., m. 12

Rex Roberto de Roppell salutem. Si Simon de Turrevill habuit in prepositura Leircestrie centum solidat. reddit. per annum tempore Roberti comitis Leircestrie et tempore Sahery de Quency comitis Wintonie postquam dictus R. comes mortuus est etc. illas ei habere faciatis secundum tenorem carte sue quam inde habet de predicto Roberto comite. Teste me-ipso apud Dunest. ij die Nov. per ipsum regem.

Ibid., m. 11

Rex baronibus etc. Mandamus vobis quod de finibus quos Saherus de Quincy comes Wintonie nobiscum fecit pro terris que fuerunt Roberti comitis Leicestrie tam de comitatu Leicestrie quam de honore de Hynkelay et de aliis terris suis in Anglia capiatis vos ad ipsum Saherum de medietate illorum finium computatis eidem S. in medietate illa hiis quos inde postea pacavit et unde habuit literas nostras de quietancia et concessimus ei quod de residuo illius medietatis reddat ad instans scaccarium sancti Michaelis anno regni nostri ix cc marc. et ad scaccarium Pasche proximo sequens cc marc. et sic de scaccario ad scaccarium cc marc. quousque illa medietas persolvatur. Et ideo [etc.]. . . . Teste W. de Briw. apud Merleberg. xxvij die Nov. per etc. . . . (In rotulo finium.)

Ibid., m. 10

Rex etc. baronibus etc. Computate Roberto de Roppell quadraginta libr. quas pacavit in camera nostra apud Geldef. de exitu terre Simonis comitis Leicestrie die beatorum Inno-centum anno etc. ix. Teste Ricardo de Marisco apud Geldef. xxviij die Dec. anno etc. ix.

Ibid., m. 7

Rex Roberto de Roppell etc. precipimus tibi quod sine dilatione facias habere monialibus de Pratell. consuetam elemosynam quam percipere solebant a comite Leircestrie apud Leircestriam. Teste me-ipso apud Winton. xv die Feb. per breve domini regis de privato sigillo suo.

H

Ibid., m. 6

Rex etc. Roberto de Roppell custodi terre que fuit quondam comitis Leircestrie etc.   Mandamus tibi quod faciatis habere in pace monialibus de Pratell. elemosynam ass. quam habere solebant ad scaccarium Leircestrie et si quid inde non venit in manum nostram de terminis preteritis id eisdem monialibus sine dilatione reddi facias.   Teste domino P. Winton. episcopo apud Merleberg xvij die Marcii. per eundem.

Rex baronibus de Scaccario etc.   Sciatis quod die Lune proxima ante festum beati Benedicti anno regni nostri ix recepimus in camera nostra apud Merleberg per manum Roberti de Roppell centum marcas de exitu terre Simonis comitis Leircestrie et ideo vobis mandamus quod ipsum inde quietum esse faciatis.   Teste Ricardo de Marisco apud Merleberg xvij die Marcii. per eundem.

Pipe Roll, 9 John, m. 19

Saierus de Quenci reddit compotum de mm et d marc. scilicet de medietate de mmmmm marc. per quas prius finiverat sicut continetur in rotulo vij in Norhamtescira pro habenda tota terra de honore de Grentemaisnil cum pertinentiis sicut continetur ibidem et de medietate de m marc. per quas finiverat ut rex committat ei totam terram que fuit comitis Leicestrie in tota Anglia sicut continetur in rotulo vi in Warrew. et Leicestr. et est summa istarum medietatum mmm marc.   Ita ut ei computetur quicquid ei perdonatum est in predictis comitatibus per breve regis et quicquid reddidit in thesauro sicut continetur in brevi quod rex misit baronibus quod est in forulo marescalli.   Ita videlicet ut ad predictam summam de mmm marc. respondeat quia rex perdonavit ei aliam medietatem scilicet mmm marc. per predictum breve.   In thesauro nichil et in perdonis ipsi Saero ccc marc. per breve regis et debet mm et dcc marc. de quibus debet reddere per annum cccc marc. ad duo scaccaria.   Idem reddit compotum de eodem debito.   In thesauro cc marc.   Et debet mm et d marc.   De quibus debet reddere per annum cccc marc. ad duo scaccaria. . . .

Saerus de Quenci comes Wintonie lx li. de catallis Fulberti

de Doure que requirebantur a Willelmo Bewre sicut continetur in compoto ejusdem Willelmi pro Devenesira. . . .

Simon de Muntfort comes Leycestrie debet lx li. de eisdem catallis sicut supra continetur.

Pipe Roll, 10 John, m. 3

Seiherus de Quenci reddit compotum de iij optimos caszuros (sic) pro habenda medietate suburbii Leircestrie quod partitum fuit per juratam legalium hominum ultimam factam per preceptum regis.   In thesauro nichil.   Et ipsi R. iij chacur.

(Note, the Close Rolls for 10, 11, 12, and 13 John are missing with the exception of a fragment for the twelfth year.   The Patent Rolls for 11, 12, and 13 John are also missing.)

Pipe Roll, 11 John, m. 2d.

Compotus terrarum Simonis de Muntfort comitis
Leycestrie a festo Purificationis anno viij
usque ad festum sancti Nicholai anni sequentis.

Robertus de Roppellay reddit compotum de iiij li.–viij s. de arerag. redditus prepositure Leircestrie de predicto termino Purificationis et de l s.–ix d.–ob. de arerag. cujusdam redditus extra portam orientalem de eodem termino.   Et de ij marc. de redditu pontium de eodem termino.   Et de xl d. de Gilda fullon. de eodem termino.   Et de ij s.–iij d. de quodam novo fefamento.   Et de vj li.–iij s.–ij d. de arerag. cujusdam taill. facti per eundem comitem.   Et de lxvj s.–j d. de arerag. j scutag.   Et de iiij li.–iiij s.–xi d. de arerag. perquisitorum. Et de xxxix s.–vj d.–ob. de arerag. herbagium.   Et de xxxv s. de arerag. vilenagium de Hinkelay de eodem termino.   Et de xxxix s.–viij d. de redditu burgi de Hinkelay.   Et de ij s.–ij d. de baillio de Hinkelay.   Et de iiij s.–iiij d. de essartis de Barewell.   Et de xx s. de redditu de la Wike.   Et de vj d. de arerag. taill. de Hinkelay.   Et de lxvj s.–iiij d.–ob. de firm. ville de Baggewurde.   Et de xlv s.–vij d. de firm. de Dereford de eodem termino.   Et de ix s. de arerag. taill. ejusdem ville. Et de iiij s. de melle vend.   Et de lxix s.–vj d.–ob. de firm. de Selton.   Et de x d. de firm. de Hecton.   Et de iij s.–xj d. de firm. de Stanton Ysabel.   Et de xviij s.–viij d. de firm. de

Belegrave. Et de xix s.–vj d. de fine Tome de Haddone.
Et de xiiij li.–vj s.–j d. de furnis Leircestrie et suburbio extra
portam orientalem et de redditibus de Belegrave et de Deresford antequam predicte terre assignarentur Saiero comiti
Wintonie. Et de c et xvij li.–xv d. de firm. prepositure ville
Leycestrie de anno ix. Et de x li. de dominico ville Leicestrie
posito ad firm. de eodem anno. Et de iiij li. de firm. pontium.
Et de xxxvj li.–xiij s.–iiij d. de firm. molendinorum Leircestrie.
Et de x s. de Gilda fullon. Et de xvj s.–viij d. de novo fefamento. Et de xviij d. de redditibus piperis. Et de lvj s.–v d. de
redditibus suburbii extra portam orientalem. Et de iiij s.–
ij d. de redditibus gallinarum. Et de c et vj li.–ij d. de taill.
ville Leircestrie. Et de x li. de perquisitionibus ejusdem ville.

Et de xj li.–v̲j̲ s.–viij d. de bobus vend. Et de xviij d. de toris

vend. Et de ij s. de fructu vend. Et de c et v s.–iij d.–ob. de
pasnag. Et de x li.–xij s. de herbag. Et de xv s.–v d.–ob. de
portitoribus fasciculorum. Et de ccc et viij li.–xj s.–ix d.–ob.
de bosco vend. per maneria de (toto) predicto tempore. Et de
c et viij s. de firm. villenag. de Hinkelay de predicto anno ix.
Et de c et xix s. de firm. burgi de Hinkelay. Et de vj s.–vj d.
de firm. de baillio. Et de lx s. de firm. de la Wike. Et de
xiij s.–ij d. de essartis de Barewude. Et de xiiij li.–vj s.–viij d.
de duobus taill. de soca de Hinkelay. Et de c et xix s. de
perquisit. Et de iij s.–ix d. de fructu vend. Et de x li.–vj s.–
vij d.–ob. de .redditibus de Baggewrde de anno ix. Et de
xiiij li. de duobus taill. ejusdem manerii. Et de iiij li.–vj s.–
xj d. de perquisit. ejusdem manerii de toto predicto tempore.
Et de c et xij s. de redditibus de Schelton. Et de vilj li. de
duobus taill. ejusdem manerii. Et de xl s.–j d. de perquisit.
Et de vj li.–vj s. de redditibus de Deresford. Et de ix li.–ij s.
de ij taill. Et de xxx s.–viij d. de perquisit. Et de iij s.–j d.
de melle vend. Et de ij s.–vj d. de firm. Osmundi de Hocton.
Et de xij s.–ix d. de firm. de Stanton Ysabel. Et de xx s. de
firm. Willelmi de Senevilla. Et de c s. de fine Tome de
Haddon. Et de iiij li. de fine Hugonis filii Willelmi. Et de
cc et xx li.–ix s.–x d.–ob. de redditibus predictorum maneriorum
de anno preterito. Et de xix s. de fructu vend. de eodem
anno. Et de iiij li.–xvij s.–ob. de pasnag. Et de c et xviij s.–

iij ob. de herbag. Et de c et lxiiij li.–vij s.–iiij d. de redditibus predictarum terrarum de duabus partibus hujus anni. Et de xxj li.–vij s.–v d. de pasnag. Et de x li.–vj s.–xj d.–ob. de herbag. Et de xxij s.–xi d. de predictis portitoribus. Et de c et xv s.–vj d. de lxxvij porcis vend. Et de iiij s.–j d. de redditibus unius essart. de termino sancti Michaelis.

S.–M et CC et XXIII li.–VIII s.–I d. In thesauro nichil. Et ipsi regi in camera dccc et xxij li.–viij d. per xj brevibus regis.

Et in decima constit. priori de Ware lxiij s.–j d. de decima pasnag. predictorum nemorum de toto predicto tempore. Et eidem prioi xxx li.–xvij s.–ij d. de decima boscorum venditorum de toto predicto tempore. Et eidem liij s.–ix d.–ob. de decima herbagii de predicto tempore. Et eidem lxx s. de decima portitorum fasciculorum. Et in elemosyna const. canonicis Leircestrie iiij li. de terminis Purificationis et Pentecost anni viij de vj li. quos solebant percipere de prepositura ad certos terminos per annum. Et eisdem xx s. de termino sancti Michaelis ejusdem anni de medietate que pertinet ad comitem Simonem. Et eisdem vj li. de eadem medietate de anno ix et x de v terminis. Et eisdem v s.–iiij d. in terra Radulfi Lit[l]e-child de eisdem terminis. Et eisdem xxvij d.–ob. de dono Simonis clerici de eisdem terminis. Et clericis servientibus in capella sancte Marie de Castello ij marc. de terminis Pasche et Pentecost anni vilj antequam terra partiretur inter comitem Simonem et Saierum de Quenci. Et eisdem xx s. de parte comitis Simonis de vj terminis sequentibus. Et monialibus de Pratell. x marc. de predictis duobus terminis. Et eisdem x li.–xj d. de parte comitis Simonis de predictis vj terminis. Et fratribus sancti Lazari dim. marc. de duobus premis. terminis. Et eisdem x s. de predictis vj terminis. Et eisdem iiij s.–v d. de firm. pontium de predictis ij terminis. Et eisdem dim. marc. de predictis vj terminis. Et fratribus leporosis Leircestrie xiij li.–iiij s. de utraque medietate de toto predicto tempore de parte comitis Simonis. Et eisdem xvij s.–viij d. de predicto tempore [ad] p̄bendam carettarii trahentis ligna eorum. Et priori de Ulveseroft viij s.–x d.–ob de predictis ij terminis. Et eidem j marc. de predictis vj terminis de decima Sopar. et Hunfrido capellano et Roberto clerico xxx s.–ij d. de predictis ij terminis de decima furnorum. Et eisdem xiij s. de predictis vj terminis. Et priori de Ware xlviij s.–x d.–ob. de decima molendinorum de predictis ij terminis. Et eidem v marc. et dim. de vj predictis terminis. Et Simoni de Turevilla x marc. de iiij terminis per breve regis. Et predicto priori de Ware xxxj li.–xij s. de decima prepositure de toto predicto tempore. Et fratribus hospital. de Estbrigg viij s.–x d.–ob. de ij predictis terminis. Et eisdem j marc. de predictis vj terminis. Et magistro Gileb. de Aquila v marc. de predictis ij terminis. Et eisdem c s. de predictis vj terminis per breve regis. Et in pastu porcorum iiij s.–viij d. per idem breve. Et in quiet. terrarum v forestariorum lxxij s. de toto predicto tempore. Et debet cc et lv li.–xvij s.–x d.–ob.

Idem reddit compotum de eodem debito. In thesauro nichil. Et in emptione ferri xx marc. per breve regis. Et debet cc et xlij li.–xi s.–ij d.–ob.

Idem reddit compotum de eodem debito. In thesauro nichil. Et predictis fratribus leporosis Leircestrie viij li. de firm. de Hinkelay de toto predicto tempore. Et priori de Hinkelay vij li.–xj s. de predicto tempore. Et monialibus de Wrokeshal xxx s. de eodem tempore. Et debet cc et xxv li.–x s.–ij d.–ob.

Idem reddit compotum de eodem debito. In thesauro xxx li. Et debet c et quater xx et xv li.–x s.–ij d.–ob.

Pipe Roll, 12 *John*, *m.* 9*d*

Compotus terrarum Simonis de Muntford de anno integro a die qua Willelmus de Cantelupe suscepit custodiam terrarum illarum.

Willelmus de Cantelupe, Philippus de Kinton pro eo, reddit compotum de c et lxxij li.–iiij s.–iiij d. de redditibus ass. ville de Leircestria cum molendinis et aliis redditibus sicut comp. in rotulo precedente. Et de xv li.–vj s.–viij d. de redditibus ass. de Hinkelai cum pertinentiis. Et de x li.–vj s.–vij d.–ob. de redditibus ass. de Baggewrde. Et de c et xij s. de redditibus de Scheltone. Et de vj li.–vj s. de redditibus ass. de Deresford. Et de ij s.–vj d. de firm. Osmundi de Hocton. Et de xij s.–ix d. de firm. de Stanton Ysabel. Et de xx s. de firm.

Willelmi de Senevilla. Et de c s. de fine Tome de Haddon.
Et de iiij li. de fine Hugonis filii Willelmi.

S. CC et XX li.–IX s.–X d.–ob.–Et de ccc marc. de taill.
ville Leircestrie. Et de c li. de fine heredis Henrici Costen.
Et de xix li.–xi s.–x d. (de perquisit.) Et de xxj li.–ix s. de
taill. predictorum maneriorum. Et de c et vj li.–j marc. de
bosco vend. Et de viij li.–xv s.–iiij d. de herbagiis. Et
de ix li.–ij s. de pasnag. Et de xij s.–vj d. de fructu vend.
Et de xxv s. de portitoribus fasciculorum.

S. DC et quater XX et VII li.–XVIII s.–X d. In thesauro
ccc li. per burgenses Leircestrie et Henricum Costen.

Et priori de Ware de decima const. de venditione boscorum
x li.–j marc. Et eidem xx s. de decima herbagii et portitorum.
Et eidem xviij s.–ij d. de decima pasnag. Et in elemosyna
const. canonicis Leircestrie lx s. Et eidem (sic) ij s. de terra
Rad. Litlechild. Et eisdem xvj d. de domo Simonis clerici.
Et clericis de castell. x s. Et monialibus de Pratell. c s.–xx d.
Et fratribus sancti Lazari v s. Et eisdem xl d. de firm.
pontium. Et fratribus leporosis Leircestrie iiij li.–xix s.–iij d.
Et eisdem iij s.–vj d. ad p̄bendam carettarii sui.

Et priori de Ulveseroft dim. marc. Et Unfrido capellano
et Roberto clerico xxij s.–viij d. Et priori de Ware xxxvj s.–
viij d. de decuna molendinorum. Et Willelmo de Turrevilla
c s. Et predicto priori de Ware xi li.–xvij s. de decima prepositure. Et fratribus hospital. de Estbrigge dim. marc.
Et magistro Gileb. de Aquila l s. Et fratribus leporosis
Leircestrie lx s. de firm. Hinkel. Et priori de Hinkel. lvj s.–
vij d.–ob. Et monialibus de Wrokeshal x s. Et in quiet.
terrarum forestar. xxx s. Et in pastu porcorum et cignorum
xvj s. Et in superplus quod habet in compoto suo pro
Wirecestria xvij li.–xij s.–ij d. Et debet ccc et xj li.–xvj s.–
viij d.–ob.

Idem reddit compotum de eodem debito. In thesauro nichil
et in stipendiis servientium et necessariis expensis per maneria
xx li. Et debet cc et quater xx et xj li.–xvj s.–viij d.–ob.

Idem reddit compotum de eodem debito. In thesauro cc
et xxiiij li.–ij s.–viij d. Et debet lxvij li.–xiiij s.–ob. De quibus
ix li.–vij s.–ij d.–ob. sunt super Robert. de Turneham. Et
debet predictus Willelmus lvij li.–vij d.

Idem reddit compotum de eodem debito. In thesauro nichil. Et in vasto Sopar. Leircestrie pro combustione xiiij marc.–viij d. Et debet xlvij li.–xiij s.–iij d.

Idem reddit compotum de eodem debito. In thesauro lib. et quietus est.

Pipe Roll, 13 *John*, *m.* 11*d.* Compotus terrarum
Simonis de Muntfort

. . . S. tocius ccc et xl li.–xviij d.–ob.

Pipe Roll, 14 *John*, *m.* 15. Compotus earundem

. . . S. ccc et lxv li.–xviij s.–ij d.–ob. (This includes "xxv li. de exitibus terre comitisse Petronille de uno termino in Wiltes. et Dorset.")

Pipe Roll, 15 *John*, *m.* 16. Compotus earundem

. . . S. tocius ccc et xl li.–xviij d.–ob.

Patent Roll, 17 *John*, *m.* 19

Rex Willelmo de Cantilupo salutem. Sciatis quod commisimus dilecto et fideli nostro R. comiti Cestrie totam terram comitis Simonis de Monteforti cum foresta et omnibus pertinentiis suis custodiendam ad opus ejusdem Simonis. Et ideo vobis mandamus quod eidem R. predictam terram cum foresta et omnibus pertinentiis suis sine dilatione habere faciatis. Et in hujus etc. vobis inde mittimus. Teste ut supra anno eodem. [scilicet apud Oxon. xxj die Julii anno regni nostri xvij].

Close Roll, 1 *Henry III*, *m.* 6

Mandatum est vicecomiti Berkes. quod sine dilatione plenam saisinam habere faciat R. comiti Cestrie de manerio de Saudon cum pertinentiis quod est de feodo comitis Simonis de Monteforti. Et qm. etc. Teste comite ut proximo supra. [scilicet apud Lameth. iij die Octobris].

Patent Roll, 2 *Henry III*, *m.* 3

Mandatum est omnibus ballivis et fidelibus etc. quod manuteneant protegant et defendant homines res terras redditus

et omnes possessiones que fuerunt comitis Leicestrie que sunt
in custodia Philippi de Albiniaco nullam eis etc. addita clausa
"Volumus etiam quod terre predicte et possessiones habeant
easdem libertates quas habuerunt tempore comitis Roberti
filii Petronille." Teste comite apud Newerc xxij die Julii.

Patent Roll, 3 Henry III, m. 5

Similar writ dated 10th of January.

Patent Roll, 2 Henry III, m. 2

Rex omnibus militibus et libere-tenentibus et aliis de honore Leicestrie qui contingebat comitem Simonem de Monteforti in comitatibus Warewici et Leicestrie salutem. Sciatis
quod commisimus Stephano de Segrave et Ricardo de Brom
clerico omnes terras que contingebant comitem Simonem de
Monteforti de honore Leicestrie in comitatu (sic) Warewici et
Leicestrie ad respondendum de exitibus earundem ad scaccarium nostrum quamdiu nobis placuerit. Et ideo vobis
mandamus quod eisdem Stephano et Ricardo tanquam ballivis
nostris in omnibus sitis intendentes et respondentes. Et in
hujus etc. Teste comite apud Bannebiry xxvj die Julii anno
etc.

Rex vicecomiti Wiltesire salutem. Scias quod comes Simon
de Monteforti sicut pro certo audivimus mortuus est. Mittimus
igitur in partes tuas Galfridum le Sauvage et Philippum de
Langerg ad custodiendum omnes terras que fuerunt ipsius
comitis in baillia tua et tibi precipimus quod eisdem Galfrido
et Philippo sine dilacione plenam saisinam habere facias de
omnibus terris que fuerunt predicti comitis in baillia tua cum
bobus vaccis ovibus et porcis et aliis instauris que fuerunt
ipsius comitis. Teste comite apud Crandun xxvj die Julii
anno etc. secundo.

Close Roll, 2 Henry III, m. 3

Rex Willelmo de Cantilupo salutem. Audivimus quod
comes Simon de Monteforti in fata concessit. Et ideo vobis
mandamus quod sine dilatione faciatis habere dilecto et
fideli nostro Stephano de Segrave plenam saisinam de
omnibus terris in balliva vestra que ipsum Simonem heredit-

arie contingebant de honore Leicestrie cui commisimus custodiam earundem terrarum ad respondendum nobis ad Scaccarium nostrum de exitibus earundem. Teste ut supra. [scilicet apud Walingeford xxviij die Julii. (See also Fine Roll, pt. 1, m. 3, and pt. 2, m. 3.)].

Fine Roll, 2 Henry III, pt. 1, m. 3, and pt. 2, m. 3

Mandatum est Philippo de Albiniaco quod plenam saisinam habere faciat Willelmo de Cantilupo vel certo nuncio suo litteras domini regis deferente de omnibus terris que fuerunt comitis Simonis de Monteforti com. Leicestrie custodiendis quamdiu domino regi placuerit. Teste comite apud Caversham vij die Aug.

Close Roll, 2 Henry III, m. 2

Dominus rex concessit P. Winton. episcopo custodiam terre que fuit comitis Simonis de Monteforti quamdiu ei placuerit et mandatum est Petro de Maulay quod ei sine dilatione plenam saisinam habere faciat de terra predicta cum pertinentiis in ballia sua. Teste comite apud Winton. xxvj die Augusti.—Idem in rotulo finium.[1]—Eodem modo scribitur W. com. Sarr. et Philippo de Albiniaco.

Close Roll, 3 Henry III, m. 7

Rex Philippo de Albiniaco custodi honoris Leicestrie salutem. Mandamus vobis quod habere faciatis Roberto de Stanton xx solidos ad preposituram Leicestrie quos habere debet de dono comitis Roberti et unde cartam suam habet. Teste ut supra. [scilicet xix die Junii].

Close Roll, 4 Henry III, m. 7

Rex vicecomiti Sumerset salutem. Scias quod Johannes de Cromhal est in servicio nostro per preceptum nostrum ad custodiendum honorem Leicestrie in comitatu Wiltesire. Et ideo tibi precipimus quod ipsum Johannem non ponas in assisis in comitatu tuo quamdiu fuerit in servicio nostro ad predictum honorem custodiendum in predicto comitatu. Teste H. etc. apud Westmonasterium xxiiij die Julii.

[1] Pt. 1, m. 3; and pt. 2, m. 2.

Ibid., m. 2

Rex Philippo de Albiniaco salutem. Sciatis quod concessimus R. comiti Cestrie et Lincolnie quod habeat talem saisinam de honore Leicestrie cum pertinentiis quamdiu nobis placuerit qualem inde habuit die qua iter peregrinacionis sue versus terram sanctam arripuit. Et ideo vobis mandamus quod eidem comiti de predicto honore plenam saisinam sine dilatione habere faciatis. Teste ut supra. [scilicet iiij die Octobris].

Eodem modo scribitur vicecomiti Leicestrie, vicecomiti Dorsetie, vicecomiti Wiltescire.

Patent Roll, 4 Henry III, m. 1

Rex omnibus militibus libere-tenentibus et aliis de honore Leicestrie salutem. Sciatis quod concessimus R. comiti Cestrie et Lincolnie quod talem habeat saisinam de honore Leicestrie cum pertinentiis quamdiu nobis placuerit qualem inde habuit die qua iter peregrinacionis sue versus terram sanctam arripuit. Et ideo vobis mandamus quod eidem comiti sitis in omnibus que ad honorem illum pertinent intendentes et respondentes quamdiu nobis placuerit sicut predictum est. Et in hujus etc. Teste ut supra, [scilicet iiij die Octobris] anno etc. iiij. per eundem et consilium domini regis.

Patent Roll, 11 *Henry III, m.* 6

Dominus rex concessit R. comiti Cestrie et Lincolnie totam illam partem [honoris Leicestrie cum pertinentiis quam prius tenuit de ballio predicti j. regis][1] patris domini regis cum omnibus escaetis que inde decetero excidere poterunt habendam et tenendam sibi ad totam vitam suam [hoc modo quod dominus rex non admittet ad pacem suam comitem Leicestrie ad quem predicta pars pertinet][1] ita quod partem illam ei reddat nisi predictus comes Cestrie et Lincolnie pacem invenire possit versus regem Francorum ita quod recuperet terram suam in Normannia quam amisit in servicio predicti j. regis patris domini regis. In cujus etc. Teste rege apud Westmonasterium xviij die Maii.

[1] Expanded by collation with the preceding grant.

AMAURY COUNT OF MONTFORT TO HENRY III
Angleterre, II, No. 14 (5)

Excellentissimo domino suo Henrico, Dei gratia illustri regi Anglorum, Amalricus comes Montisfortis et Leycestrie salutem in eo qui dat salutem regibus et cum omni subjectione tam debitum quam devotum ad obsequia famulatum. Vestre regie majestati multotiens supplicavi humiliter et devote ut mihi terram meam et jus meum quod habeo et habere debeo in Anglia, quod bone memorie pater meus de vestro tenuit et tenebat dum decessit pacifice ac quiete, mihi vestro militi redderetis; quod quia dominationi vestre non placuerit hucus- que facere, adhuc vestre majestati supplico humilitate qua possum quatinus hac vice mihi vobis servire parato sicut decuerit reddere dignemini terram; et si hoc vobis non placu- erit, ego ad pedes dominationis vestre transmitto Simonem fratrem meum qui de domino rege Francie nichil tenet, cui si eam reddideritis me pro bene pagato tenerem. Datum Parisius, mense Febuario.

(A thirteenth-century roll preserved in the Bibl. Nat. de France. Printed in Layettes du Trésor des Chartes, no. 2088: printed also from the Carte MSS. in Bibl. Bodl. by Rymer, Foedera R.C., i, p. 202.)

Patent Roll, 14 *Henry III, m.* 6

De honore Leicestrie reddendo—Rex omnibus ad quos pre- sentes litere pervenerint salutem. Sciatis quod ad petitionem et dimissionem Aumarici de Monteforti filii et heredis Simonis de Monteforti quondam comitis Leicestrie nos et heredes nostri tenemur reddere Simoni de Monteforti filio predicti comitis Simonis et fratri ipsius Aumarici omnes terras cum pertinentiis quas ipse Simon comes aliquando tenuit in Anglia de honore Leicestrie cum tercio denario comitatus Leicestrie quem ipse comes Simon percepit nomine comitis Leicestrie et cum senescalcia quamcito predicte terre deliberabuntur de manu dilecti et fidelis nostri R. comitis Cestrie et Lincolnie qui eas tenet de ballio nostro per cartam nostram. In cujus rei testimonium has literas nostras patentes ei fieri fecimus. Hiis testibus: H. de Burgo &c, R. comite Cestrie et Lincolnie, W. comite Marescallo, S. de Sedgrave, Philippo de Albiniaco, Radulfo filio Nicholai et aliis. Date per manum R. Cycestrensis episcopi cancellarii nostri apud Westm. vj die Febuarii.

Close Roll, 14 *Henry III, m.* 12

Rex Simoni de Monteforti salutem. Noveritis quod Amaricus de Misternum miles vester quem ad nos pro negotiis vestris misistis in Angliam ea que fuerunt eidem a vobis injuncta diligenter nobis exposuit. Quibus intellectis ut in servitio nostro stare velitis tam in Anglia quam alibi concessimus vobis quadringentas marcas annuas de scaccario nostro donec comitatum Leicestrie receperitis secundum quod provisum fuit cum essetis ad nos in Anglia. Rogamus igitur vos quatinus dictum annuum censum quadringentarum marcarum recipere et in servitio nostro stare velitis. Teste rege apud Rading viij die Aprilis.

Close Roll, 15 *Henry* III, *m.* 6

Rex cepit homagium Simonis de Monteforti de tota terra quam Simon de Monteforti pater ejus quondam comes Leicestrie de rege tenuit de honore Leicestrie et que ipsum Simonem jure contingit hereditario. Et mandatum est vicecomiti Leicestrie quod de tota predicta terra cum pertinentiis in ballia sua eidem Simoni sine dilatione plenam saisinam habere faciat. Teste rege apud castrum Matildis xiij die Augusti.

Eodem modo scribitur vicecomitibus Suhamptonie, Dorsetie et Wiltesire.

Ibid., *m.* 3

Rex cepit homagium Simonis de Monteforti de tota terra quam Simon de Monteforti quondam comes Leicestrie pater ejus cujus heres ipse est de rege tenuit in capite de honore Leicestrie. Et mandatum est vicecomiti Leicestrie quod de tota terra que fuit predicti Simonis de Monteforti in balliva tua (sic) predicto Simoni filio suo talem saisinam habere faciat qualem predictus Simon pater ejus inde habuit die quo egressus est terram Anglie et qualis inde saisina postea devenit in manum Johannis regis etc. post recessum predicti

Simonis a terra Anglie. Teste rege apud Elmel. xxij die Septembris.

Eodem modo scribitur vicecomitibus Suhamptonie, Wiltescire et Dorsetie.

AMAURY COUNT OF MONTFORT TO HENRY III
Angleterre, II, No. 14 (4)

Karissimo domino suo Henrico Dei gratia regi Anglie illustri Amauricus comes Montisfortis, Francie constabelarius, salutem in eo qui dat salutem regibus et debitum famulatum. Sicut per alias literas nostras jam vestre significavimus majestati nos concessimus karissimo fratri nostro Simoni de Monteforti terram nostram de Anglia et jus nostrum et adhuc concedimus, vos rogantes quatinus de omni jure nostro quod habemus et habere debimus in Anglia saisietis eundem, et cum de ipsa saisitus fuerit nos absolvimus vos super hoc et quitamus salvo jure nostro et heredum nostrorum si sine herede decesserit frater noster et si ipsum de jure nostro in hominem receperitis hac vice qua ad vos proficiscitur in presenti. Datum apud Floriacum anno Domini mcc tricesimo primo mense Augusto.[1]

(A thirteenth-century roll preserved in the Bibl. Nat. de France. Printed in Layettes du Trésor des Chartes, no. 2151 : printed also from the Carte MSS. in Bibl. Bodl. by Rymer, Foedera R. C., i, p. 206.)

Close Roll, 16 *Henry III, m.* 17

Mandatum est vicecomiti Leicestrie quod occasione precepti domini regis quod (ei) fecit de facienda Symoni de Monteforti tali seisina de omnibus terris que fuerunt Symonis de Monteforti quondam comitis Leycestrie patris sui et que ipsum hereditarie contingunt in balliva sua qualem idem Symon comes pater ejus inde habuit die quo egressus est terram Anglie tempore domini Johannis regis patris nostri non disseisies Margaretam comitissam Wyntonie de suburbio Leicestrie versus orientem vel de furnis Leycestrie vel de maneriis de Belegrave et de Glenesfeld vel de redditibus

---

[1] Datum apud Parisiis A.D. 1232 mense Augusto (Foedera).

centum et xix sol. in Weston et xl sol. in Deresford de quibus ut dicitur postquam primo facta fuit particio honoris Leycestrie inter Saherum de Quency comitem Wyntonie et ipsam comitissam Wyntonie uxorem ejus et predictum comitem Symonem tempore predicti Johannis regis patris nostri ipse Saer et comitissa uxor ejus recuperaverunt seisinam coram justiciariis postea assignatis per preceptum dicti patris nostri ad particionem inde secundo faciendam de voluntate ipsius comitis Symonis et ad instantiam predictorum Saheri et comitisse uxoris sue conquerentium injustam prius eis factam fuisse particionem et pro qua particione facienda per predictos justiciarios idem comes Symon ante recessum suum de Anglia attornavit quendam militem suum ad particionem suam ad opus suum recipiendam per extentam factam de predicto honore Leycestrie per predictos justiciarios post recessum suum ab Anglia. Teste ut supra. [scilicet x die Januarii].

Patent Roll, 16 *Henry III, m.* 6

Rex omnibus etc. salutem. Sciatis quod de voluntate nostra et ad petitionem Aumarici comitis de Monteforti primogeniti fratris dilecti et fidelis nostri Simonis de Monteforti reddidimus eidem Simoni totam terram cum omnibus pertinentiis suis que fuit Simonis de Monteforti quondam comitis Leicestrie in Anglia patris predictorum Aumarici et Simonis et que ad ipsum Aumaricum jure hereditario pertinebat et inde homagium predicti Simonis cepimus. In cujus etc. Teste rege apud Salop. xxvij die Maii.

Patent Roll, 16 *Henry III, m.* 5

Rex omnibus ad quos presentes littere pervenerint salutem. Sciatis quod concessimus dilecto et fideli nostro Simoni de Monteforti quod cum decetero escaete alique de terris Normannorum acciderint de feodo suo in Anglia quas nos et antecessores nostri in manu nostra retinere vel dare consuevimus ipse liberam inde habeat amministrationem retinendo eas in manu sua vel pro voluntate sua conferendo donec terra nostra Anglie et terra Normannie communes fuerint. In cujus rei testimonium &c. Teste rege apud Wudestok xv die Junii.

THE IRREGULAR GRANT TO SIMON DE MONTFORT
Angleterre, II, No. 14 (1)
Cotton Vesp. D., x, *fol.* 132

Noverint universi presentes et futuri quod nos Amalricus[1] comes Montisfortis, Francie constabelarius, dedimus et concessimus et hac presenti carta nostra confirmavimus Simoni de Monteforti comiti Leycestrie fratri nostro totam terram que fuit bone memorie Simonis patris nostri in Anglia et quicquid ad ipsum Simonem patrem nostrum accidere potuit de hereditate Amicie heredis et sororis comitis Roberti Leycestrie primogenite cum Senescalcia Anglie totius[2] habendum et tenendum eidem[3] Simoni et heredibus suis de uxore sua desponsata exeuntibus de Henrico illustri rege Anglie et heredibus suis cum omnibus pertinentiis libere (et[4]) pacifice et hereditarie faciendo inde dicto regi[5] Anglie servitium quod ad dictam terram pertinet et ut nos vel heredes nostri in predictam terram cum pertinentiis versus predictum Simonem vel heredes suos de uxore sua desponsata exeuntes nullum clamum[6] de cetero habere possimus presenti (nostro[7]) scripto sigillum nostrum apposuimus hoc retento quod si dictus Simon frater noster sine herede de uxore sua genito decederet tota terra predicta cum senescalcia[8] ad nos et heredes nostros libere et sine difficultate aliqua reveniret. Actum Parisius anno Domini mcc tricesimo secundo (mense Junio[9]).

(No. 1 is a thirteenth-century roll preserved in the Bibl. Nat. de France. No. 2 is a thirteenth-century transcript, temp. Edward I, preserved in the British Museum.)

(Printed in Layettes du Trésor des Chartes, No. 2190; printed also from the Carte MSS. in Bibl. Bodl. by Rymer, Foedera, R.C., i, p. 205.)

Charter Roll, 23 *Henry III, m.* 4, *No.* 32. (By Inspeximus, dated April 17th, 1239)

Sciant presentes et futuri quod ego Amauricus comes Montisfortis Francie constabularius in presencia Henrici

---

[1] Amaricus, no. 2.　　[2] tocius Anglie, no. 2.　　[3] eisdem, no. 2.
[4] omit, no. 2.　　[5] regi dicto, no. 2.　　[6] clamium, no. 2.
[7] omit, no. 1.　　[8] senescallia, no. 2.　　[9] omit, no. 2.

illustris regis Anglie filii regis Johannis apud Westmonasterium die Lune proxima post quindenam Pasce anno regni ipsius Henrici regis vicesimo tertio recognovi concessi et quietum clamavi de me et heredibus meis dilecto fratri meo Simoni de Monteforti comiti Leycestrie totam partem honoris Leycestrie cum omnibus pertinentiis in regno Anglie adeo plene et integre sicut comes Simon pater noster vel comes Robertus Leycestrie illam unquam melius plenius et liberius tenuerunt habendam et tenendam eidem Simoni fratri meo et heredibus suis de corpore suo procreatis de predicto domino Henrico rege et heredibus suis libere et quiete in perpetuum cum omnibus escaetis et aliis que inde accidere possent de eodem honore faciendo inde eis debitum servitium ad illam partem pertinens tam in senescalcia domini regis Henrici predicti quam in aliis servitiis salvo tamen jure meo et heredum meorum si forte contigerit quod idem Simon frater meus sine heredibus de corpore suo procreatis obierit vel heredes sui de corpore suo procreati forte obierint sine heredibus de corpore ipsorum procreatis. Et ut hec mea recognitio concessio et quieta clamatio stabiles et firme secundum quod predictum est permaneant inperpetuum huic scripto sigillum meum apposui. Hiis testibus Ricardo comiti Cornubie fratre domini regis, Johanni de Lascy comite Lincolnie et constabulario Cestrie, H. de Bohun [comite] Herefordie et Essexie, Willielmo de Ralegh thesaurario Exon., Johanne de Monemue, Henrico Alditheley, Petro de Malo-Lacu, Henrico de Trublevill, Roberto de Quincy, Johanne filio Galfredi, Ricardo de Gray, Stephano de Setgrave, Hereberto filio Mathei, G. vicedomino Pincon., Guidone et Harveo de Caprosia fratribus, Amaurico de Meten, Amaurico de sancto Amando, Gaufrido Dispensatore. Actum apud Westmonasterium in presencia dicti domini regis et presente venerabili patre domino Ottone Dei gratia sancti Nicholai in carcere Tulliano diacono cardinali apostolice sedis legato anno et die prenominatis.[1]

(Printed from transcripts only in Layettes du Trésor des

[1] See also Duchy of Lancaster, Great Cowcher, vol. ii, fol. 45d, no. 5.

Chartes, no. 2789 ; also very inaccurately by Rymer, Foedera R.C., i, p. 204.)

Charter Roll, 23 Henry III, m. 4, No. 34

Rex archiepiscopis episcopis etc. salutem.   Sciatis quod recognitionem concessionem et quietam clama[1] {nciam} (cionem)[2] quas Amauricus comes Montisfortis, Francie constabularius, in presencia nostra fecit dilecto fratri et fideli nostro Simoni de Monteforti comiti Leicestrie per cartam suam de tota parte honoris Leicestrie cum omnibus pertinentiis in regno nostro Anglie habenda et tenenda eidem comiti Simoni et heredibus suis de corpore suo procreatis adeo plene et integre sicut comes Simon pater eorum comitum Amaurici et Simonis vel Robertus comes Leicestrie illam unquam melius plenius et liberius tenuerunt ratas et gratas habemus pro nobis et heredibus nostris Quare volumus et firmiter precipimus pro nobis et heredibus nostris quod predictus frater noster comes Simon et heredes sui de corpore suo procreati habeant et teneant inperpetuum predictam partem predicti honoris cum omnibus pertinentiis suis bene et in pace libere et quiete cum omnibus libertatibus et liberis consuetudinibus ad eam pertinentibus sicut carta predicti comitis Amaurici quam idem comes Simon inde habet rationabiliter testatur.   Hiis testibus venerabilibus patribus E. Cant. archiepiscopo, ʃ. Bathon, W. Exon., H. Eliens., R. Linc., W. Wigorn., et W. Karleol. episcopis ; ʃ. comite Linc. et constabulario Cestrie, W. comite Warrenn., W. comite de Ferar., H. comite Heref. et Essex., Willelmo Lungesp., W. de Vescy, Hugone Wak., Stephano de Segrave, Johanne filio Galfridi, Bertram. de Cryoill., Amaurico de Sancto Amando, Galfrido Dispensar., et aliis. Data per manum regis apud Westmonasterium xvij die Aprilis anno regni nostri xxiij.

[1] An erasure.   [2] An interlineation.

CHAPTER IV

THE EVOLUTION OF THE HEREDITARY
STEWARDSHIP IN THE HANDS OF
SIMON EARL OF LEICESTER

IN order to appreciate the evolution of the hereditary
stewardship during the reign of Henry the Third we
must again take up the history of the other seneschals, the
king's ordinary household stewards, the provincial governors
and so forth.

During Richard's reign the normal number of household
stewards in attendance was still two, and their usual style
became *senescallus* or *senescallus regis* (which was also the
proper style of the hereditary stewards): this style was
maintained during the next two reigns, but the number of
stewards became ultimately reduced to one. This household
office was increasing in importance, and during the thirteenth
century acquired extensive judicial powers.

The various French provinces from time to time held by
the English kings during the period 1189–1272 were uni-
formly placed under the control of seneschals who had viceregal authority. Their proper style was *senescallus Normannie*,
senescallus Pictavie, or as the case might be.[1] They were
nominated by the king and held office during his pleasure,
with, however, one important exception. On the 24th June,
1200, John made William des Roches hereditary seneschal
of Anjou,[2] Maine and Touraine: this baron transferred his
allegiance to Philip Augustus, and continued seneschal of
Anjou under the new régime.[3] It is noticeable that the

---

[1] See the Close, Patent, Norman and Charter Rolls passim.

[2] Rotuli Chartarum, R.C., p. 72. Compare the appointment of
Geoffrey de Cella as seneschal of Poitou, ibid., p. 59b.

[3] Delisle, Cat. des Actes de Philippe-Auguste, nos. 848, 849;
note also ibid., no. 562.

French king, after some hesitation,[1] ended by abolishing the more recent stewardship of Normandy; he however retained William de Humez as hereditary constable of that duchy.[2] Poitou and Gascony were occasionally placed under the same seneschal. The three dioceses of Limoges, Perigord, and Cahors, ceded to England by the treaty of 1258, were first placed under the control of the seneschal of Gascony,[3] but a separate seneschal for these was appointed in 1260.[4] Ireland was treated differently, and placed under a justiciar: naturally in this case the English system was preferred.[5]

The chief officer of state in England, until the death of John, was still the chief justiciar. On the accession of the infant Henry, William Marshal, earl of Pembroke, took control of the administration; and, no doubt in deference to precedent, began by styling himself justiciar of England.[6] The Marshal certainly intended to govern; but he cannot have intended either to oust Hubert de Burgh from, or even to share with him, the ordinary judicial duties of his office. Still, to have two justiciars, one the subordinate of the other, was not then a very satisfactory arrangement: accordingly, about the middle of November, 1216, the Marshal changed his style to *rector noster et regni nostri*,[7] and under this designation the earl continued to govern with Hubert as his justiciar.

On the death of the Marshal the justiciarship recovered for a short time only its former supremacy. In April, 1234, Stephen de Segrave, the then justiciar, was removed from his post, and the office was allowed to fall into abeyance.

Enters at this stage Simon de Montfort, ambitious to a degree, marvellously capable, earl of Leicester and yet a penniless adventurer, brother-in-law to the king of England but without English supporters. A most unstable synthesis,

---

[1] Delisle Cat. des Actes de Philippe-Auguste, nos. 817b, 825a.
[2] Ibid., no. 1011, etc.
[3] For a list of seneschals of Gascony see Henry III, Royal Letters, Rolls Series [27], vol. ii, pp. 399–400.
[4] Close Roll, 44 Henry III, pt. i, m. 2d.
[5] See Cal. of Docts., Ireland, vol. i, p. 582.
[6] Close Roll, R.C., p. 293; Patent Roll, R.O., i, pp. 1–3 passim.
[7] Patent Roll, R.O., pp. 3 et sqq. passim.

this omnipotence of the man, the impotence of his circumstances.

The same year (1239) which saw Simon established in his earldom and chief man in the king's council also witnessed his utter downfall. His friendship with earl Richard, that dispensation from the Pope and other similar commodities represented a heavy sum of borrowed money. His creditor unfortunately was under a vow, for the breach whereof he excused himself to the Pope: "he was very sorry but until Simon paid his debts he really could not go crusading." Perhaps Rome, when she heard the excuse, had a twinge or two of conscience at the thought of where most of this money had been spent. At all events fierce and quick came the papal fulminations: a day for settlement was named, in default, excommunication.[1] Simon, in dire distress, having neither cash nor credit, appears to have raised the money to pay the debt from Thomas of Savoy by naming Henry, without his authority, as surety for the amount.

For the time being, however, all was well in England and nothing known. The queen, whom they had feared sterile, bore a son to her lord, and great were the rejoicings. The earl of Leicester attended the christening.[2] In August the queen was to go to her churching and the earl and countess of Leicester were summoned for the event. But between the invitation and the day of the ceremony Henry heard the whole story. Thomas presumably had applied to Henry for payment.

When the earl and countess arrived for the ceremony Henry was beside himself with anger: bade them begone; used ugly words, shameful and hard to relate. He called Simon excommunicate, the seducer of his sister, whom but for imminent scandal to the nation he should never have married—this before all the court. Then cursed him for obtaining at Rome a cloak for his transgressions by perjury

[1] See Dehaisnes, Inventaire de l'ancienne Chambre des Comptes de Lille, p. 270; Bémont, Simon de Montfort, appendix no. 1. Letter giving directions as to Simon's excommunication.

[2] Matthew Paris, Rolls Series, iii, p. 540.

and wholesale corruption, and for his crowning iniquity in naming Henry as surety for his debts.[1]

The earl and countess wept: the king was unmoved.[2] Simon and his lady withdrew, and thought to take refuge in the palace of the late bishop of Winchester, lent them by the king. Henry gave orders for their instant ejectment; and it was only through the intervention of the earl of Cornwall that these orders were not duly executed.[3] Simon saw matters had reached a hopeless pass. The following evening,[4] in the gathering darkness, he and his wife then great with child dropped down the tideway of the Thames in a little boat, and straightway fled to France.[5]

In April, 1240, Simon returned to England. Apparently the catastrophe to the Christian arms at Gaza in November, 1239, was the pretext for a reconciliation which perhaps both sides desired. Anyhow Simon was cordially welcomed by the king. The earl had not returned to stay, but merely to prepare for the crusade to avenge Gaza: Simon's family honour was concerned, for Amaury his brother was among the prisoners captured on that occasion.

With this crusade we are not concerned. That Simon gave striking proofs of his power and capacity may be inferred from the proposal to make him governor of Jerusalem.[6] Simon left the Holy Land, and when Henry made his mad attempt to renew the war with France he joined him in Poitou. How the French attacked at the bridge of Taillebourg, how the English fell back upon Saintes, the prowess of Leicester, Salisbury and Norfolk are matters of general history and have, moreover, no bearing upon the subject

---

[1] Matthew Paris, Rolls Series, iii, p. 566.

[2] Et cum flentes et ejulantes reverterentur, veniam flagitantes, regiam iram non sedarunt (ibid.).

[3] Compare Matthew Paris with Simon's own account of the affair in Bémont, Simon de Montfort, appendix no. 34.

[4] The time and sequence of events are somewhat obscure.

[5] . . . cum dies inclinasset, per Tamensem in cimba minima cum uxore tunc gravida et pauca familia ad mare festinanter declinans continuo transfretavit. Matthew Paris, iii, p. 567.

[6] MS. Cotton Vesp. F., i, fol. 114; printed Manners and Household Expenses, Roxburghe Club, p. xix, n. i.

under consideration; but one instructive incident is told of the subsequent council of war in Saintes.

Henry, as we know, wanted to defend the place: Simon and every clear-headed person present realised that resistance at this juncture meant envelopment, and either surrender or annihilation. Simon confronted the council and said what he thought: " as for the king," he concluded, " treat him like Charles the Simple; there are iron-barred rooms at Windsor well adapted for his residence."[1] The English forces withdrew to Bordeaux: the French, checked by the formidable defences of Blaye, decimated by disease, achieved nothing further. A five years' truce was concluded in April, 1243.

Perhaps we should infer from the affair at Saintes that Simon was already bent on dominating Henry and ruling England, and that at a critical moment he gave a premature glimpse of a settled policy. Be this as it may, the earl could not then head an opposition to Henry. Between his plans and their fulfilment his poverty raised a formidable barrier. Only by fostering friendly relations with Henry could he hope to become rich; and so, during the years 1242 to 1248, he was constantly begging of Henry and constantly receiving money and estates.[2] But their friendship was merely superficial: the events related above had caused a breach between them never to be closed.

In 1248 Simon de Montfort was appointed seneschal of Gascony.[3] The story of this period belongs to the history of Europe and need not be told here, but it behoves us to summarise what took place. Did Simon, think you, during his governorship, afford early proof of that passionate regard for constitutional liberty which won him a martyr's crown at Evesham? Did he summon, do you imagine, the estates of Gascony to attend his councils; and, by a popular administration and an equitable judicature, restore peace and prosperity to that distracted province? Nothing could be further from the facts. The whole story is one of ruthless

[1] Bémont, Simon de Montfort, appendix no. 36; printed from Bibl. Nat. MS., lat. 9016, no. 5.
[2] See Bémont, Simon de Montfort, p. 17, n. 2, for some details.
[3] Patent Roll, 32 Henry III, m. 2.

repression, wholesale imprisonment, execution and forfeiture without the vestige of legal process.

True, Gascony was a nest of bandits: her chief men were such by trade, Gaston de Béarn, the vicomte de Gramont, Raimond de Fronsac and a host of others. The petits seigneurs, the chevaliers du Labour and such-like followed the example of their betters, though in humbler fashion. The former raided, the latter merely robbed. Simon out-briganded the brigands. Some drew sword against him and perished by the sword, others submitted and were put to ransom; many languished long years in prison, untried and forgotten. The tale is pitiable in the extreme. But whether Simon should be censured for what he did is another matter: perhaps, in view of the pass things had come to before his arrival, he should be praised, but not, I think, much praised; Gascony was cowed by him, not pacified.[1]

Nevertheless, whatever we may think of the matter, the earl's exploits undoubtedly gained him a great reputation in France, and led to his receiving a singular offer.

The story of the French seneschalship has been related above—its humble origin, its rapid rise to inordinate power, how it challenged the royal supremacy, how it declined somewhat at the close and was in effect suppressed in 1191, though the fiction of a mere vacancy survived the thirteenth century. In 1253 Simon de Montfort visited France and received an apparently genuine offer of this same seneschalship of France, provided, presumably, he would throw up his allegiance to Henry.[2] Under the circumstances this was a most significant

---

[1] For these events see Bémont, Simon de Montfort, chap. ii and appendices; also an article by the same writer in Revue Historique, iv, pp. 241–77.

[2] Comes autem ne precibus pulsaretur ut rediret, cessit in Franciam, ubi magnates regni Franciae libentur ipsum retinuissent, proponentes ipsum sibi et regno ad consulendum regno desolato et multum desperato propter absentiam regis et mortem Blanchiae reginae, ut esset eis, quia strenuus fuit et fidelis, pro senescallo. Quod constanter renuit comes, ne videretur proditor extitisse, secundum illud Apostolicum, ab omni specie mali abstinete vos. (Matthew Paris, Rolls Series, vol. v, p. 366.)

Instante vero festo Paschali, magnates Francorum, considerantes

episode. How, we may wonder, did the offer originate? Possibly Leicester unburdened his mind to the magnates of France; told them he had no scope for his energies in England, that his Gascon stewardship was at an end, that he ought by hereditary right (so he thought) to be steward of England with similar powers, but Henry would not have it so. And then, perhaps, the French nobles answered: " As you may not be seneschal of England, be seneschal of France; we are leaderless now and desire a leader; you are of French not English stock, throw in your lot with France." Something of the kind must have occurred.

Simon declined the offer, and his refusal has been counted to him for virtue; but surely it would have been folly for him to accept. He would have staked his whole future in the venture: the promised interest was no doubt high, but the security absolutely nil.

On his return to England the earl of Leicester assumed in his charters the style of steward of England (*senescallus Angliae*).[1] Now this style had never been assumed by his predecessors in title, and its adoption undoubtedly signified

regnum Franciae consilio destitutum imminere periculo, tum propter regis in terra sancta Deo militantis absentiam, tum propter dominae Blanchiae reginae mortem, tum propter optimatum Franciae casum in terra sancta subversorum, conspicientesque comitis Legrecestriae Simonis fidelitatem et magnificentiam, qui per omnia studuit patris, sare, ipsum quoque jam fuisse a custodia Wasconiae absolutum-postulabant ipsum devote ut, apud ipsos commorans, unus foret custodum coronae ac regni Franciae, et ipsi honores ei condignos accumularent pro merito. Sciebant enim, ut asserebant, quod regnum Francorum ab antiquo, sicut et pater ejus Simon qui pro ecclesia contra Albigenses dimicaverat, praecordialiter dilegebat, nec est a sanguine Francorum alienus. Hoc jam secundo missis literis et nuntiis solempnibus Franci comiti memorato significaverunt, quod constanter comes, ne transfuga videretur, renuebat. (Ibid., pp. 371-2.)

Tunc quoque temporis, comes Legrecestriae Symon, qui in senescallum Franciae, ut praetactum est, postulabatur propter sui fidelitatem et strenuitatem, sed noluit consentire, quia nemo potest duobus dominis sibi adversantibus commode famulari, venit in Wasconiam ad regem Angliae. . . . (Ibid., p. 415.)

[1] See Bateson, Records of the Borough of Leicester, nos. xxii, xxiii, etc.

on the part of Simon de Montfort a deliberate policy of self-aggrandisement. He might, to be sure, have plausibly defended the style by producing the charter (which must have been in his possession) making Robert, *le Bossu, dapifer Angliae et Normanniae.*

But whatever *dapifer Angliae* may have portended in 1155, the style *senescallus Angliae* in 1255 had a very definite and special connotation. It implied viceregal power and precedence; it implied that Simon claimed to be in England what he had been in Gascony; it suggested a dignitary in every respect comparable to the late seneschals of France. The king regarded Simon as *senescallus regis* (*de feodo*), and there was all the difference in the world between the two styles. At the same time, the assumption of the style *senescallus Angliae* had the precedents of the constable and marshal to support it. Probably any magnate of the first rank invested with the office of steward would sooner or later have attempted the same style.

That the recognised though menial duties attaching to the office were not dropped we know from letters patent of Henry dated St. Edward's Day, 1260.[1] By these the king made notification that Henry of Germany had been received as Leicester's deputy, to perform at that day's feast the services properly appertaining to the stewardship.

From 1255 to 1265 the political changes are kaleidoscopic :

[1] Patent Roll, 44 Henry III, pt. i, m. 2; printed Rymer, Foedera R.C., vol. i, p. 402. Pur le Cunte de Leycestre. Henri par la grace Deu, roys de Angleterre, etc. a tuz ceus qui cestes lettres verront saluz en nostre Seigneur. Sachez toz que nus receumes le jur seint Edward le an de nostre corounement xliiij a nostre feste ke nus tenimes alors a Westmonstier Henri le fiz le roi dalemaigne nostre nevou la torne Simon de Muntfort conte de Leycestre a servyr pur li a la vuantdite feste si com il apent au servise de la senescaucie. E entesmoyne de ceste chose nus avons fet ade susdit Simon icestes nos lettres overtes par le conseyl de nos hauz homes de nostre conseyl. E ceste chose fu fete lan e le jur avant diz.

Ista littera lecta fuit et approbata coram domino rege in garderoba sua, presentibus Edwardo filio regis, Hugone filio regis Allemannie, comite Glovernie, comite Oxonie, Henrico le Bygod justiciario, Johanne Mansel et Roberto Walerand et aliis, et per preceptum ipsorum sigillata.

from the Sicilian affair to the Purveyance of Oxford; the un-accountable submission to Louis, the mise of Amiens and the papal bull; the victory of Lewes, the superb fiction of a full parliament, the awkward reality of Simon's committee of public safety; the speedy but inevitable disaster of Evesham where the dissimulating, ruthless, excommunicated autocrat perished gloriously for the liberties of England. The general course of public affairs must be kept in mind in tracing the development during these ten years of the stewardship of England.

One result of the mailed parliament of 1258 was the re-appointment of a justiciar. Hugh Bigod was selected, but he did not remain long in office.[1] In October, 1260, Hugh the Despencer was appointed justiciar by the barons; and in April (?), 1261, the king, on his part, appointed Philip Basset.[2] For a short time these two justiciars acted concurrently for their respective parties. During the following year relations between the king and the opposition became less strained and the Despencer retired, but in 1263 the barons were in arms and he was reinstated.

In 1261 the differences between Henry the Third and Simon de Montfort were submitted to the arbitration of the king of France, and some, at all events, of the written plead-ings on both sides have been preserved. As regards his stewardship, Simon pleaded: "e de la seneschaucie pluseurs draiz me retient, e sovent l'ei requis q'il me feist drait, mes unqore ores ne m'en a rien fet." And again, at the end of one of his defences to the king's allegations relative to his administration of Gascony, Simon adds as if by way of counterclaim: ' Fet a remembrer de Grainelle, et des draiz de la seneschaucie.' This is striking evidence of the potential importance of that office in the opinion of Simon.[3]

The reappointment of justiciars must have directed the attention of Leicester to the relative position of the two

---

[1] The date of Hugh Bigod's retirement is uncertain; he did not finally retire until some time after Despencer's appointment.

[2] It was not until August that he received his patents of appoint-ment. (Patent Roll, 45 Henry III, no. 13.)

[3] Bémont, appendices nos. 34-8.

offices. Hitherto he had possibly not taken much account of a vacant post, assuming that the seneschal, in England as elsewhere, was ex officio chief minister. Face to face with a justiciar he may have found that his views required reconsideration. Ultimately, at all events, we have the clearest evidence that he made careful inquiries into the matter.

At times Simon seems to have hesitated about asserting his office, for in the letters to the pope from the " communitas " of England concerning Sicily and the see of Winchester he subscribes as plain earl,[1] though the Bigods style themselves, respectively, Marshal of England and Justiciar of England.[2] In 1263, however, in the letters patent of the barons referring all matters in dispute to Louis—the submission which resulted in the mise of Amiens—Simon figures as seneschal of England immediately before Hugh the Despencer, justiciar of England.[3]

On the 23rd of January, 1264, the mise of Amiens quashed the Provisions of Oxford, but reserved the previous rights of the English people. Simon had sworn by the sacred gospels[4] to abide by the award: once made, however, he instantly took up arms to resist it. In so doing he most emphatically broke his oath, and has moreover severely taxed the ingenuity of his latter-day apologists, who one and all apparently have subscribed to the dogma that Simon valued his oath more than his life. The simple truth is that Simon had loaded himself with many and quite incompatible oaths, so that from time to time some had to be jettisoned. On this particular occasion he most wisely selected to break the most foolish.

On the 14th of May the earl of Leicester fought the decisive battle of Lewes which placed the king and all England in his power. Simon thus became, in sober truth, viceroy of England ; and as he constantly figures during this period as seneschal of England in official documents bearing

---

[1] There is ample evidence that Simon hesitated to assert his office when associated with the earl of Gloucester.

[2] Matthew Paris, vi, pp. 400–5; and Rymer, Foedera R.C., i, p. 373.

[3] Rymer, Foedera R.C., i, p. 434.

[4] " tactis sacrosanctis evangeliis," ibid.

the great seal,[1] we have all the necessary conditions present for a repetition in England of the history of the French dapifership. It can hardly be doubted that, had Simon de Montfort succeeded in finally establishing his government, he would have sought to define and regularise his position by recourse to the supposed rights and privileges of his hereditary office. Simon's supremacy, however, was too short-lived, and all he can be said to have done in this direction before his death was to institute careful inquiries about his office. On the 29th of April, 1265, Simon in Henry's name sent letters close to a certain recluse, named Lauretta, who is alleged by Camden to have been Lauretta countess of Leicester, relict of the last Beaumont. They run as follows :—

The king—to the recluse of Hakinton greeting. Because you know better than others, so it is said, what rights and liberties appertain to the stewardship of England in right of the earldom and honour of Leicester; we, wishing to be more fully certified on these matters by you, diligently require and command you forthwith to expound the said rights and liberties in the presence of our well-beloved in Christ the abbot of St. Augustine's, Canterbury, and the prior of Christchurch in the same town. . . .[2]

The recluse's answer is probably not in existence; in any event it could hardly have afforded Simon de Montfort much assistance or satisfaction. There were no rights or privileges

---

[1] See the Patent Roll 49 Henry III passim; a few instances are given in Rymer, Foedera R.C., i, pp. 454-6. The following occur on the Charter Roll 49 Henry III : (Westminster) *30th Jan.*, *1st March*, 20th March, 29th March, *14th April;* (Hereford) *12th June, 16th June.* On the dates italicised Simon attests as seneschal, his attestation immediately preceding that of Despencer as justiciar.

[2] Rex recluse de Hakinton salutem. Quia vos nostis pre ceteris ut dicitur que jura et libertates pertinent ad senescalciam Anglie racione comitatus et honoris Leycestrie, nos volentes super hiis per vos plenius certiorari vos attente requirimus et rogamus quatinus in presentia dilectorum nobis in Christo abbatis sancti Augustini Cantuariensis et priori (sic) ecclesie Christi ejusdem ville dicta jura et libertates exponatis, et ea coram eis distincte ac aperte scribi et sub sigillis eorundem abbatis et prioris ad nos mittere faciatis. Mandavimus etiam ipsis quod ad certum diem quem ipsi

belonging to the office other than those which Simon was aware of; and, whoever this recluse may have been, she could have told him nothing whatever beyond the negative fact that there was nothing whatever to tell. The mere circumstance, however, that such a request for information was sent clearly shows that Simon still thought otherwise.

So much for the stewardship in the hands of Simon earl of Leicester. After all it was a very secondary matter, occurring at a time when mighty issues were at stake. In June, 1264, we have the committee of three (Leicester, Gloucester and the bishop of Chichester), and the council of nine; afterwards the full parliament. Ostensibly Simon had the nation at his back. But, meanwhile, French armies were preparing for invasion; there were royalist leaders in the west where the Welsh were mustering on the border; and the Pope excommunicated Simon and his followers. Before the full parliament had finished its session the ultimate defection of Gloucester became obvious. In April, 1265, Simon was holding royal court at Odiham; but none the less his short day was over, events were everywhere hurrying him to the final catastrophe.

It should be noted, to avoid mistake, that on the Patent Rolls of this period the authority for affixing the great seal is occasionally stated in the following form: " Per Regem. comitem Leicestrie. justiciarium . . .", neither the name nor even the initial of the justiciar being given. This has led to extraordinary confusion, and induced one writer to attribute Simon's fall, in part at any rate, to the unjustifiable proceeding of appointing himself justiciar. Simon never did anything of the kind: the supreme authority had been assumed

et vos ad hoc duxeritis providendum vobis ad hoc personaliter assistant. Teste ut supra [scilicet xxix die Aprilis]. Et scribitur eidem priori quod una cum prefato abbate ad certum diem quem ipse et dicta reclusa duxerint providendum ad eam personaliter accederit, et ea que sibi de juribus et libertatibus supradictis exponet in presencia ejusdem recluse, cui rex super hoc scribit, distincte et aperte scribi faciat, et ea sub sigillis suis eidem liberet ad regem mittenda prout rex ei injunxit. Teste ut supra. (Close Roll, 49 Henry III, m. 6d. See Patent Roll, 20 Henry III, m. 13, Cal., p. 133; and chapter vi, appendix.)

by him ; the Despencer was his close ally and chief minister, and continued to act as such under the title of justiciar of England until he fell by the earl's side at Evesham. When letters patent are represented as emanating or proffered—per comitem Leicestrie, justiciarium, etc.—this simply means that they were approved or vouchered both by the earl of Leicester and by Hugh the Despencer.[1]

In May, Edward escaped from custody and was joined by Gloucester. Hostilities began at once. Simon was at Hereford. The strategy of the royalists was masterly : so rapidly and successfully did they strike that Simon found himself trapped in Wales with the eastern bank of the Severn held strongly against him. On the 19th of June the earl made a treaty with Llewellyn which secured him some additions to the altogether inadequate forces at his disposal. He then marched to Newport by way of Monmouth, and attempted to force a passage of the Severn before Bristol. The attempt was defeated and Simon turned northwards to Hereford again.

On the 2nd of August he succeeded at last in crossing the river, and shortly after reached Evesham, but with a very attenuated following. He expected reinforcements from his son, but these had been already defeated near Kenilworth, and the whole royalist forces were marching southwards to crush him before further help could arrive.

On the 4th of August Simon de Montfort was attacked. The heavens that day, it is said, were black with cloud and there was a great storm. The battle was little better than a massacre. The Welsh lost heart and fled. Simon was soon unhorsed and surrounded, but he fought desperately to the end. His assailants closed ever closer round him : " Traitor, yield thee," they hissed ; and, as Simon struggled grimly on, one stole behind him and pricked him to the heart under his armour. " Dieu merci," he breathed, and sank to the ground. So he died, and men wreaked their miserable vengeance on a lifeless body.

The stewardship of England during Simon de Montfort's tenure of it claimed to be and was in course of becoming the

---

[1] See appendix to this chapter.

first great office of state. The chief obstacle to such an augmentation of rank was the existence of the justiciarship. However, after the battle of Evesham the latter office was finally abolished; and under these circumstances, had the stewardship fallen into strong hands, that office would probably have acquired all the more important functions of the other. As will be seen the stewardship fell into weak hands, with the result that it was the steward of the household who acquired such of the justiciar's ordinary powers as were not transferred to the newly created official, the Chief Justice of the King's Bench.[1]

APPENDIX TO CHAPTER IV

THE ALLEGED USE OF THE STYLE "JUSTICIAR" BY SIMON DE MONTFORT

The view that Simon de Montfort on various occasions during the captivity of Henry the Third assumed the title of justiciar appears to be almost universally accepted, and several somewhat remarkable conclusions have been founded upon it. Thus Professor Shirley has written of the parliament which met on the 20th of January, 1265 :—[2]

They appear to have appointed Simon de Montfort to the office of Justiciar of England, and to have thus made him in rank what he had before been in power, the first subject in the realm. . . . Montfort at all events had now gone so far, he had exercised such

---

[1] Fleta. ed. Selden, p. 66. De differentiis curiarum : cap. 2 :—
Habet enim rex curiam suam in concilio suo in parliamentis suis, praesentibus praelatis, comitibus, baronibus, proceribus et aliis viris peritis, ubi terminatae sunt dubitationes judiciorum, et novis injuriis emersis nova constituuntur remedia, et unicuique justicia prout meruit retribuetur ibidem. Habet etiam curiam suam coram senescallo suo in aula sua, qui jam tenet locum capitalis justiciarii regis, de quo fit mentio in communi brevi de homine replegiando, qui proprias causas regis terminare consuevit, et falsum judicium ad veritatem revocare, et conquerentibus absque brevi justiciam exhibere, cujus vices gerit in parte idem senescallus hospitii regis, cujus interest de omnibus actionibus contra pacem regis infra metas hospitii. . . .

[2] Quarterly Review (1866), vol. cxix, p. 55.

extraordinary powers, he had done so many things which could never really be pardoned, that perhaps his only chance of safety lay in the possession of some such office as this.

In passing I must observe that not a single statement in the above extract appears to me to be warranted by the existing evidence, however that evidence is construed. Simon, even on the professor's reading of the records, was justiciar before the meeting of parliament. The justiciarship, like the modern office of prime minister, conferred power and not rank.[1] Simon's appointment to the first-named office could not have added one tittle to his rank, but it might in some small measure have legalised the powers he was exercising. Pauli, or at all events his translator, puts forward similar views :—[2]

During this parliament the power he had grounded upon wisdom and energy reached its climax. As if seeking for a designation which should in some measure justify it, he assumed the title of count justiciar in addition to his hereditary dignity of seneschal of England, although Hugh Despencer continued to hold the post of great justiciary.

Foss ventures the following opinion :—

Brady quotes three records on May 10th, June 7th, and June 8th, 1265, in which the earl of Leicester is styled ' justiciarius," and during that interval no document occurs in which Hugh le Despencer uses the title.[4] In Leland's Collectanea there is an account of a short disagreement between them about this time during which it is possible, but not likely, that the one threw up the office in anger and the other assumed it for the time that it might not appear to be vacant. If, however, for that may be doubtful, the word really meant the same as " justiciarius Angliae," by which Bigod, Basset and Despencer had been specially designated, the title would have been merely nominal and was undoubtedly only temporary, for the

[1] A special rank, however, has quite recently been conferred on the prime minister.
[2] Simon de Montfort, 1876, p. 180.
[3] Judges of England, vol. ii, pp. 154–5.
[4] This statement is quite untrue; there are, in fact, many such documents. The Charter Roll contains five, dated at Hereford the 15th, 15th, 20th, 20th, and 20th of May respectively. I have found five on the Patent Roll and one on the Fine Roll.

K

earl never acted and Hugh had resumed it before the battle of Evesham, on August 4th, when he fell by the earl of Leicester's side.

Mr. Prothero is less doubtful than Foss in his account of the matter. He says :—[1]

A far less justifiable proceeding was the appointment of himself as justiciar. (There is some doubt about this. Foss does not give the earl's name as justiciar, but the evidence from writs signed by him as justiciar seems too strong to reject.) The object of this act is hard to discover, especially as Hugh Despencer was at hand to undertake the duties he had already twice before discharged. Such an accumulation of power was most unwise, it was a needless challenge to the opposition.

Mr. Round apparently adopts in part the conclusion of Foss.[2]

Lastly, I would examine the title of "Justiciar" which Simon de Montfort appends to his signature at the foot of these royal proclamations. . . .

And then, after considering and commenting upon the statements of the previous writers cited above,[3] he expresses this opinion :—

It will, I think, be found . . . that Hugh's name does not occur in any document in which Simon styles himself justiciary. We may indeed have in this fact a hint that with his characteristic love of constitutional forms, Simon, in order to give his writs every appearance of legality, assumed the style of justiciary *pro hac vice*, whenever Hugh Despenser was *not* at hand.

Let me remark parenthetically that Simon never tests or signs royal proclamations as justiciar, or at all. The question at issue is whether such proclamations are ever expressed to emanate from him as justiciar, which is a very different thing.

[1] Simon de Montfort, p. 322.
[2] Antiquary, ix, pp. 17–19. See also Mr. Round's article on Hugh Despencer in the Dictionary of National Biography.
[3] See also the Report on the Dignity of a Peer, i, p. 154 : " From this and other writs it appears that the earl of Leicester had been made justiciary."

There is clearly a superabundance of modern authority in support of Simon de Montfort's style. Nevertheless the whole story is absolutely without foundation. The record evidence shows plainly that the style in question is throughout used by the regular justiciar, and not once by the earl of Leicester.

I must begin my argument with a few general remarks for the benefit of those unfamiliar with original records.

Royal letters patent at this period are expressed to be tested by the king if he is in England, by the justiciar if the king is abroad, and by no one else. These documents, however, are not signed, but are authenticated by sealing with the great seal, and nothing more was required to give them every appearance of legality. The recipients of these writs and the general public looked to the great seal only.

But the chancellor or keeper who affixed the seal was in a very different position. The king could not always be present at the sealing of a prerogative writ, nor could the keeper always be present at the council table with the engrossed documents directed to be issued by order in council. Sometimes a writ of privy seal would sufficiently authenticate the royal commands, but the chancellor had often to be satisfied with something much less formal. A few members, or even a single member of council would attend, hear the engrossed document read out, and approve it on behalf of the king or council simply by word of mouth.

Now, besides the original writ bearing the great seal, the chancery even at this time always made a copy, which was entered on the appropriate roll to be carefully preserved ; and on these rolls the scribe occasionally states, at the foot of an enrolment, the authority for affixing the great seal. In later times "per breve de privato sigillo" became the commonest authority, but there was always a great variety of others, such as : "per ipsum regem"; "coram justiciarlo"; "per justiciarium"; "per Robertum Walerand"; "per consilium"; "per Robertum Walerand et alios de consilio"; "per ipsum regem oretenus" ; "per regem, nunciante comite Herefordie"; etc., etc. In many cases, however, and, at the time we are considering, in most cases, no authority is stated.

Probably there was deliberate method in all this, but that is a question too foreign to the subject-matter in hand to be discussed here. I will merely observe that during Henry the Third's minority it became a common practice to give the authority for a writ; this practice was almost entirely dropped when the king attained his majority,[1] but was to some extent revived at certain periods of this reign which appear to correspond with the periods when the king was in trouble with his barons. During the temporary ascendency of a baronial opposition the clerk of enrolments had obvious reasons for being careful.[2]

Now the chancery enrolments were not written out in full, but elaborate time-saving abbreviations were used. Thus if the authority for a writ was the justiciar of England, the clerk soon got tired of writing " per Hubertum de Burgo justiciarium Anglie" even in an abbreviated form, but commonly wrote "p justic"; or, for example, "p dom Wynꝑ & justic", if, as sometimes happened, the writ had the twofold authority of the bishop of Winchester and the chief justiciary.

Having said this much by way of preface, it only remains to cite illustrative extracts from the enrolments made during the final periods of the baronial ascendency.

Winchester, 6th July, 1258. (Patent Roll,
42 Hen. III, m. 4.)

Per comitem Leycestrie. comitem Gloucestrie. comitem Marescallum. Hugonem le Bigod justiciarium. Johannem filium Galfridi. Johannem Mansell & alios de consilio regis.

Clarendon, 1st October, 1258. (Patent Roll,
42 Hen. III, m. 2.)

Ista litera processit de precepto H justiciarii Anglie & Egidii de Argentem senescalli regis.

---

[1] The earlier Patent Rolls of this reign have been printed in full, and therefore precise information on this point is within reach of everyone.

[2] See the Patent of July 30th, 1260, cited below. Between the enrolment of two writs, dated February 24th, 1260–1, the scribe notes :—Hic recessit dominus H. de Malo-Lacu a curia.

Westminster, 26th December, 1258. (Patent Roll,
43 Hen. III, m. 13.)

Per Petrum de Sabaud. Robertum comitem Gloucestrie.
H justiciarium & alios de consilio regis.

Westminster, 18*th February,* 1258–9. (Fine Roll,
43 Hen. III, m. 10.)

Per Justiciarium & consilium regis.

Windsor, 16*th August,* 1259. (Patent Roll,
43 Hen. III, m. 3.)

Per Justiciarium.

Westminster, 18*th June,* 1260. (Fine Roll, 44 Hen. III, m. 6.)

Per Regem & Justiciarium.

Westminster, 5*th July,* 1260. ⟨Ibid.⟩

Per ipsum Regem. Justiciarium. . . .

Westminster, 30*th July,* 1260. (Fine Roll,
44 Hen. III, m. 4.)

Per ipsum Regem. Comitem Gloucestrie & Justiciarium.

Westminster, 30*th July,* 1260. (Patent Roll,
44 Hen. III, m. 5.)

(Letters patent—" pro Rogero de Mortuo Mari.") . . .
Teste Rege apud Westmonasterium xxx die Julii. Et scien-
dum quod litera predicta die predicto in camera prioris apud
Westmonasterium emanavit de assensu R comitis Gloucestrie
R comitis Marescalli H comitis Herefordie ꞃ comitis Warrenne
H le Bygod justiciarii (Anglie)[1] Philippi Basset Johannis
Mansell & Roberti Walerand in quorum presencia predicta
litera lecta fuit et acceptata. Teste ut supra.

Memorandum quod ista littera per regem et consilium processit et in absencia cancellarii sigillata fuit set postea Edwardus filius regis coram magnatibus de consilio reclamavit
contra remissionem predictam.

[1] Interlined.

Windsor, 26th September, 1260. (Fine Roll,
44 Hen. III, m. 2.)

Per ipsum Regem. Johannem Mansell & Robertum Wale-
rànd. Justiciarium. Comitem Gloucestrie & Philippum Basset.

Westminster, 25th November, 1260. (Patent Roll,
45 Hen. III, m. 21.)

Per Justiciarium.

Tower of London, 13*th February,* 1260–1. (Patent Roll,
45 Hen. III, m. 17.)

Per Regem Romanorum. Justiciarium Hugonem le Bygod.
Johannem Mansell Thesaurarium Eborum & Robertum
Walerand.

Westminster, 15*th November,* 1262. (Patent Roll,
47 Hen. III, No. 54.)

Teste Philippo Basset justiciario regis.

Westminster, 26th August, 1263. (Fine Roll,
47 Hen. III, m. 2.)

Per Justiciarium.

St. Albans, 24th September, 1263. (Patent Roll,
47 Hen. III, m. 3d.)

Teste H le Despenser justiciario Anglie apud Sanctum
Albanum xxiiij die Septembris. per eundem justiciarium.

Westminster, 25th October, 1264. (Fine Roll,
48 Hen. III, m. 2.)

(Pro Radulfo de Cameys) Per Regem. H le Despenser
Justiciarium. Petrum de Monteforti. Adam de Novo Mercato. Egidium de Argentenn et alios de consilio.

(Pro Henrico de Bromfeud) Per Justiciarium ad instanciam
Humfridi de Bohun.

(Pro Petro de Monteforti) Per Regem. Justiciarium &
alios ut supra.

Woodstock, 24th December, 1264. (Patent Roll,
49 Hen. III, No. 110.)

Per ipsum Regem. Episcopum Londonie. Justiciarium
& alios de consilio regis.

Westminster, 5th January, 1264-5. (Patent Roll,
49 Hen. III, m. 26d.)

Per Regem. Justiciarium & alios de consilio.

Westminster, 17th January, 1264-5. (Patent Roll,
49 Hen. III, No. 106.)

Per Regem. Comitem Leicestrie. Justiciarium & Rogerum
de Sancto Johanne.

Westminster, 5th February, 1264-5. (Patent Roll,
49 Hen. III, No. 104.)

Per comitem Leicestrie.
(On this date Despencer as justiciar of England witnesses
a charter at Westminster.)

Westminster, 16th February, 1264-5. (Patent Roll,
49 Hen. III, No. 101.)

(De inhibicione torneamenti) Rex dilectis et fidelibus suis
Simoni de Monteforti comiti Leycestrie Gilberto de Clare
comiti Gloucestrie Roberto de Veer comiti Oxonie Hugoni
le Despenser Justiciario Anglie . . . salutem. . . . Teste Rege
apud Westmonasterium xvj die Febuarii. Per Regem. Justiciarium. Episcopum Londonie & Magistro Th de Cantilupo.

Westminster, 5th March, 1264-5. (Patent Roll,
49 Hen. III, No. 93.)

Per Justiciarium. Petrum de Monteforti. Adam de Novo
Mercato.
(On this date Despencer as justiciar of England witnesses
a charter at Westminster.)

Westminster, 6th March, 1264-5. (Patent Roll,
49 Hen. III, No. 93.)

Per Adam de Novo Mercato.

Northampton, 23rd April, 1265.   (Fine Roll,
49 Hen. III, m. 4.)

Per Regem.   Justiciarium & Rogerum de Sancto Johanne.

Hereford, 16th May, 1265.   (Patent Roll,
49 Hen. III, No. 63.)

Per Consilium & comitem Leicestrie.

Hereford, 20th May, 1265.   (Patent Roll,
49 Hen. III, No. 61.)

Per Regem.   Comitem Leicestrie.   Justiciarium. . . .
(On this date Despencer as justiciar of England witnesses
a charter at Hereford.)

Hereford, 30th May, 1265.   (Fine Roll, 49 Hen. III, m. 2.)

Per Regem.   Comitem Leicestrie . . . reclamante H le
Despenser justiciario Anglie.

Hereford, 12th June, 1265.   (Patent Roll,
49 Hen. III, No. 49.)

(Simon is referred to in the body of this patent as
" senescallus Anglie.")   Per Regem.   Comitem Leicestrie.
Justiciarium. . . .
(On this date Simon as seneschal of England and Despencer
as justiciar of England witness a charter at Hereford.)

Hereford, 19th June, 1265.   (Patent Roll,
49 Hen. III, No. 48.)

This refers to Despencer as justiciar of England.

Hereford, 19th June, 1265.   (Fine Roll, 49 Hen. III, m. 2.)
Per Regem & Justiciarium.

Besides these enrolments there is one original document
which it may be useful to notice.   On Tuesday, the 18th
December, 1263, the following letters patent were sealed at
London :—

Universis presentes litteras inspecturis Henricus Londoniensis,
Walterus Wygorniensis episcopi, Simon de Monteforti comes Ley-

cestrie et senescallus Anglie, Hugo le Despenser justiciarius Anglie.
. . . Et in testimonium premissorum nos Londoniensis et Wygorniensis episcopi, justiciarius et Ricardus de Grey, predicti, vice
et mandato omnium predictorum presentibus sigilla nostra apposuimus. Datum London. [etc.][1]

These letters patent are sealed, as stated, with four seals,
the third being the little seal of Hugh the Despencer, justiciar
of England.

No further argument is called for, the records speak for
themselves. Rymer and others have printed two or three
letters patent expressed to be expedited: " Per Regem.
Comitem Leicestrie. Justiciarium . . ."; but omitting the
full-stop which appears, tolerably plainly in most cases, after
"Leicestrie." The absurd supposition that earl Simon assumed
the style of justiciar rests solely on this evidence. It is an
extraordinary blunder; but so long as our chief collection of
English records consists of so inaccurate and unscholarly a
work as the " Foedera," such blunders are inevitable. I can
hardly hope that this work of mine is free from similar errors,
but I have saved myself from at least some very serious ones
by, whenever possible, collating printed documents with the
originals, and by studying the character and form of other
contemporary records of a like nature.

[1] Printed in Layettes du Trésor des Chartes, iv, no. 4886. Cf.
ibid., no. 4888, where Despencer attests as "justiciarius Anglie"
without name or initial. This is also an original document with
Despencer's seal attached.

For further evidence see Close Rolls, R.O., 1231–4, pp. 181,
182, 187, 188, 193, 227: in each case the justiciar is Segrave, and
not the bishop of Winchester.

CHAPTER V

THE LANCASTRIAN STEWARDS

AFTER the battle at Evesham the great house of Montfort perished altogether. Many coveted their estates
and counselled Henry accordingly. These spoils of the
royalist victory were speedily distributed. Edmund, the
king's son, was put in possession of the honour of Leicester,
and invested with the earldom of that county and the
stewardship of England. These grants were first embodied
in letters patent bearing date the 25th of October, 1265:[1]
senescalcia Anglie is the term used in referring to the stewardship, and that office is expressed to be conferred on Edmund
and his heirs. Thus the style, steward of England, adopted
by Simon de Montfort receives official recognition, and the
French precedent is followed of conferring this post on a
near relative of the crown. But a grant in fee of an already
dangerous office was a piece of gratuitous folly, and probably Edward objected. At all events, a formal charter
bearing date the 26th of October, 1265, was prepared and
attested; but it was never delivered, and remained an
escrow.[2]

The honour of Leicester was then granted afresh to
Edmund, on the same day, by an amended charter which

[1] See Appendix.

[2] Hitherto no one appears to have appreciated this fact, and
error upon error has resulted. For example, the Complete Peerage
says of Edmund (s.v. Lancaster): "He was created 26th Oct.,
1265, Earl of Leicester and Seneschal or High Steward of England."
This statement is quite untrue. Edmund is, however, styled earl
of Leicester in an original charter of Henry III, dated 12th
January, 51 Henry III; see Royal Charters, Duchy of Lancaster,
no. 108.

makes no mention of the stewardship.[1] The letters patent
of the day before should have been and probably were
surrendered for cancellation, but the entry on the Patent Roll
remains uncancelled to this day. However, further letters
patent were subsequently issued conferring the stewardship
of England on Edmund for his life only.[2] These are dated
the 9th of May, 1269, and are perhaps purposely expressed
so as not to bind Henry's heirs. Strictly speaking, therefore,
the stewardship expired on the death of Henry the Third.
Edmund, however, appears to have claimed an estate of
inheritance in the office at the coronation of Edward the
First: no documentary evidence could be produced in support of the claim; and evidently, as a matter of right, the
claim was disallowed. As a special favour Edmund was
permitted to hold the office for the remainder of his life, but
probably only on condition that he executed the deed, dated
the day after Edward's coronation, in which he renounces
for himself and his heirs all hereditary pretensions in that
direction.[3] Edmund was not a man of great parts, and
probably had neither the wit nor the wish to exploit the
stewardship; but if he had by chance any hopes of emu-
lating the stewards of France, these hopes had not the

[1] See Appendix. It is not certain that even this charter passed,
although it is enrolled; and it must shortly afterwards have been
cancelled. It was superseded by a charter of 1269 (original, sealed;
and Charter Roll, 53 Henry III, m. 11), which was inspected on
the 17th of August, 13 Edward I, and not long afterwards produced
in evidence (Assize Roll, 544, m. 36, Middlesex, 22 Edward I).
There was also an intermediate charter dated July 12th, 1266
(original sealed: Inspeximus Original, and Charter Roll, 4 Edward
III, no. 19), a provisional grant—"donec inde sibi escambium
racionabile fecerimus in aliis terris nostris ad valorem," etc.; and
certain letters patent which are all quite irreconcilable with the
existence of any such earlier grants. The documents in question
are set out in full in the appendix to this chapter.

[2] See Appendix.

[3] See Appendix. Edward no doubt was merely following a
custom already established in France, where, it appears, oaths
against hereditary claims were habitually exacted from the great
officers; e.g., Ego Johannes marescallus domini Ludovici regis illustris notum facio universis praesentes litteras inspecturis me super
sacrosancta jurasse ipsi domino regi quod non retinebo equos nec

smallest prospect of fruition under the strong rule of the man men have called the English Justinian. So we hear nothing of the stewardship during this period; it simply relapsed into obscurity. Probably Edmund continued to perform the functions of a dapifer[1] on state occasions; but

palefridos nec roncinos redditos ad opus meum ratione ministerii mei quod habeo de dono ipsius domini regis, nec ego nec heredes mei reclamabimus marescalliam jure hereditario tenendam et habendam. In cujus, etc. (Soissons, 1223; Martène, Ampliss. Collect., i, 1175).

The grant of the stewardship to Edmund for his life was not formally made until the 27th February, 1275. See Appendix.

[1] Let me repeat that there is nothing surprising in an earl, even of the blood royal, delighting in the performance of these menial duties on state occasions. Other earls were ready enough to perform precisely similar services for humbler individuals. Compare the following instances :—

Inthronization of the archbishop of Canterbury.—The fees of the hye stewarde and cheefe butler of the feast of coronization as it appeareth by composition betwixt Boniface archbyshop of Canterburie on th'one partie and Richarde de Clare earle of Glocester and Hartforde on th'other partie of certayne customes and services whiche the foresayde archbyshop claymeth of the aforsayde earle; vidz of the manors of Tonybridge, and Hall of Veilstone, Horsmond, Meliton and Pettis, etc., for the whiche the aforesayde archbyshop asketh of the aforesayde earle that he should do hym homage and service of iiii knightes suite of the court of the sayde archbyshop for the aforesayde manors. And that he shoulde be the hye stewarde of the sayde archbyshop and of his successors at their great feast when it shoulde fortune the sayde archbyshoppe to be intronizated, and that he shoulde be also the hye butler of the sayde archbyshop and his successors with divers other suche services for the manors aforesayde. (Ex Bibl. Bodl. Arch. A., Rot. no. vi; printed Monasticon Anglicanum, vol. i, p. 118. An enrolment of the original document, dated 42 Henry III, May 1st, is preserved in the Record Office, s.v. Chancery Miscellanea 16/1.)

Compositio inter Episcopum Exonie et Comitem Devonie super Homagio et Servitio ipsius Comitis ac Feodis sibi debitis tempore Inthronizationis Episcopi Exonie.—Noverint universi quod cum inter dominum Walterum de Stapledon Dei gratia Exonie episcopum ex parte una et dominum Hugonem filium et heredem domini Hugonis de Courtenaye ex altera, discordie materia fuisset exorta super eo quod dictus dominus Hugo clamavit et clamat tenere manerium de Slapton in comitatu Devon cum pertinentiis de eodem domino episcopo per homagium et servicium, occasione cujus tenure asseruit

small wonder if the chroniclers, busied with recording mighty warfare, now west of the Severn, now north of the Tweed, omitted to relate even those special occasions when the king's own brother waited on his sovereign at the royal banqueting table. Edmund, it should be mentioned, was made earl of Lancaster by Edward the First: he died on the 5th of June, 1296, and the stewardship once more became extinct. Edmund's son Thomas succeeded to the titles and estates.

On the 7th of July, 1307, Edward the First died at Burgh-on-Sands by Solway Water, and the Prince of Wales came

dictus dominus Hugo quod debuit esse senescallus dicti domini episcopi in festo intronizationis sue et ipse et heredes sui similiter in quolibet festo intronizationis cujuslibet episcopi Exonie, et ponere homines ad beneplacitum suum in quolibet officio in dicto festo et aliqua feoda percipere ibi et alibi occasione senescalcie predicte; tandem die et loco confectionis presentium, communibus amicis intervenientibus, super dicta senescalcia et feodo occasione dicte senescalcie percipiendo necnon et positione hominum dicti domini Hugonis et heredum suorum in officio in dicto festo et etiam omnibus aliis dictam senescalciam tangentibus in forma subsequenti convenit perpetuis temporibus servatura, viz : quod predictus dominus Hugo ratione predicti manerii de Slapton quod de dicto domino episcopo tenet nomine senescalcie et servicii de dicto manerio de Slapton dicto domino episcopo debiti die intronizationis cujuslibet episcopi Exonie suo tempore intronizandi et heredes sui qui plene etatis fuerint post ipsum, die intronizationis cujuslibet episcopi Exonie futuri, obviabunt dicto episcopo extra portam orientalem in descensu palefridi sui ad tardius, et ex tunc inantea ducent latus ejus dextrum ipsumque a concursu et oppressione populi pro viribus conservabunt quousque ducatur in chorum ecclesie cathedralis Exonie intronizandus : Et subsequente ipso die in majori refectione ponant personaliter totum primum ferculum coram dicto domino episcopo, et percipiant tantummodo quatuor discos argenteos de illis quos posuerunt coram episcopo in dicto primo ferculo, duo salsaria et unam cuppam de qua bibet episcopus ad mensam in dicta refectione, unum salsarium, unum picherium ad vinum, unum coclear et duas pelves de quibus lavit dominus episcopus predicto die, et hec omnia vasa debent esse argentea. . . . Datum apud Nyweton priorem de Plympton die dominico in crastino beati Thome apostoli anno Domini millesimo trecentesimo octavo et anno regni regis Edwardi filii regis Edwardi secundo Presentibus [etc.]. . . . (Brantyngham Register, vol. ii, fol. 36 b; printed Oliver, Monasticon Exon., p. 323.)

to the throne. At this king's coronation (February 25th, 1307–8) the Gascon favourite Gaveston took the chief place in the pageant and carried the crown; but the earl of Lancaster bore the sword "Curtana," a circumstance to be noted, and it is fairly probable that he claimed and was allowed to act as steward at the feast in Westminster Hall.[1] At all events, shortly after the coronation, Edward the Second by letters patent conferred the stewardship of England on Thomas and his heirs in tail, as being an office appurtenant so it was said, to the earldom of Leicester.[2] The stewardship now undergoes a curious development.

In many respects Edward the Second was not unlike his grandfather Henry the Third, and the course of events during the two reigns have many striking features in common. Both kings were foolish and grievously extravagant; both had a most awkward predilection for unpopular foreigners. Simon de Montfort led the opposition party under Henry the Third; his successor in title became the coryphæus of discontent under Edward the Second; both earls gained some measure of success; both ultimately came to a violent end at the hands of the king's party. Moreover, each earl enjoyed a scarcely merited apotheosis, was regarded as a martyr, worked according to local report many notable miracles with his corpse. And yet, in many ways, it is invidious to compare Simon with Thomas. Simon started his English career as a French pauper: Thomas was by inheritance the richest and most powerful nobleman in the kingdom. The former

---

[1] Baronibus pro rege. Quia rex quibusdam de causis vult certiorari que et cujusmodi feoda quondam comites Leycestrie, temporibus quibus ipsi comites senescalli progenitorum regis quondam regum Anglie de feodo extiterint, ratione senescalcie illius percipere consueverunt, et que et cujusmodi feoda ad eandem senescalciam pertinuerunt temporibus supradictis: rex mandat baronibus quod, scrutatis rotulis, libris et aliis memorandis de dicto scaccario per que super premissis poterunt melius informari, regem de eo quod inde invenerint reddant distincte et aperte sub sigillo ejusdem scaccarii certiorem, hoc breve regi remittentes. Teste rege apud Lenton. xxx die Septembris anno primo. Per ipsum regem. (Exchequer Memoranda Roll, L.T.R. Brevia Mich., 1 Edward II, m. 16d.; printed Madox Exchequer, vol. i, p. 52n.)

[2] See Appendix.

achieved what he did achieve by sheer force of character and strenuous activity : the methods of the latter have been aptly characterised as sulky inaction.

During Edward the First's reign the king represented the law and the constitution, and the people gave little thought to politics ; but the popular political principles evoked by Henry the Third's bad administration revived under his grandson's similar rule, and patriotic feeling turned once again to the barons in opposition to the king. There was also, no doubt, some reaction on the part of the barons themselves against the stringent pressure by which Edward the First had kept them in order.

Concisely stated, the position of affairs was this : the people had various specific constitutional grievances which they desired to have redressed ; the barons had their own personal grievances, and were exasperated by the offensive behaviour of Gaveston. All parties appear to have been agreed as to the remedy for their complaints : the king must never be without wise counsellors in attendance on his person ; moreover, in all difficult and arduous matters he must also have the advice of the national council in parliament. Who, in England, would not have assented to these political platitudes ? The difficulty was to discover by what perennial system of procedure the cure could be enforced. Furthermore, seeing that any efficient system of procedure must needs involve some amount of coercion, it remained to find some formula, some acceptable political cry to justify such measures.

Now the leader of the opposition in Henry the Third's reign, and also in the reign of Edward the Second, was in each case the hereditary steward. Again, the commission of reform appointed in 1258 had included, besides the steward, both the hereditary constable and the hereditary marshal. The fuglemen of the solitary political crisis under Edward the First were the hereditary constable and the hereditary marshal.[1] While, against Edward the Second and his

---

[1] This occurred in 1297 and ended by the king being compelled to confirm the great charters. According, however, to Hemingburgh (ii, 121), the action taken by the constable and marshal had no very creditable origin. When required by the king to lead his

minions, Lancaster's chief supporter was the earl of Hereford, the constable. Under these circumstances it is hardly surprising that some persons should have sought to establish the principle that, when the king erred, it was the business of these hereditary officers to correct his errors.

This principle is unequivocally enunciated in two very curious documents closely connected with the period under consideration. One document is the well-known *Modus tenendi Parliamentum*, the other is a tract setting out the functions of the stewardship of England. Possibly only the last-mentioned document was actually composed in the reign of Edward the Second; but, in both, the powers claimed as belonging ex officio to the stewardship are unmistakably derived from certain events of Edward the Second's reign. These events are so well known that the briefest mention of them will be sufficient.

In 1309 the barons under Lancaster and Hereford compelled the king to consent to the appointment of a committee of peers to redress the national grievances. The committee, known as the Lords Ordainers, was accordingly appointed and consisted of seven prelates, eight earls and six barons : the result of their deliberations was the production of certain ordinances, beneficial no doubt to the kingdom, but highly derogatory to the king; amongst other things the banishment of Gaveston was decreed. The king, unable to resist, signed and published the ordinances, but with the fixed intention not to observe them one moment longer than was necessary. Gaveston did, in fact, leave England, but soon after rejoined the king in the north. The barons, finding

---

armies into Gascony they excused themselves : they were ready to accompany the king but not to go without him. The earl marshal was pressed again and again to go. He said : "Willingly with you, Sire, and in the front rank of your army, as by hereditary right I am bound to do." To this the king : "Even without me you will still go with the others."—"I am not bound," said the earl, "nor is it my pleasure to undertake the expedition without you." The king's wrath was kindled. "By God, earl marshal, either you go or you hang."—"By the same oath, O King," replied the other, "I will neither go nor hang"; and without waiting permission he withdrew from the king's presence.

themselves flouted, collected an army and, headed by the steward and constable of England, marched against the king and his favourite.

Eventually Gaveston took refuge in Scarborough, the king in York. Lancaster placed the bulk of his forces between York and Scarborough, detaching Surrey and Pembroke to besiege Gaveston in Scarborough castle. The favourite soon realised that the place was untenable, and he surrendered to Pembroke upon conditions which guaranteed his personal safety. Pembroke then marched south with his prisoner, intending to convey him to Wallingford, Gaveston's own castle. All went well till they reached Dedington, where Gaveston was lodged for the night in the custody of Pembroke's servants; but before dawn next day he received a peremptory order to prepare for instant departure; and on leaving his chamber he found himself confronted, not by his former custodians, but by men in the livery of his arch-enemy Warwick. Gaveston must have known at once that his fate was sealed. They hurried him to Warwick castle, where he vainly pleaded for mercy from Lancaster and Hereford. His death was promptly decided upon. Whether judgment was previously passed upon him by his peers (he was earl of Cornwall, be it remembered), or by others, it is idle under such circumstances to inquire. They took him to Blacklow hill within the jurisdiction of the earl of Lancaster, and he was beheaded in the presence of the baronial leaders.

The king, when he heard of it, was quite incapacitated with rage and grief. The country as a whole was decidedly scandalised, and Pembroke, who deeply resented the kidnapping of his private prisoner, seceded from the opposition.

Nevertheless Lancaster maintained his position and influence; a reconciliation with the king was effected under stress of Scotch alarms; and in the year 1316 Thomas was made president of the king's council on his own conditions, which included amongst other things the provision that unprofitable counsellors should be removed from time to time by authority of parliament. According to the earl of Lancaster, the ordinances, and more particularly the removal of bad advisers, summed up the requirements of every situation; and we find him continually harping upon this one theme, in parliament and out of parliament, in letters and speeches, in season and out of season.

After Gaveston came the Despencers, and their ascendency soon brought on another and similar crisis. Lancaster and Hereford backed by their numerous adherents scored the first success. In 1321 the Despencers were proceeded against in parliament[1] upon accusations represented to have been framed by the prelates, earls, barons and other peers together with the commons. The alleged misdeeds of the Despencers were found by examination, though in the absence of the persons accused, to be notorious and truly asserted; and, in the presence of the king, the peers of the realm sentenced the Despencers to disherison and banishment. This judgment was recited in a statute passed in the first year of the reign of Edward the Third; the recital runs as follows:—[2]

Come Hugh le Despenser le piere et Hugh le Despenser le fitz, nadgairs a la suyte Thomas adonqes counte de Lancastre et de Leycestre, seneschal d'Engleterre, par commune assent et agard des piers et du poeple du roialme et par l'assent du roi Edward, piere nostre seigneur le roi que ore est, come treitres et enemys du roi et de poeple feussent exilez, desheritez et bannis hors du roialme pur touz jours. . ..[3]

This appears to be the first instance where a steward of England, so styled in a formal record, took part in the trial of a peer in parliament. Whether, however, earl Thomas himself pronounced the judgment, or even presided at the trial, does not appear from the contemporary record of the proceedings on the Close Rolls.

The Despencers submitted to the decree of parliament and left England.

---

[1] These proceedings are more fully dealt with in a subsequent chapter.   [2] Statute 1 Edward III, preamble.
[3] It is important to note that this recital is quoted more than once in the rolls of Parliament. See Rot. Parl., vol. ii, p. 256; and vol. iii, p. 366. It must always be borne in mind that the recorded circumstances, and not the actual circumstances, are what influence future procedure.

Now with these facts before us we will consider the two documents which purport to give an account of the steward's powers and duties. The passage in the "Modus" is entitled *De casibus et judiciis difficilibus*, and runs somewhat as follows :—

When any dispute, question, or difficult case, whether of peace or war, shall arise in or out of the kingdom, the case shall be related and recited in writing in full parliament and be treated of and debated on there among the peers of the parliament, . . . and if by disagreement between them and the king and any magnates, or perchance between the magnates themselves, the peace of the kingdom be disturbed, or the people or country troubled, so that it seem to the king and his council expedient that this matter be treated of and amended by the consideration of all the peers of his realm, or if the king and kingdom be troubled by war, or if a difficult case arise before the chancellor of England, or a difficult judgment has to be rendered before the justices and so forth ; and if by chance in such deliberations all or at least the greater part cannot agree, then the earl steward, the earl constable, and the earl marshal, or two of them, shall elect twenty-five persons from all the peers of the realm, namely two bishops, and three procurators for the whole clergy, two earls and three barons, five knights of the shires, five citizens, and [five] burgesses, making twenty-five, and those twenty-five may choose twelve of their number and delegate their powers to these, and these twelve may delegate to six, and the six to three, but the three may not further delegate their powers except by license from the lord king, and if the king consents the three may delegate to two, and, of these two, one may delegate to the other, and thus at last his ordinance shall stand above the whole parliament; and thus by delegation from twenty-five persons to a single person (unless a larger number agree and ordain) at length a single person as aforesaid who cannot disagree with himself shall ordain for all ; preserving to the lord king and his council their right to examine and amend such ordinances after they have been written, if they can and care to do so, in such a way that it be done there and then in full parliament, and with the assent of parliament and not otherwise.[1]

[1] See Appendix. There has been considerable divergence of opinion as to the date when this document was first compiled. Stubbs attributed it to the middle of the fourteenth century. Bémont (Mélanges Julien Havet) believes it to have been written soon after the accession of Richard II. Hardy assigns it to the period

The tract on the office of the stewardship is entitled *Hic annotatur quis sit senescallus Angliae et quid ejus officium.* I subjoin a substantially verbatim translation of it :—[1]

The stewardship of England appertains to the earldom of Leicester, and has appertained thereto from ancient times.

And it should be known that his office is to supervise and regulate, under and immediately after the king, the whole realm of England and all the officers of laws within the said kingdom in times of peaces and wars, in manner following.

The manner how and when he ought and is bound to exercise his office by service and oath of homage and fealty is such : When any man or woman shall come to the court of the lord king, whatever court it be, and possibly to the king, to have and obtain remedy for injustice done, and he or she shall not be able in due season to obtain remedy, then the steward of England ought and is bound to receive such petitions and complaints and to keep them until the next parliament thereafter to be holden, and to give and assign unto such complainants, if they so desire, a day there for prosecuting their petitions, and, in full parliament in the presence of the king, apprehending and charging that officer or those officers, whoever they be, who so have failed in doing of justice, and to call them to account in respect thereof, unto whom in such cases everyone throughout the kingdom is bound to answer, the king only excepted. And if the chancellor of England have failed to make original remedy, and the justices, treasurers, barons and chamberlains of the exchequer, steward of the king's house, escheators, coroners, sheriffs, clerks, bailiffs and other officers, of what localities or places soever they be, shall fail or desist in their processes, judgments, executions of judgments, and justice to be done, to the favour of one and loss of the other party, for gifts, bribes or other procurements ; and further if any justices, when both parties pleading before them have come to judgment, shall by such suborned procurements defer such judgments contrary to justice and the law and custom of the realm ; and if the chancellor of England, in such case, or any other of the officers of law, shall allege in parliament

1294-1327. For the French version see Archæological Journal, xix, pp. 259-74. See also Round, Commune of London, ch. xv.

[1] For the Latin text see Appendix.

Compare this tract with the De senescallo ducis et ejus officio in the Grand Coutumier de Normandie (Appendix).

and say for their excuse that in such case such hardness and ambiguity of the law did arise when the same was heard before them, that neither he nor the court of Chancery, nor any other courts wherein he is an officer, were able or knew how to attain unto the safe determination of the law, then shall he declare the same ambiguity and doubt in parliament. If then it be found that the law was doubtful in that case, the chancellor and such like officer shall be held excused; and then shall the steward of England together with the constable of England in the presence of the king and others of the parliament make choice of five and twenty persons, more or less, according as the case, together with other similar cases referred to the same parliament, shall require, amongst whom shall be earls, barons, knights of the shires, citizens and burgesses, who there shall ordain, found, and establish remedy of law in all such cases for ever after to endure. And these laws shall then be recited, written, and approved in full parliament, and sealed with the great seal, and delivered to all places of justice from thenceforth to be holden for laws, and to public places, where it shall be thought expedient for the commonalty, to be proclaimed and divulged, as everyone is held to know common laws and especially statute laws publicly proclaimed.

And if it so happen that there was in such case either common law or statute law, so that the king, the steward, and others of the parliament may understand and perceive that such default and delays in processes and judgments occur and take place through such officers, whence the subornation or malice of such officers plainly and often may be presumed, then shall he be removed from office and some other fit officer shall be appointed in his place; and if the presumption is against the justices and such like officers, but they for excusing themselves shall say that they have not heretofore known themselves, or the courts whence they are, take cognisance of such cases, or that by chance they were negligent; then ought they to be admonished by the steward on behalf of the king and parliament, that they study and search better the common laws that no such ignorance nor negligence be found in them in the like or other cases afterwards; and if it shall happen again, then they shall be removed from their offices, and others more discreet and diligent shall be appointed by the king and his council.

Likewise, it is the steward's office [to intervene], if the king have evil counsellors about him who advise him to do such things as are plainly and publicly to his dishonour or disherison, and to the public hurt, and destruction of his people; [and] then the steward of England, taking with him the constable, and other magnates, and others from the commons of the realm of England, shall send to such counsellor of the king, that he desist from thus leading and counselling the king, making mention of such evil counsels of his previously given to the king, and that he withdraw from him and his presence, and not abide with him to his dishonour and the public loss as aforesaid, which if he shall not do, they shall send to the king to remove him from him and not to hear his counsels, for the reason that by the whole people he is presumed to be an evil counsellor between the king and his people. Which if the king shall not do, again and often shall they send as well unto the king as unto him; and if at the last neither the king nor such counsellor have regard to such missions and supplications, but rather shall neglect to comply, then for the public good it is and shall be permissible for the steward and constable of England, the magnates and others of the commons of the realm, with banner raised in the name of the king and realm, to take such counsellor as the public enemy of the king and kingdom and keep his body in safe custody until the next parliament, and in the meantime to seize his goods, rents, and all his possessions till he shall attend and undergo judgment by consideration of the whole realm in parliament, as it happened to Godwin earl of Kent, in the time of King Edward the immediate predecessor of William duke of Normandy the conqueror of England, who for such like evil deeds and counsels was adjudged to lose his earldom and banished from the whole realm of England, the said earldom escheating to the said king; and afterwards, by the mediation of the king, the same Godwin by the grace of the magnates returned to England and again incurred forfeiture. Likewise concerning Hubert de Burgh earl of Kent, in the time of King Henry son of King John, who for his evil deeds and other such like counsels of his was taken by the steward and other magnates and adjudged to lose the same earldom by the consideration of the whole parliament. Likewise concerning Peter de Gaveston, who in the time of King Edward son of King Henry for such like deeds and counsels was banished from all the dominions of the King of England as well beyond as this side the seas; which Peter afterwards, on the mediation of the King, by the grace and permission of the magnates returned to England and had by gift of the king the earldom of Cornwall; and afterwards for his evil deeds and counsels was again banished by the magnates and commons, the said earldom escheating to the king. And afterwards he returned without the consent of the magnates of England, and attached himself to the king, which when perceived by the steward and constable and other magnates of England, he was taken by them, and, as a public enemy of the king and realm, beheaded at Blacklow in the county of Warwick.

The *Modus tenendi parliamentum* need not be discussed here, but the tract on the stewardship has a direct bearing on the history of the steward's various jurisdictions, and merits far more attention than it has hitherto received. The original version of this last-named tract may with fair certainty be assigned to a period, subsequent of course to the death of Gaveston, but prior to the banishment of his successors; and it was very possibly composed for the purpose of justifying the proceedings instituted against the Despencers in parliament by Lancaster and Hereford.

As an historical account of the office in question the tract is not entitled to the smallest credit: the author's reference to Godwin and Hubert de Burgh is more valorous than discreet; and, apart from these two instances, the document is nothing more than an assertion of abstract principles of right founded more or less closely on the concrete political events of Edward the Second's reign. The interest of the tract, however, lies not in the past but in the future: this particular document clearly forms the root of title to the jurisdiction conferred on or assumed by the steward of England in the reign of Richard the Second. Eventually this dignitary acquired settled functions very different from those claimed by Thomas, but only by a modification, gradual and easily traced, of the prerogatives asserted in the tract.

Regarded as a device for the foundation, or at least the aggrandisement of an office, the document lacks originality: Henry the Second's claim to be hereditary steward of France was founded upon a precisely analogous composition which asserted equally unrecognised powers.[1] Even as a formula

---

[1] The following are the judicial prerogatives of the steward of France according to Hugh de Clers: Item, quando erit in Francia, quod et curia sua judicaverit firmum erit et stabile. Si vero contentio aliqua nascetur de judicio facto in Francia, rex mandabit quod

for dealing with irresponsible kings, this Lancastrian tract was by no means unique. The Great Charter contained similar provisions for electing twenty-five persons, and for compelling the king *vi et armis* to redress grievances. Matthew Paris states in his chronicle that the earl of Chester carried the sword *curtana* at the coronation of 1236 to indicate that he was earl-palatine with power to coerce the king when he erred, an authority Lancaster, as bearer of that sword at Edward's coronation, might have cited in self-justification.[1] Moreover the reign of Edward the Second produced a rival tract ascribed to the younger Despencer.

Homage and oath of allegiance regard the crown more than the king's person [the first sentence is the keynote of the formula], and are due to the crown rather than to the person, and this is manifest in that before the estate of the crown be descended no allegiance is due to the person. Wherefore, if the king by chance be not guided by reason in exercising the rights of the crown, his lieges are bound by their oaths to the crown to lead the king and the estate of the crown back again to reason, otherwise the oath would not be kept. The question then arises, how the king is to be brought back, whether by suit of law or by force. By suit of law no man can do it, because he can have no other judges but the king's; in which case, if the king's will be not according to reason, the error will only be maintained and confirmed. Wherefore it is needful in order to save the oath, that when the king will not redress or remove an evil matter damaging to the people and the crown it must be removed by force; for by their oaths both the king is bound to govern his people, and his lieges are bound to govern in aid of him and in his default.[2]

comes veniat illud emendare; et si pro ea mittere noluerit, scripta utriusque partis comiti transmittet, et quod inde sua curia judicabit firmum erit et stabile.

[1] Matthew Paris, Rolls Series, vol. iii, p. 337. Comite Cestriae gladium sancti Ædwardi qui Curtein dicitur ante regem bajulante in signum quod comes est palatii, et regem si oberret habeat de jure potestatem cohibendi, suo sibi scilicet Cestrensi constabulario ministrante, et virga populum, cum se [in]ordinate ingereret, subtrahente. . . .

[2] Close Roll 15 Edward II, m. 30d.; and see Close Roll Cal., 1318–23, p. 492.

The Lancastrian party made this composition the first count against the younger Despencer in the proceedings for his banishment: they alleged that it had been written for the purpose of accroaching sovereign power, and had been employed to cow the king into submission. An interesting example this of thief catching thief. More interesting still is the conclusion from such and similar evidence, that these were times when pamphleteering was considered scarcely less effective than the ordinances as a means for reducing the king to impotence.

If earl Thomas had been a man of Simon de Montfort's character and ability, he might have ruled England, and Scotland also, in whatever capacity he chose; as chief of the council, as steward, perhaps as king. But in character Thomas was treacherous, cruel and selfish: his ability is an unknown quantity. More than once he obtained supreme control of the government, but he never governed. He was given supreme command over the English armies, but he never commanded or led them. Gaveston's capture was perhaps a necessary adventure, but his kidnapping and execution by Lancaster was a grossly dishonourable blunder. The banishment of the Despencers was a clean and vigorous performance, ably executed, but it was Lancaster's last success. Very soon after came pitiful tragedy. Edward had a burst of energy; Lancaster and Hereford fled northward, vainly hoping for assistance from Scotland; Harcla of Carlisle, the northern watch-dog, intercepted them. Hereford was slain at Borough Bridge; Lancaster was made prisoner and brought to his own castle of Pontefract. There he was condemned to a traitor's death, but being of the blood-royal the sentence was commuted to beheading. In sorry guise he was ridden to his execution; men pelted him with mud on his last journey. Arrived at the place of death, Lancaster knelt for the end facing eastward; but brutally they turned his face to the north: "You look for help," they said, "not from God, but the Scots." Then the headsman did his business, and the office of steward of England once more became vacant.

APPENDIX TO CHAPTER V

Patent Roll, 49 *Henry III, m.* 2

Rex militibus liberis-hominibus et omnibus aliis tenentibus de comitatu et honore Leycestrie senescalcia Anglie et de omnibus terris et tenementis que fuerunt Simonis de Monteforti quondam comitis Leycestrie salutem. Sciatis quod dedimus et concessimus Edmundo filio nostro karissimo predicta comitatum honorem senescalciam terras et tenementa que fuerunt prefati Simonis inimici nostri exceptis dominicis nostris habenda et tenenda de nobis et heredibus nostris eidem Edmundo et heredibus suis imperpetuum faciendo servicium inde debitum et consuetum. Et ideo vobis mandamus quod eidem Edmundo tanquam domino vestro in omnibus que ad predicta comitatum honorem senescalciam terras et tenementa pertinent de cetero intendentes sitis et respondentes sicut predictum est. In cujus etc. Teste ut supra. [scilicet apud Cantuar. xxv die Octobris].

Register Munimentorum, Liber A.,[1] *fol.* 190

Henricus Dei gratia rex Anglie dominus Hibernie et dux Aquitanie archiepiscopis episcopis abbatibus prioribus comitibus baronibus justiciariis vicecomitibus prepositis ministris et omnibus ballivis et fidelibus suis salutem. Sciatis nos dedisse concessisse et hac carta nostra confirmasse Edmundo filio nostro karissimo comitatum et honorem Leycestrie senescalciam Anglie et omnes terras et tenementa que fuerunt Symonis de Monteforte quondam comitis Leycestrie inimici et felonis nostri per quem guerra in regno nostro mota fuit necnon omnes terras et tenementa que fuerunt Nicholai de Segrave inimici et rebellis nostri qui eidem Simoni et imprisis suis [tempore] guerre predicte adhesit ad exheredationem nostram et destructionem corone nostre usque ad bellum inter nos et dictos inimicos et rebelles nostros [apud Evesham] commissum et quorum inimicorum

[1] A register temp. Edward I of documents in the custody of the crown.

etiam rebellum terre et tenementa per forisfacturam eorum de communi consensu et consilio magnatum ac fidelium regni nostri ad nostram ordinationem et dispositionem salvis capitalibus dominis homagiis et servitiis suis hac vice pertinent habenda et tenenda eidem filio nostro et heredibus suis de capitalibus dominis feodi illius sive nobis vel aliis cum omnibus ad predicta comitatum honorem senescalciam terras et tenementa spectantibus dum tamen terre et tenementa predicta non fuit (sic) de dominico corone nostre faciendo inde omnia servitia debita et consueta ita quod occasione hujus donationis nostre nichil capitalibus dominis predictis in wardis releviis aut rebus aliis ad eos pertinentibus depereat imperpetuum. Quare volumus et firmiter precipimus pro nobis et heredibus nostris quod predictus Edmundus et heredes sui comitatum honorem senescalciam terras et tenementa predicta cum omnibus pertinentiis suis habeant et teneant de capitalibus dominis feodi illius sive nobis vel aliis dum tamen terre et tenementa predicta non sint de dominico corone nostre faciendo inde omnia servitia debita et consueta sicut predictum est imperpetuum. Et volumus et precipimus pro nobis et heredibus nostris quod nullus ratione juris quod sibi per predictos Symonem et Nicholaum hereditarie competere posset actionem vel clamium ullis temporibus habeat de cetero in predicto comitatu honore senescalcia terris et tenementis sed ab omni jure actione et clamio penitus excludatur imperpetuum. Et nos et heredes nostri hanc nostram donationem defendere et conservare tenemur sicut nos et antecessores nostri alias donationes nostras et feoffamenta conservare et defendere consuevimus et sicut ea conservare et defendere tenemur. Hiis testibus—Venerabili patre W. Bathon. et Wellen. episcopo, Hugone le Bigod, Philippo Basset, Rogero de Leyburne, Roberto Walerand, Willelmo Belet, Waltero de Burges, Galfrido de Percy et aliis. Data [per manum nostram apud] Cantuar. xxvj die Octobris anno regni nostri xlix.[1]

---

[1] (In margin) Carta per quam H. rex dedit Edmundo filio suo comitatum [et] honorem Leycestrie senescalciaṁ Anglie et omnes terras et tenementa [que] fuerunt Symonis de Monte [fort]e et omnes terras et tenementa [que] fuerunt Nicholai de Segrave.

(Printed by Rymer, Foedera, i, p. 465, where, instead of giving the regnal year as xlix in numerals, the word "quinquagesimo" occurs. Note that a modern hand has crossed out "xlix" in red chalk and inserted "50" in the margin. The true date is October 26th, 1265, but the regnal year depends on whether the 19th or the 28th of October, 1216, is treated as the commencement of the reign. This charter never passed.)

Charter Roll, 49 *Henry III, m.* 1

[Pro Edmundo filio] regis.—[H. Dei gratia rex Anglie etc. archiepiscopis etc. salutem. Sciatis nos dedisse] concessisse et hac carta nostra confirmasse Edmundo filio nostro karissimo {comitatum et*} honorem Leycestrie et omnes terras et t[enementa] cum pertinentiis que fuerunt Simonis de Monteforti inimici et {rebellis*} (felonis†) nostri (cui†) {qui complicibus et fautoribus suis*} inimici{s*} nostri{s*} et imprisis suis adhes{it*}(erunt†) tempore guerre nuper {habite*} in regno nostro mota fuit per ipsum Simonem et dictos imprisos suos ad exheredacionem nostram et destructionem corone nostre usque ad bellum inter nos et dictos inimicos et rebelles nostros commissum etquorum inimicorum et rebellium nostrorum terre et tenementa per forisfactum eorum de communi consensu et consilio magnatum et fidelium regni nostri ad nostram ordinacionem et disposicionem salvis capitalibus dominis homagiis et serviciis hac vice pertinent habenda et tenenda (cum feodis militum advocacionibus ecclesiarum libertatibus et omnibus aliis ad dicta honorem terras et tenementa pertinentibus†) etc. Dum tamen comitatus honor terre et tenementa non sint de dominico corone nostre faciendo inde omnia servicia debita et consueta ita quod racione illius donacionis nostre nichil capitalibus dominis predictis in wardis releviis aut rebus aliis ad eos pertinentibus depereat imperpetuum salvis nobis et heredibus nostris hiis que ad nos secundum regni nostri consuetudinem pertinent racione terrarum et tenementorum que de nobis tenentur in capite. Quare volumus et firmiter precipimus pro nobis et heredibus nostris etc. sicut predictum est et volumus et precipimus quod nullus racione juris etc.

* Erasures.   † Interlineations.

Et nos et heredes nostri etc. Hiis testibus—Venerabili patre W. Bathon. et Wellen. episcopo, Hugone le Bygot, Philippo Basset, Rogero de Leyburne, Roberto Wallerand, Roberto Aguilon, Willelmo Belet, Galfrido de Percy, Bartholomeo le Bygot et aliis. Data per manum nostram apud Cantuar. xxvj die Octobris.

(This charter passed, if at all, on the 26th of October, 1265, or the same date as the escrow transcribed in the Liber A.)

Royal Charters, Duchy of Lancaster, No. 97. Original Letters Patent, Sealed.

H. Dei gratia rex Anglie dominus Hibernie et dux Aquitanie omnibus tenentibus de dominicis suis que fuerunt in manibus quondam S. de Monteforti et Nicholai de Segrave salutem. Sciatis quod ad sustentacionem Edmundi filii nostri karissimi concessimus eidem filio nostro omnia dominica nostra que fuerunt in manibus predictorum Simonis et Nicholai inimicorum nostrorum habenda sibi cum omnibus pertinentiis et exitibus suis quamdiu nobis placuerit vel donec ei in equivalenti providerimus. Et ideo vobis mandamus quod eidem Edmundo decetero intendentes sitis et respondentes sicut predictum est. In cujus rei testimonium has litteras nostras fieri fecimus patentes. Teste me-ipso apud Northampton xxviij die Decembris anno regni nostri quinquagesimo.

Royal Charters, Duchy of Lancaster, No. 98. Original Letters Patent, Sealed

H. Dei gratia rex Anglie dominus Hibernie et dux Aquitanie omnibus tenentibus de dominicis suis que fuerunt in manibus S. de Monteforti quondam comitis Leycestrie salutem. Sciatis quod ad sustentacionem dilecti filii nostri Edmundi concessimus et assignavimus eidem filio nostro omnia dominica nostra que fuerunt in manibus predicti comitis inimici nostri habenda et tenenda eidem Edmundo cum omnibus pertinentiis et exitibus suis quamdiu nobis placuerit vel donec ei in equivalenti providerimus. Et ideo vobis mandamus quod eidem filio nostro decetero intendentes sitis et respondentes sicut predictum est. In cujus rei testi-

monium has litteras nostras fieri fecimus patentes. Teste
me-ipso apud Norhampton vj die Januarii anno regni nostri
L°.

Royal Charters, Duchy of Lancaster, No. 100. *Original
Letters Patent, Sealed*

H. Dei gratia rex Anglie dominus Hibernie et dux Aquitanie omnibus ad quos presentes littere pervenerint salutem.
Cum nuper dederimus et concesserimus dilecto filio nostro
Edmundo omnes terras et tenementa que fuerunt Simonis de
Monteforti quondam comitis Leycestrie et omnes terras et
tenementa que fuerunt Nicholai de Segrave inimicorum nostrorum habenda et tenenda sibi et heredibus suis imperpetuum.
Nos eidem filio nostro gratiam uberiorem facere volentes
dedimus et concessimus eidem omnes terras et tenementa
inimicorum nostrorum de feodis predictorum comitis et
Nicholai de quibus collaciones aliquas aliquibus prius non
fecerimus faciendo inde servicia debita et consueta. In cujus
rei testimonium has litteras nostras fieri fecimus patentes.
Teste me-ipso apud Norhampton xij die Januarii anno regni
nostri quinquagesimo.

Royal Charters, Duchy of Lancaster, No. 105. (*Original, no
Seal.*) *Charter Roll, 4 Edward III, n.* 19 (*inspeximus*)

[H]enricus Dei gratia rex Anglie dominus Hibernie et dux
Aquitanie archiepiscopis episcopis abbatibus prioribus comitibus baronibus justiciis vicecomitibus prepositis ministris et
omnibus ballivis et fidelibus suis salutem. Sciatis nos dedisse
concessisse et hac carta nostra confirmasse Edmundo filio
nostro karissimo honorem Dereby castra maneria et omnes
terras et tenementa que fuerunt Roberti de Ferariis et
honorem Leicestrie et omnes terras et tenementa cum pertinentiis que fuerunt Simonis de Monteforti quondam comitis
Leicestrie inimicorum nostrorum et que per forisfacturam
eorundem ad manum nostram tanquam escaeta nostra devenerunt habenda et tenenda eidem Edmundo et heredibus
suis de corpore suo legitime procreatis de nobis et heredibus
nostris imperpetuum una cum feodis militum advocacionibus
ecclesiarum dotibus cum acciderint et omnibus aliis ad

honores castra maneria terras et tenementa pertinentibus faciendo servicia inde debita et consueta. Ita quod prefatum Edmundum vel heredes suos predictos inde non disseisiemus nec disseisiri permittemus donec inde sibi escambium racionabile fecerimus in aliis terris nostris ad valorem honorum castrorum maneriorum terrarum et tenementorum predictorum. Quare volumus et firmiter precipimus pro nobis et heredibus nostris quod predictus Edmundus et heredes sui predicti imperpetuum habeant et teneant honores castra maneria terras et tenementa predicta cum feodis militum advocacionibus ecclesiarum dotibus cum acciderint et omnibus aliis ad eadem pertinentibus faciendo servicia inde debita et consueta ita quod prefatum Edmundum vel heredes suos predictos inde non disseisiemus nec disseisiri permittemus donec inde sibi escambium racionabile fecerimus in aliis terris nostris ad valorem honorum castrorum maneriorum terrarum et tenementorum predictorum sicut predictum est. Hiis testibus—Venerabili patre W. Bathon. et Wellen. episcopo, Rogero de Mortuo-Mari, Rogero de Clifford, Rogero de Leyburn, Roberto Aguillon, Willelmo de Aett, Radulfo de Bakepuz, Stephano de Eddewurth, Bartholomeo le Bigod, et aliis. Data per manum nostram apud Kenillewurth duodecimo die Julii anno regni nostri quinquagesimo.

Royal Charters, Duchy of Lancaster, No. 122. (*Original, Sealed.*) *Charter Roll,* 53 *Henry III, m.* 11

[H]enricus Dei gratia rex Anglie dominus Hibernie et dux Aquitanie archiepiscopis episcopis abbatibus prioribus comitibus baronibus justiciis vicecomitibus prepositis ministris et omnibus ballivis et fidelibus suis salutem.[1] Sciatis nos dedisse concessisse et hac carta nostra confirmasse Edmundo filio nostro karissimo honorem villam et castrum Leycestrie et omnes terras et tenementa ejusdem honoris cum feodis militum et aliis omnibus pertinentiis suis quocunque nomine censeri possint que fuerunt quondam Simonis de Monteforti comitis Leycestrie inimici nostri et que secundum legem

---

[1] C.R. : Pro Edmundo filio regis—Rex archiepiscopis etc. salutem.

et consuetudinem regni nostri per guerram quam contra nos
ad exheredacionem nostram in regno nostro excitavit et bella
que contra nos in quorum altero apud Evesham quo tamquam
inimicus noster interfectus fuerat commisit ad nos tamquam
eschaeta nostra per predictam forisfacturam suam devenerunt
habenda et tenenda eidem Edmundo et heredibus suis de
corpore suo legitime procreatis de nobis et heredibus nostris
bene et in pace cum omnibus ad dictum honorem villam et
castrum spectantibus quocunque more vel nomine censeri
possint sicut idem Simon ea quondam tenuit et habuit
faciendo inde nobis et heredibus nostris servicia inde debita
et consueta. Dedimus eciam et concessimus eidem Edmundo
filio nostro omnes terras et tenementa que idem Simon tenuit
de baronia quondam Johannis le Viscunte in Northumbr. et
alibi et omnes alias terras et tenementa que idem Simon
hereditarie de nobis tenuit et que per supradictam forisfacturam ipsius Simonis ad nos similiter tanquam eschaeta
nostra devenerunt habenda et tenenda eidem Edmundo filio
nostro et heredibus suis predictis cum advocacionibus ecclesiarum feodis militum serviciis liberorum hominum et omnibus
aliis ad predictas terras et tenementa spectantibus faciendo
inde nobis et heredibus nostris servicia inde debita et consueta.
Dedimus eciam et concessimus prefato Edmundo filio nostro
omnes alias terras et tenementa que idem Simon tenuit de
aliis capitalibus dominis suis et que per predictam forisfacturam suam de communi consensu et consilio magnatum ac
fidelium regni nostri ad nostram ordinacionem et disposicionem sicut et terre aliorum rebellium nostrorum qui
nobiscum in bellis supradictis congressi fuerant salvis capitalibus dominis homagiis et serviciis suis hac vice pertinebant
habenda et tenenda eidem Edmundo filio nostro et heredibus
suis supradictis cum omnibus ad dictas terras et tenementa
spectantibus de capitalibus dominis feodorum illorum faciendo
eis inde omnia servicia debita et consueta imperpetuum.
Quare volumus et firmiter precipimus pro nobis et heredibus
nostris quod predictus Edmundus filius noster et heredes sui
de corpore suo legitime procreati habeant et teneant predictum honorem villam castrum et omnes terras et tenementa
ejusdem honoris cum feodis militum et aliis omnibus perti-

nentiis suis quocunque nomine censeri possint de nobis et heredibus nostris bene et in pace cum omnibus ad dictum honorem villam et castrum spectantibus sicut predictus Simon ea quondam tenuit et habuit faciendo inde nobis et heredibus nostris servicia inde debita et consueta et omnes terras et tenementa que idem Simon tenuit de baronia quondam Johannis le Viscunte in Northumbr. et alibi et omnes terras et tenementa que idem Simon hereditarie de nobis tenuit et que per supradictam forisfacturam ipsius Simonis ad nos similiter tanquam eschaeta nostra devenerunt cum advocacionibus ecclesiarum feodis militum serviciis liberorum hominum et omnibus aliis ad predictas terras et tenementa spectantibus faciendo inde nobis et heredibus nostris servicia inde debita et consueta et omnes alias terras et tenementa que idem Simon tenuit de aliis capitalibus dominis suis et que per predictam forisfacturam suam de communi consensu et consilio magnatum ac fidelium regni nostri ad nostram ordinacionem et disposicionem sicut et terre aliorum rebellium nostrorum qui nobiscum in bellis supradictis congressi fuerant salvis capitalibus dominis homagiis et serviciis suis hac vice pertinebant sicut predictum est. Hiis testibus— Venerabili patre N. Winton. episcopo, Edwardo primogenito filio nostro, Johanne de Warren comite Surrey, Willelmo de Valencia fratre nostro, Roberto Walerand, Nicholao de Yatingeden, Petro de Chaumpvent, Waltero de Percy, Willelmo Belet, Willelmo de Faukham et aliis. Data per manum nostram apud Windesor vicesimo secundo die Aprilis (anno regni nostri quinquagesimo tercio[1]).

Patent Roll, 53 Henry III, m. 15

Rex omnibus ballivis etc. salutem. Cum per cartam nostram dederimus et concesserimus Edmundo filio nostro karissimo honorem villam castrum Leycestrie et omnes terras et tenementa ejusdem honoris cum feodis militum et aliis pertinentiis suis quocumque nomine censeri possint que fuerunt quondam Simonis de Monteforti comitis Leycestrie inimici nostri et que secundum legem et consuetudi-

---

[1] C.R. omits.

M

nem regni nostri per guerram quam contra nos ad exheredacionem nostram in regno nostro excitavit et bella que
contra nos in quorum altero apud Evesham tanquam inimicus
noster interfectus fuerat commisit ad nos tanquam escaeta
nostra per predictam forisfacturam devenerunt habenda et
tenenda eidem Edmundo et heredibus suis de corpore suo
legitime procreatis imperpetuum. Nos eidem filio nostro
gratiam facere volentes uberiorem concessimus ei Senescalciam Anglie quam idem Simon quondam habuit habendam et
tenendam ad totam vitam ipsius Edmundi cum omnibus ad
Senescalciam illam pertinentibus de gratia nostra speciali.
In cujus etc. Teste ut supra [scilicet apud Windsor. nono
die Maii].

Register Munimentorum, Liber A., fol. 197b[1]

Universis Christi fidelibus ad quos presentes littere pervenerint Edmundus egregii principis Edwardi illustris regis
Anglie germanus salutem. Ad omnium vestrum notitiam
volumus pervenire quod cum in coronatione prefati domini
nostri regis officium senescalcie Anglie quo ad diem predicte
coronacionis et alia anni tempora nobis ad opus nostrum et
heredum nostrorum ex dono et concessione domini genitoris
nostri vendicaremus nos juri et clamio quod in dicta senescalcia in feodo et hereditate nobis et heredibus nostris ullo
jure competere potuit renuntiamus imperpetuum. Idem
autem dominus germanus noster dictam senescalciam Anglie
cum juribus et pertinentiis suis nobis de sua curialitate et
benevolentia ad totam vitam nostram concessit ita quod
nobis descedentibus nullus heres aut alius assignatus noster
quicquam in dicta senescalcia aut ejus pertinentiis clamare
possit imperpetuum. Concedimus etiam pro nobis et heredibus nostris quod si que carte vel instrumenta exnunc ap-
pareant per que heredes nostri jus aliquod sibi in dicta
senescalcia et ejus pertinentiis clamare possint cassa sint et
inania atque pro nullis imperpetuum habeantur. In cujus
rei testimonium huic scripto sigillum nostrum fecimus apponi.
Datum apud Westmonasterium die Lune proxima post festum

[1] A register, temp. Edward I, of documents in the custody of
the crown.

assumptionis beate Marie anno regni dicti domini regis secundo.[1]

Patent Roll, 3 Edward I, m. 30

Pro Edmundo fratre regis.—Rex omnibus etc. salutem. Sciatis quod de gratia nostra speciali concessimus pro nobis et heredibus nostris Edmundo fratri nostro karissimo senescalciam Anglie cum omnibus ad eandem senescalciam pertinentibus quam Simon de Monteforti quondam comes Leycestrie aliquando habuit habendam et tenendam eidem Edmundo quoad vixerit. In cujus etc. Teste rege apud Wyndsor xxvij die Febuarii.

Patent Roll, 1 Edward II, pt. 2, m. 12

Rex omnibus ad quos etc. salutem. Sciatis quod cum celebris memorie dominus H. quondam rex Anglie avus noster per cartam suam dederit et concesserit Edmundo filio suo avunculo nostro comitatum Leycestrie cum omnibus ad comitatum illum spectantibus habendum et tenendum eidem Edmundo et heredibus suis de corpore suo legitime procreatis de ipso avo nostro et heredibus suis imperpetuum per certa servicia inde dicto avo nostro et heredibus suis facienda. Nos volentes dilecto consanguineo et fideli nostro Thome comiti Lancastrie filio et heredi predicti Edmundi gratiam in hac parte facere specialem dedimus ei et concessimus pro nobis et heredibus nostris senescalciam Anglie ad predictum comitatum Leycestrie ut dicitur pertinentem habendam et tenendam eidem comiti et heredibus suis de corpore suo legitime procreatis de nobis et heredibus nostris cum omnibus ad senescalciam illam spectantibus imperpetuum sicut Simon de Monteforti quondam comes Leicestrie et ceteri comites comitatus ejusdem loci antea senescalciam predictam habuerunt et tenuerunt. In cujus etc. Teste rege apud Westmonasterium ix die Maii.

(Printed by Nichols, History of Leicester, i, app., p. 23; and by Rymer, Foedera R.C., vol. ii, p. 38.)

[1] (In margin) Litera per quam Edmundus germanus egregii principis Edwardi regis Anglie non vendicat officium senescalcie Anglie nisi ad terminum vite sue, non ad heredes ejus descendet.

Hic annotatur quis sit Senescallus Anglie et quid
ejus officium

Senescalcia Anglie pertinet ad comitivam[1] Leycestrie et pertinuit ab antiquo. Et sciendum quod ejus officium est supervidere et regulare sub rege et immediate post regem totum regnum Anglie et omnes ministros legum infra idem regnum temporibus pacum et guerrarum in forma que sub-sequitur.[2]

Modus quomodo et quando officio suo uti[3] debet et tenetur per servicium et per sacramentum homagii et fidelitatis sue talis est : cum aliquis vel alique[4] ad curiam domini regis venerit, quecumque curia illa fuerit, et forte ad regem, et[5] ad remedium habendum et perquirendum contra injustitiam sibi factam et idem seu eadem remedium assequi non valeant opportunum, tunc Senescallus Anglie debet et tenetur hujus-modi petitiones et querelas recipere custodiendas usque proximum parliamentum extunc tenendum, et hujusmodi querentibus diem ad hujusmodi peticiones suas si velint prosequendas dare et assignare et in pleno parliamento, in presencia regis, ministrum seu ministros illos qui ita de justitia facienda defecerint coripere et arguere, quiscunque fuerit, et eos inde ad racionem ponere. In quemlibet[6] de regno in hujusmodi casu respondere[7] tenetur, regemet[8] dum-taxat excepto, ut si Cancellarius Anglie defecerit de originali remedio faciendo et justitiarii, thesaurarii, barones et camer-arii de scaccario, senescallus hospitii[9] regis, escaetores, coronarii, vicecomites, clerici, ballivi et alii ministri de qui-buscumque locis seu placiis[10] fuerint in eorum processibus, judiciis, judiciorum execucionibus, de justitia facienda in unius partis favorem et alterius dampnum pro donis, exenniis aut aliis procuracionibus deficiant,[11] desistant; et saltim si qui justiciarii cum ambe partes coram eis placitantes in judicio descenderint per hujusmodi subornatas procuraciones hujus-modi judicia procrastinient et elongent contra justiciam et

---

[1] comitiam, N.L.	[2] sequitur, L.	[3] ut, N.L.
[4] aliqua, N.	[5] omit, N.	[6] cum quilibet, N.L.
[7] r̄ndere, V.	[8] regunet, V.	[9] de hospitio, N.L.
[10] placeis, N.L.	[11] deficient, N.L.V.	

legem et consuetudinem regni. Et si Cancellarius Anglie in hujusmodi casu seu alius minister legis alleget in parliamento et dicat pro excusatione sua quod in casu illa talis durissia et juris ambiguitas quando coram eo fuerat propositus emersit quod ipse nec curia cancellarii, seu alia curia unde idem est minister, potuerunt nec sciverunt ad deliberationem juris pertingere securam, tunc assignabit ibidem duriciam et ambiguitatem illam in parliamento ; et si ambiguitas juris comperiatur, habebitur[1] tunc Cancellarius et hujusmodi minister pro excusato ; et tunc senescallus Anglie una cum constabulario Anglie ibidem, in presentia regis et aliorum de parliamento, eligent viginti-quinque personas, vel plures vel pauciores secundum quod casus ille exegerit,[2] una cum aliis casibus consimilibus[3] in parliamento illo relatis, inter quos erunt ipsi comites, barones, milites de comitatibus, cives et burgenses, qui ibidem[4] ordinabunt, condent[5] et statuent remedium juris in omnibus hujusmodi casibus imperpetuum duraturum. Et erunt leges ille tunc recitate, scripte[6] et approbate in pleno parliamento et sigillato cum magno sigillo, et liberate ad omnes placeas legum, extunc tenenda[7] pro legibus, et loca puplica, quibus pro communitate expedire videbitur, proclamande et divulgande[8] [ut] quilibet leges[9] communes et precipue leges statutas in toto regno puplice[10] proclamatas scire teneatur.[11] Et si forte in hujusmodi casu prius fuerat lex communis vel lex statuta ita quod rex, sen[escallus] et alii de parliamento intelligere vel scire possint quod hujusmodi defectus et dilationes in processibus et judiciis interveniant et fiant per hujusmodi ministros, unde[12] subornacio vel malicia penes hujusmodi ministrum aperte et pluries presumatur,[13] tunc amovebitur ab officio et alius idoneus minister loco suo assignabitur ; et si presumat contra justiciarios et hujusmodi ministros vel[14] ipsimet se excusando dicant quod ipsi nesciverunt prius se ipsos et curias, unde sunt, in hujusmodi casubus deliberare, vel forte

---

[1] omit, N.L. [2] exierit, V. ; exit, N.L. [3] consilibus, V.
[4] ibunt, V. [5] concordent, N.L. [6] scripta, V.
[7] tenendo, N.L. [8] devulgando, N.L.V. [9] legee, N.L.
[10] publico, N.L. [11] teneantur, N.L. [12] ubi, L.
[13] presumat, L. [14] read—" sed."

negligentes fuerint, tunc puniri debent per senescallum ex
parte regis et parliamenti quod ipsi melius studeant[1] et
scrutentur leges communes, ita quod hujusmodi insipiencia vel
negligencia in personis suis in hujusmodi nec in aliis casubus
extunc alias apprehendatur; et si iterato contingat, tunc
amoveantur ab officiis suis et alii discretiores et diligentiores
ibidem per regem assignabuntur et ejus consilium.

Item officium senescalli est quod si rex habeat malos consiliarios circa eum, qui sibi dant consilia[2] ad faciendum talia
que sunt aperte et puplice ad dedicus suum aut exheredacionem suam et ad puplicum malum et destuccionem populi
sui, tunc senescallus Anglie, assumpto secum constabulario
et aliis magnatibus et aliis de communitate regni Anglie,
mittent ad hujusmodi consiliarium regis quod ipsum regem
ita ducere et consulere desistat, de hujusmodi malis conciliis
suis prius regi factis[3] mensionem faciendo et quod ab eo et
ejus presentia recedat, et moram[4] cum eo ad dedicus suum
et dampnum puplicum ut predictum est non faciat. Quod
si non fecerit, tunc mittent ad regem quod ipsum ab eo
ammoveri faciat et ejus consilia non audiat, pro eo quod a
toto populo malus consiliarius inter regem et suum populum
presumitur.[5] Quod si rex non fecerit, alias et pluries mittent
tam regi quam ei; et, si demum nec rex nec hujusmodi
consiliarius de hujusmodi missionibus et supplicacionibus
curaverint, set potius ea facere neclexerint, tunc pro bono
puplico licet et licebit senescallo et constabulario Anglie, magnatibus et aliis de communitate regni, banerio regis nomine
regis et[6] regni[7] erecto, hujusmodi consiliarium tanquam
inimicum puplicum regis et regni capere et[8] corpus ejus[9]
salvo custodire usque ad proximum parliamentum, et seisire
res, redditus et omnes possessiones suas interim donec judicium
suum attenderit et subierit per consideracionem totius regni
in parliamento, sicut[10] accidit de Godwyno comite Kancie,
tempore regis Edwardl proximi antecessoris Willelmi ducis[11]
Normannie[12] conquestoris Anglie, qui pro hujusmodi malis

---

[1] studiant, N.L.   [2] consilio, L.   [3] factus, V.N.
[4] mora, N.L.   [5] presumit, L.   [6,7] omit, N.L.
[8] omit L.   [9] et ejus, L.   [10] sicut sicut, N.
[11] duci, N.   [12] et Normannie, L.

gestis et consiliis suis fuit adjudicatus a comitiva[1] sua et bannitus a toto regno suo[2] Anglie, et predicta comitiva[3] escaeta predicto regi ; et postmodum mediante rege idem Godewinus rediit in Angliam de gratia magnatum, et iterato forisfecit. Item de Huberto de[4] Burgh comite Kancie, tempore regis Henrici filii regis Johannis, qui pro malis gestis et hujusmodi consiliis suis al[iis] captus fuit per senescallum et ceteros magnates[5] et adjudicatus de eadem[6] comitiva[7] per consideracionem tocius parliamenti. Item de Petro de Gavaston qui tempore regis Edwardi filii regis Henrici[8] pro hujusmodi gestis et consiliis fuit bannitus a tota potestate regis Anglie tam ultra maria quam citra, qui Petrus postmodum mediante rege de gracia et permissione magnatum rediit in Angliam, et habuit de dono regis comitivam[9] Cornubie, et postea pro malis gestis suis[10] et consiliis suis fuit iterato bannitus per magnates[11] et communitatem, et comitiva[12] predicta escaeta regis.[13] Et postmodum revenit[14] absque consensu magnatum Anglie, et applicuit se ad regem, quod cum perceptum fuerit[15] a senescallo et constabulario et ceteris Anglie magnatibus captus fuit per eosdem, et tanquam inimicus puplicus regis et regni decollatus apud Blaklowe[16] in comitatu Warrwici.

(Brit. Mus. MSS. Cotton. Vesp. B. VII, fol. 100 ; and Nero C. I ; also Lansdowne 522. These are noted as V., N., and L. respectively. MS. Vesp. B. VII belongs to the reign of Richard II, the others belong to the fifteenth century.)

De Officio Senescalli
De Senescallo Ducis et ejus Officio
Grand Coutumier de Normandie, Cap. IV, bis (ed. Tardif,
p. 12)

Solebat autem antiquitus quidam justiciarius predictis superior per Normanniam discurrere, qui senescallus principis

---

[1] comitia, N.   [2] omit, N.   [3] comitia, N.L.   [4] omit, L.
[5] magnatos, N.L. [6] eodem, N. [7] comitia, N.
[8] " Edwardi " in margin of V. in a modern hand.
[9] comitiam, N.L.   [10] omit, N.L.   [11] magnatos, N.L.
[12] comitia, N.L.   [13] regi, V.   [14] renuit (?), V.
[15] fuit, N.   [16] le Blakelowe, N.L.

vocabatur. Iste vero corrigebat quod alii inferiores delinque-
bant, terram principis custodiebat, leges et consuetudines
Normannie custodiri firmiter faciebat et quod minus juste
fiebat per ballivos corrigebat, querimonias ad se de ipsis
delatas audiebat et fine debito terminabat ; minores servientes
de suis delictis corrigebat et eos a serviciis principis remove-
bat, si eos videbat amovendos ; . . .

(MSS. temp. 1297–1318. Compare cap. cxxiii, s. 4,
Tardif, p. 328, MSS. temp. 1254–8.)

Modus Tenendi Parliamentum
De Casibus et Judiciis difficilibus.

Cum briga, dubitatio, vel casus difficilis sit pacis vel guerrae,
emergat in regno vel extra, referatur et recitetur casus ille in
scriptis in pleno parliamento, et tractetur et disputetur ibidem
inter pares parliamenti, et, si necesse sit, injungatur per regem
seu ex parte regis, si rex non intersit, cuilibet graduum parium
quod quilibet gradus adeat per se, et liberetur casus ille clerico
suo in scripto et in certo loco recitare faciant coram eis casum
illum ; ita quod ipsi audirent et considerent inter se qualiter
melius et justius procedi poterit in casu illo, sicut ipsi pro
persona regis et eorum propriis personis, ac etiam pro personis
eorum quorum personas ipsi representant, velint coram Deo
respondere, et suas responsiones et avisamenta reportent in
scriptis, ut omnibus eorum responsionibus, consiliis et avisa-
mentis hinc inde auditis, secundum melius et sanius consilium
procedatur, et ubi saltem major pars parliamenti concordet.
Et si per discordiam inter eos et regem et aliquos magnates,
vel forte inter ipsos magnates, pax regni infirmetur, vel
populus vel patria tribuletur, ita quod videtur regi et ejus
consilio quod expediens sit quod negotium illud tractetur et
emendetur per considerationem omnium parium regni sui, vel
si per guerram rex et regnum tribulentur, vel si casus difficilis
coram cancellario Angliae emergat, seu judicium difficile
coram justiciariis fuerit reddendum, et hujusmodi, et si forte
in hujusmodi deliberationibus omnes vel saltem major pars
concordare non valeant, tunc comes senescallus, comes constabularius, comes marescallus, vel duo eorum eligent viginti-

quinque personas de omnibus paribus regni, scilicet duos episcopos et tres procuratores pro toto clero, duos comites et tres barones, quinque milites comitatuum, quinque cives et burgenses, qui faciunt viginti-quinque; et illi viginti-quinque possunt eligere ex seipsis duodecim et condescendere in eis, et ipsi duodecim sex et condescendere in eis, et ipsi sex adhuc tres et condescendere in eis, et illi tres in paucioribus condescendere non possunt nisi optenta licencia a domino rege, et si rex consentiat illi tres possunt in duos, et de illis duobus alter potest in alium descendere; et ita demum stabit sua ordinatio supra totum parliamentum; et ita condescendendo a viginti-quinque personis usque ad unam personam solam, nisi numerus major concordare valeat et ordinare, tandem sola persona, ut est dictum, pro omnibus ordinabit, quae cum se ipsa discordare non potest; salvo domino regi et ejus concilio quod ipsi hujusmodi ordinationes postquam scriptae fuerint examinare et emendare valeant, si hoc facere sciant et velint, ita quod hoc ibidem tunc fiat in pleno parliamento, et de consensu parliamenti, et non retro parliamentum.

(The Modus Tenendi Parliamentum immediately precedes the tract on the stewardship in the three MSS. from which the last-mentioned tract has been printed above. MS. Vesp. B. VII belongs to the period of Richard II.)

CHAPTER VI

THE LANCASTRIAN STEWARDS (*continued*)

THE Lancastrian party was far from crushed by the execution of earl Thomas and the death of the constable. Henry de Lancaster, the next brother of Thomas, rapidly acquired a position of great influence in the country. In 1323 he petitioned the king and council in parliament for a restoration of the earldoms of Lancaster and Leicester, and his brother's forfeited estates. About March in the following year he was given seizin of the Leicester fiefs, and on the 10th of May, 1324, the king in council decided to allow him the name and honour of earl of Leicester. It is interesting to find it stated in the roll recording these proceedings[1] that Thomas "went the way of all flesh," without leaving lawful issue, and never a suggestion that he was assisted along that road by the axe of the king's executioner. The Lancastrian rebels, if you please, were no longer rebels but "contrariants." Still, as regards their defunct leader, it was necessary to follow a most august precedent and set a watch about his tomb,—more nequissimi Pilati jussit imponi custodes, says one chronicler,[2]—not to prevent a theft of the body, but to stop the sick, the lame, the blind and so forth from being miraculously cured by it. Such saintly acts, however imaginary, were not conducive to a reconciliation of the opposing parties.

Henry de Lancaster had not long to wait to avenge the death of his brother. When the queen Isabella landed with

---

[1] Fine Roll, 17 Ed. 2, m. 10; printed in Parliamentary Writs, vol. 2, ii; Appendix, pp. 252-3.

[2] Flores Historiarum [95], iii, p. 214.

See also Close Roll, 16 Ed. 2, m. 2d., letter to the bishop of London, printed in Rymer, Foedera R.C., vol. ii, p. 525.

an armed force in September, 1326, he at once joined her, took part in declaring prince Edward guardian of the king-dom, and on the 27th of October, 1326, assisted in the trial and condemnation of the elder Despencer. Immediately afterwards he went in pursuit of the king. Both Edward and the younger Despencer soon fell into his hands, and the latter was tried and executed at Hereford in November.[1]

On the accession of Edward the Third, Henry petitioned for and secured a reversal of the attainder against his brother Thomas,[2] and he thereupon became earl of Lancaster and Leicester ; but, not being an heir of the body of Thomas, he had no apparent right to the stewardship of England ; at all events he could not claim under the grant in tail to his brother.

For the first few years of Edward the Third's reign Henry earl of Lancaster was nominally the chief of the king's council and guardian of the royal person : in reality the government of the country was entirely under the control of the queen-mother and her paramour, Mortimer earl of March. This state of things lasted till the year 1330, when the favourite was proceeded against in parliament, condemned to death, and executed at Tyburn. This event materially improved the position of the earl of Lancaster ; and directly afterwards he appears to have taken steps to establish a title to the stewardship of England, with a view probably to officiating at the coronation of the queen.

Robert de Veer, earl of Oxford, was at the same time claiming a right to the chamberlainship for the same purpose. Of the de Veer claim, which was allowed by the king, we possess ample information,[3] but there is little direct evidence of the claim to the stewardship. On the 5th of December, 1330,[4] the earl of Lancaster obtained a charter of inspeximus

---

[1] A roll containing an account of these proceedings is preserved at the Record Office. See Misc. Rolls Chancery, 18/3, and the account in Knighton, Rolls Series [92].

[2] See below, appendix to chapter ix.

[3] Liberate Roll, 4 Edward III, m. 7 ; see below.

[4] Royal Charters, Duchy of Lancaster, no. 258 (original inspexi-mus) ; Charter Roll, 4 Edward III, no. 19.

and confirmation of the honour, etc., of Leicester granted (12th of July, 1266)[1] by Henry the Third to Edmund. This grant certainly makes no mention of the stewardship of England, but there is no grant to Edmund on the Charter Rolls which does mention it. If, however, the office really was appurtenant to the Leicester fiefs it might be reasonably considered that the office passed under the general words of the grant in question. This view is not inconsistent with the letters patent granting the stewardship to earl Thomas in tail; on the contrary, it is the last-mentioned grant which has an operative part inconsistent with its own recitals. The recitals in the letters patent imply that the right to the stewardship was in the heirs of the body of Edmund, while the operative part limits the office to the heirs of the body of Thomas.

On the 18th of February, 1330–1, Philippa the consort of Edward the Third was crowned queen; and on the 20th of the same month the earl of Lancaster figures in the Charter Roll for the first time as steward of England, attesting as such immediately after Thomas earl of Norfolk and marshal of England.[2]

The inferences to be drawn from these facts are not very clear, but we may at least safely conclude that, at or about the time of queen Philippa's coronation, the earl of Lancaster's right to the stewardship had been admitted. The earl became blind about this time: he died on the 22nd of September, 1345, and was buried at Leicester.

The stewardship of England at this period possesses a vague glamour, perhaps, of ancient greatness about it, but it is not an office of the smallest political consequence. The relative importance of the three great offices of state—the marshal, the constable, and the steward—in the sphere of practical politics may be accurately gauged by the relative frequency with which these styles are added to the names of

---

[1] Royal Charters, Duchy of Lancaster, no. 105 (original). This is the provisional grant mentioned in the previous chapter.

[2] Charter Roll, 5 Ed. 3, m. 31. This appears to be the only occasion on the Charter Rolls where he is so styled. I have examined the earlier Charter Rolls of this reign with some care.

their respective holders in formal contemporary documents. Judged in this way the marshal stands by a long way the first, the steward unquestionably last.

Henry earl of Derby (nicknamed Tortcol), only son and heir of Henry the late earl, succeeded his father as earl of Lancaster and Leicester and steward of England. His martial exploits figure prominently in the general history of Edward the Third's reign, but as steward of England he did nothing worthy of notice; indeed, the only occasion on which he is represented as performing the functions of steward was during his father's lifetime. In 1344 Edward's love of pageantry led him to emulate king Arthur and institute festivities similar to those which that legendary prince is said to have delighted in. It was at the establishment of a round table in Windsor that the earl of Derby, as steward of England[1] and bearing a wand of office, took part in a royal procession.

In recognition of his many services Henry, in 1351, was made duke of Lancaster. He died of the plague on the 13th of March, 1360-1, and without male issue. The dukedom accordingly became extinct; but Henry's other honours and vast possessions descended to his two daughters, the lady Maud and the lady Blanche, as co-heiresses. Maud the elder had married William of Hainault; Blanche the younger was wife to John of Gaunt the king's son. In these circumstances a partition was necessary; and this, roughly speaking, resulted in the Lancaster fiefs being allotted to John of Gaunt's wife, the Leicester fiefs to William of Hainault's wife. There was, however, one substantial piece of property in the county of Leicester, which went to the lady Blanche: this was the manor of Hinckley.[2]

[1] Qua celebrata exivit dominus rex a capella, quem praeibant dominus Henricus comes Derby, tanquam seneschallus Angliae, et dominus Willelmus comes Sarisburiae, tanquam mareschallus Angliae, utroque colore officii sui virgam in manu gestante, et ipso domino rege sceptrum regale in manu tenente. (Murimuth, Rolls Series [93], p. 232.)

[2] The partition is entered on the Fine Roll, 35 Edward III, m. 23. The entry is headed :—Particio terrarum et tenementorum que fuerunt Henrici nuper ducis Lancastrie defuncti que de rege

On the Fine Roll the division is punctiliously equalised down to the uttermost farthing.[1] I trust, therefore, that I shall not be accused of disputing an authoritative record if I observe that there was a limit even at that time to what the king's son could obtain in a partition suit. To have acquired both the Lancaster and the Leicester honours would have been impossible: the former under these circumstances was naturally selected by John of Gaunt, but unfortunately this certainly did not carry with it the stewardship of England. The difficulty was evidently not considered to be insuperable, for another tract on the stewardship now makes its appearance.[2] In this account the office is said to

tenuit in capite inter heredes et participes hereditatis predicte vide-licet.—(Propars comitis Richemond et Blanchie uxoris ejus unius filiarum et heredum predicti ducis.) . . . [This includes] manerium de Hynkeleye cum balliva ibidem et aliis pertinentiis suis in comitatu Leicestrie in valorem quadraginta et septem librarum undecim solidorum et duorum denariorum . . .—(Propars Matill. alterius filiarum et heredum ejusdem ducis.) . . . [This includes] castrum et manerium de Leycestria cum membris et aliis pertinentiis suis. . . .

[1] The earl of Richmond is to pay to Matilda of Hainault in respect of the excess value of his share—septem libras quinque solidos unum obolum et medietatem unius quadrantis.

[2] See Appendix. The three accounts there set out are obviously not independent.

It should be borne in mind that, since the death of Thomas, no one had been in a position to claim the office by grant; and to claim by tenure was no longer easy. For a long time prior to the partition, Hinckley had been treated as a parcel of the Leicester honour; and the tenure of the honour was not serjeanty, but knight-service. Chancery Inquisitions p.m., 1 Edward III, no. 88, file 6, m. 36.

. . . Thomas nuper comes Lancastrie tenuit in dominico suo ut de feodo, die quo obiit, de domino Edwardo nuper rege Anglie patre domini regis nunc, castrum et honorem Leycestrie in comitatu Leycestrie . . . per servicium due feode (sic) et medietatem feodi unius militis.

. . . Predictus comes tenuit die obitus sui in dominico suo ut de feodo manerium de Hynkle in comitatu predicto, de predicto domino Edwardo patre domini regis nunc, tanquam parcellum predicti castri per servicium supradictum.

Hence, doubtless, the claim at Richard the Second's coronation "as earl of Leicester." A most unconventional claim, but sufficiently supported for practical purposes by the Red Book of the Exchequer and other similar records.

be annexed, not to the earldom of Leicester, but to the honour of Hinckley; and a history of the devolution of the stewardship is given, containing a really ingenious conglomerate of fact and fiction. It is unhappily my business to bury this myth, not to praise it; but the tale has been almost universally accepted by subsequent writers, ancient and modern, who mention the subject; and surely no greater tribute could be paid to the ingenuity of the fraud.[1]

I regret to record that the tract was quite thrown away, for the elder co-heiress conveniently died without issue. It was common talk that she died of poison, administered with the object of preventing the splitting up of a great inheritance. If so, the object was attained, for thereupon the whole of the

[1] See, for example, Hearne, Antiquarian Discourses, vol. ii, which contains short essays on the origin of the stewardship of England, by Sir Robert Cotton, Camden, Agard and others: a large number of MS. copies of these essays are preserved among the Cottonian, Harleian and other collections. See also Thoms, Book of the Court; Walter Scott, Ivanhoe, etc. Nichols' History of Leicester, The Complete Peerage, and some other authorities hesitate to accept the story.

Here is Sir Robert Cotton's account: " For it appears out of our English story that among many worthy persons that came in with the Conqueror one, Sir Hugh of Grantmesnil, a Norman of noble descent, so valiantly behaved himself [that] the king rewarded him, not only with great store of lands and manors in the shires of Gloucester, Northampton, Leicester, Nottingham and Suffolk, but also richly married him to one, Adeliza, a great inheritrix of a noble family, and at the solemnisation thereof gave him the office of lord high steward of England. By this Adeliza he had two daughters, Petronilla or Pernell the eldest, and Adeliza the second who married Roger Bigod, a Norman. All the inheritance of the said Sir Hugh Grantmesnil was divided betwixt those two daughters, saving that in the partition the lordship of Hinckley and office of High Steward of England fell to Pernell, because she was the eldest. This Pernell married Robert ove les blanches-maines . . . the son of Robert le Bossu earl of Leicester. . . . So that this Robert was the first of the house of Leicester in whom this office took root."

This narrative ingeniously elaborates the original myth by attempting, with a magnificent disregard for chronology, to explain the dispute between the Beaumonts and the Bigods.

estates belonging to the late duke of Lancaster passed to John of Gaunt and his heirs in right of his wife.[1]

John of Gaunt was created duke of Lancaster in 1362, and at or about the same time was recognised as earl of Leicester and steward of England.[2] We are not concerned with the general history of this man's life, a history of immense opportunities and irredeemable mediocrity. Suffice it to recall that in 1373 the Black Prince, his health completely broken, practically retired from public life, and died three years later, leaving an infant son as heir to the throne: meanwhile the martial spirit of the old king flickered out, and he too retired, abandoning war and politics for a life of senile voluptuousness. Under these conditions the reins of government inevitably fell into the hands of John of Gaunt; and, notwithstanding his conspicuous lack of ability, the failure of his undertakings, his unpopularity with all classes, he remained almost continuously to the day of his death by far the most influential personage in England.[3]

On the death of Edward the Third, Lancaster assumed control of the preparations for crowning Richard. Probably every detail of the ceremonies required careful reorganisation: there had been no coronation for nearly fifty years, and, so far as we can judge, no coronation records for the last hundred years worth looking to for precedents. Details relating to the crowning of Edward the Second are entered in the Close Roll;[4] these are of little value; they attest the

---

[1] The writs to the escheators directing them to take possession of the lands of the late "duchess of Bavaria," issued at Westminster on the 24th April, 36 Edward III. (Fine Roll, 36 Edward III, m. 5.) On the 6th of May the escheators were ordered to give John "earl of Lancaster" seizin of the aforesaid moiety which had been allotted to Matilda, late "duchess of Bavaria and countess of Hainault." (Ibid., m. 20.)

[2] See, for example, Patent Roll, 38 Edward III, pt. 1, m. 6 (July 1st). Confirmation by king of a grant by John of Gaunt, in which he styles himself steward of England.

[3] For a detailed account of the duke's career see Armitage-Smith, John of Gaunt.

[4] Close Roll, 1 Edward II, m. 10d., printed Rymer, Foedera, vol. ii, p. 36. Rymer has also printed the extant coronation roll of Edward II, which, however, relates almost exclusively to the religious ceremony.

paramount influence of Gaveston, and suggest that vested rights received perfunctory treatment. The coronation of Edward the Third took place under distressing circumstances, and no very elaborate preparations seem to have been made. The only extant official record of the event is a sort of postscript on the dorse of the roll containing the proceedings against the Despencers.[1] The ceremony for the sacring of Philippa of Hainault may have been better organised, but there is no evidence of special preparation for it.

At the coronation of Richard the Second, Lancaster established a precedent for all future occasions. He issued a proclamation directing all persons who claimed to perform offices or receive fees at the coronation to bring their bills and petitions before him or his deputies. Numerous claims were thereupon put in, and these Lancaster in person heard and determined, sitting for that purpose in the White Hall of the palace of Westminster. In the account of these proceedings,[2] which was enrolled by the duke's order, it is represented that Lancaster presided over the court as steward of England (*tanquam senescallus Angliae*). This has led various persons to infer that the court of claims, presided over by the steward, was at that time a well-established institution. The same words, however, (*tanquam senescallus Angliae*)[3] are used to describe the part played by Lancaster's father-in-law at

---

[1] Misc. Rolls Chancery, 18/3.

[2] Et memorandum quod prefatus dux, die Jovis proximo ante coronacionem predictam, sedebat de precepto regis tanquam senescallus Anglie in alba aula regii palacii Westmonasterii prope capellam regalem, et inquirebat diligenter que et qualia officia seu feoda dicto die per quoscunque facienda vel optinenda fuerant, et cum hoc eodem die Jovis publice proclamari fecit quod tam magnates quam alii qui alia officia ad coronacionem predictam facere seu feoda aliqua optinere clamare vellent billas et peticiones suas clamea sua continentes coram ipso senescallo vel ejus in hac parte locum tenentibus proferri facerent indilate. Super quo diversa officia et feoda, tam per peticiones quam oretenus, coram ipso senescallo exacta et vendicata extiterunt in forma que subsequitur. . . . (Close Roll, 1 Richard II, m. 45.)

[3] This may mean merely that the duke wore the steward's robes and carried the steward's staff. He is represented doing the latter in a contemporary illustration.

N

the institution of the round table in Windsor by Edward
the Third : the expression is no evidence of pre-existing
or vested right.   Details about previous coronations are
mostly very meagre ; but, such as they are, they negative
rather than support the existence of a steward's court of
claims.

At the coronations of John, Henry the Third and Eleanor
the right to the office of steward was in dispute; and, from
the elaborate record of the last-mentioned ceremony which
is preserved in the Exchequer Red Book, it is plain that
nothing in the nature of a steward's court of claims was then
in existence.   If there were claims to be determined when
Edward came to the throne, it is most probable that he dealt
with them in person, almost inconceivable that Edmund was
entrusted with this duty in right of an office which the king
had decided to suppress.   At the coronation of Edward the
Second the office was virtually extinct; moreover, had the
court in question been instituted on this occasion, the Close
Roll could hardly have failed to mention the circumstance.
Before the accession of Edward the Third the office had
again become extinct; but at this king's crowning the fees
for services, and perhaps the services themselves, were considered and allowed by the king's council, of which Lancaster
was the nominal president.[1]   This was owing to the king's
minority.   So far as I can discover there is only one extant
claim for services and fees relating to the coronation of queen
Philippa, that is the claim of the earl of Oxford[2] to be

[1] Rot. Parl., vol. ii, p. 96 ; see below.
[2] Liberate Roll, 4 Edward III, m. 7.   Pro Roberto de Veer
comite Oxon.   Rex thesaurario et camerariis suis salutem.   Supplicavit nobis dilectus et fidelis noster Robertus de Veer comes Oxon
quod cum ipse jure hereditario camerarius regine Anglie que pro
tempore fuerit die coronacionis sue esse debeat et ipse et antecessores sui comites Oxon officium camerarie diebus coronacionum
reginarum Anglie que pro tempore fuerunt a tempore cujus contrarii
memoria non existit facere et exercere et pro feodo suo eodem die
lectum ipsius regine et calciamenta sua ac tres pelves argenteas
per quas eidem regine die predicto deserviebat, unam videlicet pro
locione capitis sui et duas pro locione manuum suarum percipere
consueverunt : velimus ei hujusmodi feodum pro die coronacionis
Philippe regine Anglie consortis nostre carissime, quo die idem

chamberlain. The claim was made by petition to the king and was allowed. In the face of these facts we may fairly safely conclude that, before the accession of Richard the Second, no steward of England, as such, had ever held a court for coronation claims.[1] John of Gaunt was in the same position at the close of Edward the Third's reign as Henry of Lancaster was at its commencement; and, steward or no steward, John of Gaunt was the proper person to settle coronation services. The fact that this court at once became an established institution and definitely associated with the office of steward must not be attributed solely to the action of John of Gaunt. Undoubtedly an important contributory circumstance was the subsequent accession to the throne of his own son Henry. The court has survived to this day, and it retains a certain picturesque charm borrowed from the ceremonies to which it is a prelude; but its powers and jurisdiction are of the most trivial character, its decisions do not bind the king nor any future court of claims.

The services at the coronation of Richard the Second were many and various. Classification is impossible : all we can say is that some are technically described as grand serjeanties, others perhaps as petit serjeanties; and that the

comes camerarius ejusdem regine fuit, facere liberari ; nosque pro eo quod per diversas evidencias nobis per prefatum comitem exhibitas plenius apparebat quod idem comes et antecessores sui officium illud diebus coronacionum reginarum predictarum habere et hujusmodi feodum percipere consueverunt, prefato comiti ut camerario ejusdem consortis nostre die predicto calciamenta ipsius consortis nostre et tres pelves argenteas pro feodo suo liberari fecimus, volentesque ei de lecto supradicto satisfacionem exhiberi, concessimus ei centum marcas pro lecto supradicto percipiendas de thesauro nostro. Et ideo vobis mandamus quod eidem comiti dictas centum marcas liberetis de thesauro nostro, recipientes a prefato comite litteras suas acquietancie receptionem dictarum centum marcarum testificantes. Teste rege apud Wodestok, secundo die Aprilis.

[1] We have also, it must be remembered, the negative evidence afforded by the famous tract on the stewardship. If the court of claims was in existence at the time when that tract was composed, how came it that the tract makes no reference whatsoever to any such jurisdiction ? A little tincture of truth is so useful in political pamphlets, it will cover such a multitude of lies.

greater part, but not apparently all of them, are incident to the possession of certain lands or liberties.[1]

The history of court offices and serjeanties in England presents us with countless services, ranging along the whole flight of steps which separates the sublime from the ridiculous. The constableship and marshalship of England, for example, were undoubtedly posts of the highest distinction; but the king's lenten cock-crower was a character too strange for fiction. The last-named official remained in existence till the accession of the House of Hanover. Unfortunately, on the first ensuing Ash-Wednesday when chanticleer according to custom marched into the dining apartment and crowed the hour, the heir-apparent, half frightened, half suspecting some intentional affront, made such a scene that it was deemed advisable to discontinue the office.

Many very curious services incident to land tenure are to be met with. A certain house in St. Margaret's parish, London, once owned by Isaac the Jew of Norwich, was granted by John to the earl of Derby by the service of waiting on the king at dinner, the head uncovered, the hair

---

[1] The following attempt at classification has been made: "There are offices of three kinds; those which are hereditary, those which are an appanage to a title, and those which are performed owing to the tenure of lands by grand serjeanty. Of the first kind there are five officers, the lord high steward, the lord great chamberlain, the lord high constable, the earl marshal, and he who carries the spurs. . . . Of the second kind there were never more than four, the sewer . . . and the bearers of the three swords. Of the third kind there were seventeen. . . ." I can hardly conceive a worse classification. The *original* sewer, or dapifer, was of course the subsequent lord high steward, who, in John's reign at all events, was treated as holding that office as a serjeanty incident to the tenure of the honour of Leicester, the service becoming on partition of that honour annexed to the elder moiety. In several documents mentioned above the stewardship is apparently claimed as an appanage to the earldom of Leicester. Such a claim, whether in respect of the stewardship or any other office, is not worth serious consideration. The office of constable of England was frequently enjoyed as an hereditary office, but at certain periods of its history it was none the less a service incident to tenure by grand serjeanty. Thus, in Edward the First's time, Caldecote and Wockesei manors

bound with a girdle of the breadth of the little finger.[1] One estate has been held by the service of housing the king's concubines; this, to be sure, was only petit serjeanty. The duty incident to the tenure of Archer's court was holding the king's head when the channel crossing was rough.[2]

In the pageant of a mediæval coronation the hereditary champion was perhaps the most striking figure, but his duties can only be described as mere stage-play. His principal appearance was at the coronation banquet after the conclusion of the first course. Armed at all points, mounted

---

were held by this service (Cal. Inq. p.m., no. 131). See also Dyer's Reports, pt. 3, 285b, no. 29, the Duke of Buckingham's case. On the other hand the office was frequently granted during pleasure or for life. The marshalship is often referred to as a serjeanty; for example ". . . Rogerus Bygot comes Norfolk et marescallus Anglie tenet xx libratas terre per serjanciam mareschallie in Hamstede . . ." (Assize Rolls, Berks, Michaelmas, 12 Edward I, no. 48). The marshalship is referred to as a serjeanty in a writ of Edward II (County Placita, divers counties, no. 2, 8 Edward II): this is a writ to the Exchequer to ascertain whether any widows of marshals have held the office of marshal of England, and generally whether other women have held serjeanties in consimili casu; the return to the writ is appended. In the time of Richard II we have this description: "Marescalcia autem est quedam magna seriantia regis comiti Norfolk in feodo commissa . . ." (MS. Cotton Dom., 18, fol. 23). According, however, to later distinctions between grand and petit serjeanty, the marshalship was partly petit serjeanty, for we find the holder regularly appointing deputies to discharge particular functions which he is under no obligation to discharge in person. The seventeen serjeanties mentioned in the classification that I am criticising may be all properly described as hereditary offices, but whether they were all grand serjeanties is a difficult question. Even the office of champion would in its inception have been described as petit serjeanty by some authorities. Could Littleton have consistently described "ad inveniendum unum militem " as grand serjeanty? (See Inq. p.m. 7 Edward I, no. 33.)

[1] Grant dated 26 June, 15 John; Duchy of Lancaster, Great Cowcher.

[2] Inquisition post mortem 31 Ed. I, 34; Inquisition post mortem, Sir M. Browne, 4 and 5 Ph. and M.; Hasted, ix, 440; Elton, Tenures of Kent, p. 227. The manor of Seaton was held by the service of going, or providing a man to go, as leader of the king's greyhounds whenever the king went to Gascony "until he had worn out a pair of shoes worth 4d. bought at the king's cost." Elton, op. cit., p. 226.

on a horse trapped in black housings embroidered with silver lions, he was escorted into the hall by the constable and marshal; and his herald of arms proclaimed a challenge against all who denied the feasting sovereign to be rightful inheritor of the realm—this was repeated a second and a third time in different parts of the hall. Then the king drank his health in a golden bowl; the champion received the same bowl as his fee, drained the remaining contents exclaiming, " Long live the king!", and backed his horse out of the building with as much grace as he could command. We never hear of the champion being called upon to defend his sovereign's title.[1]

The offices and serjeanties connected with the king's coronation were none of them unduly absurd. By reason of their antiquity we are inclined to regard those which have survived as highly dignified. John of Gaunt claimed several services at the coronation of Richard the Second. Notably, as earl of Leicester he claimed the office of steward of England,[2] as duke of Lancaster the right of carrying the principal sword *curtana*, and, as earl of Lincoln, the right of

---

[1] The service is incident to the tenure of Scrivelsby (Inq. p.m., 7 Ed. I, no. 33.)

[2] Decedente de nutu summi Preceptoris felicissimo strenuo et potenti rege Anglie et Francie domino Edwardo tercio post conquestum vicesimo primo die mensis Junii anno Domini millesimo trecentesimo septuagesimo septimo et anno regni sui quinquagesimo primo, successit ei rex Ricardus secundus filius Edwardi nuper principis Wallie primogeniti dicti regis Edwardi, et cum tractaretur et provisum fuisset de solempniis coronacionis ipsius regis Ricardi die Jovis in crastino translacionis beati Swithuni tunc proximo sequente celebrandis, Johannes rex Castelle et Legionis dux Lancastrie coram dicto domino rege Ricardo et consilio suo comparens clamavit ut comes Leycestrie officium senescalcie Anglie et ut dux Lancastrie ad gerendum principalem gladium domini regis vocatum Curtana die coronacionis ejusdem regis et ut comes Lincolnie ad scindendum et ad secandum coram ipso domino rege sedente ad mensam dicto die coronacionis. Et quia facta diligenti examinatione coram peritis de consilio regis de premissis, satis constabat eidem consilio quod ad ipsum ducem tanquam tenentem per legem Anglie post mortem Blanchie quondam uxoris sue pertinuit officia predicta prout superius clamabat exercere, consideratum fuit per ipsum regem et consilium suum predictum quod idem dux officia

carving before the king as he sat at table on the day of his sacring. All these claims were allowed by the king and council.

The most onerous coronation service was probably that of the Mayor of London, who had to provide three hundred and sixty liveried pages, each holding a silver cup in his hand. His fee was a gold cup with a cover, and an ewer of gold enamelled.[1] In the reign of Edward the Third the city intimated a desire to be discharged from this service; but they none the less claimed it in 1377 before the steward of England. Two very notable petitions tried before John of Gaunt on this occasion were the rival claims of Dymoke and Freville to the office of champion; after a long trial with witnesses the final hearing was adjourned, interlocutory judgment being given in favour of Dymoke.[2]

predicta per se et sufficientes deputatos suos faceret et exerceret et feoda sibi debita in hac parte optineret. Qui quidem dux officium senescalcie predicte personaliter adimplevit, et eciam dictum gladium coram prefato domino rege, quousque alta missa post coronacionem ipsius domini regis celebrata fuit, in manibus suis propriis gerebat, et extunc occupatus circa officium senescalcie predicte gladium illum Henrico comiti Derbie filio et heredi ejusdem ducis coram ipso rege deferendum commisit.... (Close Roll, 1 Richard II, m. 45.)

[1] A nostre seignour le roy et a son conseil monstre Richard de Bettoyne de Loundres qe come au coronement nostre seignour le roy q'ore est, il adonqe meire de Londres fesoit l'office de botiller ove ccc e lx vadletz vestutz d'une sute chescun portant en sa mayn un coupe blanche d'argent, come autres meirs de Londres ount faitz as coronementz des progenitours nostre seigneur le roy, dont memorie ne court, et le fee q'appendoit a cel jorne, c'est asavoir un coupe d'or ove la covercle et un ewer d'or enamaille, lui fust livere par assent du counte de Lancastre et d'autres grantz qu'adonqes y furent du conseil nostre seigneur le roy, par la mayn sire Robert de Wodehouse; et ore vient en estreite as viscountes de Londres hors del Chekker de faire lever des biens et chateux du dit Richard lxxxix li.–xij s.–vj d. pur le fee avantdit, dont il prie que remedie lui soit ordeyne. . . . Et si i plest a nostre seignour le roy et a son conseil, nous payeroms volenters le fee issent qe nous soyoms descharges de la service. (Rot. Parl., vol. ii, p. 96.)

[2] The petitions were addressed in every case to the duke and styled him seneschal of England; as one petitioner commences his petition without further preface than this—A Seneschall Dengleterre monstre Johan filz Johan que; this man at least, it would seem, must have connected the jurisdiction with the office. This, however, is no evidence that such a court had ever sat before.

It was, apparently, not until the year 1386 that the office of steward of England was again brought into prominence. Commissioners were then appointed at the instance of a powerful opposition headed by Gloucester, Derby and Nottingham. These commissioners, who were entrusted with the redress of grievances, were an obvious revival of the ordainers of 1310. Lancaster was abroad at the time, meddling rashly and ineffectively in Spanish affairs. Derby, his son and heir, was representing him in England; Gloucester and Nottingham, the other leaders of the opposition, were constable and marshal of England respectively. Here we have again the great hereditary officers of state attempting to coerce the king, and there are strong grounds for supposing that the *Modus tenendi parliamentum* was at this time put forward to justify the actions of the opposition.[1] The resulting strife between the rival parties led to many peers being brought to trial before parliament: these incidents are dealt with elsewhere.

In 1397 there was a reaction, and several members of the opposition were appealed of treason by the king's party. The appealed included Richard earl of Arundel and Thomas earl of Warwick: they went through a form of trial in parliament, and both were sentenced to death. Judgment in each case was pronounced by the duke of Lancaster (styled steward of England in the report) as representing the king and the lords temporal, and by Thomas Percy the steward of the household as procurator for the clergy. It must be observed that Lancaster on this occasion is not even represented by the rolls of parliament as sitting *tanquam senescallus Angliae*, but is merely given his official style.[2]

In the following January Sir John Cobham was impeached by the commons for treason, and Lancaster took a precisely similar part in the resulting trial; but this time he is not styled steward of England in the report.[3]

---

[1] See Round, The Commune of London, p. 316.

[2] Rot Parl., vol. iii, pp. 374 et sqq. See also chap. x below.

In Arundel's case occurs the following passage: " A quel count d'Arundell fuist dit et declare par le duc de Lancastre seneschal d'Engleterre, par comandement du roy et avys de. . . ."

[3] Rot. Parl., vol. iii, p. 381.

The above-mentioned cases, as reported in the Parliament Rolls, can hardly be said to establish precedents for appointing the lord high steward to preside at trials before the House of Lords. These reports, on the contrary, favour if anything the view that Lancaster presided because he was Lancaster, and not because he was steward of England. Certainly, hitherto, there had existed no settled practice as to who ought to preside. The chancellor very commonly did so in cases not involving peril of life or limb. At other times we find the steward of the household presiding.[1] On the other hand, the chroniclers either definitely assert or clearly imply that the duty of judging in parliament belonged to the lord high steward as such, and it is at least probable that Lancaster himself with characteristic effrontery claimed to act in right of his office.[2]

The next incident which must be mentioned is the singular affair between Lancaster's son and the duke of Norfolk.[3] The former had been created duke of Hereford by the king, and both were seemingly in high favour. Hereford, it

[1] See below, chap. x.

[2] Deinde adduxerunt comitem Arundell et dux Lancastriae fuit justitiarius ibidem qui sibi exposuit appellationem dominorum et accusationem parliamenti, et jussit respondere. . . . (Eulogium, Rolls Series, 9, iii, p. 374.)

Sedente igitur pro tribunali, mox Ricardus comes Arundell sistebatur in judicio, indutus desuper toga cum capicio de scarleto. Tunc Johannes dux Lancastriae et senescallus Angliae (qui ad hoc deputatus erat) ex officio dixit domino de Nevyle: "Tollas sibi zonam et capicium." Et factum est ita. . . . Dux Lancastriae (qui et senescallus) dixit sibi. . . . Et tunc dux Lancastriae tulit in eum sententiam in hunc modum : "Ricarde, ego Johannes, senescallus Angliae, te adjudico proditorem et condempno te. . . . (Vita Ric. II, p. 136.)

Die sancti Matthaei apostoli et evangelistae productus est Ricardus comes Arundeliae ad respondendum coram rege totoque parliamento de depositis contra eum. . . . Tunc dux Lancastriae, senescallus Angliae, cui hoc ex officio pertinebat, notificavit [sibi] quod causa multarum extortionum et proditionis in regem suum fuerit arestatus . . . (Trokelowe, Rolls Series, 28, iv, p. 214.)

Et tunc dux Lancastrie mortis sentenciam sub hiis verbis tulit in eundem: "Ricarde, ego senescallus Anglie te proditorem esse judico, et. . . ." (Adam of Usk, ed. 1904, p. 14.)

[3] This case appears at great length on the Parliament Rolls.

appears, was journeying from Brentford to London and on the road overtook Norfolk. "Do you know," began Norfolk, "that we are on the point of being undone?"—"Why so?" asked Hereford. Thereupon Norfolk proceeded to recount to his friend that there was a plot on foot, to which the king was privy, for the overthrow of the dukes of Lancaster, Albemarle and Exeter, the Marquis of Dorset and them-selves. "God forbid," said Hereford when Norfolk had told his story; "it were strange if the king should assent to such designs: he has promised to be good lord to me, indeed, he has sworn it by St. Edward."—"Ah," replied Norfolk, "he has often sworn the like to me by God's body, but I trust him not the more for that."

In some way or other the king got wind of this conversation, and Hereford was ordered to lay the matter before parliament. This amounted to directing Hereford to appeal Norfolk of treason. However, Hereford had to comply, and on the 30th of January, 1397-8, he laid his charge before the parliament at Shrewsbury. The whole matter was then relegated to the parliamentary committee: Norfolk was not present, and orders were issued to compel his attendance. On the 23rd of February both Hereford and Norfolk had an audience with the king at Oswaldstre. There was an informal discussion: Hereford, of course, stuck to his story. "Sire," said Norfolk, bending the knee to his sovereign, "your cousin, if I may say so, is a liar." Richard ordered both dukes into custody.

The parliamentary committee decided that the case must be referred to a high court of chivalry. A court was accordingly convened at Windsor in April which made an order for trial by battle, and the case was then adjourned to the lists at Coventry. The 16th of September was the day assigned. With life and honour at stake neither party was willing to leave anything to chance. Hereford sent to Milan for his mail: Norfolk put his trust in Germany. On the day appointed a vast concourse assembled to witness the duel. The king took his seat on a throne, warder in hand. The two champions, fully equipped, entered the lists; the usual preliminaries of chivalry were solemnly gone through;

popular excitement was strained to the highest pitch; and then came anticlimax, sudden and complete; the king threw down his warder and stopped the fight.

Richard, it appears, had since the adjournment in April received advice from various quarters to stay all further proceedings. This no doubt influenced his conduct, but in no way excused the extraordinary capriciousness of such behaviour. Worse was to follow. To stay the course of justice may be a proper, even a laudable act, when done in exercise of the royal prerogative of mercy or pardon; but Richard had no such object in view. He summoned both champions before him, freely admitted to them that neither with prosecution nor with defence had he any fault to find, regretted the course which mature consideration compelled him to take, and then and there sentenced Hereford to banishment for a period of ten years, Norfolk to banishment for life. This outrage to justice caused universal indignation. Little pity was felt for Norfolk; but Hereford, popular enough before, at once became the idol of the nation, and his departure for the coast assumed the character of a triumphal procession.

Richard was careful at this stage to show him some consideration; he was permitted to remain a few weeks at Sandgate, and was authorised to appoint attorneys to receive his heritage in the event of his father's death. Ultimately Hereford proceeded to Paris and took up his residence at the Hôtel Clisson.

On the 3rd of February, 1398–9, old John of Gaunt died, leaving exiled Hereford heir to his vast possessions and honours. Either the temptation was too great for the king, or this was merely the looked-for opportunity. On the 18th of March the letters patent securing Henry's right to his heritage were revoked, the Lancastrian estates were confiscated, and Henry banished for ever.

This attempted ruin of Hereford speedily recoiled on the head of Richard. The king left England for Ireland: Hereford left Paris for England. The story of how Henry of Lancaster wrested the kingdom from Richard need not be related, but certain declarations of intention made by Henry at this time are recorded in contemporary chronicles, and these it is important to consider. It is asserted, doubtless by his opponents, that Henry at first disclaimed having any designs against the crown, and stated that he had merely come to claim his inheritance, including the stewardship of England, and to insist on exercising his right as such supreme judge of trying and punishing certain traitors[1] and malefactors in a parliament to be summoned forthwith to meet at Westminster. Here again we have another definite assertion by chroniclers that the steward of England was the supreme judge, or in other words the proper person to preside at a trial in parliament.[2]

[1] . . . et que il vous plaise quil ait seulement sa terre et quil soit grant juge Dengleterre ainsi comme son pere et ses predecesseurs ont este. . . . (Northumberland's message to Richard the Second, Chronique de la Traison et Mort de Richard II, Engl. Hist. Soc., p. 48.)

> Et que grand juge soit il restitue
> Dengleterre, comme lavoit este
> Le duc son pere et tout son parente
> Plus de cent ans.
> Le nom de ceulx qui seront atendans
> Le jugement vueil dire : . . .
>
> .   .   .
>
> En atendant de v[ost]re parlement
> Ou vous serez couronnez haultement,
> Roy et seign[ieu]r ;
> Et la sera comme juge greigneur
> Le duc Henry.   Sans penser a faveur
> Ceux qui aront fait mal vice ne erreur
> Ou trayson
> Seron pugniz : cest la conclusion
> De monseigneur. . . .

(MS. Harleian, no. 1319; printed in Archaeologia, vol. xx, p. 354.)

Adonc dist le conte [de Northumberland] : " Mon très chier seigneur, le duc de Lenclaistre m'envoye par devers vous pour vous dire que . . . [il] ne vous demande rien en ce monde vivant fors qu'il ne vous déplaise de le tenir pour cousin et amy, et qu'il vous plaise qu'il ait seulement sa terre et qu'il soit grand juge d'Angleterre, ainsi comme son père et ses prédécesseurs on esté; . . . " (Jean le Beau, printed Froissart, ed. Buchon, Supplement, ii, p. 71).

[2] This is like, but not identical with, the claim put forward in the " Hic Annotatur." Compare with the following indication of

On the 30th of September, 1399, Richard's resignation was accepted, and Henry then claimed and was admitted to the vacant throne. With the accession of Henry the Fourth the stewardship of England became merged in the crown. However, on or before the 4th of October, the new king appointed Thomas his second son steward of England ;[1] and, on account of this prince's youth (he was only eleven years old), Thomas Percy, earl of Worcester, was appointed deputy steward for the coming coronation. These, with the assistance of the constable and marshal of England, thereupon held a court for coronation claims, following in all respects the precedent established by John of Gaunt on the accession of Richard the Second.[2]

French procedure :—De l'ofice as mètres : Li mestre de l'ostel le roi ont plenier poïr par dessus toz autres. Et aucunes foiz avient qu'il deivent porter les granz causes pardevant le roi, comme de cels qui convient jugier par pers. (Li Livre de Jostice et de Plet, I, cap. 20, s. 1.)

[1] He was appointed, it seems, like the stewards of the household, by handing him a bâton, and not by a formal instrument.
Sabbato proximo tunc sequente, rex Henricus Thomam secundum filium suum fecit senescallum Angliae, dans ei virgam illius officii ; quia tunc affuerunt omnes qui debebant regi servitium in coronatione [sua], et illi praecipue pertinebat cuilibet allocare officium debitum in coronatione regia vel assignare. (Annales Henrici Quarti, Rolls Series, 28, iv, p. 287.)
Rex Henricus in hoc parliamento fecit secundum filium suum, dictum Thomam, Angliae senescallum. (Walsingham, Rolls Series, 28, ii, p. 238.)

[2] See Appendix.
The following entry occurs in the rolls of parliament : Et fuit ilico de dicti regis mandato publice proclamatum ibidem quod die Lune proximo post festum sancti Michaelis parliamentum ibidem teneri et celebrari deberet : quodque die Lune proximo extunc sequente, videlicet in festo sancti Edwardi, coronatio dicti regis fieret apud Westmonasterium : et quod omnes illi qui vendicare voluerint aliquod servitium se in dicta coronatione facturos, et eo pretextu aliquid sibi deberi, venirent in albam aulam palatii coram senescallo, constabulario et marescallo Anglie, die Sabbati proximo ante diem parliamenti predicti, quod in ea parte justum fuerit petituri, quibus plena justicia fieret in petitis. . . . (Rot. Parl., vol. iii, p. 423.)
The steward and his deputy appear to have played a conspicuous

At this court a Freville again contested the right of the Dymokes to the office of champion. The parties appeared by counsel, Adam of Usk, the chronicler, being briefed for the Dymokes. The hearing threatened to take some time, and was again adjourned upon terms which allowed Dymoke to act at Henry's coronation.[1]

Thomas Plantagenet, better known as the duke of Clarence, held the office of steward of England for the rest of his life.[2] During his tenure of the stewardship two coronations took place at which he was unable to attend, namely, the coronation of Henry the Fifth in 1413 and the coronation of queen Katharine in 1421. On both occasions the earl of Warwick was appointed to act as vice-seneschal.[3] The only trial at which the duke of Clarence presided took place in 1415, at Southampton, when parliament was not sitting. The persons tried were the earl of Cambridge and lord Scrope of Masham. From the enrolled commission appointing Clarence we know that he did not preside as steward of England.[4]

part in the various ceremonies with which this reign opened. For example :—

Die Lunae ex tunc sequente proximo, qui fuit dies sanctae Fidis, rex novus praesidebat in parliamento regaliter, et Henricus filius suus primogenitus secundum locum tenuit inter dominos temporales. Secundus filius, tanquam totius Angliae senescallus, virgam sui officii tenuit coram patre. (Annales Henrici Quarti, Rolls Series, 28, iv, p. 288.)

In the state procession from the Tower to Westminster—Dominus Thomas Percy portavit virgam senescalli coram rege, vice filii sui Thomae, quem dudum diximus senescallum. (Ibid., p. 291.)

At the beginning of this reign the steward of the household was Thomas Rempston (styled senescallus hospitii domini regis). Many modern writers dealing with this period still confuse the two offices.

[1] Usk, p. 34. See also the Annales Henrici Quarti, p. 288 : Tandem res finem sortitur hujusmodi, ex responso vice-senescalli, constabularii et marescalli ; quod quia praesens causa sine deliberatione majori non potuit terminari, propter vicinitatem regiae coronationis, expectaret diem. . . .

[2] He is repeatedly so styled in formal documents ; and he describes himself as such in his last will and testament. It remains doubtful whether his father's intention was to give him an estate of inheritance in the office, for he died without issue, leaving Henry V his heir-at-law.   [3] See Appendix.

[4] This trial will be discussed at length in a subsequent chapter.

Clarence, it will be remembered, fell at the fatal battle of Beaugé, the victim of his own rashness. After his death the stewardship of England was never again regranted except for particular occasions. Thus closes the history of the regular stewards of England.

It only remains now to consider in what condition the stewardship was left by the death of the last holder.

The chief function of the steward in earlier times, of supervising and waiting at the royal table on special feast days, appears in course of time to have become limited to similar services to be performed only on the occasion of a king or queen's coronation. The steward's connection with the coronation became crystallised by the famous and much-consulted entry in the Exchequer Red Book for queen Eleanor's coronation : but, if his services at other times were seldom required, he was probably always regarded as one of the persons who could be called upon to play master of the ceremonies in any great pageant. There is, for example, the case of the earl of Derby at the institution of the round table at Windsor.

The steward's court of claims first made its appearance on the occasion of Richard the Second's coronation; but Henry the Fourth very naturally followed his father's precedent; and, long before the stewardship as a permanent office had ceased to exist, not only had this recently acquired function become thoroughly established, but also the practice of appointing a deputy-steward for the particular occasion if disability or absence prevented the permanent steward from discharging his duties.

In addition to the above matters, the steward had certainly on various occasions asserted formidable powers and privileges; had in the year 1397, if never before, presided at the trial of peers in parliament, and had in the year 1415 presided at the trial of peers when parliament was not sitting. But it cannot be seriously suggested that, even in the case of trials before the House of Lords, the steward possessed as yet any recognised functions.

We should hardly on simple inspection have looked for such a conclusion. We know that to this day, when a peer is accused of treason or felony, it is the rule to appoint a lord high steward to preside, in the lord's house if parliament is sitting, and, if there is no parliament in session, in a court known as the lord high steward's court. Knowing this, we should naturally expect to find both precedents well established before the office in question fell into abeyance. We should expect as much for the simple reason that it would seem a strange step to revive this extinct official for the purpose of entrusting him with unprecedented functions.

Be this as it may, it is quite clear that the mediæval steward of England began and ended his career somewhat ingloriously. We will attempt elsewhere to explain his posthumous judicial pre-eminence.

APPENDIX TO CHAPTER VI

Harleian MSS. 1808, *fol.* 20b ;[1] *and* 2386, *fol.* 30.[2]
Genealogia Comitum Leycestrie.

Robertus comes Mellenti anno Domini millesimo centesimo secundo, regnante rege Henrico primo, post mortem Simonis comitis adeptus est comitatum Leycestrie, qui genuit ex uxore sua Isabella filium et heredem Robertum le bosszu. Hic fundavit abbatiam de Leycestre et postea assensu uxoris sue canonicus factus est ibidem, et Amicia uxor sua filia Radulfi de Monteforti facta est monialis apud Etonam quam prius fundaverat. Et habuerunt inter se filium primogenitum nomine Robertum ove lez blaunchemeyns qui desponsavit Petronillam filiam Hugonis de Grantmene cum qua habuit honorem de Hynkeleye cum senescalcia Anglie ex dono dicti Hugonis; De qua tres filios et duas filias procreavit, videlicet, dominum Robertum dictum Petronell, dominum Rogerum apud sancti Andree in Scotia, dominum Willelmum leprosum fundatorem sancti Leonardi Leycestrie, dominam Amiciam desponsatam Simoni Mountford et dominam Marga-

---

[1] MS. on parchment, fifteenth century, temp. Henry VI.
[2] MS. on paper, late fifteenth century and apparently a transcript from no. 1.

retam desponsatam domino Saero de Quincy, (postea[1]) comiti Wintonie. Dictus Robertus filius Petronelle comes Leycestrie Loram filiam domini Willelmi le Brewes duxit in uxorem de qua nullum suscitavit prolem. Qui postquam magnum Soldanum in armis regis Ricardi per hastiludium bellicum prostraverit rediit in Angliam et sepultus est apud Leycestre. [(Et[2]) nota (quod[2]) Malcolmus rex Scotie, frater Willelmi regis, habuit filiam nomine Ezabell, que fuit mater Roberti de Quincy, qui Robertus genuit Saerum de Quincy; Saerus genuit Rogerum de Quincy; Rogerus (vero) genuit Margaretam comitissam de Ferrers, que fuit mater Roberti comitis de Ferrers. Robertus genuit Johannem comitem de Ferrariis et fundavit abbathiam de Myryvalle anno gratiae mclii.[3]]

Particio hereditatis

Dominus Symon Mountford per uxorem suam habuit medietatem comitatus et honoris de Hynkeleye et factus est a rege comes Leycestrie et senescallus Anglie, et dominus Saerus de Quincy factus est comes Wyntonie et habuit medietatem dicti comitatus. Simon comes genuit de uxore sua Simonem et Amaricum, qui Amaricus a Turcis captus et mortuus est. Simon vero pater ejus propter suam inobedientiam a rege exheredatus est et cum filiis suis ab Anglia exulatus. Simon filius suus post patrem mortuum, gratiam regis adeptus, comitatum Leycestrie et senescalciam recuperavit, et duxit Elianoram sororem regis Henrici, que prius voverat castitatem, de qua sex filios et unam filiam genuit, Henricum, Ricardum, Amaricum, Guidonem, Symonem, Thomam et Alianoram quam desponsavit Leulinus princeps Wallie. Iste Simon insurrexit contra regem et fuit occisus in bello apud Evesham et datus est comitatus Leycestrie domino Edmundo filio regis.[4]

---

[1] An interlineation in no. 1. [2] Not in no. 1.

[3] This is a footnote in no. 1 but is incorporated into the text of no. 2.

[4] No. 2 has been printed down to this point in Knighton, Rolls Series [92], i, pp. 62–6.

Pars hereditatis Comitis Wyntonie

Dominus Saerus de Quincy

.   .   .   .   .

Genealogia Comitum Lancastrie

Post mortem Simonis de Monteforti, illustris comes Lancastrie Edmundus filius regis Henrici tercii ex dono regis
Henrici patris sui comitatum Leycestrie (Derbeye[1]) et
honorem de Hynkeleye cum senescalcia Anglie est adeptus ;
dominam Blanchiam reginam Navarrie (sororem comitis de
Artoys[2]) desponsavit et ex ea tres filios procreavit Thomam,
Henricum et Johannem. Thomas comes Lancastrie post
mortem patris sui Edmundi in hereditatem succedens
{Agnetam[3]} (Alesiam[4]) filiam domini Henrici de Lacy
comitis Lincolnie et Wintonie desponsavit, sed quia inter
illos nulla proles remansit superstes ideo post mortem
ejusdem Thome apud Pontefractum in domino requiescens.
(sic) frater ejus Henricus dictus de Grisemount sibi in hereditate successit. [. . .[5]], Dominus Henricus de Grysemount,
post mortem fratris sui Thome, comes Lancastrie et Leicestrie
et senescallus Anglie effectus. . . . Dominus Henricus Lancastrie post mortem Henrici patris sui dux Lancastrie, comes
Derbeie, Lincolnie et Leycestrie et senescallus Anglie effectus.
. . . Johannes de Gaunt comes Richemundie post mortem
domini Henrici ducis Lancastrie effectus e[6] jure uxoris sue
dux Lancastrie, comes Derbeye, Lincolnie, Leycestrie et
senescallus Anglie. . . . [After a short notice of Henry IV
and Henry V this genealogy concludes as follows :] . . .
Et genuit ex Katherina filia regis Francie unicum filium

----

[1] No. 2 has "comitatus Lancastrie, Leycestrie et Derbeie." In
no. 1 "Derbeye" is an interlineation.

[2] Interlined in no. 1.

[3] An erasure in no. 1.   [4] An interlineation in no. 1.

[5] A marginal note in no. 1 is here incorporated into the text of
no. 2.

[6] est in no. 2.

Henricum nunc dei gratia regem Anglie hujus nominis sextum.[1]

(The differences in spelling between no. 1 and no. 2 are very numerous but of no apparent importance. The spelling in No. 1 has been adhered to throughout.)

Chronicon Henrici Knighton (Rolls Series [92], i, *pp.* 62–6)

Robertus comes Molenti venit cum Willelmo in Angliam, cui Roberto datus est comitatus Leycestrensis. Iste Robertus re-aedificavit ecclesiam Sanctæ Mariae de castro Leycestrensi, et posuit in eadem canonicos seculares et restituit eis terras possessiones et ecclesias. Robertus Bossu filius ejusdem Roberti de Mollent de consensu Alexandri episcopi Lincolniensis anno gratiae millesimo centesimo xliii fundavit monasterium Beatae Mariae de Pratis Leycestriae in honorem assumptionis ejusdem gloriosae virginis, et de ecclesiis terris et possessionibus antedictorum canonicorum secularium cum multis aliis supererrogatis tam ecclesiis aliisque possessionibus et redditibus luculentur dotavit, et eas in usum canonicorum regularium transformavit. Qui etiam in eodem monasterio de consensu Amiciae uxoris suae canonicus regularis factus est, et annis quindecim in habitu regulari ibidem Christo militans canonicus vitam finiens obdormivit in pace, in latere ibidem chori dextro sepultus, scilicet anno gratiae millesimo centesimo lxvii. Iste Robertus fundavit abbathiam de Gerondona monachorum et monasterium sanctimonialium de Etona, in quo Amicia uxor ejusdem Roberti ex mutuo assensu viri sui facta est sanctimonialis de residuo vitae suae Deo serviens, unde ipse factus est canonicus regularis et illa sanctimonialis. De quibus processit Robertus ou les blancmeines filius eorum, comes Leycestrensis tertius post conquestum, qui desponsavit Petronillam filiam Hugonis Grantmenyl, cum qua accepit totum honorem de Hyncley una cum senescalatu Angliae ex dono ejusdem Hugonis. Quae Petronilla construxit magnam navim ejusdem ecclesiae abbathiae Leycestrensis, et in choro coram magno altari

---

[1] No. 2 has "unicum filium dei gratia regem Anglie hujus nominis sextum Henricum." The word "nunc" is omitted.

est humata : quae etiam comam capitis sui ad modum funis composuit, et ad cordam unius lampadis in choro posuit, unde more instrumenti cum eadem coma crinium subtrahendi sursumque levandi diuturnus usus dabatur. Et predictus funis in eodem monasterio in devotam predictae dominae memoriam non obliviscitur sed memoriter servatur. Iste Robertus Mellent etiam hospitalitatem de Bracheleye fundavit et dotavit, ubi cor ejusdem Roberti de Mollento adhuc integrum in plumbo sale servatum habetur. Robertus ou les blancmeyns genuit de dicta Petronilla Robertum dictum filium Petronillae haeredem, Rogerum sancti Andreae in Scotia episcopum et Willelmum leprosum fundatorem hospitalis sancti Leonardi Leycestriae, et Amiciam desponsatam Simoni de Monteforti, et Margaretam desponsatam Sayro de Quinci. Iste Robertus tertius comes peregre profectus Ierosolymam ac rediens apud Duraco in Graecia anno gratiae millesimo cxc obiens sepultus est. Robertus filius Petronillae iiii comes Leycestrensis in terram sanctam profectus peregre postquam magnum Soldanum in armis Ricardi regis Angliae per hastiludium bellicum prostravit et strenue interfecit, in Angliam rediens in abbathia Leycestrensi mortuus sepultus est, et tunc partita est haereditas inter duas sorores, scilicet Amiciam et Margaretam, deficiente semine fratrum nec illo habente filium. Symon de Monteforti per Amiciam seniorem filiam cum medietate comitatus Leycestriae et honoris de Hyncleye factus est comes Leycestrensis et pro honore de Hyncleye jure haereditario senescallus Angliae. Scirus de Quinci per minorem filiam Margaretam cum altera medietate comitatus Leycestrensis factus est comes de Wynchestria. Dominus Simon de Monteforti postea propter inobedientiam suam erga regem exhaeredatus et exlegatus cum filiis suis, et comitatus Leycestrensis cum honore de Hinkleye datus est Ranulfo comiti Cestrensi. Set Simon filius dicti Simonis de Monteforti post mortem patris sui in Angliam rediens ex dono regis recuperavit haereditatem suam de comitatu et honore praedictis. Sed rex reservavit sibi et haeredibus suis solum patronatum abbathiae Leycestrensis et prioratus de Kynelworthia. Iste Simon junior accepit uxorem Elianoram sororem regis Henrici, quae prius voverat castitatem, et anulum ut sponsa Christi de manu sancti Edmundi Cantuariensis acceperat. De qua genuit nobilissimam prolem, sed cito de hoc mundo transituram, scilicet filios et unam filiam Elianoram quam postea desponsavit Lewlinus princeps Walliae. Iste Symon patrissare volens, super quibusdam constitutionibus observandis inter regem Henricum 3m et barones regni se ingessit ut capitaneus eorum, unde duo bella mortalia ingruerunt in Anglia, unum apud Lewes et aliud apud Evysham, ut infra plenius patebit. In quo ipse Symon et filius ejus una cum multis aliis ex parte baronum ceciderunt. Et sic Henricus dedit comitatum Leycestriae cum honore de Hyncleye et senescalatu Angliae Edmundo filio suo. De quo Edmundo et haeredibus suis historia prolixius patebit in antedicta abbatia Leycestrensi; similiter de Sciro de Quinci scilicet comite Wyntoniensi et ejus haeredibus ibidem plenarie copia habetur.[1]

(This part of the Chronicle was probably written not later than 1366, for the narrative at this date breaks off abruptly, the next entry referring to events of the year 1377.)

British Museum, Add. MS. 29,502.[2]

Robertus Blaunchemeynes comes Lerecestrie post conquestum Anglie tercius dominam Petronillam filiam domini Hugonis de Grauntemenil accepit uxorem, de qua tres filios et duas filias procreavit videlicet dominum Robertum dictum Robertum Fitzpernell, dominum Rogerum episcopum Sancti Andree in Scocia et dominum Willelmum leprosum fundatorem hospitalis Sancti Leonardi Leicestrie, dominam Amiciam postea desponsatam domino Simoni de Monteforti et dominam Margaretam postea desponsatam Saero de Quinci.

[3] Iste Robertus le Blaunchemeynes cum dicta uxore sua domina Petronilla totum honorem de Hinkleye una cum

---

[1] The writings to which Knighton is here referring would appear to be none other than the original source of the Harleian transcripts. If this is the case the genealogies in question must have been added to after Knighton's time, a by no means unlikely occurrence.

[2] A parchment roll: the handwriting is late fifteenth century.

[3] In the MS. wide spaces are left between each paragraph.

senestatu†[1] Anglie ex dono dicti Hugonis adeptus est: Iste
dictus Robertus Blaunchemeynes in Grecia diem clausit
extremum: Robertus filius Petronille comes Leicestrie post
conquestum Anglie quartus dominam Loram filiam domini
Willelmi de Brewes accepit uxorem et que post mortem viri
sui Haklington. juxta Cantuariam anchorita effecta usque
ad diem obitus sui. Et quia inter Loram predictam et ipsum
Robertum soboles est extyncta et de duobus fratribus suis
predictis nulla ulterius suscitata, ideo partita est toto† here-
ditas inter Amiceam† et Margaretam sorores supradictas.
Quarum seniorem silicet† Amiciam postea desponsavit dominus Simon de Monteforti cum prima medietate hereditatis
predicte, Margaretam vero sororem juniorem desponsavit
dominus Saerus de Quinci cum altera medietate et factus est
a rege comes Wintonie: Simon predictus factus est comes
Leicestrie et senescallus Anglie, de uxore sua procreavit duos
filios Simonem et Amaricum, quiquidem Amaricus captus
apud terram sanctam a paganis et incarceratus ibidem
mortuus est. Iste autem Simon propter inobedienciam suam
erga regem a predictis honoribus est exheredatus: et tam
ipse quam filii sui ab Anglia exules sunt effecti: Anno
domini millesimo [cc] s[ex]to.[2] Et advocacio abbathie
Leicestrie sui patronatus ad manus domini regis Johannis
per forisfacturam Simonis predicti devenit. Radulphus
autem comes Cestrie predictos honores de consensu regis
inde optinuit et annis plurimis occupavit.

Simon Junior de Monteforti supradictus postquam annis
aliquibus elapsis in partibus transmarinis vassalus famosissimus est proclamatus, post mortem patris sui gratiam regis
Anglie adeptus est et honores Leicestrie et Hynkley predictos recuperavit sed rex reseravit† sibi et hereditibus† suis
solum patronatum abbathie Leicestrie et patronatum de
Kenylworthe. Iste†

Iste autem Simon junior dominam Elienoram filiam regis

---

[1] The obelus is used to avoid repeating the word "sic." Obviously
the correct reading is "senescalatu."

[2] This is a possible reading, but "s[e]c[und]o" is much more
probable. It may be that "ccv." is the correct reading of the
original from which the scribe copied.

Johannes† et sororem regis Henrici tercii, [que] prius voverat castitatem et Anulum ut sponsa Christi de manu sancti Edmundi tunc Cantuarienɫ† archiepiscopi acceperat, desponsavit, de qua prolem nobilissimam, sed cito de hoc mundo migravit, sex post† filios et unam filiam procreavit, Henricum, Ricardum, Amaricum et Welliseborum†, Wgydon[em]†, Simonem, Thomam et Elienoram Mounfort† quam postea desponsavit dominus {Willelmus†} (Leolinus[1]) princeps Wallie.

Iste autem Simon postquam hereditatem paternam est adeptus et comes Leicestrie est effectus cupiens de carcere redimere fratrem suum uterinum Amaricum supradictum modicum borcum†[2] vendidit Abbathie Leicestrie et duplum hospitali Jerosolomitane pro magna summa pecunie: sed Amaricus morte perventus est ante adventum Simonis supradicti.

Iste vere Simon in Angliam tres filios Amaricum, Welisseborum, Simonem supradicti reversus et p[atr]issare volens super quibusdam constitucionibus observandis inter Henricum regem tercium et barones regni ingessit se: ut capud† ex parte baronum: unde duo bella mortalia ingruerunt, unum apud Lewes aliud apud Evysham. In quo ipse Simon et filius ejus una cum multis aliis ex parte baronum ceciderunt. Et sic ex dono regis Henrici datus est comitatus Leicestrie cum honore de Hynkley et senestatu† Anglie nobilissimo domino Edmundo comiti filio suo et fratri illustrissimi principis Edwardi de quo quidem Edmundo et heredibus suis inferius prosecutum.[3]

Coronation Roll of Henry the Fourth

In parliamento ad mandatum domini regis Ricardi secundi post conquestum anno Domini millesimo trecentesimo nonogesimo nono, anno vero ipsius regis vicesimo tertio apud Westmonasterium convocato ultimo die mensis Septembris,

---

[1] A subscript in a modern hand.
[2] The correct reading is probably "boscum."
[3] Here follows, in the same hand, an account in English of the battles of Lewes and Evesham. The roll appears to be incomplete and ends in the middle of this account.

cessione et resignatione ejusdem regis prelatis proceribus et communitati totius regni publice notificatis, et ab eisdem admissis, ac ipso rege propter sua demerita deposito ; successit eidem Henricus dux Lancastrie, comes Derbie, Lincolnie, Leycestrie, Herefordie, Northamptonie, senescallus Anglie. Et cum tractaretur et provisum fuisset de solempniis coronationis ipsius regis Henrici die Lune in festo translationis sancti Edwardi regis et confessoris tunc proximo sequente celebrandis, dictus dominus noster rex ut in jure comitis Leycestrie, cui officium senescalli pertinet, idem officium commisit Thome filio suo in coronatione predicta faciendum ; quod quidem officium, tam in propria persona sua quam in persona domini Thome Percy comitis Wigornie, qui propter etatem juvenilem predicti Thome filii regis, eidem assignatus erat in auxilium, et predictum officium exercuit de precepto predicti regis Henrici, et feoda eidem consueta clamabat et percepit in coronatione prefati domini Henrici, dicto die Lune apud Westmonasterium solempniter facta et celebrata. Et memorandum quod prefatus Thomas filius regis die Sabbati videlicet quarto die Octobris ante coronationem predictam sedebat de precepto regis, tanquam senescallus Anglie, in alba aula regii palatii Westmonasteriensis prope capellam regalem et inquirebat diligenter que et qualia officia seu feoda dicto die per quoscumque facienda vel optinenda fuerunt. . . .

(Printed by Rymer, Foedera, vol. viii, o.s., p. 90.)

Patent Roll, 1 Henry V, pt. 1, m. 36

Rex carissimo consanguineo suo Ricardo comiti Warwice salutem. Sciatis quod nos de industria et cicumspectione vestris plenius confidentes asignavimus vos ad omnia et singula que ad officium senescalli Anglie ad coronationem nostram pertinent hac vice tantum faciendum et exercendum. Et ideo vobis mandamus quod circa premissa diligenter intendatis et ea faciatis et exequamini in modo et forma debite antiquitus usitatis. In cujus, etc. Teste rege apud Westmonasterium secundo die Aprilis. Per ipsum regem.

(Printed by Rymer, Foedera, vol. ix, o.s., p. 2.)

Close Roll, 8 Henry V, m. 4d

Rex vicecomitibus Londonie salutem. Precipimus vobis firmiter injungentes quod statim visis presentibus in singulis locis civitatis predicte et suburbiorum ejusdem ubi expedire videritis publice ex parte nostra proclamari faciatis quod omnes et singuli qui alique servitia diebus coronationum reginarum Anglie ratione tenure sue seu alio modo debent aut facere tenentur sint coram dilecto et fideli consanguineo nostro Ricardo comite Warrwice locum tenente carissimi fratris nostri Thome ducis Clarencie senescalli Anglie de ordinatione nostra die Lune proximo futuro apud Westmonasterium in aula alba ad petendum per petitiones suas servitia sua die coronationis Katerine nunc regine Anglie consortis nostre carissime cum omni honore et reverentia quibus decet ibidem more solito fieri et exerceri. Et hoc nullatenus omittatis. Teste.

(Printed by Rymer, Foedera, vol. x, o.s., p. 63.)

PART II

THE TRIAL OF PEERS

CHAPTER VII

JUDGMENT OF PEERS, EARLY PRINCIPLES
AND MAGNA CHARTA

THERE are two principles of great antiquity underlying the privilege popularly expressed in the phrase—"the right of being tried by your peers." One principle is that a man ought to be tried only by the members of his own community—the vassal of this or that lord by vassals of the same lord, the citizen of this or that chartered town by his fellow-citizens of the same town, and so forth. The other principle is that a superior ought not to be tried by an inferior; an intelligible though aristocratic principle, but obviously dangerous if carried too far. The two principles are quite distinct and must not be confused.

The former principle was part and parcel of the feudal system: the growth of the latter principle was slow and unsystematic, in some cases altogether abortive. There exist several early enunciations of both doctrines which deserve to be cited and commented upon.

In the year 856 Charles le Chauve granted a charter of liberties to his revolted subjects :—

Et si aliquis de nobis in quocumque ordine contra istum pactum incontra illum [scilicet regem] fecerit, si talis est ut ille inde eum ammonere voleat ut emendet, faciat ; et si talis est causa ut inde illum familiariter non debeat ammonere et ante suos pares illum in rectam rationem mittat, et ille qui debitum pactum et rectam legem et debitam seniori reverentiam non vult exhibere et observare, justum justitiae judicium sustineat.[1]

[1] Monumenta Germaniae Hist., Capitularia, ed. Boretius and Krause, vol. ii, p. 281.

Here, it seems, we have an undeveloped example of the first principle. It is the king who gives judgment, but peers are to be present as assessors.

An ordinance of Conrad the Salic in 1037 provided: "ut nullus miles, . . . tam de nostris majoribus valvassoribus quam eorum militibus, sine certa et convicta culpa suum beneficium perdat, nisi secundum consuetudinem antecessorum nostrorum et judicium parium suorum. . . ."[1] That is to say, no knight, be he tenant-in-chief or only under-tenant, is to be disseised except in accordance with precedent and the judgment of his peers; and this provision is further defined by the same ordinance as follows: "Si contentio fuerit de beneficio inter capitaneos, coram imperatore definiri debet; si vero fuerit contentio inter minores valvassores et majores de beneficio, in judicio parium suorum definiatur per judicem curtis." This must mean that in the case of tenants-in-capite the matter is to be determined *coram imperatore;* while in the case of under-tenants the matter is to be determined in the court of the mesne lord by the judgment of the under-tenant's peers.

Illustrations of the first principle might be multiplied indefinitely: the second principle is less frequently asserted.

The judges ought to be of a rank equal to the litigants. If therefore the vassal litigating with the lord is earl or baron, undoubtedly the peers of the court . . . ought to be earls or barons.[2]

In this case the peers of the court in question evidently include persons of lower rank than earls and barons. Not every one of the baron's peers may try him, only earls or

[1] Monumenta Germaniae Hist., Constitutiones, ed. Weiland, vol. i, p. 90.

[2] Jacobinus de S. Georgio, cited by Ducange, s.v. "Par": Pares curiae seu curtis dicuntur convassalli, qui jurarunt fidelitatem eidem domino pro aliis feudis quae tenent ab eo. Sed si essent vassalli qui non praestitissent sacramentum fidelitatis eidem domino, non dicerentur esse de paribus curiae. Et est advertendum quod isti pares curiae qui habent cognoscere de causa feudali debent esse illius qualitatis cujus sunt vassalli litigantes; et ideo si vassallus litigans cum domino est comes vel baro, certe pares curie qui habent cognoscere de causa feudali debent esse comites vel barones.

barons. Whether an earl must be tried only by such of his peers as are earls is not clear.

There is a law upon the subject ascribed to David of Scotland which certainly does not lack precision: "No man shall be judged by his inferior who is not his peer; earl shall be judged by earl, baron by baron, vavassor by vavassor, burgess by burgess; but an inferior may be judged by a superior."[1] Here we have the second grafted on to the first principle: a man's inferior is not his peer. In the other instance cited the two principles were, on the contrary, distinguished.

In England there is an early reference to both principles contained in the compilation called the laws of Henry the First—"Unusquisque per pares suos judicandus est et ejusdem provinciae: peregrina vero judicia modis omnibus submovemus . . . nec summorum quispiam minorum judicatione dispereat."[2] These laws are a hybrid collection of little authority; the central curia regis is outside the scope of the work; they illustrate, however, the generality of these doctrines. It should be noted that while the judges of the local courts are, in the above extract, required to be the peers of the parties, they are elsewhere in the same work more particularly defined: "Regis judices sunt barones comitatus, qui liberas in eis terras habent, per quos debent causae singulorum alterna prosecutione tractari; villani vero vel cotseti vel ferdingi, vel qui sunt viles vel inopes personae non sunt inter legum judices numerandi."[3]

It was not everywhere that these principles found acceptance. Germany could afford to pity Hungary: "quod si aliquis ex comitum ordine regem . . . offenderit . . ., nulla sententia a principe, sicut apud nos moris est, per pares suos exposcitur, nulla accusato excusandi licentia datur, sed sola principis voluntas apud omnes pro ratione habetur."[4] But even those who allowed judgment by peers were wont to place limitations on the right to claim it.

[1] Cited by Pollock and Maitland, Hist. English Law, vol. i, p. 173.
[2] Leges Henrici, c. 31, s. 7; c. 32, s. 1.
[3] Leges Henrici, c. 29.
[4] Otto of Frisingen, Gesta Friderici, ed. Waitz, p. 40.

The sovereign was more than the peer of all his subjects.[1]
What possible application had either principle to a case tried
coram rege? If we may resort to the precise language of
later legists like Bracton the answer is simple : there must be
three parties to every judgment, plaintiff (or accuser), defendant (or accused), and judge. Therefore between vassal
and vassal the sovereign may judge ; but between vassal and
sovereign the peers of the sovereign's court must judge.[2]
This theory, where admitted, obviously cuts a mighty cantle
from the scope of the original doctrine.

Until the beginning of the thirteenth century, judgment by
peers, as a duty to the accused, as a principle enforced for his
protection, cannot be clearly illustrated by actual cases tried
in the court of a sovereign. It was indeed in danger of
becoming altogether obsolete by being merged in a very
different principle. The proper administration of justice was
ever one of the most arduous and difficult functions of
monarchy, and one which could not be adequately performed
without much assistance. The mediæval king was lord
paramount with vastly more judicial business to transact
than any mesne lord. Even the mesne lord found it necessary
to exact suit of court from his feudal tenants, much more so
the sovereign. What every king habitually did for his own
convenience cannot be legitimately imputed to, nor is it
conducive to the development of a principle which purports
to be solely concerned with the protection of the subject.

In the year 864 Bernard, grandson of William de Gellone,
lay ambushed in a wood with intent to assassinate certain
vassals of Charles le Chauve, or, as others asserted, with

---

[1] Quia dominus rex nullum habere potest parem, multo minus
superiorem. . . . (Glanville, Lib., vii, cap. 10.)
. . . ita habet rex in regno suo ordinariam in temporalibus, et
pares non habet neque superiores. (Bracton, fol. 412.)
[2] Preterea si de feudo inter duos vassallos controversia sit, domini
sit cognitio, et per eum controversia terminetur. Si vero inter
dominum et vassallum lis oriatur per pares curie a domino sub debito
fidelitatis conjuratos terminetur. (Fredc. I, imp., Nov., 1158;
Mon. Germ. Hist., Leges, ed. Pertz, ii, p. 114. Cf. ibid., pp. 169,
173, 178. See also Constitutiones, ed. Weiland, i, pp. 248-9, 402-3,
415.)

designs against the person of the king. The plot was discovered and Bernard took to flight. He was thereupon
convicted and disseized of his honours by judgment of the
king's feudatories: " Unde judicio suorum fidelium honores
quos ei [Bernardo] dederat rex recepit, et Rodberto fideli
suo donavit."[1] Observe that Bernard is stated to have been
judged by persons who are not styled Bernard's co-feuda-
tories but the king's feudatories. This case therefore indicates a sovereign's practice rather than a subject's privilege.

There is a letter written by Eudo II, count of Chartres, to
Robert of France with reference to a judicial commission
entrusted to Richard duke of Normandy. The duke, writes
the count, had refused a demand of Robert to pronounce
judgment against the count involving confiscation, on this
ground: "nec sibi competere dicebat ut me ad talem judicium
exhiberet sine conventu parium suorum."[2] If the last word
had been "meorum," and not "suorum," this would have
been a definite assertion of the privilege of judgment by
peers. The letter as it stands amounts to nothing of the
kind.

In England during the reign of William the Conqueror
we commonly find the magnates of the realm summoned to
the assistance of the king or his justiciars for the trial of
important cases; but I venture to think that monarch would
have been mightily surprised if anyone had suggested that
their concurrence was necessary to the validity of his judgments. According to Ordericus Vitalis it would seem that
Odo bishop of Bayeux was sentenced to imprisonment by
the Conqueror in person, the magnates present resolutely
declining to take any part in the proceedings. It was on
this occasion that Odo made his famous protest, and William
his no less famous retort. " I am a clerk and God's minister!" exclaimed the prelate; "it is not lawful to condemn

---

[1] Annales de S. Bertin, Soc. de l'Hist. de France, p. 138. The
case of Pépin, traitor and apostate, was disposed of in the same
" Placitum": primum a regni primoribus . . . et demum generaliter
ab omnibus ad mortem dijudicatur. (Ibid., p. 137.)

[2] Bouquet, H. F., vol. x, pp. 501-2; Revue Historique, t. 54,
p. 37.

P

a bishop without the judgment of the pope." And to this came the reply, " I condemn not the clerk, but my earl."[1]

In the reign of William Rufus, bishop William of St. Carilef was accused of treason. The bishop offered to purge himself as a bishop; the king insisted on compurgation *laicaliter.* Neither would give way. Eventually the prelate was brought before the king's court consisting of the king, archbishops, bishops, earls, barons and others. Various preliminary points were decided against the prelate, who thereupon alleged an appeal to the pope. And when the bishop withdrew from the court, and on being summoned returned, Hugh de Beaumont rose and addressed the prelate: " My lord bishop, the court of the king and these barons justly adjudge that you forfeit your fief on the ground that you decline to reply to these matters concerning which the king by me has appealed you, but invite him to submit his suit to the decision of Rome." The bishop replied: " In every place where not violence but justice holds sway I am ready to prove my innocence of crime and perjury ; and this, which you have here recited by way of judgment, I will demonstrate in the Roman Church to have been falsely and unjustly pronounced." To this Hugh rejoined: " I and my compeers are ready to confirm our judgment in this court."[2]

[1] ". . . et frater meus, cui totius regni tutelam commendavi, violenter opes diripuit, crudeliter pauperes oppressit, frivola spe milites mihi surripuit, totumque regnum injustis exactionibus concutiens exagitavit. Quid inde agendum sit caute considerate, et mihi, quaeso, insinuate."

Cumque omnes tantum virum timerent, et sententiam in illum proferre dubitarent, magnanimus rex ait : "Noxia temeritas semper comprimenda est, nec uni ad detrimentum reipublicae pro aliquo favore parcendum est. Hunc ergo virum, qui terram turbat comprehendite, et, ne in deterius praevaleat, solerter custodite." Cumque nullus in episcopum auderet injicere manum, rex ipse primus apprehendit eum. Illo autem reclamante : "Clericus sum, et minister domini ; non licet pontificem damnare sine judicio papae"; providus rex ait : "Ego non clericum nec antistitem damno, sed comitem meum. . . ." (Ordericus Vitalis, vol. iii, p. 191 ; see also Bigelow, Placita Anglo-Normannica, p. 291, App. B.)

[2] Cumque episcopus egrederetur et vocatus regrederetur, Hugo de Bellomonte surgens dixit episcopo, "Domine episcope regis curia et barones isti vobis pro justo judicant, quando sibi vos

The expression "peer" and "baron," it will be observed, are treated as synonymous; and here again the presence of the peers is not referred to as a privilege enjoyed by the accused, for the words used are "compares mei" and not "compares tui."

We need not pursue this line of inquiry any further. Such evidence as exists all points in the same direction, and we must conclude that, up to about the end of the twelfth or the beginning of the thirteenth century, the principle of judgment by peers for the protection of the subject in the king's court existed, if at all, only in the background of practical politics. No urgent need to evoke the principle had arisen : there was no apparent reason why the need ever should arise; the king habitually summoned the barons of his court, and summoned them for his own assistance; more than this, it was the king who was always insisting, the barons who were always reluctant to fulfil an irksome obligation.[1]

Between principle number one and the regular crown procedure there was no likelihood of conflict; it was quite otherwise with principle number two. The prudent king probably took care to include among the members of his court some persons of rank not inferior to the litigants; but there is no evidence earlier than the thirteenth century to

respondere non vultis de hiis de quibus vos per me appellavit, sed de placito suo invitatis eum Romam, quod vos fedum vestrum inde forisfacitis"; et episcopus respondit; "in omni loco in quo non violentia sed justicia dominetur, de scelere et perjurio me purgare paratus sum; et hoc, quod hic pro judicio recitasti, in Romana ecclesia falsum et injuste dictum esse monstrabo." "Ego," inquit Hugo, "et compares mei parati sumus judicium nostrum in hac curia confirmare." (Ex Bibl. Bodl. MS., Fairfax; printed in full in Monasticon Anglicanum, vol. i, pp. 244–50; see also Bigelow, op. cit., App. D., p. 307.)

[1] Chapter xi of the Constitutions of Clarendon declares that : Archiepiscopi, episcopi, et [sicut] universe persone regni qui de rege tenent in capite, habent possessiones suas de domino rege sicut baroniam, et inde respondent justiciis et ministris regis, et sequuntur et faciunt omnes rectitudines et consuetudines regias, et sicut barones ceteri debent interesse judiciis curie domini regis cum baronibus usque dum perveniatur in judicio ad diminutionem membrorum vel mortem.

show that, either in France or England, the king was under
any obligation to include persons of equal rank or to exclude
persons of inferior rank. Some limits, however, to this latitude
can be traced.

In a treaty of alliance made in 1109 between Henry
the First and Robert of Flanders the following passage
occurs :—

Ipse comes illuc ibit et regem Henricum per fidem juvabit . . .
nec dimittet quin eat, donec rex Franciae judicari faciat comiti
Rotberto, quod non debeat juvare dominum et amicum suum
regem Angliae cujus feodum tenet : et hoc per pares suos qui eum
jure judicare debent.[1]

And in a treaty of 1163, to which Henry the Second and
Thierry count of Flanders were parties, almost identical
words are used.[2] Now the count of Flanders was recognised
in the thirteenth century as *par Francie*, his only peers were
the other members constituting the famous college of twelve.
What, then, was count Thierry claiming in 1163? Was he
claiming to be peer of France and privileged accordingly?
Was he asserting principle number two? There is very
little ground for supposing that he was asserting anything
more than principle number one.[3]

By virtue of the treaty of 1185 Flanders ceded the Amiénois
to Philip Augustus, a transfer of territory which converted
many of the count's liegemen into vassals of France. One
of these persons, who had no love for his quondam lord, took
occasion to say to the count : "Domine comes, hactenus

---

[1] Rymer, Foedera R.C., i, p. 7. Compare the claim of the duke
of Aquitaine in 1128 : si sic judicaverint regni optimates, fiat, sin
aliter, sicut. (Suger, Louis le Gros, ed. 1887, p. 110.)

[2] Rymer, Foedera R.C., i, p. 22.

[3] In 1153 the court of Louis the Seventh tried the celebrated
suit between the bishop of Langres and the duke of Burgundy—
congregatis multis archiepiscopis, episcopis atque baronibus. The
names of the persons present are given. According to thirteenth-
century ideas the two litigant feudatories were peers of France,
but there was no peer of France among the judges. The case is
printed by Langlois, Textes relatifs à l'Hist. du Parlement, no. 11,
pp. 18-21.

homo vester fui, nunc autem, Deo volente, par vobis factus sum, et vobiscum in curia domini regis habeo judicare."[1]

The reign of Stephen caused a break in the continuity of England's constitutional development. If Henry's demise had been followed by a strong but lawless despotism (take Montfort's administration of Gascony as a type) the privilege under discussion might conceivably have become the war-cry of a baronial reform party: the anarchy which in fact supervened necessarily had a contrary result; the authority of the king's court as such waned and vanished, while ecclesiastical jurisdiction flourished like a green bay tree.[2] The first business of Henry fitz-Empress was to restore the power and prestige of the curia regis, and clip the claws of the church; and the only means by which he could hope to effect this object was by adopting the policy indicated in the Constitutions of Clarendon,[3] a policy which quite overshadowed the

---

[1] Gislebert de Mons, Chronicon Hanoniense, ed. Vanderkindere, p. 185.

[2] Note, for example, the trial of the earl of Hereford for unlawfully imprisoning and putting to ransom certain knights, and for sacrilege. There appears to have been no evidence of sacrilege. He was tried by the archdeacon of Worcester, on the complaint of Gilbert de Lacy and R. de Worcester, and acquitted. The bishop of Hereford who wished to try the case himself was much disgusted and obtained an order from the king to re-try it. The earl pleaded res judicata and appealed to the papal legate. The bishop thereupon sent his version of the affair to the legate: the earl, he thought, ought to be condemned, he had done the same sort of thing before, he was very friendly with William de Beauchamp who was excommunicate, things had been told about him in the confessional. (See Letters of Gilbert Foliot, ed. Giles, vol. i, pp. 171, 175-8, 181, 186-8.)

[3] De caetero magno frequentique commonemur imperio duci Normannorum assistere et sibi placitis obtemperare. (Letters of Gilbert Foliot, ed. Giles, vol. i, p. 189.) Sic igitur ecclesiae geminata potestas est ut hinc Regi caelesti serviat, hinc terreno principi quod ad eos spectat exhibeat; ejusque ministros efficit potestas, hinc a Deo collata pontifices, hinc a rege suscepta comites aut barones. Potestas haec est, qua magnum in palatio obtinet ecclesia principatum, cum in omnibus regni judiciis, praeterquam si de vitae periculo tractetur aut sanguine, locum habeat ipsa praecipuum: haec regi nos obligat, ut affirmant, ut ab ipso citati debeamus assistere, et singulorum causas universi discu-

converse traditional privilege.[1] However, the complete success of Henry's efforts soon left him free to pursue whatever policy he pleased.

On the main outlines of Plantagenet jurisprudence the treatise of a Norman law-writer compiled at the close of the twelfth century is no mean authority. " Assisie vero tenentur per barones et legales homines. Par per parem judicari debet: barones igitur *et milites*, legis statuta scientes et Deum timentes, possunt judicare unus alium, et subditum eis populum ; rustico enim non licet, vel aliis de populo, militem vel clericum judicare."[2] According to modern ideas judgment by

tere et judicare. Nam qui in his quae ad Deum sunt gradu quodam distinguimur, ut superiores quidam inferiores alii reputemur et simus, nos in hoc pares aestimant, ut si de fundis ad ecclesiam libertate regia devolutis, inter nos aut in nos fuerit oborta contentio, apud regem quae spectant ad singulos universorum definiat pronuntiatio. (Ibid., pp. 277–8.)

Mandatum domini papae suscepimus, quatinus Hugonem comitem de Norfolchia districte conveniremus, et nisi canonicis de Panteneia villam ipsam de Panteneia, et caetera quae sibi ablata queruntur, admonitus restitueret, ipsum et totam terram suam interdicto subjiceremus, et nisi vel sic infra quadraginta dies resipisceret, eum excommunicationis innodare sententia non differemus. In hoc vero nobis regia se graviter opponit auctoritas, asserens ad summam regni sui spectare dignitatem, ut dum cuique adversus comitem vel baronem suum super terris aut feudis querelam habenti, plenam paratus fuerit exhibere justiciam, ipsum nec archiepiscopus, nec aliquis regni sui episcopus aut interdicto premat, aut excommunicationi subjiciat. (Ibid., p. 244.)

[1] To the church I apologise, for I write as a layman. The following letter from the pope to Becket is, I suppose, sufficient to convict me of a canonical error.

Quod minor majorem judicare non possit, et eum praesertim cui jure noscitur praelationis subesse, et obedientiae vinculo tenetur astrictus, tam Divinae quam humanae leges demonstrant, et praecipue sanctorum patrum statutis id manifestius declaratur. Haec siquidem nos, quorum interest errata corrigere. . . , sententiam ab episcopis et baronibus Angliae, quoniam ad primam regis citationem tui copiam non fecisti, adversum te praesumptuose prolatam, in qua tibi jam dicti episcopi et barones omnia mobilia tua tam contra juris formam quam contra ecclesiasticam consuetudinem abjudicarunt, (Praesertim cum nulla mobilia praeterquam de bonis ecclesiae tuae habueris) irritam penitus esse censemus, et eam apostolica auctoritate quassamus. (Materials, vol. v, p. 178.)

[2] Coutumiers de Normandie, ed. Tardif, p. 24.

peers thus defined amounts to very little, but this is not in the least an exceptional instance. Compare, for example, the following passage : " Tous ceaus qui sont de la haute cour, chevaliers homes liges dou roy, sont pers, qui que il soient, hauz ou bas, povres ou riches . . . , et porte au tel force le dit des uns come des autres."[1]

As a principle of practical importance for the protection of the subject, judgment by peers received a momentous recognition in England by being introduced into the Great Charter of John in language remarkable for its ambiguity. The foremost provision on the subject is of course the following :—

Nullus liber homo capiatur vel imprisonetur aut dissaisiatur aut utlagetur aut exuletur aut aliquo modo destruatur nec super eum ibimus nec super eum mittemus nisi per legale judicium parium suorum vel per legem terre.[2]

The other clauses in John's charter which make reference to a judicium parium were mostly ephemeral, and did not finally become part of the statute law. These, however, will have to be considered, for without their assistance it would be impossible to arrive at the true meaning of the clause in question. It is an elementary rule for ascertaining the right construction of a written instrument that such instrument must be construed as a whole, and there is nothing in the case of the Great Charter to make it an exception to the rule.

No portion of this famous document can possibly be described as a good piece of drafting; but it seems that centuries of familiarity with and reverence for this cornerstone of English liberties has, until quite recently, disarmed hostile criticism. From the language of Coke in his Second Institute we might conclude that the whole common law of his day was merely an inadequate commentary on this stupendous achievement. The charter, in truth, was the golden idol which had brought the English out of bondage, and it is not till our own time that iconoclasts appear on the scene. Of legal and historical exegesis there has been an abundance

[1] Assises de Jerusalem, ed. Beugnot, vol. i, p. 448; see ibid., p. 458; compare Beaumanoir, Coutumes du Beauvoisis, Soc. de l'Hist. de France, vol. i, p. 29; etc.   [2] Magna Carta, cap. 39.

during the last few years. Many erroneous interpretations have been exposed and discarded, and the leading modern authorities have ultimately arrived at contradictory and wholly inconclusive conclusions.

Until comparatively recently historians accepted the popular view that chapter xxxix of the Charter—as the provision we are principally concerned with has since been called [1]—pointed to that cherished privilege of Englishmen, trial by jury in criminal cases.[2] This myth has been successfully assailed. The negative results of the higher criticism of this chapter have been excellent, but the positive results have been singularly meagre and disappointing; in fact, latter-day views may be very briefly summed up and contrasted. Thus one writer observes :—[3]

It is often asserted, and still more often assumed that the judgment of a man's peers, in the case of a person of lower estate than that of a peer of the realm, must have been, in some way, the equivalent of trial by jury. It is absolutely impossible, for two distinct reasons, that the words can have had any such sense. In criminal cases trial by jury had not even been instituted, and the only modes of trial were by ordeal, by compurgation and by battle. From the time when trial by jury first commenced, either in civil or in criminal cases, to this present end of the nineteenth century, no jury ever did or could give judgment on any matter whatsoever. . . . King John bound himself in such a manner as to show that "judgment of peers" was one thing, the "law of the land" another. . . . The "law of the land" included all legal proceedings, criminal or civil, other than the judgment of peers. The judgment of peers had reference chiefly to the right of land-holders to their lands, or to some matters connected with feudal tenure and its incidents. . . . It can hardly be doubted that when judgment by peers was mentioned in the charter the earls and barons interpreted it to mean that in cases of alleged treason and felony, when forfeiture or escheat was involved, they should be judged only by earls and barons.

[1] The division of the Charter into chapters is a modern device to facilitate reference.

[2] See Pollock and Maitland, Hist. of Eng. Law, vol. ii, p. 625 n., for the early history of the myth, which still flourishes in elementary books of reference and other popular works.

[3] Pike, Constitutional History of the House of Lords, p. 169.

Another writer discusses the clause as follows :—[1]

In passing, a commentator should observe that in mediæval Latin "vel" will often stand for "and." . . . The wording of the charter leaves open the question whether a man can ever be imprisoned or disseised by the law of the land without having had the judgment of his peers. In the second place it is now generally admitted that the phrase *judicium parium* does not point to trial by jury. For a legal instrument to call the verdict of recognitors a judgment would have been as gross a blunder[2] in 1215 as it would be at the present time. . . . Thirdly there can hardly be a doubt that this clause expresses a claim by the barons for a tribunal of men of baronial rank which shall try even the civil causes in which barons are concerned.

The historian of the criminal law, well qualified by training if not by research to discuss the Charter, makes the following remarks :—[3]

The famous passage in Magna Charta about the "legale judicium parium suorum" appears to me to refer to the trial of peers in the king's court rather than to trial by jury. The 21st Article of Magna Charta has a similar expression : "Comites et barones non amercientur nisi per pares suos et non nisi secundum modum delicti." I do not think the expression "trial by jury" would have been used or would have been intelligible in King John's time. It would have been described rather as the taking of an inquisition by an assize or by lawful men, and is I think referred to by the words "vel per legem terrae." These would include not only inquests taken by jurors on the execution of commissions of eyre, gaol delivery, and oyer and terminer, but also trials by combat or by ordeal, each of which was part of the lex terrae at the date of Magna Charta. In short I should be inclined to construe "nullus liber homo" distributively—"no freeman shall be taken, &c., except (if he is one of the vassals of the king's court) by the lawful judgment of his peers, or (if he is not such a vassal) by the law of the land, in the ordinary course of justice."

[1] Pollock and Maitland, Hist. of Eng. Law, vol. i, p. 173 n.
[2] Trial by jury took the place of the ordeals in criminal cases. Ordeal was habitually described as a judgment. The jury are habitually said to be judges of fact.
[3] Stephen, Hist. of the Criminal Law of England, vol. i, p. 162.

The most recent commentator[1] seems to have committed himself to the interpretation that—chapter xxxix secures to every freeman both a lawful trial and a lawful judgment by his equals; that is to say, lex terre is used in a more or less technical sense, and "vel" must be construed "and." He rejects the antithesis between "judicium parium" and "lex terre" drawn by one of the writers quoted above—"because the two things may be and indeed must be combined. The trial by a law and the judgment by equals were complementary of each other. The peers appointed the test and decided whether it had been properly fulfilled."[2]

The above passages have been cited, partly to contrast the opinions of modern writers and show that, while they may be agreed as to what the famous clause does not mean, they differ essentially as to what it does mean; but also because the authority of most of the writers is such that their views cannot be passed over in silence. I do not, however, propose to discuss these views, the problem must be considered entirely de novo.

A preliminary word about current translations is desirable. Chapter xxxix is commonly rendered into English as follows :—

No freeman is to be taken or imprisoned or disseized or outlawed or exiled or in any way destroyed, nor will we go upon him nor will we send upon him, except by the lawful judgment of his peers or by the law of the land.

Many have strained at the words "go" and "send"; few

---

[1] McKechnie, Magna Carta.

[2] Ibid., p. 443 n.; see generally under chap. xxxix, and pp. 443–4. I wonder what John would have thought of this theory? Over and over again in his charters he refers to the test or trial as a *judgment.* —Cum judicio ferri, aque, ignis et duelli (Rot. Cart. R.C., p. 81 ; see ibid., pp. 71, 79, et passim). On the other hand, there are scores of charters of John containing passages identical with or similar to the following: et quod nullus de misercordia pecunie judicetur nisi secundum antiquam legem burgi (Charter to Cambridge) ; or—nisi secundum legem hundredi (Charter to Dublin); or—nisi secundum legem liberorum burgorum nostrorum (Charter to Ipswich).

have failed to swallow the word "destroyed."[1] Several of the words are certainly uncouth and the general effect crude, but in every instance those who have strayed from a literal rendering in search of more polished language have grievously blundered. Interpretation under the guise of translation is in this case an inevitable snare. The only admissible translation (if any) is the one I have given.

Now if we desire to discover in what cases it was intended by those who drafted the Charter that a man must be tried by his peers, or what else was intended, we are bound to confine ourselves as strictly as possible to the information afforded by the Charter itself; and we must be very cautious about resorting to any extrinsic evidence, except for the purpose of ascertaining the meaning of the terms employed.

There are several other clauses which refer to judgment by peers and several which refer to the law of the land: these certainly throw considerable light on the meaning of chapter xxxix. Thus chapters lii, lvi, and lvii[2] provide for the restitution of lands disseised without lawful judgment of peers by either king John, his father, or his brother. Where Henry or Richard were the disseisors the right of restitution is limited to lands which king John either retained or was bound to warranty, but there is no express limitation

---

[1] McKechnie gives the following translation (?): "No freeman shall be arrested, or detained in prison, or deprived of his freehold, or outlawed, or banished, or in any way molested; and we will not set forth against him nor send against him, unless by the lawful judgment of his peers and by the law of the land."

The Statutes Revised, i, p. 49, give the following translation of the parallel passages in the confirmation of 1297: "No freeman shall be taken or imprisoned or be disseised . . . or be outlawed or exiled or any otherwise destroyed; nor will we not pass upon him nor condemn him ([alternatively] deal with him) but by lawful judgment of his peers or by the law of the land."

Pike, Constitutional Hist. of the House of Lords, translates the clause: "No freeman is to be taken, or imprisoned, or disseised, or outlawed, or in any way destroyed, nor will we proceed against him, or direct proceeding against him, except in accordance with the judgment of his peers, or in accordance with the law of the land." The words "aut exuletur" are, perhaps merely through inadvertence, passed over altogether.

[2] See Appendix.

in cases where John himself was the disseizor: this, however, is a minor point. The chief circumstance to notice is that lawful judgment of peers is the only process recognised by these clauses in cases of disseizin; there is no mention so far of the law of the land, either as an alternative or as a concomitant process. But the same clauses further provide for the settlement of disputed claims to restitution: claims against John are to be decided by the twenty-five barons; Welsh claims against him are to be determined in the Marches by judgment of peers according to the laws of England, the Marches or Wales as the case might be; with regard, however, to claims against John's predecessors, the king is to do full justice, and to the Welsh full justice according to their laws. A bad piece of work this. If the injustice is correctly stated, the appropriate and sufficient remedy was, in each case, lawful judgment of peers. Either one of the remedies is plainly inappropriate, or "justice according to the laws of the Welsh" connotes, in the case of disseized Welshmen, the same thing as "lawful judgment of peers."[1]

On the other hand, chapters lvi and lix[2] also prove that, whatever judgment of peers may mean, it does not mean judgment by equals in rank. If king John had been disseized without lawful judgment of peers by the Welsh, they were to make restitution; also justice was to be done to the king of Scots in John's court by the judgment of his peers. At this rate why should not a knight, provided he was a tenant-in-capite, be the peer of any mere earl or baron?

A reference to chapter ix of the Charter still further warns us against allowing judgment of peers any very technical meaning, for that chapter fully recognises the right of the king or his bailiffs to disseize a debtor of his lands when his chattels are insufficient. It would be repugnant to the Charter to suggest that the king's right to land properly

---

[1] While the Great Charter in chapter lii refers only to "judgment of peers," and makes no mention of the "law of the land," other charters do exactly the opposite. For example, the charter of Henry II to London provides: De terris suis et tenuris quae infra urbem sunt, rectum eis teneatur secundum legem civitatis.

[2] Appendix.

seized for debt could be challenged under chapter lii. Therefore the ordinary procedure employed against debtors during the reigns of Henry the Second, Richard and John satisfied the requirements of a judicium parium.

If we refer to chapter xlii we see that imprisonment and outlawry are effected by the "law of the land": outlawry entitled the king to seize the outlaw's property, and was by far the commonest punishment inflicted in England for treason and felony. Outlawry, moreover, was the antithesis of trial; and therefore this clause is fatal to the view that trial is meant when the expression "the law of the land" is employed.[1]

I express no opinion as to whether a man reduced to penury by exorbitant amercements was *destructus* within the meaning of that colloquial expression in chapter xxxix; but chapter xxi provides that earls and barons shall not be amerced except by their peers (nisi per pares suos) and proportionately to the offence. It is admitted that this chapter introduced nothing new; it merely confirmed a pre-existing right.[2] Chapter lv provides redress for past wrongful amerce-

---

[1] Compare chapter xlii of the Charter with Bracton, fol. 1286: utlagatus rite et secundum legem terre; and Glanville, Lib. vii, cap. 17: cum quis vero per legem terre fuerit utlagatus. See Appendix.

[2] Stubbs says that "the judicium parium which is mentioned in Magna Charta . . . covers all cases of amercement in the county, the hundred and the manorial courts. . . ." (Const. Hist., i, p. 664.) The Great Charter, however, does not expressly allow the mere freeman to be amerced by his peers. By chapter xx it is provided that the freeman shall be amerced—per sacramentum proborum hominum de visneto; this is something substantially different to amercement by the peers of the court, if we mean by peers the persons having the judicium. The principle is no doubt extended to manorial courts by chapter lx, and was very widely adopted; but we find some exceptions to the rule. See, for example, Borough Customs, Selden Soc., p. 241: Et si quis gratis se ad illam inquisitionem absentaverit, amercietur ad voluntatem ballivi et non per pares suos. (Hereford, temp. Edward I (?)); see ibid, p. 265: Et si faciant, pro perjuriis habeantur vel ad voluntatem ballivi amercientur et non per pares suos. The rule appears in Glanville, Lib. ix, cap. xi. For the practice of the crown with regard to amercements see Rot. Cur. Reg., i, pp. 169–70; Select Pleas of the Crown, Selden Soc., case 44; also appendix to chapter ix, infra.

In Normandy there was already, it would appear, a fixed scale for amercements. Cap. lvi of the Très Ancien Coutumier provides:

ments, but, exhibiting what we may describe under the circumstances as a very charming versatility of language, defines such wrongful amercements as—*amerciamenta facta injuste et contra legem terre.*

We may sum up this part of the argument by saying that the Charter affords quite sufficient internal evidence to prove that the framers used "lawful judgment of peers" and the "law of the land" as to some extent convertible terms. In fact, what the barons of England required of the king is fairly adequately and very felicitously summed up in a passage of Matthew Paris : [*quod*] *omnes homines suos secundum justa curiae suae judicia judicaret, quodque singulis redderet jura sua.* By "lex terre" they claimed "*justa* judicia," while by "legale judicium parium suorum" they meant simply "justa *judicia.*" Excellent this for the layman, but not precise enough for the lawyer.

If we now turn again to the Charter we shall find it throws some further light on the requisites of a justum judicium. Chapter xviii provides as follows :—

> Recognitiones de nova dissaisina, de morte antecessoris et de ultima presentatione, non capiantur nisi in suis comitatibus et hoc modo; nos, vel, si extra regnum fuerimus, capitalis justiciarius noster, mittemus duos justiciarios per unumquemque comitatum per quatuor vices in anno, qui cum quatuor militibus cujuslibet comitatus electis per comitatum capiant in comitatu et in die et loco comitatus assisas predictas.[1]

(1) Barones jurati faciunt venire servientes de vicecomitatu et quinque milites legaliores patrie, vel duodecim, vel viginti, juxta magnitudinem baillie, ad cognoscendum sacramento catalla eorum, qui in assisia illa [in] misericordia ducis ceciderunt. (2) Si comes vel baro vel archiepiscopus vel episcopus vel abbas, c. libras dabit; miles vero ad minus dabit xx vel ***; rusticus vel alius de populo, v. solidos vel nichil. (Coutumiers de Normandie, ed. Tardif, i, p. 45.)

Walter Map, De Nugis Curialium (Camden Soc.), p. 225, makes the following assertion : Cum quis comes aut magnorum principum ex judicio cadebat in regis ut dici solet misericordiam, multum erat dare c. solidos, quos tamen infra triennium persolvebat, et de querelis prius ortis pax in foro regio cuicunque sub misericordia constituto. Walter Map wrote about 1180–90.

[1] Compare cap. xxviii of the Très Ancien Coutumier : Tres vel quatuor milites, vel barones, electi sunt ad assisias tenendas ; . . . (Coutumiers de Normandie, ed. Tardif, i, p. 25).

And chapter xix provides :—

Et si in die comitatus assise predicte capi non possint, tot milites et libere tenentes remaneant de illis qui interfuerint comitatui die illo, per quos possint judicia sufficienter fieri, secundum quod negocium fuerit majus vel minus.

Two justices and four knights of the shire are to take these assizes; that is to say, they are to constitute the bench. For the days when the county is in session no further provision is made; but for subsequent days so many knights and freeholders must remain—per quos possint judicia sufficienter fieri. The intent of chapter xix is obvious; its object is to provide for the presence of recognitors : their verdict and the consequent sentence together form the essential requirements of a judgment within the meaning of this chapter.

An assize taken in accordance with chapters xviii and xix must, for the reasons given above, be treated as satisfying the requirements of a judicium parium; therefore, for the purposes of these assizes, justices and knights were the peers of any man.

The position of the recognitors at the assizes is not sufficiently defined by the Charter to justify a conclusion either for or against the view that recognitors were regarded as quasi-judges and might be challenged by a litigant if they were not his peers. Not many years later the question became an important one, and a more or less affirmative conclusion was arrived at.

Next to the meaning of a judicium parium the most controverted question relating to the construction of the Charter arises from the use of the word "vel" in chapter xxxix. I have shown that the Charter treats judgment of peers and the law of the land as to a great extent convertible terms. A large area was covered by both, but their boundaries were by no means quite conterminous. There is not the smallest doubt that prior to the Charter (and subsequently) judgment was not a condition precedent to the arrest and imprisonment of a felon caught flagrante delicto; on the contrary, the law of the land, no less than the most elementary principles of public safety, required that such persons should be instantly captured and secured. The law of the land, in other words, overlapped judgment of peers; and the converse proposition is equally true. It is perhaps problematical whether exile was a punishment which the law of the land was competent to inflict;[1] but the phrase "super eum ire" had especial reference to proceedings vi et armis[2] which were plainly extra-judicial. The question consequently arises: Did the famous clause xxxix intend to alter this and impose a double test; to insist upon a judicium parium for everything therein specified, to prohibit everything outside the scope of the law of the land? Or to state the case more concisely, must we change "vel" into "et"?

With extraordinarily misplaced zeal various commentators have set themselves to show that the word "vel" is not invariably used as a disjunctive, "in mediæval Latin 'vel' will often stand for 'and.'" To the lawyer, as distinguished from the theorist, such an argument seems the acme of absurdity, it is a violation of the most elementary principles. It is a fact, and I should imagine it is also common knowledge, that in modern English "or" will often stand for "and";[3] this particular blunder is by no means confined to the mediæval Latin writer. But whosoever asserts that such a blunder has been made in any particular instrument must

---

[1] In Pollock and Maitland the following statement is made (vol. ii, p. 518): "True exile is unknown, but the criminal who has taken sanctuary abjures the realm, and occasionally, by way of grace, other criminals are allowed to do the like."—"Bracton, fol. 136, § 4," they add in a note, "speaks in romanesque terms of exile." Perhaps, but so does the Chancery of John. See appendix.

[2] See appendix.

[3] "You will find it said in some cases that 'or' means 'and'; but 'or' never does mean 'and.' There may be a context which shows that 'or' is used for 'and' by mistake. Suppose a man said: 'I give the black cow, on which I usually ride, to A. B.'; and he rode a black horse. Of course the horse would pass, but I do not think even a modern annotator of cases would put in the marginal note 'cow' means 'horse.' You correct the wrong word by the context" (per Jessel, M.R. in Morgan v. Thomas 51 L.J., Q.B., p. 557). See also Stroud, Judicial Dict., s.v., "Or read as And"; and Theobald on Wills, 6th ed., pp. 400, 674–6.

prove it from the instrument itself. The Great Charter affords no justification for doing violence to the natural meaning of chapter xxxix, quite the reverse, for the suggested construction involves at least one gross absurdity, namely, that a judgment of peers must always precede arrest. Under these circumstances we are forced to allow that this chapter means what it says; it requires compliance either with one condition or the other, lawful judgment of peers or the law of the land, not both.

To complete our evidence as to the meaning of the terms *judicium parium* and *lex terre* we may and must have recourse to extrinsic evidence. The term peer was at this period a very common word used to describe many different things: it was by no means a technical word. This fact is important, — it makes a wide and not a restricted interpretation the more probable. Those meanings of the word which have obviously no possible connection with judicature we need not deal with;[1] but, having excluded these, the rest must be closely examined.

The word peer was still primarily used to designate co-vassalship pure and simple without restriction as to rank or condition.[2] Even the villein who purchased land was said by one writer to have for his peers the other tenants of the lord of his fee: "Nus ne doit douter se li hons de poeste tient fief de son droit, et aucuns plede à li de ce que au fief apartient, que il ne doie estre demesné par ses pers, aussi comme s'il estoit gentix hons."[3] Conversely we find negative definitions excluding the lord.[4] The Grand Coutumier de Normandie gives the following: "Pares enim sunt cum unus alii non subditur homagio, dominatione vel antenatione."[5]

---

[1] Glanville, perhaps, ought not to be passed over.—Omnes filie erunt pares ad hereditatem patris. (Lib. vii, cap. 3.)—Quia dominus rex nullum habere potest parem, multo minus superiorem . . . (Lib. vii, cap. 10.)

[2] See Libri Feudorum, Antiqua, ed. Lehmann, passim; Assises de Jerusalem, i, passim; Beaumanoir, Coutumes des Beauvoisis, passim; Pierre de Fontaines, ed. Marnier, pp. 228–9, 234–6, 254.

[3] Beaumanoir, Coutumes des Beauvoisis, xlviii, 11.

[4] Ibid., i, 15.

[5] Tardif, p. 328. Compare, however, ibid., p. 202, cap. lxxxv, s. 5:

Q

In a large number of communities and at many feudal courts the word peer was becoming a title of office or honour, conferred upon a select body of burghers who exercised certain civil and criminal jurisdictions, or upon a few of the chief vassals of a particular county or district.[1] In 1216 we

... versus autem dominum sexta manu in curia domini sui; si autem in curia domini superioris placitaverit, se tercia manu disraisniabit versus dominum, et dominus versus hominem suum simili modo; in curia enim domini superioris placitando sunt quasi pares.

[1] In 1145 we hear of the twelve peers of Valenciennes; Cluny, Recueil des Chartes de l'Abbaye de Cluny, Doc. Ined., vol. v, p. 449, no. 4099. The peers of Lille are mentioned in 1173: et precipue militum ejusdem loci qui pares dicuntur. . . . (Cartulaire de S. Pierre de Lille, i, pp. 41-2, no. 33.) See Borough Customs, Selden Soc., p. 167:—Burgensis si de pari sacramentum acceperit, nisi de debito in forisfacto erit; si de altero quam pari quietus erit. (A.D. 1194, Pontefract, cap. xviii.) See ibid., p. 172:—Item si aliquis burgensis queritur de aliqua re et alius adversus eum negaverit, et querens per judicium nominabit duos testes et ex illis habebit unum ad diem et ad terminum, et ipse potest habere quemcunque legalem hominem testem et alium burgensem ad legem ponere; defensor autem contra burgensem ad jusjurandum ponetur tercia manu per pares suos. (Preston, cap. viii, twelfth century.) Compare ibid., pp. 140, 181, 188, 241, 265. For the twelve peers of Flanders, see Hist. des Comtes de Guines, in Mon. Germ. Hist., Scriptores 24; and Bibl. de l'École des Chartes, t. 60, p. 83, n. 4. A charter of the countess Eleanor, circa 1184, and a royal charter dated 1195, confirming the former, contain the subjoined reference to the peers of Vermandois:—Cum primum communia acquisita fuit omnes Viromandie pares qui tunc temporis majores habebantur et omnes clerici, salvo ordine suo, omnesque milites, salva fidelitate comitis, firmiter tenendam juraverunt. (Livre Rouge de S. Quentin, Bouchot et Lemaire, p. 320; Ordon. des Rois de Fr., xi, p. 270.) The commune of Rouen was regulated by a charter of John:—De centum vero paribus eligentur viginti quatuor assensu centum parium, qui singulis annis removebuntur; quorum duodecim eschevini vocabuntur, et alii duodecim consultores. Isti viginti quatuor, in principio sui anni jurabunt se servaturos jura sancte ecclesie et fidelitatem domini regis atque justiciam, quod et ipsi recte judicabunt secundum suam conscienciam. . . . (Giry, Les Etablissements de Rouen, App. s. 2. Cf. ibid., s. 14 and s. 22.) For the expression "peers and other nobles" see Gislebert de Mons (ed. 1904), p. 119:—Quid autem faciendum inde esset, dominus comes [Hanoniensis] fidelium suorum, Jacobi [de Avethnis] scilicet, parium et aliorum nobilium, judicio commisit. (A.D. 1175.)

are introduced to that notable college of eminent feudatories, the [12] peers of France.[1]

Peer and baron very commonly, and peer and justice or baron and justice occasionally are treated as synonymous terms. About the year 1170 the following statement is made in a charter of Philip of Flanders and Vermandois: "Rorgo Radulfum adduxit, qui nullam ei guarandiam tulit, nec judicium curie et parium suorum Viromandensium super hoc volens audire absque licentia de curia recessit; Rorgo autem, taliter a suo domino derelictus, judicio baronum Viromandensium qui astabant, quia guarantiam sicut debuerat non habuit, michi adjudicatus est."[2] Instances of this kind are numerous; they illustrate the two points of view; the vassal speaks of his peers, the lord of his barons.[3] That peer and justice or baron and justice should sometimes be treated as convertible terms is merely a further development of this

---

[1] Layettes du Trésor des Chartes, i, pp. 431–2, no. 1182. Only six persons are styled peers of France in this document. (See further on this subject infra chap. viii.)

[2] Extract from the Cartulaire Noir de Corbie, Bibl. de l'École des Chartes, t. 60, p. 82.

[3] Thus Louis VIII in 1225: De quibus et aliis feodis de regno Francorum moventibus fuit abjudicatus Johannes quondam rex Anglie, per judicium parium suorum Francie, baronum nostrorum. (Annales Ecclesiastici, t. 20, p. 482.) Thus Louis's ambassadors to Rome in 1216: "Consuetudo est in regno Francorum quod rex habet omnimodam jurisdictionem in homines suos ligios; et rex Angliae erat suus homo ligius, tanquam comes et dux; ergo licet esset alias rex inunctus, tamen tanquam comes et dux erat de jurisdictione domini regis Francorum. Sed si comes et dux in regno Francorum delinqueret, posset et deberet judicari ad mortem per pares suos. Immo si non esset dux vel comes vel homo ligius regis Franciae, et deliquisset in regno Franciae, ratione delicti in regno perpetrati, potuerunt barones eum judicare ad mortem. . . ." (Matthew Paris, ii, p. 657.) Compare the case of bishop William of St. Carilef, supra, p. 210. Duodecim pares vel barones castro Ardee appenditios instituit. (Hist. des Comtes de Guines in Mon. Germ. Hist., Scriptores, 24, p. 614.) Ut hereditario jure cum duodecim Flandrensis curie paribus et baronibus sedeat et judicet. . . . (Ibid., p. 619.) See also Delisle, Catal. des Actes de Philippe Auguste, no. 1739; and Langlois, Textes, p. 33; and generally Lot, Revue Historique, t. 54, p. 36; and Guilhiermoz, Bibl. de l'École des Chartes, t. 60, p. 81 n.

dual aspect. A singular instance is furnished by one of John's charters to the Jews: complaints by Christians against the Jews were to be judged *per pares Judei*,[1] and there cannot be the least doubt as to the persons thus indicated: they were the justices or custodes of the Jews. With the "barons" of the Exchequer we are all familiar.

With regard to the phrase "lex terre," modern authorities have expressed various views. One writes in this manner: "The expression 'per legem terre' simply required judicial proceedings according to the nature of the case; the duel, ordeal, or compurgation in criminal cases, the duel, witnesses, charters, or recognition in property cases."[2] Another states the case cautiously in his text: "No freeman could be punished except in accordance with the law of England. These often-quoted words were used in Magna Carta with special though not perhaps exclusive reference to the narrow technical meaning of 'lex' which was so prominent[3] in 1215." In a note, however, the following comment is to be found: "It has already been shown that the right of 'standing mute,' that is, virtually, of demanding ordeal, was only abolished in 1772. . . . Five and a half centuries were thus allowed to pass before the criminal law was bold enough, in defiance of a fundamental principle of Magna Carta, to deprive accused men of their 'law.'"[4] The pro-

---

[1] Rot. Cart. R.C., i, p. 93; the charter is dated 10th April, 1201. See also Select Pleas of the Jews, Selden Soc.

Robertus de Tatteshala reddit compotum de una marca ut scribatur in magno rotulo quod disrationavit in curia regis apud Westmonasterium coram W. Rothomagensi archiepiscopo, Ricardo Londoniensi episcopo, Galfrido filio Petri et aliis justiciariis domini regis, villam de Wutton versus Willelmum filium Hervei; et quod idem Willelmus recognovit coram predictis baronibus prefatam villam de Wutton cum pertinentiis esse jus et hereditatem ipsius Roberti. (Pipe Roll, 6 Richard I, cited Madox, Exchequer, i, p. 200.)

[2] Bigelow, Hist. of Procedure, p. 155 n.

[3] This is absurd; probably it is an illogical inference from the action of the Lateran Council forbidding clergy to take part in the ordeals. Technical legal terms are not prominent in time of war. The ordeals were subsequently lamented as the *judicium ignis et aquae*. Note Book, no. 592, Foedera R.C., vol. i, p. 154.

[4] McKechnie, Magna Carta, p. 440.

position is unsound, the corollary untenable; even the expression "law of England" is singularly infelicitous· Intrinsic evidence alone sufficiently proves that the "lex terre" of the Charter has the same vague popular signification which the words "law of the land" bear at the present day;[1] while extrinsic evidence shows that "lex terre" was, even by lawyers,[2] quite as commonly used in this sense as in any other.[3]

[1] Compare chapter lv of the Charter: Omnes fines qui injuste et contra legem terre facti sunt nobiscum, et omnia amerciamenta facta injuste et contra legem terre omnino condonentur. . . . The parallel passage in the Articles is clause 37 : Ut fines qui facti sunt pro dotibus, maritagiis, hereditatibus et amerciamentis injuste et contra legem terre omnino condonentur. . . . Chapter xlii of the Charter : . . . exceptis imprisonatis et utlagatis secundum legem regni. . . . Chapter xlv of the Charter : Nos non faciemus justiciarios, constabularios, vicecomites vel ballivos, nisi de talibus qui sciant legem regni et eam bene velint observare; and clause 42 of the Articles : Ut rex faciat justiciarios, constabularios, vicecomites et ballivos de talibus qui sciant legem terre et eam bene velint observare. Chapter lvi of the Charter refers to the lex Anglie, lex Wallie and lex Marchie. Contrast with chapter xxxviii of the Charter where lex is used without any addition and obviously in a technical sense.

[2] Thus Glanville in his Tractatus (ed. 1604).

(Prologus) Leges namque Anglicanas licet non scriptas leges appellari non videtur absurdum, cum hoc ipsum lex sit quod principi placet et legis habet vigorem. . . .

(Lib. i, cap. 2, fol. 1) Crimen quod in legibus dicitur crimen lese majestatis.

(Lib. ii, cap. 3, fol. 15) Et ille campio tanquam victus omnem legem terre amittet . . . et preterea legem terre amittet.

(Lib. ii, cap. 19, fol. 22) . . . legem terre amittentes.

(Lib. v, cap. 5, fol. 36) Quia si quis prius nativus hoc modo ad libertatem perductus contra extraneum aliquem ad diracionationem faciendam produceretur in curia vel ad aliquam legem terre faciendam. . . .

(Lib. v, cap. 6, fol. 37) . . . villenagio eo ipso legem terre tanquam nativus amittit.

(Lib. vii, cap. 1, fol. 44) . . . secundum leges Romanas. Cf. Lib. vii, cap. 15, fol. 57.

(Lib. vii, cap. 5, fol. 51) . . . libera enim dicitur esse cujuscunque ultima voluntas secundum has leges sicut et secundum alias leges.

Note continued on next page.

(Lib. vii, cap. 16, fol. 58) . . . lege usurarii . . .

(Lib. vii, cap. 17, fol. 59) . . . cum quis vero per legem terre fuerit utlagatus.

(Lib. x, cap. 3, fol. 77) . . . et si in tali crimine obierit damnabitur tanquam usurarius per legem terre.

(Lib. x, cap. 5, fol. 79) . . . ante legem vadiatam. . . .

(Lib. x, cap. 14, fol. 85) Quippe generaliter verum est quod conventio legem vincit.

(Lib. xiv, cap. 1, fol. 112, 113) . . . per legem apparentem purgandus est. . . . Si vero per hujusmodi legem super capitali crimine fuerit quis convictus . . . . . . et lege victi censeatur.

(Lib. xiv, cap. 2, fol. 114) . . . ob infamiam autem non solet juxta legem terre aliquis per legem apparentem se purgare licet aliter per assisam fieri possit.

Now turn to the Très Ancien Coutumier.

Chapter lxiii is entitled De Legibus and is as follows :—

Deinde placitores populo plures leges faciebant vadiare, licet per unum repta[men]tum et uniloquium reptati fuissent. Quod non licet, quia, si aliquis de pluribus rebus per unum reptamentum reptatus fuerit, per unam legem se purgabit, excepto tamen quod, si contigerit per hec verba plura duella posse vadiari, plures leges vadiabuntur.

The following chapter recounts how a man was accused of carrying " in collo suo xl. hestres."—" De hoc voluerunt placitores quod de unoquoque hestre unam legem vadiaret."

In chapter 1 :—". . . mulier vero fustata recedat et legem testimonii vir amittat."—". . . omnis enim per duellum convictus [legem] testimonii amittit."

The ordeals are always referred to as "judicia." See chapters xxxviii, xxxix, l, and li. And note the following uses of "lex."

(c. 15.) . . . Vulneratus vel ejus adversarius deliberabit se per jus jurandum juxta legem patrie.

(c. 40.) . . . sacramento se purgabit juxta morem patrie.

(c. 26.) . . . legis statuta scientes. [The custumal is called "Statuta et consuetudines Normannie."]

(c. 82.) Quicunque . . . exoniationes suas salvaverit per legem superius scriptam . . .

Note finally chapter lxxxv :—". . . vadiata recognitione."

[3] John of Salisbury in his Polycraticus constantly and invariably uses the word "lex" in the popular sense. For example Lib. iv, cap. 6 :—Quod debet legem Dei habere prae mente et oculis semper. Lex occurs here passim. Also Lib. vii, cap. 20 :—De legibus secularium principum. And Lib. viii, cap. 8 :—De sumptuariis legibus.

Note continued on next page.

Compare the following: . . . fiscalis ratio seu publicae rei necessitas a lege communi eximit. (Letter of Hubert archbishop of Canterbury, 1194-8, printed Giles; Letters of Peter of Blois, vol. ii, p. 18.) Legum vero scientia impudica est. Denique pro parte maxima leges ab ethnicis institutae sunt: Deus autem dedit legem vitae et disciplinae. . . . Et quis, quaeso, spiritus hodie in legum professoribus dominatur? (Letter of Peter of Blois, ibid., p. 38.)

In the collection of the letters of Gilbert Foliot "lex" is once used in a technical sense:—Audio in curia domini abbatis Radingensis tibi legem adjudicatam esse, ut manu duodecima jures te nunquam vel predecessores tuos de terra de Samefeld ecclesiae de Lumin quinque solidos, quos a te quaesit, reddidisse. (Vol. i, p. 128.) But the same prelate frequently uses the word in its popular sense, e.g.: Quod pro eo adversus abbatem de Gevesten pronuntiavimus, juris et legum observantia fuit. (Ibid., p. 296.) Immo quod ipsi formam legum secuti et canonum, multis nobis assidentibus, et judicavimus et judicatum executioni legitimae mandare curavimus. (Ibid., p. 306.)

To conclude our evidence upon this point we will call in Wendover, and note each instance when he mentions the word "lex" while describing the events of 1215 :—

p. 113. . . . petierunt quasdam libertates et leges regis Edwardi . . . prout in charta regis Henrici primi et legibus praedictis adscriptae continentur; asserebant praeterea quod . . . illas leges et libertates antiquas promiserat . . .

p. 114. De principalibus exactoribus legum et libertatum.

p. 115. . . . quae essent leges et libertates quas quaerebant. At illi nuntiis praelibatis schedulam quandam porrexerunt, quae ex parte maxima leges antiquas et regni consuetudines continebat . . .

Capitula quoque legum et libertatum . . . partim ex legibus regis Edwardi antiquis excerpta . . .

p. 118. . . . leges et libertates quas petebant . . .

p. 119. Tandem igitur . . . rex Johannes . . . leges subscriptas et libertates concessit et charta sua in hunc modum confirmavit.

p. 135. . . . quod leges et libertates praedictas observarent . . . sicut in charta continebantur.

p. 138. . . . exigentes ab eo [Johanne rege] quasdam leges et libertates iniquas . . .

p. 141. (Quoting the pope's letter which quashed the Charter.) . . . ita quod . . . in curia sua per pares eorum secundum leges et consuetudines regni suborta dissensio sopiretur.

p. 143. (Quoting the papal letter to the barons.) . . . eodem rege parato in curia sua vobis per pares vestros secundum leges et consuetudines regni justitiae plenitudinem exhibere . . .

The citations are from Rolls Series [84], vol. ii.

None the less, the fact that " lex " had at that time various other meanings is a circumstance to be taken into account. In its narrowest sense, it was the technical term for compurgation ;[1] it had a broader meaning which included the ordeals,[2] and certain other meanings which it is safer to illustrate than attempt to define.[3]   On the other hand it must be noted that

[1] Customs of Newcastle, Stubbs, Select Charters, p. 112 : Si quis burgensis de re aliqua appellaverit non potest super burgensem pugnare, sed per legem se defendit burgensis.   Compare Giry, Etablissements de Rouen, app. s. 14 : et si conviciatus non habet testes de paribus, querela ejus deducetur lege terre. The context shows that compurgation is meant ; see ibid., s. 22 and s. 46.

Select Pleas of the Crown, Selden Soc., case 61 (A.D. 1202) : . . . defendat se xii manu in adventu justiciariorum.   Vadiavit legem.   Plegius de lege Willelmus filius Ascelini.   See also ibid., case 82 (A.D. 1200), and case 178 (A.D. 1225.)

[2] Dialogus de Scaccario, ii, 7 : . . . leges candentis ferri vel aquae.

Rotuli Curiae Regis, ii, 173 (A.D. 1200) : . . . consideratum est quod Warinus defendat se judicio ferri.   Vadiavit legem.

[3] Compare Glanville supra.   The following instances are noteworthy : Propositis igitur legibus Anglicanis secundum tripartitam earum distinctionem, hoc est Merchenslage, Denelage, Westsaxenlage, quasdam reprobavit, quasdam autem approbans, illis transmarinas Neustriae leges, que ad regni pacem tuendam efficacissime videbantur, adjecit.   (Dialogus de Scaccario, i, 16.)   Et quod terre et tenementa infra predictum burgum et hundredum tractentur per legem Bretolli et legem baronye et legem Anglescherie secundum quod terre et tenementa solent tractari per predictas leges. (Charter of John to Shrewsbury, Rot. Cart., p. 142.)   Et de terris de quibus ad me clamaverint rectum eis tenebo lege civitatis. (London Charter, s. 10, Borough Customs, Selden Soc., p. 231.)   Nul homme de la cité ne doit estre mis par plus ke par xii bons pleges selun la lai de la vile. (London Add. MS., xxiii, s. 2, ibid., p. 19.)   Leges et jura regni. (Hoveden, iv, p. 12.)   Secundum antiquam legem civitatis.   (Charter of Richard to Winchester, Foedera R.C., i, p. 51.)   Quod nullus de misericordia pecunie judicetur nisi secundum legem quam habent cives nostri Lundoniarum. (Charter of Richard to Lincoln, ibid., i, p. 52.)   The following examples may be added : Alioquin si modo predicto probare non poterit, tunc secundum legem terre adjudicabitur. (Fordwich, s. 15, Borough Customs, Selden Soc., p. 60 (fourteenth century).)   Nul home ne put autre namer pur dette ne pur rente ke seyt venu al cunté ou al levé ou al mandement l'apostoille par ley de tere. (Exeter, s. 35, ibid., p. 104 (circa 1282).)   Son aversere eit son defens sulump lei de tere.   (Winchester, s. 49, ibid., p. 202 (circa 1280).)   See also Pollock and Maitland, Hist. of English Law, i, p. 175 ; Thayer, Evidence, pp. 199–200.

the addition of the word "terre" or the like is very uncommon in England when "lex" is being used in a technical sense, and that the Charter Roll of John habitually uses the word *judicium*—not *lex*—to describe the ordeals, and constantly employs the word *lex* in its popular sense.[1]

With these materials before us let us reconsider the meaning of judicium parium in chapter xxxix of the Charter. To begin with, it may be observed, there are in reality at least three quite distinct questions which we have to answer: "When a man can claim to be judged by his peers?" is one, "Who are a man's peers?" is another, and a third question is "What constitutes a sufficient quorum?"

The answer to question number one is simple enough. The man must be a freeman, in loco defendentis, and the matter must either be one where the law of the land requires a judgment, or one to which the law of the land does not extend.

The answer to the second question is not so simple. Take the particular case of an under-tenant tried in the king's court for murder. His only peers in the primitive feudal sense of co-vassalship are the other tenants of his mesne lord, but in the king's court they are not recognised as his peers, and he certainly cannot claim to be judged by them. It is shown conclusively by chapter lx that the rights of an under-tenant, as such, in the court of his mesne lord are outside the scope of chapter xxxix, therefore the mere freeman in a large proportion of the cases coming within the provisions of chapter xxxix has no peers in any feudal sense of the word. In fact, every meaning of peer but one is quite inapplicable to the under-tenant; and, so far as he is concerned, we must answer this question in the words of the Grand Coutumier de Normandie: "pares sunt cum unus alii non subditur homagio dominatione vel antenatione."[2] So far as the tenants in capite are concerned there is no reason why peer should be given any other than its primary feudal meaning of co-vassalship. The necessity for some such

[1] See above, p. 218, n. 2.
[2] In another passage of the Grand Coutumier the expression *quasi pares* is used, see above, p. 226.

classification in construing the Charter must have been perfectly obvious at the time ; but the actual classification which the draftsman had in his mind was evidently not that of under-tenant and tenant-in-chief, which would have been more theoretical than practical ; but freeman on the one hand, earls and barons on the other. This is borne out by the provisions for affeering amercements. The freeman is to be amerced by men of probity from the vicinage, amercement by peers would not have given him what he wanted ;[1] earls and barons, however, are to be amerced by their peers. Here, again, the Grand Coutumier affords an admirable key to the true interpretation of chapter xxxix. "Barones autem per pares suos debent judicari ; alii vero omnes per eos qui non possunt a judiciis amoveri." How far the under-tenant had the right to exclude his mesne lord we are not concerned with here. That an earl or baron, either in criminal or civil cases, had any right to exclude all persons who were not, strictly speaking, earls or barons there is no evidence whatsoever ; no such right existed before the Charter, and there is nothing in the Charter to confer it.

The third question raises many points of considerable interest. Every earl, baron and freeman is to have the judgment of his peers, not of one or some of them, but of his peers generally. It is not, however, contemplated that in every case the whole body of peers must take part in the judgment. Even if disseizin, par excellence, requires a judgment of peers, two justices and four knights constitute a sufficient bench for hearing all assizes of novel disseizin. The sufficiency of a judgment in this respect must be tested by precedent, the law of the land and the requirements of each case. A judgment of the whole body of peers is unexceptionable ; but when some peers only give judgment, clearly the onus is on the king to show that such judgment is lawful and sufficient. On the 27th of June, 1215, writs were issued to the sheriffs to seize the lands, tenements and chattels of all contrariants. "Et hoc provisum est," the writs conclude, "per

---

[1] Note Glanville, Lib. ix, cap. xi : Est autem misericordia domini regis qua quis per juramentum legalium hominum de visineto eatenus amerciandus est ne aliquid de suo honorabili contenemento amittat.

judicium domini Cantuariensis archiepiscopi et baronum regni nostri."[1] Here is a judgment which cannot claim to be a lawful judgment except by virtue of the concurrence of the whole body of peers.[2]

The sudden and extraordinary prominence given to the judicium parium by the Great Charter is perhaps partly to be explained as an unconsidered example of a not uncommon natural phenomenon. At a crisis in the affairs of England somebody produces a charter of liberties attributed to Henry the First: immediately the laws and customs of Henry[3] are turned to as the one fertile source from which long-lost liberties may be regenerated, and a new charter is conceived. After a short but bitter period of gestation the Great Charter is brought forth. Some of the parent laws referred particularly to this *judicium parium*, and when the offspring appears this phrase is a predominant feature.

---

[1] Patent Roll, 17 John, m. 21 ; printed by Rymer, Foedera R.C., vol. i, p. 134.

[2] Obviously to constitute a *legale judicium*, the law of the land, if there is any on the point, must be complied with ; but a judgment in which all the barons of the realm concur must needs be lawful, because none has authority to overrule it.

[3] In hac autem absolutione juravit rex Johannes quod . . . bonas leges antecessorum suorum et precipue leges Edwardi regis revocaret, et iniquas destrueret. . . . (Wendover, Rolls Series, ii, p. 81 (A.D. 1213).)

In hoc colloquio, ut fama refert, archiepiscopus memoratus, convocatis seorsum quibusdam regni proceribus, coepit affari eos secretius in hunc modum ; "Audistis," inquit, "quomodo tempore quo apud Wintoniam regem absolvi, ipsum jurare compulerim quod leges iniquas destrueret et leges bonas, videlicet leges Edwardi, revocaret et in regno faceret ab omnibus observari. Inventa est quoque nunc carta quaedam Henrici primi regis Angliae per quam, si volueritis, libertates diu amissas poteritis ad statum pristinum revocare. . . ." (Ibid., p. 84.)

Rex tenuit curiam suam ad Natale Domini apud Wigorniam vix per spatium unius diei ; deinde cum festinatione Londonias veniens, apud Novum Templum hospitio sese recepit. Venientesque ad regem ibidem supradicti magnates, in lascivo satis apparatu militari, petierunt quasdam libertates et leges regis Edwardi cum aliis libertatibus sibi et regno Angliae et ecclesiae Anglicanae concessis confirmari, prout in carta regis Henrici primi et legibus predictis adscriptae continentur. . . . (Ibid., ii, p. 113 (A.D. 1215).)

Had the Great Charter always been reissued with no substantial omissions, chapter xxxix would have been less easily misunderstood. After a critical examination of the whole original document there can be no reasonable doubt as to the true meaning of this chapter; but, standing alone or with the limited context of subsequent reissues, its meaning is decidedly obscure. It is most important to realise this fact. What the chapter did mean is a question very interesting no doubt to the antiquary and even to the historian, but of no practical moment. It was the obscurity of the chapter when reissued, the fact that it might mean so many things—which supplied the congenial soil wherein the principle of trial by peers was able to expand and grow to maturity. Indeed, the Charter as a whole became the Bible of the constitution, the oracle which men might appeal to and construe, now this way, now that, according to the exigencies of the moment.

APPENDIX TO CHAPTER VII

A COMPARATIVE ANALYSIS OF THE LANGUAGE AND PROVISIONS IN CHAPTER THIRTY-NINE OF MAGNA CHARTA

Nullus liber homo capiatur vel imprisonetur aut dissaisiatur aut utlagetur aut exuletur aut aliquo modo destruatur nec super eum ibimus nec super eum mittemus nisi per legale judicium parium suorum vel per legem terre. (Magna Carta, c. 39.)

Rex omnibus ad quos litere presentes pervenerint salutem. Sciatis nos concessisse baronibus nostris qui contra nos sunt quod nec eos nec homines suos capiemus nec dissaisiemus nec super eos per vim vel per arma ibimus nisi per legem regni nostri vel per judicium parium suorum in curia nostra donec· . . . Apud Windesor x die Maii anno regni nostri xvj. (Rot. Pat. R.C., p. 141.)

Ne corpus liberi hominis capiatur nec imprisonetur nec dissaisietur nec utlagetur nec exuletur nec aliquo modo destruatur nec rex eat vel mittat super eum vi nisi per judicium parium suorum vel per legem terre. (Articles of the Barons, c. 29.)

(Capiatur) (Concedit rex Johannes quod non capiet hominum absque judicio nec aliquid accipiet pro justitia nec injustitiam faciet.—See Eng. Hist. Rev., viii, 288 ; ix, 117, 326.)

(Capiatur) Item quod non capiantur sine judicio nec detineantur contra vadium et plegium nisi in casibus secundum formam in carta domini patris nostri contentam. (Inspex. Charter of William Marshal, Charter Roll, 5 Edward III, no. 46,/4.)

(Capiatur) Item burgensis captus a ballivo dimittatur per vadia et plegios nisi sit pro morte hominis captus et per judicium hundredi deducatur de hoc quod ad hundredum pertinet. (Ibid., 2.)

(Capiatur) Est autem mos burgi quod pro accusatione non debet capi aliquis burgensis a domino vel a preposito si plegios sufficientes habeat. (Preston, 44, twelfth century ; Borough Customs, Selden Soc., p. 19.)

(Capiatur) Et qui invenietur per sacramentum predictorum rettatus vel publicatus quod fuerit robator vel murdrator vel latro vel receptor eorum . . . capiatur et eat ad juisam aquae . . . (Assize of Clarendon, s. 2.)

(Capiatur) Item in criminalibus causis ubi sequi debet capitale judicium, vita videlicet vel mutilatio membrorum, non sequitur attachiamentum aliquod sed corpus talis, quicunque fuerit ille, ab omnibus arrestetur qui sunt ad fidem domini regis, sive inde praeceptum habuerit sive non habuerit. (Bracton, Rolls Series [70], vi, p. 506.)

(Capiatur) Et juratores testantur quod idem Thomas semper post factum illud venit et rediit ad domum suam et terram suam coluit et non fuit captus nec terra sua capta fuit in manum domini regis nisi pridie contra adventum justiciariorum. Et ideo ad judicium de vicecomite. (Select Pleas of the Crown, Selden Soc., no. 153. A.D. 1221.)

(Capiatur vel imprisonetur) Si vero qui fidem se dedisse non diffitetur die nominata venerit nec satisfecerit, si dominus est, ad scaccarium quamdiu sederit detinebitur, fide data in manu marescalli, sicut supra diximus, quod a leugata villae nisi baronum licencia non recedet : soluto vero scaccario illius termini, si nondum satisfecerit, in loco tuto sub libera custodia collocabitur, quousque rex ipse si praesens fuerit, vel praesidens cum aliis assidentibus, quid de ipso agendum fuerit decernat qui fidem se dedisse de satisfaciendo confessus nullo modo satisfecit ; quod si miles vel alius ejus oeconomus venerit nec satisfecerit, pro fide laesa comprehenditur, et marescallo custodiendus tradetur, post solutum scaccarium licite vinculandus, et in carcere mittendus, sive miles fuerit sive non. Miles vero super debito proprio non satisfaciens, cum tamen de satisfaciendo fidem dederit, post solutum scaccarium, non in carcere sed infra septa domus carceralis libere custodietur, fide corporaliter praestita quod inde sine regis vel praesidentis licencia non recedet. (Dialogus de Scaccario, xxi.)

(Capiatur vel imprisonetur) Et si aliquis vicecomes mandaverit alio vicecomiti quod homines fugerint de comitatu suo in alium comitatum pro roberia vel pro murdro vel latrocinio vel receptione eorum vel pro utlagia vel pro retta forestae regis, ille capiat eos : et etiam si per se vel per alios sciat quod tales homines fugerint in comitatum suum, capiat eos et custodiat donec de eis habeat salvos plegios. (Assize of Clarendon, s. 17.)

(Capiatur vel imprisonetur) Et quod nullus burgensis capiatur nec imprisonetur aliqua de causa dum plegios possint et velint invenire. (Warton, c. 9; A.D. 1246–71. Borough Customs, Selden Soc., p. 19.)

(Capiatur vel imprisonetur) Et quod nullus de burgensibus nostris predictis capi nec imprisonari debeat in castro nostro predicto pro aliquibus eis tangentibus dum manucapcionem seu plegiagium ad exteriorem portam ejusdem castri possent invenire nisi in casu felonie cum manuopere tantum capti fuerint, seu pro aliquibus nos aut familias nostras specialiter tangentibus. (Charter of H. le Despencer to Cardiff, A.D. 1340. See Eng. Hist. Rev., xv, p. 517.)

(Capiatur vel imprisonetur) Et Hugo Fullo captus fuit pro morte illa et in gaola positus eo quod predictus Johannes occisus fuit in domo suo. [Hugo is acquitted at the trial.] (See Select Pleas of the Crown, Selden Soc., No. 74, A.D. 1203.)

(Dissaisiatur) Si quis fuerit disseisitus vel elongatus per nos sine legali judicio parium suorum de terris castellis libertatibus vel jure suo statim ea ei restituemus et si contentio super hoc orta fuerit tunc inde fiat per judicium vigintiquinque baronum de quibus fit mentio inferius in securitate pacis: de omnibus autem illis de quibus aliquis disseisitus fuerit vel elongatus sine legali judicio parium suorum per Henricum regem patrem nostrum vel per Ricardum regem fratrem nostrum quae in manu nostra habemus vel quae alii tenent quae nos oporteat warantizare respectum habebimus usque ad communem terminum cruce-signatorum, exceptis illis de quibus placitum motum fuit vel inquisitio facta per preceptum nostrum ante susceptionem crucis nostrae: cum autem redierimus de peregrinatione nostra, vel si forte remanserimus a peregrinatione nostra, statim inde plenam justitiam exhibebimus. (Magna Carta, c. 52.)

(Dissaisiatur) Si quis fuerit disseisitus vel prolongatus per regem sine judicio de terris libertatibus et jure suo statim ei restituatur, et si contentio super hoc orta fuerit tunc inde disponatur per judicium xxv baronum: et ut illi qui fuerint dissaisiti per patrem vel fratrem regis rectum habeant sine dilatione per judicium parium suorum in curia regis: et si rex debeat habere terminum aliorum cruce-signatorum tunc archiepiscopus et episcopi faciant inde judicium ad certum diem, appellatione remota. (Articles of the Barons, c. 25.)

(Dissaisiatur) Si nos dissaisivimus vel elongavimus Walenses de terris vel libertatibus vel rebus aliis sine legali judicio parium suorum in Anglia vel in Wallia eis statim reddantur; et si contentio super hoc orta fuerit tunc inde fiat in Marchia per judicium parium suorum, de tenementis Anglie secundum legem Anglie, de tenementis Wallie secundum legem Wallie, de tenementis Marchie secundum legem Marchie. Idem faciant Walenses nobis et nostris. (Magna Carta, c. 56.)

(Dissaisiatur) De omnibus autem illis de quibus aliquis Wallensium dissaisitus fuerit vel elongatus sine legali judicio parium suorum per Henricum regem patrem nostrum vel Ricardum regem fratrem nostrum que nos in manu nostra habemus vel que alii tenent que nos oporteat warantizare respectum habebimus usque ad communem terminum cruce-signatorum illis exceptis de quibus placitum fuit vel inquisitio facta per preceptum nostrum ante susceptionem crucis nostre: cum autem redierimus vel si forte remanserimus a peregrinatione nostra statim eis inde plenam justiciam exhibebimus secundum leges Wallensium et partes predictas. (Magna Carta, c. 57.)

(Dissaisiatur) Si rex Wallenses dissaisierit vel elongaverit de terris vel libertatibus vel de rebus aliis in Anglia vel in Wallia eis statim sine placito reddantur; et si fuerint dissaisiti vel elongati de tenementis suis Anglie per patrem vel fratrem regis sine judicio parium suorum rex eis sine dilatione justiciam exhibebit, eo modo quo exhibet Anglicis justiciam, de tenementis suis Anglie secundum legem Anglie et de tenementis Wallie secundum legem Wallie et de tenementis Marchie secundum legem Marchie: idem facient Wallenses regi et suis. (Articles of the Barons, c. 44.)

(Dissaisiatur) Por quel coze que li sires prengne en se main ce dont il trueve son home saizi et vestu, s'il ne le prent par jugement de ses pers, il est tenus à resaisir son home tout à plain avant que li hons respondre en cort à coze que ses sires li demande. Et quant il sera resaisis il sires pot propozer contre li ce qu'il li bee à demander, en la presence de ses pers; et li hons doit metre ses deffenses encontre, et puis doit atendre droit par les pers dessus dis. (Beaumanoir, Coutumes du Beauvoisis, c. 2, s. 5 : Soc. de l'Hist. de Fr., i, p. 47.)

(Dissaisiatur) Si quis aliquem sine judicio dissaisiet, ut de feodo et jure suo, vicecomes per judicium debet adunare aldermannum et vicinos de vicineto et ab eis inquirere per juramentum et fidem quam domino regi debeant utrum ille sine judicio dissaisiatus fuisset....(Liber Albus, 114; London add. MSS. xix ; Borough Customs, p. 231 ; post A.D. 1166.)

(Dissaisiatur) Item quod terras et empticia sua et teneuras et vadimonia sua in pace teneant, et ego faciam eis reddi debita sua, si fuerint in pace et justicia mea; et si aliquis post mortem regis Henrici dissaisitus fuerit, faciam eum ressaisiri si fuerit in pace et justicia mea. (Charter of Henry duke of Normandy; Chéruel, Hist. de Rouen, i, p. 243; circa A.D. 1150.)

(Dissaisiatur) J. Dei gratia rex Anglie etc. Sciatis nos dedisse concessisse et hac carta nostra confirmasse regi Kunnoc, totam terram Kunnoc cum omnibus pertinentiis suis habendam et tenendam sibi et heredibus suis de nobis et heredibus nostris quamdiu nobis bene servierint ita quod inde sine judicio curie nostre non debeant dissaisiri. . . . Data [&c.] . . . apud Dovr. xiij die Septembris anno regni nostri decimo septimo. (Rot. Cart. R.C., p. 219.)

(Dissaisiatur) *De libertatibus.*—Rex vicecomiti Lincoln. Scias quod provisum est in curia nostra coram nobis quod decetero nullus homo captus pro morte hominis vel pro alia felonia pro qua debeat imprisonari dissaisietur de terris tenementis vel catallis suis quousque convictus fuerit de felonia de qua rettatus fuerit . . . (Close Roll, 18 Henry III, m. 10d.)

(Dissaisiatur) Et quod terre et tenementa infra predictum burgum et hundredum tractentur per legem Bretolli et legem Baronye et legem Anglescherie secundum quod terre et tenementa solent tractari per predictas leges. (Charter of John to Shrewsbury; Rot. Cart. R.C., p. 142.)

(Utlagetur) Liceat unicuique de cetero exire de regno nostro et redire salvo et secure per terram et per aquam salva fide nostra, nisi tempore gwerre per aliquod breve tempus propter communem utilitatem regni, exceptis imprisonatis et utlagatis secundum legem regni et gente de terra contra nos gwerrina et mercatoribus de quibus fiat sicut predictum est. (Magna Carta, c. 42.)

(Utlagetur) Rex etc. archiepiscopis etc. Sciatis quod nolumus quod aliqua recognitio fiat in Hybernia nisi in curia nostra neque aliquis sit uthlagatus nisi per curiam nostram. Quare vobis mandamus et prohibemus ne de hiis de cetero vos intromittatis. Teste me-ipso apud Berkelay xxviij die Oct. (Rot. Cart. R.C., p. 99.)

(Utlagetur) Cum quis vero per legem terre fuerit utlagatus et postmodum. . . . (Glanville, lib. vii, cap. 17.)

(Utlagetur) Utlagatus rite et secundum legem terre. . . . (Bracton, fol. 1286.)

(Exuletur) Vult etiam dominus rex quod ipsi qui facient legem suam et mundi erunt per legem, si ipsi fuerint de pessimo testimonio et publice et turpiter diffamati testimonio

R

multorum et legalium hominum, forasjurent terras regis, ita quod infra viij dies mare transibunt, nisi aura eos detinuerit, et cum prima aura quam habebunt postea mare transibunt et ultra in Angliam non revertentur nisi per misericordiam domini regis: et ibi sint utlagati, et si redierint capiantur sicut utlagati. (Assize of Clarendon, 14.)

(Exuletur) Et apud Northamptoniam additum est pro rigore justitiae quod dexterum similiter pugnum cum pede amittat et regnum abjuret et infra quadraginta dies a regno exulet. Et si ad aquam mundus fuerit inveniat plegios et remaneat in regno nisi retatus fuerit de murdro vel alia turpi felonia per commune comitatus et legalium militum patriae; de quo si predicto modo retatus fuerit quamvis ad aquam salvus fuerit nihilominus infra quadraginta dies a regno exeat. . . . (Assize of Northampton, 1.)

The following are distinguishable :—

(Exuletur) . . . et si forte dampnati fuerint homines eorum ad mortem vel ad membrorum perdicionem vel in exilium perpetuum. . . . (Charter of John, A.D. 1199; Rot. Cart., p. 18.)

(Exuletur) Johannes etc. Sciatis quod quantum ad nos pertinet perdonavimus Rogerio de Swereford fugam et foris-banistram in eum promulgatam. . . . (Charter of John, A.D. 1200; ibid., p. 99.)

Exile had also a technical meaning :—

(Exuletur) Volumus et concedimus quod invadiamentum dilecti et fidelis nostri Roberti de Turnham quod fecit Hugoni Oisel de manerio de Boutone cum pertinentiis stabile sit et firmum quousque . . . ita tamen quod idem Hugo predictum manerium teneat cum pertinentiis suis sine vasto et exilio usque ad terminum suum. . . . (Charter of John, A.D. 1200; ibid., p. 46.)

(Exuletur) *Justiciario Hibernie pro rege.* . . . Nullum etiam vastum venditionem vel exilium faciatis aut fieri per-mittatis de predictis terris domibus parcis vivariis boscis vel aliquibus rebus aliis que fuerunt predicti comitis [scil. Pem-brokie] in Hibernia. . . . (Close Roll, 18 Henry III, m. 23.)

(Destruatur) Et si dixerit illi cui res tolluntur quod male eum destruat et contra legem et justiciam, tunc. . . . Et si . . .

tunc veniant 3 de ipsis qui praeside sua dicant et pro pares suos sunia nuntiant. (Mon. Germ. Hist., Pertz, Leges, ii, p. 11 ; A.D. 561–84.)

(Destruatur) Si autem aliquis homo destructus fuerit per judicium, sive sit fugitivus, sive bannitus, dux Normannie habet proventus totius terre sue per unum annum, et ille de cujus feodo terra movet habet terram post annum. (Ex reg. Philippi Augusti : cited by Delisle, Bibl. de l'école des Chartes, ser. 3, t. 3, p. 102, n. 4.)

(Destruatur) (Exilium) *De abbata sancti Edmundi.* . . . et quia predicta pars dicti bosci destruitur per terram et factum est ibi exilium et solum redactum est in culturam contra tenorem carte sue predicte, preceptum est vicecomiti quod faciat venire huc dictum abbatem a die sancti Martini in quindecim dies ad respondendum de destructione et exilio predicto. (Exchequer Treas. of Rec., Forest Proceedings, 13, m. 23 ; 20 Edward I.)

(Super eum ibimus) Sciant presentes et futuri quod Galfridus de Turre devenit homo ligius domini Johannis illustris regis Anglie pro feodo centum et l librarum Turron. per annum ab ipso rege percipiendo, hoc modo quod ipse Galfridus ibit in propria persona sua cum ipso domino rege super quoscumque ierit preterquam super Petrum comitem Britannie quamdiu civitatem Nacietar. habebit. . . . Si vero comes Britannie ierit super regem Anglie, dictus Galfridus in propria persona sua ibit ad ipsum dominum regem in ejus subsidium . . . et si rex ierit super comitem Britannie prefatus Galfridus ibit in proprio persona sua ad. . . . (Charter Roll, 16 John, m. 8d ; Rot. Cart. R.C., p. 209.)

(Super eum ibimus) *De judicio reddito contra L. filium Griffini.* Concordatum est de communi consilio omnium predictorum prelatorum comitum baronum et aliorum quod dominus rex predictam peticionem ipsius L. non exaudiat nec ejus excusationes prenotatas admittat set quod eat super ipsum L. tanquam super rebellem suum et pacis sue perturbatorem. . . . (Close Roll, 4 Edward I, m. 1d., 13th October, 1276 ; see Parl. Writs, i, p. 5.)

(Super eum mittemus) Prohibemus etc. ne quis justiciarius vicecomes vel forestarius vel aliquis alius ballivus exceptis ballivis ipsius regine in predicta manum mittat vel de aliquo se inde intromittat nisi de voluntate et assensu ipsius regine. . . . (Dower Charter of Queen Isabel, 5th May, 1204 ; Rot. Cart., p. 128.)

(Super eum mittemus) Et precipimus et volumus quod nullus vicecomes vel minister ejus se unquam de eis intro- mittat vel ad maneria illa vel ad hundreda predicta vel ad homines in eis manentes manum mittat in aliquo. . . . (Charter to Hugh archdeacon of Wells, 25th April, 1204 ; Rot. Cart., p. 129.)

(Super eum mittemus) Quare volumus et firmiter preci- pimus quod ipsi omnia predicta habeant integre et plenarie . . . ita quod nullus de ministris nostris se inde intromittat nec disturbet eos. . . . (Whitby Charter, 1st March, 1203–4. Rot. Cart., p. 121).

(Super eum mittemus) J. Dei gratia rex Anglie etc. Sciatis nos concessisse et hac carta nostra confirmasse civibus nostris Herefordie in Wallia . . . civitatem nostram Herefordie . . . habendam et tenendam . . . ita quod nullus vicecomitum nostrorum in aliquo se intromittat super eos de aliquo placito vel querela vel occasione vel aliqua re alia ad predictam civitatem pertinenti sicut carta regis Ricardi fratris nostri quam habent rationabiliter testatur salvis nobis et heredibus nostris imperpetuum placitis corone nostre que attachiari debent per eosdem cives nostros usque in ad- ventum justiciariorum nostrorum. (Charter of John, dated 10th of July, 1215 ;[1] Rot. Cart., p. 212.)

(Per judicium parium suorum) (vide supra passim, and compare the following): Nos faciemus Alexandro regi Scottorum de sororibus suis et obsidibus reddendis et liber- tatibus suis et jure suo secundum formam in qua faciemus aliis baronibus nostris Anglie nisi aliter esse debeat per cartas quas habemus de Willelmo patre ipsius quondam rege Scottorum, et hoc erit per judicium parium suorum in curia nostra. (Magna Carta, c. 59.)

(Per legem terre) (vide supra passim).

---

[1] Compare the charter of the empress to Geoffrey de Mande- ville (A.D. 1141): Non mittam aliam justiciam super eum in comi- tatu illo, nisi ita sit quod aliquando mittam aliquem de paribus suis qui audiat cum illo quod placita mea juste tractentur.

CHAPTER VIII

JOHN LACKLAND AND THE PEERS OF FRANCE— JUDGMENT BY PEERS IN FRANCE IN THE THIRTEENTH CENTURY

AS soon as the Great Charter of England had been sealed and delivered, measures were taken for enforcing its provisions, and the twenty-five barons referred to in the security for peace were elected. These twenty-five were apparently intended to sit as a more or less permanent court of appeal for the redress of grievances, but fierce civil war supervened, and this phantom tribunal vanished away.

At this point the evolution of judgment by peers in England is unmistakably influenced by the development of that principle in France. To appreciate the one it is essential that a survey of the other should be undertaken, including the proceedings against John, king of England. The history of judgment by peers in France will be found by no means devoid of interest.

Prior to the year 1216 the expression "peer" was, as we have seen, in common use to denote co-vassalship, community and so forth; but there is not one atom of authentic evidence testifying the existence in France during this period of any persons formally styled "peers of the realm" or "peers of France"—nothing but an apocryphal procès-verbal for the coronation of Philip Augustus, and a forged letter purporting to have been written in 1171 by a certain prior of Grandmont.[1] But there was in existence a genuine popular tradition concerning twelve peers of France which figured in many a famous chanson de geste.

> " Par ceste barbe que veez blancheier
> Li duze Pers mar i seront jugiet." [2]

---

[1] Luchaire, Revue Hist., t. 54, pp. 382–91.
[2] Chanson de Roland, vv. 261–2.
See Flach, Origines de l'Ancienne France, vol. i, p. 253.

According to this tradition the epic twelve (which included the archbishop of Reims, the duke of Burgundy, the duke of Normandy and the count of Anjou) were undoubtedly pre-eminent among their fellows. Hitherto, however, the principle of judgment by peers and the French king's court had been quite unaffected by the tradition, which after all merely gave twelve more or less unspecified feudatories a particular name, and connected them with romantic Carolingian legends not unlike our legends of king Arthur. But at the beginning of the thirteenth century a series of events occurred which com-pletely changed this state of things, gave actuality to poetic fable, and brought into prominence a body, partly ideal, partly real, of twelve peers of France.[1] It consisted of six lay peers : the dukes of Normandy, Burgundy[2] and Aquitaine, and the counts of Flanders,[3] Toulouse and Champagne ;[4] and six ecclesiastical peers : the archbishop of Reims,[2] and the bishops of Laon,[5] Langres,[2] Beauvais,[2] Noyon[2] and Châlons.[2] The circumstances connected with the appearance in history of these twelve peers are shortly as follows :—

In 1202 John was summoned as count of Anjou and duke of Aquitaine to appear before the French courts on the appeal of the counts de la Marche and d'Eu :[6] he was, it appears, deliberately, not summoned as duke of Normandy on account of special privileges claimed in respect of that duchy.[7] John

---

[1] The first formal document enumerating the complete college of twelve is dated A.D. 1275. See Langlois, Philippe III, p. 423.

[2] First mentioned as a peer of the realm in 1216 : Langlois, Textes, no. 19.

[3] Trial of countess of Flanders as such in 1224 : post, p. 271.

[4] Succession to the comté tried in 1216 ; ibid.

[5] Present as peer of the realm at trial of count of Flanders, A.D. 1237 ; post, p. 272.

[6] Rigord ; Oeuvres de Rigord et Guillaume le Breton, Soc. de l'Hist. de France, vol. i, p. 151. William le Breton ; ibid., vol. i, pp. 207, 209-10. Ralph de Coggeshall, Rolls Series, pp. 135-6. Gervase of Canterbury, Rolls Series, vol. ii, pp. 93-4. Letters of Innocent III ; Migne, Patrol. Lat., ccxv, cols. 182-4.

[7] Ralph de Coggeshall (loc. cit.) : Rex autem Angliae, respondens se ducem esse Normannorum, allegabat se nequaquam debere ad ullum colloquium Parisius procedere, sed solummodo inter utrosque fines, regni scilicet et ducatus, ad colloquium regis occurrere : quia

demurred to this form of citation, and declined to appear or
in any way submit to the jurisdiction. There were several
adjournments of the court, but John refused to give way.
Under these circumstances Philip acted as Edward the First
did in like case with Llewelyn : on the advice of his magnates
he declared war.[1] One chronicler, however, Ralph de Coggeshall, asserts that a judicial sentence was previously passed,
and that this was a sentence of forfeiture involving all John's
French possessions.[2] The assertion as it stands is wholly
unsupported by any other contemporary authorities, and is

sit antiquitus inter ducem et regem decretum et scriptis authenticis
confirmatum erat. Rex autem Philippus allegabat nequaquam justum
esse ut jus suum, quod ad comitatum Aquitanicum spectabat, amit-
teret, si idem esset dux Normanniae qui et comes Aquitaniae.

[1] Sed quoniam rex Angliae ad diem praefixum, nec in propria
persona venit, nec responsalem sufficientem mittere voluit, habito
rex Franciae cum principibus et baronibus suis consilio, collecto
exercitu Normanniam ingressus, munitiunculam quamdam quam
Boutavant vocabant funditus evertit. (Rigord, loc. cit.)

Verum cum rex Angliae Johannes injunctum sibi non compleret
mandatum, . . . habito cum suis consilio, rex Franciae subito incan-
duit, et exiliens archiepiscopum Cantuariensem praecepit abire ;
quem armatus et militibus vallatus a tergo subsequens, castrum de
Butavant succendit et diruit. (Gervase of Canterbury, loc. cit.)

Letter to John, dated October 29th, 1203 : . . . Cumque, communi-
cato cum baronibus et hominibus suis consilio, certum tibi terminum
statuisset, ut in ejus praesentia compareres, quod jus dictaret sine
retractatione facturus, licet esses ligius homo ejus, nec ivisti tamen
ad diem statutum nec misisti aliquem responsalem, sed mandatum
ejus penitus contempsisti. Consequenter vero personaliter te convenit. . . . Verum cum nec sic satisfacere voluisses, licet te de
baronum et hominum suorum consilio difidasset, mota tamen guerra,
ad te quatuor ex militibus suis misit, volens certificari per eos si
velles ea quae in ipsum commiseris emendare. Alioquin notum tibi
esse volebat quod ex tunc contra te foedus cum hominibus tuis ubicunque posset iniret. . . . (Innocent III, loc. cit.)

[2] Tandem vero curia regis Franciae adunata adjudicavit regem
Angliae tota terra sua privandum, quam hactenus de regibus Franciae
ipse et progenitores sui tenuerant, eo quod fere omnia servitia eisdem
terris debita per longum jam tempus facere contempserant, nec
domino suo fere in aliquibus obtemperare volebant. Hoc igitur
curiae suae judicium rex Philippus gratanter acceptans et approbans,
coadunato exercitu, confestim invasit castellum Butavant (pp. 135–6).
See also M. Bémont in the Revue Historique, t. xxxii, pp. 301–11.

therefore not entitled to serious consideration. It is highly improbable that the French court would have gone through the solemn farce of passing a judicial sentence which could only be enforced, if at all, by extra-judicial process. But making allowance for monkish ignorance of court formalities the error is rather a natural one, and in itself quite trivial; no lawyer of the period, I think, would have been misled by the statement.

The explanation is simply this, that in the common parlance of the time a resolution of the king in council to make war on a subject was a *judicium;* it was, in fact, to use words consecrated by our charter of liberties, a *judicium super eum ire*.[1] That a judgment of this description was passed is quite clear from other authorities; it is, of course, equally clear that in principle there was as much difference between this judgment and a judicial sentence as there is, for example, between bill of attainder and impeachment.

---

[1] Compare the case of Llewelyn : Close Roll, 4 Edward I, m. 1d : De judicio reddito contra L. filium Griffini. Concordatum est de communi consilio omnium predictorum prelatorum, comitum baronum et aliorum, quod dominus rex predictam peticionem ipsius L. non exaudiat, nec ejus excusationes prenotatas admittat, set quod eat super ipsum L. tanquam super rebellem suum et pacis sue perturbatorem. . . .

Cotton, Rolls Series, p. 154 : Eodem anno dominus Edwardus rex tenuit parliamentum suum generale in quindena Paschae, et cum vocatus fuisset ante Lewelinus princeps Walliae ut veniret et faceret homagium domino regi et responderet de pluribus transgressionibus, quia non venit, fuit provisum quod rex cum exercitu suo iret super eum.

William of Rishanger, Rolls Series, p. 86 : Post parliamentum vero, rex, ut Lewelino principi Walliae liberior ad se pateret accessus, Cestriam usque, quae in confinio Walliae sita est, progreditur; missisque iterum nunciis, homagium exigit ab eodem. Quo mandatis regiis parere detrectante, rex exercitum convocat, disponens principem sibi denegantem homagium, de suo feodo expugnare.

Trevet, Engl. Hist. Soc., p. 293 : Post parliamentum rex, ut principi liberior ad se pateret accessus, Cestriam usque, quae in confinio Walliae sita est, progreditur, missisque iterum nuntiis homagium ab eo exegit : quo regis mandatis parere detrectante, rex exercitum convocat, disponens denegatum sibi homagium de suo feodo principem expugnare.

Hemingburgh, Engl. Hist. Soc., ii, p. 5 : Quo audito, statim

The loss of John's French provinces swiftly followed the declaration of war, and John's quondam subjects were called upon to swear fealty to Philip Augustus. It will be remembered that during the war Arthur duke of Brittany fell into the English king's hands, and never escaped alive.[1] According to the popular story, John first made an unsuccessful attempt to have the youth mutilated at Falaise : then, by his orders, Arthur was transferred to the citadel of Rouen, and there, on Maundy-Thursday, the king being drunk and possessed of the devil, slew his nephew with his own hand, and flung the body, weighted with a great stone, into the waters of the Seine.[2]

Now after the conquest of Normandy a difficulty was raised by the Norman bishops about swearing fealty to France ; and Philip, as appears from a letter of Innocent III,

guerram movit in Wallia ipse Leulinus, devastans gladio et igne succendens quaecunque manus ipsius contingere potuerunt : divertitque rex ibidem cum exercitu copioso, et in tantum arctavit eum quod pacem quaerere compulsus est. . . .

The chronicles of Edward I and Edward II, Rolls Series, 76 ; the Flores Historiarum, etc., are all absolutely silent as to the judgment on Llewelyn. Except for the entry on the Close Roll, how easy it would have been to maintain that Edward never proceeded to judgment against this prince at all!

[1] John might quite properly have ordered Arthur's instant execution ; he had been captured fighting against his feudal lord, and was not even entitled to trial and judgment. Perhaps John hoped by sparing him to win him over to his side. His murder was a piece of gratuitous folly. The popular legends connected with the manner of Arthur's death are not entitled to the smallest credence. His murder, or at least his mutilation, was said to be necessary because he was the true heir to the throne, but his title to the throne was purely mythical. By a custom prevalent in Western Europe Arthur would have succeeded to Henry II before John, but a brother had a better right than a nephew to succeed to Richard. See Très Ancien Coutumier de Normandie, cap. xii ; Beaumanoir, Coutumes du Beauvoisis, i, 238, 240; Close Roll, 13 Henry III, m. 14d.

[2] The following has some claim to be considered a semi-official account of Arthur's death: Anno mcciiij Arthurus dux armoricanorum britonum in carcere regis Johannis obiit vel aut alii volunt occisus est. Philippus rex Francie normanniam dolo consulum et baronum terre ditioni sue subjugavit. (Domesday, Exch. Miscel. K.R., no. i, p. 18.)

met their objections with the assertion that "justitia praeeunte per sententiam curiae suae Normanniam acquisivit";
whereupon the bishops appealed to the pope for advice.[1]

As I read the assertion it means that "justice having
been previously offered (and declined), Philip in pursuance
of a decision of his court took possession of Normandy (by
force)." If this is the meaning, then we know that the
assertion is literally true. The only reasonable ground for
doubt is that Innocent goes on to say that he cannot advise
the bishops as to the sufficiency of Philip's answer—"quia
vero nec de jure nec de consuetudine nobis constat, utpote
qui causam, modum et ordinem aliasque circumstantias
ignoramus." This letter was written on March 7th, 1205.

We know from an earlier letter of Innocent[2] that he was,
in fact, fairly well informed as to what had taken place;
indeed, we are bound to assume that Philip had taken care
to inform the pope of all facts telling in his own favour,
John to be sure having done as much for himself. Therefore
either Innocent was dissembling when he professed ignorance (which is not *prima facie* improbable, for it was
obviously to his interest to evade, if he could, a direct
answer to the Norman bishops), or the pope must really
have thought that the facts so far as he knew them did not
justify Philip's assertion.

There can be little doubt that Philip had on the facts
a remarkably weak case. He had chosen for his own convenience not to cite John as duke of Normandy, and now
he was asserting the validity of his conquest of that duchy
on the ground of John's contempt of court.[3] It was obviously open to John to say that, however much he might

---

[1] Letter dated March 7th, 1205; printed Migne, Patrol. Lat.,
ccxv, col. 564. See also Transactions of the Royal Hist. Soc.
N.S., xiv, p. 63.

[2] Letter of October 29th, 1203, cited supra.

[3] It has been asserted by one publicist (Bibl. de l'École des
Chartes, t. 60, p. 46) that Normandy was *hors de cause* in 1202.
In view of the fact that it was Normandy which Philip invaded in
execution of the judgment, this statement is absurd on the face of
it. It is also, of course, in direct conflict with the statement of
Ralph de Coggeshall.

have been in contempt as count of Anjou and duke of Aquitaine, as duke of Normandy at all events he had committed no contempt. Such being the facts Philip is scarcely likely to have given the pope very precise information on the subject; but in any event there is nothing in Innocent's letter which a statesman and a Christian could not have written under the circumstances.

Until a few years ago historians accepted without question the fact that John was judged by the French court in 1202. It was, however, apparently assumed that the judgment was a judicial sentence. This at all events was an error. But the existence of any judgment in 1202 has been disputed by a recent writer,[1] who puts forward the view that no judgment was given, but that Philip, when confronted with the scruples of the Norman bishops, sought to obviate the difficulty by promulgating a bold myth to the effect that Normandy had been by a sentence of the French court declared forfeit to the crown. The argument in substance rests solely on the professed ignorance of the pontiff.

Even assuming we had only Philip's ipse dixit as evidence of the judgment, I, for my part, could not believe the French king guilty of such stupidity as to invent a non-existing judgment for the purpose of setting at rest the question of fealty, when that very question obviously afforded him a perfect opportunity for then and there obtaining a legal decision confirming his conquests, assuming, of course, that a legal decision was what was required.

The obvious course would have been to take proceedings to enforce fealty and service from some Norman baron in a prepared test case. Whatever technical flaws existed in Philip's title, he would none the less have obtained without the least difficulty an unexceptionable judicial decision in his favour. This method was well known; it had been resorted to, for instance, by Henry the Second in proceedings directed against Robert III, earl of Leicester, after his re-

[1] Miss Norgate in Transactions of the Royal Hist. Soc. N.S., xiv, pp. 53–67.

bellion.[1]   If, therefore, it was a case of a king's word against
a prelate's, I should believe the former. Philip had no dis-
cernible motive for lying, and not the smallest prospect of
being believed if he did lie. However, for the reasons I
have already stated, there seems no ground whatever for
doubting the word of either.

On the 1st of October, 1207, a son was born to John who
afterwards became Henry the Third. John's position and
prospects nevertheless went from bad to worse, and in 1213
the pope intervened. He excommunicated John and com-
missioned Philip Augustus to dethrone him.

Philip prepared for invading England ; and at Soissons,[2]
in the beginning of April, John was a second time subjected
to a *judicium super eum ire* by the king and the assembled
magnates of France.[3] This time the judgment was of a

---

[1] Council at Northampton, 1177.   In eodem vero concilio
Willelmus de Chahannes intimaverat regi, quod ipse deberet de
eo tenere in capite baroniam suam, quam de Roberto comite
Leicestriae tenebat.   Haec autem dicebat pravo usus consilio, quia
regi placere voluit, qui dominum suum odio habebat.   Cumque
praedictus comes Leicestriae ad diem sibi statutum per regis summonitionem venisset et cum omnia quae adversus eum loquebantur
auscultasset, respondit, quod quamvis praedecessores sui, proavus
scilicet et avus suus, et pater suus et ipsemet haberent cartas et
privilegia regum Angliae, Willelmi scilicet et Henrici primi, de
terris suis, et nominatim de baronia illa, et quamvis praedecessores
Willelmi de Chahannis baroniam illam de praedecessoribus suis
semper inconcusse tenuissent ; noluit tamen contra regis voluntatem,
neque de eo neque de alio tenemento placitare ; sed concessit,
ut id et omnia alia tenementa sua essent in misericordia regis.
Cumque rex audisset eum ita pie loquentem, commotus pietate,
reddidit ei omnia tenementa sua in integrum, sicut ea habuit
quindecim diebus ante gwerram ; sed rex retinuit in manu sua
castellum de Munsorel et castellum de Pascy. . . . (Benedict of
Peterborough, Rolls Series, i, p. 133.)
    It would have been necessary, probably, to send a formal sum-
mons to John. See Glanville, Lib. xii, cap. 8.
[2] It is no doubt a mere coincidence that all the ecclesiastical
peers of France were situated in close proximity to this town !
[3] Eodem anno convocavit Philippus rex concilium in civitate
Suessionensi, in crastino Dominice Palmarum [8th April, 1213] cui
interfuerunt omnes proceres regni. . . . Ibidem igitur tractatum fuit
de transfretando in Angliam et placuit sermo iste baronibus universis,

much more serious and far-reaching character : it was directed against John's person, his kingdom of England and all his possessions, and the grounds of the judgment included the murder of Arthur and other infamous acts. No mention, however, is made of any prior judicial sentence against John,

et spoponderunt auxilium et quod etiam personaliter transfretarent cum ipso. . . . (William le Breton, i, p. 245.)

Causa que Philippum regem magnanimum moverat ad hoc ut vellet in Angliam transfretare fuit . . . ut ipsum regem Johannem qui nepotem suum Arturum occiderat . . . vel pene condigne subjiceret, vel a regno prorsus expellens, secundum agnominis sui interpretationem omnino efficeret sine terra. (Ibid., p. 253.)

Compare the account in the Philippide. As in the case of Llewelyn, the secondary chronicles do not suggest anything in the nature of a judgment. For example :—

En cele année assembla li rois Phelippe un concile à Soissons lendemain de Pasques flories. À ce concile furent tuit li baron du roiaume et . . . En ce concile fu traitié de passer en Angleterre, et plut ceste chose à toz les barons qui là furent, et promistrent au roi leur confort et leur aide en totes manieres, que il meismes passeroient ovec lui en propres persones. (Chroniques de S. Denis, Bouquet H.F., vol. xvii, p. 400.)

Li rois manda toz les haus barons de sa tierre à parlement, si lor requist que il venissent o lui en Engletierre pour le regne conquerre. (Hist. des Ducs de Normandie, Soc. de l'Hist. de Fr., p. 120.)

After the events of 1216, the judgment of John is stated in stereotyped language : Johannes autem Arthurum apud Mirabellum cepit, ceterisque per obsides liberatis, ipsum, ut fertur, latenter peremit ; super quo a baronibus apud regem Francie accusatus, cujus vassallus erat, cum comparere nollet, post multas citationes per judicium parium exheredatus est. (Vincent de Beauvais (died 1264), Douai, iv, p. 209 ; Guillaume de Nangis (died ante 1304), Soc. de l'Hist. de Fr., i, p. 118, etc.)

Apparently the last-mentioned writer believed that John was twice condemned for the murder of Arthur, for he gives the following account of the proceedings at Soissons :—

Philippus rex Franciae, prelatis et baronibus regni sui Suessionis convocatis, dedit ibidem Mariam filiam suam, relictam Philippi comitis Namurcii, duci Brabantiae in uxorem. Fuit etiam ibidem de transfretando in Angliam, consentientibus baronibus, ordinatum. Causa vero quae regem movebat haec erat : ut . . . regem ipsum Johannem, qui nepotem suum Arturum comitem Britanniae occiderat, qui etiam plurimos parvulos obsides suspenderat et innumera flagitia perpetraverat, vel poenae condignae subjiceret, vel a regno prorsus expellens, secundum interpretationem agnominis sui, sine terra efficeret. (Ibid., p. 142.)

which is inexplicable if anything of the kind had taken place.

It would be absurd, in my opinion, to attempt to consider the constitutional aspects of this "judgment." The affair was an international one, and altogether outside the scope of jurisprudence.[1] It so happened too that these proceedings proved abortive. John made his peace with the pope by an act of abject submission, and a crushing naval defeat was suffered by the French.

It was not till 1216 that the invasion of England was seriously attempted; this time, not by Philip, but by his son, and at the invitation, not of the pope, but of the revolted English barons. Rome indeed was determined if possible to blast the enterprise, and Walo as papal legate was sent to France for that purpose. It was a difficult mission: the legate when he presented his credentials to Philip Augustus was at once rebuffed. To the remonstrances of the pope the monarch, it is said, incontinently replied as follows:—[2]

The kingdom of England never was the patrimony of Peter, nor is, nor shall be. John forsooth, in days long past, seeking unjustly to deprive his brother Richard of the kingdom of England, and

---

[1] Nevertheless an apologist has, apparently in all seriousness, cited the following extract from Durand, Speculum Juris Lib., iv, De Feudis, s. 2, no. 33 : Eo enim ipso quod aliquis est homo meus ligius, hoc ipso est jurisdictioni mee subjectus et sum ejus judex. . . . Et omnia bona ejus que non habet ab alio in feudum . . . sunt mihi subjecta ratione jurisdictionis, licet illa non teneat a me in feudum. Eo enim ipso quod personam suam michi principaliter subjecit, videtur per consequens omnia bona sua subjecisse. If this statement of the law could be applied to the case under discussion, then, assuming the validity of the judgment, Philip became absolutely entitled to John's English possessions to the exclusion of all other claimants. See further on the subject of forfeiture infra.

[2] "Regnum Angliae patrimonium Petri nunquam fuit, nec est nec erit. Rex enim Johannes, multis retroactis diebus, volens fratrem suum regem Richardum a regno Angliae injuste privare, et inde de proditione accusatus et coram eo convictus, damnatus fuit per judicium in curia ipsius regis; quam sententiam pronunciavit Hugo de Pusaz episcopus Dunelmensis. Et ita nunquam fuit verus rex, nec potuit regnum dare. Item si aliquandò fuit verus rex, postea regnum forisfecit per mortem Arthuri, de quo facto condemnatus fuit in curia nostra." Item dixit quod nullus rex (vel

being accused of the treason and convicted, was condemned by the judgment of that king's court. . . . Therefore never was John true king, nor able to assign his realm. Even if he ever was true king, afterwards he forfeited his kingdom by the death of Arthur, for which deed he was condemned in our court. Again, no king or prince can assign his kingdom without the assent of his barons whose duty it is to defend such kingdom, and if the pope has decided to uphold this error, he is setting a very evil example to all nations.

The magnates are said to have loudly applauded this speech. It only contains one statement which calls for special comment here. John, it is contended, regnum forisfecit per mortem Arthuri, etc. It would appear from these words that forfeiture at the date of the crime, and not at the date of the judgment, is what is asserted. This was certainly the general custom. Property lawyers of the period speaking from their own standpoint would describe committing murder as committing a forfeiture.[1] The relevancy of this comment will become apparent in due course.

On the following day Louis appeared in court. The king adopted a judicial attitude:[2] "Verily if Louis claims any rights for himself in respect of the kingdom of England, let him be heard; and let what is just be conceded to him." A legal argument then took place. Louis appeared by counsel —"miles quidam quem Ludovicus procuratorem suum constituerat." The murder of Arthur was again mentioned:—[3]

princeps) potest dare regnum suum sine assensu baronum suorum qui regnum illud tenentur defendere; et si papa hunc errorem tueri decreverit, perniciosissimum regnis omnibus dat exemplum. (Wendover, Rolls Series [84], ii, pp. 176–7; Matthew Paris, Rolls Series [57], ii, pp. 650–1.)

[1] Ballivi ducis capiebant homines alicujus *** qui aliquod forisfactum fecerat, vel furando, vel aliquem occidendo. (Très Ancien Coutumier de Normandie, cap. 61.)

[2] "Veruntamen si jus aliquid sibi Ludovicus de regno Angliae vendicat, audiatur, et quod justum fuerit concedatur eidem." (Wendover and Matthew Paris, loc. cit.)

[3] "Domine rex res notissima est omnibus, quod Johannes dictus rex Angliae, pro Arthuri nepotis sui proditione, quem propriis manibus interemit, in curia vestra per judicium parium suorum ad mortem sit condemnatus, ac postmodum a baronibus Angliae pro multis homicidiis et enormitatibus aliis quas ibidem fecerat, ne

My lord king, it is a notorious fact, that John the said king of England, for the treacherous murder of his nephew Arthur whom he slew with his own hands, was condemned to death in your court by the judgment of his peers; and afterwards, on account of the many homicides and other enormities which he had perpetrated, was rejected by the barons of England from reigning over them; wherefore the same barons took up arms against him that they might expel him for all time out of the kingdom. Moreover the aforesaid king, without the consent of his magnates, conveyed England to the lord pope and the church of Rome, that he might receive it again at their hands rendering therefor an annual tribute of a thousand marks. But if he could not without the barons assign the crown of England to anyone, nevertheless he could divest himself of it; therefore immediately he surrendered the kingdom he ceased to be king. A vacant realm ought not to be disposed of except by the barons; accordingly the barons elected the lord Louis on account of his wife; whose mother, that is to say the Queen of Castille, alone of all the brothers and sisters of the king of England was then living.

The legate is reported to have used one argument only: John was cruce-signatus. The reply was directed to this point. The legate expressed himself dissatisfied with the reasons advanced by Louis, and finally vetoed the expedition under pain of excommunication. However, about the 20th of May Louis embarked for England at Calais and landed in Thanet. He was joined by large numbers of the English baronage and carried all before him. Nothing but the sudden death of John and the hostility of the pope saved England from annexation.

regnaret super eos, reprobatus; unde iidem barones guerram contra eum jam moverunt ut ipsum a solio regni immutabiliter depellant. Praeterea rex saepedictus, praeter assensum magnatum suorum, regnum Angliae domino papae contulit et ecclesiae Romanae, ut iterum illud reciperet ab eis tenendum sub annuo tributo mille marcarum. Et si coronam Angliae sine baronibus alicui dare non potuit, potuit tamen dimittere eam; quam statim cum resignavit, rex esse desiit, et regnum sine rege vacavit. Vacans itaque regnum sine baronibus ordinari non debuit; unde barones elegerunt dominum Ludovicum ratione uxoris suae; cujus mater, regina scilicet Castellae, sola ex omnibus fratribus et sororibus regis Angliae vivens fuit." (Wendover, ii, pp. 177-9; Matthew Paris, ii, pp. 651-3.)

To assist his enterprise Louis issued in England a portentous manifesto[1] which contained the following allegations: (1) That John had been tried by his peers of England under Richard and found guilty of treason. Consequently at the death of Richard the crown devolved on Louis as heir to the queen of Castille. (2) That John had been cited by his peers to the court of the king of France in respect of the murder of Arthur, and had subsequently by the same peers been lawfully condemned; to this murder he had many times confessed, and by this condemnation, in accordance with the customs in force, he forfeited all his goods wheresoever and whencesoever. Thus again the crown devolved on Louis as true heir, especially as John was then without heirs of his body. As to the treaty afterwards concluded between our dearest lord and parent, we were no party to it, etc.[2] (3) That by the common consent of the realm, John having been adjudged unworthy of ruling for certain specified reasons, we Louis have been elected king.

In a document of this sort we can scarcely expect un-

---

[1] Printed, Rymer, Foedera R.C., i, p. 140.

[2] Preterea satis notum est, quomodo de murdro Arthuri nepotis sui in curia karissimi domini regis Francie, cujus ambo erant homines ligii, per pares suos citatus et per eosdem pares tandem fuit legitime condempnatus, quod quidem murdrum ejusdem temporis pluribus in Anglia et pluries predictus Johannes est confessus, per quam condempnationem bona sua, ubicunque essent aut undecunque ea haberet, per usitatas consuetudines forisfecit, et tunc iterato nobis tanquam vero heredi cessit jus regni Anglie, maxime cum adhuc de carne sua heredem non haberet. Nos vero pro jure nostro ex tunc eidem Johanni gwerram movimus, quam contra ipsum continuavimus absque omni interruptione pace vel treuga . . . usque ad dies istos. De (treuga) enim que postmodum inter karissimum dominum et genitorem nostrum et ipsum facta fuit, nec fuimus requisiti nec alium requisivimus, licet presentes essemus, unde nec crucis assumptio nec aliqua conditio postmodum, lite pendente, suscepta poterit ipsum tueri, quin contra ipsum jus nostrum prosequimur. In the transcript from which the above has been printed, i.e. Cotton, Julius D., ii, fol. 121, the word which I have placed in brackets is plainly "gwerra," and not "treuga." This, however, is clearly a mere clerical slip. The manifesto is also transcribed into the chartulary of St. Augustine's, Canterbury. There too the word is "gwerra."

s

varnished truth. The first argument gives a very partial and inaccurate account of what took place in the days of Richard: the second is not entirely convincing. It is improbable that John frequently confessed to the murder of Arthur; but then who could possibly prove the contrary? The alleged citation by peers had perhaps some foundation in fact. It is worth noting that the word "tandem" used in describing John's condemnation suggests a considerable interval between citation and judgment. The statement that John at that time had no issue is only true if the time referred to is the forfeiture and not the judgment. In this case, however, not only would no useful purpose have been served by misrepresenting the date of the judgment, but the reference to a treaty (in the singular) proves that nothing of the kind was intended. By this treaty must necessarily be meant the last treaty, that is, the one concluded in 1214: the judgment therefore cannot be antedated, and forfeiture is the only possible date consistent with the argument.

The legal aspect of the second argument deserves attention. The first assertion (cujus ambo erant homines ligii) is clearly designed to show jurisdiction. Citation by peers was never required by English law, but if true was worth stating. John's default is not referred to; it was unnecessary to do so; the words "legitime condemnatus" covered everything. A writer, to whom we shall have to refer more than once, observes: "Dans la procédure de forbannissement contre un contumace, ce qui sert de preuve, et de preuve unique, suffisante et absolue, c'est la contumace elle-même."[1] There was a tendency to limit this rule: Bracton held that in outlawry at the king's suit something more or less equivalent to conviction was required: confession was quite sufficient. Forfeiture is asserted to have taken place by virtue of the judgment. We may take it to have been the general rule that such forfeiture related back to the date of the crime; and disinherited, not only the man himself, but also his heirs, or rather all persons claiming through him whether born or

---

[1] M. Guilhiermoz, in Bibl. de l'École des Chartes, t. 60, p. 56.

unborn at the date of forfeiture.[1] This rule, however, in John's case would have operated with every bit as much force against Louis as against Henry. If one was excluded so was the other, so unquestionably was everyone else. The rule, shall we say, was not framed to meet the case of criminous kings and ought not to be pressed. If we may concede so much, we may no doubt the more readily exclude Henry on the ground that he was not in existence at the date of the forfeiture. At this point, of course, the argument inevitably breaks down : the claim of Louis to be next heir was preposterous on the face of it.

Here for the moment we may take leave of the argument. It is, to be sure, quite unsound in at least one essential particular ; but, considering that it was merely designed for political purposes, I venture to describe it as a highly creditable performance.

Fortunately for England, the pamphleteering of Louis weighed little against the ecclesiastical veto, and the prince found himself in evil plight. John was lawfully damned for disobeying the citations of his feudal lord?—the merest peccadillo. Louis was about to enforce the sentence by defying the injunctions of the vicar of God. The situation was intolerable : envoys were sent hot haste to Rome to beguile the holy father with the story of Louis's just claims, and thus avert the wrath to come.

St. Albans has preserved the only extant account of what occurred at Rome : this purports to be a more or less verbatim report of a legal discussion between the pope and

---

[1] . . . retrotrahitur tempus ad perpetrationem feloniae. . . . Propriis autem haeredibus forisfacit haereditatem suam propriam propinquis et remotis, scilicet quicquid tenuit tempore feloniae perpetratae et qualitercunque et secundum quod tenuit. (Bracton, Rolls Series, ii, p. 350.) See also Pollock and Maitland, i, p. 477.

Compare the rule in Glanville :—

Preterea si quis de felonia convictus fuerit vel confessus in curia, eo per jus regni exheredato terra sua domino suo remanet escaeta. Notandum quod si quis in capite de domino rege tenuerit, tunc tam terra quam omnes res mobiles suae et catalla penes quemcunque inveniantur ad opus domini regis capientur sine omni recuperatione alicujus heredis. (Lib. vii, cap. 17.)

the envoys of Louis. There is no reason to doubt the genuineness of the document or the general accuracy of its statements.[1]

The first proposition formulated against John was: "quod Arthurum nepotem suum propriis manibus per proditionem interfecit, pessimo mortis genere, quod Angli murdrum appellant. Pro quo facto idem rex condemnatus fuit ad mortem in curia regis Francorum per judicium parium suorum."

The pope demurred: John was an anointed king; the barons of France, tanquam inferiores, had no jurisdiction. "It is a custom in the kingdom of the French," the envoys replied, "that the king has complete jurisdiction over his liegemen, and John was the king's liegeman. But if he was not, the king still had jurisdiction, otherwise such an one might do murder with impunity, even as it was with Arthur." The last perhaps was a necessary plea; war severed the feudal tie.

At this point Matthew Paris interpolates a confused argument of his own. "The truth is," he says, "John was not rightly deprived of Normandy." What had Normandy, however, to do with the discussion? Then the chronicler relates how John sent Eustace of Ely and Hubert de Burgh to Philip claiming restitution, and offering to appear at Philip's court if a safe-conduct was granted him. "In pace salvo veniat," said Philip. "Domine, et redeat," urged the bishop. "Ita sit," came the reply, "si parium suorum judicium hoc permittat." The king, pressed for a more favourable reply, grew wrathful: "per sanctos Franciae, non nisi mediante judicio." John, when these terms were reported to him, was unwilling to accept—"maxime cum timeret ut ei de turpissima morte Arthuri objiceretur." The chronicler adds: "Magnates tamen Franciae nichilominus processerunt in judicium, quod rite non debuerunt facere; ex quo judicandus abfuit, qui adesse voluit si posset. Unde si rex J[ohannes] abjudicatus fuit per adversarios suos, non rite abjudicabatur."

The magnates, that is to say, *subsequently* proceeded to

[1] See Wendover, ii, pp. 183–90; and Matthew Paris, ii, pp. 657–63.

condemn John *for the murder of Arthur*, which they had no right to do; therefore, if John's forfeiture *of England* was founded on this judgment, such forfeiture was invalid. Obviously the forfeiture of Normandy has nothing to do with the matter; it is merely mentioned by way of necessary preface to the story. The above facts may be true enough; but Matthew Paris is not a contemporary authority, and all the circumstances bear a suspicious resemblance to the case of Henry the Third versus Hubert de Burgh.

We now return to the argument at Rome: "Secunda objectio contra regem fuit quod saepe citatus non personaliter juri pariturus comparuit, nec sufficientem responsalem pro se ad curiam regis Franciae destinavit." The pope thereupon disputed the right to condemn John to death, and showed that he was acquainted with the alleged custom that a duke of Normandy could not be cited to appear except on the border (in marchiam).

The next point raised is of vital importance: "Item dicit Papa quod si sententia lata fuit contra regem Angliae, non tamen mandata fuit exsecutioni; quia non fuit occisus; unde proles quam suscepit postea debet ei in regno succedere; quia rex Angliae non commisit crimen laesae majestatis, nec crimen haereseos, pro quibus tantum filius exhaeredatur pro delicto patris. Ad haec nuncii responderunt; 'Consuetudo est in regno Franciae quod ex quo aliquis est damnatus ad mortem, quod proles suscepta post sententiam damnationis succedere non debet; geniti tamen ante sententiam succedere debent.' Sed tamen super hoc nuncii litigare noluerunt."

If this report is correct there is, seemingly, a serious discrepancy between the facts set out above and the argument which took place in Rome in 1216. The pope is reported to have made a statement, which showed him to be under the impression that the sentence had been pronounced prior to the birth of Henry[1]: the French envoys, it appears, took advantage of this by alleging a custom which excluded issue born after sentence while admitting persons born before sentence; then, realising perhaps the insecurity of their position, were unwilling to pursue the argument. This at

---

[1] Perhaps he was confusing the two judgments.

first sight is the explanation which suggests itself. We might to some extent get rid of the discrepancy by supposing that, per incuriam, sentence is the word used when forfeiture (virtute sententiae) is what was really meant. This, or some similar solution, is at all events infinitely more probable than that John was in fact condemned to death prior to the birth of Henry, an hypothesis for which not a single item of evidence can be produced; or that it was not the events of 1213, but a wholly fictitious judgment which was being asserted. We are not yet, however, in a position to attempt a final solution of the difficulty, for by no means all the material circumstances have yet been stated.

It has been concluded from subsequent statements in the report that the envoys were fully prepared to lie, and did lie in the course of the proceedings: if this is so, any discrepancy between fact and argument scarcely calls for explanation; but a closer examination of the matter discloses a singular situation. Admit the facts and custom apparently alleged by the report, and while the argument then becomes intelligible, the hesitation of the envoys becomes inexplicable. On the other hand, if persons born before John's forfeiture (or sentence) were also excluded, neither Louis nor anyone else claiming by inheritance could possibly make a good title. It so happens, however, that a custom admitting persons born before forfeiture (or sentence) is absolutely fictitious, nothing of the kind existed in France.[1]

[1] Philippe de Beaumanoir, Les coutumes du Beauvoisis, xxx, 2 (ante 1283): Quiconques est pris en cas de crieme et atains du cas . . . il doit estre trainés et pendus, et si meffet tout le sien quanques il a vaillant, et vient le forfeture au segneur desoz qui il est trouvés; et en a çascuns sires ce qui est trouvé en sa segnorie. Très Ancien Coutumier de Normandie, cap. 88, s. 1 (circa 1199–1230): Si aliquis ad mortem condempnatus fuerit per judicium propter delictum suum vel subterfugiens justiciam forisbannitus fuerit, . . . omnia bona ejus sunt regis . . . et terra ejus tenetur in manu regis usque ad annum et diem, et deinceps domino feodi terra illa redditur, et heredes ipsius exhereditantur, ita eciam quod non possunt recuperare illam hereditatem, neque per donum domini neque per commutationem neque per contractum, neque alio modo. Section 3 specially notices that the king cannot restore the outlaw to his inheritance. The reason is plain: the king may not show

Except for this one passage (I will deal with the alleged lie in due course) the envoys could not fairly be accused of

mercy at the expense of the vested rights of the mesne lord. See also Loisel, Institutes, vi, 2, 19. In May, 1224, Louis as king of the French directed letters patent to the burgesses of Limoges containing the following preamble : Noverit universitas vestra quod Johannes, quondam rex Anglie, communi et concordi judicio parium et aliorum baronum Francie fuit abjudicatus imperpetuum de tota terra quam ipse tenuit citra mare Anglie de karissimo genitore nostro Philippo quondam rege Francorum, priusquam Henricus qui nunc dicitur rex Anglie natus esset, et ex tunc tota terra illa cessit in jus dicti patris nostri. (Printed Petit-Dutaillis, Règne de Louis VIII, p. 516.) This, I contend, clearly refers to the first judgment of John in 1202; but even if it does not, by necessary implication it altogether negatives the right of persons born before this forfeiture to succeed to John's forfeited estates. Philip of course had already asserted the same thing : justitia praeeunte per sententiam curiae suae Normanniam acquisivit. See also Li Livres de Jostice et de Plet, xviii, 24, s. 19, p. 279 : De murtre de traïson d'omecide et de rat, qui en est atainz est pendables. De toz les fez dom hom prent mort par juigement, toz les meubles que il a en sa possession el jor del juigement sont le roi, et tuit si héritage; sauf le doere à la feme. Et quant la feme sera morte, li doeres remaint au roi. Cf. ibid., s. 66, p. 283. Aucune foiz avient que li propre heirs est forclos, et que la borse le roi a l'éritage, si comme quant li père est dampnez d'aucun griéz criminel; et por ce n'a pas li fiz droiture en sa chose. (Ibid., xi, 20, s. 1, p. 247.)

M. Petit-Dutaillis, however (op. cit., p. 84 n.), observes : Ici les hésitations des agents de Louis se comprennent encore moins que leur ordinaire aisance à mentir. Quoi qu'en dise M. Bémont (Rev. Hist., t. 32, p. 67) l'exhérédation des enfants nés après la forfaiture du père semble avoir été une coutume admise à cette époque. He then refers to the case of Simon de Dammartin (infra). M. Guilhiermoz also (op. cit., p. 54) : M. Bémont avait aussi mis en doute l'existence d'une coutume alléguée par les envoyées de Louis en vertu de laquelle les enfants d'un condamné à mort nés après la condamnation étaient incapables de succéder. He quotes M. Petit-Dutaillis and concludes : Nous dirons à notre tour qu'il n'y avait pas de coutume plus avérée, ainsi qu'en témoigne notamment Philippe de Novarre. (Assises de Jérusalem, i, pp. 497–8.) I cannot pretend to appreciate the ratiocination of these eminent French publicists; but, if they imagine the authorities cited by them in any way support the case of Louis in 1216, they are vastly mistaken. Here is the first authority. Ludovicus, etc. Ad regiam pietatem pertinere dinoscitur illos vel illas qui sunt minus legitime nati quantum ad successionem hereditatis restituere natalibus, et successioni hereditarie

misrepresenting either the facts or the law. They had a
weak case, a hopeless case if you will, but they argued it

si regie placuerit majestati. Ad haec noverint universi presentes
pariter et futuri, quod veniens ad nos dilecta et consanguinea nostra
Maria comitissa Pontivi, nobis humiliter supplicavit, ut filios et filias
quos susceperat a Simone fratre comitis Ren. Boloniensis, post
interceptiones quas idem Simon fecerat adversus pie recordacionis
regem Philippum genitorem nostrum, et adhuc erat susceptura,
materne restitueremus successioni. Nos igitur motu pietatis ducti
ejusdem consanguinee nostre precibus nostrum animum inclinantes,
filios et filias a dicto Simone ipsi comitisse natos et nascituros
materne duximus successioni jure hereditario restituendos. . ..
Nos autem . . . concedimus et volumus quod filii et filie comitisse
sicut recti heredes succedant ei in tota hereditate de qua ipsa
comitissa erit tenens et saisita die qua decederet. . . . Actum, etc.
(Chinon, 1225; printed Martène, Ampl. Coll., i, 1198.) See also
Layettes du Trésor des Chartes, no. 1713. Now Marie de Ponthieu
was not a bastard, even if none of her three children, Jeanne,
Philipette and Marie, was born in time, she had scores of collaterals
who, if the custom alleged by Louis existed, had acquired contin-
gent interests in the estates in question by virtue of Simon's forfeiture. What power had Louis to disinherit these people? Why
should Louis from motives of piety commit an act of gross injustice?
It is perfectly plain that Louis contemplated nothing of the kind:
he was releasing his own claims to those estates, not the claims of
others; and the Charter so far from supporting is fatal to the
existence of the custom.

This is what Philippe de Novarre says: Mais si le requeror fust
engendré et né avant que son ancestre fu forjugié, là peut aveir
grant plait: car le seignor peut dire que toutevoie est il engendré
et descendu de celui qui est forjugié, et *que il entent que ce est assise
ou usage* que l'eir engendré et descendu de celui qui est forjugié est
aussi bien deserité comme est l'air de celui qui vent son fié par
l'assise. Le requeror peut dire que il estoit engendré et né avant
que celui jugement fu fait . . . et il est heir dou conqueror dou fié
et de part lui le requiert; et avant que ce avenist que l'om dist du
forjugiement de son ancestre estoit-il heir . . . et que ce soit voir
que l'om soit heir vivant son ancestre, les privileges le garentissent
où il se contient: " Je doing et otroi à toi et à tous heirs que tu as
et que auras." En cestui cas peut l'on aleger assés d'une part et
d'autre, *mais je n'en vi onques esgart faire, ne faire ne l'en veull*, tant
puis je bien dire vraiement que devant la gerre . . . avoie je oï
dire à moult de gent tousjours que les heirs engendrés et nez
avant que lor ancestre fust forjugié ne devoient pas estre deserités.
(Cap. xxiv, pp. 497-8.) Chapter xxv contains the same argument
about collateral heirs. This writer admits the prevailing custom

with great ability and straightforwardness. Let us take up the argument where we dropped it.

Again the pope says, that admitting the king of the English had been condemned to death, and also that the sons begotten by him [were excluded], still Blanche ought not to succeed, but his nearer relations, for example issue of an elder brother, and therefore the sister of Arthur, or Otho, who was the son of an elder sister. And if it is argued that the queen of Castille ought to succeed and thus her daughter Blanche, it is not true; because the male is to be preferred, that is the king of Castille, and if there was no male the queen of Léon ought to be preferred as the elder. To these things the envoys replied: "Sons of a brother ought not to succeed when at the date of the sentence (tempore latae sententiae) the brother was not living, and therefore the niece, the sister that is of Arthur, ought not to succeed, because she is not in the descending line, since she is the daughter of a brother. Similarly at the date of the sentence the mother of Otho was not living, therefore she did not succeed, therefore Otho ought not to succeed. But the queen of Castille was living, and was a sister, and therefore she succeeded; therefore on the death of the queen of Castille[1] her offspring succeeded and ought to succeed." To this the pope says, that the king of Castille ought to succeed, being a male, or the queen of Léon as the elder. The envoys replied, that when there are many heirs who ought to succeed to anyone, and he who has the prior right is silent or neglects to take the inheritance, the remoter heir, if he so desires, ought according to approved custom to be admitted to the inheritance, saving nevertheless the right of the other if he makes a claim.

(assise ou usage); he admits that he knows of no decision to the contrary; he seems to be merely advocating less harsh rules of forfeiture as a desirable innovation, although, if his arguments were accepted, forfeiture to the lord could never occur unless the criminal happened to be a bastard without issue; and, even in this case, there could be no forfeiture as distinct from escheat unless the criminal survived his sentence and left after-born issue living at his death. This, if you please, is the authority cited to support the allegations of the French envoys in 1216. I hope it will have been noticed that Philippe de Novarre is not discussing either French or English laws; and, finally, let me apologise for attempting a serious reply to so frivolous an argument.

[1] Eleanor of Castille died 31st October, 1214. See Schirrmacher, Geschichte Castiliens, ss. 320–2.

It cannot be said that (after excluding the issue of John) the queen of Castille's right to succeed was indisputable, but the weight of authority was certainly in favour of Louis on this point. It was the rule in England and Normandy that a younger brother succeeded before the son of a deceased elder brother, and it appears that originally this rule applied equally in the case of females. There was a tendency, however, to place sisters in a less favourable position, and Richard introduced the rule into Normandy that nephews, being sons of sons, were to be preferred to sisters.[1] The practice of admitting a remoter heir to the inheritance, without prejudice to subsequent claimants with a better title, was common enough in England : it will be sufficient to recall the two cases of Margaret de Beaumont under John, and Simon de Montfort under Henry the Third.

The rest of the discussion is not very material until we come to the last objection put forward by the pope :—

Item dicit Papa, quod rex Francorum et Ludovicus filius ejus, post sententiam a baronibus Franciae in regem Angliae latam, ipsum " regem " appellaverunt, et ipsum pro rege habuerunt, et cum eo tanquam cum rege Angliae treugas statuerunt. Ad haec nuncii responderunt, quod post latam sententiam a baronibus in regem nunquam illum pro rege habuerunt ; sed ipsum "regem depositum " appellaverunt sicut abbas depositus, et quilibet alius, dici solet.

Here, it is said, we have incontestable proof of bad faith ; the agents deliberately lied. According to M. Bémont : " Les agents répondirent . . . que les actes officiels n'ont jamais désigné Jean que ' comme roi déposé, comme on dit un abbé

---

[1] Très Ancien Coutumier de Normandie, cap. xii, s. 1 : Filius licet postgenitus heres propinquior est hereditatis patris sui quam nepotes, filii fratris sui primogeniti.—s. 2 : Postea vero in tempore guerre, Ricardo rege possidente, filie portionem non potuerunt habere aliquam [de] hereditate habenda succedente de morte patris contra nepotes qui erant filii fratris sui.

Compare Beaumanoir, Coutumes du Beauvoisis, i, 238, 240. This custom, however, was certainly not universal in France.

The following occurs on the Close Roll, 13 Henry III, m. 14d : Non est consuetudo vel lex in terra nostra Anglie quod filia fratris alicujus primogeniti fratrem juniorem patri suo succedentem hereditarie . . . super hereditate sua possit vel debeat impetere.

déposé, ou toute autre personne.' "[1] If such was the tenor of their reply without doubt they lied, but this is placing a most unwarranted construction on their words. The true construction is prima facie something quite different. Stated in oratio recta the reply of the envoys was this : " After sentence passed by the barons against the king, *we* have never held him to be king, but have called him a deposed king [etc.]." A disingenuous reply perhaps, but it can hardly be challenged. Louis had already in his manifesto taken up the sound legal attitude that the acts of Philip could not prejudice him. Is it credible that the envoys abandoned this well-fortified position for the precarious refuge of a lie? Indubitably they were clever men, far too clever to lie where there was not the smallest reason for so doing.[2]

There is one other point deserving attention. The pope speaks of treaties in the plural. Between 1203, the supposed date of Arthur's murder, and the year 1216 several treaties had in fact been entered into by the rival kings, but only one was posterior to John's second condemnation.[3] This confirms the view that the pope antedated the sentence in question. Louis, it will be remembered, had on the contrary referred to one treaty only in his manifesto, and by so doing had as against himself fixed the date of John's sentence within very narrow limits.[4]

We are now in a position to attempt a final solution of the

---

[1] Revue Historique, t. 32, p. 69.

[2] We find John himself treating Philip and Louis as distinct persons in connection with the subject of peace and treaties. See the Flanders Charter in Charter Roll, 15 John, m. 4d. Printed Rot. Cart., p. 197.

[3] For the treaty of 1214 see Delisle, Cat. des Actes de Ph. Aug., no. 1506; and see generally Petit-Dutaillis, Règne de Louis VIII, pp. 81-2.

[4] The last occasion, so far as I am aware, when Louis can be said to have styled John "king of England," actually occurred at Soissons in April, 1213, at the time of the famous assembly. In the Act which provides for the eventuality of John's dethronement and the crowning of Louis we find—si vero regem Anglie capi contigerit, [etc.]. (Delisle, op. cit., no. 1437.) Therefore either the agents of Louis lied or John's second condemnation took place between 1213 and 1214.

only real difficulty which Louis's case presents, that is to say, the argument excluding John's issue. It is, under the circumstances which have been detailed, well-nigh incredible that the envoys either invented or accepted a false date for John's judgment, and then invented a non-existing custom to fit that date. It is clear from the manifesto that this was not the case Louis was setting up; the date of Henry's birth was introduced as an important but not a vital factor in his argument. The most probable construction to be placed on the report is this. The pope urged that John's issue ought to succeed: that he described such issue as born after sentence has no bearing upon the main argument. The envoys very justly replied that customary law excluded issue in such a case. They then added that, notwithstanding the custom, persons (other than issue) born before the forfeiture ought to succeed. The last point, naturally enough, they were unwilling to discuss: the difficulty underlying such a contention has been already indicated. This construction does not necessarily involve doing any violence whatever to the language of the report. The envoys were not concerned to do more than meet word for word the actual objections raised by the pope. If "sentence" was, in fact, the word used, they certainly meant "forfeiture," merely using the former word because the pope used it. But it is perhaps more probable that the report is in error on this point: it must be a condensed account of what took place, and the scribe in drawing it up may, carefully or carelessly, have made answer correspond with question.

The second condemnation of John has occasioned a vast amount of controversy. Until comparatively recently historians accepted the view that John had been sentenced to death within a year of Arthur's murder. Then in 1886 M. Bémont published an essay[1] in order to demonstrate that no such judgment ever took place; he did not, however, direct his attention to the events of 1213. M. Bémont's conclusions were universally adopted, and the controversy was regarded as closed until, in 1899, M. Guilhiermoz, in an article

[1] Revue Historique, t. 32, pp. 33 and 290.

contributed to the Bibliothèque de l'École des Chartes,[1] attempted to reinstate the earlier opinion. This last-mentioned writer maintained that John was condemned to death by a judicial sentence passed in April, 1203, his main argument being that Philip and Louis could never have asserted, as they did in 1216, the fact of John's condemnation if the whole story had been a mere fiction, that so impudent a lie must inevitably have been unmasked. The latter writer certainly succeeded in invalidating some of the minor and less carefully considered arguments of the former, but he was unable to produce one single unequivocal item of evidence in support of a condemnation in 1203.

Notwithstanding M. Guilhiermoz, historians still regard M. Bémont's conclusions as substantially unshaken. In my opinion the problem has been entirely misconceived, and the facts are as I have stated them.[2]

In July, 1216, Philip Augustus cited Blanche de Navarre and her son Thibaud IV to appear before his court at the suit of Erard count of Brienne, who claimed the comté of Champagne. An original act of Philip is preserved,[3] dated at Melun, which states that judgment was delivered :—

a paribus regni nostri videlicet A. Remensi archiepiscopo, W. Lingonensi, W. Cathalaunensi, Ph. Belvacensi, Stephano Noviomensi episcopis, et O. duce Burgundie, et a multis aliis episcopis et baronibus nostris videlicet [G.] Altissiodorensi, R. Carnotensi, G. Silvanectensi, et J. Lexoviensi episcopis, et Guillelmo comite Pontivi, R. comite Drocarum, P. comite Britannie, G. comite Sancti Pauli, W. de Ruppibus senescallo Andegavensi, W. comite Jovigniaci, J. comite Bellimontis, et R. comite de Alenceon, nobis audientibus et judicium approbantibus . . .

---

[1] t. 60, pp. 45-85.

[2] For a bibliography on this subject see Viollet, Instit. de la France, vol. iii. If M. Bémont's hypothesis is correct, how came it that so many lies were told and not a single document forged in support of those lies? Disciples of M. Bémont have actually cited cases of forgery by kings to show that economy of truth is not astonishing in sovereigns. The economy of deceit involved by M. Bémont's thesis I find decidedly astonishing.

[3] Langlois, Textes, no. 19.

This is the first recorded appearance in French history of persons styled peers of the realm, and it coincides very curiously with the assertions at Rome and in England concerning John's condemnation by his peers. It seems most improbable that this coincidence was purely fortuitous.[1] Let me recapitulate the leading facts. In the year 1202 John was subjected to a "judicium super eum ire," and later on Philip relied upon this judgment to silence the scruples of the Norman ecclesiastics. On this occasion the pope neither admitted nor denied the validity of the process. In 1213, by a similar process, something much more serious was attempted against John, nothing less, in fact, than condign punishment for murder and confiscation of his kingdom. Then, in 1215, England obtained her Great Charter with its frequent references to judgment of peers, including one provision offering judgment by peers to the king of Scotland, and another constituting a semi-judicial, semi-executive tribunal of twenty-five magnates. In 1216 the judgment of John by his peers of France was asserted, and objected to on the ground that the barons of France were not John's peers. Lastly, in the same year we are introduced to a select body of French magnates consisting of peers of France and twelve other barons, representing quite possibly part of an ideal court of twenty-four magnates. These sequences are truly remarkable, but no very convincing explanation can even be conjectured. Perhaps the countess of Champagne took advantage of Philip's predicament to claim a hitherto unrecognised privilege: perhaps Philip Augustus took advantage of

---

[1] Prior to the Champagne case, let me repeat, there is no record whatsoever of a trial by peers of France: but of this particular trial we are given a superabundance of testimony. By special invitation (see Langlois Textes, no. 19 bis) each noble present advertises the occurrence by separate letters patent under his own hand and seal; and, what with originals and contemporary transcripts, scores of these documents are still preserved. Why this extraordinary publicity? And why, if you please, did Manasses bishop of Orleans have the bad taste and temerity to slander the whole affair? . . . Contra judicium baronum Francie ad quos pertinent hujusmodi judicia locutus est. Super qua temeritate in presentia nostra et parium predictorum . . . idipsum nobis et paribus emendavit. (See Delisle, Cat. des Actes de Ph. Auguste, no. 1739.)

a pending dispute to fortify his special pleading *in re* Jean Sans-Terre by a bit of ex post facto evidence. Be that as it may, from 1216 onwards the reported decisions affecting peers of France are numerous ; the cases, during the thirteenth century, mostly representing attempts to expand these privileges resisted and defeated by the crown.

In the year 1224[1] an attempt was made by the peers of France, at the trial of the countess of Flanders, to exclude the household officers, the chancellor, butler, chamberlain and constable from taking part in the proceedings. The attempt

[1] Cum esset contentio inter Johannam comitissam Flandrie ex una parte, et Johannem de Nigella ex altera, idem Johannes appellavit comitissam de defectu ad curiam domini regis. Dominus rex fecit comitissam citari coram se per duos milites. Comitissa ad diem comparens proposuit se sufficienter non fuisse citatam per duos milites, quia per pares suos citari debebat. Partibus appodiantibus se ad judicium super hoc, judicatum est in curia domini regis quod comitissa fuerat sufficienter et competenter citata per duos milites, et quod tenebat et valebat submonitio per eos facta de comitissa. Item, comitissa proposuit quod Johannes de Nigella pares habebat in Flandria, per quos debebat judicari in curia comitisse, et quod parata erat ei facere jus in curia sua per pares ipsius Johannis, nec idem Johannes dicebat quod comitissa defecerit ei de jure per pares ipsius Johannis, per quos judicari debebat in curia comitisse : et ita requirebat comitissa curiam suam de Johanne de Nigella. Johannes de Nigella e contrario respondebat quod ad curiam comitisse nullo modo reverti volebat, quia ipsa defecerat ei de jure et de defectu juris appellaverat eam ad curiam domini regis, ubi paratus erat eam convincere de defectu juris ad considerationem curie domini regis. Super his judicatum est quod Johannes de Nigella non debebat reverti ad curiam comitisse et quod comitissa debebat ei respondere in curia domini regis, ubi eam appellaverat de defectu juris. Preterea cum pares Francie dicerent quod cancellarius, buticularius, camerarius, constabularius Francie, ministeriales hospitii domini regis, non debebant cum eis interesse ad faciendum judicia super pares Francie, et dicti ministeriales hospitii domini regis e contrario dicerent se debere ad usus et consuetudines Francie observatas interesse cum paribus Francie ad judicandum pares, judicatum fuit in curia domini regis quod ministeriales predicti de hospitio domini regis debent interesse cum paribus Francie ad judicandum pares ; et tunc judicaverunt comitissam Flandrie ministeriales predicti cum paribus Francie apud Parisius anno Domini MCCXXIV. (Langlois, Textes, no. xxi ; Martène Ampl. Coll., i, 1193 ; Actes du Parlement, i, p. 303, c. ii.)

failed. This case is in other respects remarkable. It was an appeal by a vassal of Flanders against the countess *de defectu juris*, and according to later ideas should not have been tried by peers of France at all.

In 1237 the case of the count and countess of Flanders was heard by a court at which three peers only were present, namely, the bishops of Laon, Langres and Noyon.[1]

In the year 1259 the archbishop of Reims was the defendant in an action of ejectment. The case was tried by Julien de Péronne and other justices (maistres); the decision was adverse to the prelate. The archbishop, much concerned, consulted with his advisers who assured him the judgment was bad for want of jurisdiction : " pour ce qu'il n'est pas faiz ne rendus pas vos pers ; et vous iestes pers, si devez estre jugiez par eus." The archbishop accordingly moved the king for a new trial, and his case was argued by counsel as follows : " Par foi, sire, li arcevesques est pers de France, si doit estre jugiez par ses pers. Cis jugemens n'est pas faiz par ses pers ; si ne veut pas que il li griet. . . ." The justices advised that the judgment was good, " car la querele dont li jugemenz estoit faiz n'estoit pas de la perie et pour ce convenoit-il qu'il fust tenuz." The archbishop took leave of the court weeping bitterly.[2]

This last case should be compared with two others, an earlier one and a later one. In 1210 the bishop of Orleans had stated publicly before the king that he ought not to be judged except by the bishops of France, and had thereupon left the court.[3] In 1267 the bishop of Châlons also pleaded, not that he was a peer, but that he was *presbiter et episcopus*. On the other side it was contended that the bishop should answer—*cum sit baro et par Francie et homo ligius domini Regis*, and the bishop's demurrer was overruled by the court.[4]

In 1293 Edward of England was cited as duke of Aquitaine to appear before the court of peers. Edward, alarmed at the prospect of a conviction, sent Edmund of Lancaster to

---

[1] Teulet, Layettes du Trésor des Chartes, ii, 355–7.
[2] Les Olim, i, 454, no. 18 ; Langlois, Textes, nos. xxxii, xxxii bis.
[3] Langlois, Textes, no. xviii.   [4] Les Olim, i, p. 666, no. iii.

place the duchy completely at the disposal of the French king.[1]

On the 29th of March, 1295, Valenciennes affected to choose Guy count of Flanders as its feudal lord. Philip was extremely angry, Guy decidedly contumacious; the count was summoned to Paris, and Flanders distrained for his contempt. The case came before the king in council.[2] Guy protested that it was contrary to right and reason that the king, by himself or his council, should be judge in his own cause; and that he would recognise no judges but the peers of France, for the question at issue concerned the seizin of the whole of his peer's fee. (This was not true.) The king overruled these pleas: judgment was pronounced by the chancellor, to the effect that the supreme judicature of the realm was in the king and council, and that it was for them to decide when it was necessary to have recourse to the peers. The general issue was also decided against the count, and he was ordered to surrender Valenciennes.

On the following 9th of January Guy delivered his famous *diffidatio*.[3] This was a very different matter, and the count was at once summoned to appear before the tribunal of peers. When served with the summons he is reported to have said: " I will appear to this on the frontiers of Flanders." He certainly disobeyed the summons; and a court, at which some peers were present, found no difficulty in condemning him.[4]

By the end of the thirteenth century the principles obtaining with regard to judgment by peers of France were briefly

---

[1] The principal documents relating to this matter are printed in Rymer, Foedera R.C., vol. i, pt. 2; see also Engl. Hist. Rev., vol. x, p. 227.

[2] Nobis ipsi comiti [Flandrensi] jus super hoc facere offerentibus, eodem comite proponente non ad nos set ad pares suos pertinere reddere jus super istis; altercato diutius coram nobis an ad nos per nostrum consilium, vel per pares, pertineret decernere quis, cujus esset jurisdictio, deberet judicare, pronunciatum fuit, per curie nostre judicium, pertinere ad nos — per nostrum consilium — decernere cujus sit jurisdictio in premissis. (Les Olim, ii., p. 396, no. 23; Langlois, Textes, no. cxiii.)

[3] Kervyn de Lettenhove, Hist. de Flandre, ii, p. 559.

[4] These proceedings are printed by Kervyn de Lettenhove, ii, 574-8.

these. The presence of a single peer was sufficient to
support the judgment of the king's court. It was not
necessary to summon the peers at all unless the whole of
a peer's fee was in issue. It was for the king's court to
decide when recourse to the peers was necessary.[1] These
are the chief principles; but there are secondary questions
of procedure, at this time under discussion, which are well
worth mentioning.

Thus we find Philip le Bel by the treaty of Athis-sur-Orge
laying down rules for the composition of the tribunal of
peers. The right of state officers and other magnates to
be present is definitely stated, but the king concedes to the
count of Flanders that in his case the court shall be
restricted to peers and twelve others.[2] By a subsequent
concession the composition of the tribunal was restricted
to peers and officers of state, a concession limited in terms
to the joint lives of the contracting parties. The count,
moreover, was not to incur forfeiture except in accordance
with the general law of the land relating to lord and
vassal.[3] The connection of these concessions with the cases
of 1216 and 1224 should be noticed. Apparently it was
on the authority of the former that the right to associate
twelve magnates with the peers was claimed, while on
the latter was based the claim of the state officers to be
present.[4]

On or about the 30th of June, 1315, the count of Flanders,
in default of appearance to a summons by Louis the Tenth,
was sentenced to forfeit his title and estates. Judgment was
pronounced by a court consisting of six peers (including the
countess of Artois) and eleven other magnates. Edward the
Second of England was summoned to sit as a peer of France

---

[1] See Luchaire, Manuel des Instit. Fr., p. 560.

[2] This treaty is printed in Archives de la Ville de Bruges, i, 285.
The date of the treaty is June, 1305.

[3] Letter of 19th July, 1312; original preserved in Bibl. Nat.,
Mél. Colb., 348, no. 86; printed Funck-Brentano, Études dédiées
à G. Monod, p. 358.

[4] Would it be rash to conclude that, then as now, these two were
the earliest records available concerning the composition and jurisdiction of the court of peers?

for this trial, but he essoined himself on account of the Scotch war.[1]

Artois, Anjou and Brittany had been added to the French peerage in 1297. From the close of the thirteenth century onwards such fresh creations became fairly frequent: Poitou was added in 1315, la Marche in 1317, and so on. The avowed object of the first creations was to fill the vacancies in the original college caused by the extinction of the peerages of Normandy, Toulouse and Champagne; but, if there was ever any idea of always limiting the college to twelve, that idea was soon abandoned.

The principle of judgment by peers in France was not reduced to precision until the year 1458, when the duke of Alençon was accused of high treason. Parliament, after searching the records, gave the following ruling:[2] When any peer of France is accused of a crime which touches or may touch his body, his person and estate, the king presides in person, the peers of France and the other lords holding by peerage are summoned, and these assisted by other notables of the realm, prelates and others of the king's council ought to have cognisance of the case.

The position, during the thirteenth century, of earls and barons of France who were not peers need not be discussed. They retained for some considerable time privileges analogous to those enjoyed by the peers of France: relatively perhaps these privileges were nearly the same at the outset; but it goes without saying that, neither relatively nor absolutely, were they ever any greater.

[1] See Funck-Brentano, op. cit., pp. 359–60, and authorities there cited.
[2] See generally Viollet, Inst. de la Fr., vol. iii, pp. 301–7, and the authorities there cited.

CHAPTER IX

JUDGMENT OF PEERS IN THE THIRTEENTH AND FOURTEENTH CENTURY

IN a former chapter I have attempted to define as accurately as possible the nature of the concession set forth in clause 39 of the Great Charter. This clause affords two alternative guarantees for the liberty of the freeman—the lawful judgment of peers, or the law of the land—but these are treated as being in many respects coextensive. At the beginning of Henry the Third's reign the Charter was reissued in a modified form, which did not, however, tend to make the intention of the clause in question any clearer. Meanwhile, too, the phrase judicium parium was undergoing a change of meaning which was bound sooner or later to influence the construction of these words in the Charter. The pamphleteering of Louis, the legal argument at Rome, and later the presence of a large number of Frenchmen at the English court, persons well acquainted with the recent development of these doctrines in France; all these circumstances helped to infuse fresh life into the principle and direct its development into aristocratic channels.

In 1233 the matter came up for discussion before Henry the Third, when it was boldly stated in the king's presence that several of his subjects had been illegally condemned without judgment of peers.[1] The bishop of Winchester hotly

---

[1] Matthew Paris, Rolls Series, iii, p. 251 : Plures autem qui praesentes erant regem humiliter rogabant in Domino quatinus pacem faceret cum baronibus suis et nobilibus. Et aliae favorabiles personae, utpote fratres Praedicatores et Minores, quos rex solito venerabatur et exaudivit, eum attentius hortabantur, ut ipse debita dilectione homines suos naturales studeret amplexari, quos absque judicio parium suorum coegerat exulare extorres, villas eorum cremaverat, silvas et pomeria succiderat. . . . Ad haec respondens

disputed the allegation. There were no peers in England, he said, comparable to the peers of France, therefore the king's justices were the peers of any man.[1] This assertion caused quite a scene at court ; some very plain speaking was indulged in, and the bishop, we gather, had to listen to remarks about himself which were the reverse of flattering. But, although the prelate's opinions were exceedingly unpopular, it by no means follows that they were bad in law.

Viewing the question dispassionately we must admit that there was something to be said on both sides. The statement of Peter des Roches was paradoxical, on simple inspection it certainly seems to be a " perverse misrepresentation of the English law." His opponents, however, were in a worse case. They were questioning the jurisdiction which had been exercised by the king's justices in an appeal of robbery against the earl of Pembroke, Gilbert Basset and others. The real if not the avowed act of robbery was the abduction of Hubert de Burgh from sanctuary. The respondents had not appeared and had been outlawed. Outlawry, we know, could be effected by the " law of the land," both the Charter and Bracton tell us so distinctly : at the same time outlawry was a judicial act involving a judgment. Assuming the law of the land had been in other respects complied with, could the bishop's opponents maintain that such judgment should have been, and yet was not, a judgment of peers ? They certainly could not define judgment of peers in such a way as to exclude the justices, and still assert that every judgment must be a judgment of peers : they had to face the recognised jurisdiction of the Exchequer and Bench as separate courts. This fatal inconsistency could only be got over by admitting the bishop's contention, or

P[etrus] Wintoniensis episcopus dixit, quod non sunt pares in Anglia sicut in regno Francorum ; unde licet regi Anglorum per justitiarios, quos constituerit, quoslibet de regno reos proscribere et mediante judicio condempnare. Episcopi vero haec audientes quasi una voce comminabantur, quod nominatim excommunicarent principales regis consiliarios iniquos. See also Wendover, Rolls Series, iii, p. 58.

[1] Compare the rule of Loisel : serjent à roi est pair à comte ; see Établissements de S. Louis, vol. i, p. 193.

by limiting the scope of the principle.[1] If, however, they asserted that all judgments in suits to which the king was a party must be judgments of peers (justices excluded), they would be asserting a distinction, familiar no doubt in some countries, but scarcely known at that time to the jurisprudence of England, and little satisfaction would they derive from such a shift. The jurisdiction of the Bench was disposed of but not that of the Exchequer; and a more fatal objection, the narrower claim would not cover the case under discussion for the king was not a party to it. The opposition were trying to preserve old wine in new bottles, and the task was beyond their powers.

For his attitude on this occasion Henry's minister has been roundly abused, not only by his contemporaries, but also by posterity; he has been accused of an impudent attempt to support illegal convictions obtained by the king; Dr. Stubbs has called him an ignorant blunderer. For my own part, I see no reason for doubting that this acute lawyer, equally familiar probably with both French and English law, was expressing a perfectly genuine opinion, and one which he well knew could not be safely controverted.

The king at this time was neither strong enough to enforce the bishop's opinion, nor so weak as to be compelled to adopt a contrary view. Henry had received a lesson from France in these matters, and he did to others as Philip Augustus was alleged to have done to his father.[2] The magnates, whose treatment led to the discussion related, had, when threatened with the alternative of trial by battle or outlawry, demanded judgment of peers[3] and a safe-conduct

---

[1] Doubtless many still considered it to be a legal axiom that every judgment ought to be a judgment of peers. Probably only a few clearly perceived the inroads which the development of royal justice was making upon the principle. The separation of the Bench was the work of the Charter, although it may be that nothing similar to the actual court of common pleas at Westminster was ever dreamed of. An instance of the ordinary formula, that one court is not to follow another, will be found in Rot. Cart. R.C. at p. 168.   [2] See above, p. 260.

[3] They appear to have made the same demand in respect of several previous charges brought against them. See Matthew Paris,

to and from the king's court. If the latter claim had been granted the king would probably have had to submit to an unpalatable definition of the former claim. Henry offered the magnates in question a safe-conduct to his court provided they came singly and unattended; as regarded the safe-conduct from his court, that must be subject to such judgment as his court might pronounce. The offer was not accepted, and they were all outlawed. In 1234, when the reform party were again in the ascendant, the sentences of outlawry were quashed.[1] The question of judgment by peers was only

Rolls Series, vol. iii, p. 257. Ad haec respondens Marescallus fratri Agnello dixit: "Ad primum quod dicunt, debeo, quia terram regis invasi, non est verum; quia rex ipse, cum semper paratus essem stare juri et judicio parium meorum in curia sua, et per internuntios plures pluries petii illud quod ab ipso mihi semper extitit denegatum, terram meam violenter ingressus contra omnem justitiam invasit." See also ibid., vi, p. 63: answers of Laurence of St. Albans to the charges against Hubert de Burgh, 1st July, 1239. Cum dies datus esset Huberto de Burgo comiti Kantiae in octabis sancti Johannis Baptistae anno regni xxiij, ad respondendum domino regi, quales emendas ei faceret, eo quod non deliberavit ei maritagium Ricardi de Clare, ad diem ab eodem domino rege sibi datum, secundum conventionem inter eos factam vel secundum considerationem parium suorum, et dominus rex peteret ab eo, quod ei emendas faceret et non fecit; propositae fuerunt ei ex parte domini regis transgressiones subscriptae, simul cum praedictis ut ad eas responderet. Ad quod respondit idem comes quod ad haec nullum diem habuit; sed et dixit quod ad diem certum et rationabilem satisfaceret domino regi vel inde staret ad considerationem parium suorum, et petiit quod dominus rex in scriptis ei ostenderet super quibus articulis tenetur respondere. Ad hoc respondit comes, quod ad singulos dies ei a domino rege datos idem comes venit, nec in aliquo quaesivit dilationem, sed semper recepit diem ad voluntatem domini regis. Unde videtur ei quod omnes dies ei dati, postquam fuit apud Kenintone, pro uno die sibi debent allocari. Et semper paratus est stare ad considerationem parium suorum, quod. . . . Et si hoc non sufficit, dicit aliud; et super hoc paratus est facere quod pares sui considerabunt. . . . De utlagatione unde dicitur, dicit quod talem conventionem non fecit, neque debet talis conventio aliqua reputari; quia nullus probus homo et fidelis potest utlagari ex conventione, quia utlagatio est paena malefactoris et non bene operantis, et sequitur ex malefacto illius qui non vult stare recto. Ipse vero non fuit talis quia semper rogavit et optulit stare judicio parium suorum. . . .

[1] See Bracton's Note Book, case 857: . . . Et super hoc venit

incidentally mentioned; there were excellent technical grounds for declaring the outlawry a nullity.

The controversy raised by the bishop of Winchester's statement does not appear to have been ever revived. In course of time and as the result of differently developed ideas the point became quite obsolete; but in the meanwhile that statement continued to represent the position taken up by the crown, and it was a position from which the crown never completely receded. To this day the king's justices, in cases of misdemeanour, are competent to try the premier duke of the realm. The Hubert de Burgh case teaches us nothing definite, it decided nothing; but we may gather from it that the meaning of judgment by peers and the scope of the privilege was already debatable ground, and that both sides were struggling for a definition favourable to themselves. We are also in a position to appreciate the difficulties in the way of any logical solution.

We can now begin to trace the development of a new and quite distinct line of construction for the thirty-ninth chapter of the Charter, based on the circumstance that judgment of

dominus rex et cognoscit et recordatur quod predicti Marescallus Gilebertus et alii ante utlagationem illam multociens per nuncios sollempnos (sic) et per litteras pecierunt misericordiam vel ut per salvum conductum adiri (sic) possent curiam domini regis et stare ibidem judicio parium suorum, quod quidem illis fuit denegatum, nisi in forma tali, scilicet quod unusquisque per se et solus veniret et rediret nisi judicium illum incumbaret. Et plures episcopi et alii quamplures presentes hoc idem testati fuerunt. Et quum predicta abduccio Huberti facta fuit occasione gwerre, et preterea cum nullus utlagari deberet nisi aut per appellum racionabile, aut per sectam domini regis ubi fama patrie accusaret aliquem, vel de seditione domini regis vel alia manifesta transgressione contra pacem domini regis, et hoc tempore pacis, et predicta fuerunt tempore gwerre, et preterea quia testatum fuit quod predictus campio non appellavit eos de aliqua robberia sibi facta, sed tantum pro transgressione facta domino regi, et quia appellavit pro comitatu Wiltes. de transgressione eis facta, scilicet de predicto Huberto abducto que quidem transgressio pertinebat ad dominum regem, et quia dominus rex cognoscit quod ipsi semper obtulerunt per litteras et per nuncios veniendi ad curiam et standi recto, Consideratum est quod utlagatio illa nulla est et pro nulla habeatur de cetero. . . . (A.D. 1234, anno regni 18.)

peers and the law of the land are mentioned disjunctively. It may be stated in this way. The king's justices had full authority to administer the law of the land, but their jurisdiction, though commensurate with, was strictly limited by such law: neither on their own initiative nor by virtue of any royal mandate could they exercise unprecedented jurisdiction; cases raising questions of this kind must be determined by the peers of the party or parties concerned. In other words the king must proceed by the law of the land; or, if that fails him, then by judgment of peers.[1] We do not find any statement precisely to this effect, but in many cases such a principle is unmistakably indicated. Here is an example:—

In or about the year 1234-5 the earl of Chester was made defendant in an important civil suit connected with the descent of the Chester estates. The writ was served on him in the county of Northampton, but the subject-matter of the suit was property situate in the earl's palatinate where the king's writ did not run. The earl demurred to the jurisdiction and claimed the judgment of his peers. The court overruled the objection on the ground that there were precedents for such procedure.[2]

[1] Also, judgment by peers is one thing, judgment by justices another; although the meaning of the former expression still lacks definition.

[2] Bracton's Note Book, case 1213. . . . J. comes Cestrie et Huntingdone summonitus fuit ad respondendum Hugoni de Albyniaco, W. comiti de Ferrariis et Agneti uxori ejus et Hawisie comitisse Lincolnie quare deforciat eis racionabilem partem suam que eos contingit de hereditate Rannulfi quondam comitis Cestrie et unde ipse obiit seisitus in comitatu Cestrie. . . . Et comes alias respondit quod noluit ad hoc breve [respondere] nisi curia consideraverit et sine consideratione parium suorum per summonitionem factam in comitatu Northamptone [de] terris et tenementis [in] comitatu Cestrie ubi brevia domini regis non currunt. Et quia ita usitatum est hucusque quod pares sui et alii qui libertates habent consimiles sicut episcopus Dunholmensis et comes Marescallus respondent de terris et tenementis infra libertates suas per summoniciones factas ad terras suas et tenementa extra libertates suas, ideo consideratum est quod respondeat. . . . (A.D. 1236, anno regni 21.)

The same principle appears even more clearly in a later case, the celebrated dispute between the earls of Hereford and Gloucester in the reign of Edward the First. The king had appointed special justices to hear this case, and had directed that evidence was to be taken on oath from the magnates as well as the commoners who had knowledge of the facts. Certain magnates thereupon were duly summoned and presented with the book; but they all declined to be sworn, asserting that there was no legal precedent for making them give evidence on oath (which was admittedly true). The justices replied to the effect that they were not proceeding by law, but under a prerogative mandate from the king. The magnates rejoined by claiming the judgment of their peers upon the question.[1]

One more instance may be mentioned, a forest case of the year 1286. An inquisition found that the bishop of Coventry and Lichfield had made a park in his wood of Heywode and two saltoria within the metes of the forest of Cannock, also another saltorium in his own park of Brewode, but on the

---

[1] Voluit idem dominus rex pro statu et jure suo per ipsos justiciarios quod inde rei veritas inquiretur per sacramentum tam magnatum quam aliorum proborum et legalium hominum de partibus Wallie et comitatibus Gloucestrie et Herefordie per quos rei veritas etc. cujuscunque condicionis fuissent, ita quod nulli parceretur in hac parte, eo quod res ista dominum regem et coronam et dignitatem suam tangit. . . . Dictum est ex parte domini regis Johanni de Hastinges et omnibus aliis magnatibus supranominatis quod, pro statu et jure regis et pro conservacione dignitatis corone et pacis sue, apponant manum ad librum ad faciendum id quod eis ex parte domini regis injungetur; qui omnes unanimiter respondent quod inaudatum (sic) est quod ipsi vel eorum antecessores hactenus in hujusmodi casu ad prestandum sacramentum aliquod coacti fuerunt. . . . Et licet prefatis Johanni et aliis magnatibus expositum fuissent quod nullus in hac parte potest habere marchiam,—dominus rex qui pro communi utilitate (per) prerogativam suam in multis casibus est supra leges et consuetudines in regno suo usitatas,—ac pluries eisdem magnatibus ex parte ipsius regis conjunctim et separatim libroque eis porrecto injunctum est quod faciant sacramentum; responderunt demum omnes singillatim quod nichil inde facerent sine consideracione parium suorum. (See Duchy of Lancaster Misc., 6/5; Welsh Roll, 20 Edward I; Rot. Parl., vol. i, p. 70; Abbreviatio Placitorum, p. 227b.; Morris, Welsh Wars of Edward I; etc.)

boundaries of the forest. On this finding a judicial writ was issued summoning the bishop to attend. The bishop was allowed to appear by attorney: he denied the trespass, pleaded that he was seized of the lands and woods in question as part of his barony with power of taking venison, etc., and that he was not bound to answer *sine brevi domini regis vel sine paribus suis baronibus Anglie*, a plea to the jurisdiction based on the statute of Marlborough. A day was thereupon given to the bishop to appear before the king in Parliament, but nothing was done in the matter on this adjournment. Eventually a decision in eyre was given against the bishop, and the lands in question taken into the king's hands.[1]

Obviously, in ordinary cases, there was no need to invoke the principle under consideration. If there was any doubt about the jurisdiction you could appeal, baron or no baron. The right of appeal was a wider and more comprehensive remedy.

The construction of the Charter indicated by these decisions once adopted, it is quite clear that any lawyer writing a treatise on the laws of England has nothing whatever to do with judgment by peers: it is only when the laws of England cease that the privilege of judgment by peers arises. Indeed, the *judicium parium* now figures, not as a legal principle at all, but merely as a check on the royal prerogative. This, I

---

[1] See William Salt, Arch. Soc., vol. v, pt. 1, p. 167, pleas of the forest A.D. 1286: Manwood, Forest Laws. For a similar plea to the jurisdiction see Abbreviatio Placitorum, p. 201 (A.D. 1281): Gilbertus de Clare comes Gloucestrie qui clamat tenere terras suas in Glamorgan sicut regale quamvis per consilium regis cosideratum fuit quod responderet in placito. Nichilominus dicit quod tenet predictas terras et libertates de suo et antecessorum suorum conquestu unde videtur ei quod de hiis sine consideratione parium suorum Anglie et Marchesium Wallie qui eisdem libertatibus in terris suis Wallensibus gaudent non debet inde alicui respondere.

In this case the plea of the earl of Gloucester is not: I am an earl, and must be judged by earls; or, I am a lord marcher, and must be judged by lords marchers; but simply this: I hold by conquest sicut regale, the king's writ does not run in the lands in question, and by the law of the land the king cannot claim jurisdiction; therefore, etc. See also Glamorgan Charters, vol. i, p. 192; and Coram Rege Roll, 10 Edward I, Mich., m. 35.

think, sufficiently accounts for the silence of Bracton upon the subject; it was not a matter which came within the scope of his work.

At this stage a new and not very prepossessing idol of the law is allowed to occupy the vacant shrine of English liberties. No man, it is now asserted, not even the king, may be judge in his own cause; and under cover of this principle it is sought to enforce judgment by or with the assistance of peers of the realm in cases of high treason. We have met with this principle elsewhere,[1] but hitherto there has been little trace of its influence on English jurisprudence.[2]

Bracton sets out the matter in this way. The king himself, he writes, cannot be judge in cases of treason, because he would then be prosecutor and judge in his own cause. Nor can the justices judge, because they represent the person of the king. Who, then, should judge? Without prejudice to a better opinion it would seem that the court and (the) peers should judge. Bracton then points out that there were different degrees of treason, which did not always amount to felony. The light cases, punishable only by fine, the justices might deal with without the assistance of (the) peers; but in the graver cases, where the penalty approached disherison, (the) peers should be associated with the justices in giving judgment.[3]

---

[1] See chap. vii, p. 208, n. 2.

[2] This plea is tentatively raised in the Siward v. Gloucester appeal: see Glamorgan Charters, vol. i, p. 91. The same case is also remarkable for the following plea: Et Ricardus [Siward] venit et respondit et defendit totam feloniam et totum factum ut predictum est, et posuit in judicio comitatus si debeat de predictis respondere versus dictum Stephanum Baucen sicut non est de comitatu nec par suus.

[3] Bracton, Rolls Series, vol. ii, p. 264: Et tunc videndum quis possit et debeat judicare, et sciendum quod non ipse rex, quia sic esset in querela propria actor et judex in judicio vitae membrorum et exhaeredationis, quod quidem non esset si querela esset aliorum. Item justiciarii? Non, cum in judiciis personam domini regis, cujus vices gerit, representet. Quis ergo judicabit? Videtur, sine praejudicio melioris sententiae, quod curia et pares judicabunt ne maleficia remaneant impunita, et maxime ubi periculum vitae fuerit

I should observe in passing that the passage in Bracton is somewhat obscure : the word *pares* may mean *the peers*, or simply *some peers ;* and it is not quite certain whether this writer really means to divide treason, for the present purpose, into three or only into two classes : if the latter, then by the court he merely means the justices. However, there can be no question as to what Bracton's disciples thought he meant.

et membrorum vel exhaeredacionis, cum ipse rex pars actrix esse debeat in judicio. . . . Si autem tale sit factum quod debeat ibi majis transgressio quam felonia denotari, remanebit duellum, sed tunc videndum utrum transgressio illa quae tangit regem gravis fuerit vel levis, sive sibi sive uxori et pueris. In suis vero poterit rex injuriari. Si autem levis fuerit transgressio quae poenam infligat pecuniariam tantum et levem, bene possunt justiciarii sine paribus judicare. Si autem gravis fuerit transgressio et proxima exhaeredacioni, quod redemptionem inducat, ibi debent pares justiciariis associari, ne ipse rex per seipsum vel justiciarios suos sine paribus actor sit et judex.

Compare this with chapter xxxix of the Dictum of Kenilworth (printed in the Statutes of the Realm, vol. i, pp. 12–17, and Stubbs, Select Charters, p. 425): Si quis eciam non velit dictum istud tenere, vel judicium curiae domini regis per pares subire, et sic exhaeredati qui se dicunt tales, nullum jus habeant ad recuperandum terras. . . .

Li Livres de Jostice, XVI, i, s. 1, states the French rule thus: Uns des pers de France s'otroie à juigier pardevant le roi par ceus qui juigier le doivent, et dit que li rois, ne si conseux, ne le doivent pas juigier : mès il ne dit pas bien. Mès li rois, ne son consoil, sanz autres, ne le puet pas juigier, c'est-à-dire que si per i doivent estre. And ibid., I, xvii, s. 4 : Duc, conte, baron, chastelain sont de lor choses de la jotice au prévost. . . . Prévoz puet prandre des choses aus barons amonétez por rendre, ou por recréance avoir de ce que li devantdit conte, duc prendra de cels que li prévoz ara à governer ; et l'en entent de ce que droiz ne doit sofrir. Duc, contes, barons ne devent pas estre tret en plet devant prévost dou fet de lor cors ne de lor demeine : quar chascune tele persone ne doit estre jugiez que par le roi, qui li doit foi, ou par ses pers.

Dudum lite mota coram hominibus judicantibus in curia comitis de Drocis in castro de Dommart inter Andream de Rambures militem, ex una parte, et Bernardum d'Alliel militem, filium et heredem domine quondam de Vaucheles, ex altera . . . dicti homines judicaverunt . . . a quo quidem judicato tanquam falso et pravo fuit per ipsum Bernardum ad nostram curiam appellatum. . . . Dicebat . . . quod pecierat ferri sententiam et jus sibi dici per pares suos solum judicantes in dicta curia, et non per alios homines ligeos, cum a dicto comite de Drocis teneret in paragio

The next legist to be considered is the author of the work called *Fleta*, said to have been written in the Fleet prison, and certainly compiled about A.D. 1290. In *Fleta*, treason cases are only divided into two classes: (1) felonies and grave misdemeanours, to be judged *coram curia et paribus;* and (2) light misdemeanours determinable by the justices. Bracton is merely expressing an opinion; *Fleta* states the rule as if it was settled law.[1]

Next comes the work called Britton, written about A.D. 1291, a curious compilation purporting to represent a declaration of the law by the sovereign himself.

With respect to the jurisdiction he may say that he is not bound to answer in a place where the judge is a party, since in every judg-

alias *en paarrie*, et sic de consuetudine patrie in castellaniis in quibus sunt pares et homines judicantes, sicut erant in castro de Dommart predicto, per pares solum judicari debebat, et dicti homines cum paribus contra ipsum tulerunt judicatum suum predictum contra consuetudinem predictam. . . . Ex adverso . . . dicti homines et pares judicantes . . . dicebant . . . quod de usu et consuetudine patrie a longinquis temporibus observata, ex quo litigium erat pro mobilibus et captalibus, homines cum paribus vel homines solum sine paribus poterant judicare seu jus reddere in causa mota inter parem et aliam quamcunque personam. . . . Per judicium nostre curie fuit dictum dictos homines et pares bene judicasse. (Arrêt du Parlement, A.D. 1326. Extracted by M. Guilhiermoz, Bibl. de l'École des Chartes, t. 60, p. 81 n.)

 Dou droit au ber [i.e. baron] d'estre jugié par ses pers: Si li bers est apelez en la cort le roi d'aucune chose qui apartaigne à heritage, et li die: "je ne vueil pas estre jugiez fors par mes pers de ceste chose," adonc si doit l'en les barons semondre à tout le moins jusques à iii; et puis doit la joutise feire droit o ces et o autres chevaliers. (Établissements de S. Louis, Livre i, cap. 76, vol. ii, p. 124.) This text is derived from the customary law of Touraine-Anjou; see ibid., vol. iii, p. 31.

[1] De crimine laesae majestatis. (s. 11): Et cum accusatus, propterea non sit dimittendus, quaeri poterit ubi terminari debet hujusmodi culpa; non enim coram rege, cum non deceat ipsum in amissione vitae vel membrorum actorem esse et judicem; nec etiam coram justiciariis, cum personam regis in judicio praesentent: sed revera distinguendum est, nam si sit felonia vel transgressio gravis proxima exhaeredationem quaeque redemptionem ad minus inducat, tunc coram curia et paribus procedere debet judicium; et si transgressio levis sit, liceat justiciariis dumtaxat judicare. (Fleta, ed. Selden, cap. xxi, p. 31.)

ment there ought not to be less than three persons, to wit a judge, a plaintiff, and a defendant; and in cases where we are party our pleasure is that our court, to wit the earls and barons in time of parliament, shall be judges. [1]

Of the three writers Bracton always and deservedly possessed an unshaken pre-eminence; but, if the other two were admittedly less authoritative, their comparative conciseness probably made them much more popular with legal practitioners. The influence of all of them on the trial of peers is well marked. Britton's argument is, of course, a reductio ad absurdum of Bracton's. If the rule was valid in treason, it was equally valid in *quo warranto* or any civil case where the king was litigant. Moreover, by the end of the thirteenth century it was well recognised that the king was a party to all criminal cases other than appeals.

In the eyre of Henry the Third's reign, held in the presence of all the prelates, earls, barons and lesser dignitaries of the county, the principle of Bracton and his disciples was doubtless sufficiently satisfied. But the later systems, for example the criminal administration of the professional justices acting under commissions of oyer and terminer and gaol delivery, could not be reconciled with it. Nevertheless the principle must have been a popular one, and the conflict with practice sufficiently obvious. [2]

[1] . . . et quant a la jurisdiccioun put il dire, qe il n'est mie tenu a respoundre en place ou le juge est partie, desicum nul jugement ne se put fere de meyns qe de iii persones, ceo est a saver de un juge, de un pleyntif, et de un defendaunt, et en cas ou nous sumus partie, voloms nous qe nostre court soit juge, sicum countes et barouns en tens de parlement. (Britton, ed. Nichols, Livre i, cap. xxiii, s. 8, p. 102.)

[2] The practice so common during the fourteenth century of inserting the names of one or two earls and barons in the commissions of oyer and terminer is perhaps attributable to the influence of Bracton. We have here a problem in which it would be absurd to look for consistent developments. The developments, in fact, are manifold and illogical. It is the same in France. Here, for instance, is a remarkable argument from the pen of a Reimish jurist: Utrum rex habeat cognitionem in causa ipsum et comitem Flandrie tangente. In negocio regis et comitis Flandrie, reputavi arrestum bonum quod rex debet habere primum judicium; scilicet

At last, in an odd way, comes the reconciliation of crown procedure with Bracton and with chapter xxxix of the Great Charter. A new point is reached. To some extent, no doubt, Bracton himself paved the way for it when he committed the "gross blunder" of referring to the verdict of jurors as a judgment.[1] At the beginning of the four-teenth century we have a reported case upon the new point.[2] The case is a prosecution for rape at the king's suit. The prisoner at the bar is a knight named Sir Hugh. Foreseeing probably that counsel would be denied him at his trial, he took legal advice beforehand, and came into court primed with every possible plea. He began by claiming benefit of clergy. "Sir," said he to the justice, "I am a clerk and ought not to answer without my ordinary." The ordinary then came forward and claimed him. But the justice, who seems to have known something of the prisoner's family, objected. "You are a bigamist," he said, "for you have married a widow; tell us if you say she was a virgin when you married her, but you may as well admit the truth at once for we can find out in a moment from a jury." Sir Hugh was not going to lose any chance for want of a lie, and said she was a virgin. "We will soon see," said the justice. So he charged the jury, who found that she was a widow when the prisoner married her. The justice there-upon decided Sir Hugh must answer as a layman, and told him to agree to the verdict of the twelve good men present. Upon this Sir Hugh answered, "Sir, by them I am accused,

qui cognitionem et jurisdictionem haberet, eo quod rex est judex simpliciter et generaliter, sine contestacione et determinatione et restrictione. Et hoc est verum, si partem non faceret. Sed quia faciebat partem, nec ipse judex erat competens, nec pares; sed ipse judices dare debebat. (Liber Practicus de Consuetudine Remensi; Varin, Archives législatives de la ville de Reims, Coutumes, i, p. 85.)

[1] Bracton, Rolls Series, vol. iv, p. 392 : Eodem modo potest jurator falsum facere judicium et fatuum, cum judicare teneatur per verba in sacramento contenta. . . . Et si justiciarius secundum eorum judicium pronunciaverit, falsum faciet pronunciationem. There are other instances cited by Pollock and Maitland, ii, p. 625 n.

[2] Year Book, 30-1 Edward I, p. 529.

I will not agree to them: moreover, sir, I am a knight and ought not to be judged *except by my peers.*" The justice replied: "Because you are a knight we are willing that you should be judged by your peers."[1] A jury of knights was accordingly empanelled, and ultimately Sir Hugh was acquitted.

In this way trial by jury gradually came to be accepted by the commoner as the promised *judicium parium;* and, so interpreted, it afforded a complete answer to Bracton's objection that the king, neither by himself nor by his justices, should be judge in his own cause. In the case of the commoner, at least, the jury were the associated peers.

The resulting effect on the construction of the Great Charter we are not yet in a position to discuss. We have still our main task before us—to consider the influence of these developing ideas on procedure against the nobility.

In all civil cases, and in all cases of mere misdemeanour (transgressio), prelates, earls and barons were tried, and judgment was pronounced against them by the king's justices.[2] They were up to this point dealt with in the same way as the ordinary freeman. Even the various compulsory processes in aid of jurisdiction, distraint, imprisonment and so forth, were (with some exceptions, in civil cases)[3] equally available against the man of rank and the mere commoner. The justices gave judgment, they enforced their judgments, but the penalty they had nothing to do with. The appropriate punishment for misdemeanours and the like (amercement) was not assessed by them or under their supervision. Earls and barons were always amerced during the reign of Henry

---

[1] (Hugo) . .. Item, domine, ego sum miles et non debeo judicari nisi per meos pares.—(Justiciarius) Quia vos estis miles, volumus quod vos sitis judicati per vestros pares. Et nominabantur milites.

Compare the privilege enjoyed by peers of having knights on the jury in civil cases. See Year Book, 12-13 Edward III, Rolls Series, p. 290; and Pike, Hist. of the House of Lords, pp. 258-9.

[2] Cases illustrative of the procedure adopted against men of rank, have been collected in the appendix to this chapter.

[3] See Pike, Hist. of the House of Lords, cap. xix. Such privileges are outside the scope of this work.

the Third either by the barons of the Exchequer or *coram rege:*[1] this was the practice before the Great Charter and

[1] Countesses and baronesses were amerced in the same way as earls and barons. See Appendix.

Bracton, Rolls Series, vol. ii, p. 242 : Comites vel barones non sunt amerciandi nisi per pares suos, et hoc per barones de scaccario vel coram rege.

Note that when for any reason a case could not be disposed of in eyre, and an earl or baron was implicated, it appears to have been the practice at one time to adjourn the case coram rege; and, if untried, for trial as well as judgment. Thus at the Hertford Eyre (15 Edward I) we find the following procedure fairly consistently adopted. If the defendant in *quo warranto* pleaded prescription or the like, he was adjourned to hear judgment before the barons of the Exchequer. If, however, he vouched to warranty a commoner, he was given a day at Westminster and a jury was awarded: but if he vouched to warranty a baron, a day was given *coram domino rege* at Westminster and a jury was awarded. (See Roll 328, m. 40d, where Thomas Gereberd vouches the earl of Hereford.) For a quo warranto case in which John king of Scotland is the defendant see Roll 544, m. 36d. (22 Edward I): John puts in a special plea and is adjourned coram rege.

French examples of the general principle have been cited above, pp. 285–6. But even peers of France had no right to be amerced by their peers.

(Archives Legislatives de Reims, i, p. 327.) No. cdxxii: Quid jus habent pares Francie. Jus parrie effectum habet, quod pares judicentur per pares; in exercitum proximum locum post regem optineant. No. cdxxiii: Utrum questione pendente inter comitem Flandrensem et homines parrie, rex vel pares debeant judicare. Contra comitem Flandrie . . . , Gandenses, Duacenses, Brugenses faciebant requestas. Comes dicebat se velle deffendere requestas, sed dicebat quod non tenebatur ingredi judicium, quia spoliatus toto comitatu, nisi prius restitutus. Unde supplicabat regi extra judicium, quod eum ressaisiret, vel paratus erat recipere judicium per pares; et si dubium esset (an) pares debeant de hoc esse judices, petebat fieri declarationem per pares. Sed dicebatur ex parte regis, cum quod non ageretur de feodo, nec ad admissionem feodi, sed ad emendam pecuniariam propter inobedienciam, rex (debebat) esse judex, et hoc ipse offerebat, scilicet facere justiciam ; offerebat eciam se jus facturum, si [ad] ipsum cognitio et judicium pertinerent. Et judicatum fuit, et bene, quod rex primum haberet judicium, quia rex est superior et judex comitis simpliciter ; pares non nisi secundum quidem, scilicet in questione feodi.

(Li Livres de Jostice et de Plet, ut supra.) Duc, conte, baron, chastelain sont de lor choses de la jotice au prévost.

was continued by Henry the Third, apparently because it was to his manifest advantage to do so, rather than because there was any legal difficulty in the way of amercing earls and barons in the counties.[1] Eventually a fixed scale of amercements came into use; and the privilege, if any, of special assessment was gradually superseded and forgotten.[2]

There is no evidence whatever that earls and barons desired to have a tribunal of peers to try the civil causes in which they were concerned. Instances could perhaps be produced where some baron, looking vainly for a tabula in naufragio,

---

[1] Rot. Claus. R.C., p. 383 b. (3 Henry III): Rex justiciariis itinerantibus in comitatu Kancie salutem. Mandamus vobis quod omnes loquelas planas que fuerint sine contencione et coram vobis venerint teneatis, et omnes illos qui coram vobis inciderint in misercordia de communibus loquelis amercietis, exceptis comitibus et baronibus qui coram consilio nostro amerciandi sunt; omnes autem demandas que coram vobis fuerint quas homines exigunt de libertatibus, videlicet quas dominus Cantuariensis archiepiscopus, G. comes de Clara vel alii exigunt, in respectum ponatis usque in xv dies post festum sancti Hyllarii coram consilio nostro apud Westmonasterium: si q. et loquele ardue coram vobis emerserint que coram vobis sine difficultate terminari non possint, nec sine consilio consilii nostri, eas similiter in respectum poni faciatis usque ad predictos diem et locum. Teste Comite apud Turrim London, ix die Decembris.—coram domino Winton. episcopo.

Compare ibid., p. 387 b. (3 Henry III): *De amerciamentis.* Rex H. Lincoln. episcopo et sociis suis justiciariis itinerantibus in comitatu Lincoln., Nottingham., et Dereby, salutem. Mandamus vobis quod nullum comitem vel baronem amercietis occasione misericordiarum in quas inciderint coram vobis vel aliquem alium pro aliquo unde magnum amerciamentum debeat pervenire, set hujus▪ modi amerciamenta consilio nostro reservetis. Teste domino W. Coventr. episcopo apud Westmonasterium v die Febuarii.

[2] The Mirror of Justices, Selden Soc., p. 150: Peine peccunielle appelluns nous amerciementz . . . qe ascuns pointz sont en certein e en ascuns pointz nient. En certeins amerciementz sunt en certeins ascuns foiz solum les dignitiez de gentz, sicom est de contes et des barrons. Car cum tenaunt contie enteree est amerciable a c li. quant meins est amercie. E baron de baronie en entere a c marz. E qi meins entenent ou plus, solom la quantite de sa tenure.

See also ibid., p. 36: Les ij chevalers soleient estre appelez ij barons pur affoerer les amerciementz des countes et des barouns, e de tenaunz counties et baronies si qe nul ne fust affoere forque par ces piers. See finally, Madox, Exchequer, cap. xiv, s. 1.

asserted this right. I have discovered no such case: the instances usually quoted have been already explained, not one of them supports the discussion.

In dealing with the graver misdemeanours there exist excellent examples of the procedure which was probably partly the cause, partly the consequence of those principles which Bracton, *Fleta* and *Britton* attempted to lay down. The justices had full power to try such cases and proceed to conviction. If conviction resulted the justices might imprison or admit to bail pending final judgment, but they themselves did not pronounce final judgment against prelates, earls or barons: these in Bracton's time were commonly sent coram rege, while in *Britton's* time we usually find them adjourned to appear before the king at the next parliament.[1] We may say that *a fortiori* the man of rank could not be *judged* by the ordinary justices for treason or felony, but we have no ground for saying that he could not be *tried* by them for these crimes.

At the beginning of the year 1290 a fierce private war was in progress between the earls of Gloucester and Hereford, the seat of hostilities being certain disputed territory in the Welsh marches.[2] Under ordinary circumstances private war was treason, felony or anything the king chose to consider it. We must however concede, in extenuation of the acts in question, that the marcher lords claimed then, and always had claimed, that private war was a privilege of the march. The king's chief object all through was to break this custom. On January 25, 1289-90, a royal mandate was issued inhibiting hostilities. The result was an immediate raid by Gloucester's tenants into Brecknock: men were killed, cattle lifted, much booty secured; a third of the loot was received

---

[1] For examples see appendix to this chapter. For further evidence of the use of the expression, and as to its meaning, see Statute 13 Ed. I, c. 24, Close Roll, Cal. (1272-9), pp. 137, 200, 268, (274), (305), 363, 375, (380), 427, 450, 462, (465), 466, 470, (521), 528, 570; and the Close Rolls during the rest of this reign passim: also Pike, History of the House of Lords, pp. 47-50.

[2] This was by no means the first instance of such private war between these two earls. See, for example, Close Roll, Cal., 1272-9, p. 504.

by Gloucester himself. Two more raids subsequently took place from the same quarter, Hereford meanwhile remaining passive in compliance with the king's order. Then Edward struck hard. An originating writ of *sci. fa.* was issued, and special commissioners appointed, consisting of a bishop, an earl and two regular justices. These were directed to proceed with the inquiry notwithstanding any attempt by the earls to settle the dispute; and, for the purpose of the inquiry, magnates as well as others were to be summoned to give evidence upon oath—*eo quod res ista dominum regem et dignitatem suam tangit.*

The commissioners sat on the day appointed, when Hereford appeared but not Gloucester. A two days' adjournment was ordered. When the court reassembled after the adjournment Gloucester was still absent. The commissioners then proceeded to empanel a jury, and in accordance with their instructions attempted to swear in certain of the marcher lords. These, for reasons already referred to, resolutely declined to take the oath, and finally a jury of commoners was collected which found a verdict implicating Gloucester. The judges, after repeating the inhibition against hostilities, adjourned the proceedings and reported to the king.

Edward decided that he and his council would hear the case at Abergavenny at Michaelmas. Meanwhile more raids took place, but this time without the cognisance of either earl. Hereford's men for once had the advantage, and secured a large amount of Gloucester's cattle found pasturing on the disputed territory. At this point Hereford committed a blunder. A civil suit, it appears, was pending between him and Gloucester to decide their claims, but apart from this the whole matter was clearly sub judice. Notwithstanding this, Hereford directed that the cattle should be retained until security had been given that his right to the land would be recognised. This was from any point of view a manifest contempt of court.

Both Hereford and Gloucester appeared at the hearing before the king; and a jury was empanelled as before to prove the new facts, which have been already stated. The earls were then put upon their defence, and Gloucester raised various objections to the finding at the first hearing. The council decided that the commissioners had proceeded perfectly properly, and that judgment might duly be pronounced in this and similar cases on such and similar inquisitions. Both earls were eventually sentenced to imprisonment and forfeiture of certain lands. The judgment was pronounced on behalf of the whole council consisting of king, prelates, earls, barons and others.[1]

The original offence in this case appears to have been treated as treason-trespass, and perhaps for this reason peers were associated with the justices in taking the inquisition : more probably the peers were appointed for purely practical reasons. The matter came before the king as one which had been tried but not judged : it so happened that certain further events had taken place which necessitated a further finding, but that is a detail. The earls were subsequently brought up before parliament when Edward was graciously pleased to mitigate their sentences. Certain other persons were sentenced by the king in council at the same time that judgment was passed on the earls; and the whole proceeding, owing no doubt to the adjournment above mentioned, is recorded on the rolls of parliament.[2]

In 1305 Nicholas Segrave, a baron, was arraigned at Westminster on a charge of high treason. The circumstances were somewhat peculiar.[3] Segrave and Cromwell had been serving with the king in the Scottish campaign, during which Segrave brought an accusation against Cromwell, presumably in the king's military court, and wager of battle

---

[1] For references to the reports of this case, see supra, p. 282.

A similar case against John Giffard is recorded in the Coram Rege Roll (104), Pasch., 15 Edward I, m. 31, but the report breaks off abruptly in the middle of the argument of the attorney for the crown.

The trial of Theobald de Verdun (a baron) on a serious charge of giving false evidence is set out in the appendix.

[2] Rot. Parl., vol. i, pp. 70 et sqq.

[3] See Memoranda de Parliamento, 1305, Rolls Series [98], pp. 255 et sqq. The same roll contains the record of proceedings against another baron, Almaric de St. Amand, for high misdemeanours. See also Rot. Parl., vol. i, pp. 172–4, 181 ; and Flores Historiarum [95], iii, pp. 121–2.

appears to have been joined. It was the usual practice throughout Europe to forbid duelling during a campaign, and Edward had evidently issued either general or particular orders applying to the present case. Segrave thereupon challenged his adversary to fight him in the court of the king of France, and, with never so much as a by-your-leave to king Edward, he withdrew himself for the purpose from the English army.

Segrave was brought up for trial before the king, the primate, and divers earls, barons and others of the king's council *in full parliament*. This to us seems something like a contradiction in terms: before long, no doubt, divers of the king's council did not constitute a full parliament, then it was evidently otherwise. Segrave pleaded guilty, and the council on being asked said that the punishment in such case was death. The king, however, of his grace accepted an undertaking from seven sureties that he would render himself to prison if called upon to do so.[1]

[1] . . . Et Nicholaus de Segrave modo venit in pleno parliamento in praesentia ipsius domini regis, archiepiscopi Cantuariensis et plurimorum episcoporum, comitum, baronum et aliorum de consilio domini regis tunc ibidem existentium.

Et Nicholaus de Warrewike qui sequitur pro ipso domino rege acculpavit praedictum Nicholaum de Segrave de eo quod . . . et hic offert pro ipso domino rege verificare prout curia consideraverit etc.

Et praedictus Nicholaus de Segrave . . . omnia antedicta in forma sibi imposita expresse cognovit, et voluntati domini regis de alto et basso inde se submisit.

Et super hoc dominus rex, volens habere avisamentum comitum, baronum, magnatum et aliorum de consilio suo, injunxit eisdem in homagio, fidelitate et ligiantia quibus ei tenentur, quod ipsum fideliter consulerent qualis poena pro tali facto sic cognito fuerit infligenda. Et interim idem Nicholaus committatur prisonae ad Turrim.

Qui omnes . . . dicunt quod hujusmodi factum meretur poenam amissionis vitae, etc.

Et licet idem Nicholaus de Segrave per considerationem praedictam judicium vitae subire deberet, dominus rex tamen, de gratia sua speciali, pietate motus . . . remittit eidem Nicholao judicium vitae et membrorum et concedit [etc.]. . . . (Memoranda de Parliamento, Rolls Series [98], pp. 255-8.)

We may conclude from the above and similar cases [1] that, in the reign of Edward the First, judgment in " parliament" was habitually accorded to men of rank in criminal cases of a serious nature; but in some instances, at all events, the case was only adjourned to be so judged after a trial and verdict differing little, if at all, from that vouchsafed to the commoner.

In passing it should be noticed that we are arriving at a classification which has no relation whatever to the matters enumerated in chapter xxxix of the Charter. Take the privileges actually enjoyed by earls and barons at any given period from the time of John to the present day : at no time on any intelligible principle of construction can those privileges be directly deduced from the language of the Charter. They are, on the contrary, largely if not entirely the outcome of ideas derived from wholly different sources, juridical ideas which have perhaps little vitality of their own, but, as parasites, are going to thrive lustily on the dead root of English liberties.

A turbulent period followed upon the accession of Edward the Second. England became split up into rival factions; and although, as the natural results of internal disorder, the period has many causes célèbres, these for the most part merely represent the triumph of one political party over the other. As each side gained the ascendency it sought to secure its position, on the one hand by taking the life and lands of the leaders opposed to it, on the other by annulling as far as possible the work done by these same opponents during their period of power. The one business was carried out by judgments for treason, which certainly exhibit the minimum regard for legal formalities : the other was achieved by legislative acts, reversing these judgments for errors of law and procedure.

The case of Gaveston we need not consider : his banishment was the result of a political bargain, his death an ill-advised, badly-planned coup d'état, both worthless as precedents for how peers should be tried.

---

[1] For other cases see the appendix to this chapter.

The first proceedings against the Despencers took place in parliament with a considerable show of formality. Prelates, earls, barons and other peers together with the commons are represented as having framed the accusation. The trial, however, was conducted in the absence of the persons accused, and simply consisted of a finding by the peers of the realm that their alleged misdeeds were notoriously true ; whereupon the peers of the realm, earls and barons in the king's presence passed sentence of forfeiture and banishment upon them.[1]

It is obvious that this was not a judgment in accordance with the law of the land : indeed, it was part of the contrariants' case that process of law was impossible under the circumstances.[2] The law of the land indubitably required that the defendants should be present, that they should be arraigned, that they should plead, and if they denied the charge that they should be put to answer. By the law of the land, then, the award was illegal in many particulars : could it, however, be supported as a valid judgment of peers? The question must be answered in the negative.

Before long the Despencers, who had left England in consequence of the judgment, returned from exile and obtained an Act reversing the sentence on the ground of error. This Act was passed in the fifteenth year of Edward the Second, and is enrolled on the Close Roll for that year.[3] It is a verbose and unskilfully prepared instrument, but valuable notwithstanding. The following are the principal errors recorded : the judgment was contrary to the tenor of Magna

---

[1] See Calendar of Close Rolls (1318–23), pp. 492–5.

[2] Statutes of the Realm R.C., vol. i, p. 185. The contrariants defined their intention as follows : quod super hiis fiat unum statutum in praesenti parliamento ad perpetuam rei memoriam et exemplum consiliatorum perversorum. . . . (Chronicles of the reigns of Edward I and Edward II, vol. ii, p. 65 et sqq.) A fertile idea, the precursor of fifteenth-century attainders, but insufficiently elaborated.

[3] The Calendar of Close Rolls gives a verbatim translation of the whole proceedings. There is also a transcript of the proceedings entered subsequently on the Parliament Rolls, see Rot. Parl., vol. iii, pp. 360–7. The material parts for our purpose are set out in the appendix.

Carta, the Despencers were not called into court nor put to answer, the matters contained in the award were not duly proved, the magnates came armed to parliament, the magnates were both prosecutors and judges, the king was not in reality a party to the judgment, and the prelates, who are peers of the realm in parliament, did not assent. It was not and could not have been contended that the judgment was not a judgment of peers. This Act does not appear on the Statute Roll or on any contemporary parliament roll, although the repeal of the subsidiary pardon granted to the prosecutors is duly enrolled.[1] The principal Act in question was in its turn reversed by Edward the Third, but only to be restored by Richard the Second. In these vicissitudes, however, there is nothing to suggest that the errors found by the Act were open to dispute.

Thomas earl of Lancaster's case is the next we have to consider.[2] This earl, after his defeat at Borough-bridge, was brought before the king at Pontefract. There were several magnates in attendance, but nothing in the nature of a trial seems to have taken place. The earl's crimes were recorded, and sentence was pronounced on behalf of the king.[3] The peers who were present are not stated in the record to have been in any true sense parties to this judgment, but whether they were or were not in fact parties is of no present importance. The judgment was tried and found wanting on the record alone, and was reversed for error by an Act of Edward the Third. This was granted on the petition of Henry of Lancaster, and the errors he alleged were these: that whereas every liegeman of the king taken for felony in time of peace ought to be arraigned of the crime laid to his charge and put to answer, and ought to be convicted thereof by law, etc., before he is adjudged to death; nevertheless,

---

[1] Printed in Statutes of the Realm, R.C., vol. i., p. 185.

[2] Roger Damory, a baron, was tried and sentenced, some little time before the battle of Borough-bridge, in the court of the Constable and Marshal. This case is given in the appendix to chap. xi, in which the jurisdiction of the military court over peers of the realm is considered at some length.

[3] See Appendix.

although earl Thomas was a liegeman of the late king taken in time of peace, the said king *recorded* that Thomas was guilty of the crimes contained in the said process without arraigning him thereof or putting him to answer: Moreover, since Thomas was one of the peers and magnates of the realm, and Magna Carta provides that no free man shall be taken, etc., except by lawful judgment of his peers or by the law of the land, the said Thomas was erroneously adjudged to death by record of the king as aforesaid in time of peace without arraignment or answer or lawful judgment of his peers contrary to the law, etc., and contrary to the tenor of Magna Carta. By reason of " the errors aforesaid and others " in the record and process, annulment is decreed by " the king, proceres, magnates and the whole community of the realm." These proceedings are enrolled on the Close Roll, and there is also an inspeximus and exemplification entered on a subsequent Patent Roll, but no similar entry occurs on any existing Parliament or Statute Roll.[1]

Four other well-known barons, namely the Mortimers of Chirk and Wigmore, Bartholomew de Badlesmere and Henry Tyes, were sentenced for treason about the same time.[2] In each case the method pursued was the same: a writ was issued to certain persons enjoining them to visit the prisoner and pass judgment upon him according to the tenor of a document scheduled to the writ; this document differs not at all from a common-form judgment except that, instead of rehearsing the prisoner's confession or conviction, it contains the formula that his crimes are notorious and the king records the fact; thereupon the commissioners thus appointed visited the prisoner and read aloud to him the words of the schedule. That was all. In the four cases mentioned none was tried, none of the commissioners appointed was a peer of the realm.

The judgments against the Mortimers and Badlesmere were

---

[1] Appendix.
[2] These proceedings as they appear on the Coram Rege Roll are all set out at length in the appendix to vol. ii, pt. 2, of the Parliamentary Writs. For the original records of the proceedings against the Mortimers, see Exchequer Miscellanea, 24/12.

also severally reversed for error on the accession of Edward the Third.[1] There is no entry on the Parliament or Close Rolls, but the grounds for reversal are set forth in letters of inspeximus and exemplification enrolled on the Patent Rolls. Thus in the case of the Mortimers :—

And because after examination it was found that they were so sentenced without having been admitted to answer any of the charges brought against them, and that in time of peace when the king was not riding with banners displayed, and when the chancery of the king and the justices of either bench were sitting, and without legal judgment of their peers which is contrary to the law and custom of England and the tenor of the aforesaid charter, it was determined by the king that now is and his council in full parliament that all the said judgments against them should for the errors aforesaid be wholly annulled and revoked.

Here we have the principle unmistakably asserted that a peer in such case must be judged according to the law of the land and also have the judgment of his peers. At the same time we must notice the very suggestive circumstance that these interpretations of the Great Charter never appear either on the Parliament or on the Statute Rolls.

The case of Andrew Harcla, earl of Carlisle, differs considerably from the previous ones, for it was no mere political faction, but the king and his entire realm who regarded Harcla as a traitor. The circumstances are somewhat obscure. This man had been created earl, not so much for services rendered at Borough-bridge, though these counted for much, as for his strenuous activity on the Scotch border : then, in the height of his fame, he made treasonable overtures to England's northern foe. Success must have unhinged his mind.

At the outset the king appears to have acted very properly. On being informed of Harcla's treason he summoned him to his presence to give a personal explanation of what had occurred ; and then, as this summons was disobeyed, issued orders for his arrest. The earl was taken and imprisoned at Carlisle. Thereupon the king issued a special commission

[1] Appendix.

to Edmund earl of Kent, John de Hastings (a baron), three knights (king's justices) and Scrope (the chief justice), or any five, four, three or two of them, not to try the earl, but to deprive him of his dignities and pass judgment upon him according to the tenor of a document scheduled to the commission. The victor at Borough-bridge receives in his turn the same treatment as the vanquished: this document is his judgment, it contains the common formula of the time to the effect that the earl's crimes are notorious and the king records the fact;[1] there is no mention on the Coram Rege Roll of any trial whatsoever; the ready-made, prerogative judgment was pronounced by the justices in presence, it would seem, of all the commissioners, and Harcla was degraded and executed.[2]

It was a most iniquitous proceeding, no doubt, this judgment without a trial; but how far it was contrary to the law of the land or against the form of the Great Charter is a different matter. The law, as we have seen, required that the prisoner should be arraigned, but only for the purpose of establishing his guilt. The same law laid down the rule that the record of the king was conclusive evidence of the facts recorded. Harcla's guilt was therefore already established, and consequently it might be argued there was no need for a trial. To us, of course, this argument seems absurd; the annulment of those other judgments, *in pari materia* upon this point, utterly disposes of it; so much for the law of the land. With regard to the Charter and the *judicium parium*

---

[1] . . . les quieux sont notoires et conuz en le roialme, et nostre seigneur le roi le recorde, por quoi agarde ceste courte qe por la dite treson soietz treisne, pendu et decolle . . .

In the case of Bartholomew de Badlesmere the formula is slightly different: . . . les queus traysouns, arsouns, homicides, robberies, chevachez ove banere desplaietz, sont notoires as countes, barouns et autres grauntz et petitz de son roialme, et nostre seigneur le roi de son real poer la recorde; por quey agarde ceste court qe pur la traysoun soyetz trayne et. . . .

[2] The record of the process is printed in full from the Coram Rege Roll, Hil., 18 Edward II, in Parliamentary Writs, vol. ii, pt. 2, app., pp. 262–3. See also Rymer, Foedera; and Placitorum Abbreviatio. The presence of the two peers is by no means certain, although the earl of Kent was the person ordered to return the record of the judgment.

it may be observed that to this day only one peer is required
for passing judgment on another peer in the court of the lord
high steward: the other peers who are summoned merely
attend to perform the functions of a jury and establish the
facts. In this case, but for the wording of the commission
which permits, so to speak, the absence of both peers, we
might conclude that Edward deliberately constituted the
commission so as to comply with the requirements of Bracton
as interpreted by *Fleta*—that in treason cases involving peril
of life and member peers should be associated with the
justices. Perhaps this is the true conclusion notwithstanding
the form of the commission.[1]

The judgment on Harcla is only less remarkable than the
petition for its reversal.[2] It is in this petition that we first
find the claim put forward to a *jury* of peers. The petition
does not assert that Harcla was condemned without judgment
of peers: in fact, the only error alleged is that he was not
"atteint par enquest de ses piers." The case still stands, but
it would be absurd to pretend that it is of any great importance as a precedent: still it is one of the few cases in the
fourteenth century where a peer has been judged for treason
elsewhere than in parliament; this fact alone gives it a certain
value.

At the end of the reign of Edward the Second the
Despencers fell into the hands of the queen's party, and
first one, then the other, was condemned and executed as
a traitor. Both cases were so clearly the acts of a revolu-
tionary party that it seems idle to consider what formalities
were observed: neither Despencer, it may be mentioned, was
tried in parliament.[3]

The position of the spiritual lords with reference to trial

---

[1] Compare this commission with the series issued a few months
later (July 18th, 1323), where special words were inserted to secure
the presence of at least one peer; see Cal. Pat. Rolls, 1321–4, pp.
260, 371–2.

[2] See Appendix.

[3] A detailed account of these proceedings is given by Knighton,
Rolls Series [92], i, pp. 436–41; and see Misc. Rolls Chancery, 18/3.

by peers has proved a highly controversial subject.[1] Saving the higher right of the church, they appear to have considered themselves equally entitled with lay peers to the benefits (whatever they might be) of chapter xxxix of the Charter; but this saving clause bade fair to cut away, or perhaps we should say to supersede, the greater portion, if not the whole, of such benefits. In high crimes and misdemeanours, in matters involving peril of life or member, the church claimed complete exemption from lay jurisdiction, and this privilege was recognised and confirmed by a statute of 9 Edward II.[2] With lesser transgressions excluded from

---

[1] The famous case against the archbishop of York in the reign of Edward I seems to me to have no direct bearing on the question. This case appears on the Parliament Roll (printed, Rot. Parl., vol. i, p. 102), the K.R. Memoranda Roll (22 Ed. I, m. 12), etc.

[2] The church to be sure probably regarded the matter in this way. There were two estates in the body politic, clergy and laity; and of these each had its grades : of the laity there were king, lords and commons. The bishop was a lord and a great deal more. The peers of a bishop included no layman, not even the king. Therefore, under Magna Carta no less than under the divine ordinances of holy church, no bishop could be judged for a crime except in an ecclesiastical court.

Between the "clerici rettati" of 1164 and the statute of 9 Edward II the authority asserted by the temporal power over criminous clerks had undergone striking modifications and developments : even the canon law had received significant interpretations. Gratian was quite out of date. Gratian indeed! Nullus episcopus, neque pro civili neque pro criminali causa, apud quemvis judicem, sive civilem sive militarem, producatur vel exhibeatur. Clericus apud saecularem judicem si pulsatus fuerit, non respondeat aut proponat. But even in the days of a universal ordinary, the primæval law of self-preservation would occasionally prove antagonistic to and stronger than the whole corpus juris canonici. Here is a cause célèbre of the twelfth century: Causae quidem ejus quae inter Osbertum Eboracensem archidiaconum et S. clericum vertitur initium prosecutio et finis, appellatione ille suspensus est, quem ex literis legati vestri domini Cantuariensis archiepiscopi plena potest veritatis luce sublimitas vestra cognoscere. Has quidem et diligenter inspeximus et omnes causae ipsius articulos in eum processisse modum, quo literis designantur eisdem, plane testificamur. S. enim predictum archidiaconum super morte Willelmo archiepiscopo veneno ut dicebat illata et quibusdam criminibus aliis impetens, in ipsum vinculum inscriptionis arripere et coram judice

the category of offences punishable only by judgment of peers, little was left in the whole scale of crime worth claiming privilege of peerage for.

Under Edward the Third it became settled law that in treason there was no benefit of clergy. Unfortunately privilege of peerage could scarcely be claimed by spiritual peers in this case without abandoning their higher claim " to the prejudice of God and Holy Church." We are not in the least concerned here with ecclesiastical exemption; but nevertheless some mention of two important cases against prelates, occurring during the reign of Edward the Second, seems desirable in deference to former controversies. These cases, however, decide nothing.

Walter Langton, bishop of Coventry and Lichfield, was arrested on various vague charges made against him as treasurer of the late king.[1] He was imprisoned first at Windsor, then in the Tower, and a special commission was issued to four justices to try him. The offences alleged against the bishop were definitely described as trespasses. Langton was released eventually on the interposition of the pope. No objection was at any time raised to the jurisdiction of the justices.

The case of Adam Orleton, bishop of Hereford, is more important. This prelate was attached on the finding of a special inquisition which charged him with being concerned in levying war on the king. The order for his attachment seems to have been irregular: no day was given him to

ecclesiastico agere recusabat. Quumque in tanta multitudine parentum et amicorum archiepiscopi defuncti solus ipse staret, et nullis fulta testimoniis verba funderet, laminam candentis ferri in praedictum archiepiscopum eo tutius offerebat quo ecclesia Dei probationem hujusmodi nullatenus admissuram attendebat. Ipsumque ad regis audientiam eo confidentius provocabat, quo ad judicium hoc apud cinctum judicem de jure celebrare non posse avertebat. Quumque judicis animum in eo non oporteat versus quemquam moveri, quod non potest ostendi, pro jam dicto archidiacono preces sublimitati vestrae porrigimus, ne apud vos incurrat iram. . . .
(Letters of Gilbert Foliot, ed. Giles, vol. i, pp. 152–3.)

[1] See Patent Roll, 1 Edward II, pt. 1, m. 8d., Calendar, p. 40; chronicles of the reigns of Edward I and Edward II, Rolls Series [76], i, pp. 257, 264; Trokelowe, Rolls Series [28], pp. 63–4.

appear, either before the justices making the order, or otherwise. According to the records of the court of King's Bench[1] he was arraigned before that court on or after January 23rd, 1323-4; and, on being asked by the justices how he would acquit himself, he said that he was bishop of Hereford at the will of God and the supreme pontiff, that the matters laid to his charge were so weighty that he ought not to answer them in that court, nor could he do so without offence to God and holy church. He was thereupon ordered to appear in person from day to day to hear judgment. The record then, without any intermediate announcement, states what took place on the 24th of February. The bishop appeared before the king in full parliament. The matter was rehearsed: the bishop was asked whether he had anything more to say, and he made answer as before. The archbishop of Canterbury then claimed him as one constituted in the episcopal dignity. The claim was allowed; but the archbishop was ordered to produce the bishop in court on the Monday next before Mid-Lent, for which day the sheriff of Hereford was ordered to summon a jury. The archbishop, the bishop and the jury came into court on the day appointed. The jury found a verdict in the terms of the indictment; and judgment was given that the bishop should remain in the custody of the archbishop as a clerk-convict, and his temporalities be seized into the king's hands. This record is obviously defective in many matters of ordinary routine procedure, and on these grounds was reversed for error early in the reign of Edward the Third.[2] Upon the face of the record, however, the inquest of office taken by a jury of Hereford was quite regular. It is therefore very curious to find it stated in letters close of the first year of Edward the Third that—"licet idem episcopus in inquisitionem aliquam inde faciendam se non posuisset, nihilominus prefati justiciarii

---

[1] See Coram Rege Roll, Hilary, 17 Edward II, m. 87 (printed Placit. Abbrev. R.C., p. 345), and Patent Roll, 3 Edward III, pt. 1, m. 33 (printed Rot. Parl., ii, p. 427).

[2] Patent Roll, 3 Edward III, pt. 1, m. 33. The errors of procedure are very fully set out in this document.

x

ad inquisitionem predictam capiendum processerunt."[1]   In
short, if we were not dealing with the "authoritative records
of the Court of King's Bench," as one writer has called them,
we might suspect that they were not telling the plain truth.
Now a contemporary chronicler named Blaneforde has given
us a detailed account of these events which, if true, would
fully explain the whole position.[2] Let us confront Blaneforde
and the records.   It should be stated by way of preface that
the magnates of England had been summoned for a "colloquium" on the 20th of January, 1323-4; this was followed
by a parliamentary summons for the 23rd of February
following.[3] Now the monk's story is somewhat as follows:
The bishop of Hereford was arraigned before the king and
all the magnates of the realm, and charged with high treason.
He listened patiently to the indictment; then objected.
"My lord king," he said, "with all due respect to your royal
majesty, I, an humble minister and member of God's sacred
church and a bishop consecrate (licet indignus), refuse and
am bound to refuse to answer aught to the weighty matters
laid to our charge without the authority of the archbishop
of Canterbury, . . . and the consent of my other peers, the
bishops."[4] Upon this the archbishops and other suffragans
rose and humbly besought the royal clemency.   But as the
king was in no way appeased or his anger mitigated, the
whole clergy claimed the said bishop as a consecrated member of the church.   And so he was delivered to the archbishop until such time as he should, at the king's pleasure,
answer to the matters charged and to be charged against
him.   Then, on a certain day not long after, the king, as
before, summoned the bishop.   A rumour of this reached
the ears of the archbishops.   The archbishops of Canterbury,
York and Dublin, and ten suffragans, hastened with uplifted
crosses to the place of judgment; took their brother, who

---

[1] Close Roll, 1 Edward III, pt. 1, m. 13 (printed Rot. Parl., ii,
p. 429).
[2] Printed Rolls Series [28], p. 140.
[3] Full details of these matters are printed in the Parliamentary
Writs, R.C., vol. ii.
[4] "et aliorum parium meorum, episcoporum, consensu."

was standing alone and forlorn, under their protection ; and, without any answer given, carried him away, enjoining all present in the name of God and on pain of anathema that none should presume to lay violent hands upon him. When the bishop had been taken away, the king, enraged at the audacity of the clergy, ordered an inquisition to be taken. The country was accordingly convened ; and the jury, fearing the vengeance of their earthly rather than their heavenly king, found the *absent*[1] bishop guilty of all the matters charged against him.

Certainly Blaneforde's account affords a very convincing explanation of the errors of ordinary procedure appearing on the face of the record. It was the king in person who was virtually conducting this prosecution. Again, if it was the fact that an inquisition was ordered after Hereford had left the court, and that contrary to the entry on the Coram Rege Roll this inquisition was taken in the bishop's absence, then an irregularity had been committed quite sufficient to account for the mysterious entry on the Close Roll.

Unfortunately very little is known about Blaneforde; we do not know what value to attach to his story. Perhaps from the unsorted documents at Hereford fresh evidence may some day be forthcoming. At present the real truth is somewhat conjectural; but at least we have some evidence for thinking that what the modern constitutional lawyer calls claiming privilege of clergy, Adam Orleton would have described as claiming the trial by his peers accorded by Magna Carta.[2]

---

[1] This, of course, is a flat contradiction of the Coram Rege Roll.

[2] The following official explanation was sent to the pope : Vice reproba et ingrata, inimicis et rebellibus nostris nuper in dicto regno more guerrimo contra nos insurgentibus, effectualiter adhaesit, consensit et auxilium praestitit ; ipsos in maneriis suis receptando, et eis, in sua rebellione persistentibus, de hominibus ad arma, equis et armaturis subsidium faciendo ; sicque participando eisdem in crimine laesae majestatis, prout haec omnia nedum fama volatili vel assertiva, set processu legitimo, in pleno parliamento nostro, praesentibus archiepiscopis, episcopis, proceribus et aliis magnatibus regni nostri, secundum legem et consuetudinem ejusdem regni declarata fuerunt. Et licet contra ipsum potuissemus rigorius processisse, ipsum tamen de criminibus supradictis,

At this point we may sum up our investigations, so far as they have gone, with the briefest observations. By the end of Edward the First's reign the practice in trial of peers was being rapidly reduced to precision : the serious cases were judged in full council or parliament. During Edward the Second's troubled administration uncertainty and confusion arises : parliament and the council are becoming distinct organisms; there are precedents, like Harcla's case, opposed to the practice of Edward the First. It has become a question how far such precedents will, in the future, be approved and followed. As to the position of the spiritual lords, at the end of the latter reign, with regard to trial by peers, we have nothing to say ; if trial by peers when applied to them meant trial by lords temporal as well as spiritual, apparently they cared for none of these things.

APPENDIX TO CHAPTER IX

Assize Roll, Hertford, 10 *Richard I, m. 2d.; printed Rot. Curiae Regis, vol. i, pp.* 168–70

Amerciamenta de Hertford. . . . Gerard de Furnivall. amerciand. ad scaccarium pro disseisina. . . . Reginald de Argenton amerciand. ad scaccarium pro disseisina.   C m.

Assize Roll, Hereford, Pasch. et Trin., 1 *John, m.* 6 ; *printed Placitorum Abbreviatio, p.* 24

Per assisam Philippus de Stapilton et Emma uxor ejus recuperant seizinam suam de libero tenemento suo in Dor-
misericordia   minton et in Bricwarestr. versus Herbertum filium
baro est   Herberti. Ideo Herbertus in misericordia.

ob reverentiam episcopalis ordinis, in foro ecclesiae reliquimus judicandum, et temporalia episcopatus predicti in manum nostram seiziri facientes, ea decrevimus prout de jure licuit suo perpetuo retinenda sicut alias sanctitati vestrae scripsisse meminimus. . . . (Chertsey, 28th May, 1325 ; Roman and French Roll, 18 Edward II, m. 1. Printed by Rymer, Foedera R.C. ii, p. 601.)
The above was not, of course, an occasion on which we should expect impartiality or truth.

Curia Regis Roll, 17, 4 *John ; printed Selden Soc.,*
Select Pleas of the Crown, vol. i, p. 20

Mercatum de Undele est remotum de die dominica usque
misericordia diem sabbati. Et mercatum est abbatis de Burgo.
apud Westm. Ideo in misericordia.
Juratores dicunt quod mercatum de Rowell. est remotum a
misericordia die dominica usque in diem sabbati. Et mercatum
apud Westm. est comitis de Clara. Ideo in misericordia. . . .

Curia Regis Roll, 42, *m.* 4*d.,* 7–8 *John*

Oxon.—Assisa venit recognoscere si Alanus filius Rollandi
injuste et sine judicio disseisivit Laur. de Scace de communi
pastura sua in Abbefeld infra assisam. Juratores dicunt quod
disseisivit [sine] judicio. Alanus in misericordia et Laurent.
habet saisinam suam. Dampnum iiij s. amerciandus
coram rege
est coram rege.

Northumberland Eyre Roll, 40 *Henry III ; printed*
Surtees Soc., 88, *p.* 74

Juratores presentant quod Robertus de Cregling et Jacobus
le Escoc., duo extranei, capti fuerunt pro suspicione latrocinii
per ballivos Willelmi de Valencia et imprisonati in prisona
ejusdem Willelmi apud Rowebyr. Et predictus Robertus
postea evasit de prisona illa usque ad ecclesiam de Rowebyr.
et cognovit ibi latrocinium et abjuravit regnum coram Willelmo
de Baumburg tunc coronatore. Nulla habuit catalla. Et
Jacobus liberatus fuit vicecomiti. Ideo vicecomes respondeat
de eo. Et ad judicium de evasione super Willelmum de
Valencia. . . .

Ibid., p. 103

De faltis dicunt quod Willelmus de Feugers, Simon de
Monteforti comes Leycestrie, Johannes de Ballyoll . . . comes
Malcolmn, comes de Fyf . . . non venerunt primo die coram
justiciariis. Ideo in misericordia.

Huntingdon Eyre, 1265 ; *printed Selden Soc., Select Pleas of the Forest, p.* 13

Presentatum est per forestarios et viridarios quod Ricardus cocus domini Ricardi comitis Gloucestrie, Willelmus marescallus et Walterus clericus de camera ejusdem comitis in eundo de Huntindon versus Stanford, ad parandum hospicium domini sui, die Veneris proxima ante festum sancti Andree, quando dictus comes ivit versus Ebor. ceperunt unam damam cum leporariis suis. Quod factum forestarii domino comiti statim intimaverunt, qui factum illud bene advocavit. Et ideo coram rege.

coram rege

Northamptonshire Eyre, 1255 *; printed ibid., p.* 34

Presentatum est per eosdem quod die nativitatis beate Marie anno tricesimo quinto R. de Clare comes Glocestrie fuit apud Rowell. Et post prandium ivit ad boscum suum de Miklewod spaciaturus, et ibidem fecit decopulare duos brachettos qui invenerunt unum cervum in eodem bosco ; et illum fugaverunt usque in campum de Deseburg supra Rowell et ibi captus fuit. Cujus capcioni interfuit Robertus de Mares cum tribus leporariis, Robertus Basset cum tribus leporariis, Robertus de Longo Campo et Johannes Lovet viridarius qui comederant cum dicto comite eo die : ideo de dicto comite coram rege, et ad judicium de predicto Roberto, Roberto, Roberto et Johanne . . .

coram rege
ad judicium

Northamptonshire Eyre, 1272, *printed ibid., p.* 40

Presentatum est et convictum per . . . qui dicunt super sacramentum suum quod inter bellum de Lewes et Evesham tempore quo Petrus de Monteforti habuit custodiam castri et parci de Norhamt. Robertus comes de Ferar. cum familiaribus suis vi et contra voluntatem et sine scitu ipsius Petri fregit murum parci versus Moleton et intravit eum cum canibus et leporariis suis et cepit quatuor feras et asportavit sine waranto. Coram rege quia baro.

coram rege

Presentatum est etc. quod Reginaldus de Grey cum aliis de familia et societate sua intravit parcum predictum tempore quo idem habuit custodiam ejusdem parci et fugavit in eodem

pro voluntate sua et cepit quinque feras ad minus, cuniculos
eciam et lepores tam in parco quam in warenna, unde certus
numerus non potuit inquiri. De eo coram rege
coram rege quia baro.

*Exchequer Treasury of Receipt, Forest Proceedings, 12,
m. 6d., 5 Edward I*

[Dominus Robertus filius Walteri] venit et super hoc convictus et quia coram justiciariis minabatur forestariis et
viridariis qui eum indictaverant adjudicatur prisone et habet
diem coram rege. . . . Et predictus Robertus filius Walteri
finivit coram domino rege cc m. per plegios Ranulphi de
Monte Canisio [etc.]. . . .

*Northumberland Eyre Roll, 7 Edward I; printed
Surtees Soc., 88, p. 327*

Juratores presentant quod Radulphus filius Rogeri tenet
manerium de Dicheburn in capite de domino rege in baronagio
per servitium feodi unius militis et levavit ibidem furcas xx
annis elapsis. Et Radulphus venit et requisitus quo warranto
levavit predictas furcas dicit quod ipse et antecessores sui
semper habuerunt. Et dicit quod ceciderunt semel et illas
relevavit sicut ei bene licuit. Et de hoc ponit se super patriam
et juratores dicunt super sacramentum suum quod predictus
Radulphus levavit predictas furcas viginti annis: et quod
nullus antecessorum suorum habuit furcas in predicto manerio
donec predictus Radulphus levavit illas: levavit injuste etc.
Ideo ad judicium de eo.

Ibid., p. 379—Amercements

De Radulpho filio Rogeri quia levavit furcas sine
baro warranto. . . . [No amercement is entered on the
roll in this instance.]

Ibid., p. 332

Juratores presentant quod Robertus quondam episcopus
Dunelmensis appropriavit sibi quandam piscariam in aqua
de Eysworth juxta mare unde homines domini regis de
Warnemue piscari solebant, ita quod nullus eorum ausus est
ibidem piscari sine licentia dicti episcopi ad dampnum et
prejudicium etc. Ideo ad judicium de eo.

Ibid., p. 385—*Amercements*

De episcopo Dunelmense pro eodem [scil. purprestura in aqua de Tine]. . . . [No amercement is entered against the bishop.]

Ibid., p. 372

Gilbertus de Humfravill comes de Anegos alias coram Galfrido de Agwillum et Philippo de Welebi indictatus de hoc quod deberet levasse quandam warennam apud Balbington sine warranto. Et similiter de hoc quod deberet attraxisse ad libertatem suam de Reddesdal placita corone de Coketmore que ad dominum regem pertinere debent et solent. Et de hoc quod deberet receptasse infra libertatem suam predictam quendam Johannem filium Willelmi utlagatum in libertate de Extelsham. Et de hoc quod deberet receptasse quendam Walterum Demas latronum notorium cum sociis suis in castro suo de Prodhou et apud Hirbotel. . . . Venit et defendit totum etc. et quidcunque est contra pacem domini regis. Et quoad warrenam dicit quod. . . . Et quod non sit culpabilis de predictis transgressionibus sibi impositis ponit se super patriam de bono et malo, salvo sibi beneficio de tempore regis Henrici eo quod hec omnia predicta fieri deberent tempore ejusdem regis Henrici. Et juratores tam citra Coket quam ultra Coket videlicet tam de illis qui fuerunt juratores coram prefatis Galfrido et Philippo quam de illis qui modo electi fuerunt ad coronam dicunt super sacramentum suum quod predictus comes in nullo est culpabilis de predictis trangressionibus sibi impositis. Ideo inde quietus.

Exchequer, Treasury of Receipt, Forest Proceedings, 161, *m.* 4, 8 *Edward I*

Episcopus
Wynthon.
coram Rg.
loquendum

Presentatum [est] per eosdem et convictum quod Nicholas episcopus Wynton. venit de manerio suo . . . et cepit unum cervum et unum damum. . . . Unde loquendum cum domina regina.

(For other cases where the queen is similarly referred to see Forest Proceedings, 231, 8 Edward I.)

Ibid., m. 9

Presentatum est per eosdem et convictum quod predictus Johannes de Sancto Johanne, Galfridus de Lucy, Thomas Paynel et Johannes Boun venerunt in foresta de Wolvemere . . . et ceperunt unum feconem bisse et asportaverunt sine warranto. Et quod predictus Galfridus de Lucy, Johannes de Boun et Johannes de Percy venerunt . . . et ceperunt unam bissam et unum feconem bisse. . . . Et non venerunt nec fuerunt attachiati. Ideo mandatum est vicecomiti Surrey et Sussex quod faciat venire predictos. . . . Postea venerunt predicti Johannes de Boun et Johannes de Percy et adjudicantur prisone. Johannes de Sancto Johanne . . . Johannes de Bouhun (et) Johannes de Percy per breve domini regis habent diem usque ad parliamentum prox. post Pasch.

(margin: Coram rege ad parliamentum)

(On m. 12, there is a hunting case in which the bishop of Winchester is again implicated. The report concludes: " de predicto episcopo coram rege." And in the margin, "coram rege.")

Exchequer Treasury of Receipt, Forest Proceedings, 30, m. 11, 10 Edward I

Presentatum est etc. quod Humfridus de Boun (modo) comes Herefordie et quidam Blakeng. qui tunc fuit ventarius suus (et alii de familia sua) venerunt de domo predicti comitis de Wytenhurst die sancti Petri ad Vincula anno predicto et cum leporariis suis ceperunt duas damas et asportaverunt apud grangiam de Ardlaunde ubi jacuerunt illa nocte et in crastino redierunt ad domum dicti comitis apud Wytenhurst et non venerunt nec fuerunt attachiati. Ideo mandatum est vicecomiti Wiltes. quod faciat venire predictum comitem die Veneris prox. post mediam quatragesimam. . . . Postea venit predictus Humfridus coram justiciariis et adjudicatur prisone. Et invenit manucaptores [ad habendum] eum coram domino rege in proximo parliamento suo videlicet a Pasch. in unum mensem ad satisfaciendum eidem de transgressione predicta videlicet Grimbaldum Pauncefot et Walterum de Baskerville milites.

(margin: mand.)

(margin: coram rege)

(On m. 5 there is a report of proceedings against the earl of Warwick, who is summoned in respect of the improper release by him of certain prisoners; he appears by attorney, but has no valid defence. The report concludes: "Ideo de eo coram rege." And in the margin: "loquendum de comite Warrwici. Coram rege.")

Eyre Roll, 46, Berks, m. 22, 12 Edward I

Robertus clericus de Hayele captus fuit pro latrocinio et imprisonatus in castro de Wallingford Edmundi comitis Cornubie et a prisona ejusdem evasit. Ideo ad judicium de evasione super predictum comitem Cornubie.

Eyre Roll, 46, Berks, Amercements, 12 Edward I

baroñ	Milicent de Monte Alto pro eodem [scil. defalto]. . . .
baro	Reginaldo filio Percy quia non reparavit pontem [etc.]. . . .
baro	Rogero episcopo Coventry et Lichfield pro injusta detencione. . . .

Eyre Roll, 86, Cambridge, Amercements, 14 Edward I

baroñ	Elena la Zouche pro fuga Patricii [de Galeweye] qui fuit de mauu sua. . . .
baroñ	Dionisia de Monte Caniso pro defalta . . . habet breve.
comes	Rogero le Bygot comite Norf. marchall. Angl. pro fuga Willelmi quondam messar. sui. . . .

Eyre Roll, 63, Bucks, Amercements, 14 Edward I

baro	Henrico de Lacy comite Lincoln pro fuga ejusdem Willelmi. . . .

Eyre Roll, 280, Gloucester, Amercements, 15 Edward I
(See also ibid., m. 33)

baro	Godefrido Giffard episcopo Wygorn pro subtractione cujusdam secte. . . .

Eyre Roll, 278, Gloucester, Amercements, 15 *Edward I*

cõĩa   Ela comitissa Warrwici pro defalta. . . .

Eyre Roll, 925, Sussex, Amercements, 16 *Edward I*

baro   Abbate de Hyde pro [etc.]. . . .

Exchequer Treasury of Receipt, Forest Proceedings, 5,
m. 13, 13 *Edward I*

Presentatum est et convictum per eosdem quod dominus Robertus de Brus paī. et cum eo dominus Johannes de Seyton fuerunt in foresta domini regis de Inglewod ad capiendum decem damos quos dominus rex ei dederat per breve suum anno predicto; unde predictus Robertus cepit in presencia sua tres damos et unam damam de qua predictus Robertus fuit calumpniatus eo quod ceperat illam damam que fuit bestia alia quam continebatur in breve quietus per   suo, et. . . . Et quia baro domini regis ideo breve regis   loquendum est cum rege.

(See Close Roll, 14 Edward I, m. 8; Cal., p. 380, for the writ.)

{in re-
spectum   Presentatum est et convictum per eosdem quod
usque ad par- dominus Rogerus de Lancaster . . . cepit. . . .
liamentum¹}
loquendum   Et quia baro loquendum cum rege.
cum rege

Exchequer Treasury of Receipt, Forest Proceedings, 127,
m. 2, 15 *Edward I*

Presentatum est et convictum etc. quod Johannes comes Warren. die Martis prox. ante festum sancti Nicholai anno predicto interfuit per forestam de Shirewod in Langedale et ibi permisit currere leporarios et cepit duas damas et unum priketum dame et asportavit secum et predictus comes non venit nec prius attachiatus sed testatum est quod habet terras in comitatu Ebor. Ideo preceptum est vicecomiti etc.

{coram   Postea est prefatus comes redemptus ad xx li,
rege¹} xx li. coram baronibus de scaccario.

¹ Erased on the roll.

Ibid., m. 2d

Presentatum est et convictum etc. quod dominus Edmundus frater domini Edwardi regis interfuit per forestam die Lune prox. post festum sancti Hillarii anno predicto [secundo] . . . et cepit . . . et non venit. Ideo coram rege. Postea est idem dominus Edmundus frater {coram regis redemptus coram baronibus de scaccario rege[1]} xx li. ad xx li.

Ibid., m. 4

The case of Robert de Everyngham concludes with "ideo ad judicium coram rege." And in the margin "coram rege." Compare the Close Roll Cal., 1277-88, p. 404.

Ibid., m. 14

The archbishop of York is attached to appear before the justices of the forest for taking vert within the metes of the forest: an inquisition results in a doubtful finding. "Et quia predicta inquisitio est ambigua ideo loquendum est cum domino rege et datus est dies predicto (Johanni) archiepiscopo ad proximum parliamentum post proximum adventum domini regis in Anglia coram ipso domino rege."

Note the following: "et de predicto Almarico [de sancto Amando] coram rege quia est in Wallia in servicio domini regis." Forest Proc., 12, m. 5, 5 Ed. I. "Willelmus de Leybourne . . . quia est in servicio domini regis. Ideo de eo ponitur in respectum donec coram rege." Forest Proc., 45, m. 4, 14 Ed. I. "Egidius de Fenes . . . ajornatur coram rege eo quod est de hospicio suo." Forest Proc., 13, m. 8, 20 Ed. I.

Eyre Roll, 302, m. 32. Coram Rege Roll, Mich., 19-20, Edward I, m. 51d.

Wallia. Placitum de Consilio missum per Gilbertum de Robys clericum de Consilio.

Theobaldus de Verdun allocutus et ad racionem positus coram ipso domino rege et ejus consilio qualiter et quomodo se velit acquietare de hoc quod eidem Theobaldo nuper

---

[1] Erased on the roll.

videlicet a die sancti Michaelis in unum mensem proximo
preteritum ex parte domini regis dictum fuit quod haberet
coram ipso domino rege et ejus consilio apud Westmonasterium
in crastino Epiphanie proximo preterito Philippum Vaghan
. . . [et alios] . . . homines de terra sua de Ewyas Lascy et
infra terram suam predictam manentes et commorantes prout
dominus rex intellexit ad respondendum ipsi domino regi de
quibusdam contemptu et transgressionibus sibi per predictum
Philippum et alios factis videlicet de hoc quod cum idem
dominus rex nuper assignasset vicecomitem suum Herefordie
qui nunc est et Rogerum de Amphill justiciarios suos ad
inquirendum de quibusdam transgressionibus contra pacem
suam factis in terris predictis de Ewyas Lacy et prefati justiciarii certis die et loco per ipsos constitutis premissa per preceptum domini regis facere voluissent et incepissent predicti
Philippus et alii cum multitudine Wallensium tam equitum
quam peditum predictos justiciarios de loco ubi sedebant et
patriam coram eis venire fecerunt vi et armis amoverunt et
extra terras illas de Ewyas Lacy fugaverunt in contemptum
domini regis decem mille libr. Et super hoc predicto Theobaldo in presencia sua ex parte domini regis dictum fuisset
ut predictum est quod haberet corpora predictorum Philippi
et aliorum ad prefatum terminum ad respondendum domino
regi de contemptu predicto. Et idem Theobaldus hoc idem
manucepit et assumpsit si iidem Philippus et alii in terris suis
superstites essent et inveniri potuissent. Predictus Theobaldus
ad predictum crastinum Epiphanie falso et in decepcionem
curie et contra homagium et fidelitatem coram ipso domino
rege et ejus consilio testatus fuit quod quidam proditorum
Philippi et aliorum non sunt inventi . . . [etc.] ad dampnum
ipsius domini regis viginti mille libr. et in exheredacionem
ipsius quia in decepcionem curie et contra homagium et fidelitatem suam in presencia ipsius domini regis falso testatus
fuit etc. Et predictus Theobaldus in propria persona sua
defendit quicquid ei imponitur falso et in decepcionem curie
domini regis et contra homagium et fidelitatem et dicit quod
quicquid . . . testatus fuit . . . bene et fideliter testatus fuit
. . et hoc paratus est verificare qualitercumque domino regi
placuerit et curia sua consideraverit. Ideo preceptum est

coronatoribus comitatus Herefordie quod venire faciant coram
ipso domino rege a die Pasch. in xv dies ubicumque etc.
xxiiij tam milites quam alios liberos et legales homines de
comitatu etc. per quos etc. . . . (The jury find in favour of
the accused baron.)

Exchequer Treasury of Receipt, Forest Proceedings, 13 *m*. 12*d*.,
20. *Edward I*

Ricardus episcopus London habet canes et leporarios in
foresta currentes et capit leporem vulpem et catum per
_{misericordia} adventus suos ad maneria sua in comitatu Essexie.
_{coram rege} . . . Et de ipso coram rege eo quod non ostendit
inde warantum videlicet in proximo parliamento post Pasch.

Abbatissa de Cadomo habet canes et leporarios currentes
in terris suis in manerio suo de Felstede et capit
warantum leporem vulpem et catum et habet cartam regis H.
de warenna habenda ibidem.

misericordia   Nicholas de Cyney tenet leporarios et capit
xx s.   leporem in foresta sine waranto. Ideo in misericordia et leporarios amoveantur etc.

coram rege   Robertus de Ver comes Oxon habuit canes et
leporarios currentes in foresta unde nullum ostendit warantum.

Abbatissa de Berkynges habet canes et leporarios currentes
in foresta per antiquam tenuram ut dicit et eciam per cartam
regis H. proavi cujus tenor est in rotulis cartarum. Ideo inde
ponitur in respectum usque ad proximum parlia-
coram rege mentum post Pasch. vl coram domino rege.

misericordia   Dyonisia de Monte Canisio habet canes et
coram rege leporarios currentes in foresta et non ostendit
warantum. Ideo etc.

c s.   Johanna de Huntyngfeld habet canes et leporarios currentes in foresta et non ostendit warantum. Ideo etc.

Johannes comes Warenne per adventus suos ad manerium
suum de Roygne habet canes et leporarios etc. et non
misericordia ostendit warantum. Et venatores sui portant
coram rege arcus et sagittas contra assisam. . . . Et de comite
coram rege in proximo parliamento post Pasch.

Exchequer Memoranda Roll, King's Remembrancer,
21 *Edward I*

(m. 12) *Baronibus pro Humfrido de Bohun comite Herefordie et Essexie*

Rex mandat baronibus quod illas m marcas per quas idem comes finem fecit cum rege in ultimo parliamento regis pro quibusdam transgressionibus quas fecisse dicebatur et quas per suṁ scaccarii exigi fecerunt ad opus regis ab eodem ponent in respectum donec rex aliud inde preceperit et districciones si quas ei ea occasione fieri fecerint interim relaxari faciant eidem. Teste rege apud Berewik super Twed xxv die Octobris anno xx.

(m. 23d.) *Baronibus pro Theobaldo de Verdun*

Rex volens Theobaldo de Verdun gratiam facere specialem mandat baronibus quod demandam quam ei per suṁ scaccarii ad opus regis fecerunt de d marcis ad quas coram coram (sic) rege in parliamento regis nuper amerciatus fuit pro quadam transgressione regi et quibusdam de suis per ipsum illata supersederi mandent videlicet ad voluntatem regis. Datum sub privato sigillo apud Robur. xxiij die Julii anno xx.

(m. 26d.) *De iiij talliis sub nomine Philippi Marmyun*

Memorandum quod Rogerus de Coningesby exec. testamenti Philippi Marmyun venit coram baronibus iij die Junii anno xxj et tulit iiij tall. . . . Item protulit j tall. contra Robertum de Cheddewurth vicecomitem Lincolnie de xx li. de Philippo Marmyun convicto de capcione venacionis pro redempcione.

Exchequer Treasury of Receipt, Forest Proceedings, 188, *m.* 4*d.*

Presentatum est et convictum quod die Lune prox. (in) septim. Pentecost. anno E. x Rogerus de Somery cucurrit in chacia sua de Baggerugg que est infra forestam de Canok et cum canibus suis movit quendam cervum qui fugit versus forestam de Kenefar. Supervenit Thomas filius Walteri de Womburin cum arcubus et sagittis et ipsum cervum bersavit coram canibus predictis qui fugit in forestam et cecidit mortuus in foresta. . . . Et venacionem asportaverunt ad

domum dicti Rogeri. . . . Et non venit nec fuit attachiatus
ideo preceptum est vicecomiti quod faciat eum

preceptum
venire de die in diem. Postea venit predictus
Rogerus et propter receptamentum predictum adjudicatur
prisone et attornatur coram rege in proximo

coram rege
parliamento post festum Pasch. Et quia idem
Rogerus non satisfecit domino regi de transgressione predicta ad diem predictam redimatur ad ducentas marcas si
placeat domino regi.

Exchequer Treasury of Receipt, Forest Proceedings, 188,
m. 5

Presentatum est per eosdem et convictum quod Philippus
de Marmyun, Willelmus de Hondesare qui mortuus est,
Johannes venator ejusdem Philippi et alii de familia sua
venerunt in ballivam de Alrewas die Mercurii prox. ante
festum sancti Petri ad Vincula anno predicto cum leporariis
ejusdem Philippi [et] ceperunt unum sourum damẏ et venacionem secum asportaverunt ad domum predicti Philippi. . . .
Et non venerunt nec fuerunt attachiati ideo mandatum est
vicecomiti [etc.]. . . . Predictus Philippus venit et adjudicatur
prisone et de eo coram rege ad proximum parliamentum. . . .
Et quia idem Philippus Marmyun non satisfecit regi ad parliamentum predictum ponitur ad cc libr. si placeat

cc li.
domino regi pro transgressione. . . .

Exchequer Treasury of Receipt, Forest Proceedings, 188,
m. 9*d.*

Presentatum est et convictum quod Nicholas baro de
Stafford cepit unum cervum et unum feconem bisse in brueria
de Calnheth [in] vigil. exaltacionis sancte crucis anno regni
regis Edwardi xiij in foresta. . . . Et idem Nicholas venit
coram justiciariis apud Huntindon et adjudicatur prisone.
Et quia dominus rex est extra regnum coram quo deberet
redimi quia tenet per baroniam ponitur ad ducentas

cc m.
marcas si placeat domino regi.

*E Registro Domini Godefridi Giffard Wygorniensis Episcopi,
fol. 351b; printed by the Hampshire Record Society,
Crondal Records, p. 414*

Indictamentum contra Godefridum episcopum Wygorniensem pro Colingrugge. Rogerus de Moles, Adam Gurdune et
Johannes filius Thomae vicecomiti Suthamptonie salutem.
Ex parte domini regis tibi mandamus quod distringas Godefridum episcopum Wygorniensem per omnes terras et catalla
in balliva tua ita quod ad ea manus non apponet donec a
domino rege aliud habueris mandatum, et quod de exitibus
earundem domino regi respondeas, et quod habeas corpus
ejusdem episcopi coram domino rege in crastino assumpcionis
beate Marie virginis ubicunque fuerit in Anglia ad satisfaciendum domino regi de transgressione venacionis unde est indictatus coram nobis in comitatu predicto, et ad habendum
ad eundem diem ibidem Augerum nepotem suum, Willelmum
Salvage pincernam suam, Henricum venatorem suum, Johannem garsonem ejusdem Henrici et Radulphum Sprenggehuse
manupastos suos de transgressione venacionis indictatos ad
respondendum domino regi pro transgressione predicta, et
habeas ibidem tunc hoc breve. Datum apud Wyntoniam
die dominica proxima ante festum translacionis beati Thome
martyris anno regni regis Edwardi vicesimo primo.

*Writ of Replevin; printed, e registro predicto, Crondal
Records, p. 414. Close Roll, 21 Edward I, m. 3*

(Edwardus Dei gratia rex [etc.] . . . dilecto et fideli suo
Rogero de Moles salutem. Mandamus vobis[1]) quod manerium
venerabilis patris G[odefridi] episcopi Wygorniensis de Ichulle
quod nuper capi fecistis in manum nostram[2] pro transgressione
quam ipsum episcopum fecisse dicitur capiendo unum cervum
in foresta nostra[2] de Collingrugge[3] sine licencia nostra[2] et unde
indictatus fuit coram vobis[4] et (dilecto et fideli nostro[5]) Adam
Gurdune justiciariis nostris[2] ad inquirendum de transgressionibus in forestis chaciis et parcis nostris[2] factis in diversis

---

[1] C.R., Mandatum est Rogero de Molis.   [2] C.R., R.
[3] C.R., Colingerigge.   [4] C.R., eodem Rogero.
[5] Omitted in C.R.

y

comitatibus regni nostri[1] assignatis eidem episcopo per manucapcionem suam propriam usque ad instans parliamentum
nostrum sancti Michaelis replegiari facias[2] ita quod tunc stet
recto in curia nostra[1] de transgressione predicta. Et habeatis[3]
ibi hoc breve. Teste me-ipso[1] apud Bristol. xxx die Septembris anno regni nostri vicesimo primo.[4]

Close Roll, 22 Edward I, m. 13

Pro G. Wigorniense episcopo manucapiendo. Mandatum
est vicecomiti Wygorniensi quod si venerabilis pater G.
Wygorniensis episcopus inveniat sibi duodecim probos et
legales homines de balliva sua qui eum manucapiant habere
coram rege videlicet corpus pro corpore in octab. sancti
Hillarii ubicunque tunc rex fuerit in Anglia ad respondendum
regi de contemptu et transgressione sibi per eum illatis ut
dicitur (et ad faciendum et recipiendum ulterius quod curia
·regis inde consideraverit[5]) tunc omnes terras et tenementa
ipsius episcopi que hac occasione per preceptum regis cepit
in manum regis una cum omnibus inde perceptis interim
replegiari faciat per manucapcionem predictam et quod
habeat ibi nomina manucaptorum et hoc breve. Teste ut
supra [scil. apud Westmonasterium vj die Decembris].

Patent Roll, 15 Edward II, part 2, m. 14; printed by Rymer, Foedera R.C., vol. ii, p. 478

Placita corone coram domino Edwardo rege filio domini
regis Edwardi tenta in presentia ipsius domini regis apud
pontem Fractum die Lune proximo ante festum Annuncia-
tionis beate Marie virginis anno regni sui quinto decimo.

Cum Thomas comes Lancastrie captus pro prodicionibus
homicidiis incendiis depredationibus et aliis diversis feloniis
ductus est coram ipso domino rege presentibus Edmundo
comite Kancie, Johanne comite Richemund, Adomaro de
Valencia comite Pembrok, Johanne de Warrenna comite
Surrey, Edmundo comite Arundel, David comite Athol,

[1] C.R., R.   [2] C.R., faciat.   [3] C.R., quod habeat.
[4] C.R. adds—per ipsum regem nunciante H. de Veer.
[5] Interlined.

Roberto comite d'Anegos, baronibus et aliis magnatibus regni, dominus rex recordatur quod idem Thomas homo ligius ipsius domini regis venit apud Birton super Trentam simul cum Humfrido de Bohun nuper comite Hereford proditore regis et regni, invento cum vexillis explicatis apud Pontem Burgi in bello contra dominum regem et ibidem interfecto, et Rogero Damory proditore adjudicato, et quibusdam aliis proditoribus et inimicis regis et regni cum vexillis explicatis ut de guerra hostiliter resistebat et impedivit ipsum dominum regem homines et familiares suos per tres dies continuos quominus pontem dicte ville de Birton transire potuerunt prout debuerunt et quosdam homines ipsius domini regis ibidem felonice interfecit . . . [the earl's crimes are recited at some length]. . . . Que quidem proditiones homicidia combustiones depredationes debellationes hostiles cum equis et armis et vexillis explicatis manifeste sunt et notorie et note comitibus baronibus et aliis magnatibus et populo regni. Et ideo consideratum est quod predictus Thomas comes pro predicta proditione trahatur et pro predictis homicidiis depredationibus incendiis et roberiis suspendatur et pro predicta fuga in hac parte decapitetur . . . [hereupon follows a lengthy recital of the earl's past misdeeds]. . . . Unde dominus rex habito respectu ad tanta dicti Thome comitis facinora et iniquitates et ejus maximam ingratitudinem nullam habet causam ad aliquam gratiam eidem Thome comiti de penis predictis super ipsum adjudicatis pardonandis in premissis faciendam: quia tamen idem Thomas comes de parentela excellenti et nobilissima procreatus est dominus rex ob reverentiam dicte parentele remittit de gratia sua speciali predicto Thome comiti executionem duarum penarum adjudicatarum sicut predictum est scilicet quod idem Thomas comes non trahatur neque suspendatur sed quod executio tantummodo fiat super ipsum Thomam comitem quod decapitetur. . . . [Sentence is then passed on other traitors.] . . . In cujus etc. Teste rege apud Ebor. ij die Maii.

Repeal of the Process against the Despencers.   Scheduled
to Close Roll, 15 *Edward II, m.* 14

. . . A queu parlement a Everwyk les ditz Hugh le fitz et
Hugh le piere estoient menetz devant nous en court et pur-
suirent lour quereles susdites et prierent que nous les feissoms
dreit en ceste partie.   Et le dit Hugh le fitz pur luy monstra
et allegga les errours en le proces du dit agarde come est
susdit.   Et ensement le dit Hugh le pere proposa et allegga
meismes les errours pur luy meismes, et prierent les ditz
Hugh et Hugh severalement et jointement que desicome le
dit agard se fist voluntriement erroinement et torcenousement
countre les leis et les usages du roialme et countre commune
droit et resoun que nous vousissome le dit agard anenter et
defere et que eux soient remis et recounciletz a nostre foi
et a tiel estat come eux aveint et en tiel estat come eux
estoient avaunt le temps del dit agard selom droit et resoun.
Et sur ceo oies les resouns les ditz Hugh et Hugh feismes
le dit proces examiner en plein parlement a Everwyk en
presence des prelatz countes barouns chivalers des countez
et le poeple que estoit venutz par enchesoun du dit parlement; et trovasmes que le dit agard se fist sauntz appeler les
ditz Hugh et Hugh en respouns, et que cel agard se fist
sauntz lassent dez prelatz qui sount piers du roialme en
parlement, et countre la tenur de la graunt chartre des
fraunchises Dengleterre en laquele est contenu, Qe nul fraunc
homme ne soit exile ne en altre manere destruit forsque par
leal jugement de ses piers ou par la ley de terre, et que les
ditz Hugh et Hugh n'estoient appelletz en court ne a respouns sicome est susdit.   Et pur les errours avaunteditz,
et pur ceo que les causes contenu en le dit agard ne feurent
pas duement approvetz; et estre ceo eauntz regard a ceo que
nous feismes somondre nostre dit parlement a Westmonstier
en due manere et mandasmes as ditz grauntz par nos briefs
de venir duement a ceu parlement, et sovent en temps devaint
avions comande et defendu que alliance ne assemble se feist
des gentz armetz ne as armes dount nostre pees poet estre
troble et greinur mal avenir, et que les ditz grauntz nient

eiauntz regard a nostre mandement vindrent armetz (a) nostre
parlement a Westm. as chivaux et armes et a tote lour force
sicome est susdit, de la quele nous ne y esteÿmes devaunt
aparceu : et qaunt les ditz grauntz estoient en tiele manere
venutz a Loundres eux tindrent lour conseil a Loundres et
lour assemble sauntz venir a nous a Westm. sicome eux
estoient somouns, et sur ceo mandasmes a eux qils feussent
venutz a nous a Westm. a parlement come resoun fust, eux
venir ne voleint ne faire asavor a nous lour volonte ne les
causes dut dit agard, puis que nous avioms comence nostre
dit parlement et tenu par xv jours et plus et avioms fait
venir devaunt nous prelatz et aucuns countes barouns et
chivalers des countez et autres que vindrent pur la commune
du roialme et fait publier que touts yceux qui voleint liverer
peticiouns les feissent liverer ; et apres criee de ceo faite null
petitioun nesteit livere ne pleint faite devers les ditz Hugh
et Hugh tant que les ditz grauntz vindrent en la manere
susdite et lour conseil del dit agard de tut devers nous
celerent jeskas alhour qils vindrent a Westm. a force et
armes et noun duement et firent lour dit agard countre
resoun come de chose trete e accode entre eux meismes de
lour auctorite propre en nostre absence, et ensi purpristerent
les ditz grauntz sur nostre real poer jurisdictioun et conis-
saunce de proces et de jugement faire des choses que a
nostre real dignite appendent. Par quei nous ne poeismes
adonk arestier le dit agard ne droit faire as ditz Hugh et Hugh
sicome a nous appendent. Et estre ceo eauntz regard a ceo
que les ditz grauntz apres le dit agard fait prierent a nous
pardoun et reles de ceo que eux sentre-allierent par serement
escript ou en altre manere santz conge de nous et en pur-
suauntz les ditz Hugh le fitz et Hugh le pere avoient
chivauchetz a baners desplietz de nos armes et de lour armes
et pristrent et occuperent chasteux villes maners terres tenementz,biens et chateux et ensement pristrent et emprisonerent
gentz de nostre ligeaunce et autres et ascuns reindrent et
ascuns tuerent et autres plusours choses fesoient en destruantz
les ditz Hugh et Hugh en Engleterre Gales et aillours dount
aucuns choses purreient estre ditz trespas et aucuns felonies :
et ensi apercerent les ditz grauntz qil estoient adversairs et

malvoillauntz as ditz Hugh et Hugh en temps du dit agard et devaunt, dount eux ne devoient par resoun estre juges sur les ditz Hugh et Hugh en lour pursuite demene ne record aver sur les causes del dit agard. Et nous par le serement que nous feismes a nostre coronement sumes tenutz et obligez de faire droit a toutz nos subgitz et de tortz a eux faitz redresiere et faire amendre quant nous en sumes requis : et que en la dite graunt chartre est countenutz, Qe nous ne nieroms ne delaieroms a nuli droit ne justice; et auxi chargeauntz le counseil et la requeste des ditz prelatz queux nous fesoient pur salutz de nostre alme et pur peril eschuire et auxint a la requeste des ditz countes et pur toller malveis ensaumple du temps avenir de tieles emprises et jugementz faire en cas semblable countre resoun enblemissemeint de nostre corone et (a) grant damage dautres. Par quei nous veantz et sachauntz les ditz proces et agard faitz en la manere sus dite estre aux bien en prejudice de nous et en blemissement (de nostre corone e) de nostre reale dignete countre nous et nos heirs come countre les ditz Hugh et Hugh et par plusours autres enchesouns resonables,—De nostre poer real en plein parlement a Everwyk par le counseil et lassent des prelatz countes barouns chivalers des countez le commune du roialme et altres a nostre dit parlement a Everwyk estauntz le dit agard de tut anentissoms et defesoms del exil les ditz Hugh et Hugh et de lour desheritaunce et quant que cel agard touche, et meismes ceux Hugh le Despenser le fitz et Hugh le Despenser le pere remettoms et recouncilloms plenerement a nostre foi et a nostre pees et a lestat qil avoient et en tiel estat come eux estoient avaunt le dit agard en toutz pointz, et agardoms que eux reeient seisine de lour terres et tenementz biens et chateux etc. Et voloms et comandoms que qaunt qest enroule en les places de nostre court del dit agard soit chauncelle et anenti pour toutz jours.

Close Roll, 1 *Edward III, pt.* 1, *m.* 21*d*
Patent Roll, 2 *Edward III, pt.* 1, *m.* 17. (*Inspeximus and Exemplification*)

De adnullacione Processus contra Thomam comitem Lancastrie

Placita coram domino rege et consilio suo apud Westmonasterium in presencia ipsius domini regis, procerum et magnatum regni in parliamento suo ibidem convocato in crastino purificacionis beate Marie anno regni regis Edwardi tercii post conquestum primo. *Henricus de Lancastria* frater et heres Thome quondam comitis Lancastrie venit in parliamento isto et exhibuit coram ipso domino rege proceribus et magnatibus regni et consilio ipsius domini regis tunc ibidem existentibus quandam peticionem in hec verba: *A nostre seigneur le roi* et son conseil prie Henry de Lancastre frere et heir Thomas jadis counte de Lancastre que come le dit Thomas nadgair(e)s devant sire Edward jadis roi Dengleterre piere nostre seigneur le roi qore est et son conseil a Pountfrett l'an de son regne quinzime no(u)nresonablement estoit jugge a la mort(e) par un proces erroyne co(u)ntre lui adonqes fait par quel juggement il fuist mis a la mort(e) et par cause de mesme le juggement ses heirs desheritez dont le record et proces sont en Chancellerie: Qil pleise a nostre seigneur le roi commander au Chanceller qil face venir le record et proces del juggement ava(u)ntdit cy en parlement et qils soient recitez et examinez issint qe errour si nul y soit duement soit redresse et au dit Henry come (a) frere et heir le dit counte droit en(t) soit fait et son heritage a lui livere. *Pretextu* cujus peticionis dictum fuit cancellario per ipsum dominum regem quod scrutatis rotulis domini regis Edwardi patris domini regis nunc de cancellaria sua de anno predicto deportare faceret hic in parliamento &c. recordum et processum predicta. Qui quidem cancellarius postea recordum et processum predicta protulit hic in hec verba.... [The process against Thomas earl of Lancaster is set out verbatim.] ... *Et* super hoc in presencia ipsius domini regis et procerum et magnatum regni et aliorum hic in parliamento &c. existencium recitatis et lectis recordo et processu predictis quesitum est a predicto Henrico ob quam causam venire fecit hic recordum et processum predicta. Qui dicit quod ipse est frater et heres predicti comitis et ob errores in eisdem recordo et processu interventos quos petit corrigi &c. venire fecit hic recordum et processum predicta. Et dictum est ei quod ostendat errores &c. Qui dicit quod erratum est in hoc quod cum quicunque homo ligeus domini regis pro sedicionibus homicidiis roberiis incendiis et aliis feloniis tempore pacis captus et in quacunque curia regis ductus fuerit de hujusmodi sedicionibus et aliis feloniis sibi impositis per legem et consuetudinem regni arrenari debet et ad responsionem poni et inde per legem &c convinci antequam fuerit morti adjudicatus. Licet predictus Thomas comes homo ligeus predicti domini regis patris &c. tempore pacis captus et coram ipso rege ductus fuisset, dictus dominus rex pater &c. recordabatur ipsum Thomam esse culpabilem de sedicionibus et feloniis in predictis recordo et processu contentis absque hoc quod ipsum inde arrenavit seu ad responsionem posuit prout moris est secundum legem &c. Et sic absque arenamento et responsione idem Thomas erronice et contra legem terre tempore pacis morti extitit adjudicatus. Unde cum notorium sit et manifestum quod totum tempus quo impositum fuit eidem comiti predicta mala et facinora in predictis recordo et processu contenta fecisse et etiam tempus quo captus fuit et quo dictus dominus rex pater &c. recordabatur ipsum esse culpabilem &c. et quo morti extitit adjudicatus fuit tempus pacis maxime cum per totum tempus predictum cancellaria et alie placee curie domini regis aperte fuerunt et in quibus lex cuicunque fiebat prout fieri consuevit nec idem dominus rex unquam in tempore illo cum vexillis explicatis equitabat, predictus dominus rex pater &c. in hujusmodi tempore pacis contra ipsum comitem sic recordari non debuit nec ipsum sine arenamento et responsione morti adjudicasse. Dicit etiam quod erratum est in hoc quod cum predictus Thomas comes fuisset unus parium et magnatum regni et in magna carta de libertatibus Anglie contineatur quod nullus liber homo capiatur imprisonetur aut disseisiatur de libero tenemento suo vel libertatibus seu liberis consuetudinibus suis aut utlagetur aut exuletur aut aliquo modo destruatur nec dominus rex super ipsum ibit nec super eum mittet nisi per legale judicium parium suorum vel per legem terre, predictus Thomas comes per recordum regis ut predictum est tempore pacis erronice morti fuit adjudicatus absque arenamento seu responsione seu legali judicio parium suorum contra legem &c. et contra tenorem magne carte predicte. Unde petit errores predictos corrigi et predictum judicium tanquam erronium adnullari &c. et ad hereditatem suam ut frater et heres ipsius Thome admitti &c. *Et quia* inspectis et plenius intellectis recordo et processu predictis ob errores predictos (et alios in) eisdem recordo et processu compertos consideratum est per ipsum dominum regem proceres magnates et totam communitatem regni in eodem parliamento quod predictum judicium contra predictum Thomam comitem redditum tanquam erronicum revocetur et adnulletur et predictus Henricus ut frater et heres ejusdem Thome comitis ad hereditatem suam petendum et habendum debito processu inde faciendo prout moris est admittatur et habeat brevia cancellarie et justiciariorum in quorum placeis dicta recordum et processus irrotulantur quod eadem recordum et processus irritari faciant et adnullari &c.[1]

(An inaccurate transcript of the above is printed in vol. 2 of the Rotuli Parliamentorum exactly as if these proceedings were enrolled on a parliament roll. This is a most serious and misleading blunder.)

Patent Roll, 1 Edward III, part ii, m. 3. (Inspeximus and Exemplification)

Adnullacio Processus facti contra Rogerum de Mortuomari le Neveu

Rex omnibus ad quos &c. salutem. *Inspeximus* recorda et processus habita in parliamento nostro apud Westmonasterium

---

[1] The Patent Roll omits the heading, beginning and concluding as follows:—

Rex omnibus ad quos &c. salutem. Inspeximus recorda et processus habita in parliamento nostro apud Westmonasterium ultimo convocato in hec verba—Henricus de Lancastria . . . adnullari. Nos autem ad majorem securitatem ipsius Henrici predicta recordum et processus tenore presencium duximus exemplificanda. In cujus &c. Teste rege apud Ebor. tercio die Marcii.

ultimo convocato in hec verba. *Tenor petitionum* per Rogerum
de Mortuomari le Neveu portatarum coram domino rege
Edwardo tercio post conquestorem et consilio suo in pleno
parliamento suo convocato apud Westmonasterium post festum
purificationis beate Marie anno regni sui primo : *A* , nostre
seigneur le roi prie Rogier de Mortemer de Wiggemor qe
come en le record et proces et jugementz renduz sur Rogier
de Mortemer de Chirk son uncle qui heir il est devant Mons.
Wautier de Norwy et ses compaignons justices sire Edward
nadgaires roi Dengleterre piere nostre seigneur le roi qore est
a ceo assignetz lan de son regne sezisme errours diverses
soient trovez come purra plus pleinement apparir par mesmes
le record et proces qe demoerent en chauncellerie par maun-
dement le roi fait au tresorer et chaumbelleins de les faire
venir hors de la tresorie illuqes et qe pleise faire venir les ditz
record et proces devant vous et vostre conseil et les errours
leinz trovez faire anientir.   En mesme la manere prie le dit
Rogier . . . [a similar petition with reference to the judgment
against himself]. . . . *Pretextu* quarum petitionum mandatum
fuit cancellario quod venire faceret coram ipso rege et consilio
suo in parliamento suo recorda et processus de quibus peticiones
predicte faciunt mencionem qui quidem cancellarius (ea) coram
predictis domino rege et consilio in eodem parliamento venire
fecit in hec verba . . . [The proceedings against the Mortimers
are set out verbatim.]. . . . *Et modo* venit predictus Rogerus de
Mortuomari le Neveu in parliamento (predicto) et quesitum
est ab eo qua de causa venire fecit recorda et processus predicta : Dicit quod ob errores in eisdem : Et dictum est ei quod
ostendat errores si qui &c. et predictus Rogerus de Mortuomari
le Neveu d[icit quod] in recordis et processibus predictis sic
redditis tam contra ipsum quam (dominum) Rogerum luncle
cujus heres ipse est error inest manifestus in hoc videlicet quod
cum aliquis de *** regis tempore pacis deliquerit erga
dominum regem vel alium per quod debeat vitam vel mem-
brum perdere et super hoc coram justiciis in judicium ductus
f[uerit] primo debeat poni rationem et super delicto sibi imposito responsiones ipsius audiri priusquam procedatur ad
judicium de eo.   Set in recordis et processibus predictis continetur quod [dicti] Rogerus et Rogerus coram justiciis ducti

adjudicati fuerunt judicio tractus et suspendii et postea perpetue prisone adjudicati et mancipati absque hoc quod ipsi fuissent arrenati seu quod ipsi ad aliqua eis imposita possent respondere quod est contra legem et consuetudinem regni &c. per quod ad judicium de eis erronice processum est: Dicit etiam quod in recordis et processibus predictis continetur quod dominus rex recordabatur versus ipsos Rogerum et Rogerum quod ipsi hostiliter equitaverunt cum Humfrido de Bohun comite Herefordie et aliis inimicis domini regis contra ipsum dominum regem et populum regni sui diversa mala et facinora perpetrandis quare judicia predicta super eisdem [lata] fuerunt, cujusmodi recordum non est domino regi facere nisi de inimicis suis tempore guerre et hoc scilicet quando dominus rex equitat cum vexillis [explicatis] et non tempore pacis, set eo tempore dominus rex non equitavit cum vexillis explicatis nec fuit tempus guerre cancellaria domini regis et justicii placearum de [utroque banco] sedebant ad justiciam unicuique conqueri volenti et persequenti faciendum per quod ad judicium de eis ut predictum est erronice processum est: Dicit etiam quod erratum est [in hoc] quod cum in magna carta de libertatibus Anglie contineatur quod nullus liber homo capiatur aut imprisonetur aut de libero tenemento suo disseisiatur vel libertatibus vel liberis consuetudinibus suis aut utlagetur aut exuletur aut aliquo modo destruatur nec quod dominus rex super eum ibit nec super ipsum mittet nisi per legale judicium parium suorum vel per legem terre set in recordis et processibus predictis continetur quod predicti Rogerus et Rogerus singillatim judicio tractus et suspendii adjudicati fuerunt et etiam [postea] perpetue prisone adjudicati et mancipati absque legali judicio parium suorum ad hoc vocatorum et contra legem terre per quod ad judicium de eis ut predictum est erronice processum est: Et petit quod recorda et processus predicta videantur et examinentur et ob errores predictos revocentur et adnullentur. *Et quia* inspectis recordis et processibus predictis diligenterque recitatis et examinatis compertum est in eisdem quod predicti Rogerus de Mortuomari le Neveu et Rogerus de Mortuomari luncle *** enti judicio tractus et suspendii adjudicati fuerunt et eciam postea perpetue prisone adjudicati et mancipati absque hoc quod ipsi ad aliqua eis vel eo imposita possent respondere et hoc tempore pacis et absque hoc quod dominus rex equitavit cum vexillis explicatis et cancellaria regis et jus- ticiariis de utroque [banco] sedentibus ut predictum est et absque legali judicio parium suorum quod est contra legem et consuetudinem regni Anglie et tenorem carte predicte: *Consideratum est* per dominum regem nunc et ejus consilium in pleno parliamento predicto quod omnia judicia predicta tam contra dictum Rogerum le Neveu quam contra prefatum Rogerum luncle [sic] data et promulgata ob defectus et errores predictos et alios in dictis recordis et processibus compertos penitus adnullata sint et revocata et pro nullis et revocatis habeantur et predictus Rogerus de Mortuomari le Neveu ad communem legem restituatur et rehabeat terras et tenementa sua &c. et heres predicti Rogeri de Mortuomari luncle habeat hereditatem suam &c. *Nos* autem ad majorem securitatem ipsius Rogeri le Neveu predicta recorda et processus tenore presencium duximus exemplificanda. In cujus &c. Teste rege apud Hayden xxiiij die Julii.

Patent Roll, 2 Edward III, pt. ii, m. 11. (*Inspeximus and Exemplification*)

De adnullacione judicii super Bartholomeum de Badelesmere redditi

. . . Et dictum est ei [scilicet Egidio filio et heredi Bar- tholomei] quod ostendat errores si qui etc. qui dicit quod error inest manifestus in hoc videlicet quod cum aliquis de regno regis tempore pacis deliquerit erga dominum regem vel alium per quod debeat vitam vel membros perdere et super hoc coram justiciariis in judicium ductus fuerit primo debet poni ratione et super delicto sibi imposito responsiones ipsius audiri priusquam procedatur ad judicium de eo set in recordo et processu predictis continetur quod predictus Bar- tholomeus coram justiciariis ductus adjudicatus fuit judicio tractus suspensionis et decollacionis absque hoc quod ipse fuit super aliqua felonia arenatus seu quod ipse ad aliqua ei im- posita posset respondere quod est contra legem et consuetu- dinem regni etc. per quod ad judicium de eo erronice est processum etc. Dicit etiam idem Egidius quod in eisdem recordo et processu continetur quod prefatus dominus rex pat' etc. recordabatur versus prefatum Bartholomeum quod ipse hostiliter equitavit cum Thome nuper comite Lancastrie etc. . . . quare judicium predictum super eundem Bartholomeum redditum fuit. Cujusmodi recordum non est domino regi faciendum nisi de inimicis suis tempore guerre et hoc quando dominus rex equitat cum vexillis explicatis et non tempore pacis set eo tempore dominus rex non equitavit cum vexillis explicatis nec fuit tempus guerre presertim cum cancellarius domini regis et justiciarii de utroque banco sedebant ad justiciam unicuique conqueri volenti et persequenti faciendum per quod ad judicium de eodem Bartholomeo ut predictum est erronice est processum. Dicit etiam idem Egidius quod erratum est in hoc quod cum in magna carta de libertatibus Anglie contineatur quod nullus liber homo capiatur aut imprisonetur aut de libero tenemento suo disseisiatur vel libertatibus vel liberis consuetudinibus suis aut utlagetur aut exuletur aut aliquo modo destruatur nec quod dominus rex super eum ibit nec super eum mittet nisi per legale judicium parium suorum vel per legem terre, set in recordo et processu predictis continetur quod predictus Bartholomeus judicio tractus suspensionis et decollacionis adjudicatus fuit absque legali judicio parium suorum ad hoc vocatorum et contra legem terre per quod ad judicium de eodem Bartholomeo ut predictum est erronice est processum. Et petit idem Egidius quod recordum et processum predicta videantur et examinentur et ob errores predictos revocentur et adnullentur. Et quia dictis recordo et processu inspectis et diligenter recitatis et examinatis compertum est in eisdem quod predictus Bartholomeus coram justiciariis ductus et judicium tractus et suspensionis et decollacionis adjudicatus fuit absque hoc quod ipse ad alique ei imposita potuit respondere et hoc tempore pacis et absque hoc quod dominus rex equitavit cum vexillis explicatis cancellario regis et justiciariis de utroque banco sedentibus ut predictum est et absque legali judicio parium suorum contra legem et consuetudinem regni et contra tenorem carte predicte. *Consideratum est* per ipsum dominum regem nunc et consilium suum in pleno parliamento predicto quod dictum judicium contra ipsum Bartholomeum sic pronunciatum et redditum ob errores predictos adnullatum sit et revocatum et pro nullo et revocato habeatur imperpetuum. Et quod heres predicti Bartholomei ad hereditatem suam habendum debito processu admittatur. *Nos* autem recordum et processum predicta ad majorem notitiam revocacionis et adnullacionis predicti judicii sic erronice pronunciati et redditi tenore presencium duximus exemplificanda. In cujus &c. Teste rege apud Wyndesore xix die Novembris.

Ancient Petitions, No. 2500, File 50

A nostre seigneur le Roi et a son conseil prie Henri neveu et heir sire Andrew de Harcla. Sicome les terres et tenements le dit sire Andrew fueront seisi en la mayn le roi Edward pier nostre Seigneur le roi q'or est comes terres forfaites par la forfeture le dit sire Andrew *** [nonobstant q'il] *** ne fuist attaint par enquest de ses piers ne des autres de nule mauvaite mais fuist mys a la mort par jugement par cette cause *** [qe le dit roi] *** Edward pier nostre seigneur le roi q'or est recorda sur lui q'il fuist son enemy et aydaunt a ses enemyes : destotz q'il *** [plaise a nostre seigneur aver] *** regard a ceo q'il ne fuist unqes atteint par enquest des ses piers ne des autres du dit mauvaite que lui fuist sur **** dit jugement done sur tiel record et encountre ley de tut temps usee soit anentie e q'il poese estre inherite del heritage du dit sire Andrew e ceo pour Dieu et pour deliver le alme le dit pier nostre seigneur le roi de perile desicome il est pres de servir au roi *** son estat et come ses auncestres sunt servi les auncestres nostre seigneur le roi puis le conquest ***

(Endorsed) Coram rege et magno consilio
Suie de faire venir le record et proces du dit jugement entre cy et le primer parlement.

CHAPTER X

TRIAL OF PEERS IN THE FOURTEENTH CENTURY

THE accession of Edward the Third was followed almost immediately by an Act reversing the attainder of Thomas earl of Lancaster. This has been already dealt with. Nothing less would have served to secure the stability of the new administration. Unfortunately fresh troubles were brewing. The nominal chiefs of the council found they had no voice whatever in matters of state: at the real head of affairs was Mortimer earl of March, with no better credentials to show for his position than a shameless intimacy with the queen-mother.

Edmund earl of Kent was the first victim of this unsatisfactory political situation. For some reason, not known, Isabella and her paramour appear to have come to the conclusion that Edmund's death was a necessary measure for their protection, and they deliberately inveigled him into a treasonable correspondence. He was arraigned before the parliament at Winchester in March, 1329–30, confessed his guilt and was condemned to death.[1] Not long after, as the

---

[1] The record of this trial is not preserved among the parliament rolls. For an account of the trial sent to the pope on Edward's behalf see Rymer, Foedera R.C., ii, 2, p. 783. For the earl's confession see Murimuth, Rolls Series [93], p. 253; Walsingham, Rolls Series [28], ii, p. 351. Among chronicles the Brute Chronicle gives the fullest account (Harley, MS. 2279, printed by Thompson in his notes to Baker at p. 221). See also Chron. de Lanercost, p. 264, Baker, ed. Thompson, p. 44, etc. See also Close Roll, 4 Ed. III, m. 37; Calendar, p. 17. There was some difficulty, it is said, in finding an executioner for the condemned earl. One has it that a "yonge fermer" smote off his head (Brute); another that the earl must needs wait outside the castle gate until the hour of vespers, when a ribald criminal from the Marshalsea (in consideration of a pardon) volunteered for the business (Knighton).

result of a counter-conspiracy to which the youthful king was privy, Mortimer himself was seized in Nottingham castle. He was tried in parliament, but without being arraigned, and condemned by the earls and barons as peers and judges of parliament.[1] He was executed at Tyburn.

The judgment of the earl of Kent appears to have been legal enough, notwithstanding its being the result of an infamous conspiracy. On the other hand, it is quite clear that Mortimer was illegally condemned. Accordingly, on the subsequent petition of Edmund's widow and heir, their respective rights to dower, title and estates were allowed notwithstanding the judgment;[2] but the result of a petition in Mortimer's case was the reversal of that judgment for error.[3]

Mortimer was not the only person dealt with by the parliament of 1330: certain of his associates, though not peers, were also condemned, but only after a notable protest by earls and barons to the effect that they were not bound to sit in judgment on any but peers of the realm. The king admitted the justness of the protest, and it was agreed by

---

[1] Rot. Parl., vol. ii, p. 52. . . . Lesqueux countes, barouns, et peres, les articles par eux examinez, reviendrent devant le roi en mesme le parlement et disoient tres touz *par un des peres* que totes les choses contenues es ditz articles feurent notoires et conues a eux et au poeple; et nomement l'article tochant la mort sire Edward, piere nostre seignur le roi que ore est. Pour quoi les ditz countes, barouns et pieres, come juges du parlement par assent du roi en mesme le parlement, agarderent et ajugerent: Que le dit Roger, come treitur et enemy du roi et du roialme, feust treyne et pendu. Et sur ce estoit comande a counte mareschal a faire l'execution du dit jugement. . . .

Baker, ed. Thompson, p. 47. Per suos pares fuit morti condigne adjudicatus, non tamen venit coram eis nec responsioni ratiocinatus, quoniam a morte comitis Lancastrie, Wintonie, et Gloucestrie, et Cancie, non solebant nobiles ratiocinio deputari, set sine responsione atque legitima conviccione perierunt; unde comes iste jure quod in alterum statuit usus extitit, et juste eadem mensura quam aliis mensus fuerat erat eidem remensum.

[2] Rot. Parl., vol. ii, p. 33; ibid., p. 55.

[3] Ibid., pp. 255–6: Et sur ceo eue bone deliberation et avis od grant leiser par nostre seigneur le roi, prelatz, prince, et ducs, countes et barons avant ditz, il piert clerement que meismes les juggementz et record sont erroignes et defectives en touz pointz.

the king and magnates in full parliament that the judgments then passed on commons were not to be treated as precedents, by reason whereof the said peers might be charged to judge other than their peers contrary to the law of the land. A most infelicitously worded resolution, which might but obviously does not mean that the persons tried could in such cases take exception to the jurisdiction.[1]

The fall of Mortimer, coupled with the death of Edward the Second, cleared the political atmosphere for some time to come. However, the ex-king's mysterious demise could not be simply ignored, and Thomas de Berkeley, a peer, who had been Edward's custodian, was brought before parliament and arraigned on a somewhat vague charge of being concerned in the affair. He defended every word of the charge, and for good and evil put himself upon the country: in other words, he claimed trial by jury. A jury was awarded for the octave of St. Hilary, and on this day Thomas de Berkeley came before the king in full parliament; there came also twelve jurors, all knights, who found Thomas not guilty of the death of Edward. As, however, the ex-king was admittedly murdered by the servants of the accused, a day was assigned in the next parliament for Thomas to appear and hear judgment; meanwhile he was given into the custody of the steward of the household. Here, although the case was commenced in parliament, we have trial by knights, judgment by peers; a singular and unfruitful precedent,

---

[1] Et est assentu et acorde par nostre seigneur le roi et touz les grantz en pleyn parlement qe tut soit il que les ditz peres, come juges du parlement, empristrent en la presence nostre seigneur le roi a faire et a rendre les ditz jugementz par assent du roi sur ascuns de ceux qui n'estoient pas lur peres, et ce par encheson de murdre de seigneur lige . . . que par tant les ditz peres que ore sont, ou les peres qui serront en temps a venir, ne soient mes tenuz ne chargez a rendre juggement sur autres que sur leur peres, ne a ce faire, mes eient les peres de la terre poer einz de ce pour touz jours soient dechargez et quites. Et que les avantditz jugementz ore renduz ne soit tret en ensaumple n'en consequencie en temps a venir par qoi les ditz peres puissent estre chargez desore a jugger autres que lur peres contre la lei de la terre, si autiel cas aveigne que Dieu defend. (Rot. Parl., vol. ii, p. 54.)

z

well illustrating the tentative development in practice of an indefinite and ill-considered principle.[1]

In the year 1341 the trial of peers again occupied the attention of parliament. The French war had placed Edward in dire financial difficulties: there was also an epidemic of lawlessness in England which was being dealt with by the not over lawful commissions of trailbaston. Under these circumstances the king's officers had every inducement and every opportunity for exacting heavy amercements from high and low throughout the country. Edward in France was assailed with complaints against the extortions of his officials, but the time could scarcely have been less opportune: he himself was engaged in chiding these same officials for the shortage of his revenues.

Edward, apparently, of a sudden came to the conclusion that extensive malversation might be the cause of both his and his people's complaints: quite unexpectedly he returned to England, had several persons in authority arrested, and appointed special commissioners to inquire into all cases of alleged extortion by his ministers. The commissioners of course sat, inquired and obtained large fines which were paid to the king. Edward must have been very simple-minded if he thought such procedure would gratify anyone but himself. Nevertheless the avowed object of these commissions was to appease the people: in the king's own particular interests the machinery of the exchequer was set vigorously in motion for the purpose of enforcing payment of the supplies voted.

This was not all. One of the king's first actions on arriving in England was to make certain charges against his ex-chancellor, Stratford archbishop of Canterbury, complaining in particular of his not having provided for the payment of certain foreign merchants. Admittedly there were no sufficient assets in the treasury for the purpose, but this the king contended was due to the wilful default of the primate and his other ministers in not promptly and rigorously collecting the supplies voted.

[1] See Rot. Parl., vol. ii, p. 57; Report on the Dignity of a Peer, vol. i, p. 300.

The king summoned Stratford to appear before him, but the prelate declined to obey the summons, although a safe-conduct was offered him: he did, however, express his willingness to clear himself before a parliament.[1] The primate then embarked upon a deliberate policy of opposition to the king, which we need not go into. Edward got very angry and made other and far more serious charges against Stratford, which drew from the latter a reminder that, if the offence alleged against him was treason, no king or temporal lord was competent to judge him.[2]

A parliament was summoned and met on Monday after the quinzaine of Easter, that is, on the 23rd of April. Stratford received his summons in due course,[3] and attended. The events which then took place are related, and faithfully enough in all probability, by a contemporary monk named Birchington;[4] none the less this writer's account has been misunderstood, and grossly misrepresented by a host of mediæval and modern writers.[5] The story can only be briefly told here.

[1] Patent Roll, 15 Edward III, pt. 1, m. 48; Rymer, Foedera R.C., ii, p. 1146. Roman Roll, 15 Edward III, m. 4; Rymer, Foedera R.C., ii, pp. 1152-3.

[2] The archbishop's reply is given by Birchington (printed Wharton, Anglia Sacra, pt. 1, pp. 27-36). . . . Quia praemissa proditionis crimen in caput nostrum retorquere videntur, quo casu rex nullus vel dominus temporalis judex noster competens esse potest, sicut satis superius est ostensum; protestamur palam et publice per praesentes, quod per dicta vel dicenda in nullo statui nostro praejudicare intendimus in hac parte, sed judicis cujuscunque secularis examen totaliter declinare. (Op. cit., p. 34.)

[3] Close Roll, 15 Edward III, pt. 1, m. 37d.: Report Dig. Peer, vol. iv, p. 529.

[4] See Anglia Sacra, pt. 1, pp. 38-9.

[5] For example, the Political History of England revives the absurd suggestion that Edward wished to have the primate tried for treason in the court of Exchequer. At the present day such an error, an error which must be terribly disconcerting to any intelligent student, ought to be impossible; but it is obvious that until some system of annotation, similar to that adopted in barristers' chambers, is employed in all reference libraries, these mistakes will continue to be made by even the most careful and competent writers.

The substantial charge against Stratford, as already stated, was wilful default in collecting the revenue. As a matter of fact, a very few hundred more sacks of wool collected would have made all the difference to the king, and he would have escaped the humiliating necessity of leaving the earl of Derby in pawn abroad.[1] Stratford, if you please, at this particular juncture was himself in default to the extent of forty-five sacks and fifty-seven pounds of wool, due in respect of wools lately granted by parliament; at any rate the Exchequer alleged the debt and were taking proceedings against the primate to enforce payment.[2] The debt was not a very great one, a fourteenth of the amount required to free the earl of Derby, and it was certainly disputed: all the same this was a singularly damaging incident; it would have afforded, as the lawyers say, very useful material for cross-examination. I think anyone would have been justified in telling the archbishop that, until he had disposed of this claim, his protestations of innocence were somewhat premature.

Now according to Birchington, on the morrow of St. George's Day, that is, on Tuesday, April the 24th, the archbishop came with the intention of forcing his way into parliament; but at the entrance to the great hall, Stafford steward

---

[1] Idem archiepiscopus ad dicti subsidii collectionem et aliorum nobis necessariorum subministrationem interim promisit efficaciter interponere partes suas. (Letters of the king to certain bishops and others; see Close Roll Cal., 1341–3, p. 102; Rymer, Hemingburgh, Avesbury, etc.)

As to the position of the earl of Derby see Close Roll Cal., 1341–3, pp. 13, 24, 32, etc.

[2] Exchequer Memoranda Roll, K.R., Hilary, 15 Edward III, Brevia Retornabilia: Rex vicecomiti Kancie de venire faciendo archiepiscopum Cantuar. de xlv saccis iiij petris j lb. Mr. Pike, Hist. of the House of Lords, p. 191, makes the following statement in a marginal note: "The Rolls of the Exchequer show that Stratford merely appeared there in relation to a trivial matter of account by attorney"; and in his text: "Reduced into the actual words of the Exchequer it is neither more nor less than fifteen sacks and fifty-seven pounds of wool." If he had not misread the record, perhaps the word "trivial" would have been omitted. The amount was not trivial.

of the household and Darcy the king's chamberlain barred his passage, and he was ordered, in the king's name, to answer the case against him in the Exchequer before coming into parliament. Birchington asserts that Stratford did go twice into the Exchequer, and I see no reason whatever to doubt that he did. He did not of course, in legal phraseology, appear in person to argue his case, but employed a well-known attorney of the period named Wadeworth who had a large practice in the Exchequer court. But even litigants who employ attorneys commonly have to be personally present. Stratford obtained successive adjournments of his case, first to the Trinity, then to the Michaelmas, and finally to the Hilary sittings.[1] So much for the Exchequer proceedings, which were, after all, merely a side issue. So far as parliament was concerned Stratford acted with prudent obstinacy, and insisted upon attending: on Tuesday, Wednesday and Friday he took his seat; but the king was equally obstinate, and on Saturday the serjeants-at-arms received orders to exclude him. The primate came as expected, the serjeants-at-arms were polite but firm, for the moment perhaps Stratford was disconcerted; then Darcy came up, and a rather remarkable scene appears to have followed. The primate indulged in misplaced heroics, thought himself a second Becket, and professed himself ready for a martyr's death. He was brought to his senses by the laconic rejoinder: "Non tu ita dignus, nec nos ita fatui"; he then

---

[1] Archiepiscopus Cantuariensis attachiatus fuit ad respondendum domino regi de xlv saccis iiij petris et j lb. lane quas regi debet de lanis nuper per prelatos, religiosos et quosdam alios de clero in parliamento apud Westmonasterium in crastino purificationis beate Marie anno duodecimo tento concessis et juxta ratam (etc.). . . . Et predictus archiepiscopus per Eliam de Wadeworth attornatum suum venit et dicit se sufficienter posse ostendere curie quod de lanis predictis onerari non debet sed dicit quod evidencias suas inde jam non habet in promptu et petit diem ulterius super hoc ei prefigi etc. et datus est ei dies hic in octab. sancte Trinitatis ad ostendendum quod pro se habet in exoneracionem etc. Ad quem diem venit per dictum attornatum suum et habet diem in octab. sancti Michaelis etc. . . . . Ad quem diem venit et habet diem in octab. sancti Hillarii. . . . (Exchequer Memoranda Roll, K.R., 15 Edward III, Pasch. Adhuc Recorda, Kent.)

reverted to his previous attitude of dignified obstinacy, and the same day saw him occupying his usual place in the painted chamber.

The heat of the main controversy had become somewhat dissipated by the beginning of May; Stratford made his peace with the king, and after this can hardly have considered himself as standing accused of anything more than certain vague misdemeanours, but of these he wished to clear himself by arraignment and answer before the peers in parliament. The king seemed willing to accede to the primate's wish subject to the more pressing business of parliament being first disposed of.[1]

But Stratford was not the only magnate with a grievance born of the events recorded; and the king was petitioned by the peers as a body to give them due protection in the future by decreeing that, even in cases of misdemeanour, they should only be proceeded against in parliament. The king very properly refused his assent. The peers then requested that a committee of bishops, earls and barons, with certain sages of the law, should be appointed to report on the privilege of judgment by peers; and a committee was nominated consisting of four bishops, four earls and four barons, but no sages of the law were appointed.[2] The committee were

[1] Et le dit ercevesque se humilia a nostre seignur le roi, enquerant sa bone seignurie et sa bienvoillance; et nostre seignur le roi lui resceut a sa bone seignurie: dont les prelatz et autres grauntz lui mercierent tout come il savoient ou purroient. Et puis pria l'ercevesque au roi, q'il pleust a sa seignurie, que desicome il est diffamez notoirement par tut le roialme et aillours, q'il puisse estre aresnez en pleyn parlement devant les pieres, et illoeqes respoundre, issint q'il soit overtement tenuz pur tiel come il est. Queu chose le roi ottreia. Mes il dit, q'il voleit que les busoignes touchantes l'estat du roialme et commune profit fusses primes mys en exploit, et puis il ferroit exploiter les autres. (Rot. Parl., vol. ii, p. 127.)

[2] Et pur ce que entre autres choses contenues en la prier des grauntz est fait mention, qe les piers de la terre, officers ne autres, ne serront tenuz de respondre de trespas que lour est surmys par le roi, fors que en parlement: queu choses fust avys au roi que ce serroit inconvenient et contre son estat: si prierent les ditz grantz au roi, q'il voloit assentir que quatre evesques, quatre countes et quatre barons, ensemblement ove ascuns sages de la leye, fussent esluz de trier en queu cas les ditz piers serroient tenuz de respon-

instructed to inquire in what cases peers ought to be arraigned in parliament, and in what cases not.

The committee eventually reported[1] that peers of the realm ought not to be arraigned or brought to judgment except in parliament and by their peers; moreover, a peer who was or had been chancellor, treasurer, or the holder of any other office was none the less entitled to be so tried as aforesaid in respect of all matters, whether they did or did not concern his office. Upon this finding they made a declaration of right which was embodied, practically verbatim, in a statute passed in the same parliament. The clause in question runs as follows:—

Item, because in times past peers of the land have been arrested and imprisoned, and their temporalities, lands and tenements, goods and chattels seized into the hands of kings, and some put to death, without judgment of their peers: it is accorded and assented that no peer of the land, officer or other, by reason of his office or matters touching his office, or for any other reason shall be brought to judgment to lose his temporalities, lands, tenements, goods or chattels, or be arrested, imprisoned, outlawed, exiled or forejudged, or made to answer or be judged except before the said peers in parliament; saving always to the lord the king and his heirs in other case the laws rightfully used and by due process, and saving also

dre en parlement et nulle parte aillours, et en quel cas nemy; et de reporter lour avys a lui. Et furent esluz a ceste chose faire les esvesques de Excestre, (Cicestre), Baa, Loundres; les countes d'Arundel, Sarum, Huntyngdon et Suffolc; les seignurs de Wake, Percy; Monsr. Rauf de Nevill et Monsr. Rauf Basset de Drayton. Lesqueux douze reporterent lour avys en pleyn parlement le Lundy preschein suant, en une cedule dont la copie s'ensuit en ceste forme. . . . (Parliament Roll, 15 Edward III, m. 5, no. 6.) Referring to this passage, Mr. Pike observes (Hist. of the House of Lords, p. 195): "The committee, however, did not, as is commonly represented, consist exclusively of peers. It included four bishops, four earls, and four barons, 'together with some sages of the law.'" The passage has been misread by the writer: what "is commonly represented" happens in this instance to be true. I have examined the original roll: except that the word "Cicestre" is an interlineation, the printed copy is identical with the roll. I fear Mr. Pike has been in this matter a blind leader of the blind; several persons have followed him into the ditch.

[1] See Rot. Parl., vol. ii, p. 127.

the suit of parties:[1] And in case any peer of his own accord is willing to reply or be judged elsewhere than in parliament, this shall not prejudice the other peers or himself in other case. Provided always that if any peer is a sheriff or farmer of fee or has been an officer or has received money or chattels on behalf of the king, by reason of which office or receipt he is bound to account, that such person account by himself or his attorney in the accustomed places. Provided that the pardons heretofore made in parliament remain in force."[2]

The king only permitted the statute to be sealed because it was imperative for him to obtain supplies. Once these had been voted, Edward announced that he had dissembled in the matter of this enactment, and purported to revoke it by order in council.[3] Dissimulation is certainly not a praiseworthy quality in sovereigns, but Edward in this case has received from historians more than his fair meed of blame. If he erred in assenting and then revoking his assent, the peers of the realm erred infinitely more in seeking to obtain such a statute; had it remained law the result must have been disastrous to the constitution. The judges, or at least some of them, appear throughout to have protested against this statute; they must indeed have regarded it with nothing less than dismay, and probably felt perfectly sincere when they said that their oaths of office might preclude their giving effect to it.[4]

The statute was repealed by the king in the following parliament,[5] and need not therefore be discussed in any detail. A few points should be noticed. The proviso excepting the suit of parties from judgment by peers affords fairly conclusive evidence that this was considered settled law; consequently

[1] et salve auxint la suite des parties.

[2] See Appendix. The statute also contains provisions relating to other matters.

[3] Close Roll, 15 Edward III, pt. 2, m. 1d.; Statute Roll, m. 19d. (Printed in Rymer, Foedera, vol. ii, pt. 2, p. 1177; Statutes of the Realm, R.C., vol. i, p. 297.)

[4] See Rot. Parl., vol. ii, p. 131 (no. 42).

[5] Rot. Parl., vol. ii, p. 139: the king, in response to a petition to maintain the statute, announced its repeal.

a peer appealed of felony had no right to be judged differently to a commoner. Again, the circumstance that bishops were put on the committee, the assertion by Stratford that when life or limb were in peril he could not be tried by any secular tribunal whatever, coupled with his demand in this particular instance to be arraigned in parliament, afford sufficiently consistent and clear evidence of the attitude of the church. The clergy as a body claimed in cases of treason and felony absolute exemption from secular jurisdiction; but in cases of misdemeanour the spiritual peers now desired judgment by peers temporal and spiritual in Parliament.

It may be mentioned in passing that the king prudently evaded Stratford's request to be arraigned before the peers in parliament;[1] instead, a committee of two bishops and four earls was appointed to hear his replies, but they were not to proceed further.[2] Eventually the same parliament which repealed the obnoxious statute annulled the process against the primate.

In the year 1344 it was enacted that no archbishop or bishop should be proceeded against for any crime before the king's justices without a special order from the sovereign.[3] This no doubt was intended, and was considered by the church to be a concession. The Act, however, clearly implies that, except in so far as privilege of clergy could be claimed, king's justices armed with a special order had full power to *try* bishops.

---

[1] Selden, Stillingfleet, Jeremy Collier and others have asserted that he was tried by the peers : there is not the smallest foundation for such assertion.

[2] Et ex tunc praelatis et aliis data fuit licentia recedendi; sed assignati fuerunt episcopi Dunelmensis et Sarisburiensis, comites [Arundel,] Sarisburiae, Warewikiae et Northamptoniae ad audiendum excusationes archiepiscopi super sibi impositis et ad referendum regi in proximo parliamento. Et cum archiepiscopus offerret se paratum statim se immunem ostendere et docere, dicti episcopi et comites asseruerunt sibi tunc vacare non posse; sicque remansit illud negotium in suspenso. (Murimuth, Rolls Series [93], p. 120.)

[3] Quant au primer article, il est avis que en cause de cryme nul ercevesque ne evesque soit empeschez devant les justices si le roi ne le comande especialement, tan que autre remedie soit ordeynez. (Rot. Parl., ii, p. 152.)

About the year 1355 William lord Greystoke appears to have been tried and condemned to death for the loss of Berwick. He seems to have been tried by a court consisting of peers and others, presided over by Sir Walter Manny who pronounced judgment.[1] I have not been able to discover any record of the trial. Assuming this peer was condemned as stated, it is quite clear that he subsequently received the king's pardon.[2]

In the year 1376 William lord Latymer and several others who were not peers were impeached in parliament by the commons for high misdemeanours affecting the state. Latymer was sentenced by the prelates and peers to suffer certain penalties, but who presided at the trial is not stated.[3] The others were also dealt with, and there is no suggestion of any protest by the peers against judging commoners. Impeachment was not at this time a technical term, the action of the commons was practically unprecedented, and a protest might have been reasonably expected. According to strict constitutional principles, however, the procedure adopted can be readily justified. There was clearly no remedy for the

---

[1] . . . baron de Greystok q'estoit seigneur et un des piers du roialme . . . estoit ajugge par l'advis du dit aiel [Edward III], le roi de Chastel que si est, les nobles duc et countes queux Dieux assoile Henri jadys duc de Lancastre, les countes jadys de Northampton et Stafford, et sire Wauter de Manny, que la dite ville estoit perduz en defaut du dit baron, et par celle cause il averoit juggement de vie et de membre, et que y deusse forfaire quant qe il avoit : et a celle juggement rendre avoit le dit sire Wauter les paroles par comandement du dit aiel. . . . (Rot. Parl., vol. iii, pp. 11-12.)

[2] For particulars of this branch of the Greystoks see Newminster, Surtees Soc., vol. lxvi passim. Inquisition post mortem of William de Greystok, baron Greystok, taken at Sadby 21 Sept., 1359, Durham Cursitor's Records Reg., vol. ii, fol. 62 ; also various inquisitions p.m., Chancery, 33 Edward III, no. 43.

Baker (ed. Thompson, p. 126) mentions the loss of Berwick as follows : Et Calesiam reversus, audivit rex quod Scoti furtim intrarunt et ceperunt villam Berewici, barone de Greistoke non invitato cum rege militante, cui tamen committebatur cura ville jam capte. This writer says nothing about the baron's trial. His appointment to Berwick is entered on the Scotch Roll, 28 Edward III, m. 5.

[3] Rot. Parl., vol. ii, pp. 324-7.

grievances of the commons except in parliament. They were an estate of the realm which could neither sue nor be sued at law. For cases outside the scope of the law of the land, the magnates of the realm (in parliament) constituted the sole but recognised judicial tribunal. This was a popular principle, and the institution of impeachments was by no means its first practical application. Time was when this principle existed as one of the great formative ideas of the English constitution and made the judicature of the country a living prolific organism; but inevitably with the growing power and fecundity of the legislature, the judicature became more and more sterile.

The impeachment of Latymer and the others was a tentative process. Shortly after there came a political reaction; and in the next parliament the commons petitioned that Latymer might be restored to his offices, seeing that he had been ousted from them without due process. A preposterous petition: constitutional conservatism was evidently of no account to the political factions of this period. Edward, of course, granted the petition.[1]

After the accession of Richard the Second impeachment by the commons became a recognised procedure and was frequently resorted to. It is needless to refer to these cases in detail, but it is not unimportant to notice who presided at them. In some instances this is not stated. We know, however, that at the trials of John Sire de Gomeniz and William de Weston it was the steward of the household who in each case arraigned and sentenced the prisoner.[2] Sir Robert

---

[1] Rot. Parl., vol. ii, p. 372 (no. 75): Item prient les communes a nostre dit seigneur le roi et as nobles seigneurs de parlement, que come al derrain parlement, par meins vrai suggestion et sanz due proces, le seigneur de Latymer qu'est un des pieres del roialme . . . estoit oustez de toutz offices et des privez conseilx entour le roy, q'il soit ore par agard de ce present parlement restitut a son primer estat et degree. . . .

[2] A quel jour de Vendredy les ditz Johan et William amesnes par le dit conestable devant les seigneurs avant ditz en plein parlement seantz en la Blaunke Chambre, ils sont severalement aresonez a comandement des ditz seigneurs par sire Richard le Scrop, chivaler, seneschal de l'hostel nostre seigneur le roi, en manere come s'ensuyt . . . . (Rot. Parl., vol. iii, p. 10.)

Fulmere, on the other hand, tried in 1383, was sentenced by the chancellor,[1] and the same official presided on the impeachment of the bishop of Norwich.[2]

In the year 1387 the king made a vain attempt to free himself from the control of the greater magnates, but his hopes were blighted in the bud by the defeat of de Vere at Radcot Bridge. From the battlefield the victorious army of the five lords marched straight to London. Usk, the chronicler, relates how he saw them file through the city of Oxford on their way to the capital; Warwick and Derby led the van, Gloucester the main body, Arundel and Nottingham brought up the rear. The confederate lords received the keys of the city from the mayor of London on the 26th of December, and on the 27th of December the Tower and the king of England were in their possession. A parliament was summoned to meet in February. At this parliament the five lords took proceedings against Alexander Neville, archbishop of York, Robert de Vere, duke of Ireland, Michael de la Pole, earl of Suffolk, Sir Robert Tresilian, Chief Justice, and Sir Nicholas Brembre. The proceedings purported to be an appeal of high treason against the persons named.

The appellants had lodged their appeal with the king; and he, by the advice of his council, then named a day for the respondents to appear before parliament. Service of this order was effected by proclamation through all the counties of England. On the day named Brembre was in custody, the others still very much at large. The absent respondents were called and did not appear. The appellants prayed the king and peers to record their default, and proceed to judgment. The king and peers, however, desired time to consider the matter, and the case was adjourned until the following day.[3]

The five lords had certainly taken a strange course. Appeals of treason were not unknown to the common law, and were presumably subject to the same rules of pleading

---

[1] Rot. Parl., vol. iii, p. 152.
[2] Ibid., p. 153.
[3] Ibid., p. 229.

and so forth as other appeals.[1]   The court which more
commonly took cognisance of these cases was the constable
of England's court of chivalry, where the procedure was
according to the civil law.[2]   Again, there were no reliable
precedents for trying such a case in parliament; and, as
appeals were at the suit of a subject, there was some ground
for contending on principle that parliament ought to decline
to try them.

Owing, it would seem, to the circumstances just stated, not
only justices, serjeants and sages of the common law, but
also persons learned in the civil law were asked to advise.
These, after considering the matter, stated that they well
understood the tenor of the appeal and were of opinion that
it did not comply with the requirements either of the common
law or of the civil law.[3]

Upon this the lords made a counter-declaration to the
effect that, in the case of any high crime touching the king's
person and the state of the realm perpetrated by peers of the
realm with others, the cause ought not to be determined
elsewhere than in parliament, or by any other law but the
law and procedure of parliament. It was the ancient privilege
of the lords of parliament to be judges in such cases with the
king's consent. England never was and never should be
subject to the civil law, nor should parliament (which was
the highest court) be controlled by the procedure of the
lower courts of the realm. The lords thereupon adjudged,
with the consent of the king, that the appeal was duly made
and affirmed and the process conformable to the law and
practice of parliament.[4]

[1] For examples of appeals of treason see the case of William
Douglas v. Gilbert de Humfraville, Coram Rege Roll, 51-2
Henry III (no. 131), m. 28d.; Bain, Calendar, i, 2452; Surtees
Soc., 88, p. 147n.   Robert le Eyr v. Nicholas de Wantham,
Twyne MS., iv, p. 617, Eyre Roll, A.D. 1285; Oxford Hist. Soc.,
18, p. 204.   Compare, Select Pleas of the Crown, Selden Soc.,
vol. i, no. 115; etc.
[2] As regards the constable's jurisdiction, and the court of
chivalry, see post, chap. xi.
[3] Rot. Parl., vol. iii, p. 236.
[4] Ibid.

Whether the lords were right or wrong in making such a declaration is a question which scarcely admits of a definite answer. No statute denied the peers this jurisdiction; no other court in England had authority to overrule them; but, on the other hand, the peers did not consider themselves bound by their own decisions, and were not unwilling to pass a solemn judgment one year and denounce it the next as a flagrant breach of the customs of the kingdom. Under such conditions the judicial decisions of parliament at this time cannot altogether be rejected as bad law, even when they failed to stand the test of time and the caprice of future parliaments; nor, merely because they survived such test, can they be accepted *ab initio* as good law.

After another adjournment the appeal of the five lords was proceeded with in accordance with the peers' declaration stated above, and the prayer that the default of the four respondents might be recorded was renewed. At this point the spiritual peers rose from their seats. They were forbidden by the canons of holy church in any manner to take part personally in such judgments as were likely to be passed. The archbishop of Canterbury produced a written document which he read to the house :—

In the Name of God, amen.—Whereas by the law and custom of the realm of England it belongeth to the archbishop of Canterbury for the time being, and all and singular his suffragans, brethren, fellow bishops, abbots, priors and other prelates whatsoever holding of our lord the king by barony to be personally present in all the king's parliaments whatsoever as peers of the realm as aforesaid, and together with the other peers and others having the right to be there present to advise, treat, ordain, establish and determine concerning the affairs of the realm. . . .

and so forth. In such matters, the primate protested, the prelates intended to be present in manner accustomed, saving the rights of their order. But since certain matters were coming under discussion at which they were by the sacred canons forbidden to be personally present, they intended to retire, saving always the rights of their peerage; and this protest was made in order that their absence might not invalidate the judgment about to be delivered. Durham and

Carlisle made similar protests on their own behalf, and then all the prelates withdrew from the house.[1]

At the request of the appellants, and after a lengthy examination of the articles of appeal, the temporal lords proceeded to judgment. The absent respondents were found guilty of treason; and, with the exception of the archbishop, sentenced accordingly.[2] Tresilian, who had been in hiding, was shortly afterwards apprehended and brought before the lords; having nothing to say in arrest of judgment, he was hurried to execution. The others were beyond the reach of their enemies. Suffolk was in Paris, the duke in Holland. A humble but happy fate was reserved for the archbishop; he obtained a small curacy and died a village priest.

[1] Rot. Parl., vol. iii, p. 236. The northern primate, being one of the appealed, and a refugee, was not in a position to protest on behalf of his province; hence the interposition of Durham and Carlisle.

[2] Rot. Parl., vol. iii, p. 237. Sur quoy les ditz seigneurs temporels par commandement du roi nostre dit seigneur examineront les articles du dit appell, et le coupe des ditz Ercevesque d'Everwyk, duc, counte et Robert Tresilian, appellez come devant en celle partie, par grant labour et diligence, et par continuance de diverses jours tan que le Joedy le xiij jour du dit moys de Feverer. Et par lour avisement et bone deliberation firent declaration et ajuggeront que le primere, le seconde, [etc.] . . . articles sont treson. . . . Et troveront par deue examination et par proeve et information par touz les voies q'ils purroient lour conscience deuement enformer que les ditz ercevesque, duc, counte et Robert Tresilian appellez coment devant feuront coupables notoriement en ycelles . . . et ajuggeront les ditz . . . coupables et convictz dez tresons contenuz en les ditz articles, declarez pur treson come devant, et agarderont que mesmes les duc, counte et Robert Tresilian, appellez come devant, feussent treynez et penduz . . . et que les ditz ercevesque, duc, counte et Robert Tresilian, appellez come devant, et lour heires feussent desheritez toutz jours, et que lour terres, tenementz, biens et chateux feussent forfaitz au roi nostre dit seigneur, et les temporaltees du dit ercevesque d'Everwyk de l'ercevesque d'Everwyk seisiz es mains le roi nostre dit seigneur. Et pur ce que tiel cas n'ad mye este veu en le roialme touchant le persone de ercevesque ou evesque, les ditz seigneurs de parlement se vorroient aviser. . . . Compare the case of the archbishop with that of the bishop of Chichester, impeached in the same parliament. (Rot. Parl., vol. iii, pp. 243-4.) In neither case did the lords venture to pass sentence of death. The bishop of Chichester was sentenced to exile.

Brembre, the remaining respondent, who had been some little time in custody, was the last to be dealt with.[1] He was arraigned in full parliament and showed a fine spirit, pleaded not guilty, angrily flung down his gauntlet and claimed to defend with his body. A dramatic episode in a great tragedy : not only the appellants, it is said, were ready to answer this challenge; scarcely a peer present but plucked forth a glove and flung it on the floor of the house.[2] Nevertheless it was decided that trial by battle did not lie : Brembre was found guilty and led away to his death.

The lust of the "merciless" parliament was not yet sated ; several other persons, including the bishop of Chichester, were impeached by the commons and found guilty by the lords ; but, on the intercession of the spiritual peers, many of the sentences were commuted to banishment.

After all this was over the lords spiritual and temporal renewed (in somewhat different shape) their previous demands. They claimed that matters of great moment touching peers of the realm debated in the then present or any future parliament should be determined by the course of parliament, and not by the civil law or the common law as administered in inferior courts. This claim the king allowed and approved in full parliament.[3]

In 1397 the king took his revenge. His first actions for securing it were ingenious but somewhat unkingly. There was, to begin with, the little dinner-party which Warwick alone was fool enough to attend; he was sent to Tintagel. The earl of Arundel was beguiled into surrendering and lodged at Carisbroke. The king then paid a visit to Gloucester at his seat in Essex, with the result that Gloucester left England for Calais in the custody of the earl of Nottingham. A council was held on the first of August when

---

[1] This case seems to have been in progress when Tresilian was brought to the bar (Rot. Parl., vol. iii, p. 238). The chief justice, it is said, trusting to an inadequate disguise, had imprudently looked out of a neighbouring window to see what he could of the trial. He was recognised and seized.

[2] This tumultuous acceptance of Brembre's challenge rests on very slender authority.

[3] Rot. Parl., vol. iii, p. 244.

strict retaliation was decided upon. The appellants of 1387 should be the appealed in 1397. A Bill was accordingly presented to the king by the earls of Rutland, Kent, Nottingham, Somerset and Salisbury, Thomas lord Despencer and Sir William le Scrope appealing Gloucester, Arundel and Warwick of treason, and a day was assigned for the accused peers to answer in the parliament summoned to meet in September.

When this parliament met various preliminary preparations were made for the coming reprisals. The speaker of the commons petitioned[1] the king that whereas judgments and ordinances made aforetime had been annulled because the estate of the clergy had not given their consent, that the prelates might appoint a procurator to represent them during their absence. (This, it will be remembered, was one of the errors for which the judgment against the Despencers was set aside.[2]) A further petition was made that all pardons, general or private, granted to the duke of Gloucester and the earls of Arundel and Warwick might be recalled. These petitions were granted in full parliament.

The commons further protested that they intended by the king's leave to impeach anyone they would whenever seemed good to them during that session of parliament, and Richard gave his consent. These requests do not appear to have

[1] Item mesme le Marsdy les communes monstrerent au roy coment devant ces heures pluseurs juggementz, ordenances, faitz en temps des progenitours nostre seigneur le roy en parlement ount este repellez et adnullez pur ceo que l'estat de clergie ne feust present en parlement a la faisaunce des ditz juggementz et ordenances. Et pur ceo prierent au roi, que pur seurte a sa persone, et salvation de son roialme, les prelatz et le clergie ferroient un procuratour, ovec poair sufficeant pur consenter en leur noun as toutz choses et ordenances a justifiers en cest present parlement, et que sur ceo chescun seigneur espirituel dirroient pleinement son advis. (Rot. Parl., vol. iii, p. 348.)

[2] The case against the Despencers came up for review before this selfsame parliament, and the whole process appears on the rolls of parliament (Rot. Parl., vol. iii, pp. 360-7). The danger of proceeding in the absence of the prelates could not be disregarded. It was quite certain that they would not consent to be present in person when the appeal was disposed of.

2 A

been made by the commons of their own motion, but obviously in obedience to palace suggestions; they are none the less important on that account. Richard was not going to let the butcher's work he had in contemplation lack finality for want of attention to a few legal technicalities.

The clergy, by means apparently of a formal legal document, duly appointed Thomas Percy, steward of the household, their procurator with sufficient power to assent in their name to the business in hand.[1]

The commons opened the campaign of revenge by impeaching Thomas archbishop of Canterbury. The primate is represented as having then confessed and put himself upon the king's grace. Be this as it may, the king, the temporal lords and Percy procurator for the clergy found the matters confessed to be high treason, and the primate was ultimately sentenced to banishment.

On Friday the 21st of September Edward earl of Rutland and the other appellants appeared in parliament robed in red silk banded with white and powdered with letters of gold. They set forth their appeal and gave sureties to prosecute it. The duke of Lancaster was directed by the king to preside. Richard earl of Arundel was then brought before the house by Nevill, constable of the Tower, and put upon his trial. He too appeared in a robe of red, with a hood of scarlet, belted as an earl. Lancaster observed this at once, and turning to Nevill said, "Take off his hood and belt." The

---

[1] Nos Thomas Cantuar. et Robertus Ebor. archiepiscopi, ac prelati et clerus utriusque provincie Cantuar. et Ebor., jure ecclesiarum nostrarum et temporalium earundem habentes jus interessendi in singulis parliamentis domini nostri regis et regni Anglie pro tempore celebrandis, necnon tractandi et expediendi in eisdem : quantum ad singula in instanti parliamento pro statu et honore domini nostri regis, necnon regalie sue, ac quiete pace et tranquilitate regni judicialiter justificandum, venerabili viro domino Thome de Percy militi nostram plenarie committimus potestatem, ita ut singula per ipsum facta in premissis perpetuis temporibus habeantur. (Rot. Parl., vol. iii, p. 348 ; Vita regis Ricardi II (ed. Hearne), pp. 134-5.) The general custom of appointing proxies in parliament was well established and of wide extent. See Pike, Hist. of the House of Lords, pp. 243-4.

constable obeyed instantly. Then they unfolded to the earl the articles of accusation.

We have an eye-witness's account of this trial,[1] interesting enough but not edifying. The earl pleaded not guilty and relied on the general pardon granted in the eleventh year of the current reign, saying that he claimed the benefit of it and would never withdraw himself from the king's grace. "Traitor," said Lancaster, "that pardon is recalled."—"In truth thou liest," said Arundel; "never was I a traitor."— "Then for what purpose the pardon?" said Lancaster. But Arundel had a ready answer: "To close the mouths of mine enemies of whom thou art one."

This repartee between the judge and his forejudged prisoner was scarcely seemly. Richard interposed. "Answer to the appeal," he said.

It was a strange trial in strange surroundings. Westminster Palace was rebuilding: parliament was assembled in a large temporary structure, open at the ends, but glorious and solemn, passing anything previous kings had known.[2] Outside might be seen rank behind rank of Cheshire bowmen to the number of four thousand guarding the building.[3] Arundel surveyed his accusers and then addressed himself to the king. "I see well," he said, "that these persons accuse me of treason by showing appeals. In sooth they lie every one of them. Never was I traitor. I insist upon the benefit of my (own particular) pardon, which, within the last six years, you being of full age and with will unfettered did of your own volition

---

[1] This account is taken from Adam of Usk, but several other chroniclers give detailed descriptions of what occurred.

[2] In qua gloriosus et solemnius sedebat, quam unquam aliquis rex istius regni residere consuevit. (Vita regis Ricardi II, ed. Hearne, p. 131.) See also Annales Ricardi II, Rolls Series [28], p. 209: Erexit autem rex quamdam domum amplissimam in palatio West-monasterii, quae pene totum spatium palatii occupavit; in qua sibi thronus parabatur altissimus, et pro cunctis regni statibus locus largus, atque pro appellantibus in uno latere locus specialiter deputatus, et in alio latere locus reis pro responsis assignatus; seorsum vero pro militibus parliamenti, qui non fuerunt electi per communitatem, prout mos exigit, sed per regiam voluntatem.

[3] Usk, p. 11; and see Vita R. Ricardi II, p. 134.

grant me."—"I granted it," said the king, "saving it were not to my prejudice."—"So," said the duke of Lancaster, "that pardon holds not good."

Then the speaker, Sir John Bushy,[1] must needs take part in the wrangle. "That pardon is recalled by the king, the lords and us his faithful commons."—"Where," asked the earl, "be those faithful commons? Not here! They, I know, are sore grieved for me, but thou hast ever been false." Upon this there was an outcry. "See," exclaimed Bushy, "how this traitor strives to stir up discord between us and the commons who abide at home."—"Liars every one of you," Arundel reiterated. "I am no traitor."

And then the earl of Derby must have his say. "Did you not," he said, addressing the prisoner, "say to me at Huntingdon, where first we gathered in revolt, that it would be better first of all to seize the king?"—"Earl of Derby," replied Arundel, "you lie at your peril. I never had thought concerning our lord the king save what was to his welfare and honour." And then the king joined in. "Did you not say to me, at the time of your parliament, in the bath behind the White Hall, that my knight, Sir Simon Burly, was for many reasons worthy of death, to which I answered that I knew no cause of death in him; but none the less thou and thy following did treacherously slay him?" Arundel answered not a word.

They asked him then if he had nothing further to say in his defence, but he remained silent. So the Chief Justice of the King's Bench declared to him the law, and the penalties he would undergo if he pleaded nothing else, which only set the earl insisting upon his pardon again: therefore the appellants prayed judgment.

The king took up his sceptre and indicated to the duke of Lancaster that he was to pronounce judgment. "Richard," said the duke, addressing Arundel, "I John, seneschal of England, do adjudge thee traitor, and by sentence and judgment condemn thee to be drawn, hanged, beheaded and quartered, and that thy lands entailed and unentailed be forfeit."

---

[1] vir crudelissimus, ambitiosus supra modum, atque rei alienae cupidus. (Annales R. II, p. 209.)

Arundel was led away and beheaded the same day on Tower Hill. So perished one of England's greatest sea-captains, a man well loved and honoured by the people. "May I," wrote Adam of Usk, "be found worthy to rest with his soul in bliss, for assuredly he is gathered to the company of the saints."[1]

The official account of Arundel's trial, entered on the rolls of parliament, suggests that there was perhaps more formality and dignity about the proceedings than the chroniclers have acknowledged. The judgment on the record deserves particular attention.

Sur quoi le dit duc de Lancastre par comandement du roy et toutz les seigneurs temporeles et Monsieur Thomas Percy, aiant poair suffisant des prelatz et clergie du roialme d'Engleterre come piert de record en le dit parlement, par assent du roi agarderent le dit count d'Arundell coupable et convict de toutz les pointz dont il est appellez. Et partant lui adjugerent traitour au roi et au roialme, et q'il soit treinez, penduz, decollez et quarteres. Et a cause que les dits tresons furent si hautz; et pour avoir susrendu lour homage liege, et depose le roi de sa corone, regalie, estat et dignite, et que le leve de guerre fuist si notoire, le dit duc de Lancastre, par comaundement du roi et les autres seigneurs temporeles sus ditz piers de la terre, et le dit Monsieur Thomas Percy, eiant poair come desus est dit, par assent du roi agarderent que toutz les chastiels, manoirs [&c.] . . . soient forfait au roi et ses heirs, de dit count d'Arundell et de ses heirs quiconques, pur toutz jours, solonc l'estatuit en cest present parlement en tiel cas fait. . . .[2]

This case possesses two special features of interest. Lancaster (styled steward of England in the record)[3] presided,

[1] The accounts furnished by contemporary chroniclers of the manner of this man's death are more likely to provoke a smile than a tear. "After he had pardoned the headsman his death and given him the kiss of peace, he besought him not to prolong the torture, but study to sever the head with a single blow. With his own fingers he felt the edge of the blade which was to strike him. ' 'Tis sharp enough,' he said; 'do what thou hast to do.' With one stroke the man beheaded him; but the decapitated trunk rose to its feet, and stood erect, none supporting it, for about the space of time it takes to say the Lord's prayer, then fell prone to the earth."

[2] Rot. Parl., vol. iii., p. 377.

[3] "le duc de Lancastre, seneschal d'Engleterre." (Ibid.)

and is said by certain of the chroniclers to have presided in right of his stewardship.[1] Also a proctor, appointed by the prelates, took part in the trial as representing the clergy.

The duke of Gloucester was not brought before parliament. The return to the writ for his production stated that he was dead; and he had, in fact, been assassinated in Calais, on behalf of the king, after a long written confession had been obtained from him. He was found guilty of treason and his estates were forfeited. The report of this judgment, mutatis mutandis, is the same as in the previous case, except that the duke of Lancaster is not mentioned as taking part in it.[2]

Warwick was then brought before parliament and arraigned. He was a very old man, but, it seems, absolutely terrified at the prospect of death. He made an abject confession, weeping and wailing like a woman. It was a most pitiable exhibition of senile cowardice. The king commuted his sentence to banishment in the Isle of Man.[3] (Shortly after this same earl was outlawed for another matter altogether, a sentence which was annulled for error in the reign of Henry the Fourth.[4])

The appellants, we are informed, wished to include Sir Thomas Mortimer in their appeal, but—there being obviously most serious objections to such a course—the commons interposed and impeached him.[5] Mortimer was at the time in Ireland. A day was therefore assigned to him by proclamation setting out the penalties for default. Writs were also issued for his apprehension. Mortimer successfully evaded capture; and, on the day assigned, judgment in default of appearance was passed upon him according to the tenor of

[1] Vide supra, chap. vi, p. 185.
[2] See Rot. Parl., vol. iii, p. 378; Usk, p. 15; &c.
[3] Item comes Warwyci scistebatur in judicio, ablatoque sibi capicio et lecta appellacione, quasi misera et vetula, fatebatur omnia in appellacione contenta, plorando et lacrimando et ululando per ipsum, tanquam proditorem esse perpetrata; . . . (Usk, p. 16.)

Le comte Warvycq confessa de sa pure volenté toute la trahison en plain parlement devant tous et en criant merci au roi afin qu'il eust de lui pitié. Lequel lui sauva la vie . . . . (Le Beau, p. 11.)
[4] See Appendix.   [5] Rot. Parl., vol. iii., p. 380.

the proclamation, and with the same formalities as had been observed in Arundel's case, the earl of Wiltshire on this occasion acting as procurator for the clergy, and Lancaster presiding.[1] The commons also in the course of these same proceedings impeached Sir John Cobham, who was convicted, but afterwards received a qualified pardon.[2]

The last case of importance during the reign of Richard the Second was the Hereford *v.* Norfolk appeal, which was remitted by the parliamentary committee to a court of chivalry. The facts of this cause célèbre have been previously stated : its importance in the history of trial of peers will very shortly become apparent.

In 1399 Richard the redeless was deposed, and Henry of Lancaster usurped the crown.

APPENDIX TO CHAPTER X

Anno 15 *Edwardi III.* A.D. 1341

Statute Roll, m. 19

Me[d] quod istud statutum revocatum est per dominum regem prout patet per tenorem cujusdam brevis irrotulati in dorso istius rotuli

Nostre Seygneur le Roy Edward tierz apres le conquest a son parlement tenutz a Weistmonstier a la quinseyne de Pasche lan de son regne quinsisme desirant que la pees de la terre et les leis et les estatutz avant ses houres ordeines soient gardes et meintenus en toutz pointz al honour de dieux et de seint esglise et al comun profit du poeple par assent des prelatz countes et barouns et autres grantz et de tote la commune du roialme Dengleterre al dit parlement somonz ordeina et establist en mesme le parlement les articles southescriptes les queux il voet et grante pur luy et pur ses heires qils soient fermementz gardez et tenutz a toutz jours.

.   .   .   .   .

Item pur ceo qe avant ses houres piers de la terre ount este arestutz et emprisonnez et lour temporaltes terres et tenementz biens et chateux seisis en mains des Rois et

---

[1] Rot. Parl., vol. iii., p. 380. [2] Ibid., p. 381.

ascunes mys a la mort santz jugement de lour piers Accorde
est et assentuz que nul peres de la terre officer ne autre pur
cause de son office ne des choses touchauntz soun office ne
pur autre cause soit menez en jugement a perte de lour tem-
poraltez terres tenementz biens et chateux ne estre arestutz
nemprisones utlagez exulez ne forsjugez ne respoundre
ne estre jugez sinoun par agarde des dites peres en parlement Sauvez totefoitz a nostre seigneur le Roi et a ses heires
en autres cas les leis dreiturelment usees et par due process
et sauvee auxint seute des parties. Et si per cas nul peres
de soun gree voille aillours respoundre ou estre jugez forsqen
parlement qe cella ne tourne en prejudise des autres peres
ne a lui mesmes en autre cas: forpris si nul des piers soit
viscount ou fermer de fee ou ad este officer ou eit resceu
deniers ou autres chateux le Roi par cause de quele office ou
reseite il est tenutz dacompter qe mesme celuy acompte par
luy ou soun atturne es lieus acustomes. Issint qe les par-
douns eins ses houres faites en parlement se tiegnent en lour
force.[1]

. . . . .

(Printed Statutes of the Realm R.C., vol. i, p. 295.)

Coram Rege Roll, Easter, 1 *Henry IV, Rex, m. 8d*

Cornub.—Alias scilicet termino sancti Michaelis anno regni
domini Ricardi nuper regis Anglie secundi post conquestum
(xxij[2]) preceptum fuit vicecomiti quod exigi faceret Thomam
de Bello Campo comitem Warr. de comitatu in comitatum
quousque etc. utlageretur si non veniret et si veniret tunc
eum caperet et salvo etc. ita quod haberet corpus ejus coram
prefato nuper rege in octab. sancte Trinitatis tunc prox.
sequent. ubicumque etc. ad satisfaciendum prefato nuper regi
de redempcione sua occasione capcionis et detencionis cor-
poris David Tregoys unde per inquisitionem patrie in quam
inde se posuit convictus est. Ad quem diem vicecomes
retorn. quod ad comitatum tent. apud Launceston xx die
Januarii anno regni prefati nuper regis vicesimo secundo

---

[1] This statute also appears on the Parliament Roll, printed Rot.
Parl., vol. ii, p. 132.   [2] Interlined.

predictus Thomas de Bello Campo comes Warr. primo exactus fuit et non comparuit et sic exactus fuit de comitatu in comitatum usque ad comitatum tent. apud Lostwythyell duodecimo die Maii anno regni ejusdem nuper regis (supradicto) quo die predictus Thomas de Bello Campo quinto exactus fuit et non comparuit. Ideo in presencia coron. utlagatus fuit. Et super hoc inquiratur de bonis et catallis suis etc. Et modo scilicet die Lune proximo ante festum restencionis Domini isto eodem termino coram domino rege apud Westm. venit predictus Thomas et reddidit se prisone marescalcie domini regis occasione utlagarie predicte qui committitur marescallo et statim per marescallum ductus venit et dicit quod in recordo et processu predictis manifeste est erratum et non intendit quod utlagariam predictam sic in eum erronice promulgatam ipsum nocere debet. . . . [The earl produces in court two writs of Henry the Fourth which are set out in full. He further pleads error in that he was at the time of the outlawry imprisoned in the Isle of Man, and also—] in hoc quod ubi per communem legem terre nullum breve de exigendo versus aliquem parem regni Anglie in placitis communibus et personalibus adjudicari deberet ad utlagandum et predictus comes par regni fuit et est (et) per nomen paris in predicto brevi de exigendo nominatur; et in hoc quod ipse per nomen paris in placito predicto quod placitum personale existit utlagatus fuit est erratum. Et petit. . . . [The outlawry is annulled for the errors pleaded.]

CHAPTER XI

TRIAL OF PEERS IN THE FIFTEENTH CENTURY:
THE COURT OF CHIVALRY

IN France, the suppression of the stewardship led naturally
and inevitably to an extension of the power and authority
of the constable. An analogous phenomenon is observable
in the history of England, due in the first place to the failure
of the stewardship, even under the favourable conditions
afforded by Richard the Second's reign, to rise to a position
of any real importance, and in the second place to the fact
that the office though not suppressed was allowed to fall into
abeyance on the death of Clarence. Moreover, by a strange
irony of circumstance, the steward of England must have
come to be regarded as a royal hostage to constitutional
government; for the stewards had never ranged themselves
on the king's side, but had, on the contrary, chiefly identified
themselves with parliamentary opposition to autocracy. The
royal prerogative wanted a pander, not a keeper; and it was
the constableship of England which supplied the want.

A military court,[1] nominally, at all events, under the
control of the constable and marshal of England, is in existence at least as early as the reign of Edward the First.
The nature of its jurisdiction at the end of the thirteenth
century is not easy to define: apparently very few of its
records have been preserved. Some of the placita de spata
or placita gladii of the twelfth century were necessarily entrusted to a tribunal of this kind.[2] For the twenty-fourth
year of Edward the First we have the roll of a military court

---

[1] In Latin, "curia militaris"; in Anglo-French, "court of
chivalry."
[2] Particularly the Placita de summonitione exercitus; see Rot.
Chart., p. 19.

attached to the army in Scotland: crimes and other matters of a miscellaneous nature are tried before it.[1]

In the reign of Edward the Second, Roger Damory, a baron, was tried for high treason before this court. Fulk fitz-Warin, constable, John de Weston, marshal, and Geoffrey Lescrop presided. The act of treason alleged was levying war on the king. The accused was sentenced to death, but the king directed execution to be respited.[2] Having regard to subsequent legislation the importance of such a precedent is obvious.

By the time of Richard the Second this court had developed apace, and in 1379 the commons petitioned against appeals of treason and felony done in England being brought by Bill before the constable and marshal, contrary to the law of the land and against the form of the Charter; but the lords declined to deal with the matter on that occasion.[3]

In the thirteenth year of Richard the Second a statute[4] was passed to check these encroachments on the common law. This Act defined the jurisdiction of the court as follows:—

---

[1] Placita exercitus Regis, 24 Ed. I., a roll of several membranes in excellent condition preserved among the Scotch documents in the Record Office. I subjoin the first case entered on the roll—a fairly typical one.

Willelmus de Wytingham attachiatus fuit per Johannem de Wygeton militem apud Dalton et per ipsum liberatus prisone quia dictus fuit quod fuit insidiator regni Scocie et quod subtraxit se . . . ne deserviret domino regi in guerra sua contra Scottos; et quod est de affinitate Johannis Redecomyn inimici domini regis Anglie.

Et Willelmus venit et dicit ad sectam domini regis quod in nullo est culpabilis et de hoc ponit se etc.

Et juratores dicunt quod (sic) per sacramentum suum quod verus est et fidelis et in nullo super ea imposita est culpabilis. Ideo quietus. [2] See Appendix.

[3] Rot. Parl., iii, p. 65b. The reason given is this: Pur ce que les heirs qi cleiment l'office de conestable sont de tendre age, et en la garde nostre seignour le roi, et la chose demande grant deliberation, et tuche si haute matire, et l'estat de la corone nostre seignour le roi, et le parlement est pres a fyn; les seigneurs de parlement ne poent ne ne oesent en faire finale discution quant au present.

[4] See Rot. Parl., iii, p. 265; Statute, 13 Richard II, cap. 2.

To the constable it pertaineth to have cognisance of contracts touching deeds of arms and war out of the realm, and also of things that touch arms and war within the realm which cannot be determined nor discussed by the common'law, with other usages and customs to the same matters pertaining, which the constables have heretofore duly and reasonably used in their time, joining to the same that every plaintiff shall declare plainly his matter in his petition before that any man be sent for to answer thereunto. And if any will complain that any plea be commenced before the constable and marshal that might be tried by the common law of the land, the same shall have a privy seal of the king without difficulty, directing the said constable and marshal to surcease the plea in question, until it be decided by the king's council if that matter ought of right to pertain to that court, or otherwise to be tried by the common law of the realm.

Notwithstanding this statute the business of the court of chivalry continued to increase. If the most transparent legal fiction was sufficient to give the exchequer jurisdiction in debt, why should not a similar device be employed by the constable? The commons grumbled and petitioned, but the court of chivalry took cognisance of actions for debt *causa fidei lesionis pretense*,[1] and also continued to deal with appeals of treason and felony on practically the same simple and comprehensive pretext.

In some cases a defendant would take exception to the jurisdiction and apply to the king under the Act cited above; but there was as a rule little to be gained by such a course. A defendant who submitted to the jurisdiction was held, even by parliament, to be bound by the result;[2] but, if defeated,

---

[1] See Pat. Cal., 1381–5, p. 507 : Salisbury *v.* Montague (Nov. 29th, 1384); Pat. Cal., 1388–92, p. 130 : Asthorpe *v.* Dynham (Nov. 6th, 1389); etc. Courts Christian originally exercised jurisdiction in these matters. See Glanville, lib. x, cap. 12 : . . . creditor ipse, si non habeat inde vadium, neque plegium, neque aliam diracionationem nisi solam fidem, nulla est hec probatio in curia domini regis; verumtamen de fidei lesione vel transgressione inde agi poterit in curia Christianitatis. For an action of debt tried, "super fidei lesione et sacramenti violatione," in the ecclesiastical courts, A.D. 1218, see Record Office Transcripts, 140 A, no. 338.

[2] Salisbury *v.* Montague: Pat. Cal., 1385–9, pp. 67–8 (Nov. 28th, 1385).

an appeal to the king was, generally speaking, open to him, and meant that his case would be retried by a committee of the king's council sitting with doctors of the civil law under a special commission for that purpose.[1] A defendant disputing the jurisdiction under the Act could not proceed otherwise : he must appeal to the king in person, and his demurrer would ordinarily be heard by a similarly constituted court of appeal. It was, we must conclude, a rare favour for the appellant to get his case transferred to the court of Exchequer Chamber.[2] From and after (if not before) the

[1] See, for example, the Commission to hear the Appeal in Asthorpe *v.* Dynham : Pat. Cal., 1388–92, p. 45 (June 3rd, 1389); Brynkele *v.* Earle: ibid., p. 47 (May 28th, 1389); Lescrope *v.* Grosvenor: ibid., p. 159; for a detailed account of the last case see Nicholas, Scrope and Grosvenor Controversy, vol. i ; Henry bishop of Norwich *v.* William Baron de Hilton : Rymer, Foedera O.S., vii, pp. 688–9 (A.D. 1390); also commission in Merton *v.* Hoo: Pat. Cal., 1388–92, p. 508 (Nov. 20th, 1391); etc.

[2] For illustrations of the procedure see Pat. Cal., 1381–5, p. 425 : Waldeshef *v.* Wawe (April 2nd, 1384); ibid., p. 595 (March 17th, 1385); ibid., p. 594: Merton *v.* Stykeney (March 10th, 1385); ibid., pp. 595–6 : Whitchurch *v.* Calverly (April 16th, 1385). The case of Pounteney *v.* Borney, heard in the Exchequer Chamber and reported Year Book, Mich., 13 Henry IV, no. 10, is well worth citing in extenso.

Un Adam Pounteney suist encountre M[atthew] Borney chivaler en le court de Constable et Marshal et demaunde £1020 par un obligacion que il montre avant portant la date en Burdeux que est en Gascoigne, et l'obligacion voille quas de mutuo etc., et declare hors de sa bille libelant que coment il aver pay le dit summe as souldiers de le dit Matthew a Burdeux, et montra coment chescun summe fuist pay et a queux persons, et sur ce en temps le roy Richard un letter desouth le privy seale fuist direct a le court de surcesser par force de le statute fait de le jurisdiction de mesmes le court l'an xii[i] de mesmes le roy, sur quel le pl[aintiff] suist a councell de mesmes le roy et un breve fuist grant de proceder pour qu'ils procederont avant en le plee, tanque a ce que il avoit judgement de recover. Et nota que le procedendo fist mencion des trestouts les nosmes des evesques et chivalers que fueront del councel le dit roy, mes il ne fist mencion que ascun justice fuist en presence al temps que cest procedendo fuist grant, et ore tarde John Tiptoft et auters que sont tenants des terres de dit seignior Matthew sueront un lettre south le privie seale direct a les dits Constables etc. de surcesser d'execution, et sur cest matter fuist suite fait a le councel le roy, et par le councel commit as justices et ore en l'Eschequer Chamber : *Fulthorpe* chivaler qui

reign of Richard the Second the proceedings seem to have been exclusively in accordance with the civil law. Trial was by witnesses, or failing sufficient evidence by battle.

est le south constable dit que si cest matter ne soit my determinable par le common ley donques est ce aremittable a nostre court arere, car le statute voit, si etc., issint ne fait cest point, p. q. etc. *Thirning*: Non sir, et nous veioroms s'il appartient a vostre jurisdiction car s'il ne appent a vostre court, ne a le court le roy, donques vous n'averes procedendo come sont plusors cases en nostre ley en queux convient a un home que vouldera aver acc[ount] de ceux que il eit fait come lou debt sera maunde v[ersu]s executors, et lou home est a demaunder terre par formedon en le rem[ainder] et sans fait, en ceux cases et en autres semble home n'avera my action en nostre ley, et uncore si tiel action soit conceive en vostre court et breve de supersedeas agarde, vous n'averes breve de procedendo pour que nec hic, et a multo fortiori icy par ce que le plaintiff poit recevoir bien et aver s'acc[ount] par le common ley sur cest obligacion a Burdeux p. q. etc. *Gascoigne*: Verement si ceo fuist le primer supersedeas q'issint ne voudra dire communer que de reason nul procedendo issera. *Culpeper*: Si un obligacion fuist fais a Caleis ou serra ceo plede? quasi diceret "a le common ley a Caleis." *Fulthorpe*: Nous ussomes de le pleder en nostre court, par les clerks del dit court, si peradventure sir M. se ala en Gascoigne et n'avera riens en Gascoigne, que purra estre mis en execution illonques? le party plaintiff n'avera unques avantage par ce suit pas illonques a faire, mais serra fait en nostre court car nous purromus faire execution. *Thirning*: Nesme le reason purra estre fait, lou home de Burdeux est lye icy par obligacion, et puis ala a Burdeux, et riens lessa des biens icy, et per consequens le suit serra fait en vostre court, quod falsum est, p. q. etc. *Fulthorpe*: Si home fuit en quarres del evesque de Rome ou as auter quarres ou en pilgrimage, et il apprompt biens d'ascun de ses compaignions, et de cel il fait un obligation portant le date illonques, ce convient estre plede en nostre court, et si le party defendant le dedit, le plaintiff, s'il n'eit preuves que voudra tesmoigner que ce est le fait le defendant, convient a le plaintiff gage en nostre court de combattre ove le defendant en preuve que son dit suit soit veray. *Hank.* : Ceo serra trope grievous que un home combate pour un det. *Fulthorpe*: Sir, le gager del battaille et combat serra sur ce que le defendant ad fauxement enfreint son foy en son defence. Et nota que ascun homes teignent diversitie lou tiel fait deins le poyar del roy est fait, en quel case le suite serra termine par le commen ley, et lou il est fait hors de le poyar le roy, en quel case il est triable en le court de Constable. *Ireby* dit coment liege home fuit tue par auters des lieges nostre seigneur le roy en le terre de Escoce, et le feme de cesty que fuit tue suist appeal de son mort en court de Constable cy en Engleterre, etc.

The Black Book of the Admiralty contains a tract, composed by or on behalf of Thomas duke of Gloucester, constable of England, in the reign of Richard the Second, and this tract gives several precise details about the procedure.

In first the quarrel and the bills of the appellant and defendant shall be pleaded in the court before the constable and marshal, and when they may not prove their cause by witnesses, nor by any other manner, but determine their quarrel by strength . . . . the constable hath power to join battle.

. . . .

And if the said battle be of treason, he that is convicted and discomfited shall be disarmed in the lists by the commandment of the constable, and a corner of the lists broken in reproof of him, by the which he shall be drawn out with horse from the same place where he is so disarmed, through the lists unto the place of justice, where he shall be beheaded or hanged after the usage of the country; the which appertaineth to the marshal, and to oversee and perform his said office and to put him in execution, and to go or ride and to be always with him till it be done and all performed, and as well of the appellant as of the defendant; for good faith and right and law of arms will that the appellant incur the same pain that the defendant should do if he were convicted and discomfited. And if the cause be for another crime, he who is convicted and discomfited shall be disarmed and led out of the lists to the place of justice, to be hanged or to have his head cut off, the appellant equally as the defendant as aforesaid, according to the usage of the country, but he shall not be drawn out except by cause of treason.

· Also, if it be a deed or action of arms, he who is convicted or discomfited shall be disarmed as aforesaid, and put out of the lists without any other judgment inflicted upon him.[1]

It was to this court of chivalry that the case of Hereford v. Norfolk was remitted by parliament: an ominous precedent. One of the first acts of Henry of Lancaster, when he returned to England to seize the crown, was to have Scrope earl of Wiltshire tried and executed by a court purporting to be

[1] See Monumenta Juridica, the Black Book of the Admiralty, Rolls Series [55], i, pp. 301–30. Compare the tract (printed ibid.) De Materia Duelli; and see also Dugdale, Origines Judiciales (1671), pp. 79–86.

a court of the lord high constable.[1] By the middle of the fifteenth century we find this court has become the recognised tribunal for procuring the judicial assassination of peers of the realm.

It is, of course, easy enough to say harsh things of this court, but its jurisdiction was by no means universally feared or disliked. It had its good and it had its bad traditions. At its best it was, if anything, too popular. It enabled the nobility and gentry to decide their affairs of honour under most pleasing conditions.[2] The duel was fought at the king's expense with all the splendid rites and circumstances of mediæval tourney. With this aspect of the tribunal we are not concerned. One of its bad aspects will be found set out in the forty-fourth article of the indictment brought

---

[1] Existebant tunc in castro eodem [scil. Bristol] dominus Willelmus Scrope comes Wiltschiriae et thesaurarius Angliae, dominus Henricus Grene et dominus Johannes Busch locutor ultimi parliamenti milites, qui fuerunt maxime consiliarii dicti regis Ricardi ad mala praemissa perpetranda. Tandem capti sunt et inviti ducti extra castrum in campum ad ducem Lancastriae. Et primo quidem arrestati sunt, deinde in crastino coram judicibus, viz. constabulario et marescallo, judicio sistuntur. Et de proditione et mala gubernatione regis et regni convicti, dampnati et decollati sunt. (Vita R. Ricardi II, ed. Hearne, p. 153.)

[2] On the subject of trial by combat see Selden, Opera, iii, pp. 58–83 ; Lea, Superstition and Force; Neilson, Trial by Combat. It is quite clear that at certain periods the courts of common law found themselves in the position of having to compete with the court of chivalry for the confidence and consequent patronage of the public. In the course of this rivalry some side-lights are thrown on the current abuses of legal procedure. Even juries were not immaculate. See, for example, Ordinances of the Privy Council, vol. i, pp. 77–8 : . . . qe plese vostre tres hautisme seignurie charger sir Ric. Waldegrave chivaler et Laurence Drew esquier denvoyer . . . touz les matiers et processe qeux le dit Richard ad mys sur le dit Johan, devaunt eux pendauntz, direct al court de conestable et mareschal illoesques pur estre determinez; qar, tres redoute seigneur, si la matier et processe de lappel avant dit serroit determine a la commune ley, le dit Johan neusse que mort par une enqueste de dousze homes deins la fraunchise du dite citee par procurement et brocage des certeins persones, les queux persones ne vorroient pur cynk mille livres que la verite du dite appel fusse overtement conuz.

against Richard in the year 1399.[1] Up to the end of the fourteenth century the constable's court had not been called upon to assist the crown in dealing with a constitutional crisis. In 1388 and 1397 parliament, by permitting appeals of treason to be tried before the lords, had offered all the facilities that could be desired for political reprisals. It was Henry of Lancaster who first made systematic use of the constable's court for purging the realm of his political enemies.[2]

In the first year of Henry the Fourth a statute was passed prohibiting appeals in parliament: thenceforth all appeals to be made of things done within the realm were to be tried and determined by the good laws of the realm made and used in the time of the king's noble progenitors, and all appeals to be made of things done out of the realm were to be tried and determined before the constable and marshal.[3] This statute was effectual so far as it vetoed appeals in parliament; but, contrary no doubt to what its framers intended, it only gave a fresh impetus to the court of chivalry.[4]

[1] Rot. Parl., iii, p. 420b.: Item quamvis statutum fuerit et ordinatum ac etiam hactenus confirmatum, quod nullus liber homo capiatur [etc.] . . . tamen de voluntate mandato et ordinatione dicti regis quam plures ligeorum suorum maliciose accusati, super eo quod debuissent aliquid dixisse publice vel occulte quod cedere poterit ad vituperium scandalum seu dedecus persone dicti regis fuerant capti et imprisonati et ducti coram constabulario et marescallo Anglie in curia militari. In qua curia dicti ligei accusati ad aliud responsum admitti non poterant nisi respondendo se in nullo fore culpabiles et per eorum corpora et non aliter se justificarent et defenderent: non obstante quod accusatores et appellatores eorum essent juvenes fortes et sani et illi accusati senes et impotentes mutulati vel infirmi: unde non solum destructio dominorum et magnatum regni sed etiam omnium et singularum personarum communitatis ejusdem regni verisimiliter sequi posset.

[2] Certainly Edward the Second made use of the court of chivalry for trying peers of the realm (see Appendix). As, however, he more frequently issued commissions to his ordinary justices for this purpose, and in every way showed the minimum regard for legal privileges and legal formalities, the fact that he also gave similar employment to the constable scarcely entitles him to be considered the pioneer of this movement.

[3] Statute, 1 Henry IV, cap. xiv.

[4] The statute of 13 Richard II was, of course, a law of the realm, but not made by one of Henry's progenitors.

2 B

Frequently, during Henry the Fourth's reign, the commons presented petitions on the subject. The case of Benet Wilman was, at their instance, transferred to the common law; but in spite of opposition the constable's court steadily developed.[1]

We may now return to the general history of trial by peers. So far as the constable's court is concerned, it will be sufficient to deal with the cases tried before it as they arose.

The first case of importance in Henry's reign[2] was the impeachment of peers implicated in the appeal of 1397, namely Edward duke of Albemarle, Thomas duke of Surrey, John duke of Exeter, John marquis of Dorset, John earl of Salisbury and Thomas earl of Gloucester. The accused peers defended themselves, "each man severally by himself before the king and all the estates of Parliament." Each alleged in effect that he was no stirrer of the bill of appeal and wist naught of it till it was showed to him, and excused himself on the ground of coercion and constraint. Henry adjourned the case to the following morning, when the accused were again put

---

[1] Rot. Parl., iii, p. 473 (2 Henry IV); ibid., p. 499a. (4 Henry IV); ibid., p. 530ab. (5 Henry IV); ibid., p. 625b. (11 Henry IV). For some of the cases tried during this reign see Rymer, Foedera O.S., viii, pp. 168–70, 176 (Kighlee v. Scrop); ibid., pp. 210, 227, 346 (Count of Denia's case). For a special commission to Henry de Percy, earl of Northumberland, as constable of England see Pat. Cal., 2 Henry IV, p. 458 (Feb. 4th, 1401).

[2] The following petition, made by the commons in the first parliament of Henry IV, is of considerable importance : . . . Et outre ceo monstrerent au roy, que come les juggementz du parlement appertiegnent soulement au roy et as seigneurs, et nient as communes sinoun en cas que s'il plest au roy de sa grace especiale lour monstrer les ditz juggementz, pur ease de eux, que nul record soit fait en parlement encontre les ditz communes q'ils sont ou serront parties as ascunes juggementz donez ou a doners en apres en parlement. A qoi leur feust responduz par l'ercevesque de Canterbirs, de comandement du roy, coment mesmes les communes sont petitioners et demandours, et que le roy et les seigneurs de tout temps ont eues et averont de droit les jugementz en parlement en manere come mesmes les communes ount monstrez. Sauve q'en estatuz a faires ou en grantes et subsides ou tiels choses a faires pur commune profit du roialme le roy voet avoir especialment leur advis et assent : et que cel ordre de fait soit tenuz et gardez en tout temps advenir. (Rot. Parl., vol. iii, p. 427.)

to answer, "none of them waiting or hearing the other," so that the truth might be discovered. What they then said is not recorded. William Thyrning, the chief justice of the common bench, delivered judgment "par commandement du roi et par avis et assent des seigneurs de parlement." This is the official version,[1] but the Cotton Julius B 2 manuscript says he—"hadde the wordes for the Styward of Englond."[2] He sentenced the accused peers to the loss of certain lands and dignities. It was an elaborate judgment; and the following statement made by Thyrning, after rehearsing the facts, is worth noting:—

Upon which the king and his temporal lords thought that this appeal [of 1397] and the matter contained therein was so great and so high, and so much harm and mischief fell thereof . . . and all bygone and proceeded out of the course of the common law, so that by the course of the common law of the crown and of the land it might not well be redressed or punished but by the king and his lords peers of this land in his high court of parliament.

Thomas Merkes, bishop of Carlisle, appears to have been implicated in the earl of Kent's rebellion of the year 1400. He was indicted of high treason before a commission of oyer and terminer; and, subject to a compliance by letters close[3] with the statute of 18 Edward III, cap. i,[4] he was tried like any commoner. The bishop on being arraigned demurred, not as a peer but as a bishop, to the jurisdiction of the justices. The demurrer was overruled on the ground that, the crime being high treason, he could not claim privilege.[5]

---

[1] Rot. Parl., vol. iii, pp. 449–52.
[2] Chronicles of London (ed. Kingsford), p. 59. Compare the statement in the Annales Henrici Quarti, pp. 314–15: Die Lunae proxima post festum omnium Sanctorum datum est judicium contra dominos qui dicuntur "appellantes," Willelmo Thernyng verba prosequente jussu regis quia Thomas Percy vice-senescallus infirmabatur qui hoc ex officio debuerat pronunciasse.
[3] Dated 28th January and addressed to Thomas Beauchamp, earl of Warwick, and other justices assigned to hear and determine treasons and felonies, etc., directing them to proceed against archbishops and bishops indicted before them notwithstanding the statute of Westminster. (Printed in Rymer, Foedera O.S., viii, p. 123.)   [4] Rot. Parl., vol. ii, p. 152.
[5] See statute, 25 Edward III, cap. vi, s. 4.

The bishop thereupon, saving his ecclesiastical liberty and under protest, pleaded not guilty, and for good or evil put himself upon the country. A jury brought in a verdict of guilty; but the justices, being doubtful as to the judgment they ought to pronounce, simply remanded him to the Tower. No judgment was, in fact, ever delivered, for Merkes obtained the king's pardon.[1] This case is instructive, but not conclusive.[2] Who may judge a spiritual peer is the crucial point to be decided; we cannot say for certain that the question who may try is even relevant to the issue.

On the 27th of May, 1405, Scrope archbishop of York, and Mowbray, son and heir of the exiled duke of Norfolk, raised the standard of revolt in the north. Marching to Shipton Moor beneath the banner of the Five Wounds of Christ, they there encountered the royal forces under Westmoreland and John of Lancaster. Westmoreland, with inferior numbers, dared not risk a battle; but duplicity succeeded where force would almost certainly have failed. The details are somewhat obscure; but at all events Scrope and Mowbray, believing they had secured honourable terms from the king, disbanded their forces, only to find themselves immediately afterwards placed under arrest.[3] On the 6th of June the prisoners were taken to Bishopsthorpe, and two days later they were brought up for trial before a court consisting of Stanley the steward of the household, the earl of Arundel deputy constable *pro hac vice*, Beaufort deputy marshal *pro hac vice* and a commission of peers and justices.[4]

[1] Recorded in Placita Coram Rege, Hil., 2 Henry IV, rex m. 4.
[2] On the question of ecclesiastical privileges, compare the case stated above and the Scrope case, infra, with the following: Hiis itaque gestis, episcopus Carleolensis surrexit [scil. in parliamento], ut excusaret se de quibuslibet objectis contra eum per suspicionem, quam intendit probare fallacem. Cui rex dixit, non debere eum in illa causa judicari, sed in curia ecclesiastica fore conveniendum. Ille tamen, facta protestatione quod noluit derogare juri ecclesiae vel libertati, rogavit instantius ut excusatio sua posset audiri; declaravitque [etc.]. . . . (Annales Henrici Quarti, Rolls Series [28], p. 314. A.D. 1399.)
[3] For an account of this rising see Wylie, Henry IV, vol. ii, and Dict. Nat. Biog., s.v. Scrope.
[4] Appendix.

The constitution of the tribunal indicates that, short of a trial before parliament, the king was willing to proceed with every formality that the law could demand.[1] The constable had a special jurisdiction which could only be disputed by appeal to the king in council; the acting deputy was a peer of the realm ; and, if this was not enough, peers and justices were associated with him, in deference probably to the celebrated dictum of Bracton.[2] We are indeed definitely told that three days were spent by the council in discussing the trial.[3] The archbishop of Canterbury hurried northwards to counsel prudence, and strongly urged the king either to refer Scrope's case to the pope or at least to let it stand over for trial before parliament; while Gascoigne, the chief justice, appears to have advised very decidedly against the legality of condemning the prelate to death.

Henry perhaps had learnt to doubt the expediency of being lenient, and sterner counsels prevailed. The trial duly proceeded; both prisoners were found guilty by the court, sentenced to death and promptly executed.[4] There seems

---

[1] The popular view, that Gascoigne was told, as chief justice, to try and sentence Scrope, that he very properly declined to do so, and thereupon Scrope was subjected to a mock trial by a few laymen, is a complete travesty of the facts. This case was considered at the next session of parliament, but no definite pronouncement by the peers is recorded. (Rot. Parl., vol. iii, p. 606, set out infra.) How far the jurisdiction was strengthened by the steward of the household being joined cannot be discussed here: but, shortly stated, Scrope was tried before a full palace court, assisted by peers of the realm. A palace court had been constituted to try the persons who took part in the earl of Kent's rebellion in 1399–1400. However, on that occasion there were no peers to be tried, and the court was not specially afforced. [2] Vide supra, p. 284.

[3] Historians of York, Rolls Series [71], iii, p. 290.

[4] The accounts given by the principal chroniclers are worth comparing :—

(Chron. Angl., ed. Giles, p. 45): Sed quum dominus Joannes Gaskone, justiciarius principalis de banco domini regis, renuit sedere aut sententiam aliquam super archiepiscopum proferre, quem noverat esse patrem ejus spiritualem, et non esse juxta leges temporales judicandum, sed ad ejus judicem competentem videlicet dominum papam destinandum : et etiam sic decrevit dominus Thomas Arundelle archiepiscopus Cantuariensis : tamen qui erant consiliarii regis, non admittentes eum sic evadere ultionem, fecerunt

to be some uncertainty as to which member of the tribunal actually pronounced the judgment on Scrope, but the question is one rather of form than of substance. It was an unpleasant business : the judges doubtless saw themselves in a strait between the devil and the king, and " I pray thee have me excused " was probably the feeling of each of them. Under these circumstances it may well be the case that

duos milites, videlicet Randulphum Everis et Willelmum Fulthorpe, sedere, et per specialem commissionem eum ad mortem judicare.

(Gascoigne, Loci e Libro Veritatum, p. 226) : . . . non judici, in mandatis dedit, ut in eadem die scilicet in feria secunda septimanae Pentecostis, quae fuit octava dies Junii, sentenciam mortis in aula praefati manerii contra archiepiscopum, quem vocavit suum proditorem, proferret. Unde dum praedictus judex principalis Willelmus Gascoigne in comitatu Eboraci natus de aula exiret, praedictus Willelmus Fulthorpe in loco judicis sedit et archiepiscopum Scrop ante se adduci praecepit. Et archiepiscopo coram eo nudo capite stante hanc sententiam mortis, ipso audiente et omnibus circumstantibus, protulit : "Te Ricardum Scrope traditorem regis ad mortem judicamus, et ex precepto regis decollari mandamus."

(Historians of York, Rolls Series [71], iii, p. 290) : Et hiis regi Henrico iv nuntiatis, idem rex, . . . ad manerium archiepiscopi Eboracensis, nomine Byschopthorp, festinanter equitavit, et ibi prope civitatem Eboraci de morte praedicti archiepiscopi per tres dies tractavit, scilicet a vigilia Pentecostes usque in feriam secundam sequentem, scilicet sexto idus Junii, in quo celebratur festum sancti Willelmi archiepiscopi Eboracensis . . . et in crastino Pentecostes in praefato manerio archiepiscopi ante meridiem rex mandavit Willelmo Gascoigne armigero, in comitatu Eboraci nato, tunc principali justiciario Angliae, ut praefatum archiepiscopum, ibi existentem in eodem manerio, et in eadem die, tanquam regis traditorem, ad mortem judicaret, qui coram rege hoc veniret, et sic regi respondit : "Domine," inquit, "nullam legem habetis ad occidendum aliquem episcopum, et ideo quod vos non potestis in hac materia, ego judex talis non possum." Quibus verbis rex iratus praefatum judicem graviter redarguit. Unde quia sic constans stetit pro veritate Dei, ideo memoria ejus sit in benedictione in saeculum saeculi : sed cum hoc opus nefarium praefatus judex renuit hoc alteri viro non judici rex commisit, scilicet domino Willelmo Fulthorp militi, quem postea vidi leprosum Eboraci. (Compare ibid., ii, pp. 306-7 and p. 432.)

(Annales Henrici Quarti, Rolls Series [28], iv, p. 409) : Comes Arundeliae et dominus Thomas Beufort collateralis frater regis, accepta sententia, sederunt in judicio super eum [archiepiscopum] et comitem marescallum et condemnaverunt eos sententia proditorum ; et archiepiscopum quidem damnantes, velut apostatam,

Scrope was sentenced, as some say, by Fulthorp, a subordinate member of the tribunal; but, if so, he merely acted as the *organum vocis* of Arundel.[1] We know how the chroniclers regarded the matter: because Gascoigne protests, blessed be his memory throughout all ages; the other man, Fulthorp, wanders through York a leper as white as snow.[2]

et ordinis sui transgressorem, et eo quod captus sit armatus, regis sui necnon et regni publicum proditorem.

(Continuatio Eulogii Hist., Rolls Series [9], iii, p. 407): Et archiepiscopus Cantuariensis in praesentia cujusdam notarii dixit regi: "Domine . . . consulo vobis quod si archiepiscopus tantum deliquerit, sicut vobis suggestum est, reservetur judicio domini papae, qui talem satisfactionem vobis ordinabit quod eam judicabitis sufficientem. At si hoc non vultis, consulo ut reservetur judicio parliamenti. Absit quod judicio vestro manus vestrae ejus sanguine polluantur." Rex respondit: "Non possum propter astantes."

[1] For the use of this expression in the case of a subordinate official giving judgment in the constable's court, see Rot. Pat., 2 Henry VI, pt. 1, m. 6; Cal., p. 169.

[2] The references to the judgments on Scrope and Mowbray in the Escheators' Accounts are worth citing.

(Escheators' Accounts, 117/13): De aliquibus exitibus manerii de Benyngworth cum pertinentiis in predicto comitatu Lincoln quod Ricardus nuper Archiepiscopus Ebor. qui ratione *rebellionis sue* (cujusdam judicii versus ipsum redditi) erga regem forisfecit . . . videlicet a die Martis proximo *post* (ante) festum sancti Barnabe Apostoli accidente x die Junii dicto anno sexto quo die prefatus escaetor manerium predictum cepit in manum regis (pretextu brevis regis sibi inde directi) *eo quod tunc primo constabat ei de forisfactura predicti archiepiscopi* usque xiiij diem Junii proximo sequentem antequam prefatus escaetor liberavit (custodiam) manerii predicti. . . . (The italicised words are erased on the roll, those in brackets are interlineations.)

De aliquibus exitibus duarum parcium manerii de Eppeworth cum membris et pertinentiis suis in insula de Haxolme in predicto comitatu Lincoln, que Thomas Mowbray nuper comes marescallus, qui occasione rebellionis sue erga regem forisfecit racione judicii versus ipsum redditi, tenuit in dominico suo ut de feodo die quo forisfecit . . . videlicet ab xj die Junii dicto anno sexto quo die prefatus escaetor predictas duas partes cepit in manum regis eo quod tunc primo constabat ei de forisfactura predicti nuper comitis usque x diem Augusti proximo sequentem, antequam liberavit (predictas) duas partes. . . .

Note continued on next page.

While the revolt of 1405 was closing tragically with the execution of Scrope and Mowbray, Henry Percy earl of

(Escheators' Accounts, 18/15): . . . a viij die Junii anno regis Henrici vj, quo die [idem Thomas nuper comes marescallus] obiit, seu postea non quod per breve regis. . . .

. . . a die Lune proximo post festum Pentecostes anno vj, quo die idem Thomas obiit, seu postea non quod per breve de magno sigillo....

(Escheators' Inquisitions, Series 1, File 1107): Inquisitio capta apud Eppeworth die Jovis proximo post festum Pentecostes anno regis Henrici quarti sexto coram . . . qui dicunt super sacramentum suum quod Thomas Mowbray nuper comes marescallus qui occasione rebellionis sue erga regem forisfecit (ratione omnis quidem rebellionis quoddam judicium versus ipsum redditum fuit) tenuit in dominico suo ut de feodo die quo regi forisfecit. . . . (The words in brackets are interlineations.)

(Escheators' Inquisitions, Series 1, File 1833): Inquisitio capta apud Chepyngkyngton comitatu Warrwici die Jovis proximo post festum sancti Laurencii anno regis Henrici quarti post conquestum sexto coram . . . qui dicunt super sacramentum suum quod Thomas nuper comes marescallus et Nottyngham, qui erga dominum regem forisfecit occasione judicii contra ipsum apud Bysshopesthorp in comitatu Ebor. viij die Junii dicto anno *vj*to redditi, tenuit in dominico suo ut de feodo. . . .

Let me explain, for the benefit of those unfamiliar with the form of escheators' accounts and inquisitions, that such expressions as "ratione rebellionis sue" do not occur in cases where the validity of a judgment is unquestionable; on the contrary, this is the stock phrase for cases where there has been no judgment at all. A valid judgment, constituting as it did the escheator's root of title to the property, is always referred to. The doubts of the escheators in this instance are clearly indicated. Henry also had his doubts, and approached the lords on the subject cautiously and even timidly.

Item, en mesmes le xix jour de Juyu . . . nostre dit seigneur le roy fist demander des ditz seigneurs temporelx, peres de roialme, coment ils vorroient dire touchant le fait de Richard de Scrope, nadgairs ercevesque d'Everwyk, et Thomas Moubray, nadgairs count mareschall . . .? A quelle demande les ditz seigneurs temporelx disoient, que solonc l'enformacion a eux done de par le dit conestable, il semblast a mesmes les seigneurs peres de roialme le cas estre treason. Nepurqant les ditz seigneurs disoient q'ils, ove bon deliberacion, a lour revenue a cest present parlement dirront ensi a nostre dit seigneur le roy en cell partie, que null errour sera trove en lour fait en temps a venir. A quell temps mesmes les seigneurs prierent a nostre dit seigneur le roy de comander toutz les seigneurs temporelx peres de roialme d'estre presentz pur la cause suis dite, et que null d'eux soit absent a icell fait. (Rot. Parl., vol. iii, p. 606.)

Northumberland and the lord Bardolf escaped to Scotland. Proceedings nevertheless were commenced against these persons also by bill exhibited in the court of chivalry; but the process was then, by advice of the lords, removed into parliament. Northumberland and Bardolf were summoned by proclamation to appear on pain of conviction and attainder; successive adjournments followed, and eventually they were sentenced as in default of appearance, in the, by this time, usual course of parliamentary procedure.[1] This case illustrates the weakness of the court of chivalry. It was a recognised rule, which even at that time it was advisable not to disregard, that the constable's jurisdiction was limited to the person and chattels of the offender; the humblest criminal could not be outlawed, nor could his lands and tenements be lawfully distrained.[2] As there was no immediate prospect of effecting the arrest either of Northumberland or Bardolf, it was idle to carry their case any further in the court of chivalry. Hence the adjournment into parliament.

No other trials took place while Henry the Fourth was on the throne, either in parliament or in the constable's court or elsewhere, which call for any particular comment; but we shall have to revert later on to the fate of John Holand, earl of Huntingdon, who, during the rebellion of 1400, was put to

[1] Rot. Parl., vol. iii, pp. 604-7.
[2] The commons had quite recently petitioned the king upon this subject. See Rot. Parl., vol. iii, p. 473: Adjoustant a icell que les ditz conestable et mareschal ne delyverent en execution, par force de juggement ou sentence donez ou a doners en la dit court al suyte de nully, terre ne tenement dont ascun est seizy de franc-tenement a meyns, salvant toutfoith la dit court execution soulement de corps et biens de celly que ensy est atteinte. Et si nulles terres ou tenements soient devenuz par juggement donez en les autres courtes du roy ou par eschet hors de possession de ceux sur queux tils sentences sont donez ou a doners que les possessioners d'icell ne soient ent travaillez n'empechez en la dite court de conestable et mareschall ne oustez par eux de lour possession par cause de nul tiel sentence. . . . There was not at the time any statutory limitation to this effect, and the answer to this petition was obviously framed so as not to confer any. The form of assent was: Soient l'estatutz ent faits tenuz et gardez.

The escheators, as already explained, had their doubts in the case of Scrope and Mowbray whether such a judgment justified the

death by the king's subjects without a scintilla of legal formality.[1]

Thomas of Lancaster, duke of Clarence and steward of England, is not known to have presided at the trial of any peer during the reign of Henry the Fourth. There is no evidence of any desire to perpetuate this particular function of the steward. On the contrary the precedent of 1397 was effectually abandoned when the chief justice Thyrning was put up to sentence the first peers tried by a Lancastrian parliament, and no note made in the official record saving the rights of the youthful steward of England.

The reign of Henry the Fifth furnishes us with at least one momentous precedent. In July of the year 1415, when Henry was at Southampton preparing for the French campaign, a plot against his life was discovered. The chief persons concerned were Richard earl of Cambridge, Henry lord Scrope of Masham and Sir Thomas Grey. By the king's special order the conspirators were arrested, and given into the custody of Sir John Popham, constable of the tower of Southampton. Then, by letters patent dated the 21st of July, John earl marshal and other commissioners were appointed to inquire, by the oath of a jury of Southampton, into all treasons, felonies and so forth committed in the said county, and to hear and determine them according to the law and custom of the realm of England. On Friday the 2nd of August a jury was duly empanelled: they brought in a charge of high treason against Cambridge and Grey; Scrope they found was privy to the scheme.

seizure of lands. They had no doubts in the case of Percy and Bardolf: no judgment is mentioned in their accounts and inquisitions.

Escheators' Inquisitions, Series 1, File 1107. Inquisitio capta apud Grantham die Sabbati in vigilia sancte Trinitatis anno regis Henrici quarti sexto coram . . . qui dicunt super sacramentum suum quod Thomas nuper dominus de Bardolf, qui occasione rebellionis sue erga regem forisfecit, tenuit in dominico suo ut de feodo die quo forisfecit. . . .

Ibid.—Inquisitio capta apud Burwell die Jovis in festo sancti Barnabe apostoli anno sexto regis Henrici quarti coram . . . qui dicunt super sacramentum suum quod Henricus comes Northumb., qui occasione rebellionis sue erga dominum regem forisfecit, tenuit die quo regi forisfecit in dominico suo. . . .   [1] See chap. xii.

On this finding the three were arraigned before the commissioners. Cambridge and Grey pleaded guilty and submitted themselves to the king's mercy. Scrope said he was a peer of the realm and demanded trial and judgment by his peers according to custom. The court not being sufficiently advised with regard to the judgment which should be pronounced on Cambridge and Scrope, these two were remanded to Southampton Tower; Grey was sentenced forthwith.

The commissioners reported to the king; and Henry immediately appointed his brother, Thomas duke of Clarence, his vicegerent to hear the case against Cambridge and Scrope. Clarence was instructed to summon peers of the said earl and baron, he was to pronounce judgment *per vestrum et eorumdem parium communem assensum hac instanti die Lune* (August 5th), and see to the execution of the judgment. Henry was evidently in a great hurry. Clarence summoned two dukes, Gloucester and York; eight earls, March, Huntingdon, Arundel, the earl marshal, Dorset, Salisbury, Oxford and Suffolk; and nine barons. York for some reason did not attend personally, but appointed Dorset his proxy. This court duly sat on the same Monday, Cambridge and Scrope were brought to the bar, found guilty of treason and sentenced to death and forfeiture. There was no delay in carrying out the sentence.

A parliament met the same year under Bedford regent of England; and, in response to a petition by the commons, the Southampton proceedings were brought up for confirmation and declared by the lords spiritual and temporal to be good and lawful judgments.[1]

We may regard the Southampton trial as the true source of the court of the lord high steward.[2] There is, indeed, no substantial difference between the tribunal constituted on the spur of the moment by Henry the Fifth for the trial of Cambridge and Scrope, and the court by which in 1521 Edward duke of Buckingham was sentenced to death. Both courts were presided over by a steward of England, but

---

[1] See appendix for further details.
[2] See chap. xii.

there was this distinction : it was a mere coincidence that Clarence held that office; while Norfolk, who presided at the Buckingham trial, was specially appointed lord high steward *pro hac vice.*

In 1417 Sir John Oldcastle, lord Cobham, was tried and condemned in parliament for treason.[1] In reality he died a martyr to Lollardism. The case is of no importance in the history of trial by peers.

In the second year of the reign of Henry the Sixth, lord Talbot appealed the earl of Ormond of treason. The case was brought before John duke of Bedford as constable of England in the court of chivalry; but, eventually, as a matter of policy, the proceedings were quashed in parliament.[2]

In 1429 a petition was presented with the view of prohibiting appeals of treason done within the realm being brought before the constable's court. An evasive answer was given.[3]

In 1441 occurred the remarkable prosecution of dame Eleanor, the harlot duchess of Gloucester. A diabolical conspiracy, it was alleged, had been brewing in the Gloucester household. Bolingbroke the duke's chaplain, *clericus famosissimus*, astronomer and professor of the black arts, was the first to be attacked : he was exhibited for the delectation of the London mob on a platform before St. Paul's, tricked out, poor foredamned wretch, in the attire considered appropriate to a magician. Thereupon dame Eleanor with a lamentable lack of discretion scuttled into sanctuary at Westminster : she was, to use the parliamentary language of the day, always misgoverning herself. Inquiry and indictment speedily followed. The duchess was brought before a tribunal consisting of the king, cardinals Beaufort and Kempe, five bishops and some other ecclesiastics, and charged with being implicated in a conspiracy with Bolingbroke above-mentioned, Southwell a canon of St. Paul's, and a certain female popularly known

[1] Rot. Parl., vol. iv, p. 107.
[2] Rot. Parl., vol. iv, p. 198: the bill of complaint is, apparently, set out in full in the account of these proceedings.
[3] See Rot. Parl., vol. iv, p. 349b.

as the witch of Eye.[1] These were said, at the instigation of my lady, to have framed an image of wax fashioned to represent the king: the intention being that, as this image slowly melted before a fire, so the king by their incantations might waste away and die. The ulterior purpose was that the duke of Gloucester should thus be advanced to the crown. The duchess after some hesitation appears to have pleaded guilty to witchcraft. She was sentenced by the court to a penance, which included walking barefoot through the principal streets of London carrying a lighted taper; and was finally sent a prisoner to the Isle of Man.[2]

The nature of the charge against dame Eleanor no doubt explains the clerical character of the tribunal; but, even so, was it right that a peeress, lawfully wedded to a duke of the blood-royal, should be thus tried? The result was an Act of parliament regulating the trial of peeresses.

Item, whereas it is contained in the Great Charter, amongst other things, in the form which followeth: " No freeman shall be taken or imprisoned or disseised of his free tenement or liberties or free cus-

---

[1] Patent Roll, 19 Henry VI, pt. 2, m. 16; printed Rymer, Foedera O.S., x, p. 851.
Worcester, Rolls Series [22], p. [762]. Fabyan, p. 614.
English Chronicle (ed. Davies), Camden Soc. [64], pp. 57, 60, etc.
Chronicles of London (ed. Kingsford), p. 149.

[2] I came before the spiritualité
Two cardynals and byshoppis fyve
And oder men of gret degré
Examened me of all my lyffe
And openly I dyde me shryffe
Of alle thyng that they asked me
Than was I putt in penaunce belyffe
Alle women may be ware by me.

Thorow London in many a strete
Of them that were most pryncypalle
I went bare fote on my fette
That sum tyme was wonte to ride rialle
Fader of hevyn and lorde of alle
As thou wilt so must yt be
The syne of pryde wille have a falle
Alle women may be ware by me.
Political Songs [14], ii, pp. 205–8.

toms or outlawed or exiled or in any other manner destroyed nor will we send upon him nor will we go upon him except by the lawful judgment of his peers or by the law of the land "—in which statute is no mention made of how women, ladies of great estate in respect of their husbands peers of the land, married or sole, that is to say duchesses, countesses or baronesses, shall be put to answer, or before what judges they shall be judged upon indictments of treasons or felonies by them committed or done; in regard whereof it is a doubt in the law of England before whom and by whom such ladies, so indicted, shall be put to answer and judged: Our said lord the king, willing to put an end to such ambiguities and doubts, hath declared by authority aforesaid that such ladies, so indicted or hereafter to be indicted, of any treason or felony done by them or hereafter to be done, whether they be married or sole, that they shall be brought to answer and put to answer and judged before such judges and peers of the realm as peers of the realm should be if they were indicted or impeached of such treasons or felonies done or hereafter to be done and in like manner and form and in none other.[1]

---

[1] 20 Henry VI, cap. 9; printed in the Revised Statutes. I have in an earlier chapter produced evidence to show that no such doubts were originally entertained : even "baronesses" enjoyed the privileges of barons.

The original of this statute is in French and runs as follows :—

Item come contenue soit en la graunde chartre entre autres en la fourme qensuyt. Nullus liber homo capiatur aut imprisonetur aut disseisiatur de libero tenemento suo aut libertatibus aut liberis consuetudinibus suis aut utlagetur aut exulet[ur] aut aliquo modo destruatur nec super eum mittemus nec super eum ibimus nisi per legale judicium parium suorum vel per legem terre. En quele estatuit nest my mencion fait coment femmes dames de grande estate par cause de lour barons peres de la terre covertez ou soules cestassaver duchesses countesses ou baronesses serount mys a respoundre ou devant queux juges els seroient juggez sur enditementz de tresons ou felonies par eux faitz a cause de quelles il est une ambiguite et doute en la ley devant queux et par queux tielz dames issint enditez seront mysez a respondre et estre adjuggez : Nostre dit seigneur le roy voillant oustier tielx ambiguites et doutes ad declare par lauctorite desuisdit que tielx dames issint enditez ou on apres a enditierz de ascun treson ou felonie par eux faitz ou enapres affairez coment que eles soient covertez de baron ou soules que eles en soient mesnez en response et mys a respoundre et adjuggez devant tielx juges et peres de le roialme sicome autres peres de le roialme seroient sils fuissent enditez ou empeschez de tielx tresons ou felonies faitz ou en apres affairez et en autiel manere et forme et en nulle autre.

This statute does not define, directly or indirectly, by what modes peers are triable. It is noticeable, however, that treason and felony are the only offences mentioned: the claim to trial by peers in cases of misdemeanour is altogether abandoned.

In the year 1446 James Butler, earl of Ormond, was appealed of treason by the prior of Kilmaine. The case duly proceeded in the court of chivalry and joinder of battle was awarded. The prior, who was a man of peace, had no acquaintance whatever with the art of fighting in the lists: he accordingly took lessons, at the king's expense, of one Philip Treher, a fishmonger of London, a renowned expert in these matters; but at the last moment the king stopped the fight.[1]

When parliament assembled in January, 1450, William de la Pole, duke of Suffolk, was perhaps the most unpopular man in the whole kingdom. Anticipating attack he made a vigorous speech in self-defence at the opening of the session. The commons promptly replied by impeaching the duke, and requesting that he might be committed to ward. No formal accusations had so far been framed; and the lords, after taking judicial advice, refused to order his imprisonment. The commons then definitely charged Suffolk with making treasonable overtures to the French, and on this Suffolk was committed to the Tower. On the 7th of February formal articles of impeachment were presented, and on the 9th of March eighteen additional articles: there were, however, various adjournments, and it was not before the 17th of March that the case was disposed of.[2] On that day the king sent for all his lords, spiritual and temporal, then being in town, to come to his inner chamber in the palace of Westminster, the room with a "gavill" window over a cloister. When they were all assembled Suffolk was brought in; he appears to have kneeled continuously during the proceedings which followed.

The chancellor addressed him on behalf of the king: "Sir,

---

[1] See Ordinances of the Privy Council, vol. vi, pp. 57–9.
[2] For these proceedings see Rot. Parl., vol. v, pp. 182–3.

ye be well remembered when ye were last before the king and his lords, and of your answers upon certain articles touching accusations and impeachments of great and horrible things put upon you by the commons of the land, in this present parliament assembled, in the first bill presented by them; and how, at that time, ye put you not upon your peerage. What will ye say now furthermore in the matter?" The duke said he submitted himself wholly to the king's rule and governance to do with him as he listed.

Upon this the chancellor announced to the duke the king's will: "Sir, I conceive that, not departing from your answers aforesaid nor putting you upon your peerage, ye submit you wholly to the king's rule and governance. Wherefore the king commandeth me to say that on the first bill he holds you neither declared nor charged; and, as to the second bill put upon you touching misprisions which be not criminal, the king by force of your submission, by his own advice and not resorting to the advice of his lords nor by way of judgment, for he is not in place of judgment, putteth you to his rule and governance." The sentence thus introduced was banishment for five years.

The lord Beaumont immediately afterwards made a protest on behalf of the peers spiritual[1] and temporal that the case should not prejudice them, their heirs and successors, in time to come; but that they should enjoy their rights of peerage thereafter as freely and largely as they, their ancestors and predecessors had done in times past. As requested, this declaration was entered on the Parliament Roll.

Suffolk was not thus easily to escape the vengeance of his enemies. At the end of April he embarked for Calais. Off Dover his ship was intercepted by a vessel of the English fleet, and he was ordered on board. The last scene took place in a small boat in mid-channel: by a lewd seaman, with seven strokes of a rusty sword, the duke was delivered.

Public animosity also vented itself on the duchess of Suffolk and lord Say the ex-treasurer, Cade the "captain of Kent" taking an effective part in the proceedings. The

[1] This clearly implies that spiritual peers are entitled to the same rights of peerage as temporal peers.

duchess, lord Say and several other persons were indicted of treason at the Guildhall :[1] Say had the misfortune to be present, for lord Scales took him out of the Tower and handed him over to Cade. Say claimed to be tried by his peers, with the unsatisfactory result that he was hurried to the standard in Cheap and beheaded before he had finished shriving himself.[2] The indictment against the duchess appears to have been removed into parliament in due course. The peers tried and acquitted her. This was probably the first case of a peeress being tried in parliament since the reign of Edward the First, but no formal record of the event is known to exist.[3]

[1] The proceedings appear to have been treated as perfectly regular and legal, but in almost all cases the court party secured a verdict of not guilty at the subsequent trial. See, for example, the trial of dominus Thomas Kent clericus communis consilii domini regis. (Coram Rege Roll, Mich., 30 Henry VI, rex. m. 8.) He was indicted before lord Scales and others, according to this roll—die Sabbati proximo post festum apostolorum Petri et Pauli, anno regni nostri 28. See also the trial of Edward Grymston, ibid., rex. m. 15.

[2] See, for example, Fabyan (ed. 1811), p. 624: "Than upon the morne, beyng the thirde daye of July and Frydaye, the sayd capitayne entred agayne the cytie, and causyd the lorde Saye to be fette from the Tower and ladde unto the Guyldhall, where he was arreygnyd before the mayre and other of the kynges justyces. . .. Than the lorde Saye . . . desyred that he myghte be juged by his pyers. Wherof herynge, the capitayne sent a company of his unto the halle, the whiche parforce toke hym from his offycers, and so brought hym unto the standarde in Chepe, where, or he were halfe shryven, they strake of his hede. . . ."
Compare Chronicles of London (ed. Kingsford), p. 161 : "desired to be demyd by his perys."

[3] Et xxx die ejusdem mensis Junii Wyllelmus Ascough tunc episcopus Sarum, apud Edyngtone Wyltesire, ab insurrectoribus ejusdem comitatus interimitur. Et circa finem dicti mensis Junii, exercitu dicti regis disperso, versus Kylyngworthe progreditur. Quod audiens, communitas Kantiae iterum conglomerati sunt. Et praedictus Johannes Cade capitaneus Kantiae die Veneris (viz. iij die Julii) vi et armis London ingreditur ac domus Philippi Malpas ibidem spoliatur. Facta est itaque commissio de audiendo et terminando. Et ideo Robertus Danvers factus est justiciarius, etc. Ac etiam dux et ducissa Suffolchiae, episcopus Sarum (scilicet Askewe), dominus de Saye, Thomas Danyell, Johannes Saye et multi alii indictati sunt de proditione in Gwyhalda Londoniae. Et post hoc

2 C

A few years later Thomas earl of Devon was arraigned in parliament on a charge of high treason;[1] he was acquitted. It is stated on the rolls that the duke of Buckingham was assigned to be steward of England for the trial.[2] This was probably the first instance of such an appointment during the fifteenth century: it is not entered on either the Patent or the Close Rolls, which is fairly strong evidence of innovation. The next appointment of this kind, which occurred seven years later, figures twice on the Patent Rolls and is also transcribed into the originalia. In the same way each new appointment to this office for a coronation is duly enrolled, with the one exception of Henry the Fourth's coronation. There is no grant of the stewardship to Thomas of Lancaster or of the deputy stewardship to the earl of Worcester formally entered on any roll.

How, it may be asked, did it happen that a steward was first appointed for the trial of the earl of Devon in 1454? A conjectural explanation is all that can be offered. It was

iiii die Julii proximo sequenti, Jacobus Fynys dominus de Saye hora septima post nonam decapitatur apud le Standard in Chepe. Et eodem die Wyllelmus Crowmer, ad tunc vicecomes Kantiae per dictum capitaneum extra Algate decapitatur. (Worcester, Rolls Series, 22, iii, p. [768])

In eodem parliamento ducissa Suffolciae acquietata est per pares suos, et Johannes Say et Thomas Daniel et alii perjurati de proditione,   nde indictati fuerunt tempore insurrectionis.   (Ibid., p. [770.])[1]

[1] The proceedings against this earl were placed in the Baga de Secretis, and are not at present forthcoming. See, however, the Controlment Roll, 30 Henry VI, m. 36, which furnishes some particulars as to his indictment and arrest.

[2] Rot. Parl., vol. v, p. 249: "Be hit remembered that where the xiiij° day of Marche the said xxxij° yere in this present parlement, Thomas erle of Devonshire, uppon an enditement of high treasons by hym supposed to bee doon agenst the kyng's honourable estat and persone, afore Humfrey duc of Buckingham steward of Englond for that tyme assigned, was arraigned and of the same treasons by his peeres the noble lordes of this royaume of England being in this seid present parlement was acquited of all things contained in the seid enditement. By which enditement the right high and mighty prince Richard duc of York, lieutenant for the kyng in the said parlement, conceyved the trouthe of his alliegiance to bee emblemyshed and disteigned. . . .

obviously necessary that someone should preside; but, until the appointment of a steward had become the recognised practice, the king in person or, in his absence, the regent were the persons who would naturally direct the proceedings. It was probably considered quite immaterial who pronounced the judgment on behalf of the king and lords; this, at all events, was a matter for the discretion of the king or regent. It would perhaps have been considered improper for the king in person to sentence a peer for high treason, although in France the opposite view was maintained: this point, however, has no bearing on the present question. Under ordinary circumstances no need could possibly arise for appointing someone to preside at a trial in parliament. In Suffolk's case, the last reported trial prior to 1454, the king ostensibly presided, while the chancellor acted as his mouthpiece and delivered the sentence, such as it was, by the king's command.

In 1454 the condition of affairs was quite abnormal. Henry was insane. York had opened parliament on the king's behalf, but his position was somewhat irregular. In an ordinary case he might none the less have presided, but we learn from the Parliament Roll that the charge against the earl of Devon contained undisguised allegations of treason against York himself. The duke was a professed champion of law and order; moreover his claim to the protectorship had reached a critical stage. Under these circumstances it was practically impossible for him to preside. He might have succeeded in quashing the indictment, but to obtain an acquittal before an independent judge in a constitutional trial was infinitely preferable. The case was probably planned and was certainly treated as a test case between York and his opponents. The result was followed by a vote of confidence in York, and a few days later the lords appointed him protector.[1]

Clearly the trial of 1454 arose under peculiar conditions which required special arrangements. We may therefore reasonably conjecture that precedents were investigated and a lord high steward appointed in consequence of what was

[1] Rot. Parl., vol. v, pp. 249–50.

discovered.[1]   A fair amount of evidence, as we have already
seen, came into existence at the end of the fourteenth
century supporting the right of the steward of England
to act as judge at the trial of peers in parliament; and we
can hardly doubt that the appointment of Humphrey duke
of Buckingham, on the occasion under discussion, was considered to be in restoration of an early constitutional practice.

In the year 1459 an attempt was made by the commons
to impeach lord Stanley for not sending his men to Blore-
heath, but the matter was not proceeded with.   The articles
of impeachment appear on the Parliament Roll[2] as a bill
presented by the commons, and at the foot the significant
response, " Le roi s'avisera."

For a considerable period after this, all judicial process in
parliament, whether by impeachment or indictment, fell into
abeyance, and was, in form at all events if not in substance,
completely superseded by bill of attainder : in other words
the legislative power inherent in parliament was resorted to
in preference to the judicial power.   The transition from the
one to the other was brought about by causes which may be
traced without much difficulty.[3]   Except to the lawyers the

[1] It was not an uncommon thing to search the chronicles for this
sort of information.   See, for example, Annales Ricardi Secundi,
Rolls Series [28], p. 252.

[2] Rot. Parl., vol. v, pp. 369–70.

[3] If we except the ordinance decreeing the banishment of
Gaveston, the first precedent is furnished by a recital of the proceedings against the Despencers : Lequel agard et exil fut conferme
de comun assent par estatut en mesme le parlement.   (Rot. Parl.,
ii, p. 7 ; cf. iii, p. 365).   In the second year of Henry IV forfeiture
was pronounced by the lords temporal against certain peers and
others who had taken part in the earl of Kent's rebellion and had
been quite informally killed by the king's subjects : the legality of
the procedure in parliament was subsequently questioned on more
than one occasion.   In 1453 the notorious Jack Cade (who had
been killed while attempting to evade capture by the king's officers)
was attainted by Act of parliament.   (Rot. Parl., vol. v, p. 265.)
This person had procured, by duress, the indictment of various
eminent people : one object of the Act was to quash these indictments; another object appears to have been to legalise the forfeiture of his property notwithstanding his death.   Sir William
Oldhall was then attainted by a similar Act.   (Rot. Parl., ibid.)   He

nature of the new process was apparently not appreciated until the transition was complete, and then even the blunted national conscience of that time was unmistakably shocked. The change, it would seem, was largely due to the delays incident to the trial of absent persons, and the technical difficulties in the way of attainting dead persons.[1] The insecurity of the throne during the civil wars forbade procrastination in the matter of trial, and made the attainder of opponents who had fallen in battle a political necessity. The king for the time being had of course no wish to rob or murder the ex-king's supporters; but their conviction, forfeiture, and execution if necessary, had to be expedited. The king's ministers were the keepers of the king's conscience; it was for them to devise appropriate procedure and see to it that such procedure was legal. The attainder of the dead calls for no comment. For the rest, the first step was charmingly simple and moderately innocent. Those already captured were brought before parliament and arraigned; they might deny the charge and defend themselves if they thought it worth while. As for the others, if they chose not to surrender and stand their trial it was their own doing. Sentence was passed on all alike. In the case of the absent, an ordinary judgment would not have complied with the law of the land or with the established practice of parliament. To obviate this the judgment was drawn up and passed as a statute, the accusations being framed as recitals

had been indicted and outlawed for complicity in Cade's insurrection, and was then in sanctuary at the chapel-royal of St. Martins-le-Grand: so his attainder in parliament was a work of supererogation. Oldhall, however, had been elected speaker of the lower house in November, 1450, and the Act no doubt was intended by the commons as a demonstration of loyalty to the king, and a repudiation of their connection with such a rebel. At Coventry, on the 20th November, 1459, York, Salisbury, Warwick and others were attainted by an Act, introduced by the lords, agreed by the commons and assented to by the king, a procedure which at once became common form. (See Rot. Parl., vol. v, p. 346.)

[1] For the law relating to this matter see references given below; and see above, the preceding note. The statutes on the subject are 34 Edward III, caps. xii and xiii; 36 Edward III, cap. xiii; and 23 Henry VI, cap. xvii.

to the act. This plan had the additional merit of effectually curing all informalities in the trial of those who were tried. In its inception and in certain special cases there was something to be said in favour of attainder. It was only when a legal trial was not merely abandoned but denied that the inherent viciousness of the system became self-evident.

On the accession of Edward the Fourth a sweeping bill of attainder was passed, including Henry the Sixth, various peers and a large number of commoners. For the purpose of delivering judgment under this Act, Richard earl of Warwick was made lord high steward by letters patent dated the 3rd of December, 1461.[1] This is the first documentary precedent we possess for such an appointment.

About the same time John Tiptoft, earl of Worcester, was appointed constable of England during pleasure by a perfectly ordinary and regular instrument;[2] and, in February,

---

[1] *Pro comite Warrewici :* Rex carissimo consanguineo suo Ricardo comiti Warrewici salutem. Sciatis quod cum officium senescalli Anglie, quod in processu cujusdam actus adversus et contra tam Henricum tam Henricum nuper de facto et non de jure regem Anglie, adversarium inimicum nostrum, quam quosdam alios rebelles nostros, aliosque qui prenobilem principem et patrem nostrum Ricardum nuper ducem Eborum apud Wakefield crudelissime et proditorie murdraverunt et interfecerunt, in presenti parliamento nostro, auctoritate ejusdem parliamenti, fiendi, ex certis causis exerceri debet, jam vacat, et in manibus nostris existit: Ac nos de fidelitate probitate et provida circumspectione vestris quamplurimum confidentes assignavimus et constituimus vos senescallum Anglie habendum gerendum et occupandum officium illud in processu predicto ac ad faciendum exercendum et exequendum ea omnia et singula que ad officium predictum ex causa processus actus predicti, hac vice tantum, pertinent facienda. Et ideo vobis mandamus quod circa officium predictum intendatis et illud faciatis et exequamini in forma predicta. Damus autem universis et singulis quorum interest in hac parte tenore presentium firmiter in mandatis quod vobis in executione officii predicti intendentes sint auxiliantes consulentes et obedientes in omnibus prout decet. In cujus etc. Teste rege apud Westmonasterium tercio die Decembris. (Patent Roll, 1 Edward IV, pt. 2, m. 1; Originalia, 1 Edward IV, m. 55; printed by Rymer, Foedera O.S., xi, p. 480.)

The above entry is repeated on the Patent Roll, 1 Edward IV, pt. 3, m. 8, in identical terms, except that it is expressed to be made "per ipsum regem oretenus."   [2] See Appendix.

THE COURT OF CHIVALRY

1862, John earl of Oxford and several others were brought
before the court of chivalry, condemned by Tiptoft, and
executed on Tower Hill. These persons, says one chronicler,
were condemned by the law of Padua, an angry allusion to
the constable's legal studies on the continent.[1]

There were further proceedings in parliament in 1465, and
on the 8th of March Richard earl of Warwick was again
appointed lord high steward.[2]

[1] Worcester, ed. Hearne [lib. Nig.], ii, p. 492. Mense Febuarii
Johannes comes Oxonie, Albredus filius ejus et heres, Thomas
Tudenham miles, Johannes Clopton, Johannes Mongomere et
Willelmus Tyrrele per Johannem comitem Wigornie constabularium
Anglie arrestantur, ob suspicionem literarum receptarum domine
Margarete nuper regine Anglie, coram quo per curiam constabularii
convicti, dictus comes decollatus est, ac Clopton excusatus, et omnes
alii tracti et decollati sunt in quadam scafalda pro eis facta super
montem turris Londonie.

Warkworth, Chronicles of the White Rose, p. 108 : "And in the
fifth year of king Edward, the earl of Oxford, the lord Aubrey his
son and sir Thomas Tudenham knight were taken and brought into
the tower of London and there was laid to them high treason; and
afterwards they were brought before the earl of Worcester and judged
by law Padua, that they should be had to the tower hill, where was
made a scaffold of eight feet high, and there were their heads
smitten off, that all men might see, whereof the most people were
sorry."

[2] Patent Roll, 5 Edward IV, pt. 1, m. 23d. *Pro comite Warrewici*: Rex carissimo consanguineo suo Ricardo comiti Warrewici
salutem. Sciatis quod cum officium senescalli Anglie, quod in processibus quorundam actuum ex certis causis in presenti parliamento
nostro auctoritate ejusdem parliamenti fiendis exerceri debet, jam
vacat et in manibus nostris existat, et nos processus illos ratione
vacacionis officii illius impediri nolentes, ac nos de fidelitate probitate et provida circumspectione vestris quamplurimum confidentes
assignavimus et constituimus vos senescallum Anglie habendum
gerendum et occupandum officium illud in processibus predictis ac
ad faciendum exercendum et exequendum ea omnia et singula que
ad officium predictum ex causa predicta, hac vice tantum, pertinent
facienda. Et ideo vobis mandamus quod circa officium predictum
intendatis et illud faciatis et exequamini in forma predicta. Damus
autem omnibus et singulis quorum interest in hac parte tenore
presencium firmiter in mandatis quod vobis in executione officii
predicti intendentes sint auxiliantes consulentes et obedientes prout
decet. In cujus etc. Teste rege apud Westmonasterium viij die
Marcii.   Per ipsum regem oretenus.

Edward was none too firmly seated on the throne: the political horizon was black with wars and rumours of wars: it was essentially a time when the court of the constable of England might prove a most effective prop to a threatened dynasty. Unfortunately the jurisdiction of this court rested on very insecure foundations; it was certainly not increasing in popularity, but this latter circumstance was probably to some extent the result of the former. Whether Edward appreciated these facts and acted accordingly, we cannot say for certain; but in 1467 there was a very remarkable piece of political jugglery. The earl of Worcester surrendered his grant of the constableship, and letters patent issued conferring the office on earl Rivers for life, with remainder to his son for life. This instrument recites the previous appointment of Tiptoft correctly enough so far as it goes, but then proceeds to add a definition of the constable's duties which Stubbs describes as unparalleled. This definition plainly and unmistakably purports to be a recital of the contents of the grant to Tiptoft: the recital is therefore absolutely false, if not deliberately fraudulent. The operative part of these letters patent confers the office of constable on earl Rivers and his son successively in identical terms, which naturally enough under the circumstances are set out verbatim, instead of being conferred by reference to the recitals. The definition of the constable's powers occurs in consequence three times over in this amazing deed. A very effective advertisement![1] Whether it deceived contemporaries quite as completely as modern constitutional historians is a doubtful point.[2] In

---

[1] See Appendix

[2] Thus Stubbs, in the Constitutional Hist., iii, p. 289: "Another abuse which had the result of condemning its agents to perpetual infamy was the extension of the jurisdiction of the high constable of England to cases of high treason, thus depriving the accused of the benefit of trial by jury and placing their acquittal or condemnation in the hands of a political official. When Edward the Fourth, early in his reign, gave the office of constable to Tiptoft he invested him with unparalleled powers. . . ." The learned historian had only read the false recital in the patent of 1467. The fact that the grant is recited to have been made—"statutis, ordinationibus, actibus et restrictionibus in contrarium editis, ceterisque contrariis non obstantibus quibuscunque"—is apparently regarded as an act of shameless

1468 Tiptoft was again appointed constable:[1] his patent of appointment is quite normally framed.

About two years later the famous judge Littleton, sitting in court, uttered the following obiter dictum:—[2]

In an appeal sued against a lord of the realm he shall not be tried by the peers but like an ordinary person, and so it was decided before Fort in an appeal sued against lord Grey of Codnor, father of the present lord Grey, but on an indictment of felony or treason which is at the king's suit he shall be [tried by his peers], for the statute of Magna Charta provides—*nec super eum ibimus nec super eum mittemus*, by which is intended the suit of the king,[3] and when a lord is indicted [as aforesaid] the case shall be brought into parliament, and there the seneschal of England shall put him to reply, and he shall plead that he is not guilty, and he shall be tried by his peers, etc., and then the lords spiritual who cannot consent to the death of a man shall appoint a procurator in the parliament, etc., and then the steward must ask first the junior lord present if he is guilty, and so on separately all the lords who are there, and then, etc.

Littleton clearly took the view that a peer indicted of treason or felony could only be tried in parliament. This does not in any way exclude the jurisdiction of the court of chivalry, because proceedings in that court were not founded upon indictment. Indeed, the ordinary courts had for some time so far recognised the constable's court as to take judicial notice of its decisions in appeals of treason.[4]

autocracy. This is quite a mistake: the words mean nothing in particular, they are only inserted ex abundante cautela, and are the common-form verbiage of the period. (See the Originalia, 1 Edward IV, passim.) So too of other phrases: to the uninitiated there is a flavour of the court-martial about—"summarie et de plano et sine strepitu et figura judicii." This likewise is common-form. Compare Ord. Privy Council, i, 116.   [1] See Appendix.

[2] Year Book, Easter, 10 Edward IV, no. 17, fol. 6.

[3] Upon this point, most learned judge, you were grievously in error!

[4] Year Book, 37 Henry VI, fol. 20: . . . tiel matire append al constable et mareschal et ils determines ceo par ley civil. . ..
Nedham: A ce que vous dites que nous ne prendrons notice de ley le constable et mareschal ceo n'est issint; car ceo est la ley del terre, et le ley nostre seigneur le roy mes seroit determine devant le constable et mareschal; mais nous prendrons notice de ceo.

In October, 1470, the year of Henry's re-adeption and Edward's flight, Tiptoft earl of Worcester, the Yorkist constable, by that time popularly known and execrated as the butcher of England, was brought to trial, condemned and executed.[1] He received the measure he had meted to others. John de Vere, earl of Oxford (a most suitable person for the business), was appointed constable *pro hac vice*, and Worcester perished by the sentence of a court of chivalry.[2]

Sicome un soit appelle de mort de home, et il dit il appelle m. le home tiel jour et avoit luy devant le constable et mareschal de treason, et que nous combatames ensemble en le champ, et issint fess, et la il luy ferist, et ceo bon justification per nostre ley : ergo nous prendrons notice de ceo ley.

For references in the digests see Fitzherbert, Coron., 23 ; Brooke, Actio sur le Statut, 18 ; Trespass, 197 ; Jurisdiction, 103 ; Appeal, 129 ; Battaille, 15. Also see Year Book, 37 Henry VI, fol. 3.

[1] The date of his death is uncertain. The inquisitions post mortem taken some time after the event give various dates, viz. 24th of October, 14th of October, and die Jovis in festo sancte Luce Evang.

[2] Although we possess no direct evidence precisely to this effect, I think the statement in the text is a necessary inference from such evidence as we do possess. See, for example, Warkworth (Camden Society), p. 13 : "And thenne was taken the erle of Worcetre whiche was arested and areynede before sere Jhon Veere the erle of Oxenforde, sonne and heyre to the foreseide erle of Oxenforde whiche was behedede at the Toure Hille, as before wrytene, and so the erle of Worcetre was juged be suche lawe as he dyde to other menne. . . ." Compare the MS. City Chronicle (Cott. Vitell. A., 16, fol. 130): "And upon Sonday at nyght therle of Worceter was taken, whereof mothe people rejoysed as wel many of theym that knewe hym as other, for he was cruell in doying justice and therefore he was namyd the bowcher of England, and upon the Tuysday aftir cam therle of Oxinford to London with a fair company and was logid at the lord Hastinges place ; and upon the Satirday folowyng was therle of Worceter rayned at Westmynster in the Whyte halle and there endited of treason. And upon the Monday folowyng adjuged to go from thens upon his fete unto the tower hill and there to be heded." Modern writers differ. Ramsay, Lancaster and York, without giving any authority, says he was tried in the court of the constable ; but Nichols, History of Leicestershire, says the earl was tried in the court of the lord high steward. Nichols does not give his authority, and his statement is not worth serious consideration, although other antiquaries have made the same assertion. See, for example, MS. Harleian, 2194, which contains a list of lord high stewards and of the cases tried before them.

A few months later, after the restoration of Edward, the duke of Somerset and the prior of St. John with many others were taken prisoners at Tewkesbury: they were brought before Richard duke of Gloucester as constable of England, and the duke of Norfolk as marshal of England; they were sentenced to death and executed upon a scaffold within the town.[1]

The proceedings in the parliament of 1477 against George duke of Clarence afford us a significant example of the abuse of attainder. Either attainder in this case was unnecessary and therefore improper, or it was resorted to for the purpose of bolstering up the judgment in an irregular trial. I have not discovered any evidence that Clarence was formally indicted, but he appears to have been arrested at Westminster, in the presence of the mayor and aldermen of the city of

---

[1] Arrival of king Edward the Fourth (Camden Soc.), p. 31: "This battayll thus done and atchived and the kyngs grace thus largly shewed, it was so that in the abbey and othar places of the towne were founden Edmond callyd duke of Somerset, the prior of Seint Johns called ser John Longestrother, ser Thomas Tressham, ser Gervaux of Clyfton, knights, squiers and othar notable parsonnes dyvers, whiche all dyvers tymes were browght afore the kyngs brothar the duke of Gloucestar and constable of England, and the duke of Norfolke marshall of England theyr judges; and so were judged to deathe in the mydst of the towne Edmond duke of Somarset and the sayd prior of Seint Johns, with many othar gentils that there were taken, and that of longe tyme had provoked and continuyd the great rebellyon that so long had endured in the land agaynst the kynge and contrye to the wele of the realme."

Waurin, Rolls Series, 39, v, p. 671: Aprez ceste bataille achevee advint que en la ville de Teukesbury furent trouvez Emond appele duc de Sombresset, le prieur de Saint Jehan, sire Thomas de Tresseham, sire Gervais de Cliston, chevalliers et plusieurs autres nobles hommes, lesquelz furent prins et menez devant le duc de Glocestre frere du roy Edouard connestable d'Angleterre, ou la leur fut remoustre et declare leur rebellion et desloyaute que long tempz avoient portee envers leur souverain seigneur; puis ycelle dite remoustrance a eulz faite par le duc, ilz furent emprisonnez jusques a lendemain quon les ramena devant lui et le duc de Norfok, qui estoient commis leurs juges de par le roy, lesquelz, tout bien considere, les condempnerent a estre decapitez comme ilz furent, sur ung eschaffaut, present tout le peuple, la teste sur ung blocq dune dolloire.

London, on a charge of treason made by the king himself in
a verbose and not very dignified speech.[1]　In the ensuing
parliament Clarence was arraigned : the king, according to
the continuator of the Croyland Chronicle, prosecuted in
person: no one ventured to reply but the prisoner.　(This
last seems a somewhat unintelligent observation.)　Certain
persons were brought in by the crown presumably as witnesses, but from their conduct at the trial many thought they
were there to formulate accusations.[2]　Clarence denied the
charges, but the bill of attainder was passed by the lords
and commons and received the royal assent.[3]　The duke of
Buckingham was appointed steward of England to pass
sentence,[4] but execution was for some little time delayed : it
was, to be sure, only seemly that the king should exhibit
some reluctance about putting his own brother to death.
The commons finally paid a visit to the upper house and
requested by their speaker that the matter might be brought
to a conclusion.[5]　Shortly after Clarence was done to death.
The manner of his dying was never made public ; but the
story of the wine-butt has at least the merit of being strictly
contemporary gossip.[6]

In November, 1483, Henry duke of Buckingham was
executed for high treason against Richard the Third.　No
account of his trial appears to be extant ; but I think there
can be little reasonable doubt that he was tried and condemned in a court of chivalry[7] by Sir Ralph Ashton, who was
appointed constable in consequence of the duke's rebellion.

[1] Chron. Croyland, ed. Bohn, p. 479.
[2] Ibid.
[3] Rot. Parl., vol. vi, pp. 193–5.
[4] Patent Roll, 17 Ed. IV, pt. 2, m. 19.　See Appendix.
[5] Chron. Croyland, ed. Bohn, p. 480.
[6] Mentioned by Fabyan, ed. 1811, p. 666.
" Drowned in Malvesay." Chronicles of London, ed. Kingsford,
p. 188.
[7] He was attainted by the next parliament.　The escheators'
inquisitions are in the following form : Inquisitio capta apud
Chelmesford in comitatu Essex xviij die Marcii anno regni regis
Ricardi tercii primo coram . . . qui dicunt super sacramentum
suum quod Henricus dux Bukk fuit seisitus de . . . que quidem
maneria dominia et hundreda cum membris et pertinentiis suis

After the accession of Henry the Seventh a large number of persons were at various times attainted in parliament. Amongst these was lord Fitz-Walter, who was attainted in the parliament of 1495–6. He was previously indicted at the Berkshire sessions before Sir William Hody (chief baron of the Exchequer) and others in the Easter term of 1495, and on this indictment orders were issued for his arrest.[1]

In the year 1497 occurred the Cornish rising. The insurgents, under the command of James Touchet, lord Audeley, marched as far as Blackheath, where they encamped. Soon after, the royal army forced a general engagement and totally defeated them. Lord Audeley was taken prisoner, brought to London, and there arraigned in a court of chivalry before special commissioners (not peers), appointed *pro hac vice* to

domino regi pertinent eo quod idem nuper dux per quendam actum edictum versus eundem nuper ducem in parliamento domini regis apud Westmonasterium xxiij die Januarii anno regni sui primo tento de alta prodicione auctoritate ejusdem parliamenti attinctus existit. (Inquisitio post mortem Virtute Officii, Richard III, Chancery, no. 6; see also ibid., nos. 15, 17.)

Polydore Vergil gives the following account of Buckingham's betrayal and death :—

To these men seking owt all thinges narrowly, Humfrey Bannister, whether for feare or money yt is soom dowt, betrayed his guest Henry the duke, who brought him forthwith to Salsbury unto king Richard. The duke was dilygently examynyd and what he knew uppon demand he tould without torture, hopynge because he frely confessyd that therefor he showld have lybertie to speake with king Richerd, which he most sore desyryd ; but after he had confessyd thoffence he was beheadyd. (Cam. Soc., p. 201.)

[1] Controlment Roll, 10 Henry VII, m. 17d., Easter Term. (Berks. and Norfolk.) Johannes Ratclyff Fitzwater de Attilbourgh in comitatu Norfolk miles, alias dictus Johannes Ratclyff de Attilbourgh de Fitzwater nuper de Attilbourgh in comitatu Norfolk miles, alias dictus Johannes Ratclyff de Attilbourgh in comitatu Norfolk captus octavo Trinitatis pro quibusdam prodicionibus et feloniis personam domini regis tangentibus unde in dicto comitatu Berk indictatus est patet —— per session. comitatus Berk tent. coram Willelmo Hody milite et aliis. Anno regni regis Henrici Septimi decimo apud Grauntpount juxta Oxon.

Ibid. (Berks and Norfolk.) Johannes Ratclyff . . . [as above] . . . captus octavo Trinitatis pro quibusdam prodicionibus et feloniis personam domini regis tangentibus unde in dicto comitatu Berk indictatus —— per judicium session. supradict.

represent the constable and marshal of England.[1] By this court lord Audeley was sentenced to death. He is said to have been led to execution arrayed in a paper suit painted with his arms reversed.[2] An Act of Attainder and Forfeiture was subsequently passed in the parliament of 1503 on lord Audeley and a large number of other persons.[3]

A constitutional historian, writing immediately after Audeley's death, would have found it hard to justify the assertion that a peer of the realm had the right of being tried by his peers. In theory, no doubt, it was so: in practice no peer had for many years past enjoyed this privilege. If parliament was sitting he had no judgment at all, unless the purely ministerial sentence pronounced by the lord high steward could be so described. If parliament was not sitting a peer could be tried by the court of chivalry: and, though it was the usual custom for a peer to act as lord high constable at the trial of a peer, exceptions had occurred. The spiritual peers were in some respects more protected at this time than temporal peers, for the pope had never recognised the right of laymen to sentence to death and execute a bishop, and to do so would still have been a dangerous experiment.

Nevertheless there existed one definite statutory limitation to the *ex-officio*[4] jurisdiction of the lord high constable, a limitation which perhaps had never been plainly and deliberately overstepped. Unless it could be said that the question at issue was one of war within the realm, on no construction of the statute of Richard the Second was it possible to maintain that a court of chivalry had any *ex-officio*[4] jurisdiction to

---

[1] Appendix.

[2] The City Chronicle (MS. Cott. Vitell. A., 16, fol. 165) contains the following entry: "And the same day was the lord Audley had from the Tower to Westminster, the axe of the Tower borne before hym. And there in the White Hall areyned and adjuged, and that afternone drawen from Westminster unto Newgate and there remayned all nyght. And upon Weddensday in the mornyng about ix of the clok drawen from the said gaole of Newgate unto the Tower hill with a cote armour upon hym of paper all to torne and there his hede stryken of."

[3] Rot. Parl., vol. vi, p. 544.

[4] "Ex-officio" is used here in contradistinction to "ad instantiam partis." See Appendix.

try the case. On the other hand, in cases of war within the realm, the statute may be read as declaring that such matters ought to be tried by the constable, and cannot be determined or discussed at common law. The commons, it is true, had at least on one occasion contended for a different construction, but without success.

In 1499 it was deemed advisable to have the earl of Warwick tried and executed. Having been for some time a close prisoner in the Tower of London, he could not decently be accused of any act of war, nor was there any other pretext on which the constable's jurisdiction could be safely founded. Warwick was not tried in the constable's court but before a very different tribunal, namely a court now known as the court of the lord high steward of England. The institution of this court merits special investigation : it is, I think, quite the most interesting fraud in the whole legal history of England.

APPENDIX TO CHAPTER XI

Coram Rege Roll, 18 *Edward II, Hilary, pt.* 2, *m.* 34

Dominus rex mandavit dilecto et fideli suo Johanni de Westone nuper marescallo hospicii sui breve suum in hec verba.—Edwardus Dei gratia rex Anglie dominus Hibernie et dux Aquitanie dilecto et fideli suo Johanni de Westone nuper senescallo hospicii salutem. Quia quibusdam certis de causis certiorari volumus super recordo et processu judicii super Rogerum Damory nuper inimicum et rebellem nostrum per vos ut dicitur pronunciati, Vobis mandamus quod recordum et processum judicii predicti cum omnibus ea tangentibus nobis sub sigillo vestro distincte et aperte mittatis et hoc breve, Ita quod ea habeamus in cancellaria nostra citra festum nativitatis beate Marie virginis proximo futurum ubicunque tunc fuerit, et hoc nullatenus omittatis. Teste me-ipso apud Westmonasterium xix die Augusti anno regni nostri decimo octavo.

Tenor judicii super Rogerum Damory redditi patet in sequenti.

Placita exercitus domini regis apud Tuttebiri coram
Fulcone filio Warini constabulario, Johanne de Westone
marescallo et Galfrido Lescrop, die sabbati proxima post
festum sancti Gregorii Pape anno regni regis Edwardi
filii regis Edwardi quinto decimo.

Pur ceo qe vous Roger Damory homme lige nostre seignour le roy countre vostre fay homage et ligeance faucement
et traitrousement alastes en Gales ove baner desplye, chastels
et villes robastes et preiastes et preistes sa ville et soun chastels de Gloucestre et ylumastes sa ville de Briggenorth et
illeok tuastes ses gentz et robastes ses liges gentz et prey-
astes le pays par my la terre ou vous estes aleez a feer de
gwerre en estruant soun pople taunqe vous venistes al chastel
nostre seignour le roi a Tykehulle et ileoqes asigeastes le dit
chastel ove baner desplie come enemy nostre seignour le roi
et du realme et la tuastes et mauveiastes ses liges gentz et de
illeoqes alastes en la cumpaignye des traytours atteyntz
Thomas jadys counte de Lancastre et Umfrey jadys counte
de Hereford tauntqe a Burton sour Trente et. . . . Et si vous
Roger ussez eou a ceo la force et le power—[les quels tray-
sons arsons homicides et roberies chyvaches ove baner des-
plye] etc. sount notoires a countes barouns et a altres gentz
petiz et grauntz de soen realme agarde nostre seignour le roi
de soun real power et recorde, par quei ceste court agarde qe
pur la traysoun soiez traynez et pur les homicides arsons et
roberies pendutz : mes Roger pur ceo qe nostre seignour le
roy vous ad en temps moult amez et fuistes de sa meygne et
privez de lui et avez sa nyece esposee nostre dit seignour le
roi de sa grace et de sa realte met en respit execucioun de cel
jugement a sa volunte.

Rotulus Viagii, I-II *Henry IV*, *m.* 19 (*Patent Roll*,
No. 388)

Rex carissimo consanguineo suo Thome comiti Arundell
ac carissimo fratri suo Thome Beaufort salutem.   Sciatis
quod cum constabularius et marescallus nostri Anglie in
obsequiis nostris partibus borealibus adeo occupati existant
quod ad ea que ad hujusmodi officia constabularii et mares-

calli Anglie pertinent exercendum ad presens vacare non possunt, nos de fidelitate circumspectione et industria vestris plenius confidentes assignavimus vos prefate comes ad ea omnia et singula que ad dictum officium constabularii, vosque prefate Thoma Beaufort ad ea omnia et singula que ad dictum officium marescalli Anglie pertinent loco ipsorum constabularii et marescalli nostrorum Anglie in absencia sua faciendum et exercendum secundum legem et consuetudinem regni nostri Anglie et curie nostre militaris. Et ideo vobis mandamus quod circa premissa diligenter intendatis et ea faciatis et exequamini in forma predicta. Damus autem universis et singulis vicecomitibus majoribus ballivis constabulariis ministris et aliis fidelibus et subditis suis tam infra libertates quam extra tenore presencium firmiter in mandatis quod vobis in executione premissorum intendentes sint consulentes et auxiliantes ac vestris mandatis obedientes prout decet. In cujus etc. quamdiu nobis placuerit duraturas. Teste rege apud Bisshoppesthorpe juxta Ebor. vj die Junii. Per ipsum regem.

Rotulus Viagii, 1–11 *Henry IV, m.* 19 (*Patent Roll, No.* 388)

Rex dilectis et fidelibus suis Johanni Stanley senescallo hospicii sui, Thome comiti Arundell, Ricardo comiti Warrwici, Willelmo Gascoigne, Thome Beaufort, Willelmo domino de Ros, Ricardo domino de Grey, Willelmo domino de Wylughby, Reginaldo de Grey domino de Ruthyn, Phillippo domino de Darcy, Willelmo Fulthorp, Henrico Retford et Johanni Conyers salutem. Sciatis quod assignavimus vos duodecim undecim decem nonem octo septem sex quinque quatuor tres et duos vestrum, quorum alterorum vestrum vos prefati Willelme Gascoigne et Johannes Conyers unum esse volumus, justiciarios nostros ad inquirendum per sacramentum proborum et legalium hominum tam infra libertates quam extra per quos rei veritas melius sciri poterit de omnimodis proditionibus insurrectionibus rebellionibus et feloniis per quoscunque ligeos nostros infra regnum nostrum Anglie factis sive perpetratis et per quos vel per quemcunque quando qualiter et quomodo et de omnibus et singulis articulis et circumstanciis premissa (sic) qualitercumque convenientibus plenius veritatem et ad easdem prodiciones insurrectiones rebelliones et felonias secundum legem et consuetudinem regni nostri Anglie audiendum et terminandum. Et ideo vobis mandamus quod etc. . . . Teste ut supra [scilicet apud Bisshoppesthorpe juxta Ebor. vj die Junii].

Per ipsum regem.

Proceedings against Richard earl of Cambridge and Henry lord Scrope of Masham for High Treason A.D. 1415

[1] Memorandum quod die Veneris quinto die hujus parliamenti venit communitas ejusdem parliamenti coram domino Johanne duce Bedford custode Anglie ac dominis spiritualibus et temporalibus in parliamento illo existentibus et petiit instanter ibidem et rogavit ut judicia coram commissionariis domini regis nuper apud Suthampton contra Ricardum comitem Cantebr. de Conesburgh in comitatu Ebor. chivaler et Henricum dominum Lescrop de Masham de Faxflete in comitatu Ebor. chivaler et Thomam Gray de Heton in comitatu Northumbr. chivaler de altis proditionibus contra dominum regem et suam regiam majestatem per ipsos perpetratis apud predictam villam Suthampton convictos reddita in instanti parliamento affirmarentur et pro bonis et legalibus judiciis haberentur et tenerentur imperpetuum. Super quo postmodum venerabilis pater Henricus episcopus Wynton cancellarius Anglie recorda et processus, judicia contra proditores predictos nuper apud dictam villam de Suthampton reddita concernentia, et coram domino Thoma duce Clarencie virtute commissionis et brevis regiorum habita, que dominus rex simul cum omnibus et singulis recorda et processus illa tangentibus postea coram eo in cancellaria sua venire fecit, in parliamentum predictum de mandato dicti custodis detulit, que sequntur in hec verba.—Dominus rex mandavit carissimo fratri suo Thome duci Clarencie has literas suas patentes que sequntur in hec verba.—Henricus Dei gratia rex Anglie et Francie et dominus Hibernie carissimo fratri suo Thome duci

[1] In margin : Affirmacion de les juggements donez a Suthampton v. Richard count de Cantebrigg et autres.

Clarencie salutem. Sciatis quod nos de fidelitate industria et circumspectione vestris plenius confidentes constituimus vos locum nostrum et vicem gerentem ad audiendum recorda et processus coram dilectis et fidelibus nostris Johanne comite Marescallo et sociis suis justiciariis nostris ad omnimodas proditiones felonias conspirationes et confederationes in comitatu Suthampton audiendum et terminandum assignatis facta, et ad judicium versus Ricardum comitem Cantebrigg de Conesburgh in comitatu Ebor. chivaler et Henricum dominum Lescrop de Masham de Faxflete in comitatu Ebor. chivaler juxta id quod vobis per recorda et processus predicta constare poterit, vocatis vobis paribus predictorum comitis et Henrici, per vestrum et eorumdem parium communem assensum hac instanti die Lune reddendum et ad executionem ejusdem judicii finaliter procedendum; dantes vobis et concedentes plenam tenore presentium potestatem auctoritatem et mandatum speciale ad omnia et singula nomine nostro ibidem faciendum exercendum et concedendum que nos faceremus seu facere possemus si ibidem personaliter interessemus, promittentes nos ratum gratum et firmum habituros quicquid per vos nomine nostro factum gestum sive concessum fuerit in premissis vel aliquo premissorum. Damus autem prefatis justiciariis ac aliis quorum interest tenore presentium firmiter in mandatis quod vobis in premissis in forma predicta faciendis et exequendis intendentes sint consulentes et auxiliantes prout decet. Mandavimus insuper prefato comiti Marescallo et sociis suis predictis quod recorda et processus predicta cum omnibus ea tangentibus habeant coram vobis ad diem supradictum. In cujus rei testimonium has literas nostras fieri fecimus patentes. Teste me-ipso apud Suthampton quinto die Augusti anno regni nostri tertio. Super quo instanter dominus rex mandavit prefatis Johanni comiti Marescallo et sociis suis justiciariis suis predictis in commissione predicta contentis breve suum clausum de habendo coram prefato duce Clarencie recorda et processus predicta cum omnibus ea tangentibus in dictis literis domini regis patentibus specificata quod quidem breve sequitur in hec verba. [Here follows the writ to the commissioners informing them of the above and directing them accordingly. Also letters patent dated at

Porchester the 31st of July, 1415, appointing the commissioners and ordering the sheriff of Southampton to summon a jury for Friday, the 2nd of August.[1]] Quarum literarum domini regis patentium pretextu preceptum fuit vicecomiti dicti comitatus Suthampton quod non omittet propter aliquam libertatem in balliva sua quin venire faceret coram prefatis justiciariis [etc.] . . . Unde inter alias inquisitiones inquisitio subsequens per sacramentum xij juratorum comitatus predicti capta est que sequitur in hec verba. *Suthampton.* Inquisitio capta apud villam Suthampton coram prefatis justiciariis dicto die Veneris anno regni dicti domini regis nunc tertio per sacramentum Johannis Chonde, Johannis Lok, Johannis Steer, Johannis Veel, Roberti Upham, Laurentii Hamelyn, Johannis Welere Fyssh, Johannis Colyn, Johannis Penyton, Walteri Hore, Johannis Halle, et Johannis Snell qui dicunt per sacramentum suum quod Ricardus comes Cantebrigg . . . et Thomas Gray . . . vicesimo die Julii anno regni regis Henrici quinti post conquestum tertio apud villam Suthampton et in diversis aliis locis infra regnum Anglie falso (et) proditorie conspiraverunt et se invicem confederaverunt . . . [particulars of their treason are given] . . . et quod Henricus Lescrop de Masham . . . fuit consentiens. . . . *Ad* quem diem Veneris coram prefatis justiciariis apud Suthampton predictam predicti Ricardus comes Cantebrigg, Thomas Gray et Henricus Lescrop per Johannem Popham chivaler constabularium turris Suthampton in cujus custodiam perantea ex speciali mandato domini regis commissi fuerunt veniunt ducti, qui instanter super premissis eis impositis seperatim allocuti sunt quid adinde respondere seu se acquietare velint: predicti Ricardus comes Cantebrigg et Thomas Gray dicunt seperatim quod ipsi non possunt dedicere quin ipsi culpabiles sint de omnibus et singulis proditionibus conspirationibus et confederationibus predictis modo et forma prout ipsi superius indictati sunt. Et de hiis omnibus et singulis singillatim se ponunt et submittunt in misericordia et gratia domini regis. Et predictus Henricus

---

[1] In margin: Fait assavoir que les recordes et processes dount en ceste memorandie mencion est fait sont consutz a le dorse de ceste rolle.

Lescrop dicit et cognoscit quod predictus Thomas Gray ei primo de materia predicta narravit . . . et quo ad imaginationem mortis domini regis et fratrum suorum seu aliorum quorumcumque prout ei superius imponitur dicit quod ipse in nullo est inde culpabilis, et cum hoc dicit quod ipse est dominus et unus parium regni Anglie et petit quod ipse per pares suos regni Anglie, prout moris est, trietur et judicetur : super quo quia prefati justiciarii non avisantur ad judicium super dictis Ricardo comite Cantebrigg et Henrico Lescrop ad presens in premissis reddendum iidem Ricardus comes Cantebrigg et Henricus Lescrop remittuntur custodie[1] dicti Johannis Popham constabularii turris predicti salvo custodiendi quousque, etc. [Thomas Gray is then sentenced to death and forfeiture.] *Quibus* quidem recordo et processu virtute dicti brevis dicto duci Clarencie ut premittitur liberatis et per eundem ducem ad ea recipiendum et judicium inde reddendum necnon ad executionem judicii predicti virtute literarum dicti domini regis patentium sibi in hac parte confectarum finaliter procedendum ad tunc admissis, predicti Ricardus comes Cantebrigg et Henricus dominus Lescrop coram dicto duce Clarencie dicto die Lune apud villam Suthampton predictam per dictum Johannem Popham constabularium turris predicti venerunt ad barram ducti. Virtute cujus commissionis idem dux Clarencie instanter vocatis sibi Humfrido duce Gloucestrie fratre suo ac Edwardo duce Eborum per Thomam comitem Dorset[1] nomine et loco ipsius Edwardi ad consentiendum faciendum et judicandum cum dominis predictis in premissis coram ipso rege specialiter constituto et admisso, Edmundo comite March, Johanne comite Huntyndon, Thoma comite Arundel, Johanne comite Marescallo, Thoma comite Dorset, Thoma comite Sarum, Ricardo comite Oxon, Michaele comite Suffolk, Johanne domino de Clifford, Gilberto domino de Talbot, Willielmo domino de Zouche, Johanne domino de Haryndon, Roberto domino de Wylughby, Willielmo domino de Clynton, Johanne

---

[1] An attention mark, possibly contemporary, appears in the margin.

domino de Mautrevers, Hugone domino de Boucer, [   ]¹
domino de Botreaux, dominis et magnatibus regni Anglie et
paribus dictorum Ricardi comitis Cantebrigg et Henrici
domini Lescrop ibidem presentibus et pro viagio domini regis
ultra mare intendentibus, visisque et diligenter examinatis
recordo et processu cognitionum predictorum Ricardi comitis
Cantebrigg et Henrici domini Lescrop ut premittitur necnon
inter eosdem dominos et magnates habita inde matura et cir-
cumspecta deliberatione, Videtur eisdem duci Clarencie et
dominis qd predictus Ricardus comes Cantebrigg . . . et
quid predictus Henricus dominus Lescrop . . . qd ipsi ut
proditores domini regis et regni sui Anglie in premissis censeri debent. *Et sic* ipsi dux Clarencie et domini omnia et
singula eisdem Ricardo comiti Cantebrigg et Henrico domino
Lescrop superius imposita et per ipsos cognita ut altam
ceditionem domino regi et regno suo Anglie dampnabiliter et
nepharie imaginatam conspiratam et confederatam una voce
adjudicant et judicialiter affirmant. Per quod ex assensu et
plena deliberatione omnium dominorum et magnatum predictorum in premissis consideratum est per ipsum ducem
Clarencie ac omnes dominos et magnates predictos quod
iidem Ricardus comes Cantebrigg et Henricus dominus
Lescrop ut proditores domini regis et regni sui Anglie . . .
distrahantur suspendantur et decapitentur, et quod ipsi foris-
faciant omnia bona et catalla terras et tenementa sua. . . .
Quibus quidem recordis et processibus ac aliis premissis
coram ipso custode ac dominis predictis in parliamento ipso
lectis et per eosdem plenius intellectis, videtur curie presentis
parliamenti quod judicia predicta sic lata rite juste et legitime
reddita fuerunt : per quod iidem domini spirituales et temporales judicia illa omnia et singula versus dictos comitem
Cantebrigg, Henricum dominum Lescrop et Thomam Gray
ut premittitur lata et reddita de assensu dicti custodis affir-
marunt fore et esse bona justa et legalia judicia et ea pro
hujusmodi decreverunt et adjudicarunt tunc ibidem. [Then
follows a forfeiture clause.]

(Parliament Roll, 3 Henry V ; printed Rot. Parl., vol. iv,
p. 64.)

¹ A blank space.

The following records are sewn on the dorse of this roll :—

(1) The record of the proceedings before the king's commissioners.

(2) The record of the proceedings before the duke of Clarence.

(3) Writ appointing commissioners, dated 31st July.

(4) Writ to commissioners, dated 1st August.

(5) The panel.

(6) The inquisition.

(7) Writ appointing the duke of Clarence, dated 5th August.

(8) Consequential writ to commissioners of even date.

(9) Writ directing the duke of Clarence to lodge the records in Chancery.

Patent Roll, 1 *Edward IV*, *pt.* 3, *m.* 23. *Originalia Roll*, 1 *Edward IV*, *m.* 99

Pro comite Wygorn. Rex omnibus ad quos etc. salutem. Sciatis quod cum officium constabularii Anglie jam vacat et in manibus nostris existat ac nos de fidelitate probitate et provida circumspectione carissimi consanguinei nostri Johannis comitis Wygorn quam plurimum confidentes concessimus eidem consanguineo nostro officium constabularii Anglie habendum occupandum gerendum et exercendum officium illud in omnibus et singulis que ad idem officium pertinent quamdiu nobis placuerit cum omnibus feodis vadiis et commoditatibus eidem officio ab antiquo debitis et consuetis eo quod expressa mencio de aliis donis sive concessionibus prefato consanguineo nostro per nos perantea factis in presentibus minime facta extitit non obstante. In cujus etc. Teste rege apud Westmonasterium vij die Febuarii. Per ipsum regem oretenus.

Patent Roll, 7 *Edward IV*, *pt.* 1, *m.* 9

Pro Ricardo Wydevyll comite de Ryvers. Rex omnibus ad quos etc. salutem. Sciatis quod cum nos septimo die Febuarii anno regni nostri primo de fidelitate probitate et provida circumspectione carissimi consanguinei nostri Johannis comitis Wygorn plurimus considerantes per literas nostras patentes concesserimus eidem Johanni consanguineo nostro officium constabularii Anglie habendum occupandum gerendum et exercendum officium illud in omnibus et singulis que ad idem officium pertinerent quamdiu nobis placeret cum omnimodis feodis vadiis et commoditatibus eidem officio ab antiquo debitis et consuetis eo quod expressa mencio de aliis donis et concessionibus prefato consanguineo per nos perantea factis in literis predictis minime facta extitit non obstante, et ulterius de certa scientia nostra ac certis probabilibus et urgentibus causis nos in ea parte moventibus eidem consanguineo nostro plenam potestatem et auctoritatem dederimus et commiserimus ad cognoscendum et procedendum in omnibus et singulis causis et negotiis de et super crimine lese majestatis seu ipsius occasione ceterisque causis quibuscumque per prefatum comitem ut constabularium Anglie seu coram eo ex officio seu ad instantiam partis qualitercumque motis movendis seu pendentibus que in curia constabularii Anglie ab antiquo videlicet tempore domini Willelmi conquestoris quondam regis Anglie progenitoris nostri seu aliquo tempore citra tractari audiri examinari et decidi consueverunt aut de jure debuerunt seu deberent causasque et negotia predicta cum omnibus et singulis suis emergentibus incidentibus et connexis audiendum examinandum et fine debito terminandum etiam summarie et de plano sine strepitu et figura judicii sola facti veritate inspecta ac etiam manu regia si opportunum visum foret eidem Johanni consanguineo nostro vices nostras appellatione remota ex mero motu et certa scientia nostra predicta similiter commiserimus plenariam potestatem cum cujuslibet pene multe et ulterius cohercionis legittimeque executionis rerum que in ea parte decerneret facultate ceteraque omnia et singula que ad officium constabularii Anglie pertinerent faciendi exercendi et exequendi statutis ordinationibus actibus et restrictionibus in contrarium editis ceterisque contrariis non obstantibus quibuscunque prout in literis predictis plenius continetur. Jamque idem comes in voluntate existit literas nostras predictas nobis in cancellariam nostram restituere ibidem cancellandas ad intentionem quod nos officium predictum predilecto et fidelissimo nobis Ricardo Widevill comiti de Ryvers domino de Grafton et de la Mote patri preclarissime consortis nostre regine in forma sequenti habendum concedere dignaremus: nos nedum premissa verum etiam internam affectionem quam idem comes de Ryvers penes personam nostram habet et gerit intime considerantes ac pro eo quod idem comes Wygorn literas nostras predictas nobis in cancellariam nostram predictam ad intentionem predictam restituit cancellandas de fidelitate strenuitate probitate et circumspectione provida prefati comitis de Ryvers plurimus confidentes de gratia nostra speciali concessimus eidem comiti de Ryvers dictum officium constabularii Anglie habendum occupandum gerendum et exercendum officium illud per se vel per sufficientes deputatos suos sive sufficientem deputatum suum pro termino vite ipsius comitis de Ryvers in omnibus et singulis que ad idem officium pertinent percipiendo annuatim in et pro officio predicto ducentas libras ad receptam scaccarii nostri per manus thesaurarii et camerariorum nostrorum ibidem pro tempore existentium ad terminos sancti Michaelis archangeli et Pasche per equales portiones unacum omnimodis aliis proficuis commoditatibus et emolumentis quibuscumque officio predicto qualitercumque pertinentibus et ab antiquo debitis et consuetis, et ulterius de uberiori gratia nostra ac ex certa scientia nostra ac certis probabilibus et urgentibus causis nos in hac parte moventibus eidem comiti de Ryvers plenam potestatem et auctoritatem damus et committimus ad cognoscendum et procedendum in omnibus et singulis causis et negotiis de et super crimine lese majestatis seu ipsius occasione ceterisque causis quibuscumque per prefatum comitem de Ryvers ut constabularium Anglie seu coram eo ex officio seu ad instantiam partis qualitercumque motis movendis seu pendentibus que in curia constabularii Anglie ab antiquo videlicet tempore dicti domini Willelmi conquestoris progenitoris nostri seu aliquo tempore citra tractari audiri examinari et decidi consueverunt aut de jure debuerunt seu debent causasque et negotia predicta cum omnibus et singulis emergentibus incidentibus et connexis audiendum examinandum et fine debito terminandum etiam summarie et de plano sine strepitu et figura judicii sola facte (sic) veritate inspecta ac etiam manu regia si opportunum visum fuerit eidem comiti de Ryvers vices nostras appellatione remota, ex mero motu et scientia predicta nostra similiter committimus plenariam potestatem cum cujuslibet pene multe et alterius cohercionis legitime executionisque rerum quas in hac parte decreverit facultate ceteraque omnia que ad officium constabularii Anglie pertinent faciendi exercendi et exequendi aliquibus statutis actibus ordinationibus et restrictionibus in contrarium factis ordinatis editis seu provisis aut aliqua alia re causa vel materia quacumque non obstantibus : et insuper quamquam idem comes de Ryvers adhuc superstes sit ac dictum officium habeat et occupet ut est justum nos tamen certis considerationibus nos specialiter moventibus de gratia nostra speciali concessimus predilecto et fideli nostro Antonio Widevill domino de Scales et de Nusell filio prefati comitis de Ryvers ac fratri ejusdem consortis nostre regine dictum officium constabularii Anglie habendum occupandum gerendum et exercendum officium illud per se vel per sufficientes deputatos suos sive sufficientem deputatum suum pro termino vite ejusdem Antonii in omnibus et singulis que ad idem officium pertinent immediate post mortem sive decessum prefati comitis de Ryvers vel quamcito officium illud quacunque de causa in proximo vacare contingat percipiendo annuatim in et pro officio illo ducentas libras ad dictam receptam scaccarii nostri per manus thesaurarii et camerariorum nostrorum predictorum ibidem pro tempore existentium ad terminos predictos per equales portiones unacum omnimodis aliis proficuis commoditatibus et emolumentis quibuscumque officio predicto qualitercumque pertinentibus et ab antiquo debitis et consuetis eo quod expressa mencio de vero valore annuo officii predicti seu ceterorum premissorum aut alicujus eorundem aut de aliis donis sive concessionibus eisdem comiti de Ryvers et Antonio seu eorum alteri per nos ante hec tempora factis in presentibus minime facta existit aut aliquo statuto actu ordinatione sive provisione in contrarium factis ordinatis sive provisis non obstantibus, et ulterius de habundanti gratia nostra ac ex certa scientia nostra predicta eidem Antonio plenam potestatem et auctoritatem damus et committimus pro nobis et heredibus nostris ad cognoscendum et procedendum immediate post mortem sive decessum prefati comitis de Ryvers vel quamcito officium predictum quacumque de causa in proximo ut predictum est vacare continget in omnibus et singulis causis et negotiis de et super crimine lese majestatis seu ipsius occasione ceterisque causis quibuscumque per prefatum Antonium ut constabularium Anglie seu coram eo ex officio seu ad instantiam partis qualitercumque motis vel movendis seu pendentibus que in curia constabularii Anglie ab antiquo videlicet tempore dicti domini Willelmi conquestoris seu aliquo tempore citra tractari audiri examinari et decidi consueverunt aut de jure debuerunt seu debebunt causasque et negotia predicta cum omnibus et singulis emergentibus incidentibus et connexis audiendum examinandum et fine debito terminandum etiam summarie et de plano sine strepitu et figura judicii sola facti veritate inspecta ac etiam manu regia si opportunum visum fuerit eidem Antonio vices nostras appellatione remota, ex mero motu et scientia nostris predictis similiter committimus plenariam potestatem cum cujuslibet pene et multe et alterius cohercionis legittime executionisque rerum que tunc in hac parte decreverit facultate ceteraque omnia et singula que ad officium constabularii Anglie pertinent faciendi exercendi et exequendi statutis ordinationibus actibus et restrictionibus in contrarium ut predictum est factis ordinatis editis sive provisis non obstantibus : damus autem universis et singulis officiariis et ministris ac fidelibus ligeis et subditis nostris et heredum nostrorum quibuscumque necnon aliis quorum interest in hac parte tenore presentium firmiter in mandatis quod tam eidem comiti de Ryvers quam prefato Antonio post mortem sive decessum ejusdem comitis vel quam cito officium predictum quacumque de causa in proximo ut premittitur vacare continget in executione premissorum intendentes sint assistentes auxiliantes et obedientes in omnibus diligenter. In cujus etc. Teste rege apud Westmonasterium xxiiij die Augusti.

Per breve de privato sigillo[1] et de data predicta, etc.

(Printed Rymer, Foedera O.S., vol. xi, p. 581. Here the words "auctoritate parliamenti" occur after " de data predicta." No such words occur on the roll.)

[1] No. 2196.

Patent Roll, 10 *Edward IV, m.* 12

Pro Johanne comite Wygornie. Rex omnibus ad quos etc. salutem. Sciatis quod nos considerantes bona et laudabilia servitia que dilectus consanguineus noster Johannes comes Wygornie nobis ante hec tempora impendit ordinamus et constituimus ipsum Johannem constabularium nostrum Anglie ac officium constabularii nostri Anglie eidem Johanni damus et concedimus per presentes habendum occupandum et exercendum officium illud per se vel suum sufficientem deputatum pro termino vite sue adeo plene et integre prout ipse Johannes aut aliquis alius ante hec tempora habuit exercuit seu occupavit percipiendo et recipiendo de nobis et heredibus nostris omnia vadia feoda regarda et proficua officio illi debita et consueta ad receptam scaccarii nostri per manus thesaurarii et camerariorum ejusdem scaccarii pro tempore existentium ad festa Pasche et sancti Michaelis Archangeli annuatim durante vita sua equis portionibus: dantes et concedentes eidem Johanni plenam potestatem et auctoritatem ad faciendum exercendum et exequendum per se vel suum sufficientem deputatum omne id quod ad officium predictum pertinet: damus autem omnibus et singulis vicecomitibus constabulariis ballivis et omnibus aliis officiariis et ministris nostris [firmiter in mandatis] ut eidem Johanni et deputato suo in exequendo officium predictum sint obedientes auxiliantes assistentes et confortantes in omnibus prout decet aliquo statuto actu ordinatione seu restrictione ante hec tempora edita facta seu provisa in aliquo non obstante. In cujus etc. Teste rege apud Stamford xiiij die Marcii.

Per ipsum regem etc. et de data etc.

Patent Roll, 17 *Edward IV, pt.* 2, *m.* 19

Rex carissimo consanguineo suo Henrico duci Bukingham salutem. Sciatis quod cum Georgius nuper dux Clarencie, per nomen Georgii ducis Clarencie, de alta proditione per ipsum erga personam nostram regiam facta et perpetrata auctoritate presentis parliamenti nostri convictus sit et attinctus; ac nos considerantes quod justicia est virtus excellens Altissimo multipliciter complacens per quam regna prosperantur reges et principes regnant et gubernant omne bonum regimen policia et bonum publicum manutenentur et supportantur, quam virtutem ad Dei complacenciam pre aliqua carnali affectione sequi et ea uti intendimus ut debemus, multoque magis pro eo quod vinculo consciencie nostre et per solempne juramentum erga Deum sub pena perpetue damnationis primo pro securitate persone nostre regie et exitus nostri secundarie pro tranquilitate et defensione ecclesie Xti infra regnum nostrum Anglie et tercio pro bono publico pace et tranquilitate regni nostri predicti ac dominorum et nobilium et tocius communitatis ejusdem cujuscumque gradus et condicionis existant necnon in evitacionem effusionis sanguinis Xtiani prospicere constringimur, licet propinquitas sanguinis et internus et teneris amor quem ad prefatum Georgium in teneri etate sua habuimus et gerebamus nos ad contrarium naturaliter movent et exhortant; hinc est quod pro eo quod officium senescalli Anglie cujus presencia pro consideracione executionis judicii fiendi in hac parte requiritur ut accepimus jam vacat, ac nos de fidelitate provida circumspectione et industria vestris plenius confidentes ordinamus et constituimus vos senescallum Anglie ad officium illud ex causa predicta cum omnibus eidem officio debite pertinentibus hac vice gerendum occupandum et exercendum, dantes et concedentes vobis tenore presentium plenam [et] sufficientem potestatem et auctoritatem ac mandatum speciale ad ea omnia et singula que ad officium senescalli Anglie in hac parte pertinent et requiruntur hac vice ex causa predicta faciendum exercendum et exequendum. Et ideo vobis mandamus quod circa officium predictum diligenter intendatis et illud faciatis et exequamini in forma predicta; damus autem universis et singulis quorum interest in hac parte tenore presentium firmiter in mandatis quod vobis in executione officii predicti intendentes sint consulentes faventes auxiliantes et obedientes in omnibus diligenter. In cujus etc. Date in parliamento nostro apud Westmonasterium vij die Febuarii.

Per ipsum regem et de data predicta etc.

Patent Roll, 12 *Henry* VII, *pt.* 2, *m.* 4 (24)

Rex dilecto et fideli suo Johanni Dynham de Dynham militi thesaurario nostro Anglie ac dilectis sibi Johanni Dygby militi nostro marescallo, Willelmo Vampage militi et Roberto Rydon consilii nostri clerico salutem. Cum jam pridem Jacobus Audeley nuper dominus Jacobus Audeley de Audeley miles aggregatis sibi quampluribus de subditis nostris comitatuum nostrorum Cornubie et Devonie aliarumque parcium hujus regni nostri Anglie in ingenti numero proditorie congregati timorem Dei offensamque nostre regie majestatis postponentes nostri omniumque et singulorum [nobilium] prodicionem aliorumque fidelium subditorum nostrorum destructionem ac totius regni nostri extremam subversionem falso et proditorie machinantes et intendentes et ad suorum hujusmodi nephandissimum propositum et execrabilem intencionem perimplendum bellicis et invasionis armis induti guerram contra nos pleno campo levatis et extensis velis inierunt pugnamque et bellum letale proditorie intulerunt in nostrum maximum periculum ac lesionem majestatis et dignitatis corone nostre regie que nolumus sicuti nec debemus relinquere impunita: hinc est quod nos de fidelitatibus industriis et providis circumspectionibus vestris quamplurimum confidentes vos nostros veros et indubitatos commissarios ad tractandum expediendum et exequendum ea omnia et singula que ad officium constabularii et marescalli Anglie pertinent in hac parte facienda assignamus facimus constituimus et deputamus per presentes dantes et concedentes vobis plenam tenore presentium potestatem et auctoritatem ac mandatum speciale ad ipsum Jacobum Audeley coram vobis ad certos dies et loca quos ad hoc provideritis et ubi magis expediens videritis evocandum et venire faciendum ac ipsum de et super feloniis criminibus et delictis antedictis examinandum et responderi (sic) faciendum et compellendum ac quoscunque testes et probaciones requisitas et necessarias in hac parte producendum audiendum et recipiendum et admittendum ac diligenter examinandum ac ad veritatem in ea parte dicendum penis et multis ac aliis viis modis et mediis licitis astringendum et compellendum veritate computata ad judi-

cium secundum leges et consuetudines coram constabulario
et marescallo hactenus usitatas sine strepitu et figura judicii
sola rei veritate inspecta procedendum audiendum et terminandum ipsumque Jacobum ad penas mortis et membrorum
seu alias penas et puniciones prout opus et vobis visum fuerit
adjudicandum sentenciandum et condempnandum et debite
executionem demandandum ceteraque faciendum et perimplendum que in premissis seu circa ea necessaria fuerint seu
quomodolibet opportuna. Et ideo etc. Damus autem etc.
Teste rege apud Westmonasterium.

Per ipsum regem et de data predicta etc.

CHAPTER XII

THE INSTITUTION OF THE COURT OF THE LORD HIGH STEWARD

IF our ancient law reports, the Year Books, were to be implicitly relied upon, the first case tried before the court of the lord high steward occurred early in the year 1400. I fear even our most modern reports do not, scientifically speaking, afford first-rate evidence of either the facts or the law set forth in them.[1] However, the mediæval case which we are going to discuss is something more than unreliable: it is, as I shall endeavour to demonstrate, an absolute forgery. The following is a substantially verbatim translation :—[2]

The First Year of Henry the Fourth

Crown
How a lord
should be tried
by his peers

The earl of H. was indicted of high treason before the mayor and justices, in that he with other persons agreed to make a mumming on the night of the Epiphany, in which they agreed to kill the king then being at Windsor. And then the king made commission to the earl of D., reciting that the G. (lou G.) the earl of H. was indicted of high treason by him done against his person, and that he wished right to be done ; and, because the office of steward of England was then void, he granted that office to the said earl of D. to do right to the said earl of H., commanding by virtue of the commission all lords to be attendant on him ; and commanding also, by virtue of the commission, the constable of the Tower to attend upon him and convey the prisoner S. the earl of H. before the said earl of D.,

---

[1] That eminent body, the Incorporated Council of Law Reporting, is hardly likely to agree with this statement ; but, to persons not biassed by a legal training, it will be perfectly obvious that each judge ought at least to revise and sign the proofs of his reported cases. There is no such rule in force.

[2] See appendix for a transcript of this case collated from the various editions of the Year Books.

on such day as should be thereto assigned. And thereupon, on a certain day, the said earl of D. sat in the hall of Westminster under a cloth of estate by himself apart. And the earl of Westmoreland, and all other earls and lords there, sat by a great space from him, but not on the same bench but on other forms downward in the said hall. And all the justices and barons of the exchequer sat in the midst round a table between the said lords. And then three oyez were solemnly made by the crier, and the said commission was read. And then the justices delivered the indictment to the said seneschal, who delivered it to the clerk of the crown, who read it to the said earl of H., who confessed it; whereupon Hill, one of the king's serjeants, prayed that the said lord steward would give judgment, upon which he rehearsed the said matter, and then gave judgment that he should go to the Tower of London, and from there that he should be drawn to the gallows, and let down again still living, and that then [his entrails should be drawn out of his body and burnt, and that] he should be beheaded and quartered, and so may God have mercy on his soul. And all the justices said that, if the said Earl would have denied the treason, then the steward should demand of each lord separately and openly [when they gave their verdict] what he thought on his conscience, and he should begin first with the junior lord. And if the greater number should say guilty then the judgment shall be given as above. And no lord shall be sworn upon that, etc.

The various editions of the Year Books all agree in giving only the initials instead of the name of the earl tried, but the date and the reference to the mumming prevent any possibility of doubt as to the person indicated. The report must refer to John Holand, earl of Huntingdon. In the same way the initial given for the earl who was appointed steward of England can only stand for Edward earl of Devon.

The affair in question is commonly known as the earl of Kent's rebellion. There were altogether four earls engaged in the conspiracy, namely Kent, Huntingdon, Salisbury and Rutland.[1] An invitation for a tournament to be held at Windsor on the feast of the Epiphany seemed to offer the

[1] One of the chief conspirators was lord Despencer who had recently been deprived of his earldom of Gloucester. Rutland's share in the plot is a controverted question which cannot be dealt with here.

2 E

necessary facilities for a coup de main. Armed men were to be introduced into the castle concealed in carts laden with materials for the jousts.[1] The conspiracy appears to have been matured on or about the 6th of December. On the 4th of January Rutland is said to have revealed the plot to his father, the duke of York, who instantly informed the king at Windsor. Henry took horse the same evening and, accompanied by his sons and one or two attendants, spurred to London. On the 5th of January, writs were issued for the arrest of Kent, Huntingdon and the other rebels, and the seizure of their property.[2] On the 6th, a special mandate was despatched to Calais;[3] and on the same day Henry's military preparations were so far completed that he was able to march out of London at the head of an army mustering about 20,000 men.

Meanwhile the rebels had succeeded in capturing Windsor town and castle, but they had searched vainly for the king. It was, however, too late to draw back: they made the best of a desperate undertaking and collected what forces they

[1] For a general account of this conspiracy see Wylie, History of Henry IV, vol. i; and for an account of Huntingdon's share in it see Dict. Nat. Biog., s.v. Holand.

[2] Rex vicecomitibus Londonie salutem. Quibusdam arduis et urgentibus causis nos specialiter moventibus ac personam nostram et regnum nostrum Anglie intime tangentibus, vobis in fide et ligeantia quibus nobis tenemini et sub forisfactura omnium que nobis forisfacere poteritis precipimus et districtius quo possumus injungimus et mandamus quod Thomam comitem Kantie et Johannem comitem Huntingdonie ac quoscumque alios in comitiva sua existentes tanquam proditores nostros et regni nostri ubicumque inveniri poterunt in balliva vestra tam infra libertates quam extra, assumpto vobiscum si necesse fuerit posse ballive vestre predicte, sine dilatione arestari et capi et eos salvo et secure custodiri, ac omnia terras tenementa bona et catalla ipsorum comitum in dicta balliva vestra in manus nostras capi et seiziri et ea salvo et secure similiter custodiri faciatis, quousque aliter in hac parte duxerimus demandandum. . . . Teste rege apud Westm. v die Januarii. Per ipsum regem.

Consimilia brevia diriguntur singulis vicecomitibus per Angliam, ac vicecomiti Lancastrie. (Close Roll, 1 Henry IV, pt. 1, m. 22d.)

[3] Close Roll, 1 Henry IV, pt. 1, m. 23. (Printed by Rymer, Foedera O.S., viii, p. 120.)

could. Their first brush with the enemy took place near Maidenhead, when they effected a successful retreat in the face of superior numbers. The retreat continued as far as Cirencester, which was reached on January 7th. Kent, Salisbury and some others took up their quarters in the town; their disheartened men encamped outside. By the following morning the rebellion had become a complete fiasco; the rebel army had melted away like snow in summer; its leaders were prisoners in the abbey of the Austin Canons. It so happened that Kent and Salisbury never left Cirencester alive. A panic occurred in the town soon after their capture; a mob overpowered authority; the two earls were haled from prison and summarily beheaded in open street.[1]

The earl of Huntingdon took no part in this disastrous affair. A French account, it is true, has it that the earl was at Cirencester with the others, but escaped from a window in the darkness: this is certainly untrue.[2] Huntingdon, in fact, had been detailed to watch the progress of events in London; and, as soon as he realised that the plot had failed, he endeavoured to escape down the Thames and make for France. He embarked at Billingsgate with his retinue in a barge and a small boat, taking with him a considerable quantity of silver plate, jewels and other valuables. Unfavourable winds drove him on to the Essex shore. He first sought the friendly shelter of Hadleigh castle; then tried once more to make headway down the estuary, but escape by water was out of the question. He appears to have landed again at Leigh, in the hundred of Rochford, and was soon after

---

[1] A large amount of unpublished material exists for a history of this rebellion. See, for example, Controlment Roll, 1 Henry IV, m. 7 (Gloucester); Memoranda Roll K.R., 2 Henry IV., Hil. Adhuc. Recorda, m. 24, etc.; ibid., 3 Henry IV, Hil. Adhuc. Recorda, mm. 23-34; Memoranda Roll L.T.R., 3 Henry IV, Pasch. Adhuc. Recorda, m. 30, etc.

[2] The French version is given (inter alios) by Waurin, Rolls Series, 39, ii; the Chronique de la Traison et Mort de Richard II, Eng. Hist. Soc.; and Froissart, ed. Kervyn de Lettenhove, vol. xvi. According to Froissart, who at this period is more than usually misinformed, Huntingdon fell fighting at Cirencester, while Sir Thomas Shelley, his faithful servant, was executed before the coronation of Henry.

captured by the posse comitatus. They carried the earl north to Chelmsford, where the populace prepared to deal with him as his co-conspirators had been dealt with at Cirencester. For the moment the people were baulked of their prey by the intervention of Joan de Bohun, countess of Hereford and mother-in-law to the king. The countess succeeded in conveying him to the neighbouring castle of Pleshy, and she then despatched a messenger to inform Henry: in some accounts she is said to have added a request that the king would send the earl of Arundel to avenge him of his father's death.[1] Arundel is stated to have gone to Pleshy, and it is at least a plausible view that he had received orders from the king to bring the earl of Huntingdon to the Tower.

[1] I have not attempted to give a detailed account of Huntingdon's capture and death. Extracts from the various contemporary chroniclers, etc., relating to the last movements and fate of Huntingdon have been collected in the appendix. The best account of Huntingdon's flight, until he reached Hadleigh in Essex, is afforded by the sworn testimony of William Peion. The goods and chattels of the earl and his esquire Sir Thomas Shelley were accounted for by the king's escheator in pursuance of an inquisition held at Leigh above-mentioned. These included the earl's great and little seal. Huntingdon is said, on excellent authority, to have been captured at the house of John Pritewell, but I reject the view of Wylie (op. cit. i, 103) that this was Barrow Hall near Wakering: in face of the above inquisition it seems highly improbable that Huntingdon went so far. John Pritewell was at the time in possession of the manor of Prittlewell near Leigh, which formerly belonged to the duke of Gloucester, and was soon after restored to his widow. It is quite likely that John was residing at the chief messuage of Prittlewell and that Huntingdon was captured there. John was given possession of the manor by letters patent dated October 16th, 1399 (Originalia, 1 Henry IV, pt. 1, m. 3), at a yearly rent of £23. 6s. 8d. He was ordered to give up possession by letters patent dated October 8th, 2 Henry IV. (See generally Exch. Mem. Roll L.T.R., 2 Henry IV, Mich. Adhuc. Recorda, m. 17, and Pipe Roll, 1 Henry IV, Essex, m. 2, s.v. Nova Oblata.)
  Some of Huntingdon's portable property came to the hands of the countess of Hereford.
  Bona comitis Huntingdon.—Memorandum quod vicesimo sexto [die] Januarii anno regni regis Henrici quarti primo, Domina Johanna comitissa Herefordie liberavit consilio domini regis parcellas subscriptas de bonis Johannis Holand comitis Huntingdon

The capture of the rebel earl can hardly have been effected later than January 8th, for the king received the news on or before January 9th. I think this is a necessary inference from the peculiar circumstance that letters close issued on the last-mentioned day, directing that the countess of Hereford was to be given possession of Huntingdon's house in Thames Street.[1] On the 10th of January the archbishop of Canterbury, in a letter written from London, refers to the death of Kent and Salisbury at Cirencester, and also mentions that Huntingdon and his followers have been captured in Essex and Kent.[2] Moreover, on the same day, the king sent letters close to the constable of the Tower of London, directing him to receive the earl of Huntingdon

tanquam regi forisfactas, et ibidem per idem consilium commissas Thesaurario et Camerario salvo custodiendas. In primis unum par de trussyngcofres cordis ligatum et sigillatum. Item unum besagium continens diversa vessellamenta argentea. Item duo salaria argentea et deaurata ** cum cooperculis argenteis et deauratis pounsenez de cheres de furment. Item unum aquarium argenteum et deauratum. (Exchequer Kal. and Inv. R.C., ii, p. 85.)

[1] Close Roll, 1 Henry IV, pt. 1, m. 22 : Rex dilecto sibi Thome Knollys majori civitatis sue London salutem. Quibusdam certis de causis nos specialiter moventibus vobis mandamus quod statim visis presentibus hospicium quod fuit Johannis de Holand comitis de Huntingdon in Themestrete London cum pertinentiis in manum nostram capi et seisiri et hospicium illud Johanne comitisse Hereford liberari faciatis habendum ad voluntatem nostram. Teste rege apud Westm. ix die Januarii.

Per ipsum regem nunciante archiepiscopo Cantuar.

[2] Lit. Cantuar., Rolls Series, 85, iii, p. 74 : Hoc siquidem genus sceleris detestabilis non potuit divina potentia diu sine vindicta impunitum relinquere, sed sine morae diffugio, mentale parricidium, faetidaeque ingratitudinis piaculum, subita maledictione percussit, ipsosque sceleris auctores, ut designemus in specie, comites Kanciae et Sarum, dominos Radulphum Lomley, Thomam Blount et Benedictum Cely, ac alios sancta rusticitas, quae omnia palam facit, apud Cirencestriam comprehendit; nec solum comprehendit, sed, ne forte supervenirent qui potuerint hujusmodi captivos [mani]bus ipsorum eripere, dictos comites et Radulphum Lomley decapitavit, residuos domini nostri regis judiciis reservando; aliosque quasi a facie Dei super terram profugos, taliter *** scavit quod comitem Huntyngdon, dominum Thomam Schelley, et plures alios in Essexia et Cancia captivos detinet vis regalis. . . . Scriptum in domo habitacionis nostrae Londoniae, decimo die Januarii.

from the person who would deliver him into custody on the king's behalf.[1]

Huntingdon was not imprisoned in the Tower, nor was he given any trial. Shortly after his arrival at Pleshy he was unceremoniously and cruelly executed outside the castle walls in the presence of a great gathering of people.[2] It is said that a rough block was extemporised on the very spot where Richard the Second, on the advice of Huntingdon, had treacherously seized the duke of Gloucester. The monks buried the earl's body in the neighbouring collegiate church, but his head was taken to London and set up on London Bridge.[3]

It is not easy to fix precisely the day of the earl's death: there is considerable conflict of evidence. The dates found by various inquisitions range from the 7th to the 16th of January.[4] Two chroniclers mention a date and these agree

[1] Close Roll, 1 Henry IV, pt. 1, m. 22. (Printed by Rymer, Foedera O.S., viii, p. 121): Rex constabulario Turris sue London. et ejus locumtenenti salutem. Mandamus vobis quod Johannem comitem Huntingdonie ab eo qui ipsum vobis ex parte nostra liberabit recipiatis et in Turri predicta salvo et secure quousque aliter in hac parte duxerimus demandandum custodiatis. Et hoc nullatenus omittatis. Teste rege apud Westm. x die Januarii.
Per consilium.

[2] See Appendix.

[3] Close Roll, 1 Henry IV, pt. 1, m. 12: Order to take down head of Huntingdon from London Bridge, dated 19th February.
Ibid., m. 16. *De sepeliendo caput comitis Huntingdon:* Rex magistro sive custodi collegii ecclesie de Plessy salutem. Cum de gratia nostra speciali et ad supplicationem carissime sororis nostre Elizabeth Lancastrie que fuit uxor Johannis nuper comitis Hunting-don, qui nuper una cum aliis proditoribus nostris erga nos et ligeanciam suam proditorie insurrexit, concessimus prefate sorori nostre caput prefati nuper comitis sepeliendum : vobis mandamus quod caput predictum ab eo qui vobis illud ex parte prefate sororis nostre liberabit recipiatis et cum corpore prefati nuper comitis, ibidem ut dicitur sepulto, sepelire faciatis. Et hoc nullatenus omittatis. Teste rege apud Westm. xx die Febuarii.
Per ipsum Regem.

[4] Escheators' Inquisitions, File 1964, no. 5 (4 Henry V). Et dicunt quod prefatus nuper comes obiit vij die Januarii anno regni regis Henrici quarti primo. (A lengthy and very careful inquisition.) Ibid., no. 5a. This gives the same date. The above are not inquests

in saying that the earl was murdered on the night of the
15th of January.[1]   In my opinion it is most probable that he
died on the night of either the 9th or 10th of January, for the
writs to the escheators to seize his estates are mostly dated
the 11th of January,[2] and his death appears to have been

of office, but inquests connected with the restoration in blood and
estates of Huntingdon's heir.

Ibid., File 853, no. 4 (6 Henry IV); and Inq. ad quod damnum
(sic) 6 Henry IV, no. 15.   These give the date January 15th.

Iuq. ad. quod damnum (sic) 1 Henry IV, no. 29a (taken 16th
August, 1400).   This gives January 16th.

The earliest inquisition which I have found gives no date: see
Inq. ad quod damnum (sic) 1 Henry IV, no. 10 (taken February
5th, 1400).   The earl's widow married Sir John Cornwall and was
allowed dower out of certain of Huntingdon's lands notwithstanding
his forfeiture.   Writs issued accordingly directing an inquisition to
ascertain inter alia " qualis et quomodo et quo die idem comes obiit."
There appears to be no finding on these points, but the inquisition
is almost illegible.   See Inq. ad quod damnum (sic) 6 Henry IV,
no. 18.

[1] The Annales Henrici Quarti give nightfall on the 15th of
January—" die sancti Mauri, octavo decimo Kal. Feb."—as the time
when the crowd first collected outside Pleshy castle.   Walsingham
simply says, " die sancti Mauri," but he probably means the same
day.

[2] Fine Roll, 1 Henry IV, m. 18: Rex dilectis sibi Salamoni
Fresthorp et Johanni Asshewy ac escaetoribus et vicecomitibus
nostris in comitatibus Midd., Essex, Hertf., Bed., et Buk., salutem.
Sciatis quod cum Thomas comes Kancie, Johannes comes Huntingdon, Johannes comes Sarum, Radulfus de Lumley chivaler, Thomas
Blount chivaler et Benedictus Sely chivaler aggregatis sibi quampluribus malefactoribus contra ligeanciam suam proditorie levaverunt
et insurrexerunt ad nos et quamplures fideles ligeos nostros pro
posse suo destruendum; per quod omnia castra, dominia, terre,
tenementa, rensiones, feoda, advocationes, franchesie, libertates et
omnes alie possessiones, necnon bona et catalla quecunque, que
fuerunt ipsorum comitum, Radulfi, Thome et Benedicti, nobis foris-
facta existunt.   Assignavimus vos et duos vestrum ad omnia castra,
dominia, terras, tenementa, rensiones, feoda, advocationes, franchesias,
libertates et omnes alias possessiones ac bona et catalla quecunque,
que fuerunt eorundem comitum, Radulfi, Thome et Benedicti ac
aliorum quos vobis constare potest prefatis comitibus, Radulfo,
Thome et Benedicto in hac parte adhesisse, in comitatibus predictis,
infra libertates et extra, in manum nostram cum omne celeritate
possibili capiendum et seiziendum, ac per sacramentum proborum
et legalium hominum comitatuum predictorum infra libertates et

known at Oxford by January 12th when Sir John Blount, Sir Alan Buxhill, Sir Benedict Sely and others were tried for treason in the court of the steward of the household. The report of the Oxford proceedings is preserved.[1] Huntingdon is there referred to as "nuper comes" and is named in conjunction with Kent and Salisbury, who are similarly described and were undoubtedly dead, while the other arch-conspirator Despencer, who was still alive, is not named. No reliance can be placed on the word "nuper" by itself; but, in this particular connection, form and precedent point strongly to the fact that "nuper" is used as equivalent to defunct, otherwise indeed the record in question is bad on the face of it.

extra, per quos rei veritas melius sciri potest, juxta discretiones vestras et duorum vestrum extendendum. . . . Teste rege apud Westm. xj die Januarii.   Per ipsum regem et consilium.

Note that the name of Despencer, the quondam earl of Gloucester and one of the chief conspirators, is not mentioned: he was summarily executed by a mob at Bristol, but not until the 17th of January, 1399–1400. The above writ is entered on the Originalia Roll, 1 Henry IV, pt. 3, m. 14, where it bears the same date.

John Weever, who wrote in 1631, saw the remains of the monument to Huntingdon in the collegiate church of Pleshy. This writer states that "he was beheaded the third day after the Epiphany," i.e. January 9th; but it is by no means clear that Weever got this date from the monument. He only states that he read the following words on it: "Here lyeth John Holland, erle of Exceter, erle of Huntingdon, and Chamberleyne of England. Who dyed . . ." (See Weever, Ancient Funeral Monuments, ed. 1767, p. 393.)

[1] Placita Aulae, no. 28: Placita Aule Hospicii Domini Regis tenta in castro Oxon. de precepto domini Henrici regis Anglie post conquestum Anglie quarti et in presencia ipsius regis coram seneschallo et marescallo hospicii sui die Lune proximo post festum Epiphanie Domini anno regni ipsius regis primo [Monday, January 12th, 1399–1400]. Inquisitio capta apud castrum predictum coram prefato senescallo dicto die Lune anno supra-dicto per sacramentum Johannis Bray [etc.] . . . qui ad inquirendum de diversis proditionibus nuper in regno Anglie factis ad tunc jurati et veritatem inde dicendum onerati dicunt super sacramentum suum quod Johannes Blount chivaler, Alanus Buxhill chivaler, Benedictus Sely chivaler, . . . false nequiter et proditorie contra ligeancias suas . . . confederati fuerunt cum Thoma de Holand nuper comite Kancie, Johanne de Holand nuper comite Huntingdon, Johanne nuper comite Sarum et aliis proditoribus regis et regni Anglie. . . .

The lawless destruction of the chief conspirators saved Henry from all immediate trouble and anxiety, but such events were acts of evil example and a dangerous incentive to further lawlessness. Accordingly a minute[1] was prepared on the subject for the consideration of the great council, and this led to the issue of a stringent proclamation. The minute refers to the *destruction* of the earls of Kent, Salisbury and Huntingdon, and of lord Despencer and others, and to the fact that the commons of the realm have become so daring in consequence that they have not hesitated to destroy more of the king's lieges without process of law, while threatening to do likewise in time to come.

Notwithstanding the manner of death which befell the rebel earls, the king's escheators were, as already mentioned, directed to take possession of their estates. This was an irregularity,[2] which, however, was more or less put right by a resolution of the lords in the following parliament, declaring and adjudging that the three earls were traitors, and, as traitors, should forfeit the estates which they held in fee simple on the 5th of January, the eve of the feast of Epiphany,—"nounobstant q'ils feurent mortz sur le dit leve de guerre saunz processe de ley." Sir Ralph Lumley, who also was put to death at Cirencester, and the lord Despencer,

---

[1] Fait a remembrer de certains matires necessairs a monstrer au grant conseil du roy. . . . Item considere coment les communes du roiaume a cause de la destruccion de contes de Kent de Sarum et de Huntyndon et du sire le Despenser et autres traitours au roy sont devenuz si fiers q'ils neschuent de destruir volentrivement pluseurs des liges du roy sanz aucun processe de la loy en manaceant de faire semblablement en temps avenir dont tres-grand peril pourra avenir a tout le roialme et derogacion de lestat du roy, il semble expedient. . . . MS. Cotton, Cleopatra F, 3, fol. 9–10b. (printed, Ordinances of the Privy Council, vol. i, p. 107. The minutes are dated by the editor February, 1 Henry IV).

[2] The king none the less got a title by record, and an aggrieved party had to traverse the office. See Year Book, 43 Edward III, Ass. 28. There was a case (reported Year Book, 11 Henry IV, Hil., no. 30) arising out of the forfeiture of the earl of Northumberland. Here, however, there had also been attainder, and the plaintiff had to traverse both the office of escheator and the attainder—double matter of record. See generally Coke's Reports, ii, pp. 433–4; pt. iv, 57a. and b.

who suffered a like fate in Bristol, were included in this resolution.[1]

The various forms of the Escheators' Accounts reflect the previous irregularity and the resolution which cured it. The earlier accounts are based upon a special indictment against the conspirators, and for this reason the forfeiture is treated as occurring, not on the 5th of January, but on the 6th of December, the feast of St. Nicholas, this being the date quoted from the indictment. In the later accounts forfeiture is calculated from the 5th of January, and is stated to have taken place by virtue of a judgment in Parliament.[2] The

[1] Rot. Parl., iii, p. 459. Item fait a remembrer, que la ou Thomas Holand jadys cont de Kent, Johan Holand jadys count de Huntyngdon, Johan Montagu jadys cont de Sarum, Thomas jadis sire le Despenser et Rauf Lomley chivaler, nadgaires en diverses parties d'Engleterre soi leverent et chivacherent de guerre, traiterousement, encontre nostre seigneur le roy et encontre lour ligeance, pur destruir nostre dit seigneur le roy et autres graundes du roialme, et le dit roialme de gentz d'autre lange enhabiter, en lour dite leve de guerre par les loialx lieges nostre dit seigneur le roy feurent prisez et decollez; et partant toutz les seigneurs temporelx esteantz en parlement, par assent du roy, declarerent et adjuggerent les ditz Thomas, Johan, Johan, Thomas et Rauf pur traitours pur la leve de guerre encontre lour seigneur liege suis dit, et q'ils forfairent come traitours toutz lour terres et tenementz queux ils avoient en fee simple le quinte jour de Janver en la veille del fest de la Tiffanie nostre Seigneur Jhesu Crist, l'an du regne nostre seigneur le roy suis dit primer, ou puis, come la ley de la terre voet, ensemblement ove toutz lour biens et chatelx, nounobstant q'ils feurent mortz sur le dit leve de guerre saunz processe de ley.

[2] Escheators' Accounts, 57/1. . . . (de) exitibus manerii de Langton cum pertinentiis in comitatu predicto quod fuit Johannis nuper comitis Huntingdon et quod idem nuper comes tenuit in dicto festo sancti Nicholai dicto anno primo, quo festo idem nuper comes Huntingdon unacum prefato nuper comite Kancie et aliis diversis sibi adherentibus diu antea et postea diversis vicibus et temporibus nequiter et proditorie conspiraverunt et imaginaverunt mortem predicti nunc regis Anglie sicut continetur in [in]dictamento predicto et quod ad xlj li. extend. per annum sicut continetur in transcripto predicto videlicet a predicto festo sancti Nicholai episcopi accidente vj die Decembris quo festo idem nuper comes omnia terras et tenementa bona et catalla sua forisfecit occasione conspiracionis et imaginacionis predictarum usque predictum xxiiij diem Febuarii proxime sequentem. . . .

indictment above referred to is not forthcoming at the present
time; it is almost certain to have been consigned to the
baga de secretis[1] for the year, and seems to be irretrievably
lost.

Of the facts above related, the only circumstance which
could possibly be said to support the view that Huntingdon
was tried at Westminster, is the order sent to the constable
of the Tower of London; and I am bound to admit that
historians of no mean repute, historians too who were not
aware even of the existence of the Year Book report, have
doubted whether Huntingdon died at Pleshy simply on
account of this order to the constable.[2]   In reality the order

Escheators' Enrolled Accounts, No. 14, passim. . . . idem per
compotum de £ . . . de exitibus de . . . que Johannes de Holand
nuper comes Huntingdon tenuit in festo sancti Nicholai episcopi
adidem sexto die Decembris dicto anno primo quo festo idem nuper
comes et alii eidem nuper comiti adherentes et diu antea et postea
diversis vicibus et temporibus nequiter et proditorie conspiraverunt
et imaginaverunt mortem predicti nunc regis Anglie sicut continetur
in indictamento inde habito in banco regis in custodia clerici de
corona ibidem existente que quidem [maneria]. . .

There is a reference to the indictment on the Exchequer
Memoranda Roll L.T.R., 2 Henry IV, Adhuc Visus, Pasch., m. 9;
but neither there nor elsewhere have I discovered any further particulars concerning it.

Compare Escheators' Accounts, 80/1. This was evidently compiled before the judgment in parliament, but corrected afterwards.
Here the old date is erased and the following words inserted: . . .
quinto die Januarii . . . forisfecit vigore judicii contra ipsum
[comitem Huntingdon] in parliamento dicti regis nunc apud Westm.
anno regni sui secundo tento redditi.

Compare also the later enrolled accounts. Escheators' Enrolled
Accounts, No. 14 passim. . . . Johanni nuper comiti Huntingdon
qui proditorie insurrexit et equitavit contra regem et ligeanciam
suam predicto quinto die Januarii dicto anno et qui ea occasione
omnia terras et tenementa bona et catalla sua forisfecit eodem die
virtute judicii contra ipsum nuper comitem et alios in parliamento
regis apud Westm. in octavo sancti Hilarii anno secundo tento
redditi sicut continetur in quadam cedula . . .

[1] For frequent references to the Baga de Secretis see the Controlment Roll, 1 Henry IV.

[2] Wylie (Hist. of Hen. IV, p. 102, n. 1) says: " Similar writs were
issued to the Constable for the custody of the ' Duke of Surrey,' the
' Earl of Gloucester' and the earl of Salisbury, but of course they

in question has a perfectly indifferent bearing on the controversy. If it fits in with the theory of a trial, it equally accords with the story related by the chroniclers.[1]

We will now consider the report itself; if the case is indeed a mere forgery it would be strange to find it wholly free from blunders. In the first place the indictment against the earl, so far as it is mentioned in the report, differs entirely from the indictment as quoted in the Escheators' Accounts: the former sets up a conspiracy arranged for the night of the Epiphany, the latter alleges a conspiracy formed on the feast of St. Nicholas a month earlier. It would not be safe to insist very strongly on a discrepancy of this kind, which is more apparent than real, but this much may be justly observed: where we should fully expect corroboration if the report was genuine, we, in fact, get nothing of the kind. When, however, the report goes on to state that the office of steward of England was then void, it falls into unmitigated error. Thomas of Lancaster was at this time seneschal of England, and is repeatedly so styled in formal documents of the period in question.[2] All that can be urged in defence of the statement in the report is that Thomas was too young in the year 1400 to preside in person at such a trial.[3]

came too late"; and he cites the Close Roll, 1 Hen. IV, i, 24. This is an error; the writs in question refer to the previous proceedings before parliament, and they did not come too late.

[1] See, however, in appendix the reference to a judgment which appears upon the Memoranda Roll.

[2] It is sufficient to cite the Patent Rolls for 1399–1401, of which a calendar has been printed, viz. November 2nd, 3rd, 14th, 1399; March 5th, 1399–1400; June 1st, 1400; May 16th, June 27th, July 4th, 16th, 1401.

[3] The statement (s.v. Thomas duke of Clarence) in the Dict. of Nat. Biog. that Percy earl of Worcester "after a year's time was himself made seneschal as the prince was too young to discharge his office" is quite untrue, although derived from a contemporary source. Percy was never made steward of England: he was, however, as we have seen, appointed to assist Thomas in the discharge of his duties in connection with Henry's coronation, and at a later date was appointed steward of the household. The responsibility for the blunder in question rests with the Annales Henrici Quarti (p. 337): et dominum Thomam Percy constituit Angliae senescallum quia filius ejus junior, dominus Thomas dux Lancastriae,

In the face of these facts it seems quite unnecessary to pursue this argument any further. The earl of Huntingdon was never tried as alleged, and the only question of importance which remains to be considered is the date of this forged report.

The manuscript from which the reports of this case were printed appears to be no longer in existence. The first printed Year Book containing it was published by Tottel in or about the year 1553. Anthony Fitzherbert does not insert the case in his Grand Abridgement, published in 1514, a circumstance which fairly warrants the conclusion that this industrious legist either did not know of its existence, or did not believe it to be genuine. Brooke, it is true, also omits the case in his revised abridgement which appeared in 1568 ; but, in this instance, the omission suggests nothing, for Brooke duly inserts the report of the duke of Buckingham's trial in 1521 before the court of the lord high steward.

The trial, in 1415, of the earl of Cambridge and lord Scrope by a court of from eighteen to twenty peers, presided over by the duke of Clarence, has been already described. Between 1415 and 1499 no precedent is discoverable which has the remotest bearing on the institution of the lord high steward's court. Then in the year 1499 occurs the Warwick case, in which the official record of the proceedings is fortunately preserved.[1] The nature of the crime libelled must be specially noticed.

Edward earl of Warwick was indicted at the Guildhall on the Monday before the feast of St. Clement in the fifteenth year of Henry the Seventh. The finding of the jury appears serious enough where vague, but trivial to the point of absurdity where it is definite and specific. The earl is charged with conspiring to depose Henry and assume himself the

nondum fuit aetatis ad subeundum onus officii supradicti. Here are two atrocious blunders, one perpetuated by the biographer of Thomas, the other immortalised by Shakespeare.

Percy was acting as steward of the household at least as early as March 7th, 1400–1. See Cal., p. 475.

[1] Baga de Secretis, Pouch 2, mm. 1, 2, 3. See third report of the Deputy Keeper of the Records, app. ii, pp. 216–18.

regal dignity: the date assigned to the conspiracy is the 2nd of August, 14 Henry the Seventh; the place London, in the parish of All Saints, Barking, in the Tower ward. His fellow conspirators are, to begin with, Astwode and Cleymond, but Perkin Warbeck comes in presently. The plan of campaign is stated as follows. They were to seize the Tower, possess themselves of the crown jewels and treasure, fire the gunpowder stored in the fortress, and, while the king's lieges were busy extinguishing, take ships and away to France with the booty; lastly, a proclamation offering a shilling a day from the said treasure for recruits to make war on Henry. Truly a formidable conspiracy.

"And in order to fulfil such false and traitorous proposals," so the indictment proceeds, "Cleymond then and there said to the earl: 'My lord, you are well minded in what danger, sadness and duress you here remain; but, if you will help yourself according to the form and effect of the communication and discussion had between us, you shall come out of this prison with me; I will take you out of all danger; and leave you in surety.' And, in order to perfect his traitorous intention, Cleymond delivered a hanger to the earl to defend himself, and the earl received the hanger for such purpose."

This highly perfected plot was disclosed to the king and council by Perkin Warbeck, though how this person came to hear of it we are not informed. Cleymond then thought it was time to take sanctuary: he himself rather fancied Colchester; but, on the advice of one Thomas Ward, he decided on Westminster. Cleymond then told the earl of his intentions, and asked him to send a token to Thomas Ward "that he might be the more well affected to them." So the earl made an image of wood to be given to Ward, but he gave Cleymond a cloak and jacket of velvet.

Then the indictment begins all over again and tells a totally different story. It appears that Perkin Warbeck was lodged in the chamber immediately under that occupied by the earl; and on the 2nd of August, for the purpose this time of making Perkin king of England, Cleymond, being with the earl and by his consent, knocked on the floor and said : "Perkin, be of good cheer and comfort." Cleymond also promised to deliver him a letter from Flanders the following day. Then, when Cleymond and the earl were both in bed in the Tower, some traitorous proposals were discussed for assisting Perkin, and the wooden image was again mentioned.

On the 4th of August the earl made a hole in the vault of his chamber so that he might converse with the traitor below, and on the same day and many subsequent times spoke to Perkin, saying : " How goes it with you ? Be of good cheer." " And in this manner," the indictment concludes, " the earl, Cleymond and others aided, abetted and comforted Perkin in his treason."

On the day after the above finding (Tuesday, the 19th of November) a commission was issued by the king appointing John earl of Oxford lord high steward of England for the trial of Warwick. The steward was empowered to receive the indictment from the justices ; and, on such day and place as he should think fit, to call the earl of Warwick before him, examine and compel him to answer. He was further empowered to cause to come before him such and so many lords, *proceres et magnates*, of the kingdom of England, peers of the said earl, by whom the truth might be best known ; and to pass judgment according to the laws and customs of England.

On Thursday, November 21st, the trial took place at Westminster in the great hall of Pleas.[1] The mayor of London and the justices appeared in court and delivered the indictment to the steward. Lovell lieutenant of the Tower brought up the earl of Warwick, and the serjeant-at-arms made return that he had summoned the necessary

[1] The City Chronicle (MS. Cott. Vitell., A. 16, fol. 176) contains the following entry : Comes de Warwyk} " And upon the Tuysday next ensuyng was arayned in the greate hall at Westminster the said erle of Warwyk beyng of the age of xxiiij yeres or thereaboute, upon whome sate for juge the erle of Oxinford under a cloth of astate, where without eny presse of the laws the said erle of Warwyk for tresons by hym confessed and doon submytted hym unto the kynge's grace and mercy and so was there adjuged to be hangid drawen and quartered."

peers as commanded. Proclamation was then made for all dukes, earls and barons, who had been summoned, to appear and perform what should be enjoined them on the king's behalf. It seems that twenty-two peers in all had been ordered to attend; these were present in court and answered to their names. Warwick was brought to the bar, the indictment was read and the prisoner arraigned: he pleaded guilty. The king's serjeants-at-law, and also his attorney-at-law, prayed judgment, and the usual judgment for treason was then pronounced.[1]

This judgment was confirmed in the parliament of 1503 in an act of attainder and forfeiture affecting a large number of persons. The reference to the earl's trial is very short, but quite sufficient, according at all events to modern ideas of construction, to constitute a statutory declaration of its validity.[2]

The records we possess of the historical events of these times being by no means complete, but on the contrary very fragmentary, the fact that a particular institution is first recorded at a certain date is in itself (speaking generally) evidence neither of pre-existence nor of novelty. But in legal matters the position is somewhat different: the fact that a particular person was tried in a particular way in the year 1499 is prima facie very cogent evidence that a good precedent existed for so trying him. The reason is obvious enough in any case—an unprecedented trial is an illegal trial; but the particular instance before us is an exceptionally strong one. The nation stood aghast at the perfectly legal fate of Stanley: had it been noised abroad that the earl of Warwick was done to death by an adventitious tribunal, quite likely fear would have given place to fury. We have on investigation found a fairly good precedent

---

[1] See appendix for some further particulars.

[2] "Forasmuch as . . . for the which [said matters] the said late earl was by due course of the king's laws, by his own confession, convicted and attainted of high treason, as his deserts required in that behalf. . . . Be it enacted . . . that all the said . . . Edward late earl of Warwick . . . for their several offences above rehearsed be convicted, adjudged and attainted of high treason and forfeit to the king [etc.]. . . ." (Rot. Parl., vi, p. 544.)

dated 1415; and also a forged precedent dated 1400, the date of forgery not known, but most unlikely to have been before 1499, because Fitzherbert, writing about this time his elaborate book of precedents, does not insert it. The genuine precedent and the fictitious together adequately account for and justify the procedure in 1499; nothing less would suffice; anything more would leave the forgery without conceivable explanation. On these grounds, I think, we are justified in asserting that the lord high steward's court has an origin which is neither ancient nor obscure nor creditable.

The growing need for some such court seems plain enough. To have tried the earl of Warwick in the court of chivalry on such charges as those set out in the indictment would scarcely have been within the bounds of practical politics; the trial would have been too directly contrary to the statute of Richard the Second.[1] To have recourse in this and similar cases to proceedings in parliament was the only alternative, but one which was utterly unsuited to Tudor principles of government. Fortified by precedents (1), and with its jury of peers, the new court was fairly certain to pass muster; but its connection with the lord high steward was an ingenious detail, which the general public seems at first not to have

---

[1] Do not suppose that any Tudor sovereign, when once the steward's court had become established, had any cause to regret the court of chivalry. The civil law, pace Fortescue and constitutional historians, was considered far too tender to the prisoner, far too hard and dangerous for the prince. Here is evidence not easy to gainsay : " Where[as] pirates, thieves, robbers and murtherers upon the sea many times escape unpunished, because the trial of their offences hath heretofore been ordered before the Admiral, or his lieutenant or commissary, after the course of the civil laws, the nature whereof is, that before any judgment of death can be given against the offenders, either they must plainly confess their offences, (which they will never do without torture or pains) or else their offences be so plainly and directly proved by witnesses indifferent, such as saw their offences committed. . . ." " For reformation whereof," this statute (27 Henry VIII, cap. iv) enacts that such offences are to be determined "after the common course of the laws of the land used for felonies done and committed within the realm." (Printed Statutes of the Realm R.C., vol. iii, p. 533.) There are other statutes to a like effect.

2 F

appreciated or even noticed. The historian Hall, who died in 1547, makes the earl of Oxford preside as *constable* of England at the trial of the earl of Warwick;[1] and to this day, so little known are these undercurrents of Tudor history, that the chief modern historian of Henry the Seventh's reign repeats and emphasises the error of Hall.[2]

There is one other point which must be specially noticed. The most important and the most iniquitous part of the forged report is the assertion that a majority is sufficient for a conviction. It had long been settled law that the jury of twelve must be unanimous. If eleven agreed and one dissented there could be no judgment. The law usually took precautions to prevent disagreement by making the consequences extremely unpleasant for the dissentients, if not for the whole panel; but the rule was absolute and sacred.[3]

The rule, however, never appears to have been laid down generally by requiring unanimity; but always specifically by asserting that the prisoner's guilt must be established by the verdict of twelve, who are still further defined as twelve lawful men of the vicinage, or the like—definitions clearly inappropriate to the trial of peers of the realm. Here was opportunity for evasion. Henry the Fifth had summoned not merely twelve but as many as nineteen peers to attend the duke of Clarence, and a unanimous verdict had been given. Henry the Seventh summoned twenty-three peers in all, including the steward, and the reason seems obvious: it was the minimum number necessary to prevent any conflict

---

[1] Hall, Chronicle (ed. 1809), p. 491.
[2] Gairdner, Henry VII, pp. 174–5 (ed. 1889).
[3] See Year Book, 41 Ed. III, fol. 31, Mich., no. 36.
Pollock and Maitland, vol. ii, p. 626.
Hale, Pleas of the Crown, vol. 2, p. 297.
Thayer, Evidence at the Common Law ; etc.
If, however, we go back to the time of Glanville some justification is to be found: e.g. Lib. ii, cap. xvii, fol. 21 : De recognitionibus. . . . Sin autem quidam eorum rei veritatem sciant, quidam non, rejectis ignorantibus alii quidem vocandi sunt ad curiam donec duodecim ad minus reperiantur inde concordes. Item si quidam eorum dixerint pro uno, quidam pro alio litigantium, adjiciendi sunt alii donec duodecim ad minus in alterutram partem concorditer acquieverint.

between the new majority rule and the old verdict of twelve rule.[1]

In the year 1503 the court of the lord high steward was again called into being for the trial of Edward Sutton, lord Dudley, who had been indicted for felony at the Staffordshire assizes. I have not been able to discover any details relating to this trial which certainly ended either in acquittal or pardon.[2]

In the year 1521 took place the trial of the duke of Buckingham.[3] How it was the duke incurred the king's disfavour, who were his real enemies, whether the cardinal was one of them, are questions not easily answered. Be the truth what it may, disaster fell upon the duke suddenly and without a shadow of warning.

On the 2nd of April Buckingham received letters from the king summoning him to London: suspecting nothing, he set out for the metropolis with good speed. That he should daily see many armed men and other minions of the king journeying by the same road and in a like direction to himself appears at first to have caused him neither surprise nor disquietude; but, by the time he reached Windsor, the amount of attention he received from his fellow-travellers reached the point of impertinence.

While the duke was breakfasting at Windsor the inquisitiveness of a royal poursuivant elicited from him at last a sharp rebuke. The man replied, insolently perhaps, that he was there by the king's commandment. The truth broke on the duke with dizzy suddenness. He was going to his death, between him and this world there was to be the swift divorce of steel. For the moment his emotions mastered him; he turned ghastly pale and could not touch his food. Then his high spirits reasserted themselves; he ordered his horse and rode into London. He endeavoured to see the cardinal, but

---

[1] Would public opinion, however, have tolerated the majority rule, unless familiarity with the procedure on attainder in parliament had reconciled people to the idea? It can hardly be doubted that this was the source from which the forger evolved his principle.

[2] Appendix.

[3] For the record of the proceedings see Baga de Secretis, Pouch, 4/5.

was denied an interview on the plea of sickness. This time he showed less concern, though his worst fears were confirmed. " Well, I will yet taste my lord's wine," he said, and was conducted to his eminence's cellar with every mark of respect. A few hours later Buckingham was a prisoner in the Tower of London.

It was on the 16th of April that the duke was arrested. After this the preparations for his trial and conviction were relentlessly proceeded with. Every idle word uttered by him during the last ten years was to be laid to his charge, and this necessitated indictments in no less than five separate counties. He was indicted at East Greenwich in Kent, at Southwark in Surrey, at Bedminster in Somersetshire, at Bristol castle in county Gloucester and at the Guildhall in London. On the 11th of May Thomas duke of Norfolk, the earl marshal, was appointed lord high steward, and two days later the trial took place. Only nineteen peers had been summoned, the same number as in 1415. According to the report of this case in the Year Books, the proper number of lords to summon is twenty to eighteen, and the verdict of the majority decides the issue.[1] With so small a panel, however, the majority might consist of less than twelve; but this point did not arise, and was probably not considered by the reporter or anyone else.

The scene of the trial was Westminster Hall. There was a platform, or scaffold as it was called, for the peers; and a special canopied seat for the steward, railed and counter-railed about and barred with degrees. When the lords had taken their places Buckingham was brought in procession to the bar by Sir Thomas Lovell the constable of the Tower and Sir Richard Cholmeley the deputy lieutenant. In front of the procession was carried the axe, the edge turned away from the duke. The clerk of the crown then read the indictments to the prisoner.

---

[1] That the trial in 1415 was taken as the chief precedent is clear. These numbers cannot be mere coincidence. Including the duke of Clarence twenty peers were summoned in 1415. Excluding Clarence and the peer who did not attend, we get the number eighteen.

The general charge against Buckingham was intending to exalt himself to the crown of England, and imagining and compassing to depose the king and effect his death and destruction.   The particulars set out in the indictments were founded on the depositions of Delacourt some time chaplain to the duke, Gilbert the duke's chancellor, and Charles Knyvet a discharged surveyor.

It was Delacourt who some nine years ago had visited Nicholas Hopkins, the monk of the Carthusian priory of Henton, who feigned acquaintance with the future.   Under an oath of secrecy Father Nicholas told Delacourt that his master would *have all*, and that the duke should endeavour to obtain the love of the community.   How did he know all this ?   Why, by the grace of God !   These sayings Delacourt related to the duke, and the duke commanded him to keep the same a secret.   This wise father was consulted on other occasions, and once ventured to forecast that the king would have no issue male of his body.   Evidently the monk's prophetic soul had received no inkling of the king's latent resourcefulness for ridding himself of unprolific consorts.

Where the allegations depend on the statements of Gilbert, the indictments become somewhat cryptic.

And further, on the 20th of February, in the eleventh year of Henry the Eighth, at Bletchingly in the county of Surrey, the duke falsely and traitorously told Gilbert "that he, the duke, would delay, putting off his intentions until a more convenient time, and that the thing would be well done if the noblemen of the kingdom would mutually declare their minds to one another, but that many of them were afraid so to declare their minds and therefore this spoiled all." And the duke further told Gilbert " that all that the father of the king had done had been done in wrong": he also further traitorously said "that he, the said duke, was such a great sinner, that he was certain he wanted the grace of God, and therefore he well knew that he should be the worse for it whenever he began to do anything against the king."

There is a treasonable flavour about this conversation, quite valuable for prejudice ; but the real sting and venom of the indictment was supplied by the ex-surveyor.

And further, the duke, persevering in his said treasonable intentions, on the 4th of November in the 11th year of Henry the Eighth, at East Greenwich in the county of Kent, said to one Charles Knyvet Esquire,—that after the king had blamed him, the duke, for retaining Sir William Bulmer knight in the service of him the duke, he, the duke, thought he should ·be committed to the Tower of London.   The duke further said to Knyvet,—that if he, the duke, had understood that he should have been committed to the Tower, the chief actors therein should not profit by the same, but that he would do what his father intended to do to King Richard the Third at New Sarum in the county of Wilts, to wit that his father had made his suit to come into the presence of King Richard, having about him a concealed dagger, and that his father intended, when he should be kneeling before King Richard, to rise suddenly and plunge the dagger into the body of the said King Richard.   And the duke, thus saying, maliciously and traitorously put his hand upon the hilt of his sword, and said that if he should be so ill-treated he would do the best to fulfil his treasonable intentions, and he swore a great oath thereupon.

When the indictments had been openly read the duke is reported to have said: " It is false and untrue, and conspired and forged to bring me to my death, and that will I prove," alleging many reasons to falsify the indictments. " And," says the chronicler Hall, " against his reasons the king's attorney alleged the examinations, confessions and proofs of witnesses."   How long the duke wrestled with his indictments we are left to conjecture; but we shall be fairly safe if we assume that he urged *non multum sed multa*.   At any rate we only hear of one substantial plea of law being raised, namely that no overt act of treason was alleged.   To this Fineux, C.J., replied that between felony and treason there was a difference : there could be no felony without some act done, but to intend the death of the king was high treason, and such intention was sufficiently proved by words alone.[1]

After this Buckingham was arraigned : was he guilty or not guilty?   He said, " Not guilty."   How would he be tried? " By God and his peers."

[1] See Appendix.   Judges were present to assist the court in all questions of law and procedure which might arise.

The trial was presumably conducted with the ordinary formalities of a treason trial of that period. Unfortunately the only detailed account which we possess is quite untrustworthy upon the subject of procedure.[1] It seems that the witnesses for the crown were present and were produced; but whether anything took place similar to our present system of examination and cross-examination it is impossible to say.[2] The previous depositions of these witnesses were read in court, and without doubt considered perfectly good evidence against the prisoner. The rules of evidence now in force are of quite recent origin.

When Buckingham had concluded his defence, such as it was, the duke of Norfolk addressed him: "My lord, the king our sovereign lord hath commanded that you shall have his laws ministered with favour and right to you;

[1] Hall apparently understood very little about either the case, the tribunal or the procedure: at the very outset he exposes his ignorance. "The duke of Norfolk," he writes, "was made by the king's letters patent high steward of England to accomplish the high cause of appeal of the peer or peers of the realm and to discern and judge the causes of the peers." (See ed. 1809, p. 623.) How came Hall, an eminent lawyer, the legal hack of the court party, to describe the case as an appeal? Perhaps it was asserted at the time that the steward's court was the outcome of the statute of 1 Henry IV, which abolished appeals in parliament.

[2] Compare the statement in the Year Book: "et donq les serjeants du roy et le atturney du roy doneront evidence vers luy . . ."; and Hall: "The duke desired the witnesses to be brought forth; then was brought before him Sir Gilbert Perke, priest, his chancellor, first accuser of the same duke; master John Delacourt, priest, the duke's confessor, and his own handwriting laid before him to the accusement of the duke; Charles Knevet, Esquire, cousin to the duke, and a monk (Nicholas Hopkyns) prior of the Charterhouse (at Henton) besides Bath, which like a false hypocrite had induced the duke to the treason, and had divers time said to the duke that he should be king of England; but the duke said that in himself he never consented to it. Divers presumptions and accusements were laid to him by Charles Knevet, which he would fain have covered. The depositions were read. . . ."

Brewer appears to have been ignorant of the Year Book report, and his account is consequently not always reliable. (See letters and papers of Henry VIII, vol. iii, pt. 1; and reign of Henry VIII, vol. i.)

wherefore if you have any other thing to say for yourself you shall be heard."

Buckingham, it seems, had nothing further to add, and he was led away from the court into *Paradise*, a house so named. The lords triers then retired to consider the evidence; and on their return the verdict of each lord was taken separately, beginning with the junior, and ending with the premier peer present.[1] Every peer said *guilty*.

Buckingham was brought again to the bar to be made acquainted with the verdict and receive judgment accordingly. It was a terrible ordeal for the bravest man. Buckingham chafed and sweated in his distress, but commanded himself sufficiently to make his salutation to the court.

His grace of Norfolk, lord high steward of England, addressed the prisoner: "Sir Edward, you have heard how you be indicted of high treason; you pleaded thereunto not guilty, putting yourself to the judgment of your peers, the which have found you guilty." At this point, Norfolk, brave soldier though he was, burst into tears. "Your sentence is," he continued with faltering speech, "that you be led back to prison, laid on a hurdle, and so drawn to the place of execution, there to be hanged, cut down alive . . . your head smitten off, your body quartered and divided at the king's will. And may God have mercy on your soul." A most unsavoury sentence, which I find I cannot bring myself to set down in full: it was, of course, subsequently commuted to beheading.[2]

Perhaps Norfolk's tears helped Buckingham towards composure, for he made a very dignified exit from Westminster Hall. "My lord of Norfolk," said the prisoner, "you have said as a traitor should be said unto, but I was never one; but, my lords, I nothing malign for that you have done to me, but the eternal God forgive you my death as I do:

---

[1] Hall reverses the order, so also does Brewer; but they are clearly in error. The Year Book is against them, and the original record is conclusive: Et postea per eundem senescallum Anglie ab inferiori pare usque ad superiorem parem illorum separatim inde examinati. (Baga de Secretis, Pouch, 4/5, m. 15.)

[2] See Appendix for some additional particulars.

I shall never sue to the king for life, howbeit he is a gracious
prince, and more grace may come from him than I wish.
I desire you, my lords, and all my fellows to pray for me."
Then they turned the edge of the axe towards him, and he
was led away.   He took his death right meekly on Friday
the 17th of May at about eleven o'clock.[1]

The court of the lord high steward thus became an established institution.   Trials before it became frequent, and, time
and again, fearing earthly more than heavenly vengeance, this
noble tribunal resolutely did the will of the king.

Seeing that the steward's court rests substantially on a
fraudulent basis, it would be absurd at this stage of its
existence to attempt to define the scope of its jurisdiction ;
but we may, I think, profitably inquire whether there was

[1] Buckingham was attainted in parliament by the statute 14 and
15 Henry VIII, c. 20 : "Forasmoche as Edward late duke of
Bukyngham late of Thornbury in the countie of Gloucester the
xxiiij[th] daye of Aprill in the fourth yere of the reigne of oure
soveraigne lord the kyng that nowe is and dyvers times after,
ymagined and compassed trayterouslie and unnaturally the distruc-
cion of the moost roiall persone of oure seid soveraigne lord . . .
of the which treasons and offenses the seid late duke in the seid
counties was severally indicted.   And afterward for and upon the
same treasons the xiij daye of Maye the xiij yere of the reigne of
oure seid soveraigne lord the kyng at Westminster in the countie of
Middlesex before Thomas duke of Norfolk for that tyme oonely
beyng greate stuarde of Englande by the kynges lettres patentis,
by verdite of hys perys and by jugement of the seid stuarde
agenst the seid late duke then and there yeven after the due ordre
of the lawe and custome of England was atteynted of high treason
as by recordes therof more playnly apperith.   Wherfore be it or-
deigned, enacted and established by the kyng our soveraigne lorde
with the assent of the lordis spirituall and temporall and the
commons in this present parliament assembled and by the auctoritie
of the same, that the said late duke for the offenses above rehersed
stond and be convicted, adjugged and atteynted of hygh treason
and forfaite to the kyng our soveraigne lord and hys heires for
ever all [etc.]. . . ." (See Statutes of the Realm R.C., vol. iii,
pp. 246-58.)

There is an account of Buckingham's trial preserved among the
Lansdowne MSS. (Printed Gentleman's Magazine, 1834, vol. i,
p. 266.) It is chiefly derived from the record in the Baga de
Secretis and contains no original information.

anything in the character and circumstances of this court calculated one way or another to affect the position of the lords spiritual. Since the execution of Scrope in the reign of Henry the Fourth, for the mere lack of occasion and opportunity, the crown's jurisdiction over criminous bishops had received neither exemplification nor definition, it had remained in its original state of complete uncertainty. It is under such circumstances that quite secondary influences may determine the fate of a principle. The exercise, for example, or non-exercise by the spirituality of their right to take part in judging temporal peers might prove sufficient to turn the scale. Trials before parliament were in abeyance, but Littleton had clearly implied that there, at all events, the spiritual lords were necessary parties : there were, moreover, recorded cases where their absence had been held to invalidate the proceedings. Whoever invented the court of the lord high steward would have been rash to disregard these cases. Accordingly, when we find that the panel, both at the trial of Warwick and at the trial of Buckingham, contains the name of the prior for the time being of the Order of St. John of Jerusalem, we may safely conclude that the reason for summoning this person was to give the spirituality some semblance of representation.

There is yet one other circumstance by which we may test the set of the political current. Prelates are no longer peers of the realm, but mere lords of parliament: is not this change of style indirectly tending to exclude them from the privilege (1) of trial by peers? As counsel for the bishops we could cite excellent authority to the contrary: the Year Book which records the trial of Buckingham says clearly enough that he was tried as a lord of parliament. No definite conclusion is permissible on these data; but at least we may, up to this point, deny the assertions of those who contend that the steward's court was one of the engines for the degradation of the spiritual lords.

The moral is quite otherwise ; the truth is as clear as it is unpalatable. This court was a fraudulent device for the degradation of the nobility generally : it was intended to supersede and altogether deprive them of trial in parliament.[1] Eventually there was a complete revival of judicial proceedings in parliament; but this did not take place until some years after the Tudor dynasty had passed away.

[1] The following clause in the statute of 33 Hen. VIII, c. xx, is plainly inconsistent with the existence of two courts for the trial of peers: "Provided always and be it enacted by authority aforesaid, That if any of the peers of this realm shall happen to be accused and examined of high treason before any of the king's council, and do confess the same, and afterwards fall to madness or lunacy, as is aforesaid, that then such treasons done and committed by any peer of the realm, and by him or her confessed upon examination thereof before any the king's council as is aforesaid, and their confessions if they can write subscribed with their names, shall be inquired of by virtue of the king's commission of oyer and terminer, to be awarded in manner and form above rehearsed: And if they shall happen to be indicted of high treason by virtue of such commission, yet nevertheless their trial shall be always had by their peers before the High Steward of England to be assigned by the king's highness; and that the High Steward to be assigned by the king's majesty in every such case shall have the record of the indictment brought to him, and shall cause to be summoned to appear before him the peers of the realm as hath been accustomed at a day and place by the said High Steward to be limited, at which day and place the said High Steward, after the appearance of the peers before him, having the record of the said indictment before him, shall, in the absence of the person indicted, which shall happen to be mad or lunatick as is aforesaid, and without his or her arraignment or pleading to the indictment, cause the said indictment to be read to the peers, and in their presence cause to be declared by his discretion all manner of evidence and witness touching the treasons contained in the said indictment, and afterwards charge the said peers upon their faiths and duties of allegiance that they owe to the king's majesty to try whether the person indicted be guilty of the treasons contained in the indictments or any of them or not guilty; and if they shall find him or her guilty, that then such judgment execution and forfeitures shall be had made and done as if such person indicted had been of good memory, and personally present arraigned and pleaded to the said indictment, and had been found guilty of the treasons therein contained, the madness or lunacy of such persons in such cases as is aforesaid notwithstanding."
The next clause provides for the execution of any person who becomes mad after attainder by Act of parliament; and, generally, this Act gives the impression of being very carefully framed to meet every conceivable case.

APPENDIX TO CHAPTER XII

Exchequer Memoranda Roll, King's Remembrancer,
Adhuc Recorda de Termino Pasche anno primo Regis Henrici
Quarti, m. 23. (Adhuc Recorda)

Kanc.
Willelmus
Wankeford et
alii alloc. de
bonis et catallis
que fuerunt
Johannis nuper
comitis
Huntingdon.

Preceptum fuit Willelmo Pelon clerico de comitatu Sussex per breve sub sigillo hujus scaccarii dato xxiiij die Maii hoc termino essendi coram thesaurario et baronibus de eodem scaccario die sabbati xxix die Maii tunc proximo sequente ad respondendum certis articulis sibi ex parte regis objiciendis et hoc sub pena centum librarum quas etc. Ad quam diem idem Willelmus venit in propria persona sua. Et dictum est ei pro domino rege quod informet curiam que et cujusmodi bona et catalla que fuerunt Johannis nuper comitis Huntingdon qui versus regem forisfecit ad manus suas post forisfacturam ejusdem nuper comitis devenerunt et in quorum vel cujus manibus jam existunt et cujus precipitur eadem bona et catalla fuerunt et sunt seu ad quorum vel cujus manus aliqua alia bona seu catalla que sua fuerunt dicto tempore forisfacture sue seu postea devenerunt; qui dicit super sacramentum suum corporaliter presentatum quod tempore quo predictus nuper comes recessit ab (hospitio[1]) suo London videlicet (secundo[2]) die Januarii anno primo regis hujus ipse unacum aliis servientibus suis ivit cum eodem nuper comite usque Billyngsgate London et ibidem ceperunt quandam bargeam in qua omnes ipsi decesserunt et quod quamplura bona et jocalia que fuerunt predicti nuper comitis deinde similiter abcariata fuerunt cum eodem nuper comite in quodam parvo batello eciam cum ipso exeunte usque dum venerunt versus castrum de Hadley in Essex et ibi prope predictus nuper comes applicuit et bona ac jocalia omnia et singula supradicta in batello predicto proprius posita secum assumpsit preterquam viij discos de argento et iiij vel sex magnas chargeos unum ewer et tres pelves de argento que remanserunt in custodia cujusdam Walteri Bisshop et preterquam

---

[1] Over erasure.   [2] Written in fainter ink.

xxxij discos argenti quorum idem Willelmus Peion, Nicholas Brenthesle, Thomas Trenarke et Henricus del Chambre videlicet quilibet eorum habuit octo discos de dono predicti nuper comitis. Et dicit predictus Willelmus Peion quod postquam ipse applicuit apud Grenhyth quod fuit vij die Januarii dicto anno primo. . . .

(The rest of this witness's statement is irrelevant to this particular inquiry.)

Escheators' Enrolled Accounts (14), *m.* 43*d.* *Essex*

Nec—respondet de diversis bonis et catallis subscriptis pretii cccij li.–iij s.–iiij d. que fuerunt Johannis de Holand comitis Huntyngdon et Thome Shelle proditorum regis publice proclamatorum apud le Leye in hundredo de Roche-ford in dicto comitatu Essex scilicet—uno jakke de rubeo velvetto pretii x s., uno longo epitogo de nigro damseo furrato cum menyveer pretii xxvj s.–viij d., uno longo epitogo de viridi velvetto de mottele pulverisat. et furrat. cum foygues usitato pretii xl s., uno alio longo epitogo de russeto furrato cum cristato griseo debit. pretii xx s., uno collario aureo cum gemmis de liberata regis Francie pretii viij li., uno magno sigillo et uno parvo sigillo pretii xiiij s., duobus subligariis stipatis cum auro pretii xxiij s.–iiij d. et viij s. et ij firmaculis pretii xxiij s.–iiij d., vj grossis margaritis et viij alils margaritis pretii iiij li.–x s., uno collario de serico cum literis de margaritis pretii xiij s.–iiij d., una nigra zona de serico cum una bucula et appendice et vj stipis de auro pretii xl s., duabus aliis zonis stipatis cum auro pretii lxxiij s.–iiij d., una alia zona stipata cum auro pretii xxvj s.–viij d., ij zonis de opere paris stipatis cum argento et deauratis pretii xxiij s.–iiij d., uno cipho de auro cum pede et cooperculo ad idem pretii xiij li.–vj s.–viij d., uno alio cipho de auro cum cooperculo plano pretii x li., una magna saphiro et una parva saphiro in una bursa pretii xxvj s.–viij d., j diamante et ij parvis diamant. in una bursa pretii iiij li., uno anulo de auro cum uno saphiro, uno alio anulo de auro de opere paris, uno alio anulo de auro cum una margarita et uno monile de auro cum margaritis et una aquila operata pretii xiij s.–iiij d., uno alio monili de auro cum iij baleis una saphiro et vj margaritis pretii c s., uno alio monili cum una baleis et vj margaritis circumpositis pretii xiij li.– vj s.–viij d., una chapa unius pugionis fistulat. cum uno folio et alio auro fracto pretii xx s., vj poynt argenti deauratis cum laqueis et vj literis pro uno jakke deauratis pretil vj s.–viij d., ij ostrichfetheres de auro enamaillatis pretii vj s.–viij d., una laquea de auro et de serico pretii iij s.–iiij d., j pugione phalarato cum argento deaurato pretii vj s.–viij d., j molberye de argento deaurat. et iiij rosis de auro enamaillatis pretii xij d., uno leone de argento pretil xiij s.–iiij d., uno magno pari de patnosteres de corallo cum nigris gaudees de achate pretii xl s., uno pari paternosters de corallo pretii iij s.–iiij d., uno pari salsar. de argento cooperat. et deaurat. pretii vij li., ij peciis de argento plano pretii xl s., uno pari pelvium de argento deaurat. pretii x li., una pelvi cum una lanacro de argento plano defract. pretii cvj s.–viij d., uno lanacro de argento deaurato pretii xx s., vj parvis chargeos de argento pretii xx li., iiij magnis chargeos de argento pretil xiij li.–vj s.– viij d., xviij discis de argento de una sorte pretii xxxvj li., ij aliis discis de argento alia sorte pretii iiij li., una diamante cum uno monili de opere paris cum una aquila alba pretii xxj li., in uno sacculo sigillato xxiij li.–v s. auri et argenti in pecunia innumerata. / Item pro dicto comite una liberata Ricardi nuper regis Anglie circa brachin. pretii iiij li., uno alio monili de similitudine capitis cervi sine lapide pretii xx s., una zona de auro cum belectis pretii xx li. per estimationem, una liberata de auro regis Henrici Anglie pretii c s., uno monili de similitudine unius pellicani sine lapide pretii xl s., una liberata de cerno cum iij baleis et ij saphiris pretii x li., una liberata regis Francie cum vj baleis et vj saphiris pretii xx li., uno alio monili cum uno diamante pretii iiij li., xxxvij anulis de opere paris pretii xl s., una aquila alba enamaillata cum una baleis pretii lx s. Que quidem bona et catalla sic appreciata fuerunt per inquisitionem coram dicto escaetore inde ex officio captam et super hunc compotum liberata eo quod idem escaetor liberavit omnia bona predicta Johanni Norbury tunc thesaurario Anglie per breve regis dicto escaetori inde directum datum xxiij die Januarii anno primo. . . .

Exchequer Memoranda Roll, King's Remembrancer
Adhuc Recorda de Termino Pasche anno primo Regis Henrici
Quarti, m. 10*d.* (*Adhuc Recorda*)

Memorandum quod Willelmus Fyfhyd nuper commorans cum Johanne nuper comite Huntingdon qui versus dominum regem forisfecit presens hic in curia xvj die Maii hoc termino dedit curie intelligi quod diversa bona et catalla (que fuerunt predicti nuper comitis in quadam cedula de papiro contenta et curie per predictum Willelmum liberata in custodia hujus rememoratoris remanenda videlicet inter billas de hoc termino cujus tenor sequitur in hec verba: " Ceux sont les choses queux . . . [etc.] . . .") devenerunt ad manus Roberti Days nuper cancellarii predicti nuper comitis et quod eadem bona et catalla postea per quendam servientem dicti magistri Roberti apportata fuerunt et deliberata Ricardo Whytyngton . . . que quidem bona et catalla ratione judicii versus dictum nuper comitem redditi domino regi pertinent tanquam foris-facta.   Super quo concordatum est . . . absque hoc quod aliqua bona seu catalla de bonis in dicta cedula superius contenta seu aliqua alia bona que fuerunt predicti Johannis nuper comitis tempore judicii versus dictum nuper comitem redditi seu unquam postea. . . .

NOTE.—To anyone who wishes to maintain the genuineness of the Year Book case, notwithstanding the enormous weight of evidence which I have adduced against it, this extract will perhaps seem a veritable tabula in naufragio.   Nevertheless no drowning man ever clutched at a slenderer straw.   The few who are familiar with the memoranda of the Exchequer will simply set it down as a clerical error.   Compare, for example, the Memoranda Rolls L.T.R., 2 Henry IV, r. 45d., and ibid. Pasch. adhuc recorda, m. 9, where the earl of Kent is quite erroneously described as " convicted of treason "; and ibid., m. 32, where Despencer is similarly described. There are at least a hundred subsequent references to the forfeiture of Huntingdon on the roll from which the above extract has been taken, but the error is never repeated; on the contrary, we find on every occasion the type of formula which is employed where there has been no judgment, e.g.: " pro eo quod omnia . . . supradicta per forisfacturam predicti nuper comitis domino regi pertinent tanquam forisfacta." Again, the entry in question was perhaps not written up *before* the quinzaine of St. Hilary in the second year; consequently the entry may refer to the proceedings in parliament.

Inquisitions, 5 Henry IV; Exchequer Miscellanea, 6/28, m. 12
Confession of John Pritewell

M^d. that on the ferst Sonday of Clene Lenten last passed ther was on at Bylee in gyse of a knyght and sente for me John Pritewelle to come to hym thyder and seyde to me John Sire zoure mayster and myn and oure alder mayster our right lige-lord kyng Richard greteht zou often tyme and derelithe wel and thanketh zou hyeliche of zoure grete trouthe that ze have contened zou inne to hym ward sithen he parted fro zou, and sori is and often hath been for the defese that ze have so ofte tyme suffred for hym and for his brother of Huntyngdon yat was taken at zoure hous and often tymes he prayeth ful herteley for zou to God that. . . .

Adam of Usk (ed. 1904), p. 42

Item comes Huntingdon per Essexem ad Franciam fugere volens, per pagences captus, in eodem loco quo et dux Glowcestrie se Ricardo nuper regi reddidit, per plebeyos et mecanicos decapitatur. De quibus rex domino meo Cantuariensi scripsit; unde ipse sub isto themate: "Nuncio vobis magnum gaudium," per modum sermonis, hoc clero et populo Londoniis publicavit, et, cantato ymno, "Te Deum laudamus," Deo regraciando per civitatem cum solempni transivit processione.

Jean le Beau, ed. Buchon, p. 56[1]

Vérité est que quant le conte d'Antinton, frère du roi Richard, et son maistre d'ostel sire Thomas Stelle qui fust bon chevalier furent arrivez en escosse (sic), en une petite ville où demouroit la contesse d'Arvordre, soeur du vieil conte d'Arondel qui fut décollé à Londres, si se logèrent ces seigneurs en un ostel où ils avoient accoustumé de logier. Et sitost que la comtesse le sceust, elle commanda secrète-

---

[1] Printed as a supplement to Froissart, vol. xv, app. 2.

ment à son connestable qu'il feist armer tous ceulx de la ville pour prendre le conte d'Antinton et sa compaignie. Le connestable fist tantost le commandement de la dame et fist tant de gens assembler que de force le conte d'Antinton et sire Thomas son maistre d'ostel et Hue Credo son bouteiller, et aussi les autres tous de sa route furent prins. Quant la contesse les eust en sa prison, elle envoya une lettre au roi Henry d'Angleterre lui signiffier comment elle tenoit en sa prison le conte d'Antinton et tous ses gens. Si lui prioit qu'il lui envoyast le conte d'Arondel, son cousin, pour prendre vengeance de la mort de son père. Sur ce mandement le roi lui envoya en disant : "Beau cousin, allez à vostre ante qui vous mande, et amenez les prisonniers par deçà, vifz ou mors, hastivement." Si s'en alla le conte, et arriva devers son ante, et trouva que la dame avoit fait assembler des villains du pays bien huit mille. Et quant il eust là esté la nuit, au plus matin la dame et le conte d'Arondel son neveu firent amener le conte d'Antinton devant eulx et devant tous ces villains ; et commandèrent que devant eulx ils le tuassent ; mais pour vrai il n'y eust homme qui mal leur voulsist faire pour chose qu'on leur commandast, car moult grant pitié en avoient. . . . [Arundel upbraids Huntingdon.] . . . Adoncques vint un escuyer qui fist le bon varlet, lequel se présenta de l'occire. Adoncques commanda la dame qu'il s'en délivrast, et l'escuyer vint devers le conte une hache en sa main, et se mist à genoulx devant lui, et lui dist : "Chier sire, pardonnez moi vostre mort, car il m'est commandé de vous délivrer de ce monde. . . ." [Huntingdon cries for mercy, madame is obdurate and constrains her squire.] . . . Adoncques l'escuyer haulsa la hache et le férit parmi l'espaulle, si qu'il tomba à terre, et fut grant pitié de le voir ; car à tout ce coup le conte saillit sus et dit : "Ami pourquoi me fais-tu ainsi languir ? Pour Dieu, délivres moi légièrement." Adoncques le reférit huit coups moult honteusement qu'oncques ne sceust adrecer en la teste ; et au neufviesme coup le férit au col bien parfont ; mais ce fust grant pitié et merveille, car à tous ses coups il parla, et dist : "Hée ! Dieu mercy !" Puis ne parla ; et fut piteuse mort ; car encore lui parcoupa - il la gorge d'un coustel. Quant ainsi fut mort le conte d'Antinton, le conte

2 G

d'Arondel fist la teste bouter sur ung long baston, et le chevalier maistre d'ostel fut mené à Londres, piés et poings liés, sur ung cheval, et le bouteiller fut mené trotant à pié entre les chevaux; si vindrent à Londres le vingtième jour de janvier l'an dessus dit. . . . En ce propre jour vint à Londres le conte de Rostellen, lequel fesoit apporter devant lui la teste du seigneur Despensier. . . .

Annales Henrici Quarti, Rolls Series, 28, *p.* 326

Comes Huntyngdoniae, dominus Johannes Holand, qui prius "dux Excestriae" vocabatur, non equitavit cum predictis comitibus ad castrum de Wyndeshore, die quo meditati fuerunt peremisse regem; sed latens Londoniis expectavit rei finem, quae si juxta [vota] cessisset eisdem, paratus fuit, ut dicebatur, ad occurrendum eis et auxilia ferre cum magno numero armatorum. Sed mox ut cognovit versum in contrarium, in scapha fugere nitebatur. Qui vero ventis et mari imperat ventum contrarium sibi tam turgidum tam contrarium sibi concitavit ut nullo modo per Tamisiam fugere praevaleret. Quamobrem vectus equo velocissimo fugit in Estsexiam ad castrum de Hadle, ubi morabatur comes Oxoniae, Albredus de Veer, cum uxore sua, Oxoniae comitissa. Sed ibi diu latere non potuit propter persecutores qui propter eum omnia scrutabantur. Egressus igitur latenter a castro venit ad quoddam molendinum, sequente eum milite quodam Johanne de Schevele quem de garcione fortuna produxerat ad ardu *** paucis annis. Ibi igitur occultavit se biduo, tentans, si quomodo posset, per mare fugiendo iram domini declinare. Sed quotiens tentavit alta ponti conscendere totiens, vi ventorum repulsus, cogebatur littus repetere; donec omnino desperans de maris suffragio destitit a proposito praeconcepto. Regressus in terram igitur venit ad domum noctu cujusdam armigeri sibi noti, scilicet Johannis de Prytwelle; ubi dum esset in coena supervenerunt multi de patria, qui repente rapuerunt et duxerunt ad villam de Chelmesford, in qua censuerunt eum arbitrio communium morti turpissimae judicandum. Quo cum pervenisset, interventu dominae comitissae de Hereford, salvatus est ad horam

et ductus ad fortalicium de Plesshi, servandus per familiares
dominae, sed mediante communibus restituendus. Cumque
custodiretur ibi per dies aliquot, orientales Saxones con-
fluxerunt de cunctis villis circumjacentibus et munitionem
in qua servabatur, velut obsidendo, circumsederunt; et tandem ad hunc finem intenderunt omnes ut produceretur et,
velut regum proditor, in eodem loco decapitaretur in quo
dominus eorundem dux Gloucestriae, dum occurrisset regi
Ricardo processionaliter et pacifice, per eundem regem fuerat
arestatus.

Die igitur sancti Mauri, quae fuit octavo decimo kalendas
Febuarii, imminente jam nocte, communes petierunt dominum Gerardum Braybrok militem ut educeret proditorem.
Ille vero, juxta mandata dominae comitissae Herefordiae,
cupiens servare eum donec dominus rex cum eo colloquium
habuisset, requisivit divortia tempusque protraxit et distulit
eos audire. Qui mox, velut in mentis insaniam versi, juraverunt quod nisi ipse produceret eum sine mora, ipse morere-
tur pro eodem. Ille vero iras vulgi [metuens] promisit se
comitem producturum; jugiter reversusque, cum festinatione
tremebundus, reperit comitem atque militem, scilicet Johannem Schevelee, genuflectendo, jam dixisse commendationem
pro animabus propriis et officium mortuorum; narravitque
eis in quanto [pavore] fuerat constitutus, quia eos producere
distulisset. Comes haec audiens lamentabiliter exclamavit,
—"heu," inquit, "sumne trahendus arbitrio rusticorum et
nebulonum et mactandus juxta beneplacitum eorundem?
Sinite me," inquit, "armari deprecor, et me defendere donec
deficiam, ne tam foede mori me contingat." Gerardus et
alii e contra consulerunt ut, dismissa vindicandi voluntate,
armaret se patientia et humiliter fortunam subiret, quam
subterfugere nullo modo poterat. Cumque comes consen-
sisset eorum consiliis, vinctis a tergo manibus, eductus est
ad communes, qui steterunt super pontem hinc et inde ar-
mati lanceis, gladibus, arcubus et sagittis; nam pons longus
est ab illa turri usque ad terram contiguam, et per eorum
medium eum transire necessarium fuit. Qui ut vidit tantum
communitatis apparatum, elevata voce rogavit eos omnes ex
parte Dei et caritatis intuitu ne inordinatis clamoribus eum

stupefacerent. . . . Cumque pervenisset ad locum ubi arestatus olim fuerat dux Gloverniae, genuflectere jussus, dixit
"confiteor" in aperto, . . . rogavitque cunctos attentius ut
talis eligeretur ad decollandum eum qui foret expertus et
uno ictu decapitare sciret. Sed cum extendisset caput et
collum super breve scabellum, ganeo, qui decapitaturus fuerat
eum, vel ebrietate vel metu facti oberrans, non lictoris sed
tortoris exercebat officium, eum decem vicibus securi feriens
et miserabiliter nimis torquens. Corpus vero truncum sacer-
dotes de collegio rapuerunt et penes se collocaverunt. Caput
ejus, sicut et caeterorum qui perempti fuerunt Cyrcestriae,
Londoniis mittebatur.

Eulogium, Rolls Series, 9, iii, p. 386

Postmodum apud Prytwell in Excexce in quodam molendino Johannes Holand dux Exoniae, frater regis Ricardi ex
parte matris, se transformans in simplicem, per patriae illius
communitatem captus et usque Plasshe adductus, decollatur.

Walsingham, Rolls Series [28], i, 2, p. 245

Comes Huntyngdone, dominus Johannes Holand, non erat
cum praedictis dominis apud castellum de Wyndeshore, sed
expectavit Londoniis rei finem. Qui cum novisset rem versam
contra vota, fugere nitebatur in scapha, sed vento flante contrario repulsus est. Quamobrem equo vectus pervenit Estsexiam cum quodam milite dicto ɟ Schevele. Tentavit igitur
per mare fugisse ab illis partibus, sed quotiens voluit mare
ingredi totiens repulsus est vi ventorum, donec omnino
desperans de Neptuni suffragiis destitit ab inceptis. Tandem
reversus in terram ad domum cujusdam amici sui, dum
sederet in coena cum milite supradicto, captus est per communes patriae, et ductus primo ad villam de Chelmesfordia,
deinde ad fortalitium de Plesshi custodiendus ibidem tanquam
loco securiori. Quo confluentibus regionis communibus, die
sancti Mauri, circa solis occasum productus est et, in loco
quo dominus eorum dux Gloverniae quondam arestatus fuit
per regem Ricardum, decapitatus est, confessus prius lacry-

mabiliter se pecasse in Deum suum multipliciter et in regem suum quia, sciens consilia dictorum dominorum, regem exinde mimine praemunisset.

(See also Walsingham's Ypodeigma Neustriae, Rolls Series, p. 390.)

Otterbourne, ed. Hearne, i, p. 227

Comes Huntingdon, hoc audito, fugit et captus fuit, et ductus usque Chelmesford, deinde apud Plessy, prece comitissae Her[e]ford ad horam servatus. Sed communitas noluerunt hunc vivere ultra. Petebant namque ipsum liberari ut ibidem decapitaretur in loco viz. ubi dominus eorum dux Glouc[estriae] fuerat prius captus, vel ipsam comitissam et totam familiam suam, nisi eum sibi traderet, occiderent. Tunc illa liberavit eis, qui eum decollari fecerunt.

Vita Regis Ricardi II, ed. Hearne, p. 167

Et non multum post dominus Johannes Holont comes Huntyngdon, frater regis Ricardi ex parte matris, apud Plaschet in Estsexia per comitissam Herefordiae captus et decollatus est. Cujus captionis modum ad praesens omitto propter taedium lectorum.

Collectanea, ed. Leland, ii, p. 484

Sir John Holand duke of Excestre was taken in Estsax at a mylle by Pritelwel by communes of the cuntery and thens led him to Plaisshey, and there, in vengeange of the arresting the good duke of Glocester by king Richard, was by hedid.

An English Chronicle, Camden Society, 64, p. 21

And the same yeer at Pritwelle in Essex, in a mille, ser John Holand duke of Excestre was take be the communez of the cuntre, and unto Plasshe, where as king Richard arestid ser Thomas of Wodestoke duke of Gloucestre, and there they smoot of his hed, and yt was set on London brigge.

Chronicon Angliae, ed. Giles, p. 10

Et non multum post Johannes Hollande comes Hunting-doniae, frater Ricardi nuper regis Angliae, captus fuit per dominam comitissam Herfordiae. justa Plashe in Essexia, sine stipatu famulantium, et ibidem sine ulteriore judicio eadem domina fecit unum de militibus praefati comitis ejus caput amputare.

Lambeth MS. 306, Camden Society N.S. 28, p. 52

And in the same yere was the erle of Kent, the erle of Salisbery, be hedid at Susseter. And sir Thomas Blunt, sir Rauffe Lomney, sir John Cely and Thomas Venter were be hedyd at Oxenford. And sir John Holond and (sic) the duke of Excester were be hedyd at Plaschey. And the lord Spencer was be hedid at Bristowe.

Chronicle of London, p. 86

. . . also the erle of Huntyngton was beheded at Plasshe in Essex, the which was fled and wolde a passed the see to have brought in Frensshmen for to destroye Engelond : and he myghte have no wynd to brynge hym over, and he was take and beheded as it ys aboveseid.

Capgrave's Chronicle, Rolls Series, I, p. 276

The erl of Huntingdon herd of this and fled into Esex. And as often as he assaied to take the se, so often was he bore of with the wynde. Than was he take be the comones and led to Chelmisforth, and than to Plasche, and his hed smet of in the same place where he arestid the duke of Gloucetir.

Chronique de la Traison et Mort de Richard II, Eng. Hist. Soc., p. 96

Et quant la justice fu faicte a Oxinforde et que sire Thomas Blont fu mis a mort le roy Henry envoya le conte de Rotelan et sire Thomas Derpeghem apres le sire Despensier qui fu conte de Clocestre et fut prins et lui copa on la teste et le

conte de Rotelan le fist aussi mener a Londres. Et quant
le duc Dexcestre conte Dontinton, frere au roy Richart, et
sire Thomas Selle qui avoit este son maistre dostel, qui fu
un bon chivaler, furent arrivez en Escoce (sic) en une petite
ville ou demoura la contesse Daruorde, la suer de feu le
conte Darondel lequel avoit este decolle a Londres au grant
parlement, le duc Dexcestre et son maistre dostel si alerent
logier en lostel ou ilz avoient acoustumie destre logiez quant
ilz passoient par la, et la contesse senti que le conte Dontinton
estoit arrive. Adonc elle commanda a son connestable de
la ville que il feist assembler secretement tous ceulx de la
ville pour prendre le frere au roy Richart a tout ses gens, car
elle le vouloit avoir et prendre vengeance de son frere. Il
fu fait ainsi comme elle le commanda et la fut prins le conte
Dontinton lui iije, son chivaler, et son bouteillier lequel avoit
nom Hugue Cade. Et toute la plus grant partie de sa
chevalerie et escuierie fu prinse par tout le pais de ca et de
la quilz ne savoient quelle part chevaucher ne ou aler. Et
envoya la contesse unes lettres au roy Henry pour lui faire
savoir comment elle avoit fait prendre le conte Dontinton
et pria au roy quil lui voulsist envoyer son cousin Darondel
et quil lui venist prendre vengeance de la mort de son pere,
car elle feroit le conte Dontinton pendre et traisner. Adonc
envoya le roy le conte Darondel par dela disant: "cousin
alez a vostre ante et amenez les prisonniers par deca vifz ou
mors." Et quant le conte Darondel arriva en la ville ou le
conte Dontinton fu prins il trouva la contesse Darondel (sic)
son ante et les villains du pais qui furent la assemblez bien
viij m. ou plus. La dame avoit fait amener devant ses
villains le conte Dontinton pour le faire mourir, et pour il
navoit nul des villains la qui neust bien grant pitie de lui. . . .
[The earl's death by the unskilful hands of a young esquire
is described at great length.] . . . Ainsi fu mis a mort le duc
Dexcestre conte Dontinton frere du noble roy Richart. Et
le conte Darondel fist bouter la teste du duc sur un long
baston, et le chevalier fu liez les piez et les mains et amene
a cheval, et le bouteillier fu lie et trota a pie jusques a Londres
ou ilz arriverent le lundi xix jour de Janvier environ disner.
Et le conte Darondel vint a Londres et ses menestrelz et

trompetes devant la teste du duc Dexcestre. . . . A tel jour
mesmes arriva le conte de Rotelan lequel fist porter devant
lui la teste du sire Despensier conte de Clocestre sur un long
baton. . . .[1]

Chronicles of London, Kingsford, p. 62

And Sir John Holonde erle off Huntyngdon and Thomas
Wynter squyer weren byheeded at Plasshe in Essex, and her
heedes weren sette upon London Brigge.

Waurin, Rolls Series, 39, ii, p. 45.

(Coment le conte de Hostidonne, frere du roy Richard, fut
prins et piteusement mis a mort.   Chapter xiii.)

Ainsi comme vous oez le roy Henry et les Londriens
faisoient feste et joye, mais le conte de Hostidonne duc
d'Excestre, frere du defunct roy Richard, et messire Thomas
Saielle quy avoit este son maistre d'hostel, moult vaillant
et hardy chevallier en son temps, eulz volans, comme par cy
devant avez oy, comment les villains de Succestre avoient
uze du duc de Sudrien et des autres nobles hommes, se par-
tirent hors de la ville, ou le conte trouva son maistre d'hostel
lui douziesme avec lesquelz il prinst le chemin d'Escoce (sic),
si arriverent en une petite ville ou pour lors demouroit la
contesse d'Arondel (sic) sceur du conte d'Arondel qui avoit
este decolle a Londres au grand parlement.   Le duc d'Excestre conte de Hostidonne et sa compaignie se logerent en
une hostelerie ou autresfois avoit accoustume de soy logier
quant il passoit par la.   Alors la contesse d'Arondel (sic)
sachant le conte a privee maisnie estre en la ville, manda
secretement a son connestable quil assemblast toute la com-
munaulte pour prendre et saisir le conte de Hostidonne frere
du roy Richard et tous ceulz qui avec luy estoient, car sur lui
voulloient prendre vengance de la mort de son frere ; la quelle
chose fut faite ainsi comme elle commanda, a scavoir le dit
conte de Hostidonne, lui troisiesme de chevalliers, si furent

[1] Test the reliability of these dates by Close Roll, 1 Henry IV,
pt. i, m. 19. Writ dated January 24th directed to the Mayor of
Bristol and ordering him to send the head of Despencer to London.

fort lyez et amenez devant la contesse.   Si sachies veritable-
ment que lors ne faisoient autre chose en Angleterre que
guettier les passages, parquoy finablement furent prins le
greigneur partie des barons chevalliers et escuyers tenans la
partie du roy Richard, qui estoit moult grand pitie a veoir,
ne ilz ne scavoient quel part fuyr que tantost ne feussent
accusez comme il ny eust passage ou gens ne feussent or-
donnez pour les prendre.   Or doncques le duc d'Excestre
ainsi prins, la contesse d'Arondel (sic) rescripvi au roy Henry,
qui estoit a Londres, toute ladvenne du cas, et que prestement
luy voulsist envoier le conte d'Arondel son cousin pour veoir
prendre vengeance de son pere, car son intention estoit de
faire pendre[1] et trainner ledit conte de Hostidonne.   Le roy
Henry moult joieux de dis nouvelles, quant il eut leu les
lettres, appela le jeune conte d'Arondel et luy dist : " Beau
cousin, allez veoir vostre tante pardela, et mamenez tous les
prisonniers quelle a devers elle, mors ou vifz."   De la quelle
legation le conte d'Arondel moult joieux il monta a cheval,
si sexploita telement de chevaulchier quil vint en la ville ou
estoit la ducesse (sic) sa tante, qui avoit illec environ plus de
huit mille paysans assemblez tous armez et embastonnez, si
avoit fait amener devant eulz ledit noble conte de Hostidonne
pour le faire morir, mais pour certain il ny eut homme en
toute la compaignie quy neust de luy pitie, car il estoit ung
moult beau prince, grant et droit, bien fourme de tous mem-
bres, qui estoit la devant eulz les mains liies.   En ceste meisme
heure arriva le conte d'Arondel en la place, si salua sa tante
et vey la present le conte de Hostidonne duc d'Excestre
auquel il demanda : . . . [Arundel upbraids Huntingdon] . . .
et adonc fist mener le conte devant la bataille des villains
adfin quilz loccessient.   Le conte de Hostidonne se voiant
en ce parti, regardant moult piteusement ceulz qui le devoient
occir, leur disoit : " Mes seigneurs aiez pitie de moy car
oncques a vous ne a ceulz de ce pays ne meffis riens."   Sy ny
avoit adont nulz deulz qui eust voulloir de luy mal faire et
quy neust grant pitie de luy, excepte le conte et la contesse
d'Arondel (sic) laquell dist a ses gens : " Mauldis soyez vous

---

[1] "prendre" in Rolls edition.

tous, villains maulvaiz, quy nestes pas si hardis que de mettre ung homme a mort." Alors saprocha ung escuyer de la dame et du conte d'Arondel, qui se presenta a decoller ledit conte de Hostidonne, et la contesse luy commanda que tost le feist ; si vint lescuyer, une hace en sa main, . . . [Huntingdon's death is described at great length]. . . . Et lors le conte d'Arondel fist mettre la teste sur une longue perche. Puis les chevalliers quy furent prins avec luy eurent les mains loyees, aussi eurent les autres prisonniers, lesquelz le conte d'Arondel fist troter de pie apres luy tant quilz vindrent jusques a Londres, ou ilz arriverent le Lundy neuvieme jour de Jenvier environ heure de disner, et le conte de Arundel entra dedens Londres ses trompettes et menestrelz sonnans devant luy, et entre le dit conte d'Arondel et les menestrelz venoient lesdis prisonniers et ceulz qui aportoient la teste du duc d'Excestre conte de Hostidonne.

Chronique du Religieux de Saint Denis, vol. ii, p. 742

Comes vero de Hotinton, quondam regis Richardi frater illegitimus, cum in Scociam (sic) fugere conaretur, a gentibus comitisse Herifordie, cujus filiam desponsaverat rex Henricus, captus et incarceratus fuit. Quod audiens rex Henricus, quia sororem ejus duxerat in uxorem, mittissime sperans agere pro ipso, mandavit ut sibi remitteretur. Quod renuens remandavit quod sibi truncun vel caput solum haberet, et hec dicens ipsum decollari jussit. Sane contra predictum inexpiabili odio hucusque laboraverat, quoniam in mortem ducis Glocestrie, qui secundam filiam ejus desponsaverat, machinatus fuerat et consulerat ut ignominiose occideretur, ut dictum est. Caput autem occisi comitis ad regem, ut promiserat, transmisit per comitem Arundelli; qua eciam die comes de Rotland caput domini Dispensatoris eidem regi obtulit. Que duo capita jussit super pontem Londoniensem suspendi, et illos qui eis faverant ubique diligentissime perquiri.

MS. Gray's Inn, No. 9, *fol.* 145 (*contemporary*)

Eodem anno circa festum Epiphanie domini conspirabant quidam adversus regem Henricum non immerito ut occidere-

tur. Thomas dux Surrẏe comes Cancie qui capite est plexus
nesciente rege Henrico in villa sua a suis proditoribus apud
Surcestr. Et comes Sar. et fidelis miles Rauf Lomney cum
multis aliis nobilissimis personis similiter decapitantur. Et
dux Exon. frater regis Ricardi apud Plasshee fraudilenter est
occisus.

Year Books, 1–14 *Henry IV; First Edition published by
Tottel, n.d.* (1553?), *fol.* 1
Anno Primo Henrici Quarti[1]

I
Corone.
Coment un
seigniour
serra trie par
ses pares.

Le Countey de H. fuit endicte dell hault treason
en Londres per un commission devant le Mayre et
Justices de ceo que il ove auters parsons accord de
fayre un Mummyng en la nuycte del Epiphanie,
en quel ils entendant de tuer le Roy donques
estant all Wyndesore. Et puis le Roy fesoit commission a
le Countie de D. recitant que lou. G. le counte de H. fuit
endicte de Hault treason par luy fait concernant sa parson
et que il vouloit ceo que droit est, et pur ceo que l'office dell
Scenescall del Angleter est ore voyde il graunta cest office a
le dit counte de D. pur faire droyt all dit counte de H. com-
maundant par mesme le commission toutes seigniours de
estre attendant sur luy Et commandant auxi par mesme le
commission le Constable dell Toure pur estre attendant sur
luy, et pur conveyer le prysoner s.[2] le dit Counte de H. devant
le dit Countie de D. a quell jour ill sera a ceo assigne. Et
sur ceo a certayne jour le dit Counte de D. seyt en le sale de
Westminster south un cloth de estate a par luy Et le Counte
de Westmerlãd et toutes auters countees et seigniours la
sederñt par un graund space de luy, mes nemy sur mesme le
banke, mes sur auters formes downeward en la dit sale. Et
tous les Justices et barons del Excheker sederunt en le mulnes
circa un Table par enter les dictes seigniours. Et puis trois
Oyes fuerunt solempnemẽt faits per le Crier, et le dit commission fuit lie. Et puis les Justices deliveront lenditement

---

[1] De Termino Michaelis Anno i regni regis Henrici Quarti (ed.
1679).
[2] S. (ed. 1562–70).

a le dit[1] Scenescal, le quell ceo deliver all Clerke del Corone, le quell ceo lia a le dit Counte de H. le quel il confes, pur que Hil[2] un des seriants le Roy pria que le dit Seigniour Senescall voil doner judgement, sur quel il rehersa le dit matter et puis done judgement que il alera a le Toure de Londres et de ceo que il serra trahe a les furkes et la pend, et let down arere uncore vivant, et que donques (ses entrailes serra trahes hors de son corps et combures et que[3]) il serra decolle et quartere. *Et sic Deus propicietur animae suae.* Et touts les Justices diont que si le dit Counte voil aver denie le treason, donques le Scenescall demaundera de chescun Seigniour a par luy apartement (quant ils done[ront] lour verdict, le[3]) quel il esteme en sa conscience, et il commencera enprimes ove le puisne Seigniour. Et si le pluis nombre dira culpable, donques le judgement serra done *ut supra.* Et nul Seigniour serra jure sur ceo, etc.

(A copy of this edition is in Lincoln's Inn Library. See also, in addition to the ordinary edition of 1679, Year Books 1 Henry IV to 9 Henry V, Tottel, 1562–70; and Year Books 1 Henry IV to 9 Henry V, Thomas Wight, 1605.)

Baga de Secretis, Pouch II
Letters Patent appointing a Steward of England for the Trial of Edward Earl of Warwick

Henricus Dei gratia rex Anglie et Francie et dominus Hibernie carissimo consanguineo suo Johanni comiti Oxon. magno camerario Anglie ac admirallo ejusdem salutem. Sciatis quod cum Edwardus comes Warr. per nomen Edwardi comitis Warr. nuper de Warrewyk in com. Warr. de alta prodicione per ipsum erga personam nostram regiam facta et perpetrata coram dilectis et fidelibus nostris Nicholao Alwyn majore civitatis nostre London, Johanne Fyneux milite

---

[1] omit (ed. 1679).

[2] A Robert Hill (or Hull) was one of the worthies of this period. He became king's serjeant in 1399: in 1408 he was appointed a judge of the Common Pleas, and was one of the commission which tried Cambridge, Scrope and Grey in 1415.

[3] Not in Tottel's editions.

Thoma Bryan milite et sociis suis justiciariis nostris ad omnimodi prodiciones felonias conspiraciones rebelliones insurrectiones contemptus concelamenta forisfacturas decepciones falsitates riotas routas conventicula illicita transgressiones misprisiones et alias offensas quascunque infra civitatem predictam ac suburb. et libertatem ejusdem per quoscumque et qualitercumque facta sive perpetrata audiendum et terminandum assignatis indictatus existit: Nos considerantes quod justitia est virtus excellens Altissimo complacens eaque pre omnibus uti volumus, pro eo quod officium senescalli Anglie cujus presencia pro administracione justicie et execucione ejusdem in hac parte fiende requiritur, ut accepimus, jam vacat, de fidelitate provida circumspectione et industria vestris plenius confidentes. ordinamus et constituimus vos senescallum Anglie ad officium illud ex causa predicta cum omnibus eidem officio in hac parte debite pertinentibus hac vice gerendum occupandum et exercendum; dantes et concedentes vobis tenore presencium plenam et sufficientem potestatem et auctoritatem ac mandatum speciale indictamenta predicta cum omnibus illa tangentibus a prefatis majore, Johanne, Thoma et sociis suis predictis recipiendi et illa inspiciendi ac ad certos diem et locum quos ad hoc provideritis ipsum Edwardum coram vobis evocandi et ipsum superinde examinandi et respondere compellendi ac fine debito terminandi necnon tot et tales dominos proceres et magnates hujusmodi regni nostri Anglie ejusdem Edwardi pares per quos rei veritas in hac parte melius sciri poterit ad diem et locum predictos ex causa predicta coram vobis comparere astringendi, veritateque inde comperta ad judicium inde per hujusmodi senescallum reddendum secundum leges et consuetudines regni nostri Anglie hac vice versus prefatum Edwardum procedendi sentenciandi et adjudicandi ac execucionem inde facere percipiendi ceteraque omnia et singula que ad officium senescalli Anglie in hac parte pertinent et requiruntur hac vice faciendi exercendi et exequendi. Et ideo vobis mandamus quod circa premissa diligenter intendatis et ea faciatis et exequamini in forma predicta. Damus autem universis et singulis ducibus comitibus baronibus, vicecomitibus et omnibus aliis officiariis ministris et ligeis

nostris tenore presencium firmiter in mandatis quod vobis
in executione premissorum intendentes sint consulentes assistentes et auxiliantes in omnibus prout decet. Mandavimus
enim eidem majori, Johanni, Thome et sociis suis predictis
quod indictamenta predicta cum omnibus illa tangentibus
ex causa predicta vobis deliberent. Mandavimus eciam constabulario turris nostre London ejusve locumtenenti vel
deputato ibidem quod ad certos diem et locum quos ei scire
faciatis prefatum Edwardum coram vobis venire faciat. In
cujus rei testimonium has literas nostras fieri fecimus patentes.
Teste me-ipso apud Westmonasterium xix die Novembris
anno regni nostri quinto decimo.

Baga de Secretis, Pouch II
The Trial of the Earl of Warwick

Dominus Rex mandavit carissimo consanguineo suo Johanni comiti Oxon. magno camerario Anglie ac admirallo
ejusdem necnon senescallo Anglie hac vice literas suas
patentes in hec verba: [The earl's patent of appointment
is here set out as above.] *Mandavit* etiam idem dominus
rex dilectis et fidelibus suis Nicholao Alwyn majori civitatis
sue London Johanni Fyneux militi Thome Bryan militi et
sociis suis justiciariis ipsius regis ad omnimodi prodiciones
felonias conspiraciones rebelliones insurrectiones contemptus
concelamenta forisfacturas decepciones falsitates riotas routas
conventicula illicita transgressiones misprisiones et alias
offensas quascumque infra civitatem predictam ac suburb.
et libertatem ejusdem per quoscumque et qualitercumque
facta sive perpetrata audiendum et terminandum assignatis
breve suum clausum in hec verba—*Henricus* Dei gratia rex
Anglie et Francie et dominus Hibernie dilectis et fidelibus
suis Nicholao Alwyn majori civitatis sue London Johanni
Fyneux militi Thome Bryan militi et sociis suis justiciariis
suis ad omnimodi prodiciones felonias conspiraciones rebelliones insurrectiones contemptus concelamenta forisfacturas decepciones falsitates riotas routas conventicula illicita
transgressiones misprisiones et alias offensas quascumque
infra civitatem predictam ac suburb. et libertatem ejusdem

per quoscumque et qualitercumque facta sive perpetrata
audiendum et terminandum assignatis et eorum cuilibet
salutem Mandamus vobis quod omnia et singula indictamenta recorda et processus de quibuscumque prodicionibus
seu aliis malefactis unde Edwardus comes Warr. nuper de
Warrewyk in comitatu Warr. coram vobis indictatus est ut
dicitur carissimo consanguineo nostro Johanni comiti Oxon.
magno camerario Anglie ac admirallo ejusdem necnon hac
vice senescallo Anglie deliberetis indilate unacum hoc breve
ut ipse senescallus inspectis indictamentis recordis et processibus predictis ulterius inde hac parte fieri faciat prout
de jure et secundum legem et consuetudinem regni nostri
Anglie fuerit faciendum. Teste meipso apud Westmonasterium xx die Novembris anno regni nostri quinto-decimo.
Ac insuper mandavit idem dominus rex constabulario Turris
sue London sive ejus locumtenenti vel deputato ibidem
quoddam alium breve suum clausum in hec verba :—Henricus Dei gratia rex Anglie et Francie et dominus Hibernie
constabulario Turris sue London sive ejus locumtenenti vel
deputato ibidem salutem. Mandamus vobis quod Edwardum
comitem Warr. nuper de Warrewyk in comitatu Warr. de
alta prodicione erga personam nostram per ipsum facta et
perpetrata coram dilectis ei fidelibus nostris Nicholao Alwyn
majore civitatis nostre London, Johanne Fyneux milite,
Thoma Bryan milite et sociis suis justiciariis nostris ad
omnimodi prodiciones et alia malefacta infra eandem civitatem ac suburb. et libertatem ejusdem qualitercumque facta
et perpetrata audiendum et terminandum assignatis indic-
tatum coram carissimo consanguineo nostro Johanne comite
Oxon. magno camerario Anglie ac admirallo ejusdem necnon
hac vice Anglie senescallo ad certos diem et locum quos
idem senescallus vobis sciri faciat super premissis responsu-
rum salvo et secure venire faciatis. Et hoc nullatenus omittatis. Teste me-ipso apud Westmonasterium xx die Novembris anno regni nostri quinto decimo. *Quarumquidem*
literarum domini regis patentium predictarum prefato senescallo Anglie hac vice directarum pretextu preceptum fuit
per dictum senescallum Anglie scilicet vicesimo die Novembris anno quinto decimo supradicto prefato Nicholao Alwyn,

Johanni Fyneux militi, et Thome Bryan militi et sociis suis Justiciariis etc. quod indictamenta recorda et processus de alta prodicione persone domini regis facta et perpetrata coram eis nuper capta unde predictus comes Warrewici indictatus extitit cum omnibus ea tangentibus adeo plene et integre prout coram eis nuper capta fuerunt et penes se tunc residebant quocumque nomine predictus comes nuncupebatur in eisdem coram prefato senescallo sub sigillo suo aut unius eorum apud Westmonasterium die Jovis proximo ante festum sancti Clementis pape tunc proximo sequentem mitterent seu unus eorum mitteret ut ulterius etc. *Preceptum* fuit etiam per dictum senescallum Anglie dicto vicesimo die Novembris anno quinto decimo supradicto prefato constabulario Turris domini regis London vel ejus locumtenenti vel deputato suo ibidem quod corpus predicti comitis Warrwici in prisona domini regis sub custodia sua detentum unacum causa detencionis sue quocumque nomine predictus comes censeatur in eadem haberet coram prefato senescallo apud Westmonasterium predictum dicto die Jovis proximo ante festum sancti Clementis pape ad subjiciendum et recipiendum ea que curia domini regis de eo tunc ibidem ordinare contigerit. *Mandatum* fuit etiam per dictum senescallum Anglie dicto vicesimo die Novembris anno quinto decimo supradicto Johanni Rowdon servienti domini regis ad arma quod ipse summoneret tot et tales dominos proceres et magnates hujus regni Anglie predicti Edwardi comitis Warr. pares per quos rei veritas in hac parte melius sciri poterit quod ipsi personaliter compareant coram prefato senescallo apud Westmonasterium predictum dicto die Jovis proximo ante festum sancti Clementis pape ad faciendum ea que eis ex parte domini regis tunc ibidem in premissis injungentur. PLACITA CORAM JOHANNE COMITE OXON, SENESCALLO ANGLIE HAC VICE necnon magno camerario et admirallo ejusdem tenta apud Westmonasterium in magna aula placitorum domini regis ibidem die Jovis proximo ante festum sancti Clementis pape anno regni regis Henrici septimi post conquestum quinto decimo. Nicholas Alwyn major civitatis London, Johannes Fyneux miles et Thomas Bryan miles justiciarii etc. solempniter exacti comparuerunt et presentes

hic in curia juxta vim formam et effectum brevis domini
regis et preceptum predictum eis inde directum omnia et
singula indictamenta et recordum inde versus prefatum
comitem Warr. de prodicionibus predictis capta cum omnibus illa tangentibus adeo plene et prout coram eis et
sociis suis nuper capta fuerunt et penes eos tunc resi-
dentia coram prefato senescallo Anglie pretextu mandati
predicti hac instanti die Jovis etc. per manus suas proprias deliberaverunt terminanda. Ac etiam Thomas
Lovell miles locumtenens prefati constabularii Turris
London juxta mandatum predictum similiter exactus corpus predicti comitis tunc eodem die Jovis coram prefato
senescallo Anglie pretextu brevis domini regis et precepti
predicti paratum habuit prout sibi precipiebatur. Necnon
predictus Johannes Rowdon serviens domini regis ad arma
prefato senescallo Anglie pretextu mandati sui predicti
asseruit quod ipse omnes et singulos dominos proceres et
magnates regni Anglie predicti comitis Warr. pares per quos
etc. personaliter coram prefato senescallo ad prefatos diem
et locum compareant ad faciendum ea que eis ex parte
domini regis tunc ibidem in premissis injungentur prout
superius datum fuit sibi in mandatis etc. Super quo facta
proclamacione pro domino rege per mandatum senescalli
Anglie predicti quod tam omnes duces et comites quam
barones pares predicti comitis Warr. qui per mandatum
senescalli Anglie predicti ac summonitionem predicti ser-
vientis ad arma eis factum ad tunc in curia presentes fuerint
compareant et pro eorum nominibus responderent ad faciendum ea que eis ex parte domini regis tunc ibidem in premissis injungentur. Quiquidem duces comites et barones
tunc ibidem in plena curia existentes scilicet Edwardus dux
Bukk., Henricus comes Northumbrie, Georgius comes Kancie,
Thomas comes Surrey, Henricus comes Essex, Johannes
Kendal prior sancti Johannis Jerusalem in Anglia, Georgius
Nevill miles dominus Burgevenny, Thomas Ormond miles
dominus Ormond, Johannes Dynnam miles dominus de
Dynham thesaurarius Anglie, Ricardus Nevyll miles dominus
Latymer, Thomas West miles dominus de la Warre, Johannes
Clynton dominus de Clynton, Willelmus Blount dominus de

Mountjoy, Edwardus Hastyngs miles dominus de Hastyngs, Johannes Bourgchier miles dominus de Berners, Johannes Zouche miles dominus Zouche, Ricardus Seyntmount miles dominus Seyntmount, Willelmus Willoughby dominus de Willoughby, Edwardus Grey dominus de Wylton, Thomas Fenys dominus de Dacre, Egidius Dawbeney miles dominus Dawbeney et Robertus Willoughby miles dominus de Broke juxta vim formam et effectum proclamacionis predicte ac summonicionis predicti eis ut predicitur per predictum servientem ad arma facti ad tunc et ibidem solempniter exacti comparuerunt et per eorum nomina separatim responderunt etc. quorum presencia per prefatum senescallum recordata fuit etc. *Recordum ac Indictamenta* et processus versus prefatum Edwardum comitem Warr. de alta prodicione coram prefato Nicholao Alwyn majore civitatis London, Johanne Fyneux milite, Thoma Bryan milite et sociis suis justiciariis etc. capta et per manus suas proprias hic in curia deliberata sequntur in hec verba. ¶ London ¶ Inquisitio. . . . [The indictment is set out at length.] . . . .
. . . *Et* modo scilicet dicto die Jovis proximo ante dictum festum sancti Clementis pape coram prefato Johanne comite Oxon. hac vice senescallo Anglie apud Westmonasterium venit predictus Edwardus comes Warrewici sub custodia predicti Thome Lovell militis locumtenentis prefati constabularii turris London in cujus custodia proutantea ex causa predicta et aliis certis de causis commissus fuit ad barram hic ductus in propria persona sua, qui committitur prefato locumtenenti etc. Et statim de prodicionibus predictis sibi superius impositis allocutus qualiter se velit inde acquietare etc.: Dicit quod ipse non potest dedicere quin ipse de prodicionibus predictis sibi superius impositis est culpabilis[1] et prodiciones illas expresse cognovit. Et posuit se inde in manum domini regis. Super quo instanter serientes domini regis ad legem ac ipsius regis attornatus pro eo quod dictus comes Warrewici prodiciones predictas sibi superius impositas expresse cognovit juxta debitam legis formam petierunt versus eundem comitem judicium et executionem superinde pro domino rege versus

---

[1] (In margin) Cogn.

ipsum comitem habendum etc. Et super hoc visis et per curiam hic diligenter examinatis et intellectis omnibus et singulis premissis consideratum est quod predictus Edwardus comes Warrewici ducatur per prefatum constabularium turris London seu ejus locumtenentem usque eandem turrim et deinde per medium civitatis London usque ad furcas de Tyburn trahatur et ibidem suspendatur et vivens ad terram prosternatur et introra sua extra ventrem suam capiantur et ipso vivente comburentur et quod caput ejus amputetur quodque corpus ejus in quatuor partes dividatur et quod caput et quartia illa ponantur ubi dominus rex ea assignare voluerit etc.[1]

(Bundle in original cover indorsed—" Sess. Com. Mid. tent. apud Westm. coram Johanne comite Oxon. hac vice Senescallo Anglie, anno regni regis Henrici septimi post conquestum quinto decimo.")

Patent Roll, 19 *Henry VII, pt.* 1, *m.* 23*d.*

Rex carissimo consanguineo suo Thome comiti Surrie thesaurario Anglie salutem. Sciatis quod cum Edwardus Sutton de Dudley miles de quibusdam feloniis per ipsum ut pretenditur factis et perpetratis coram dilectis et fidelibus nostris Ricardo Lyttleton et Johanne Blounte custodibus pacis nostre ac justiciariis nostris ad diversa felonias transgressiones et alia malefacta comitatu Staffordie audiendum et terminandum assignatis indictatus existit ut accepimus. Quod quidem indictamentum coram nobis mitti mandavimus et ibidem residet. Nos considerantes quod prefatus Edwardus est unus procerum et magnatum regni nostri et quod juxta statuta et ordinationes regni nostri per pares suos et non aliter triari et adjudicari debeat et consueverit. Jamque pro eo quod officium senescalli Anglie cujus presentia pro administratione justitie et executiones (sic) ejusdem in hac parte fienda requiritur nunc vacat. De fidelitate provida circumspectione et industria vestris quamplurimum confidentes ordinamus et constituimus vos senescallum Anglie

---

[1] (In margin) T. et S.

ad officium illud ex causa predicta cum omnibus eidem officio in hac parte debite pertinentibus hac vice gerendum occupandum et exercendum, dantes et concedentes vobis tenore presentium plenam et sufficientem potestatem et auctoritatem ac mandatum speciale indictamentum predictum cum omnibus illud tangentibus vobis mitti et liberari petendi et illud recipiendi et inspiciendi ac ad certos dies et loca quos ad hoc provideritis ipsum Edwardum coram vobis evocandi et venire faciendi et ipsum superinde examinandi et respondere compellendi ac fine debito terminandi, necnon tot et tales dominos proceres et magnates hujus regni nostri Anglie ejusdem Edwardi pares per quos rei veritas in hac parte melius sciri poterit ad diem et locum predictos ex hac causa coram vobis venire et comparere astringendi, veritateque inde comperta ad judicium inde per hujusmodi senescallum reddendum secundum leges et consuetudines regni nostri Anglie hac vice versus prefatum Edwardum procedendi sententiandi et adjudicandi ac executionem inde facere percipiendi ceteraque omnia et singula que ad officium senescalli Anglie in hac parte pertinent et requiruntur hac vice faciendi et exercendi. Et ideo vobis mandamus quod circa premissa diligenter intendatis ac ea faciatis et exequamini in forma predicta. Damus autem universis et singulis ducibus marchionibus comitibus baronibus ac aliis magnatibus regni nostri predictis et aliis quorum interest in hac parte quod vobis in executione premissorum intendentes sint assistentes et auxiliantes in omnibus prout decet. Mandavimus enim justiciariis nostris ad placita coram nobis tenenda assignatis quod indictamentum predictum cum omnibus illud tangentibus ex causa predicta vobis deliberent. Mandavimus enim vicecomiti nostro comitatus predicti quod ad certos diem et locum quos ei scire feceritis prefatum Edwardum coram vobis venire faciat. In cujus etc. Teste rege apud Westmonasterium.　　　Per ipsum regem et de dato etc.

(Printed by Rymer, Foedera O.S., vol. xiii, p. 87.)

Year Book, Easter Term, 13 *Henry VIII, fol.* 11

Nota quand un Seigneur de Parlement sera arreine de treason ou felony, le roy par ses lettres patentes fera un grand et sage seigneur destre le grand seneschal d'Angleterre q le jour de l'arreinement, devant quel jour il doit faire un precept a un serjeant d'armes (q'est le serjeant a le grand senescal) pour faire venir xx siegneurs ou xviii a tiel jour, a quel jour le serjeant d'armes (le grand senescal seant sous le drap d'estat) apres le commission lie, returnera son precept, et les seigneurs seront demandez, et apres qu'ils ont apperu, et sont seants in lour lieux, le prisonnier sera demandez, et le constable del Tower luy conductera al barre ; et donq le seneschal monstrera a luy pour quel cause le roy avoit assembli les seigneurs et luy, et commande luy de respondre sans ascun timorousnes ; et donq le enditement sera leu a luy per le clerk del crown ; et apres il demandra de luy si il soit coulpable ou nemy, et s'il dira rien culpable, donque le clerk demandra luy coment il veut estre trie, et il dira par Dieu et ses pairs ; et donq les serjeants du roy et le atturney du roy doneront evidence vers luy et donc le seneschal commandra le constable del Tower de ret[i]re le prisonnier in ascun lieu pur un escape de temps, et donques les seigneurs ensembleront (mes nemy hors del lieu) et parleront secretement.   Mes icy ils ne seront my jurez *quod nota.*   Et quand ils touts, ou le grand part est agree, donq ils revertiront a leurs lieux, donques le grand seneschal demandra del plus puisne seigneur apert et seant in son lieu, s'il soit coulpable ou nemy, et il respond apert, et issint del prochein puisne tanque il ad fini ove touts separatim ; et donq le prison[nier] sera remande et aura jugement.   Et issint fuit arreine Edward duc de Buckhinham le derrain jour de terme le xiii jour de May, le duc de Norfolk donques estant grand seneschal : la cause fuit pur ceo que il avoit entend la mort de nostre seigneur le roy.   Car premierement un moine del abbey de Henton in le countie de Somerset dit a luy que il sera roy, et command luy de obtenir le benevolence del communalte, et sur ceo il donna certaines robbes a cest entente.   Donq auterfois il dit, si le roy morust sans issue male, il voulust estre roy : et auxy que

il disoit si le roy avoit luy commis al prison, donq il voulust
luy occire ove son dagger.   Mes toutes ceux matiers il denia
in effect: mes fuit trove culpable.   Or Fineux met un di-
versite parentre felony et treason: car n'est felony si ne soit
ascun acte fait: mes si un entend la mort de nostre seigneur
le roy, ceo est haut treason, car il est la teste del common
weal: et icy cest entente fuit prove per ceux paroles.   Et pur
ceo il avoit jugement come traitre, et fuit decolle le Vendredy
le feste del Pentecost, que fuit le xii jour de May avant dit.
Dieu a sa ame grante mercy, car il fuit tresnoble prince et
prudent, et mirror de tout courtoisie.

INDEX

A

Accounts of Escheators, see Escheators.

Albemarle, duke of —, see York, Edward of —.

Albini, Hugh de —, *v.* earl of Chester (jurisdiction), 281.

— William earl of Arundel, performs his office of hereditary butler, 42.

Alençon, duke of —, peer of France, ruling in case of —, 275.

Alwyn, Nicholas, mayor of London, 460 *et sqq.*

Amercement, 217, 218n, 221–2, 289–91, 308–9, 314–5, 319.

— by law of the land, common-form provision in John's charters, 218n.

— contrary to law of the land, 221–2.

— fixed scale in Normandy, 221–2n.

— statement of Walter Map, 222n.

— by peers, 221, 289–91.

— — cases of —, 308–9, 314–5.

— — exceptions to rule, 221n.

— — privilege superseded and forgotten, 291.

— of peeresses, 290n.

— — cases of—, 314–5.

— in parliament, 319.

Anfred, dapifer in Normandy, 7.

Angus, earl of —, see Umfraville.

Anjou, chronicles of —, and the stewardship of France, 66–8.

— counts of —, made peers of France, 275.

— — Fulk (the Good), 66.

— — Fulk (of Jerusalem), 39n, 67.

— — — his right to be dapifer of France recognised, 68.

— — Geoffrey (Grey-gown) and the stewardship of France, 65–7.

— — Geoffrey (le Bel), 34–7.

— — — his officers of Normandy, 35.

— — — seneschal of France, 63.

— — Geoffrey (son of Henry II) made seneschal of France, 64.

— dapifers or seneschals of —, see Tours.

— Des Roches, William, made hereditary seneschal of —, 115.

— influence on Normandy of Angevin principles, 35.

— officers of —, their precedence, 37n.

— — chief officer of state was the dapifer, 35, 37.

— stewardship of France, Angevin claim to the —, 66–8.

— — possible explanation of —, 55.

— — tract on —, 15n, 67–8.

— — comparison with Lancastrian tract, 151.

Anslech, tutor of Normandy, 9.

Appeal, suit of party, peer of realm not tried by his peers, 345, 393.

Appeals in Parliament, 348–59, 369, 439n.

— abolished, 369, 439n.

Appeals of Treason at common-law, 349n.

Aquitaine, duke of —, peer of France, 246.

Archer's Court, tenure of —, 181.

Argenton, Reginald de —, amercement, 308.

Argenton, session of Norman court at —, 27.

Arrest, 215 *et sqq.*, 223–4, 237–8, 241.

— prior to judgment, 223–4.

Arthur, duke of Brittany, death of —, 249.

— his alleged claims to the English throne, 249n.

— proceedings against John for the murder of —, 252–69 *passim.*

Articles of the barons, cap. xxix, 236–7.

Articles of the barons, cap. xxv, 239.
— cap. xliv, 240.
Artois, counts of —, made peers of
France, 275.
— countess of —, 274.
Arundel, earls of —, see Albini,
Fitzalan.
— Thomas, archbishop of Canterbury, see Canterbury.
Ashton, Sir Ralph —, constable,
396.
Assizes, the Norman —, 36n, 44n,
46n, 47n, 48n, 214, 222n.
— — barons of four counties present at —, 46n.
— the three, 222.
— — justices and knights peers of
any man for purposes of —, 223.
Asthorpe v. Dynham, 364n, 365n.
Attainder, by act of parliament,
nature and growth of —, 388 et
sqq.
— of dead persons, statutes relating
to, 389n.
Audeley, lord —, see Touchet.

B

Badlesmere, Bartholomew de —,
proceedings against for treason,
299, 301n.
— — judgment against —, reversed
for error, 299–300, 332–4.
Baga de Secretis, 386n, 427, 429n,
435n, 460, 462.
Baldwin, dapifer of France, 5n.
Bardolf, Hugh, dapifer, 40.
— Thomas, lord —, proceedings
against in the court of chivalry,
377.
— — — transferred into Parliament, 377.
Barking, Abbess of — (forest
offence, parliament), 318.
Baronesses, amercement of —, 314.
Barons of the Exchequer, 228, and
see Exchequer.
Basset, Gilbert, appealed of robbery,
277.
— Philip, 133, 134.
— — justiciar of England, 123,
129, 134.
— — tests as justiciar, 134.
Bayeux, bishops of —, Henry, chief
justiciar of Normandy, 49.
— — Odo, regent of England, 12–3,
15, 19.
— — — styled earl palatine, 15.

— — proceedings against, 209–
10.
— — Philip, 46n, 61.
— — — chief justiciar of Normandy, 47, 48n.
Beauchamp, Richard earl of Warwick, steward of England, 190.
— — patent of his appointment
for coronation of Henry V, 200.
— — locum tenens of Thomas
duke of Clarence, 201.
— Simon de —, dapifer, 33.
— Thomas earl of Warwick, appealed of treason, 184, 353, 358.
— — commission to —, 371n.
— — conviction and outlawry for
illegal detention of David Tregoys, 358, 360–1.
— — outlawry annulled for error,
361.
— William earl of Warwick (improper release of prisoners, coram
rege), 314.
Beaufort, Edmund duke of Somerset (court of chivalry, levying
war, sentence and execution), 395.
— Henry, cardinal priest, bishop of
Winchester, 380.
— John, marquis of Dorset, impeachment of —, 370–1.
— Thomas, deputy marshal for
trial of Scrope and Mowbray,
372, 374–5n.
— — — his patent of appointment,
400–1.
— — — concurrent commission of
oyer and terminer, 401–2.
— — earl of Dorset, 379, 405.
Beaumont, Amicia countess of
Montfort, 74, 80n, 89–92, 94, 112.
— — called wife of Simon IV, 192–
3, 196, 197–8.
— Hugh, pronounces judgment on
bishop William of St. Carilef,
210–1.
— John viscount —, protest on
behalf of peers, 384.
— Margaret countess of Winchester,
74, 80n, 89, 96, 110–1, 192–3,
196–8, 266.
— Robert I count of Mellent, 51,
58–60, 192.
— — obtains the earldom of Leicester, 192, 195.
— — rebuilds church of St. Mary
in Leicester, 195.
— — his other religious foundations, 196.

Beaumont, Robert II earl of Leicester, 45, 48n, 175n.
— — charter making him hereditary dapifer, 37–8, 58–9.
— — — confirmation charter, 60.
— — chief justiciar of England, 44, 48n.
— — — writ of, 45n.
— — claims to represent Fitz-Osbern earl of Hereford, 38.
— — dapifer, his position as —, 40, 42, 43.
— — — probable explanation of grant, 38–9.
— — earl of Hereford, 38n.
— — his religious foundations, 192, 195.
— — becomes a canon regular, 192, 195.
— — his death, 50–1.
— Robert III earl of Leicester, 51–2, 175n.
— — charter making him hereditary dapifer, 37, 59–60.
— — marries Petronilla de Grandmaisnil, 72–3.
— — obtains, through his wife, Hinckley and the stewardship of England, 192, 195, 197–8.
— — his children, 192–3, 196, 197.
— — revolts against Henry II, 51–2.
— — proceedings against in a test case, 251–2.
— — performs his office of dapifer, 42n.
— — carries sword at coronation of Richard I, 72, 84.
— — goes to Jerusalem, 196.
— — his death, 74, 196, 198.
— Robert IV earl of Leicester, 73–4, 80n, 89–92, 95–8, 105–6, 112–4, 192–3, 196–8.
— — contests claim of earl of Norfolk to act as steward, 55, 73–4, 83n.
— — his encounter with the Sultan, 193, 196.
— — dies without issue, 74, 193, 196, 198.
— Waleran count of Mellent, 60.
— — justiciar of Normandy, 35, 36.
— — — inquisition taken by —, 35n.
Beauvais, bishops of —, peers of France, 246, 269.
Bedford, duke of —, see Lancaster, John of —.

Benefit of Clergy, none in cases of treason, 304.
Bergavenny, George Neville lord —, 465.
Berkeley, Thomas de — (murder of Edward II, parliament, trial by knights), 337–8.
Bernard the Dane, tutor of Normandy, 9.
— styled seneschal by Wace, 16n.
Berners, John Bourchier lord —, 466.
Bigod, hereditary dapifers, 17n, 24, 33.
— hereditary marshals of England, 76.
— Hugh, dapifer, 23, 33.
— — 1st earl of Norfolk and hereditary dapifer, 40, 42–3.
— — — charter making him —, 60–1.
— — his position as dapifer, 40, 42–3.
— — ecclesiastical proceedings, against —, 214n.
— Hugh (son of 2nd earl), appears for his father to enforce the compromise in the stewardship dispute, 76.
— — — obtains a writ of fi. fa. against the earl of Chester, 77.
— Hugh, justiciar of England, 122n, 123–4, 129, 132–4.
— Roger, dapifer, 20, 22–3, 61, 87, 175n.
— Roger 2nd earl of Norfolk, 55, 73.
— — confirmed as hereditary seneschal, 72.
— — — charter, 87–8.
— — performs his office, 42n.
— — contests claim of earl of Leicester to act as steward, 55, 73–4, 83n.
— — obtains order against earl of Chester to specifically perform the stewardship compromise, 76–7.
— Roger 4th earl of Norfolk, disputes claim of Simon de Montfort to act as steward at the coronation of Queen Eleanor, 82–3.
— Roger 5th earl of Norfolk, marshal of England, 181n.
— — — (amercement), 314.
— William, dapifer, 23.
Bishops, see also Lords Spiritual.
— proceedings against, 209–11, 214n, 272, 282–3, 292, 302–8, 338–45, 371–6.

Bishops, proceedings against for any crime, not without the King's special order, 345.
— declaration of their rights of peerage, 384.
— judgment of —, by King and barons, a violation of the " judicium parium," 214n.
— what they understood by the judicium parium, 307.
— duty of —, to take part in trials and judgments, 211n.
— forced by Henry II to assist at the judgments of his court, 213-4n.
— forbidden to be present at judgments of life or limb, 350.
— they retire under protest, 350-1.
— appoint a procurator, 184, 353-4, 358-9, 393.
— how affected by institution of the steward's court, 442.
Biset, Henry, dapifer, 41.
— Manasser, dapifer, 37, 40, 60, 61.
Blanche of Navarre, and the comté of Champagne, 262-70.
Blois, Thibaud count of —, dapifer of France, 4, 54, 63-4.
Blount, John, 467.
— Sir Thomas (alias Sir John), 421n, 423n, 424, 454.
— William lord Mountjoy, 465-6.
Blundevill, Randulf, earl of Chester, see Chester.
Bohun, hereditary constables of England, 76.
— Enjuger de —, 36, 46n, 48n.
— Humphrey III de —, dapifer, 23, 33, 36n, 37, 40-1.
— — hereditary dapifer, 34.
— — — charter making him —, 57-8.
— — — charter probably never confirmed, 40.
— Humphrey IV de —, chief constable of the king, 51-2.
— Humphrey 3rd earl of Hereford (criminal proceedings against, fine in parliament), 319.
— — (forest offence, imprisonment, parliament), 313.
— — v. earl of Gloucester (king intervening, evidence on oath, jurisdiction), 282.
— — — (king intervening, private war), 292-4.
— Humphrey 4th earl of Hereford, constable of England, supports Thomas earl of Lancaster, 144-5.

— — assists at capture and execution of Gaveston, 145.
— — procures the banishment of the Despencers, 146., 151.
— — his death, 153.
— Joan countess of Hereford, see Fitzalan.
— John de —, (forest offence, imprisonment, parliament), 313.
— William earl of Northampton, present at the trial of the baron of Greystoke, 346n.
Borney, Pounteney v. — (Exchequer Chamber), 365-6.
Botreaux, William lord —, 406.
Bourchier, Henry earl of Essex, 465.
— Hugh lord —, 406.
— John lord Berners, 466.
Bracton, Henry de —, 241, 373.
— on forfeiture and escheat, 259n.
— silent on general principle of judgment by peers, 283-4.
— king may not be judge in his own cause, 284.
— peers to be associated with justices, 284-5.
— describes a verdict as a judgment, 288.
Braose, Laura countess of Leicester, 74, 89, 91-3, 95, 193.
— becomes a recluse at Hackington, 198, and see Hackington.
Braybroke, Sir Gerard —, 451.
Brembre, Sir Nicholas —, appealed of treason in parliament, 348-52.
Breszé, Louis de —, steward of Normandy, 53n.
Breteuil, Amicia de —, countess of Leicester, 38, 50-1n, 192.
— — daughter of Ralph de Montfort, 192.
— — nun at Eaton, 192, 195.
— William de —, earl of Hereford, see Fitz-Osbern.
— William de —, 38n, 58-60.
Brionne, Gilbert count of —, tutor of Normandy, 10.
Brittany, counts of —, made peers of France, 275.
— — Alan, tutor of Normandy, 10, 17n.
— duke of —, see Arthur.
Britton, three parties to every judgment, 286-7.
— judgment in parliament, 287.
Broke, Robert Willoughby lord de —, 466.

Brooke, Sir Robert, Grand Abridgement, 429.

Bruce, Robert (forest offence, baro domini regis), 315.

Bryan, Sir Thomas, 461 et sqq.

Brynkele v. Earle, 365n.

Buckingham, dukes of —, see Stafford.

Bulmer, Sir William, 438.

Burgh (Peterborough), abbot of —, amercement, 309.

Burgh, Hubert de —, justiciar of England, 116, 132.

—— earl of Kent, proceedings against, 150, 151, 167.

—— abduction from sanctuary, 277, 280n.

—— claims judgment of peers, 279n.

—— observations on his outlawry, 279n.

Burgundy, dukes of —. peers of France, 246, 269.

— seneschal of —, 53–4.

Bushy, Sir John, speaker of the commons, 356.

—— sentenced by court of chivalry, 368n.

Butler (Pincerna, Buticularius), in England, 21n, 24, 41.

— in France, 3.

— in Hainault, 43n.

— in Normandy, 6n, 17n.

— hereditary, of archbishops of Canterbury, 140n.

—— of England, 42.

Butler, James 4th earl of Ormond, appealed of treason by lord Talbot, 380.

—— appealed of treason by prior of Kilmaine, 383.

Buxhill, Sir Alan, 424.

C

Cade, Hugh, butler to earl of Huntingdon, 449, 455.

— Jack, 384–5.

—— attainder of, 388n.

Caen, castle of, session of Norman court at, 26n, 27n, 46n, 52n.

Calverly, Whitchurch v. —, 365n.

Cambridge, Richard earl of —, proceedings against for treason, 190, 378–80, 402–7, 429.

Canterbury, archbishops of —, steward at their inthronization, 140n.

Canterbury, archbishops of, John Stratford, history of his quarrel with Edward III, 338–45.

—— proceedings against in the Exchequer, 340–1.

—— wishes to clear his character in parliament, 342.

—— committee appointed to hear his defence, 345.

—— Thomas Arundel, 373, 375n, 448.

—— sentenced in parliament to banishment, 354.

—— letter referring to capture of conspirators, 421.

Cantilupe, William de —, 105, 106.

—— given custody of Leicester estates, 75n.

—— his accounts as custodian, 102–4.

—— ordered to give possession of estates to earl of Chester, 104.

Carbonel, Robert, a baron of the Norman court, 27n.

Carlisle, Thomas Merkes bishop of —, excuses of —, in parliament, 372n.

—— proceedings against for treason, 371–2.

— earl of —, see Harcla.

Cases, adjourned (coram rege, for amercement), 309.

—— (coram rege, for judgment), 310 et sqq.

—— (coram regina), 312.

—— (parliament, for judgment), 313 et sqq.

— in the court of chivalry, 185–7, 362–415 passim.

— in the ecclesiastical courts, 213n, 214n.

— in France, 212n, 245–75 passim.

— in parliament, 184–5, 294–359 passim, 370–1, 377–96 passim.

— in the court of the lord high steward, 416–70 passim.

Châlons, bishops of —, peers of France, 246, 269.

—— Conon de Vitry, unsuccessfully claims privilege as a bishop, 272.

Chamberlain, hereditary —, of England, 171, 178–9, 180n.

— office of —, in England, 21n, 24, 41, 42n.

—— in France, 3–4.

—— in Normandy, 6n, 10n, 11n, 17n, 37.

Champagne, counts of —, peers of France, 246.
— — succession judged by peers of France in 1216, 269-70.
— — — extraordinary publicity given to judgment, 270n.
— — — bishop of Orleans and the judgment, 270n.
— dapifer or seneschal of —, 53.
— and Flanders, countesses of —, contest right to stewardship of France at coronations, 55, 71.
Champion, office of —, 181-3, 190.
Chancellor of England, presides at trials in parliament, 185, 348.
Charles le Chauve, his charter of liberties, 205.
— case of Treason against, 208-9.
Chartres, Eudo II count of, judgment on —, letter concerning —, 209.
Chelmsford (Essex), 450, 452-4.
Chester, Randulf earl of —, justiciar of Normandy, 27.
— Randulf Blundevill earl of —, custodian of Leicester estates, 75-6, 104, 107.
— — ordered to assign knights' fees due to earl of Norfolk in respect of his claim to the stewardship, 77.
— — grant to him of Leicester estates, 107, 108-9.
— — obtains earldom of Leicester and honour of Hinckley, 196, 198.
— — agrees to surrender estates to Simon de Montfort, 79.
— — his death, 82.
— John Scot earl of —, Hugh de Albini and others v. — (jurisdiction), 281.
Chichester, Thomas Rushok bishop of —, impeachment, 351n, 352.
Chivalry, court of, see Court.
Chronicles, searched for information, 388n.
Civil cases, procedure in, 289-92.
Civil law, 349, 352, 366, 393n.
— too tender to the prisoner, 433n.
Claims, court of —, see Court.
Clare, Gilbert earl of Gloucester (lord marcher, regality, jurisdiction), 283n.
— — Hereford, earl of —, v. — (king intervening, evidence on oath, jurisdiction), 282.
— — — (king intervening, private war), 292-4.

— — Siward v. —, 284n.
— Richard earl of —, amercement, 309.
— Richard earl of Gloucester, hereditary steward of archbishop of Canterbury, 140n.
— — (forest offence, coram rege), 310.
Clarence, dukes of —; see George; Lancaster, Thomas of —.
Clarendon, constitutions of —, 211n, 213-4.
Clergy, exemption from lay jurisdiction, 303-4.
— procurator for —, at a trial in parliament, 184, 353-4, 358-9, 393.
Clers, Hugh de —, 70.
— — dapifer of la Flèche, 35.
— — tract on the stewardship of France, 39, 67-8.
Clifford, John lord —, 405.
Clinton, John lord —, 465.
— William lord —, 405.
Cobham, Eleanor duchess of Gloucester, proceedings against —, 380-1.
— Sir John, impeachment of —, 184, 359.
— Sir John Oldcastle lord —, 380.
Cock-Crower, 180.
Coke, Sir Edward, on Magna Charta, 215.
Colchester, and Eudo dapifer, 29.
Comes palatii, see earl palatine.
Common-law, and the Court of Chivalry, comparative popularity, 368-9n.
Commons of England, and judgment in parliament, 370n.
Compurgation, 210, 211n, 216, 228, 232.
Conrad the Salic, ordinance of —, 206.
Constable, of England, 143-4, 147, 149-50, 166-8, 172, 180-2, 184, 349, 362-415 passim.
— — constitutional position of —, contrasted with that of the steward, 362.
— — assists the steward of England in court of claims, 189, 190n.
— of France, 3-4, 55, 362.
— in Normandy, 6n, 16n, 37, 54.
— King's —, 24n, 41, 51, 54.
Constitutio domus regis, 24.
Coram Consilio, amercements —, 291n.
Coram rege, amercements —, 290-1, 309.

Coram rege, judgments —, 290n, 292, 310 et sqq.

Coram regina —, judgments —,312.

Cornwall, earls of —, Edmund (escape of criminal, judgment), 314

—— Piers, see Gaveston.

Coronations, 42n, 43, 54–5, 66, 68–73, 76, 82–4, 139–40, 162, 171–2, 176–83, 189–91, 199–201.

Cotton, Sir Robert, and the Hinckley tract, 175.

Council, the King's —, amercements before, 291n.

Countess, amercement of —, 315.

Courcy, hereditary dapifers, 17n, 24, 33.

— Robert de —, dapifer, 23, 33, 35n, 37n, 41.

—— justiciar of Normandy, 35–7, 46n.

— William I de —, dapifer, 23.

— William II de —, dapifer, 41, 50.

—— justiciar of Normandy, 41n, 50.

—— death of —, 52.

Court of Chivalry, 186–7, 298n, 349, 362–415 passim.

— appeal from —, 364–5.

—— commission to hear —, 365.

— application for supersedeas, 364–5.

—— commission to hear —, 365.

— cases tried before —, "causa fidei lesionis," 364.

— and common-law, comparative popularity, 368–9n.

—— judges took judicial notice of its decisions, 393–4.

— under constable and marshal of England, 362.

—— patent appointing commissioners for trial of lord Audeley, 414–5.

— comparison with court of lord high steward, 433n.

— cross applications for supersedeas and procedendo transferred to Exchequer Chamber, 365–6.

— jurisdiction, ad instantiam partis, 398.

——— abuse of —, by Richard II, 368–9.

—— ex officio, 398–9.

——— systematic use of —, by Henry IV, 369.

—— defendant bound by his submission to —, 364.

—— limited to person and chattels, 377.

Court of Chivalry, jurisdiction, none in outlawry, 377.

— petitions against —. 363, 370, 377n, 380.

— procedure, according to civil law, 366.

—— tract on —, 367.

—— trial by witnesses or battle, 366–7.

— roll of 24 Edward I, 362–3.

— statute of 13 Richard II, cap. 2, 363–4.

Court Christian, jurisdiction in breach of faith, 364n.

— growth of jurisdiction during anarchy, 213.

Court of Claims, 177–83, 189–91, 200–1.

— no evidence of a —, before accession of Richard II, 177–9.

— no mention of —, in Lancastrian tract, 179n.

Court of the Lord High Steward, 399, 416–70 passim.

— trials before —, 429–43, 459–70.

— comparison with court of chivalry, 433n.

— number of peers to be summoned, 432, 433, 436.

—— verdict of the majority, 417, 434–5, 460, 469,

—— verdict of the junior lord to be taken first, 393, 417, 440, 460, 469.

— intended to supersede trial before parliament, 442–3.

— statute 33 Henry VIII cap. 20, silent as to trials before parliament, 443n.

— conclusions respecting —, 441–3.

— first case reported in Year Books, 416–7, 459–60.

—— an absolute forgery, 416, 428.

—— probable date of forgery, 429.

Courtenay, Edward earl of Devon, alleged appointment as steward of England for trial of earl of Huntingdon, 416–7.

— Hugh earl of Devon, hereditary steward of bishops of Exeter, 140–1n.

— Thomas earl of Devon (high treason, trial in parliament, acquittal, steward of England presiding), 386–8.

Coventry and Lichfield, bishops of —, Roger de Meuland (judicial writ, baron, statute of Marlborough), 282–3.

Coventry and Lichfield (baron, amercement), 314.
— — Walter Langton, proceedings against —, 304.
Crassus, William, seneschal of Normandy, 53n.

D

D., the earl of —, see Courtenay.
Dacre, Thomas Fienes lord —, 466.
Damory, Roger (treason, court of chivalry), 298n, 363, 399–400.
Dapifer, Anglie et Normannie, 37, 40.
— in Anglia et Normannia, 34.
— Normannie, 11.
— sheriff so styled, 18n.
Dapifers, 4.
— Anglo-Saxon, 18–19.
— — of Edward the Confessor, 18–19.
— English, hereditary, see Beaumont, Bigod, Bohun, Lancaster, Mandeville, Montfort.
— — ordinary, of William I, 20.
— — — of William II, 22.
— — — of Henry I, 23.
— — — of Matilda, 33.
— — — of Stephen, 33.
— — — of Henry II, 40–1.
— — — commonly styled "seneschals" after accession of Richard I, see seneschal, steward of household.
— French, 3–6, 11, 22–3, 28–9, 54–6, 63–71, 120.
— — number of —, 5.
— — rapid development of office, 5.
— — not chief officer before A.D. 1070, 5.
— — honorary, 54–5.
— — at coronations, 55–6.
— — references in chronicles, etc., to hereditary office, 63–71.
— — Angevin tract on —, 67–8.
— — offer to make Simon de Montfort seneschal of France, 120–1.
— — use of expression "dapifero nullo," 3, 77.
— Norman, 7.
— — of Robert, 7.
— — of William II, 7.
— — of Henry Fitz-Empress, 37n.
— Scotch, 40n, 61–3.
Darcy, John, chamberlain, attempts to prevent archbp. Stratford entering parliament, 341
Daubeney, Giles lord —, 466.

David of Scotland, laws ascribed to —, 207.
Delacourt, John, 437, 439n.
De la Warr, Thomas West lord —. 465.
Denia, count of —, 370n.
Derby, earls of — ; see Henry IV ; Lancaster, Henry II of —.
Despencer, Hugh, justiciar of England, 123–37 passim.
— — — tests as —, 134.
— Hugh the father and Hugh the son, proceedings against in parliament, 146, 297.
— — — analogous to subsequent attainders, 297n.
— — — referred to as a statute, 388n.
— — — repealed for error, 297–8, 324–6, 353.
— — — reinstated and again reversed, 298.
— — proceedings against by the Queen's party, 302.
— — — trial and execution, 171, 177.
— Thomas, earl of Gloucester, impeachment, 370–1.
— — lord Despencer, 417n, 424–6, 427n.
— — — beheaded at Bristol, 425–6, 454.
— — — reference to his "conviction," 447.
— — — head brought to London by earl of Rutland, 450, 456, 458.
— — — order to mayor of Bristol to send head to London, 456n.
Des Roches, Peter, bishop of Winchester, see Winchester.
— William, made hereditary seneschal of Anjou, Maine, and Touraine, 115.
Destruction, use and meaning of word, 236–7, 242–3.
Devon, earls of, see Courtenay.
Digby, Sir John, marshal, 414.
Disseizin, 215, 218–20, 222–3, 234, 239–41.
— by judgment of peers, 219–20.
— by the law of the land, 220n.
Dorset, earl of —. marquis of —, see Beaufort.
Douglas, William, v. Gilbert de Umfraville, appeal of treason, 349n.
Dudley, lord, see Sutton.
Durand, Speculum Juris, 254n.

Durham, bishops of —, Robert de Insula (fishery, unlawful appropriation, judgment, amercement) 311–2.

— — William of St. Carilef, proceedings against —, 210–1.

Dynham, Asthorpe v. —, 364n, 365n.

— Sir John, lord treasurer, 414.

— — lord Dynham, 465.

E

Earl palatine (comes palatii), 13–15, 19n.

— power to coerce the king, 152.

Earle, Brynkele v. —, 365n.

Edward the Confessor, 18, 29.

— his dapifers were subordinate officers, 18.

Edward I, 138–41, 143, 162–3, 282–9, 292–6, 311–322, 362–3.

— cited as duke of Aquitaine to appear before the peers of France, 272–3.

— procedure in trial of peers becoming settled at close of his reign, 308.

— stewardship of England granted by —, to Edmund earl of Lancaster for his life, 140n, 163.

Edward II, 141–53, 163–7, 296–308, 322–6, 363.

— his coronation, 142.

— compared with Henry III, 142.

— remedies for bad government, duty of hereditary officers to coerce the king, 143–4.

— causes célèbres during reign of —, 296–307.

— his court of chivalry, 298n, 363, 369n, 399–400.

— uncertainty of procedure in trials of peers, 308.

— stewardship of England granted by —, to Thomas earl of Lancaster, 142. 163.

— summoned as peer of France, 274–5.

Edward III, 171–9, 327–47, 359–60.

— his coronation, 177.

— his death, 176, 182n.

Edward IV, 390–6, 407–13.

Edward of Langley, duke of York, etc., see York.

Eleanor of Provence, queen of Henry III, her coronation, 82–4, 191.

Eleanor of Castille, 256, 257, 265–6.

— her death, 265n.

Eleanor, sister of Henry III, countess of Leicester, 85, 117–8.

— marries Simon de Montfort after taking vows of chastity, 193, 196–7, 198–9.

Erpingham, Sir Thomas, 454.

Error, reversal of judgments for —, in parliament, 296–300, 305, 324–34, 336.

Escheators, accounts and inquisitions (lord Bardolf), 378n.

— — (duke of Buckingham), 396–7n.

— — (earl of Huntingdon), 422–3n, 445–6.

— — (lord Mowbray), 375–6n.

— — (earl of Northumberland), 378n.

— — (archbishop Scrope), 375–6n.

— — (Sir Thomas Shelley), 445–6.

— writs to seize estates of those who took part in the earl of Kent's rebellion, 423–4n.

— traversing the office of, 425n.

Essex, earls of —, see Bourchier, Mandeville.

Eu, Gilbert count of —, see Brionne.

— Ralph de Lusignan count of —, appeals John king of England, 246.

Eudo, son of Hubert de Rie, dapifer, 14–6, 20, 22–3, 29–30, 34, 56.

— — The Colchester tract on his dapifership, 15–6, 29–30, 39.

— — his dapifership conferred on Geoffrey de Mandeville, 33–4, 56–7.

— — Geoffrey de Mandeville claims to represent —, 38.

—, son of Turstin, dapifer, 20.

Everyngham, Robert de —, proceedings against, 316.

Evesham, battle of —, 127–8, 130, 154, 160, 162, 193, 197, 199, 310.

Evidence on oath, barons, jurisdiction, 282.

Evreux, Rotroc bishop of —, chief justiciar of Normandy, 48–9.

— — styled dapifer of Normandy in charter of Richard I, 49n.

Exchequer, barons of —, amercement by —, 290–1, 315–6, 319.

— court of —, in England, 51, 183n, 278, 338–41, 444–5, 447, etc.

— Norman, 28n, 49n, 52n.

Exchequer-chamber, jurisdiction of court of chivalry discussed before —, 365–6.

Exeter, bishops of —, high steward at their inthronization, 140–1n.
—— Osbern, 8.
Exeter, John Holland duke of —, impeachment, 370–1.
—— see Holand.
Exile, 224, 241–3.
Eyr, Robert le, v. Nicholas de Wantham, appeal of treason, 349n.

F

Felony, procedure in cases of —. 292 et sqq.
Ferrers, Robert earl of — (forest offence, coram rege quia baro), 310.
Fienes, Giles de — (forest offence, king's household, coram rege), 316.
— James, lord Saye, indictment and death, 384–6.
— Thomas, lord Dacre, 466.
Fife, Malcolm earl of — (default), 309.
Fitzalan, Joan countess of Hereford, seizes the earl of Huntingdon and notifies the king, 420, 449, 455–7.
—— ordered to deliver up Huntingdon, 458.
—— has Huntingdon put to death, 448–58 passim.
—— delivers up some of Huntingdon's property, 420–1n.
—— king grants her Huntingdon's house in Thames Street, 421.
— Richard earl of Arundel, appealed of treason, 184, 353.
—— tried in parliament and executed, 354–7.
— Thomas earl of Arundel, 379, 405.
—— at death of Huntingdon, 420, 449–50, 455, 457–8.
—— deputy constable for trial of archbishop Scrope and Mowbray, 372, 374–5.
—— — his patent of appointment, 400–1.
—— concurrent commission of oyer and terminer, 401–2.
— Walter, dapifer (seneschal and justiciar of Scotland), 44n.
—— charter making him hereditary seneschal, 61–3.
Fitz-Aldelm, William, dapifer, 41, 42n.

Fitz-Ansgar, William, justiciar of Normandy, 27.
Fitz-Hamo, William, seneschal of Brittany, 50n.
Fitz-Herbert, Sir Anthony, Grand Abridgement, 429, 433.
— Herbert, amercement, 308.
Fitz-John, William, 59.
—— dapifer, 41, 49.
—— justiciar of Normandy, 37, 49.
—— officer of Normandy, 45n, 46n.
Fitz-Nigel, Roger vicomte du Contentin, justiciar of Normandy, 34.
Fitz-Osbern, William earl of Hereford, 8, 11–9, 29–30, 38–9.
—— regent of England, 12–3, 15.
—— regent of Normandy, 12, 25n.
—— styled comes palatii, 13–5.
—— styled, by Ordericus and others, dapifer of Normandy, 11–2, 39.
—— no charter or contemporary evidence that he was dapifer, 13, 15.
—— styled seneschal by Wace, 17n.
—— Eudo dapifer and the Colchester tract, 15–6, 29–30.
—— Beaumont's claim to represent him, 38.
Fitz-Percy, Reginald, amercement, 314.
Fitz-Ralph, William, 49n, 54.
—— first seneschal of Normandy, 31–2, 53.
—— precedence as, 54.
—— styled dapifer in pipe-roll of 1180, 53n.
—— major procurator regis, 50n.
Fitz-Reinfrid, Gilbert, dapifer, 41.
Fitz-Richard, Robert, dapifer, 33.
Fitz-Roger, Ralph (quo warranto, judgment, amercement), 311.
Fitz-Rolland, Alan, amercement, 309.
Fitz-Walter, lord —, see Ratcliff.
— Robert (contempt, imprisonment, coram rege), 311.
Fitz-Warin, Fulk, constable, 363, 400.
Flanders, counts of —, peers of France, 246, 290n.
—— Guy de Dampierre, proceedings against in respect of Valenciennes, 273.
—— — argument of French jurist upon, 287–8n.
—— Philip, seneschal at 1st coronation of Philip Augustus, 54–5, 69.

Flanders, Counts of —, Philip, seneschal at 2nd coronation, 70.

— — — his claim to the seneschalship of France, 39, 63.

— — Robert, reference to count's peers in treaty with Henry I, 212.

— — Robert Beton, judgment against in 1315, 274.

— — Thierry, reference to count's peers in treaty with Henry II, 212.

— — — a vassal of the Amiénois, after its cession becomes the count's peer, 212–3.

— — Thomas of Savoy, proceedings against in 1237, 272.

— and Champagne, countesses of —, contest right to office of seneschal at coronations, 55, 71.

— countess of —, Johanna, trial de defectu juris, 271–2.

— — — attempts marriage with Simon de Montfort, 85.

— seneschal of —, 53.

Fleta, judgment by peers in cases of treason, 286.

— jurisdiction of the steward of the household, and the king's courts, 128n.

Forfeiture, dates from commission of crime, 255, 258–9.

— effect of —, 258–9.

— arguments excluding John's issue, 261–5.

— — views of modern critics, 263–5n.

— no custom in France limiting forfeiture to afterborn children, 262–3.

— case of Marie de Ponthieu, 263–4n.

— reflections of Philip de Novarre, 264–5n.

Fortescue, Sir John, 433n.

Foss, Edward, on Simon de Montfort and the justiciarship, 129.

Fougères, Ralph de —, seneschal of Brittany, 53.

France, dapifers (seneschals, or stewards) of —, see dapifers.

— dukes, earls and barons, how judged, 285–6n.

— officers of state in —, 3.

— — royal charters attested by them, 3–4.

— — objection taken to their judging peers of France, 271–2.

— peers of —, see peers, judgment of peers.

Fulmere, Sir Robert, proceedings against in parliament, 347–8.

Fulthorpe, Sir William, part taken by —, in proceedings against archbishop Scrope and Mowbray, 374–5, 401.

— — deputy constable, 365–6n.

Furnival, Gerard de, amercement, 308.

Fyneux, Sir John, chief justice, 438, 460 et sqq., 470.

G

Gael, Amicia de —, countess of Leicester, see Breteuil.

Garland, dapifers of France, 4, 22, 28, 55, 67–8.

— Anselm, dapifer, 67.

— Stephen, dapifer, 68.

— — deprived of dapifership, 28.

— — made chancellor, 28.

— William, dapifer, 67, 68.

Gascoigne, Sir William, chief justice, 401.

— — advises Henry IV against condemning archbishop Scrope, 373–5.

Gascony, seneschals of, 53.

Gaveston, Piers earl of Cornwall, at Edward the Second's coronation, 142, 177.

— — offensive behaviour, 143.

— — banishment of —, 144, 296.

— — leaves, and returns to England, 144–5, 150, 167.

— — besieged in Scarborough castle, 145.

— — capture and death, 145, 151, 167, 296.

George, duke of Clarence, proceedings against for treason, 395–6, 412–3.

Geoffrey le Bel; — Greygown; — son of Henry II, see Anjou.

Gerald, dapifer [England], 23.

Gerald, dapifer [Normandy], 7, 8, 54.

Germany, Otho emperor of —, 65–7.

— Henry of —, acts as deputy steward for Simon de Montfort, 122.

Giffard, John (proceedings against, private war), 294n.

Gilbert, dapifer in Normandy, 7.

Glanville, Ranulf de —, Tractatus de legibus, 221n, 225n, 229–30n, 234n, 241, 259n, 434n.

— William de, 52.

Glapion, Warin de —, seneschal of Normandy, 53n.
Gloucester, dukes of —, Humphrey, 379, 405.
— — Richard, see Richard III.
— — Thomas, constable of England, tract on procedure in the court of chivalry, 367.
— — — appealed of treason in parliament, 353, 358.
— — — assassinated, 358.
— duchess of —, see Cobham.
— earls of —, see Clare, Despencer.
— — Robert, justiciar of Normandy, 27, 28.
— — — inquisition taken before —, 28n.
Godric, dapifer, 20.
Godwin, earl of Kent, banishment and forfeiture, 150–1, 166–7.
Gomeniz, John sire de —, impeachment, 347.
Grand Coutumier de Normandie, see Normandy.
Grandmaisnil, Adeliza de —, 175n.
— Hugh de —, 7, 175n, 197.
— — his alleged grant of the stewardship of England, 192, 195, 198.
— Petronilla de —, marries Robert III earl of Leicester and brings him Hinckley and the stewardship of England, 175n, 192, 195, 197–8.
— — her religious donations, 195–6.
— — countess of Leicester, 52n, 73–4, 89, 95, 104–5.
— — her claim to the honour of Grandmaisnil, 88–93.
— — — outbidden by Saer de Quincy, 92–3.
— Honour of —, 88–93, 98.
Great Seal, authority for affixing —. 131–7.
Grey, of Codnor, Henry lord —, appeal, 393.
— Edward lord de Wilton, 466.
— Reginald de —, (forest offence, coram rege quia baro), 310–1.
— of Ruthyn, George earl of Kent, 465.
— Sir Thomas, 378–9, 402–6.
Greystoke, William baron of — (loss of Berwick, trial, Walter Manny presiding, death sentence, pardon), 346.
Grosvenor, Lescrope v. —, 365n.
Gualo, papal legate, see Walo.

H

H., the earl of —, see Holand.
Hackington, Laura the recluse of —, 125–6, 198.
— — perhaps identical with countess of Leicester, 125, 198.
— — required to state what rights appertained to the stewardship of England, 125–6.
Hadleigh, Essex, 419–20, 444, 450.
Haie, Richard de la —, 48n.
— — dapifer, 37n.
— — justiciar of Normandy, 28, 35n, 36–7.
— Robert de la —, dapifer, 23, 36n.
— — justiciar of Normandy, 26–8.
Hainault, dapifer of —, 43n.
— honorary services at the court of —, 43n.
— William of —, married to Maud of Lancaster, 173.
Hall, Edward, historian, 434, 438–9.
— — describes the proceedings against the duke of Buckingham as an appeal, 439n.
Hamo, dapifer, 20, 22–3.
— sheriff, 21.
Harcla, Andrew, 153.
— — earl of Carlisle, proceedings against for treason, 300–2.
— — petition by his nephew Henry for reversal of judgment, 334.
Harington, John lord —, 405.
Harold, 11n.
— styled seneschal by Wace, 17n.
Hastings, Edward lord —, 466.
— John de, refusal to give evidence on oath, 282n.
Heir, remoter admitted without prejudice to right heir, 265–6.
Heltho, dapifer, 20.
Henry I, 23–8, 31, 56–8, 60–1, 68, 87, 212.
— dapifers of —, 23.
— household of —, 24.
— his governors of Normandy, 25–8.
— — not styled dapifers or seneschals, but justiciars, 25.
— laws of —, 207.
Henry II (duke of Normandy), his household, 36–7.
— — — their precedence, 37n.
— — his dapifers, 37n.
— — charters conferring an hereditary dapifership, 58–60, and see 57.
— — his justiciars, 37.

Henry I (king of England), 40–55, 63–70, 87, 212–4.
— — his dapifers, 40–1.
— — precedence of his officers, 41–2.
— — hereditary dapifers summoned for coronations and feast-days, 42.
— — charters conferring hereditary dapiferships, 38, 40, 60–1.
— — establishes practice of honorary services, 43.
— — claim to the dapifership of France, 39, and see Anjou.
— — — supported by forgery, 39.
— — — enters Brittany as seneschal of France, 65.
— — — said to have served at table as seneschal, 69n.
— — — charter referring to his rights as seneschal, 70.
— — restores power of curia regis, 213–4.
— — compels bishops to assist at judgments of his court, 213–4n.
— — judgment of peers, how defined by him, 213–4n.
— — case against archbishop Becket, 214n.
— — forbids ecclesiastical courts to deal with case against the earl of Norfolk, 214n.
Henry III, 76–9, 81–6, 104–39 passim, 154–62 passim, 276–81, 289–91.
— birth, 252.
— letters patent conferring the stewardship of England on Edmund of Lancaster, 154, 161–2.
— charter (escrow) making Edmund hereditary steward, 138, 154–6.
Henry IV, (earl of Derby) 184, 348, 356.
—³— carries sword *curtana* at coronation of Richard II, 183n.
— (duke of Hereford), appeals the duke of Norfolk, 185–7, 359, 367.
— — exiled, his estates confiscated, returns to England, 187.
— — his declared intentions, 187–8.
— duke of Lancaster, etc., and steward of England, 200.
— (king of England), 179, 369–78, 400–2, 416–28, 444–60.
— — accession, court of claims, 189.
— — coronation roll of —, 199–200.
— — makes his son Thomas steward of England, 189, 200.

Henry IV, appoints Thomas Percy earl of Worcester deputy steward, 189, 200, 428n.
Henry V, 190, 200–1, 378–80, 429.
— his coronation, 190, 200.
— conspiracy against —, 378–9, 402–7.
Henry VI, 195, 380–90.
Henry VII, 397–9, 414–5, 429–35, 460–8.
Henry VIII, 435–43, 469–70.
Henry, son of Henry II, serves as seneschal of France, 54, 65, 67.
— — granted seneschalship of France as appertaining to fief of Anjou, 64, 66–7.
— — present at coronation of Philip Augustus, 69.
Hereford, bishop of —, Adam Orleton, proceedings against, 304–7.
— — — — reversed for error, 305.
— — — — Blaneford's account, 306–7.
— countess of —, see Fitzalan.
— duke of —, see Henry IV.
— earls of —, see Beaumont, Bohun, Fitz-Osbern.
— Henry de, dapifer, 41.
Herluin, dapifer, 7.
Hill (Hull), Robert, 417, 460.
Hilton, William baron de —, Bishop of Norwich v. —, 365n.
Hinckley, honour of —. 96–7, 99, 100, 102–3.
— allotted to Blanche of Lancaster on the partition of her father's estates, 173–4.
— tenure of —, was knight-service, 174n.
— tracts on the stewardship of England, 174–5, 192–9.
— — almost universally credited, 175.
Holand, John, duke of Exeter, impeachment, 370–1.
— — earl of Huntingdon, 377–8.
— — — alleged trial in court of lord high steward, report of —. 416–7, 459–60.
— — — part taken by —, in earl of Kent's rebellion, 417 et sqq.
— — — writs ordering sheriffs to arrest, 418n.
— — — flight down the Thames, 419.
— — — William Peion's account of —, 444–5.
— — — captured at house, of John Pritewell, 420n, 448, 450, 453.

Holand, John, of Huntingdon, captured at house of a friend, 452.

— — — captured at a mill at Prittlewell, 452, 453.

— — — accounts of his capture and death by contemporary chroniclers, 448–59.

— — — taken first to Chelmsford, 420, 450, 452–4.

— — — then to Pleshy, 420–2, 448–59 passim.

— — — countess of Hereford ordered to deliver him up to Henry IV, 458.

— — — order to receive him sent to constable of Tower of London, 421–2, 427–8.

— — — executed at Pleshy, on spot where Gloucester arrested, 422, 451–4.

— — — body buried at Pleshy, 422, 452.

— — — head sent to London, 422, 450, 452, 456, 458.

— — — date of his death, 422–4.

— — — writs to the escheators, 423–4n.

— — — house in Thames Street given to countess of Hereford, 421.

— — — account of his personal property seized at Leigh, 445–6.

— — — minutes of council relating to his " destruction," 425.

— — — judgment or resolution in parliament concerning, 425–6.

— — — extracts from escheators' accounts relating to —, 426–7n.

— — — indictment of —, 426–7.

— — — reference to a " judgment" against —, 447.

— — — similar erroneous references to the " conviction " of the earl of Kent and the lord Despencer, 447.

— John, earl of Huntingdon (son of above), 379, 405.

— Thomas, duke of Surrey, impeachment, 370–1.

— — earl of Kent, rebellion of —, 417 et sqq.

— — — capture of Windsor, 418.

— — — retreat to Cirencester, and death, 419, 454, 456, 459.

— — — writs, orders and other proceedings relating to this earl and his rebellion, 423 et sqq.

— — — references to his " conviction," 447.

Hoo, Merton v. —, 365n.

Hopkins, Nicholas, 437, 439n.

Howard, Thomas, earl of Surrey, 465.

— — — patent appointing him steward of England for trial of lord Dudley, 467–8.

— — duke of Norfolk, appointed steward of England for the trial of the duke of Buckingham, 436–41, 469.

Hubert, dapifer, 20.

Hubert, dapifer, 37n.

Hugh, case of Sir —, 288–9.

Humez, Richard de —, 59.

— — constable, 61.

— William de —, constable of the king, 54.

— — — his precedence, 54.

— — assumes style of constable of Normandy, 54.

— — hereditary constable of Normandy, 116.

Huntingdon, earls of —, see Holand

— countess of — ; see Lancaster, Elizabeth of —.

Hyde, abbot of — (baron, amercement), 315.

I

Impeachment, 346–8, 354, 358–9, 370–1, 383, 388.

— discontinuance of this procedure, 388.

Imprisonment, 215 et sqq., 223, 237–8, 241, 289, 292, 311 et sqq.

Innocent III, pope, letters concerning John and the conquest of Normandy, 247n, 249–51.

— — refutes the claim of Louis to the kingdom of England, 260–8.

Inquest of peers, 302, 334.

Inquisition of Escheators, see Escheators.

Ireland, placed under a justiciar, 116.

— duke of —, see Vere.

Isabella of France, queen of Edward II, 170–1, 335.

Ivo, dapifer, 22.

J

Jacobinus de S. Georgio, definition of " peers," 206.

Jerusalem, Assizes of —, definition of judgment by peers, 215.

John (count of Mortain), 72n.
—— proceedings against for treason, 254–5, 257.
— (king of England), 73–6, 80n, 83n, 88–104, 107–11, 113, 215–71 *passim*.
—— voluntary waste of Leicester estates, 75.
—— French proceedings against in 1202, 246–8.
—— first judgment against —, nature of —, 247–8.
—— captures Arthur duke of Brittany, 249, 253n.
—— loss of French provinces, 249.
—— claims restitution from Philip, offers to appear at Philip's court under safe-conduct, statements of Matthew Paris, 260–1.
—— birth of Henry, 252.
—— excommunication ; second judgment against —, in France, nature of the judgment, 252–4.
—— submits to the pope, 254.
—— his forfeiture of England alleged by Louis, 255 *et sqq*.
—— the argument at Rome, 259–68.
—— modern controversy concerning second judgment, 268–9.
John of Gaunt, married to Blanche of Lancaster, 173.
— earl of Richmond, 174n.
— duke of Lancaster, 176.
— recognised as steward of England, his influential position, 176.
— the coronation of Richard II, preparations for —, 176.
—— claims several services at —, 182–3.
—— steward of England at —, 177, 182.
—— — his court of claims, 177 *et sqq*.
— was made, in right of his wife, duke of Lancaster, earl of Derby, Lincoln and Leicester, and steward of England, 194.
— absent from England in 1386, 184.
— present at the trial of the baron of Greystoke, 346n.
— presides at the trial of the earl of Arundel and others, 184–5, 354–9.
—— styled steward of England in the official account, 184, 357.
—— stated by chroniclers to have presided in right of his stewardship, 185, 358.

John of Gaunt, his death, 187.
Judge in his own cause, no man may be —, 208, 273, 284–9.
Judgment, ordeals and battle habitually so described in John's charters, 218n.
— reversal in parliament for error, 296–300, 305, 324–34, 336.
— three parties to a —, necessary, 208, 273, 284–9.
Judgment of Peers (Judicium parium), two primitive principles, 205.
—— early illustrations of the theory, 205–8.
—— not universally admitted, 207.
—— early illustrations of the practice, 208–11.
— in Magna Charta, does not mean trial by jury, 216.
—— true meaning, 233–4.
—— whether judgment of some or all peers is necessary, 234.
—— prominence, how partially explained, 235.
— development of the principle during reign of Henry III, 276–81.
—— " The king's justices are the peers of any man," 276–7.
—— original principle inconsistent with new procedure, 277–8.
— scope of the privilege, struggle over —, 280.
—— attempt to limit, to matters outside the law of the land, 280–4.
— necessary where the king is a party, 208, 273, 284–9.
—— except in light cases, 284–6.
— committee of twelve appointed to report upon privilege, 342.
—— form of their report, 343.
—— statute passed in accordance with —, 343–4, 359–60.
—— — repealed in council, and parliament, 344.
— suit of parties excluded from privilege, 344–5, 393.
Judgment of Peers in France, 208–9, 212–3, 214, 222n, 226–7, 245–75, 277, 285–6n, 290n, 387, and see Peers of France.
Judgment of persons, not peers, protest against, 336–7.
Judgment and Verdict, confusion between, 216–7, 288–9.
—— in Bracton, 288.
—— in Magna Charta, 223.

Jurisdiction, cases (baron, evidence on oath), 282.
— — (judicial writ, baron, statute of Marlborough), 282–3.
— — (land in palatinate of Chester, service of writ in Northampton), 281.
— Ecclesiastical, growth of during anarchy, 213.
Jury, of commoners, knights upon in civil cases, 289n.
— — in criminal cases, 293–4, 310–20 *passim*, 337–8.
— of peers, 302, 334.
— trial by, claimed as the judicium parium of the Charter, 288–9.
— unanimity of —, 434–5.
— rules in Glanville for cases of disagreement, 434n.
Justicia, bench of Norman justiciars so styled, 26–7n, 31–2.
— — the barons of the court distinguished from —, 27n.
Justiciar, of England, 12–13, 19, 21, 24–5, 44–5, 51–2, 116, 137.
— — office held by hereditary steward, 44, 50–1.
— — becomes the subordinate of the regent, 116.
— — office falls into abeyance, 116.
— — reappointment of —, after parliament of 1258, 123–37.
— — alleged assumption of office by Simon de Montfort, 126–37.
— — office abolished, distribution of surviving functions, 128.
— of Ireland, 116.
— of Normandy, 14, 19, 25–8, 30–2, 43–54.
— — first attempt to convert into French and Angevin dapifer, 46–7.
— — explanation of the origin and retention of this style, 54.
— of Scotland, office held by hereditary steward, 44n.

K

Katharine of France, Queen of Henry V, 194.
— — her coronation, 190, 201.
Kempe, John, cardinal priest, archbishop of York, 380.
Kenilworth, dictum of —, 285n.
— priory of —, patronage retained by the king, 196, 198.

Kendal, John, prior of St. John of Jerusalem, 465.
Kent, earls of —, see Burgh, Godwin, Grey of Ruthyn, Holand.
— Edmund earl of —, proceedings against for treason, 335–6.
— Thomas, clerk of the king's common council, trial of —, 385n.
Kighlee v. Scrope, 370n.
Kilmaine (Kilmainham), prior of —, appeals the earl of Ormond, 383.
King, amercements affeered before, 290–1, 309.
— cases adjourned before —, for judgment, 290n, 292, 310 *et sqq.*
— more than the peer of all his subjects, 208.
Knighton, Henry, chronicler, on the origin of the stewardship of England, 195–7, and see 50–1n.
Knyvet, Charles, 437–9.

L

Lancaster, dukes of —, see John of Gaunt, and *infra*.
— genealogy of the earls of —, 194–5.
— tract on the stewardship of England, 15n, 148–51, 164–7, 179n.
Lancaster, Blanche of —, coheiress to her father's estates, 173.
— — wife of John of Gaunt, 173, 182n.
— — obtains Lancaster estates and Hinckley on partition, 173–4.
— Edmund of, 163, 172, 272.
— — has earldom of Leicester, 193–4, 197, 199.
— — has Hinckley with the stewardship of England, 194, 197, 199.
— — proposal to make him earl of Leicester and hereditary steward of England, 138–9.
— — — the letters-patent and charter, 154–6.
— — charters and letters-patent granting him the estates of Simon de Montfort and other rebels, 139, 156–61.
— — made steward of England by Henry III during their joint lives, 139, 161–2.
— — renounces all claims to an hereditary stewardship, 139, 162–3.
— — made steward of England for life by Edward I, 139, 140n, 163.

Lancaster, Edmund of, his office lapses into obscurity, 140.

— — made earl of Lancaster, his death, 141.

— — (forest offence, coram rege, redemption before barons of the Exchequer), 316.

— Elizabeth of —, countess of Huntingdon, 422n.

— — — marries Sir John Cornwall, 423n.

— Henry I of —, earl of Leicester, 170.

— — avenges his brother's death, 170–1.

— — petitions for, and secures reversal of his brother's attainder, 171, 298, 327.

— — earl of Lancaster, 171, 194.

— — — president of council at accession of Edward III, 171, 178–9, 183n.

— — — establishes his claim to the stewardship of England, 171–2.

— — — his death, insignificance of his office during his tenure of it, 172.

— Henry II of —, 194.

— — earl of Derby, 173, 340.

— — — steward of England for a pageant at Windsor, 173, 177–8, 191.

— — succeeds his father, made duke of Lancaster, 173.

— — present at the trial of the baron of Greystoke, 346n.

— — dies without male issue, 173.

— Humphrey duke of Gloucester, 379, 405.

— John of —, 372.

— — duke of Bedford, and regent of England, 379, 402, 406.

— — — constable of England, 380.

— Maud of —, wife of William of Hainault, 173.

— — coheiress to her father's estates, 173.

— — obtains the Leicester estates on partition, 173–4.

— — died without issue, 175.

— Roger de — (forest offence, baron, parliament), 315.

— Thomas earl of Lancaster, 194.

— — succeeds his father, 141.

— — carries sword at coronation of Edward II, and probably acted as steward, 142.

Lancaster, Thomas, earl of, stewardship of England granted to him and the heirs of his body, 142, 163.

— — — observations upon, 172.

— — — contrasted with Simon de Montfort, 142–3.

— — leader of the opposition, 143–4.

— — — his chief supporter the hereditary constable, 144.

— — the ordainers and the ordinances, 144.

— — marches against king and Gaveston, 144–5.

— — has Gaveston beheaded, 145, 151, 167.

— — made president of the king's council, 145.

— — removal of bad advisers his main theme, 145–6.

— — procures banishment of the Despencers, 146.

— — styled steward of England in the Act reciting these proceedings, 146.

— — captured at Borough-bridge, 153.

— — proceedings against for treason, 298, 322–3.

— — his death, 153.

— — inquisition post mortem, tenure of Leicester and Hinckley, 174n.

— — proceedings against —, reversed for error, 298–9, 327–9, 335.

— — miracles at his tomb, 170.

— Thomas of —, made steward of England, 189, 200.

— — — his court of claims for the coronation of Henry IV, 189–90, 200.

— — — holds office for rest of his life, 190, 428.

— — — Richard earl of Warwick his locum-tenens, 201.

— — " duke of Lancaster," 428n.

— — duke of Clarence, 190, 378, 429.

— — presides at the trial of the earl of Cambridge and lord Scrope of Masham, 190, 379, 402–7.

— — — patent appointing him the king's vicegerent for this trial, 379, 402–3.

— — — list of peers summoned by him, 379, 405–6.

— — his death, 191.

Lancaster, Thomas of, stewardship never granted after his death, except *pro hac vice*, 191.

Langley, Edward of —, duke of York, etc., see York.

Langres, bishop of —, peer of France, 246, 269, 272.

Langton, Walter, bishop of Coventry and Lichfield, proceedings against —, 304.

Laon, bishop of —, peer of France, 246, 272.

Lascy, Henry de —, earl of Lincoln, amercement, 314.

Latimer, Richard lord —, 465.

— William lord —, impeachment, 346–7.

— — proceedings annulled for error, 347.

Laura, the recluse of Hackington, see Hackington.

Law (lex), technical meanings of —, 228, 232–3.

— use of term, in Glanville, 229–30n.

— — in the Très Ancien Coutumier, 230n.

— popular meaning, illustrations of —, 230–2n.

— — evidence of Wendover, 231n.

Law of the land (lex terrae), meaning of in Magna Charta, 228–33.

Laws, of Henry I, 207.

— of David of Scotland, 207.

Leicester, abbey of —, patronage retained by the king, 196, 198.

— countesses of —; see Breteuil, Amicia de —; Grandmaisnil, Petronilla de —; Braose, Laura.

— earls of —, see Beaumont, Montfort, Lancaster.

— — genealogy, 192–3, 197–9.

— estates, partition of —, 74–5, 94–5, 110–1, 193, 196, 198.

— — value of —, 75, 99–104.

— — records showing devolution on death of last Beaumont, 88–114.

— — elder moiety, seizure by John and restoration, 75.

— — — custodians of —; see Cantilupe; Chester, earl of —; Ropeley.

Leigh, Essex, in the hundred of Rochford, 419, 420n, 445.

Lescrope v. Grosvenor, 365n.

Letters-Patent, authority for affixing great seal to —, 131–7.

Letters-Patent, instance where seal affixed in chancellor's absence, 133.

Lewes, battle of —, 124, 197, 199, 310.

Lex, Lex terrae, see Law.

Leybourne, William de — (forest offence, King's service, coram rege), 316.

Lincoln, Henry de Lascy earl of —, amercement, 314.

Lisieux, bishops of —, Arnulf, 45, 46n, 49n, 50n, 61.

— — chief justiciar of Normandy, 37, 43–4.

— — John, justiciar of Normandy, 26–8.

Littleton, Sir Richard, judge, 467.

— Sir Thomas, judge, on trial by peers, 393.

Llewelyn, proceedings against —, 243, 248–9n.

Loisel, the rule of —, 277n.

London, Richard of Gravesend, bishop of — (forest offence, parliament), 318.

Longchamps, Stephen, dapifer or seneschal of Richard I, 72n.

Lords Spiritual, see Bishops, Clergy.

— appoint a procurator for trials in parliament, 393.

— how affected by institution of the steward's court, 442.

Louis VIII, claims the kingdom of England, 254–69.

— — argument before the papal legate, 255–6.

— — expedition to England vetoed, 256.

— — lands in England notwithstanding, 256.

— — his manifesto, 257.

— — — legal aspects of —, 258–9.

— — the argument at Rome, 259–68.

Lovell, Sir Thomas, 465–6.

Luci, Richard de —, justiciar of England, 42n, 44, 61.

— — chief justiciar, 51.

Lumley, Sir Ralph, 421n, 423n, 425, 426n, 454, 459.

M

Magna Charta, 215–45.

— Chapters: IX, 220–1; XVIII, 222–3; XIX, 223; XX, 221n; XXI, 217, 221; XL, 326; XLII, 221, 241; LII, 219–20, 221, 239;

Magna Charta—Chapters:
LV, 221-2 ; LVI, 219-20, 239 ;
LVII, 219-20, 239-40 ; LIX,
220, 244 ; LX, 221n, 233.
— chapter XXXIX, 215, 221, 223-
5, 233-4, 236, 276, 280, 288, 296,
303, 328-9, 331, 333, 369n, 381-
2, 393.
— — modern opinions as to its true
interpretation, 216-8.
— — translations of —, 218-9.
— — "judgment of peers" does not
mean judgment of equals, 220.
— — "law of the land" does not
mean a trial or test, 221.
— — "lawful judgment of peers"
and the "law of the land" used
as more or less convertible terms,
222.
— — "vel" not to be read as "et,"
223-5.
— — offers two alternative guarantees, 276.
— — analogous provisions, 236.
Maine, David count of, 65.
Malcolm, king of Scots, charter
making Walter Fitzalan hereditary dapifer, 61-3.
Malet, Gilbert, dapifer, 41, 42n.
— Robert, dapifer, 33.
— William, dapifer, 41.
Malpalud, William de, justiciar of
Normandy, 52.
Maltravers, John lord —, 405-6.
Mandeville, Geoffrey de —, earl of
Essex, 15n, 34, 38.
— — made, by charter of the
Empress, hereditary dapifer, 33,
56-7.
— — claims to represent Eudo
dapifer, 34, 38.
— — probable explanation of his
claim to the dapifership, 38-9.
— Roger de —, justiciar of Nor-
mandy, 27.
Manny, Sir Walter, presides at trial
of baron of Greystoke, 346.
March, earls of —, Edmund, 379, 405.
— — Roger, see Mortimer.
Marche, counts de la —, made peers
of France, 275.
— — Hugh de Lusignan appeals
John king of England, 246.
Marmion, Philip (forest offence, conviction, redemption by executors),
319.
— — (forest offence, imprisonment,
parliament, redemption), 320.

Marmion, Robert, 52.
— Roger, justiciar of Normandy,
26.
— — baron of the Norman court,
27n.
Marshal, Gilbert earl of Pembroke,
appealed of robbery, 277.
— — claims judgment of peers,
279n.
— — sentence of outlawry against
—, quashed, 279-80.
— William earl of Pembroke, vicegerent of England, 116.
— — styles himself justiciar, 116.
— — changes his style to "rector
regis et regni," 116.
Marshal of England, 76, 143, 147,
168, 172-3, 180, 181n, 182, 184,
362-415 passim.
— assists the steward of England
in court of claims, 189, 190n.
— widows of marshals, their claim
to the office, 181n.
Marshalsea prison, 361.
Martel, William, dapifer, 33.
Mastac, Fulk of —, seneschal of
Poitou, 53.
Matthew Paris, chronicler, on the
condemnation of John for the
murder of Arthur, 260-1.
Matilda, the Empress, dapifers of
—, 33.
— — perhaps regent of Normandy
in 1154, 44.
— — grants by —, of hereditary
dapiferships, 33-4, 56-8.
— Queen of William I, tutor of
Normandy, 25n.
Mayor of London, 385n, 395, 416,
459.
— his coronation service, 183.
Mayors of the palace (Major,
Magister), 4, 10-1n, 15n, 18n, 23,
29, 30, 65-8.
Mellent, counts of —, see Beaumont.
Mengoti, William of —, seneschal
of Poitou, 53.
Merkes, Thomas, bishop of Carlisle, see Carlisle.
Merton v. Hoo, 365n.
— v. Stykeney, 365n.
Misdemeanours, determinable by the
justices, 284-7.
— procedure in cases of —, 289 et
sqq.
— — claim to judgment by peers
abandoned, 383.

Modus tenendi Parliamentum, 144.
— date of —, 147.
— de casibus et judiciis difficilibus, 147, 168–9.
— duties of the hereditary officers, 147, 168–9.
— connection of tract with affairs of 1386, 184.
Montague, John earl of Salisbury, 417, 419, 421, 423–7n.
— — impeachment of —, 370–1.
— — beheaded at Cirencester, 419, 454, 459.
— Thomas earl of Salisbury, 379, 405.
Montague, Salisbury v. —, 364n.
Montalt, Milicent de — (baroness, amercement), 314.
Montfort, Amaury VI, 77, 80–1, 86, 111, 114, 193, 198.
— — constable of France, 77, 110, 112, 114.
— — styles himself earl of Leicester, 77, 108.
— — letters to Henry III on behalf of Simon, 78, 81, 108, 110.
— — attempted conveyance of the Leicester estates and steward-ship, 81–2, 112.
— — visits England and formally surrenders his claims, 86, 112–4.
— — second grant to Simon, 112–4
— — — confirmation by Henry III, 114.
— — captured at Gaza, 118, 198, 199.
— — Simon raises money to ran-som him, 199.
— — his death, 198, 199.
— Amaury, son of Simon V, 193, 199.
— — styled Wellesbore or Welles-borne, 199.
— Amicia, countess of —, see Beau-mont.
— Eleanor, 193.
— — marries Llewelyn of Wales, 193, 197, 199.
— Guy, 193, 199.
— Henry, 85, 193, 199.
— Hugh, justiciar of Normandy, 26.
— Peter, 310.
— Ralph (de Gael), father of Amicia countess of Leicester, 192.
— Richard, 193, 199.
— Simon III, 74.
— Simon IV, earl of Leicester, 74, 93–114 passim, 121n.

Montfort, Simon IV, stewardship reserved to him on partition of Beaumont estates, 74–5, 94–5.
— — references to the partition, 101, 110–1.
— — deprived of his estates, 75, 80n.
— — appoints attorney for second partition, 111.
— — leaves England, 109–11.
— — accounts of his lands, 99–104.
— — estates nominally restored, 75–6.
— — — assigned to the earl of Chester on his behalf, 76, 104.
— — called husband of Amicia de Beaumont, 192–3, 197–8.
— — on the partition has Hinckley and the stewardship of England, 193, 196, 198.
— — exiled from England, 193, 196, 198.
— — his death, 76, 77, 105.
— Simon V, 78–86, 108–14, 116–37, 154–63, 266, 309.
— — comes to England, promised earldom of Leicester and steward-ship of England, receives an annuity, 78, 109.
— — ingratiates himself with the earl of Chester, 78–9.
— — does homage for the Leicester honour, 79, 109, 111.
— — difficulties in the way of his obtaining the earldom and es-tates, 79–85.
— — Amaury's irregular grant to him, 81, 112.
— — the earl of Norfolk contests his claim to the stewardship at the coronation of queen Eleanor, 82–3.
— — acts as steward at this corona-tion, 83.
— — complains that he is deprived of many of his rights as steward, 84, 123.
— — his matrimonial designs, 84–5.
— — marries Eleanor the king's sister, 85.
— — becomes, by surrender and confirmation, earl of Leicester and steward of England, and validly seized of his estates, 86, 112–4; see also, 193, 196, 198.
— — his debt and threatened ex-communication, 117.
— — raises money by fraud, 117.

Montfort, Simon V, disgrace and flight, 117-8.
— — returns to England to prepare for the crusade to avenge Gaza, 118.
— — raises money to ransom his brother, 199.
— — in Palestine, and Poitou, 118.
— — council at Saintes, 119.
— — his poverty, 119.
— — seneschal of Gascony, 119-20.
— — offered the stewardship of France, 120-1.
— — assumes the style " seneschallus Angliae," 121-2.
— — Henry of Germany acts as deputy steward for him, 122.
— — Louis arbitrates between him and Henry III, 123.
— — effect of the reappointment of Justiciars, 123-4.
— — styled seneschal of England in formal documents after the battle of Lewes, 124.
— — institutes inquiries about the stewardship, 125-6.
— — his position after the battle of Lewes, 124-7.
— — alleged assumption of the justiciarship, 126-37.
— — Evesham, 127, 193, 194, 197, 199.
— — his children, 193, 199.
— — (default, amercement), 309.
— Simon, son of Simon V, 193, 199.
— Thomas, son of Simon V, 193, 199.
Montgomery, Roger de —, 8, 9, 19.
— — tutor of Normandy, 25n.
Montpinçon, Ralph de, dapifer, 20.
Morewich, Hugh de, dapifer, 41.
Mortain, counts of —, see John, Stephen.
Mortimer, Roger of Chirk, proceedings against for treason, 299.
— — — reversed for error, 299-300, 329-32.
— Roger of Wigmore, proceedings against for treason, 299.
— — — reversed for error, 299-300, 329-32.
— — earl of March, intimacy wth queen Isabella, 335.
— — — proceeded against in parliament, and executed, 336.
— — — proceedings reversed for error, 336.

Mortimer, Thomas, impeached in parliament, judgment in default of appearance, 358-9.
Mountjoy, William Blount lord —, 465-6.
Mowbray, John earl Marshal, 378-9, 403, 405.
— John 4th duke of Norfolk, 395.
— Thomas 1st duke of Norfolk, appealed by the duke of Hereford, 185-7, 359, 367.
— Thomas, earl Marshal, his revolt, trial, sentence and execution, 372-6, and see 400-2.
— — question in parliament as to validity of the proceedings against, 376n.
Muntchensy, Denise de — (baroness, amercement), 314.
— — (forest offence, coram rege), 318.

N

Neufbourg, Robert de, justiciar of Normandy, 35-7, 43-4, 47, 50.
— — chief justiciar of Normandy, 45-6, 48n.
— — given a quasi-regal precedence, 46.
— — dapifer, 41, 46.
— — dapifer Normanniae, 46, 47n.
— — senescallus Normanniae, 47n.
— — vicecomes, vicedominus Normanniae, 48.
Neville, George lord Bergavenny, 465.
— Ralph earl of Westmoreland, 372, 417, 459.
— Richard lord Latimer, 465.
— Richard earl of Warwick, steward of England to deliver judgment on Henry VI and others, 390.
— — — his patent of appointment, 390n.
— — — reappointed steward of England, 391.
— — — his patent, 391n.
Nigel, John de —, appeals the countess of Flanders, 271-2.
Norfolk, dukes of —, see Howard, Mowbray.
— earls of —, see Bigod.
Normandy, amercements, fixed scale, 221-2n.
— assizes, 36n, 44n, 46-8n, 214, 222n.
— conquest by Philip Augustus, 249.

Normandy, bishops unwilling to swear fealty, 249–50.
—— they appeal to the pope, 250–1.
—— observations on the position, 251–2.
— Coutumiers, Très Ancien —, 26n, 30–2, 214, 230, 255n, 262n, 266n.
—— Grand —, 167–8, 225, 233–4.
— dukes of —, peers of France, 246.
—— privilege in respect of summonses, 246–7, 261.
— government of —, before the Conquest, 9–10.
—— after the conquest, 19, 25.
—— under Henry I, 25–8.
—— under Stephen, 34.
—— under Geoffrey, 35–6.
—— under Henry II, 37–54 *passim*
— judgment of peers in —, during the 12th century, 214–5.
— officers of —, 6, 36–7.
—— their precedence, 16n.
— seneschals of —, 53.
— tract on the office of seneschal, 167–8.
Northampton, William de Bohun earl of —, present at the trial of the baron of Greystoke, 346n.
Northumberland, earls of —, see Percy.
Norwich, Henry le Spenser bishop of —, impeachment, 348.
—— *v.* William baron de Hilton, 365n.
Novarre, Philip de —, his views on forfeiture, 264–5.
—— their absurdity, 265.
Noyon, bishops of —, peers of France, 246, 269, 272.

O

Odo bishop of Bayeux, see Bayeux.
Officers of the household, in France, 3, 6.
— in Normandy, 6, 16n, 35–7.
— their precedence in England, 20–1, 24, 41–2.
— Hereditary —, duty to correct the errors of the king, 143–4, 147, 168–9, 184.
—— by removing corrupt ministers, 149–51, 166–7.
Offices of the Court and Serjeanties, 180–3.
Oger, dapifer, 42n.

Oldcastle, John lord Cobham, proceedings against in parliament, 380.
Oldhall, Sir William, attainder, 388–9n.
" Or " read as ' And'," see Vel.
Ordainers, lords —, 144.
Ordeals, 216, 217–8n, 228, 232, 304n.
Ordric, dapifer, 22.
Organum vocis, 375.
Orleans, Manassé de Seignelay bishop of —, and the peers of France, 270n.
—— claims judgment by bishops, 272.
Orleton, Adam, bishop of Hereford, see Hereford.
Ormond, earl of —, see Butler.
— Thomas lord —, 465.
Osbern son of Herfast, dapifer, 7–11, 13–15.
— procurator principalis domus, 8.
Osbern, dapifer, 7.
Osbern, bishop of Exeter, 8.
Osmund, procurator, 10.
Otho, emperor of Germany, 65–7.
Outlawry, 241, 242, 377.
— by the law of the land, 221.
— and judgment of peers, 277.
— procedure in, 258.
— argument of Hubert de Burgh, 279n.
— case of the earl of Warwick, 358, 360–1.
Oxford, earls of —, see Vere.
Oyer and Terminer, names of earls and barons inserted in the commissions of, 287n, 371, 401–2.

P

Palace Courts, 373n.
Paris, Matthew, chronicler, on the condemnation of John for the murder of Arthur, 260–1.
Parliament, amercement in —, 319.
— appeals of treason in —, 348–59.
—— abolished, 369, 439n.
— attainder supersedes all judicial proceedings, 388–9.
— cases adjourned to —, for judgment, 292, 313 *et sqq.*
— court for new remedies, and redress of grievances, 128n.
— declaration of forfeiture in —, against the leaders of the earl of Kent's rebellion, 388n, 425–6.

Parliament, "full parliament," meaning of —, 295.
— impeachments in —, 346–8, 354, 358–9, 370–1, 383, 388.
— judgments in —. 287, 292, 313 et sqq.
— — of persons, not peers, protest against, 336–7.
— lords did not consider themselves bound by their own decisions, 350.
— Modus tenendi parliamentum, 144, 147, 168–9, 184.
— petitions against the court of chivalry, 363, 370, 377n.
— procedure in —, declaration of the lords as to —, 349, 352.
— — petition of the commons as to —, 370n,
— reversal of judgments for error, 296–300, 305, 324–34, 336.
— trials in —, 184–5, 305, 335–59 passim, 370–1, 377, 380, 383–96 passim.
Pascy, William de, 58–60.
Patric, William, baron of the Norman court, 27n.
Pauli, Reinhold, on Simon de Montfort and the justiciarship, 129.
Peeresses, amercement of —, 290n, 314–5.
— forest offences temp. Edward I, judgment in parliament, 318.
— statute regulating the trial of —, 381–3.
— trial in parliament, 384–6.
Peers, who were —, 225–8.
— — co-vassals, 225.
— — — freeman and villein, 225.
— — definitions excluding lord, 225.
— as a title of office or honour, 226.
— — peers of Flanders, Lille, Pontefract, Preston, Rouen, Valenciennes, Vermandois, etc., 226n.
— " and other nobles," 226n.
— of France, 226–7, and see below.
— of the Jews, 228.
— quasi peers, 226n, 233n.
— " barons " and " justices " used as synonymous terms, 227–8.
— justices and knights the peers of any man, 223, 277.
— not bound to judge any but peers, 336–7.
— claim to jury or inquest of —, 302, 334.
— not to be sworn, 282, 293, 417, 460, 469.

Peeresses of France, countess of Artois at the trial of the count of Flanders in 1315, 274.
Peers of France, 55, 226–7.
— none formally so styled prior to 1216, 245, 269–70.
— traditions concerning —, 245–6.
— the twelve —, 246.
— when first enumerated, 246n.
— amercement of, 290n.
— judgment by —, principles regulating —, 273–5, 285n, 287–8n.
— — presence of a single peer sufficient, 274.
— attempt to exclude from court the officers of the household, 271–2.
— treaties regulating composition of the tribunal, 274.
— additions to college of —, 275.
Peers Spiritual, see Bishops, Clergy, Lords Spiritual.
Peion, William, evidence on oath as to Huntingdon's flight, 420n, 444–5.
Pembroke, earls of —, see Marshal.
Percy, Henry 1st earl of Northumberland, constable of England, 370n.
— — proceedings against in the court of chivalry, 376–7.
— — — transferred into parliament, 377.
— Henry 5th earl of Northumberland, 465.
— John de (forest offence, imprisonment, parliament), 313.
— Thomas, steward of the household to Richard II, 184.
— — — procurator for the clergy, 184, 354.
— — — — joined in sentencing the primate and Arundel, 184, 354, 357.
— — earl of Worcester, assistant steward for the coronation of Henry IV, 189, 190n, 200.
— — — as vice - steward should have sentenced the lords-appellant, 371n.
— — — steward of the household to Henry IV, 428n.
— — — never appointed steward of England, 428–9n.
Perke, Gilbert, chancellor to the duke of Buckingham, 437, 439n.
Peterborough, abbot of —, amercement, 309.

Petitions, to steward of England, 183n.
— to reverse a judgment for error, 327, 330, 334.
Philip Augustus, his coronation, 54–5.
— — the count of Flanders, and not the count of Blois, acts as seneschal at —, 54–5.
— — — carries sword and serves at table, 69.
— his 2nd coronation, count of Flanders seneschal at —, etc., 70.
— v. the countess of Champagne, 269–71.
— v. John, 1st judgment against, 246–8.
— — — procedure similar to that of Edward I v. Llewelyn, 247–9.
— — conquest of Normandy, 249.
— — — bishops unwilling to swear fealty, 249–51.
— — — observations upon, 251–2.
— — refuses John a safe-conduct, 260.
— — 2nd judgment against, 252.
— — — nature of —, 252–4.
— naval defeat, 254.
— reply to the papal legate, 254–5.
Philippa of Hainault, queen of Edward III, her coronation, 172, 177.
Pincerna, see Butler.
Pirou, William de, dapifer, 23.
Pleshy, Essex, 420, 422–4, 427, 451–9 passim.
— — funeral monument to Huntingdon at —, 424n.
Poitiers, Diane de —, seneschal of Normandy, 53n.
Poitou, added to the French peerage, 275.
— seneschal of —, 53.
Pole, Michael de la —, 1st earl of Suffolk, appealed of treason in parliament, 348–51.
— Michael de la —, 2nd earl of Suffolk, 379, 405.
— William de la —, duke of Suffolk, proceedings against, 383–4.
— — does not put himself upon his peers, 384.
— — banishment and death, 384.
Ponthieu, Marie de —, 263–4n.
Popham, Sir John, constable of Southampton Tower, 378, 404–5.
Port, Adam de —, dapifer, 23.

Pounteney v. Borney (Exchequer Chamber), 365–6.
Préaux, Roger de —, dapifer or seneschal, 72n, 88.
Pritewell (Prittlewell), John, 420n.
— — confession of —, 448.
— — Huntingdon captured at his house, 420n, 448, 452–3.
Prittlewell near Leigh, Essex, 420n, 452–3.
Procedure in Parliament, declaration of the lords as to —, 349, 352.
— petition of the commons as to —, 370n.
Procurator, 8, 9n, and see Osbern, Osmund, St. John, Fitz-Ralph.
— became the popular term for the vicegerent of Normandy, 50n.
— and dapifer, 8, 9n.
— for the clergy in parliament, 184, 353–4, 358–9, 393.
Proof by Record, 298–301.
Prothero, George Walter, on Simon de Montfort and the justiciarship, 130.
Proxy, duke of York appoints the earl of Dorset his proxy for the judgment of Cambridge and Scrope, 379, 405.

Q

Queen, case adjourned before, 312.
Quincy, hereditary constables of Scotland, 76.
— Saer de —, 193–4, 196–8.
— — his claim to the Leicester estates, 74, 89–94.
— — — his claim to the honour of Grandmaisnil, 92–3, 98.
— — — his claim to the honour of Hinckley, 96–7.
— — — his claim to a moiety of the suburb of Leicester, 99–100.
— —, earl of Winchester, charter confirming to him a moiety of the Leicester estates, 94–5.
— — — the partition of the Leicester estates, 74–5, 101, 110–1, 193, 196, 198.
— — — appeals from the original partition decree, which is revised in his favour, 75, 80n, and see 110–1.
— — — legal proceedings in connection with his estates, 80n.
Quo Warranto, proceedings on —, 290n.

R

Ralph, dapifer, 23.
Ralph (Torte), tutor of Normandy, 9, 10n.
— — styled seneschal by Wace, 10n, 16n. [22–3.
Ranulf, brother of Ilger, dapifer,
Ratcliff, John lord Fitzwalter, proceedings against for treason, 397.
Recognitors, 217, 222–3.
— whether considered quasi-judges in Magna Charta, 223.
Record, proof by —, in treason, 298–301.
Redemption, 285n, 286n, 315–6, 319–20, 360.
Reims, archbishops of —, peers of France, 246, 269.
— — Thomas de Beaumetz, defendant in ejectment, claims unsuccessfully to be tried by his peers, 272.
Rempston, Thomas, steward of the household, 190n.
Richard I, 30, 72–3, 84, 115, 308.
— charter to Roger earl of Norfolk, 87–8.
Richard II, 176–89, 347–60, 363–9.
— accession, 182n.
— coronation and court of claims of —, 177, 179, 182–3.
— the revenge of 1397, 352–9.
— capricious conduct in the Hereford v. Norfolk appeal, 186–7.
— his abdication, 189, 199–200.
Richard III (duke of Gloucester), constable of England, sentences the duke of Somerset, 395.
— (king of England), 396–7, 438.
Richard I, duke of Normandy, 9.
Richard duke of York, see York.
Richmond, earl of —, see John of Gaunt.
Rivers, earl —, see Woodville.
Robert, and Geoffrey Greygown, 65–7.
— case against Eudo II count of Chartres, 209.
Robert I, duke of Normandy, his dapifers, 7.
Robert II, tutor of Normandy, 25n.
— duke of Normandy, 25.
Rocheforts, dapifers of France, 4.
Ropeley, Robert, 93, 97, 98.
— — given custody of the Leicester estates, 75n, 94.
— — — his accounts as custodian, 93, 96, 98, 99–102.

Ropeley, Robert, and the archdeacon of Stafford, custodians of the honour of Grandmaisnil, 93.
Roumare, William de —, justiciar of Normandy, 34.
Round, John Horace, on Simon de Montfort and the justiciarship, 130.
Rowdon, Robert, serjeant-at-arms, 465.
Ruffus, William, dapifer, 41.
Rutland, earl of —; see York, Edward of —.
Rydon, Robert, clerk of the council, 414.

S

S. v. Osbert archdeacon of York, 303–4n.
Sablé, Geoffrey de —, justiciar of Normandy, 26–7, 36.
St. Amand, Amaury de — (parliament, high misdemeanors), 294n.
— — (forest offence, king's service, coram rege), 316.
St. Carilef, William de —, bishop of Durham, proceedings against for treason, 210–1.
St. John of Jerusalem, in England, prior of —, 395, 442, 465.
— in Ireland, prior of —, appeals the earl of Ormond, 383.
St. John, John de — (forest offence, parliament), 313.
— William de —, 44n.
— — chief justiciar of Normandy, 49, 50.
— — — styled Normanniae procurator, 50n.
St. Martin, Alured de —, dapifer, 41.
Saintmount, Richard lord —, 466.
St. Osbert, Giles de —, dapifer of Hainault, 43n.
St. Trinité du Mont, Rouen, charter of William I to —, 13.
St. Valery, Reginald de —, justiciar of Normandy, 35–6, 48, 49n.
Salisbury, earls of —, see Montague.
— v. Montague, 364n.
Savoy, Thomas of —, 117, and see Flanders.
Saye, James Fienes lord —, indictment and death of —, 384–6.
Scales, Anthony lord —, see Woodville.
— Thomas lord —, indictments before —, at the Guildhall, 385.
Scot, John, earl of Chester, see Chester.

Scotland, hereditary dapifership of —, 40n, 44n, 61–3.

Scrivelsby, tenure of —, 182n.

Scrope, Kighlee v. —, 370.

Scrope, Henry lord Scrope of Masham, proceedings against for treason, 190, 378–80, 402–7, 429.

— — — confirmation in parliament, 379, 402–7.

— Richard, archbishop of York, see York

— Richard, steward of the household, presides at the trials of peers in parliament, 347n.

— William earl of Wiltshire, procurator for the clergy, 359.

— — tried and sentenced by a court of chivalry, 367–8.

Seal, the Great —, authority for affixing, 131–7.

Seaton, tenure of the manor of —, 181n.

Segrave, Nicholas, proceedings against in parliament for treason, 294–5.

— Stephen, justiciar of England, 116, 137.

Sely (Cely), Sir Benedict (alias Sir John), 421n, 423n, 424, 454.

Seneschals, early occurrence of —, 4.

— dapifers (q.v.) commonly so styled after accession of Richard I, 72.

— normal number became two, and then one, 115.

— increasing importance of their office, 115.

— styled finally "senescallus hospitii regis," or steward of the household, 128n, and see Steward of the household.

Seneschals of French Provinces, style and authority, 115–6.

Serjeanties, grand —, 42, 179–81.

— honorary at coronations, etc., 43.

— — their popularity, 43.

— — at the court of Flanders, 43n.

— — at the coronation of Richard II, 179–83.

— widows of serjeants, their position, 181n

" Serjent à roi est pair à comte," 277n.

Sewer, 11, 180n, and see Dapifer, Seneschal, Steward.

Shelley, Sir Thomas, 419–21n, 445–6, 448–9, 450–2, 455–6.

Sheriff, office held by dapifers, 21.

— styled dapifer, 18n.

Shirley, Walter Waddington, on Simon de Montfort and the justiciarship, 128–9.

Siward, Richard, v. the earl of Gloucester, 284n.

Soissons, council at in 1213, 252, 267n.

Somerset, duke of, —, see Beaufort.

Somery, Roger de — (forest offence, imprisonment, parliament, redemption), 319–20.

Stafford, Edward duke of Buckingham, 379, 429, 465.

— — proceedings against for treason, 435 et sqq.

— — trial before the court of the lord high steward, 436–41.

— — — report in the Year Books, 436, 439–40n, 469–70.

— — attainted by Act of Parliament, 441n.

— Henry duke of Buckingham, steward of England to execute judgment on the duke of Clarence, 396.

— — — his patent of appointment, 412–3.

— — proceedings against for treason, 396.

— — — his examination, confession and death, 397n.

— — his design to stab the king, 438.

— — attainted by Act of Parliament, 396–7n.

— Humphrey duke of Buckingham, steward of England for the trial of the earl of Devon, 386–8.

— Nicholas baron of — (forest offence, imprisonment, redemption), 320.

— Ralph, steward of the household, 340–1.

— — earl of —, present at the trial of the baron of Greystoke, 346n.

Stanley, John, steward of the household, on the commission of oyer and terminer for the trial of archbishop Scrope and Mowbray, 372, 401.

— Thomas lord —, attempted impeachment of —, 388.

Stapleton, Thomas, antiquary, his views about the stewardship of Normandy, 5–6, 13–14.

Stephen (count of Mortain), a justiciar of Normandy, 28.

— (king of England), 33, 37, 39.

— — his dapifers, 33.

Stephen (King of England), his government of Normandy, 34.
— — weakness of curia regis during his reign, 213.
— — — impetus given to ecclesiastical jurisdiction, 213.
Stewards of the archbishops of Canterbury, honorary hereditary office held by Richard Clare earl of Gloucester, 140n.
Stewards of the bishops of Exeter, honorary hereditary office held by Hugh Courtenay earl of Devon, 140-1n.
Stewards (dapifers or seneschals) of England :—
— Hereditary ; (1) Geoffrey earl of Essex (by charter), see Mandeville
— — (2) Humphrey de Bohun (by charter), see Bohun.
— — (3) Robert II earl of Leicester (by charters), see Beaumont.
— — Hugh earl of Norfolk (by charter), see Bigod.
— — (4) Robert III earl of Leicester (by charter and succession), see Beaumont.
— — Roger earl of Norfolk (by charter and succession), see Bigod.
— — (5) Robert IV earl of Leicester (by succession), see Beaumont.
— — (6) Simon IV earl of Leicester (by succession), see Montfort.
— — (7) Simon V earl of Leicester (by charters of surrender and confirmation), see Montfort.
— — (8) Thomas earl of Lancaster (by patent), see Lancaster.
— — (9) Henry earl of Lancaster (by tenure ?), see Lancaster.
— — (10) Henry duke of Lancaster (by tenure ?), see Lancaster.
— For life ; (1) Randulf Blundevill earl of Chester (?), see Chester.
— — (2) Edmund earl of Lancaster (by patents), see Lancaster.
— — (3) Thomas duke of Clarence (by livery), see Lancaster.
— By the Courtesy ; (1) William of Hainault (?), see Hainault.
— — (2) John duke of Lancaster, see John of Gaunt.
— Deputy, or Pro Hac Vice ; Henry of Germany (by patent), see Germany.
— — Henry earl of Derby, see Lancaster
— — Thomas earl of Worcester (by livery), see Percy.

— — William Thyrning (?), see Thyrning.
— — Richard earl of Warwick (by patent), see Beauchamp.
— — Humphrey duke of Buckingham, see Stafford.
— — Richard earl of Warwick (by patent), see Neville.
— — Henry duke of Buckingham (by patent), see Stafford.
— — John earl of Oxford (by patent), see Vere.
— — Thomas, earl of Surrey (by patent), see Howard.
— — — duke of Norfolk (by patent), see Howard.
Stewards of England, in the Court of Parliament, 146, 184-5, 188, 354-9, 371, 386-8, 390-1, 393, 396.
— in the Court of the lord High steward, 379, 399, 416-70 passim.
— in the Court of Claims, see Court of Claims.
— miscellaneous functions of —, 42-3, 72-3, 82-4, 122, 143-4, 147-51, 164-9, 173, 177, 189-92, 199-200.
— styles of the —, first holders styled dapifers, 56-61.
— — seneschals after the accession of Richard I, 72, 74, 86-7.
— — " seneschallus hospitii domini regis " under Henry III, 77n.
— — " seneschallus Angliae totius " by Amaury VI, 81, 112.
— — " seneschallus regis " in 1239, 113.
— — Simon V de Montfort assumes the style " seneschallus Angliae," 121.
— — " seneschallus Angliae " in formal documents under the great seal, after the battle of Lewes, 124-5.
— — " tanquam seneschallus Angliae," 173n, 177, 184, 190n.
— — " justiciarius," 185n.
— — " grand juge d'Angleterre," 188n.
— — " juge greigneur," 188n.
— tracts on the —, the Colchester Tract, 29-30.
— — the Lancastrian Tract, 144, 148-51, 164-7.
— — — an unhistorical account, 151.
— — — the foundation of future claims, 151.

Stewards of England:—
— — — comparison with other tracts, 151–3.
— — the Hinckley Tracts, 192–9.
— — — drawn up in the interest of John of Gaunt, 50–1n, 174–5.
— writ to Exchequer to ascertain fees of —, 142n.
Stewards of the Household, court of —, 128n, 424n.
— preside at trials in parliament, 185, 347.
— appointed during pleasure, 40.
— style, from latter half of 13th century, "senescallus hospitii regis," 128, 190n.
Stewards of the Household in France, connection with trial of peers, 189n.
Stewards of Scotland, 40n, 44n, 61–3.
Stigand, dapifer, 7, 8, 20, 54.
Stratford, John archbishop of Canterbury, see Canterbury.
Stubbs, William bishop of Oxford, his views about the stewardship of Normandy, 6, 12–4.
— — on the origin of the justiciar of England, 12–3, 21.
Stykeney, Merton v. —, 365n.
Succession, brothers, sisters, nephews and nieces, respective rights of —, 249n, 266.
Suffolk, Alice duchess of —, proceedings against in parliament, acquittal, 384–5, 386n.
— duke of —, earls of —, see Pole.
"Super eum ibimus," 224, 236–7, 243.
— both judgments against John were judgments "super eum ire," 248, 252, 270.
"Super eum mittemus," 236–7, 243–4.
Surrey, Thomas Holand duke of —, impeachment, 370–1, and see Holand.
— earls of —, see Howard, Warenne.
Sutton, Edward lord Dudley, lord high steward appointed for the trial of —, 435, 467–8.
Swords, carried at a coronation, 55, 69–72, 84.
— — "Curtana," carried by earl of Chester in 1236, 152.
— — carried by the earl of Lancaster at the coronation of Edward II, 142, 152.
— — — claimed by John of Gaunt at the coronation of Richard II, 182, 183n.

T

Talbot, Gilbert lord —, 405.
— John lord —, appeals the earl of Ormond in the court of chivalry, 380.
Tancarville, Ralph de —, the chamberlain, mayor of the palace, 10–1.
Tesson, Ralph, a baron of the court of Normandy, 27n.
— Ralph, seneschal of Normandy, 53n.
Three parties to a judgment, necessity for —, 208, 273, 284–9.
Thyrning, William, chief justice of the common bench, delivers judgment in parliament on the lords appellant, 371, 378.
— — — as steward of England, 371.
— — — — owing to illness of the vice-steward, 371n.
Tiptoft, John earl of Worcester, appointed constable of England, 390, 407.
— — sentences the earl of Oxford, 391.
— — surrenders his office, 392.
— — false recital of the terms of his appointment in the patent of earl Rivers, 392, 407 et sqq.
— — reappointed constable, 393, 412.
— sentenced to death by the earl of Oxford as constable of England, 394.
Touchet, James lord Audeley (court of chivalry, levying war, sentence and execution), 397–8, 414–5.
— — attainted by Act of Parliament, 398.
Toulouse, counts of —, peers of France, 246.
Tournebu, Simon de —, 52.
Tours, Joslen of —, dapifer and chief officer of state in Anjou, 37.
— S. Julien de —, charter of —, 70.
— Stephen of —, seneschal of Anjou, 53.
Treason, proceedings in cases of —, 284, 292 et sqq., et passim.
Treher, Philip, fishmonger, gives lessons on fighting in the lists, 383.
Très Ancien Coutumier de Normandie, see Normandy.
Tresilian, Sir Robert, chief justice, appealed of treason in parliament, 348–51.
— — condemned and executed, 351, 352n.

Tutores, style given to vicegerents of Normandy, 9, 12n, 25n.
Tyes, Henry, proceedings against for treason, 299.

U

Umfraville, Gilbert de —, William Douglas v. —, appeal of treason, 349n.
— —, earl of Angus (various misdemeanours, acquittal by jury), 312.

V

Valence, William de —, judgment, 309.
Valenciennes and Guy count of Flanders, 273.
Vampage, Sir William, 414.
" Vel " read as " Et," 217-8, 219n, 223-5.
— not to be so read in chapter xxxix of Magna Charta, 225.
Verdict and Judgment, confusion between, 216-7, 288-9.
— — in Bracton, 288.
— — in Magna Charta, 223.
— of junior lord taken first, 393, 417, 440, 460, 469.
— of majority, 417, 434-5, 460, 469.
Verdun, Theobald de —, proceedings against for giving false evidence, 294n, 316-8.
— — (criminal proceedings against, amercement in parliament), 319.
Vere, Aubrey 10th earl of Oxford, shelters Huntingdon, 450.
— John 12th earl of Oxford (treason, court of chivalry, earl of Worcester constable), 391.
— John 13th earl of Oxford, sentences the earl of Worcester, 394.
— — steward of England for the trial of the earl of Warwick, 431, 460-7.
— — — patent of his appointment, 460-2.
— — — styled constable of England by Hall, 434.
— Richard 11th earl of Oxford, 379, 405.
— Robert 5th earl of Oxford (forest offence, coram rege), 318.
— Robert 6th earl of Oxford, his claim to be hereditary chamberlain, 171, 178-9.
— Robert 9th earl of Oxford and duke of Ireland, defeated at Radcot Bridge, 348.

Vere, Aubrey, 10th earl of Oxford, appealed of treason in parliament, 348-51.
Vermandois, Ralph count of —, dapifer of France, 29, 54-5, 64, 68.
— — Philip count of Flanders claims to succeed to the dapifership of —, 55, 63.
Vernon, William de —, 44n, 46n.
— — a justiciar of Normandy, 35.

W

Wac, Ralph de —, tutor of Normandy, 10.
Wace, persons styled seneschal by him, 16-17n.
Waldeshef v. Wawe, 365n.
Walo, papal legate, his mission to France, 254-6.
— — forbids the invasion of England, 256.
Wantham, Nicholas de —, Robert le Eyr v. —, appeal of treason, 349n.
Warbeck, Perkin, 430-1.
Warenne, John earl of — (forest offence, coram rege, redemption before barons of the Exchequer), 315.
— — (forest offence, parliament), 318.
Warwick, earls of —, see Beauchamp, Neville.
— Edward earl of —, indicted for treason, 399, 429-31.
— — trial before the court of the lord high steward, 431-5, 460-7.
— — attainted by Act of Parliament, 432.
— — observations upon his trial, 432-5.
— Ela countess of —, amercement, 315.
Watteville, Robert de —, 60.
— — dapifer, 41.
Wavrin, Hellin de —, seneschal of Flanders, 53n.
Wawe, Waldeshef v. —, 365n.
West, Thomas lord De la Warr, 465.
Westmoreland, Ralph earl of —, 372, 417, 459.
Weston, John de —, marshal, 363, 399-400.
— William de—, impeachment, 347.
Whitchurch v. Calverly, 365n.
William the Conqueror, 5-22 passim, 29, 30, 209-10, 408-9, 411.

William the Conqueror, his dapifers, as duke of Normandy, 7, 11n.
—— as king of England, 8, 20.
— his vicegerents of Normandy, their style, 25n.
William II, 15n, 21–2, 29, 30, 210–1.
— his dapifers, 22.
William I, duke of Normandy, 9.
William, dapifer, 22.
Willoughby, Robert lord —, 405.
— Robert lord de Broke, 466.
— William lord —, 466.
Wilman, Benet, case of —, 370.
Wilton, Edward Grey lord de —, 466.
Wiltshire, earl of —, see Scrope.
Winchester, bishops of —, Nicholas of Ely (forest offence, coram regina), 312, and see 313.
—— Peter des Roches, 137.
———— asserts that the king's justices are the peers of any man, 276–7.
———— modern criticisms, 278.
———— Henry III evades deciding the point, 278–80.
—— Richard of Ilchester, chief justiciar of Normandy, 32, 52–3.
— countess of —, see Beaumont.
— earl of —, see Quincy.
Witchcraft, 380–1.
Woodville, Anthony lord Scales, patent appointing him constable of England from and after his father's death, 410–1.
— Richard earl Rivers, he and his son appointed constable of England successively for life, 392, 407–11.
—— observations upon, 392, 393n.
Worcester, Godfrey Giffard bishop of — (baron, amercement), 314.
—— (forest offence, proceedings in respect of —), 321–2.
— earls of —, see Percy, Tiptoft.
Writs, of exigent against a peer of the realm, 360–1.
— in Normandy, of faciatis habere, 26–8n, 44–5n, 49n.
—— of faciatis recognosci, 45n.
—— of faciatis tenere, 27n.
—— of teneat in pace, 45n.
— royal, naming the justiciar, 45n, 49n.
— of Arnulf bishop of Lisieux, 44n.
— of Robert de Neufbourg, 45n.
— of Rotroc bishop of Evreux, 49n.

Wytingham, William de —, proceedings against (temp. Edward I) in the military court, 363n.

Y

Year Books, first reported case of a trial before the court of the lord high steward, 416–7, 459–60.
—— evidence of it being a forgery, 416 et sqq.
— report of the duke of Buckingham's trial, 436, 439n, 440n, 469–70.
York, archbishops of —, John Romanus (inquisition, ambiguity, parliament), 316.
——— proceedings against in parliament, 303n.
—— Alexander Neville, appealed of treason in parliament, 348–51.
——— the lords did not venture to sentence him to death, 351.
—— Richard Scrope, his revolt, trial, sentence and execution, 372–6.
——— patent appointing a constable and marshal in connection with —, 400–1.
——— commission of oyer and terminer to steward of the household, peers and justices in connection with —, 401–2.
——— question in parliament as to validity of the proceedings, 376n.
—— John Kempe, 380.
— archdeacon of —, Osbert, proceedings against for murder, 303–4n.
— Edward of —, earl of Rutland, 353–4, 417–8, 450, 454, 456, 458.
—— duke of Albemarle, impeachment, 370–1.
—— duke of York, 379, 405.
— Richard of, earl of Cambridge, proceedings against for treason, 190, 378–80, 402–7, 429.
— Richard duke of York, 386n, 387.
—— death at Wakefield, 390n.
—— attainted by Act of Parliament, 389n.

Z

Zouche, Elena (baroness, amercement), 314.
— John lord —, 466.
— William lord —, 405.

PLYMOUTH : WILLIAM BRENDON AND SON, LTD., PRINTERS